Confronting Historical Paradigms

Confronting Historical Paradigms

Peasants, Labor, and the Capitalist
World System in Africa and Latin America

Frederick Cooper
Allen F. Isaacman
Florencia E. Mallon
William Roseberry
Steve J. Stern

THE UNIVERSITY OF WISCONSIN PRESS

The University of Wisconsin Press
114 North Murray Street
Madison, Wisconsin 53715

3 Henrietta Street
London WC2E 8LU, England

Library of Congress Cataloging-in-Publication Data
Confronting historical paradigms: peasants, labor, and the capitalist
    world system in Africa and Latin America / Frederick Cooper . . . [et al.].
    430 p.   cm.
        Includes bibliographical references and index.
        ISBN 0-299-13680-9   ISBN 0-299-13684-1 (pbk.)
            1. Africa—Economic conditions—1960– 2. Africa—Social
    conditions. 3. Latin America—Economic conditions. 4. Latin America—Social
    conditions. 5. Economic history—Historiography. 6. Social history—Historiography.
    I. Cooper, Frederick, 1947–
    HC800.C665   1993
    306'.096—dc20   92-39242

Contents

Preface

This book originated in a conversation between Allen Isaacman and Steve Stern about the resonance that we and other colleagues had noticed in the historical literature on major topics in African and Latin American history. We thought that this resonance constituted an underappreciated counterpoint to laments about the fragmentation of contemporary historical scholarship, and that it also suggested a rethinking of major paradigms of world history. Our initial conversation soon expanded into a larger collaboration among five coauthors. We have sought in this book to bring together broadly synthetic essays of interpretation that illuminate both the rethinking of history and paradigm that has taken place within the fields of African and Latin American history and the resonances between these fields. The first chapter introduces more specifically the intellectual context and objectives that define the larger agenda of the book and its essays.

Our approach has been flexible. We sought both to take advantage of recently published essays that would serve the needs of this book, and whose reprinting might be welcome, and to write new essays when previous publications did not seem suitable. Three essays and a postscript have been written expressly for this volume, and appear here for the first time: chapter 1 (Stern), the postscript to chapter 3 (Cooper), chapter 5 (Roseberry), and chapter 6 (Mallon). Three essays first drew attention in scholarly journals and are reprinted with permission: chapter 2 (Stern) first appeared in *American Historical Review* 93 (Oct. 1988): 829–72; chapter 3 (Cooper) first appeared in *African Studies Review* 24 (June/Sept. 1981): 1–86; chapter 4 (Isaacman) was also first published in *African Studies Review* 33 (Sept. 1990): 1–120. The essays of this book, then, come out of a rethinking of historical interpretation and paradigm in the late 1980s and early 1990s. (The only exception to this statement is the essay by Cooper, which prefigured some of the effort to chart a new scholarly synthesis in the 1980s, and which has been updated by a new postscript.) Because the essays in this book draw upon and supply order to rather massive bibliographies touching on specific topics, we thought it most useful to readers to maintain separate bibliographical lists for each essay.

A note on orthography is necessary. The hyphenated term *world-system* is associated with the important studies of Immanuel Wallerstein on the history of world capitalism. Yet the problem of capitalism as a system of world scale has engaged other influential authors as well. In general, this book deletes the hyphen to indicate this larger usage of the notion of a capitalist world system. Chapter 2, however, retains the hyphenated orthography in deference to the fact that Wallerstein's work serves as a key reference and point of departure in that essay.

Our acknowledgments are both individual and collective. Individual acknowledgments pertinent to particular essays appear separately. Here we limit ourselves to collective thanks. During the period when the book took shape, three of its authors (Cooper, Mallon, and Stern) had the good fortune to be Fellows at the Center for Advanced Study in the Behavioral Sciences in Stanford, California. The Center, under the leadership of Phil Converse and Bob Scott, provides a wonderful environment for scholarly work and reflection, both individual and collaborative. This environment greatly facilitated a day-to-day collaboration among the three of us, and the everyday contact, in turn, enhanced a five-way critique and collaboration among coauthors who were simultaneously immersed in demanding individual projects. The result, we hope, is that we were better able to shape the writing of new material that would weld the essays into a book whose whole is larger than the sum of its parts. The word-processing staff of the Center, especially Leslie Lindzey, also did a great deal of work to revamp reference styles into a consistent pattern. We are deeply grateful for this help in promoting an active five-way collaboration.

Introduction

1 *Steve J. Stern*

Africa, Latin America, and the Splintering of Historical Knowledge: From Fragmentation to Reverberation

A vast outpouring of historical scholarship has dramatically altered the epistemological and substantive foundations of historical knowledge in the quarter century since the late 1960s.[1] This introduction interprets the contributions of this book's essays within the context of that wider transformation. It reviews the changes that swept the U.S. historical profession, the splintering of historical knowledge engendered by such changes, and the significance of historical scholarship on Africa and Latin America within a larger intellectual upheaval. The essay argues that commonplace descriptions of a fragmentation that destroys larger meaning and coherence are in many respects misplaced, since they sidestep the intellectual reverberations that yielded meaningful encounters between history and theory, between particular research inquiry and larger paradigm, across apparently specialized and fragmented fields of knowledge. This essay argues further that such reverberation has been particularly strong in the African and Latin American fields, that it has yielded ongoing confrontations with major paradigms of world history, and that the fruits of this confrontation are evident in the essays of this book. In short, an ongoing process of "Third World" encounters with paradigm defines the agenda and context of this book.

The Splintering of Historical Knowledge

The turbulence in scholarship emerged in relation to a larger turbulence in politics and society. In the United States, the great expansion of the university system after World War II coincided, by the late 1960s and early 1970s, with a sense of upheaval that included both the domestic and international arenas. (The expansion of the university system, more modest in the phase of reentry of veterans into civilian life, received a special impulse from the baby-boom effect—by the 1960s, the "babies" were becoming college students.) The civil rights movement and racial violence, the rediscovery of poverty and the war mounted against it, and the beginnings of a reborn feminism and women's movement—all stirred rethinkings of U.S. history and society, all provoked intellectual ferment and political strife on as well as off college campuses. The ferment was not simply insular. The wave of decolonization and independence movements in Africa, the racial violence in South Africa, the Cuban Revolution's open defiance of U.S. power, the political polarization and violence that swept over Latin America, and most of all, the political agony and social movements that accompanied U.S. prosecution of an intractable war in Vietnam—all stirred rethinkings of world history, particularly the U.S. version of Cold War thought and leadership, and provoked additional intellectual ferment and political strife.

In many respects, of course, the intellectual and political ferment was a world phenomenon. The world regions that came to be called the Third World experienced a dramatic period of social awakening and upheaval after World War II, and the phenomenon drew attention in Europe as well as the United States. By the 1950s and early 1960s, anticolonial movements in Africa (not to mention South Asia, Southeast Asia, and the Middle East) directly implicated the British and the French, and the Algerian question had mired the French in a European version of imperial agony. In the 1960s and early 1970s, the battlegrounds between revolution, reform, and military-conservative alliance in Latin America drew world attention. The Cuban missile crisis of 1962 had warned that Latin America's drama unfolded against the backdrop of a Cold War framework that potentially endangered everyone. And Chile's struggles along the electoral road to socialism (1970–1973) seemed to encode an almost irresistible symbolism: the blending of a Western-style electoral political culture, socialist ideals and economic policies, internal polarization, and unremitting U.S. hostility exploded in a gruesome nightmare that seemed to sum up the difficulties of peaceful transformation in Third World contexts. By the late 1960s, the U.S. intervention in Vietnam provoked tremendous controversy in Europe as well as the United States. Given the dangers posed by a Cold War framework in a nuclear age, the evident frustration of U.S. expectations and control in the region, and the historical background of European colonialism in Southeast Asia, the drama of unending human suffering and destruction drew a world audience. And it could not help but deepen the sense that more endogenous approaches to history and society in the Third World might lead to more intelligent policies from the West. Finally, given the travel of news across the Third World, and the sense that many regions wrestled with the common problem of constructing a more sovereign political and economic destiny out of a colonial or neocolonial legacy, the example of social movements and interventions in one region provoked interest and debate in another. In short, intellectual ferment was dramatically evident beyond as well as within the United States. At times, the international stage of crisis and upheaval seemed almost eerily coordinated: student riots and political violence shook Mexico City and Paris as well as Chicago in 1968.

The international scale of the intellectual storms made the United States less than unique, but it did not make the U.S. version of rethinking any less vast or consequential. The United States had built a huge and expanding university system committed to a relatively inclusionary pattern of student recruitment into higher education. Its marketplace for serious books was probably the largest in the world, and sustained a large and diverse scholarly book industry. And its version of upheaval had come upon the heels of an earlier Cold War moment when benign—and even triumphant—interpretations of the United States as domestic society, world power, and world example had been fairly commonplace. To be sure, a good deal of the historical scholarship of the early Cold War period was sophisticated and complex; only some of it directly engaged the "master ideas" that supplied an overarching historical framework, and some excellent works explored the detours, roadblocks, paradoxes, and ironies that surrounded the main story. But the master ideas that defined an overall framework and the scholarly mainstream—the story lines of synthetic interpretations and textbooks—ranged from the benign to the celebratory.[2] In this vision, the domestic history of the United States had been one of unfolding freedom and remarkable consensus anchored in traditions of pragmatism and liberal political thought. Given its history of prosperity, freedom, and liberal consensus, the United States was an exceptional society, a world example to be admired, envied, or emulated. Its history was one of particularly good fortune or achievement. Its flaws (most notably, those connected to race) were anomalies and tragedies susceptible to correction, on the fringes of the main experience, certainly not so embedded in the core trajectory that they constituted the tragic flaws of Greek drama, or a basis for social indictment. Finally, the history of the United States as a world power was marked by pronounced tendencies toward isolationism, and by an eventual turn toward world involvement inspired by a blend of high ideals and a pragmatic sense of responsibility. Under the circumstances, it would have been surprising—a monument to academic segregation from society—if the upheavals in politics and society had not yielded a vast outpouring of "new" forms of historical scholarship and interpretation.

Of course, the history of intellectual contention did not all begin with a Big Bang in the 1960s. Debate on the purpose, foundations, and pertinent topics of historical knowledge preceded the 1960s and 1970s. We may find distinct approaches to history in Herodotus and Thucydides as well as more contemporary times. If one focuses on the professional practice of history outside the United States, moreover, one finds major movements that redefined the foundations of historical knowledge well before the 1960s. The development of Annales history is the most well-known European example. Even in the historical profession in the United States, debate long anteceded the 1960s and 1970s. As Peter Novick demonstrates in his splendid study (1988), a debate between historical objectivists and historical relativists cast doubt on the objectivist ideal, the "noble dream" once at the heart of professional historical scholarship, early in the twentieth century. Even in its more homogeneous and chummier incarnations, the historical profession had its dissenters and mavericks. As long as the dissenters could be categorized by critics as offbeat but brilliant, or offbeat and pernicious, and as long as their scholarship did not seem to converge with social upheaval and near civil war within the social worlds of academic life, they did not necessarily undermine the sense of a reasonably coherent, civil, and centered community.

Yet although it misreads the past to attribute unity of epistemology, interpretations, and choice of topics to the historians of earlier eras, it also misreads the past to reduce the recent sea change to one more episode of life within the club of History. The contention went beyond the criticism of elders by youths as the latter were selectively incorporated into the professional club. And it went beyond a language of polite debate where shared knowledge and common commitments to reason, civility, and significance still seemed to provide a unifying core. The scale and depth of contention and change shifted drastically in the 1960s and 1970s, and the influence of the innovations did not abate in the 1980s. This has certainly been the case in the production and consumption of professional historical knowledge in the United States.

The rupture occurred on several planes at once. On one level, it marked a new phase in the debate between historical objectivists and relativists, a final placement of the objectivist paradigm on the defensive. Historians could no longer count on wide foundations of assent among their peers if they viewed historical knowledge as the search for an objective past untainted by the historian's personal values, perspectival position, and theoretical orientation. Too many peers, too many leading historians, would respond that values, perspective, and theoretical foundation played major roles in defining pertinent historical topics and questions in the first place, and that they also helped define the array of analytical methods and insights one might fruitfully bring to the study of history and evidence.

On another level, the rupture marked a self-conscious revolt against the narrow substantive boundaries of traditional historiography. The social history movement broke with the elitism of a history focused largely on formal political life and on the men who wielded large influence over public life. It resonated strongly with the social and political movements discussed earlier. Historians could no longer assume that a community of scholars defined the pertinent more or less as the history of the powerful and the influential, or as the history of high politics and high ideas. An enormous expansion of topics and, indeed, a redefinition of research priorities, contended with earlier definitions of significance. A good deal of the substance of research asked how historical knowledge and grand paradigms shifted if one redirected the focus of inquiry to commoners rather than elites, everyday life rather than high politics, blacks rather than whites, women rather than men, the non-Western rather than the Western, and the like. Conceptually, and sometimes substantively, the new focus went beyond this. It encouraged a rethinking of grand interpretation based on the *relationships* between the formerly excluded, shadowy, or marginalized subjects of history, and the wielders of social privilege and power. To proponents, the shifts toward social history, toward interdisciplinary and theoretical self-consciousness, toward critiques of power, represented an enrichment and a potential corrective to historiography, an opportunity to reconsider and sometimes drastically alter grand paradigms and interpretations. To detractors and skeptics, the shifts represented a splintering of an earlier unity of purpose, an assault on common standards of pertinence and evaluation. By the 1980s, intellectually and politically conservative historians announced that caprice had displaced reason and objectivity, themes of lesser importance had displaced the truly significant.[3]

On yet a third level, the rupture since the late 1960s and early 1970s corresponded to a shift in quantitative scale. In an earlier era, scholarly output was sufficiently "manageable" to make less illusory the goal of a diligent scholar or graduate student to read almost all the significant published works (at least the English-language works) concerning a broad era within U.S. or European history, and to sample a good deal of the important work in fields beyond one's expertise. Debates seemed to occur, in this sense, within a community of knowing participants. By the 1980s, the sheer scale of output destroyed such illusions. Debates, when they moved beyond narrowly bounded subcommunities of specialists, might resemble "dialogues of the deaf," conversations among participants who could no longer count on sharing a common corpus of historical work and thinking—let alone similar epistemologies and theoretical inspirations.

By the 1980s, these shifts had yielded a certain "splintering" of historical knowledge. One might summarize—and simplify—the process as one of contentious transitions from epistemological objectivism to relativism, from unity of focus to competition among foci, from narrowness of historical vision to a broadening field of historical visions, from a communal to an industrial scale of published production.[4] The turn toward debate among historians on language itself—particularly the postmodern sensibilities that view language and signification as forms of power and that questioned the "fixity" or unity of meaning in texts—was perhaps the *coup de grace*. Epistemology, focus, scale, and language all seemed to have moved in concert to splinter the foundations of historical knowledge. Earlier frameworks—paradigms as epistemological foundation for all historical inquiry, and as grand historical models or interpretations that framed the significance of particular inquiries—no longer commanded paradigmatic prestige. The fragmentation that had marred or threatened the community of history in earlier times had finally broken loose and run rampant. Novick's superb study of the historical profession in the United States concludes with a nearly overpowering sense of fragmentation:

As a broad community of discourse, as a community of scholars united by common aims, common standards, and common purposes, the discipline of history had ceased to exist. Convergence on anything, let alone a subject as highly charged as "the objectivity question," was out of the question. (1988:628)

Novick saw in the historical profession the Israel that closed the Book of Judges: "there was no king in Israel; every man did that which was right in his own eyes."

The sense of fragmentation, a splintering of focus, interest, and substantive specialization that precluded community, intellectual coherence, and conversation across fields, struck many historians. John Higham constructed an arresting image. Historians of the United States and Europeanists, he wrote, dwelled in a house of history whose "inhabitants are leaning out of many open windows gaily chattering with the neighbors while the doors between the rooms stay closed." (1985:112).[5] Although Higham intended the image as a metaphor for the intellectual relationship between historians of the United States and their Europeanist colleagues, many historians would have given it a more universal application. The image of cheerful intellectual chaos captured the apparent breakdown of meaningful intellectual relations among historians of specialized fields and perspectival positions, within U.S. history and within European history as well as between the two. The growing corpus of historical research on "non-Western" history, particularly Latin American and African history, only added to the sense of intellectual splintering and solitude.

The picture of extreme fragmentation is not so much "wrong" as overstated and misleading. To be sure, the issues of epistemology, focus, scale, and language discussed above did converge to yield a sea change in the U.S. version of the historical profession, did yield more politically self-conscious and charged debate, and did contribute to a splintering of historical knowledge. These changes were on the whole salutary: a more unified sense of intellectual community often implied a certain narrowness, an agenda of significance and truth ratified by the dominant leaders of a socially rather homogeneous club of scholars. But the splintering also exacted a certain cost: the specialist-practitioners of a more enriched and diversified history might in their own way prove equally narrow. They could choose to ignore the strangers in other camps, could evade an encounter with larger paradigms and patterns of historiography that framed the meaning and method of specialized research. This kind of retreat into balkanized intellectual life, a conversion of the difficulty of expertise across fields into a near-virtue, did occur to some extent.

Yet it goes too far to lament decline into intellectual chaos, a narrowness and specialization emptied of patterned dialogue between historical camps, and with larger paradigms.[6] For not only does the discourse of declension idealize the health and vision of an earlier "community" of historical scholarship, it also ignores important counterpoints to the fragmentation effect. Alongside the process of fragmentation there also developed a process of "reverberation"— conversations within and across specialized fields and across disciplines; imperfect trackings of historiographical shift and debate; echoes of the tussles with paradigm, method, theory, and grand interpretation in other camps. Much of the "new" scholarship of the 1960s and 1970s self-consciously wrestled with "traditional" paradigms of historical research and interpretation. The sense of antagonism not only implied "debate," both latent and explicit, with more "traditional" schools of historical knowledge and interpretation. It also implied an effort to construct distinct paradigms or "frames" within which more narrowly focused research studies found (and contributed) their larger meaning. And it promoted the circulation of ideas and debates, books and journals, across the boundaries of the particular camps in which they originated. Reverberation, an important process of intellectual network and conversation, debate and echo, travel and refraction, does not quite fit the bipolar scheme of unified community versus fragmented tribalism. It mediated, however imperfectly, the specialized balkanization that is the bane of virtually all fields of contemporary knowledge. It allowed for convergences within a context of difference.

Reverberation: African and Latin American Contexts

Particularly in the development of historical scholarship of once marginal fields such as African and Latin American history, intellectual insularity made little practical sense. The graduate students of thinly staffed "peripheral" fields of history could scarcely avoid—whatever their personal inclinations—engagement with other fields. The historians who sought an enhanced institutional citizenship for African and Latin American scholarship could scarcely ignore the language of historical knowledge and persuasion in other fields. The scholar of Africa or Latin America could not help but notice the stereotyped background paradigms of backwardness and enlightenment, tradition and modernization, political innocence and vulnerability to Communism that suffused Western understandings of "tropical" peoples. (The *tropical* label is also a stereotype.) For better or worse, historians of Africa and Latin America would have to wrestle with and against these paradigms and do so in languages intelligible to Western historians and intellectuals. Obvious diaspora and migration effects, moreover, destroyed neatly bounded units of specialized interest. How easily could a historian of slavery or peoples of African descent in Latin America, for example, evince a disinterest in scholarship on the Caribbean, the United States, or West Africa? How easily could a historian of Africa evince a disinterest in the broad history of Islam, imperial Europe, or the international slave trades?

Finally, the historical field researcher could scarcely escape the necessity of intellectual dialogue and travel as a way of life. To contemplate historical research on Africa or Latin America without engaging issues of anthropology and social science, language and literature, and "native" worlds of knowledge and scholarship committed the historian to an obvious shallowness.

In short, the art of dialogue across fragmented intellectual boundaries, and a wrestling with theory and paradigm as they had been developed in the West, were preconditions of serious historical research. To recast Higham's image of the house of historian-strangers, for historians of Africa and Latin America, the neighbors in the street included anthropologists and their informants, economists and sociologists, writers of literature and cultural criticism, intellectuals and peoples of Africa and Latin America. The chatter while leaning out the windows was prelude to long ventures out into the street, recollections of ventures past. Within the house of history, moreover, the Africanists and Latin Americanists often unlocked their doors, visited the dwellers of other rooms, or passed the night talking in the kitchen. The art of dialogue and visitation across bounded fragments is so deeply embedded that the boundaries themselves sometimes crumble. This is a book about historical knowledge, but one of its authors (Roseberry) is an anthropologist, and all the authors move well beyond the disciplinary boundary of history in their patterns of citation and analysis.

Reverberation across disciplines and across fields of historical specialization, confrontation with theory and with paradigm, encouraged convergences of theme and interpretation within a massive outpouring of specialized literatures. In an age of scholarly specialization and of lament by conservative scholars that the ascent of peripheral themes and perspectival position has destroyed larger meaning and rigorous evaluation, it is especially important and striking to consider the counterpoints: the resonance and convergence effects that relieved fragmentation; the challenges to intellectually (and sometimes politically) conservative paradigms that framed and supplied larger meaning to a good deal of specialized research; the recasting of major issues in world history by specialists on Africa and Latin America. Collectively, the essays here do not deny important differences of history and historiography within and between African and Latin American fields of historical inquiry; these differences will become apparent during the course of this book. The essays *do* argue that, nonetheless, one may detect important convergences of theme, interpretation, and confrontation with paradigm in three fundamental and interrelated arenas: the historical construction and impact of the capitalist world system; the contentious organization of and struggles over labor, in grand design and in everyday life; the problem of peasantries, or more specifically, the integration of politics and consciousness into understandings of peasants as agents in history.

The attention and importance accorded these three themes is difficult to understand except in relation to the paradigms of conservative-to-moderate institutional reform that provoked disillusion and dissent. (The "moderate-to-conservative" political coloration emerged out of a process of "Third World" debates and social movements. Within "First World" political contexts, the same intellectuals and paradigms might seem "liberal.") We have already noted the background assumptions of backwardness and enlightenment, tradition and modernization, political innocence and vulnerability to external manipulation that have suffused Western understandings of Africans and Latin Americans. The more explicitly elaborated conceptual frameworks revolved around the idea of "development." What explained the poverty of Africa and Latin America, compared to the standard of living in the advanced Western countries? What explained the political and social upheavals that seemed to convulse the non-European world? How realistically might Africa or Latin America aspire to the levels of economic prosperity, national sovereignty, and political democracy of the West? The metaphor of development, understood as a condition of the advanced West to which Africans and Latin Americans aspired, captured the contrast implicit in such questions. To this day, the "development question" draws wide attention—among both "Third World" and "First World" intellectuals, policymakers, and citizens, across sharply divergent political movements and philosophies—precisely because development seems to encode so many of the crucial questions and aspirations in the Third World. (The familiar acronym *LDCs* refers to the world's "less developed countries.")

Essentially, the conservative-to-moderate paradigms approached the riddle of development by arguing for a modeling of Africa and Latin America that would allow these world regions a belated duplication of the Western experience. (Ironically, orthodox Marxist visions that saw in the expansion of world capitalism a progressive dissolution of "feudalism" and backward modes of production were in many respects compatible with these approaches.) The key themes in this approach were modernization, economic take-offs, and nation-

building. The "traditional" values associated with archaic agrarian classes—
landlords and peasants—would give way to a "modernization" of values associated with the social mobilization and expectations induced by expanding
cities, middle-class and professional sectors, and rural-to-urban migration and
cultural linkage. The ideal of stasis, the reproduction of customary right and
status, would give way before a revolution of rising expectations and maximizing behaviors. The neoclassic modeling of economic behavior that described
the logic of incentive, disincentive, and growth in the advanced West could also
describe the logic of economic backwardness and felicitous take-off in non-
Western regions. Countries that adopted the appropriate policies would benefit
accordingly. These cultural and economic transformations would allow, too,
for more effective and institutionalized nation-building in the colonized territories and newly independent nations of Africa, and in the unstable and less than
fully sovereign polities of Latin America. These transitions might be politically turbulent, even explosive, in view of the "traditionalism" of landowning
oligarchs, the historically "late" character of transition, and the vulnerability
of peasants, urban masses, and intelligentsias to external manipulation by radicals and Communists. But the paradigms of parallel development—social and
cultural modernization, economic take-off, institutional nation-building—suggested a process with a felicitous outcome, the reforms necessary to achieve
it, and the idea that wise understanding and management of the process could
fend off the worst social convulsions.[7]

The souring of these paradigms directed enormous attention to the study
of capitalism as a world system and to the history of labor and peasantries.
We have already noted the political and intellectual upheavals that shook the
West out of a stance of indifference. The paradigms of a parallel development
assisted by the West, a process of maturation well evoked in the word *modernization,* had gained urgency and attention precisely because turbulence and
revolution in the non-Western world rendered them problematic. In this sense,
the paradigms of assisted parallel development had had an embattled birth,
a politicized aspect from the start. Nor was the political dimension of such
paradigms purely academic. The paradigms of assisted parallel development
provided intellectual justifications for policy initiatives such as the Alliance for
Progress; they drew social scientists into state institutions, consulting projects,
and policy making; and they eventually entangled intellectuals in controversy
over policy-related roles in the Vietnam war and the Third World more generally. From this perspective, the paradigms of assisted parallel development
were neither benign nor neutral. From the beginning, they "dialogued" with
the nationalism evident in Africa and Latin America, with the transformation of Latin America into a battlefield among revolutionaries, reformers, and
counterrevolutionaries, with the Cold War challenge presented by revolutions
in China, Algeria, Cuba, and Vietnam, and with the forging of oppositional

and anti-imperial world views by "native" intelligensias. As dialogue heated into debate, scholars who took a more critical stance toward paradigms of assisted parallel development began to redefine the terms of inquiry and debate. They focused attention on capitalism as a system of world scale whose "underdevelopment" of colonial and neocolonial regions belied parallel development and neoclassic economic modeling. They explored the coercive and impoverished regimes of labor and material life that seemed at odds with more benign visions of modernization, social mobilization, and nation-building, and that seemed a product of historical pacts among imperial authorities, international and local entrepreneurs, and "native" agents and oligarchs. They turned also to intensive study of peasantries as peoples whose local ways of life and subsistence had been undone by the expansion of world capitalism and colonial empire, and whose transformation into political rebels fueled social revolutions that defied Western control and visions of history.[8]

In short, a cycle of debate had begun. It encompassed historians as well as social scientists, and it defined a new agenda of important topics. As we shall see, the new schemes did not "stand still." Paradigms that won approval and set a framework of inquiry in 1968 provoked too much research and debate to retain their luster in 1988.

A Cycle of Debate and Critique

The capitalist world system, labor relations, peasantries— we need not preview in detail the specific arguments on these themes that the essays in this book shall develop. Nor need we deny a certain porousness of boundaries between these arenas of research and analysis. And finally, we need not pretend that these themes constitute an exhaustive list of fruitful reverberations in the African and Latin American fields. Indeed, the concluding essay of this book points toward a more pluralized view of reverberations, including a future cycle focused on distinct themes and more directly engaged with debate over postmodernism.

Suffice it to state, for the moment, that in each of these fundamental arenas of world history, work on Africa and Latin America has challenged prevailing wisdoms, has fostered innovative "Third World" encounters of history, theory, and paradigm. The initial breaks with traditional and often conservative paradigms that erupted in the 1960s, the early efforts to develop distinct frameworks of analysis and method, the torrent of research questions and projects that flowed out of these initial ruptures and debates, the movement toward a new recasting, by the mid-to-late 1980s, founded on a generation of new research and critical of both the "traditional" paradigms and their early replacements: this process constituted a "cycle" of reverberation.

The essays in this book identify and contribute to a recasting of prevailing wisdoms that took cognizance of and built upon, yet moved beyond, the initial confrontations with paradigm in the 1960s and 1970s. On the questions of the capitalist world system and, more generally, the impact of colonialism and imperialism on economic life in the so-called Third World, the new literature acknowledged vastly unequal power within a political economy of world scale. Yet the literature has nonetheless come around to questioning the degree of explanatory dominance and theoretical unity to be assigned to the capitalist world system. The literature has pointed to more profoundly dynamic encounters and confrontations between "core" and "periphery," an endogenous underside to world-system analysis with far-reaching implications for understanding patterns of everyday life and political economy. On the question of labor, the new literature has acknowledged the grand designs dictated by imperial rule, market logic, and resident wielders of power; the ways design and practice "assigned" African and Latin American peoples to coercive categories of labor distinctive from those presumed to prevail in the more advanced North Atlantic nations; and the violation this patterning presents to views of labor history that see Europe and the West as carriers of linear progress and sequence, a transition from "coerced" to "free" labor. Yet the literature has also come around to a confrontation with the enormous heterogeneity of labor relations in the everyday life and practice of colonial and neocolonial areas; the pervasive and sometimes profound breaches with grand design and optimal exploitation; and the connections between the historical evolution and patterning of this heterogeneity, and processes of social conflict and contentiousness within the "periphery." On the question of peasants, the new literature has acknowledged the structural and economic disadvantages that have tended to silence peasant participation in politics beyond moments of outright rebellion and beyond immediate locales. Yet the literature has also come around to questioning the mechanicism that views peasants as fundamentally atomized in their politics and social existence (the "sack of potatoes" metaphor Marx applied to French peasants), and predictably parochial in their ideological outlook (the notion that peasants mainly seek land and withdrawal into their "little worlds," or that they are bound by some irreducible moral economy). The literature now underscores the necessity of integrating searching analyses of peasant economic strategies and labor processes within much more dynamic, flexible, and open-ended visions of peasant politics, social networks, and culture. The new visions of the capitalist world system, labor, and peasantries challenge the specific wisdoms that prevailed on these three topics. They also lend an air of unreality and sheer ignorance to the background assumptions of backwardness and enlightenment, tradition and modernization, and political innocence and vulnerability to manipulation that still serve as epistemological points of departure in the bulk of Western discourse on Africa and Latin America.

Confrontations with Paradigm in Historicized Perspective

The essays in this book have three fundamental purposes. First, they synthesize, order, and evaluate the significance of the enormous resonating literatures that have come to exist, for Africa and Latin America, on the themes of the capitalist world system, labor, and peasantries. No essay or set of essays can pretend to offer an "exhaustive" synthesis, given the explosion of scale in scholarly production discussed earlier. But the essays do offer broad visions of pattern and trend, synthetic critical reflections that build upon the reverberations that have informed more specialized research.

Second, the essays take up the problem of historical paradigm in the "doubled" context defined by a full cycle of reverberation in scholarship on Africa and Latin America. On one level, the essays provide a historical review and contextualization of the critical confrontations with politically and intellectually stifling paradigms that erupted in the 1960s and 1970s. This set of confrontations marked the beginnings of a cycle. It inspired an outpouring of scholarship critical of stale frameworks, experimental in the search for theoretical and interpretive alternatives, eager to fashion and deliver on a new agenda of research questions. On another level, the essays offer their own critical confrontations with the dissident paradigms that had captured the intellectual and political imagination in the 1960s and 1970s yet unraveled in many respects by the 1980s. The unraveling effect has been inspired not by retreat to the conservative assumptions of an earlier intellectual era, a simple rejection of the expansion of scholarly horizons that flowed out of a dissident "moment." The new sensibilities emerged, rather, in an unfolding process of research and debate in some ways traceable to the earlier "moment," and in some ways an expansion beyond it. By the mid-to-late 1980s, a quarter-century of social history research seemed to demonstrate that an earlier version of "new paradigms" had not captured well the full significances of human agency and struggles within Africa and Latin America. At the same time, the turn toward gender as a fundamental category of historical knowledge, and toward more "deconstructed" views of culture, discourse, and power, created an intellectual environment more deeply skeptical of all totalizing theories and paradigms.

This "doubled" encounter with the problem of paradigm, then, constitutes a second objective of the essays in this book. Together and individually, the essays place in context an earlier confrontation with historical paradigms that turned out to constitute a "foundational moment," or turning point. They make use of the unravelings and advances, themselves a partial consequence of the earlier moment of critique, to delineate the contours of a new critical confrontation with paradigms, in this instance the paradigms of early critique. And they suggest outlines of new interpretive frameworks in the study of the capitalist world system, labor relations, and peasantries in Africa and Latin America that incorporate the entire cycle of critique and research advance and unraveling.

The third purpose of this book is to historicize intellectual reverberations to the point where it becomes possible to imagine a new cycle of reverberation. In juxtaposing synthetic essays on Africa and Latin America, we seek not only to highlight the reverberations that have taken place, but to amplify them. Soft and sometimes muffled echoes become a more pressing roar, the apparent free flow of shout and response becomes a more self-conscious awareness of pattern and rhythm, antecedent and influence. One of the challenges implied by this more historicized awareness is that the growing influences of debates on postmodern approaches to culture and politics, the consolidation of gender as a fundamental category of historical knowledge, and the resurgence of ethnicity as an urgent topic of analysis are likely to spark a distinctive cycle of "Third World" confrontations with historical paradigm.[9] The beginnings of such a cycle were already evident in the 1980s, and remind us that the resonating research and debates on the capitalist world system, labor, and peasantries that constituted an important cycle of reverberations should not be taken as a closed and monopolistic circle of discussion—somehow timeless, its fundamental parameters and topics free of intellectual and political competition, change, and recasting in its own time, let alone across time.

The concluding essay of this book takes up the challenge of a more thoroughly historicized sensibility. It sets the cycle of reverberations that constituted the substantive heart of this book within the context of plurality: the plurality of the specific contexts and preoccupations that historical scholars of Africa and Latin America brought to a larger field of intellectual reverberation; the plurality implied by the emergence of distinctive networks of discussion, significant although less thickly developed, within the period when questions of capitalism, labor, and peasantries drew an enormous amount of attention. Equally important, the concluding essay asks us to imagine the possible outlines of a new cycle of major reverberations, anchored in somewhat different themes and questions. This new cycle will not "drop" the themes and debates of an earlier cycle—the issues of capitalism, labor, and peasantries will continue to demand both intellectual and political attention—but will promote dialogue between these themes and a differently flavored set of priorities and frameworks. The process of network and conversation, debate and echo, travel and refraction will yield critical and creative confrontations with the paradigms and assumptions of a "postmodern" intellectual era. And as with the problems of the world system, labor, and peasantries, the history and historians of the so-called periphery will challenge and reframe the core of the discussion.

Notes

1 The most comprehensive source (aside from personal knowledge and experience) for the characterizations of the U.S. historical profession that follow is Novick 1988. Novick's fine study is usefully complemented by historians' attempts at contemporary appraisal of specialized fields, their personal memoirs, and their debates on the trajectory of historical writing as a whole. For a sampling, see Kammen 1980; MARHO 1984; Himmelfarb 1987; *AHR* 1989; Wiener 1989; *JAH* 1989. For thoughtful commentary and critique of Novick's study, see Kloppenberg 1989; *AHR* 1991.

2 The "consensus historians" reacted against the "Progressive Historians" who had wielded great influence before World War II (see Novick 1988:332–48 for an intelligent overview). There were important differences, of course, among consensus historians. Among the three scholars identified by Novick as the most influential authors of sweeping consensus interpretations, I find Boorstin (1953, 1958) the crudest and most celebratory; Hartz (1955; cf. Hartz et al. 1964) the most cosmopolitan and even wistful; Hofstadter (1948, 1953) the crankiest and most inclined to pursue undersides of the main story.

3 See Himmelfarb 1987 (esp. 13–26, 47–49); Hamerow 1987 (esp. 201–2); cf. the comments of Himmelfarb and Hamerow in *AHR* 1989; Handlin 1979; Novick 1988:463–64, 607–11. It is wise to remember the broad context: the critiques by conservative historians resonated with a broader conservative attack on the alleged ills imposed by radicals, minority and women activists, and multiculturalism on higher education. The lament that fragmentation, declining standards, and caprice had displaced a more rigorous and centered intellectual and cultural life extended beyond the discipline of history (and, indeed, included national political figures such as William Bennett, who served the Reagan administration as secretary of education and as chair of the National Endowment for the Humanities). For a sampling of widely read books, see D'Souza 1991; Bloom 1987; Hirsch 1987 (the latter is by far the most thoughtful in the questions it raises). In D'Souza's work, the critique directly raises the subject of affirmative action in student recruitment. The unasked questions that render D'Souza's assumptions and reasoning dubious were examined in Dreyfuss and Lawrence 1979, a revealing history of the Bakke case, one of the earliest and most famous legal cases alleging reverse discrimination and declining standards.

4 It is important to remember that all such summaries exact a cost of some distortion. They at best describe shifts in tendencies and dominant patterns. Novick's book itself provides a good example. Although he traced the declining fortunes of an increasingly untenable epistemological objectivism, Novick also noted—accurately—that most historians rejected both "hyperobjectivism" and "hyperrelativism" (1988: see esp. 409–10, 415, 467, 611–12).

5 Higham's metaphor was drawn to my attention by Novick 1988:578. For evidence that Higham himself shared a sense that metaphors of a fragmentation and specialization run amuck might merit broader application, see *AHR* 1989:672 (comment by Lawrence W. Levine).

6 Here it is important to clarify that Novick did not state in his book that he considered
  the fragmentation lamentable. At most, one might say that a certain gloominess of
  tone about the issue introduced a countercurrent to an analysis sharply damaging to
  epistemological objectivism and at odds with golden-age nostalgia. What is especially revealing is that lament has been so commonplace that historians inferred it,
  in the absence of a declaration of lament, from Novick's description and gloomy
  tone. See, in this regard, the exchanges in *AHR* 1991: esp. 702.
7 The sources documenting discussions of "development," both the conservative-to-
  moderate language of modernization, institutional reform, and parallel development, and the more sharply anti-imperial critiques of colonialism, "dependency"
  and local oligarchy, are huge in number, and the chapters in this book provide detailed orientations to relevant bibliography. For a succinct sampler and intelligent
  overviews, see Klarén and Bossert 1986.
8 Again, the chapters in this book will provide detailed orientations to relevant bibliography. For a splendid and influential example of the work that merged the
  history of capitalism, local labor and material life, and peasantries into a sweeping critical vision of Third World history, see Wolf 1969; for further context, see
  Stern 1987:3–7. For an early account of the Alliance for Progress and its unraveling, see Levinson and de Onís 1970. A chilling account of the counterinsurgency
  underside that would outlive and overwhelm the original Alliance formulation is
  Langguth 1978.
      The involvement of intellectual specialists on Third World affairs and moderniza-
  tion in the design and implementation of social reform programs, the entanglement
  of this practice in the Vietnam counterinsurgency campaign, and the controversies
  provoked by the entanglement are well known to any informed intellectual who
  lived through the era. Controversy about the practice resurfaced in the 1980s in the
  heated political debates over U.S. policy and land-reform efforts in El Salvador. The
  persons under fire were not necessarily newcomers to such controversies: Roy L.
  Prosterman, a designer and defender of the land-reform program in El Salvador,
  had played a similar role in the Vietnam period. See Gettleman *et al.* 1987:163–87,
  esp. 166–68, 174–75, 186.
9 Florencia Mallon's essay (chapter 6) explores these issues in depth, and in specific
  relation to the writing of history from Third World perspectives. For a brief sampling of the new sensibilities and their general impact on historical analysis, see *AE*
  1989; Hunt 1989; Scott 1988; *Signs* 1991.

References

The following abbreviations are used: *AE* for *American Ethnologist*; *AHR* for *American
Historical Review*; *JAH* for *Journal of American History*; MARHO for Mid-Atlantic
Radical Historians Organization.

AE. 1989. "Tensions of Empire." (Thematic issue, Frederick Cooper and Ann L. Stoler,
    eds.) *American Ethnologist* 16 (Nov.).
AHR. 1989. "AHR Forum: The Old History and the New." (Commentary by Hamerow,

Himmelfarb, Levine, Scott, Toews.) *American Historical Review* 94 (June):654–98.

AHR. 1991. "AHR Forum: Peter Novick's *That Noble Dream*: The Objectivity Question and the Future of the Historical Profession." (Commentary by Hexter, Gordon, Hollinger, Megill, Novick, Ross.) *American Historical Review* 96 (June):675–708.

Bloom, Allan. 1987. *The Closing of the American Mind*. New York: Simon and Schuster.

Boorstin, Daniel J. 1953. *The Genius of American Politics*. Chicago: Univ. of Chicago Press.

Boorstin, Daniel J. 1958. *The Americans: The Colonial Experience*. New York: Random House.

Dreyfuss, Joel, and Charles Lawrence III. 1979. *The Bakke Case: The Politics of Inequality*. New York: Harcourt Brace Jovanovich.

D'Souza, Dinesh. 1991. *Illiberal Education: The Politics of Race and Sex on Campus*. New York: The Free Press.

Gettleman, Marvin E., et al., eds. 1987. *El Salvador: Central America in the New Cold War*. New York: Grove Press.

Hamerow, Theodore S. 1987. *Reflections on History and Historians*. Madison: Univ. of Wisconsin Press.

Handlin, Oscar. 1979. *Truth in History*. Cambridge, Mass.: Belknap Press.

Hartz, Louis. 1955. *The Liberal Tradition in America: An Interpretation of American Political Thought Since the Revolution*. New York: Harcourt, Brace.

Hartz, Louis, et al. 1964. *The Founding of New Societies*. New York: Harcourt, Brace, and World.

Higham, John. 1985. "Paleface and Redskin in American Historiography: A Comment." *Journal of Interdisciplinary History* 16 (Summer):111–16.

Himmelfarb, Gertrude. 1987. *The New History and the Old*. Cambridge, Mass.: Belknap Press.

Hirsch, E. D., Jr. 1987. *Cultural Literacy: What Every American Needs to Know*. Boston: Houghton Mifflin.

Hofstadter, Richard. 1948. *The American Political Tradition and the Men Who Made It*. New York: Vintage.

Hofstadter, Richard, 1955. *The Age of Reform: From Bryan to F.D.R.*. New York: Vintage.

Hunt, Lynn, ed. 1989. *The New Cultural History*. Berkeley and Los Angeles: Univ. of California Press.

JAH. 1989. "A Round Table: What Has Changed and Not Changed in American Historical Practice?" (Lead article by Wiener; commentary by Thelen, D'Emilio, Aptheker, Lerner, Lasch, Higham, Degler, Lewis; documentary appendix.) *Journal of American History* 76 (Sept.):393–488.

Kammen, Michael, ed. 1980. *The Past Before Us: Contemporary Historical Writing in the United States*. Ithaca: Cornell Univ. Press.

Klarén, Peter F., and Thomas J. Bossert, eds. 1986. *Promise of Development: Theories of Change in Latin America*. Boulder, Colo.: Westview Press.

Kloppenberg, James T. 1989. "Objectivity and Historicism: A Century of American Historical Writing." *American Historical Review* 94 (Oct.):1011–30.

Langguth, A. J. 1978. *Hidden Terrors*. New York: Pantheon.

Levinson, Jerome, and Juan de Onís. 1970. *The Alliance That Lost Its Way: A Critical Report on the Alliance for Progress*. Chicago: Quadrangle Books.

MARHO (Mid-Atlantic Radical Historians Organization). 1984. *Visions of History*. New York: Pantheon.

Novick, Peter. 1988. *That Noble Dream: The "Objectivity Question" and the American Historical Profession*. New York: Cambridge Univ. Press.

Scott, Joan Wallach. 1988. *Gender and the Politics of History*. New York: Columbia Univ. Press.

Signs. 1991. "Women, Family, State, and Economy in Africa." (Thematic issue, Bolanle Awe et al., eds.) *Signs* 16 (Summer).

Stern, Steve J. 1987. "New Approaches to the Study of Peasant Rebellion and Consciousness: Implications of the Andean Experience." In Stern, ed., *Resistance, Rebellion, and Consciousness in the Andean Peasant World, 18th to 20th Centuries*. Madison: Univ. of Wisconsin Press, pp. 3–25.

Wiener, Jonathan M. 1989. "Radical Historians and the Crisis in American History, 1959–1980." *Journal of American History* 76 (Sept.):399–434.

Wolf, Eric R. 1969. *Peasant Wars of the Twentieth Century*. New York: Harper & Row.

PART 1
Labor, Capitalism,
and the World System

2 *Steve J. Stern*

Feudalism, Capitalism, and the World-System in the Perspective of Latin America and the Caribbean

Feudalism, capitalism, the world-system—about this provocative trilogy Immanuel Wallerstein wrote a provocative book. In Volume 1 of *The Modern World-System*, published in 1974, Wallerstein argued that around the beginning of the sixteenth century Europe solved the crisis of feudalism by creating a capitalist world-economy. The new order was premised on three key elements: "an expansion of the geographical size of the world in question, the development of variegated methods of labor control for different products and different zones of the world-economy, and the creation of relatively strong state machineries in what would become the core-states of this capitalist world-economy" (38). Since, Wallerstein argued, the capitalist world-economy crossed the boundaries of various "politico-cultural" (xi) structures, the conventional unit of analysis (discrete politico-cultural structures) of historians and social scientists is mistaken. If the "world-system" as a whole exerted decisive influence on the social structures and major changes evident within the politico-cultural units it had incorporated, one could hardly gain deep insight by focusing on such units as discrete entities. For Wallerstein, "the unit of analysis is an economic entity, the one that is measured by the existence of an effective division of labor" (xi). And the division of labor created during the "long" sixteenth century (circa 1450–1640) studied by Wallerstein was laid out as follows: in the core-states of Western Europe, the rise of free wage labor (and self-employment) in agriculture, pastoral production, and industry; in the peripheries of Latin America and

Eastern Europe, the use of forced labor—either slavery or "coerced cash-crop labor" (91)—to produce bullion, sugar, and cereals; in the "semi-periphery" of Southern Europe, a necessary mediating region consisting of "former core areas turning in the direction of peripheral structures" (103), the prevalence of an intermediate labor relation, sharecropping.[1]

This complementary and interlocking structure of labor delivered to the states and privileged classes of the core the chief benefits of capital accumulation in the world-system as a whole. In Wallerstein's conception, the explanation of the distribution of particular types of production and labor relations across various regions derives from the needs of the core (or, more precisely, the capitalists and states of the core), and of the world-system as a whole:

Why different modes of organizing labor . . . at the same point in time within the world-economy? Because each mode of labor control is best suited for particular types of production. And why were these modes concentrated in different zones of the world-economy . . . ? Because the modes of labor control greatly affect the political system (in particular the strength of the state apparatus) and the possibilities for an indigenous bourgeoisie to thrive. The world-economy was based precisely on the assumption that there were in fact these three zones and that they did in fact have different modes of labor control. Were this not so, it would not have been possible to assure the kind of flow of the surplus which enabled the capitalist system to come into existence. (Wallerstein 1974: 87)

In volume 2, published in 1980, Wallerstein carried the story forward into the "long" seventeenth century (circa 1600–1750). A work fascinating in its discussion of Dutch industries and hegemony and in its innovative twist on the familiar comparison of capitalist development in Britain and France, volume 2 adds depth to Wallerstein's thesis and contributes many particular insights concerning cyclical trends and seventeenth-century developments. But it revises little of the grand paradigm sketched in volume 1, especially in its discussion of the periphery.[2] The greater Caribbean region, stretching from the southern colonies of British North America to the Northeast of Portuguese Brazil, becomes a "new" American periphery added to the "old" periphery of Spanish America. The specific discussion of events in the periphery devotes closer attention to local social conflicts, initiatives, and geography. Occasional exceptions to forced labor, as in the case of apparent wage labor in the Mexican silver mines, are noted and discussed. But the overall picture remains the same. Forced labor prevailed in the periphery (even in the Mexican mines, the mine-owners encumbered the laborers with coercive devices, including debt), and the explanation of economic and labor patterns derives either directly from the world-system or its core, or indirectly through the rational response of local American capitalists to the changing international market.[3]

The promise and limits of Wallerstein's world-system interpretation for Latin

American history and historiography constitute the central subject of this essay.[4] I will on occasion, however, refer also to the history of Caribbean slavery to round out the picture. The greater Caribbean region, after all, constituted both an important American periphery and a significant arena of Spanish colonization, and its social and economic experience with colonial slavery bears at least a family resemblance to patterns that emerged in Spanish and Portuguese America proper. Widely praised and widely criticized, Wallerstein's historical interpretation strikes an important chord among students of the so-called Third World, capitalism, and transitions to capitalism. Among scholars of early modern Europe, Wallerstein's work has stimulated discussions of high caliber.[5] Especially from students of the colonial era in Latin America, one might have expected that Wallerstein's reconceptualization of colonialism and mercantilism would have triggered a lengthy and significant debate. From the corner of Latin American history and social sciences, however, Wallerstein's provocation (in the best sense of the term) has seemed less than sharp. His is only one of several versions of the world-systems idea, and about this idea Latin Americans thought long and hard before the publication of *The Modern World-System*. In order both to understand the idiosyncrasy of Latin American responses to Wallerstein and to assess honestly the significance of his world-system for the history of Iberian America and its sister region the Caribbean, we must first move Wallerstein into a Latin American context. We must, in short, put on new spectacles and look at world history with peripheral vision.

The World-System Idea in Latin American Context

The history and mythology of the colonial period has long loomed large in the interpretation of contemporary Latin America. The feudal "diagnosis" of the colonial inheritance reaches back to the nineteenth century, although the nineteenth-century meaning of "feudalism" referred less to economic relationships than to political, social, and jural patterns (Chiaramante 1984: part 1, esp. 21–65). In the twentieth century, when analyses of the economic basis of society became more of a perceived priority, scholarly debate about the prevalence of feudalism or capitalism in colonial Latin America, and about the significance of the world economic system for any such assessment, began to assert itself as early as the 1940s. To be sure, the prevailing trend was to use feudalism or a feudal-like legacy to explain the distinctive features, particularly the agrarian question, that set Latin American societies apart from much of the modern West, especially the United States. José Carlos Mariátegui and Lesley B. Simpson in the 1920s; Luís Chávez Orozco, Gilberto Freyre, George McBride, Rodolfo Puiggrós, and Silvio Zavala in the 1930s and 1940s; Woodrow Borah, François Chevalier, and Jacques Lambert in the 1950s and 1960s—this is but a ruthlessly selective list of the prominent and otherwise diverse figures who invoked a feudal-like past to understand enduring features of Latin American life and history.[6] Important works by Richard Morse (1954, 1964), Octavio Paz (1950, rev. 1959), and Frank Tannenbaum (1946) on the Thomist political tradition of Spanish America and on the contrast between Protestant and Catholic civilizations in the Americas rarely addressed their questions in terms directly translatable into the interpretation of a colonial legacy of feudalism. Their rightly influential studies, however, proved by and large compatible with such a thesis and served indirectly to reinforce it by underscoring the persistence in Latin America of cultural traditions rooted in late medieval Europe.

Still, dissent about the place of feudalism, capitalism, and the world economic system in the interpretation of the colonial legacy appeared by the 1940s, and the dissenters were mainly resident Latin Americans. Sergio Bagú (1949), Jan Bazant (1950), Alexander Marchant (1942a), José Miranda (1941–46), and Caio Prado, Jr. (1942) all registered significant doubts about the prevailing wisdom. In their versions of colonial history, new elements drew the historian's spotlight and relegated to the shadows the traditional emphasis on aristocratic ethos and feudal involution. Description and explanation focused on the entrepreneurial drive and profit motive of the original colonizers, the evident force of mercantile exploitation as an engine structuring and restructuring economic life and social relations in Latin American hinterlands, the subordination of Iberian America to the role of provider of primary commodities and an economic surplus to the expanding world market of a Europe undergoing the rise of commercial capitalism.[7] In the Caribbean, this recasting of the colonial experience as the exploitative extension of capitalism to the New World had its analogue in the celebrated works of C. L. R. James (1938, rev. 1963) and Eric Williams (1944; cf. Ortíz 1940).[8]

These revisions of history, still very much a minority view, resonated with the broader political and intellectual environment. They constituted but one example of skeptical stirrings about the beneficence of economic relations and ideas promoted by the advanced capitalist (that is, industrialized) West. For Latin America, the beginnings of the historical critique of the feudal thesis roughly coincided with the beginnings of the social science critique of the comparative advantage theory of international trade, associated especially with the Comisión Económica para América Latina (CEPAL) and its executive secretary, the economist Raúl Prebisch.[9] As the 1950s and 1960s unfolded, several experiences—import-substitution industrialization, the cold war, the Cuban revolution, intensified political polarization—contributed to a context in which the initial dissents of the 1940s were taken up and debated extensively. The result was a complicated series of dialectics—between CEPAL-oriented intellectuals and policy makers and the mainstream West; between "moderate" Latin American advocates of development, influenced by the CEPAL idea and the promise of import-substitution, and their more "radical" Latin American critics and associates; among CEPAL-oriented colleagues, as part of a healthy process of self-evaluation; and between the orthodox left, inclined to see the necessity of a "bourgeois revolution" to transform a Latin America still encumbered by feudalism, and an innovative left, increasingly convinced that it was the historic spread of international capitalism, beginning in the Age of Discovery, that explained Latin America's poverty and apparently anachronistic economic structures.[10] These critical debates and dialogues culminated, in the 1960s, in what has come to be known loosely as "dependency theory"— full-scale critiques of neoclassical economics and modernization theory, and the construction of an alternative vision of Latin American history and reality emphasizing the external constraints and impositions of international capitalism.[11] Not surprisingly, revisionist historical and sociological studies appeared in the same period, accompanied by reprint editions of several of the landmark works of the 1940s. Their effect was to cut away at more benign views of society and historical tradition, and at the sense of disconnection between "traditional" patterns of life associated with the colonial-like countryside and more "modern" patterns associated with dynamic cities and capitalist enclaves.[12]

The literature explicating and criticizing various dependency perspectives is enormous and quickly spilled outside Latin America and the Caribbean to embrace Africa and social science theory in general.[13] For our purposes, three points stand out. First, two works written in the mid-1960s stood out as the leading theoretical and systematic efforts to construct a dependency perspective for Latin America. The coauthored book of Fernando Henrique Cardoso and Enzo Faletto on dependency and development (published in 1969, but circulated in mimeographs and oral form since the mid-1960s) and Andre Gunder Frank's study of capitalism and underdevelopment (1969a; first published in 1967) are the landmarks to which assessments of dependency perspectives inevitably return.[14] Second, the dependency idea was firmly ensconced in the historical scholarship regarding Latin America by the early 1970s. In 1969 and 1970 respectively, Tulio Halperín-Donghi and coauthors Stanley J. Stein and Barbara H. Stein published widely admired works of historical synthesis.[15] These works combined nuanced insight, deep immersion in empirical research on Latin America, and sympathetic engagement of dependency ideas. The stature of these books made it more difficult for serious historians to dismiss the dependency approach altogether as the work of radical social scientists caught up in a superficial projection of presentist theories onto the past. In the United States, whose historical profession is strongly anti-theoretical compared with those of Latin America, new college textbooks published in Latin American history reflected the continuing impact of the dependency idea.[16]

Third, despite the widespread "consumption" (Cardoso's word) of dependency perspectives in whole or in part, the dependency perspective generated very considerable debate, and this debate anticipated some of the issues arising from Wallerstein's later books. Andre Gunder Frank drew the most international and heated attention—perhaps because he published originally in English (he soon secured Spanish, Portuguese, French, and Italian translations), or because his analysis was crudely one-dimensional and unchanging compared to that of Cardoso and Faletto, or because he was Anglo rather than Latin American.[17] For Latin Americanists, Frank's thesis now appears as a kind of vulgar preview of Wallerstein's more well-researched and sophisticated work on the world-system. Frank stressed a chain of metropolis-satellite links that systematically transferred economic surpluses from the satellites (read: "periphery") to the metropoles (read: "core") and thereby caused the "underdevelopment" of the satellites. The metropolis-satellite polarization characterized relations not only between world areas (say, Western Europe and Iberian America) but also within world areas and regions, converting some metropoles (for example, Spain and Portugal vis-à-vis their colonies) into satellites (read: "semi-periphery") of more powerful metropoles (for example, the Netherlands and England). Frank's historical analysis demonstrated that the exploitative chain of the international commercial system had bound apparently "remote" and feudal-like regions of Latin America to capitalism long ago, in some regions as early as the sixteenth century. This binding had taken the form of export booms that drained Latin American regions of their wealth and left in their wake regional impoverishment and decline easily confused with feudalism. Frank contributed importantly, therefore, to demolishing the notion, prevalent in modernization theory, that Latin America was a region of "dual societies" divided between dynamic zones integrated into modern capitalism and backward zones languishing in feudal isolation. Capitalism, understood as profit-driven production of commodities for large-scale markets on unequal terms that benefited capitalists and metropoles, was the quintessential colonial legacy in precisely the impoverished regions considered "feudal" and "isolated" in the twentieth century.[18]

Scholars on the left, broadly defined, were the most disposed to confront seriously the issues and implications of dependency perspectives, and the critical assessment of Frank's work rekindled interest in the important Dobb-Sweezy debate in the 1950s on Europe's transition from feudalism to capitalism.[19] In that debate, Sweezy's critics argued that his stress on the expansion of commerce and profit making in late medieval Europe could not really account for the qualitative transformations of technique ("forces of production") and social relations ("relations of production") that gave the capitalist mode of production its distinctive historical character. Profit making and intense market activity that turned the purpose of production in wide territories toward exchange-value rather than use-value could be found in a variety of historical epochs and societies, including ancient Rome. What explained, at bottom, capitalism's unique and even revolutionary impact on economic life was its new method of organizing production on the basis of the free sale of labor-power to capitalists in exchange for a wage. Free wage labor was the relation of production that liberated entrepreneurship from the comparatively stifling restrictions of precapitalist societies. Free wage labor allowed for optimal and changing combinations of machinery and labor, a possibility that made feasible unparalleled technical experimentation and progress in production; it also encouraged the rise of mass markets for subsistence items purchased with wages, a development that expanded the scope of profitable market activity enormously. Marx's creative insight was to analyze the causes, mystifications, inner dynamics, and far-reaching consequences of this transformation of the production process. Sweezy's critics argued that, once one focused on the production rather than the circulation of commodities, the strategic issues requiring explanation shifted from the expansion of the profit motive and international commerce to the replacement of servile labor by proletarianized labor and the associated rise of home markets (that is, mass consumption of commodities). To explain the transition to capitalism therefore required close historical analysis of the social and class conflicts, expropriations of petty producers, and deterioration of subsistence strategies that underwrote the transition from servile to free labor.[20] A good deal of the Europeanists' recent debate on capitalist transition, particularly Robert Brenner's important essays (1976, 1977), follows in the tradition of the Dobb-Sweezy debate.[21]

Between Dobb and Brenner, however, came Ernesto Laclau (1971). Like Dobb, and like other critics of Andre Gunder Frank, Laclau invoked the classic Marxist emphasis on capitalism as a mode of production. To demonstrate the rise of commercial exploitation and a profit motive, as Frank had done for colonial Latin America, was insufficient to demonstrate that the Latin American economy had been "capitalist" since Cortés and Pizarro. It was obvious, observed Laclau, that mercantile exploitation used as its instrument the coercive labor relations and tributary obligations corresponding to the feudal mode of production. This was not a trivial point, since it greatly affected the explanation of Latin America's historic underdevelopment. In Laclau's scheme, underdevelopment derived not only from Europe's channeling of the colonies' economic surpluses from satellite to metropolis but also from its "fixing their relations of production in an archaic mould of extra-economic coercion, which retarded any process of social differentiation and diminished the size of their internal markets" (Laclau 1971:35). The first implication was that, in the absence of further transformations of production (transformations that could not derive simply from a process of commercialization), the feudal socioeconomic structure imposed by Europe's commercial exploitation of Latin America would have blocked capitalist development, even had Latin America retained a greater share of economic surplus. Further, material progress in twentieth-century Latin America did indeed require the breakup of the feudal socioeconomic structures that dominated many backward regions. Laclau held that Frank had confused the "mode of production" with the "economic system." It was perfectly possible, even likely, that an overarching economic system that was as a whole capitalist—that is, governed by the needs of a dominant capitalist mode of production and by the profit principle—could include several modes of production among its constituent "parts." Frank had demolished the "dual society" thesis of the modernization theorists by demonstrating that Latin America's "backward" regions had been inserted, on exploitative terms, into the world capitalist system, but this contribution hardly demonstrated that such regions were themselves capitalist.

Laclau's distinction between the economic system and its heterogeneous parts effectively undermined Frank's argument, but his assertion of the "feudal" character of the colonial economy has nonetheless remained debatable. The problem is that Latin America has so often seemed "in but not of" the capitalist economy of the North Atlantic world. In the colonial period especially, Latin America has seemed a confusing hybrid of premodern "feudal" and modern "capitalist" eras. Neither Frank nor Laclau is a historian, least of all a historian of colonial Latin America. For historians more immersed in colonial economic history and social relations, posing the choice as one between a "feudal" or "capitalist" economy may itself misconstrue the nature of the problem.

On the one hand, Latin America and the Caribbean supplied, through their colonial trades, taxation, and contraband, essential goods and economic surpluses to a European world-economy premised on the expansion of entrepreneurial profit and capital accumulation. Moreover, within Latin America, mercantile interests and the profit-investment principle constituted a powerful force reshaping urban and regional economies, restructuring the kinds and quantities of commodities produced and the technologies and social relations used to produce them. The rise of profit making and commodity production as a central principle of economic organization; the simultaneous deterioration and destruction of local subsistence economies; the impressive capital expenditures undertaken in the mines, sugar plantations, and other enterprises; and the growth of cities and mining regions, where there developed significant internal markets and relatively free forms of labor, including relations resembling wage labor—all seem to lend strength to the notion that, in the more dynamic colonial regions, the Latin American economy was never "feudal" but followed a "capitalist" logic, albeit one that reflected its special position as colony or periphery of the European world-economy.[22]

On the other hand, a long-term view of the social relations and technologies by which colonial production and social life were organized sees the rebirth on American soil of precapitalist or at least noncapitalist modes of production. Rotating labor drafts, slavery, and various forms of serfdom or peonage constituted strategic labor relations in Latin America's mines, plantations, textile workshops, and haciendas. Servile labor relations such as these resembled those of Europe before the transition to capitalism insofar as they rested on extra-economic compulsion rather than the free hiring of proletarianized laborers whose lack of subsistence drove them to sell their labor-power for a wage. In the long run, the mercantile exploitation of Latin America prevented neither the reconstitution of effective, though considerably impoverished, subsistence economies and strategies by Indian communities nor the use of "precapitalist" devices (tribute, rents, labor drafts, slavery, peonage) to extract a surplus from direct producers. Even the mining economies of eighteenth-century Mexico and Peru-Bolivia required for their profitability and expansion the reduction of relatively "free" laborers to more "bonded" status.[23] Eventually, colonial internal markets and technology stagnated. The transition to a capitalist mode of production during the late nineteenth and twentieth centuries was to require a struggle against subsistence rights that yielded land and labor arrangements more compatible with the imperatives of capitalist industry and production.[24] The long-term view, then, suggests that the colonial Latin American economy, though part of a European economic system in transition to capitalism, followed principles of economic evolution qualitatively distinct from those associated with a capitalist mode of production.

The economic patterns discussed here can lead to conceptual traps and sterile, circular debates. One can emphasize some features to find "capitalism," others to find "feudalism" (or "slavery," understood as a precapitalist mode of production). Neither characterization suffices. The dynamics of colonial labor relations, subsistence and markets, and technology were not only distinct from but in some senses antithetical to those of a capitalist mode of production. As conceptualized by Marx, a capitalist mode of production is based on the sale of labor-power for a wage, not primarily under political, social, or cultural coercion but out of economic necessity. Separated from the lands and resources needed to produce their subsistence or items that can be exchanged for subsistence goods, workers freely sell their labor-power to earn a living wage, and with their wages constitute an internal market for the sale of commodities produced in capitalist enterprises.[25] This is a phenomenon quite recognizable, despite some ambiguities and complications, by students of Latin America in the late nineteenth and twentieth centuries, but not in the colonial period. To call colonial Latin America "capitalist" thus obscures the tremendous discontinuity between the contemporary and the colonial economy, as well as the bitter traumas and conflicts associated with the transition to a capitalist mode of production in more recent times.

Yet the intensity of colonial mercantile exploitation and its associated disasters often tended to take on a destructive quality that partly proletarianized small producers and tended, also, to reduce laborers from human beings whose exploitation involved their masters in a many-sided relationship of unequal but mutual obligation to mere human repositories of labor-power used as short-term instruments of mercantile interest and bearing commodity value based on the exchange value of their exploitable labor. Slaves who were worked to death in booming tropical export sectors and drafted peasant laborers whose rotations at the mines pressed them to the limits of good health and physical endurance and virtually destroyed their customary subsistence rights serve as obvious examples. Thus to call colonial Latin America "feudal" or "seigneurial" or to equate Latin American or Caribbean slaveholding with earlier Old World slavery obscures both the intensity of mercantile exploitation inherent in the colonial system and the degree to which this very intensity led to labor relations, subsistence and market patterns, and technological developments with structure and dynamics qualitatively distinct from those of precapitalist Europe.[26]

To accept a simple choice between "feudalism" and "capitalism," then, is to walk into a conceptual trap. Laclau's brief discussion of feudal-like relations of production served, at a particular moment in an evolving debate, to expose Frank's defects. But it did not really solve the deeper conundrum posed by the interpretation of the colonial economy. In this sense, Wallerstein was right when he argued in 1974 that Laclau's was not the last word (1974:126–27). What is noteworthy, however, is the speed with which the Latin American literature moved beyond Laclau's initial statement. The 1960s and 1970s witnessed a boom in creative Marxian scholarship in Latin America.[27] Before *The Modern World-System* joined the fray, colonial studies had already yielded a series of sophisticated positions on feudalism, capitalism, and the world-economy.

We may discern four positions, each of which sought to escape the conceptual trap outlined above. One saw the original and paradoxical features of the colonial economy not as an "anomaly" to be explained away but as a basis for extending and enriching our inherited mode-of-production "categories." These scholars sought to develop theories of "colonial" and "colonial-slavery" modes of production that would complement the categories inherited from European history.[28] A second position, compatible with Laclau's theoretical stance, asserted the centrality of American "feudalism" but carefully delineated its particular features by stressing the specific historical context that joined colonial feudalism to international and local mercantile ventures, to capital accumulation, and to other modes of production. One version of this approach explored the colonial economy itself as a complex articulation of various modes of production, a unique "whole" combined of various "parts" in a specific historical context. The most successful example of this approach is Enrique Semo's (1973) pioneering interpretation of the colonial Mexican formation as a system that brought feudalism, "embryonic capitalism," and "tributary despotism" (the mode of production of indigenous communities subjected to a tributary relationship with the state) into dynamic and unequal coexistence.[29] A third position stood the inherited theoretical assumptions on their heads. This view held that to search for a dominant mode of production in colonial Latin America is misleading because the cornerstone of the colonial economy was precisely the dominance of commercial capital over production. In this line of analysis, the object of theoretically aware historical scholarship is to explore the ways commercial capital organized and exploited various relations of production, none of which served as the basis for a fully constituted mode of production in Latin America.[30]

Despite the discrepancies between these positions, they shared an important common denominator: each was quite critical of Frank's vision of colonial capitalism, and by 1974 each had advanced a theoretically sophisticated and carefully researched alternative that went well beyond the terms of Laclau's initial critique. Equally telling, perhaps, is that the pioneering works associated with these positions circulated widely in Latin America but not in English translation.[31]

A fourth position, almost certainly a minority view among Latin American intellectuals, asserted the "capitalist" character of the colonial economy, but here, too, the best works went beyond the terms staked out in the initial Frank-Laclau exchange. In 1973, for example, Angel Palerm (reprinted in 1980:65–88) argued vigorously that Spanish Mexico had constituted a "colonial segment" of the capitalist mode of production. His argument, however, relied not only on demonstrating colonial Mexico's adjustment to, and commercial exploitation by, the world capitalist economy but also on a closely reasoned and well-informed critique of Marxist theory.[32] Peter J. Bakewell's research on the silver mines of Zacatecas convinced him by 1971 of the "capitalist nature" of seventeenth-century New Spain, an economy that generally paralleled "contemporary European design" (1971:225). But he based this conclusion not on Mexico's commercial exploitation by the world-system, whose grip on Mexico had weakened in the seventeenth century, but on careful historical study of silver production in Mexico—its technology, labor relations, and capital investments—and its significance for the colonial Mexican economy as a whole.

It is against the backdrop of this debate that historians must gauge the significance, for Latin American history and historiography, of Wallerstein's historical publications on the modern world-system. Latin Americans had already expended great intellectual energy on their unequal participation in the world-system before the publication of volume 1 of *The Modern World-System* in 1974. The intensity of the debate, its fast development beyond the foundations laid by Frank and Laclau, the crystallization of relatively sophisticated theoretical positions by the early to mid-1970s, the tide of criticism that labeled Frank's thesis simpleminded and theoretically naive, all perhaps contribute to explaining "the surprisingly faint response"[33] to Wallerstein's volumes in the late 1970s and early 1980s. This is not to say that Wallerstein's important books went unnoticed, especially by U.S. scholars of Latin America and the Caribbean.[34] We may now be witnessing the delayed beginnings of a flurry of responses. But, for Latin Americans especially, the temptation to view Wallerstein as Andre Gunder Frank in more erudite garb must have been great. It was as if Wallerstein had appeared too late, after Latin Americans had staged their exhausting debate on the world-system and modes of production, after they had staked out innovative positions that handled reasonably well the paradoxes of colonial Latin America's idiosyncratic participation in the world capitalist system. And the idea of Latin America's historic dependence and manipulation by an external capitalist force, so much a part of life in Latin America, so current in the intellectual environment of the 1960s and 1970s, no longer constituted a revelation. To put it another way, the novelist Gabriel García Márquez need not have read Wallerstein to execute his brilliant portrayal of dependence in *El otoño del patriarca* (1975) (*Autumn of the Patriarch*, 1976): a Caribbean dictator, hounded by foreign creditors and the U.S. ambassador, finally succumbs to their pressure to export the Caribbean sea to Arizona, where the desalinated water will irrigate the desert! This magnificent moment of high humor and insight occurs in a work whose very language underscores the long-term continuity of subjection to plundering powers and capitalists. García Márquez interspersed the escapades of the twentieth century with passages lifted verbatim from the diaries of Christopher Columbus.[35]

The Challenge of Wallerstein's Interpretation

Nonetheless, it would be a mistake to avoid a serious evaluation of Wallerstein's work from the angle of Latin American history. To say that, in the historiographic and intellectual context of Latin America, the tendency to slight or dismiss Wallerstein *a priori* is understandable is not to say that it is advisable. For several reasons, Wallerstein's work merits a more systematic assessment. First, his impressive command of the historical literature, on Europe especially, makes his work far too rich and deep to be brushed off lightly. Wallerstein's awareness of historical complexity in the early modern "core" and "semiperiphery" surpasses that of most works adopting a dependency or world-system perspective.[36] Second, Wallerstein's is the most systematic and forceful argument that the proper unit of historical analysis since the sixteenth century is neither a state, nor a region, nor a people, but the European world-system as a whole. The challenge of this argument is not met by ignoring it. And the argument, if correct, has enormous implications for the ways historians conceptualize and practice historical research on Latin America.

Third, Wallerstein presented a direct and innovative response to the Frank-Laclau debate. His conceptualization of capitalism does not merely restate

Frank's position, and Wallerstein did not dispute the compatibility, up to a point, of feudalism and market activity. To Laclau's assertion that Latin America's servile relations of production corresponded to the feudal mode of production, Wallerstein responded that the total context surrounding particular relations of production exerts a decisive influence on their real dynamics and wider functions ("laws of motion," from the standpoint of Marxist theory). For this very reason, capitalism is best understood not as the replacement of coercive labor relations by free wage labor but rather as the rise of optimal *combinations* of free and coercive labor relations beneficial to the capitalist system as a whole. This is why, in Wallerstein's view, a vast qualitative difference distinguished the position of serfs in medieval Europe from that of sixteenth-century "serfs" subjected to feudal-like relations of production imposed by the capitalist world-economy. The reasoning behind Wallerstein's reply to Laclau is worth quoting at length:

The difference between the gleb serf of the Middle Ages and the slave or worker on an *encomienda* in sixteenth century Hispanic America, or a "serf" in [sixteenth-century] Poland, was threefold: the difference between assigning "part" of the surplus to a market and assigning "most of the surplus"; the difference between production for a local market and a world market; the difference between the exploiting classes spending the profits, and being motivated to maximize them and partially reinvest them . . . As for involvement in a capitalist world market accentuating feudalism, precisely so, but "feudalism" of this new variety.

The point is that the "relations of production" that define a system are the "relations of production" of the whole system, and the system at this point in time is the European world-economy. Free labor is indeed a defining feature of capitalism, but not free labor throughout the productive enterprises. Free labor is the form of labor control used for skilled work in core countries whereas coerced labor is used for less skilled work in peripheral areas. The combination thereof is the essence of capitalism. (1974: 126–27; cf. 1979: 8–17, 147–49)

It is for this very reason that Wallerstein considered "feudalism" a misleading concept in the sixteenth-century context and referred to servile labor under capitalism as "coerced cash-crop labor" (1974: 91). To equate Wallerstein and Frank sidesteps this argument.

Fourth, the Caribbean experience lends some historical support to Wallerstein's theoretical stance on units of analysis and capitalist combinations of free and coercive labor. The history of Caribbean plantation slavery complicates the distinction between noncapitalist modes of production founded on servile labor and a capitalist mode of production founded on free wage labor. In some extreme instances, the sugar plantation islands have seemed less like societies in their own right, whose material base rested on a noncapitalist mode of production "articulated" to the capitalist mode, than like outposts of Europe. Their absentee rulers lived and invested as an integrated part of the bourgeoisie in the metropolis, and their portfolio of investments included plantation enterprises that handled the slaves as finite repositories of labor-power to be replaced upon death or depletion by fresh African imports.[37] Under these circumstances, even Eugene D. Genovese (1969: part 1, esp. 16–17, 22–34), a scholar squarely aligned with Dobb and Laclau, equivocated.[38] One could write off the major sugar islands as an "extreme case" proving little. But extreme cases do sometimes expose otherwise hidden tendencies and relationships, and Genovese argues persuasively that the U.S. South is just as "extreme" an instance in the comparative history of American slavery.[39] To consider the Caribbean less theoretically or historically significant than the equally "extreme" U.S. South would be to make an ethnocentric assumption. Moreover, Brazil has shared more features with the Caribbean than meet the eye. In the sixteenth century, the sugar plantations were much like "islands" of commercial exploitation, narrow coastal strips of effective Portuguese control surrounded by the sea and by frontier territory. In the coffee belt of southern Brazil in the nineteenth century, the dynamic Paulista fraction of the slaveholding class acted much as Caribbean capitalists whose portfolios of real and prospective investments combined free and slave labor.[40]

Notwithstanding the prior debate in Latin America and its considerable sophistication, Wallerstein's version of the world-system idea demands serious and systematic appraisal from the perspective of Latin America and the Caribbean. For historians, critical evaluation requires that we compare case studies with the general scheme proposed in *The Modern World-System*. Yet to select a case study at random, regardless of significance, would contribute little to this process. Few will listen attentively to an exclamation such as, "After six years of careful study, my conclusion is definite: Wallerstein's model does not apply well to the case of sarsaparilla exports from Santa Rosa de la Frontera de la Oscuridad!" The closer our case studies come to the heart of the thesis, the more telling the critical evaluation. I propose that we focus on the silver mines and sugar plantations of early colonial America. These two case studies have several advantages. Silver from Spanish America and sugar from Portuguese Brazil and the Caribbean constituted the two most important exports provided by America to Europe during the long sixteenth and seventeenth centuries studied by Wallerstein. Not surprisingly, the silver and sugar sectors of Iberian America and the Caribbean also drew the most sustained and intense attention of metropolitan officials. In short, these case studies belong to the very core (if I may appropriate the term) of Wallerstein's vision of the world-system's operation in colonial Latin America and the Caribbean. If these case studies expose major problems in Wallerstein's interpretation, his entire paradigm is at risk. If, on the other hand, Wallerstein's world-system provides us genuine insights about the periphery, and core-periphery relations, these insights should become especially evident in a study of the world-system's highest American priorities.

Test Cases (I): Silver

The key questions concern description and explanation. On a descriptive level, does Wallerstein provide an adequate approximation, in the cases of silver and sugar, of the elements he himself considered essential to his argument? In other words, does the tripartite division of international labor—free labor in the core, sharecropping in the semiperiphery, and forced labor (slavery and "coerced cash-crop labor") in the periphery—succeed in describing the main features of the labor systems associated with silver and sugar production? On an explanatory level, does Wallerstein's method or reasoning account convincingly for the rise of patterns he himself considered strategic? In other words, are the main features of production, labor, and commerce in the silver and sugar sectors best explained by their functional value to the world-system, that is, as the result of optimal solutions imposed either by the world-system or by American capitalists responding to the dictates of the international market?

Let us begin with silver, the legendary American export during the long sixteenth century. The most important source of American silver during this period was Potosí, the great silver mountain on the arid Bolivian *altiplano* (see Garner 1988). Until recently, the conventional interpretation of labor in Potosí provided an almost classic illustration of Wallerstein's thesis. The earlier account runs along the following lines. Discovered for Spanish colonial purposes in 1545, Potosí first drew an anarchic rush of colonial entrepreneurs who tyrannized the Indians they reduced to slavery. As the initial plunder of rich ore sputtered in the 1560s, the colonial state moved to organize Potosí's more rational exploitation. Under the leadership of Viceroy Francisco de Toledo (1569–1581), the technology and relations of silver production changed dramatically. Enormous sums of capital financed the building of an infrastructure of lakes, dams, aqueducts, and refineries; mercury amalgamation replaced simple smelting techniques and allowed for large-scale refining of lower grade ore; and the infamous *mita* labor system, a rotating draft of Indian laborers, compelled some 13,000 peasants to work in the mines at a stipulated "wage" each year. The *mita* "wage" was so paltry, compared to the purchases and debits imposed on workers, that it represented a kind of legal fiction rather than a means of sustenance. In earlier historiography, this form of "forced paid labor" constituted the strategic labor relation, both because it provided the bulk of the labor force in the mines and because it established the cheap costs of production that underwrote Potosí's prosperity. The *mita* fixed conditions of work, productivity, and payment in a coercive mold that underpaid laborers, drew a subsidy from the peasant economy supporting drafted laborers, and maximized the surplus captured by silver producers and merchants. And the original design of technology and labor relations engineered in the 1570s held up well against the forces of erosion and secular decline. The *mita* was not abolished in Peru-Bolivia until 1812.[41] What better example could one find of a system that exploited "coerced cash-crop labor" in the periphery to serve the needs of the European world-economy?

Yet recent research corroborates only some parts of this earlier picture. The new work does not question the major investments and engineering ventures to revamp the technology of silver production in the 1570s, the inadequacy of the *mita* "wage" to support laborers, or the *mita's* economic role as a subsidy to silver production. But, on the question of labor, the conventional account breaks down.

A more subtle and well-researched history of Indian mine labor in Potosí is now available, and it recasts the *mita* labor relation into a role more modest and unintended. During Potosí's first century, three overlapping stages emerge in the history of mine labor. In a phase lasting until the early 1570s, what was remarkable was the dependence of European silver producers on conditions of work and technology defined largely by Indians. Indian mine laborers were either *yanaconas,* individual Indians who had cut or loosened ties with native ethnic-kin groups, or *encomienda* Indians, members of ethnic-kin groups "entrusted" by the Crown to particular Spanish colonizers (*encomenderos*). For the most part, the *yanaconas* floated independently from employer to employer and, in effect, leased rights to mine particular veins in exchange for providing a share of the ore to their employers. The *yanaconas* assumed responsibility for organizing, provisioning, and paying their own work parties. The *encomienda* Indians, theoretically a more subject group, in practice turned over the silver needed to pay tributes to their *encomenderos* and kept the rest for themselves. In this early period, the collaboration of the *encomienda* groups with their would-be masters was in any event a fragile matter that limited the Europeans' coercive powers. Moreover, the Indians controlled the smelting of silver. Literally thousands of *guayras,* small wind ovens, dotted the great silver mountain, and it was through the Indian ore market that crude ore was bought, refined, and resold as silver. To acquire pure silver, the Spanish had to sell the ore they received as tribute or as "shares" back to Indians.[42] As Juan de Matienzo, a keen and reliable observer, noted in 1567, the Spanish could only regain a large share of refined silver indirectly, by attempting to dominate the provision of coca leaf to Potosí. Annual coca sales absorbed about a million pesos of silver, representing roughly half the value of all market purchases.[43]

The reorganization of technology and labor in the 1570s ushered in a second phase, which dramatically altered production levels and the balance of Spanish-Indian power. In this period, the *mita* draft indeed served as the cornerstone of a profitable labor system. The *mita* rotations sent thousands of laborers to the mines and refineries for a one-year stint of poorly remunerated work assignments. The draft also facilitated the growth of a "reserve army" of voluntary laborers, since the *mitayos* (Indians on *mita* duty) brought relatives with them for their year of service, and since the *mita* itself alternated "work" and "rest" cycles (theoretically, one week working, two weeks resting) under wage and price conditions that forced "resting" *mitayos* to volunteer to sell their services in the labor market. In the 1570s and 1580s, "coerced cash-crop labor" worked wonders indeed. Silver production more than quadrupled, the peasant economy supplied workers and subsidies to the silver economy, and the European sector escaped its earlier dependence on conditions of work and smelting defined in large measure by Andean individuals and ethnic-kin groups. The *guayra* wind ovens of the Indians, inferior to mercury amalgamation except in cases of high-grade ore, slipped into a secondary role in refining.[44]

Yet, as early as the turn of the century, the *mita* assumed an altered role in overall production. The *mita* declined in importance as a *labor relation* providing workers to the silver mines and refineries but grew in importance as a subsidy, or form of "rent," that cheapened the cost of free labor. For, even as Toledo organized a state-sponsored system of forced labor, there arose a more spontaneous system of voluntary hiring. The supply of *minga* Indians, or volunteer laborers, at first drew greatly on the temporary "reserve armies" created by the *mita,* but a close reading of the evidence suggests an increasingly permanent supply of *minga* laborers by the 1600s (Bakewell 1984: 132–34). The division of labor tended to allot more primitive, dangerous, or repugnant tasks, such as carrying freshly mined ore to the surface, to the *mitayos,* and more "skilled" and highly rewarded tasks, such as ore cutting, to the volunteers. By the early seventeenth century, and perhaps earlier, the *mingas* accounted for better than half the labor supply in the Potosí mines and refineries.[45] Moreover, Indian groups and individuals and Spanish entrepreneurs had worked out arrangements whereby *mita* quotas were declared fulfilled if the Indian communities delivered not laborers but sums of money needed to hire substitute *mingas* to replace the *mitayos.* The practice probably accounted for better than half the official *mita* quotas as early as the 1630s. The conversion of *mita* labor into *mita* rent, the decline in official *mita* quotas (due to population decrease and the Indians' own use of the legal system), the stubborn resistance of Indian groups to full physical compliance with the *mita,* and the interest of colonial employers in expanding or stabilizing their labor supply and in acquiring incomes subsidizing their enterprises—all reduced the significance of the *mita* as a provider of labor but increased its significance as a form of rent, or tributary income, that reduced risks and enhanced profits in the Potosí mines.[46]

Running throughout this evolution of labor was a consistent drive by Indian mine laborers to convert relations of forced labor and of wage labor into a relation resembling sharecropping. In the early years, European social control was fragile, Indian smelters controlled the production of refined silver, and Indian traders dominated the ore market. Under the circumstances, *yanaconas* and *encomienda* Indians did not find it difficult to establish a share system, and their share in the product constituted the primary incentive for collaboration with European mineowners. The quid pro quos inherent in such arrangements began to disintegrate in the 1560s, and, not surprisingly, those years witnessed more serious interest by colonizers in a rationalized forced-labor system.[47] When, in the 1570s, the colonial state consolidated its power, reorganized the mines, and institutionalized forced labor on a massive scale, Indians nonetheless asserted a right by laborers to a share in the ore they produced. The *corpa,* the piece of ore conceded to *minga* Indians as the most attractive part of their "wage," inevitably found its way into the *mita* system. *Mitayos,* like *mingas,* established a customary "right" to the best pieces of ore encountered during the course of work, and the laborers sold their *corpa* pieces in the *qhatu,* the Indian ore market. What the *mitayos* considered a "right" that made their labors more bearable, the mineowners sometimes labeled "robbery." But, in negotiations with Viceroy Toledo on the official wage rate to be paid *mitayos,* the European miners themselves conceded that such "theft" had become a permanent and grudgingly accepted practice and that it constituted the most important part of the *mitayos'* remuneration; they pressed accordingly for its inclusion in the calculation of total "wages" received by *mita* laborers.[48] In the case of the *mingas,* a similar dialectic counterposed "right" and "robbery." What mineowners originally conceded as a right to a daily piece of good ore grew into a more systematic appropriation by laborers of high-grade ores capable of being smelted in the traditional wind ovens. This more aggressive appropriation of ore, considered a "right" by the *mingas* and "theft" by their employers, led to a major controversy about *corpa* rights and the Indian ore market in the early 1580s. Mineowners hoped to roll back the *corpa* system, in part by eliminating the *qhatu.* And no wonder. The Indian ore market accounted for some 25 percent of total production of silver ore. By the late sixteenth century, the *mingas'* customary right to appropriate shares had grown into a key strategy involving the household economy as a whole. The women received high-grade ore from their men when they brought them food at midweek. The women then proceeded to smelt the best ores in their *guayras* (by now the *guayra* sector was run by women) or to trade ore in the *qhatu.*[49]

Compared to *minga* laborers, the *mitayos* worked at tasks and under co-ercive pressures that restricted their capacity to enlarge their "share" in the product of their labors. They could inject an element of share arrangements into the forced labor relationship, but they could not really transform it. In the case of *minga* Indians, however, the balance of power contrasted sharply: "experience has shown that the metal mined with *mitayos* [*indios de cédula*] is of a higher grade than that worked by *mingas* [*indios mingados*]" (Capoche 1585: 150).[50] This observation by a well-informed contemporary, if it is to be believed, casts doubt on the common assumption that the *mingas* constituted a supply of skilled laborers more attractive to mineowners than rotations of "unskilled" draft laborers. The assumption is too crude because it fails to distinguish between "optimal" solutions in low-grade versus high-grade mines and because it fails to account for the way that lack of labor discipline might in practice undermine the theoretical advantages of "skilled" labor. In Potosí's mines and refineries, the *mingas* developed a reputation as a notoriously independent labor force—difficult to discipline, accustomed to appropriating a share of ore or silver as their "right," assertive about the hours and conditions of their work—that was grudgingly accommodated by employers for lack of a better alternative.[51] The *mingas,* especially those who worked in the underground mines, did succeed in transforming the "wage relation" initially desired by their employers into a "share relation." [52] Indeed, sometime during the late seventeenth century, when Potosí's secular decline was well advanced and the mineowners' position weak, the *mingas* expanded their right to appropriate a share of product into a form of partial possession in the mines. They established the practice of *kajcheo,* weekend raids by bands of Indians who mined for themselves the particularly rich ore sections they had encountered during the work week. *Kajcheo* grew into a customary right that plagued the mines throughout the eighteenth century. The *kajcheo* ore was processed not in the larger water-powered refineries (*ingenios*), which handled most of Potosí's ore, but in crude, human-powered mills (*trapiches*) located in the Indian fringes of the city. At the height of this activity, in 1759, some 4,000 weekend raiders accounted for only 3.3 percent of the total ore processed in Potosí, but this tiny fraction of ore in turn yielded 38.1 percent of total refined silver produced in Potosí. The "opportunity cost" of the *kajcheo* to mineowners is obvious and dramatic. For this very reason, argued Enrique Tandeter (1981a, 1981b), it was the brutal intensification of the labor regime imposed on *mitayo* laborers that made the crucial difference in Potosí's profitability and rising silver production during the late eighteenth century.[53]

Potosí and the Silver Economy in Comparative Context

How far we have traveled from the interpretation provided by Wallerstein's world-system is by now obvious. The paradigm appears badly misleading on both descriptive and explanatory grounds. During most of the long sixteenth and seventeenth centuries, Potosí's labor relations fit poorly in the mold of a periphery assigned "coerced cash-crop labor" by the world-system's international division of labor. This was the case even though the colonial state and mineowners had indeed directed enormous effort to making "coerced cash-crop labor" the centerpiece of the labor system. Except for a brief period, however, the labor system is best described as a fluctuating combination of wage relations, share relations, and forced-labor relations in which voluntary share relations predominated—both because such relations were the most numerically frequent and because their influence tended to "distort" or "twist" other labor relations in the direction of "sharecropping." [54] This description does not deny the importance of the *mita* as a coercive labor relation crucial to the reorganization of Potosí in the 1570s, or its significance as a complementary labor relation and as a form of "rent" subsidizing the mines from the late sixteenth century onward. Indeed, precisely because share relations were so dominant in the organization of labor, and so damaging to the profits of entrepreneurs, institutions of tributary rent and coerced labor sometimes mattered greatly. They could provide the marginal difference between good and poor profits, and entrepreneurs had every reason to squeeze their *mita* privileges as brutally as possible. But if scholars must stay within the descriptive categories of Wallerstein's world-system, on close inspection, labor in Potosí more closely resembles the pattern of the "semiperiphery" than that of the "periphery."

In explanatory terms, the world-system framework also fares poorly. To explain the rise of share arrangements in terms of their utility to the world-system, or to American capitalists adapting to the international market, would miss the point entirely. The twisting of wage and forced labor in the direction of share relations greatly disturbed colonial entrepreneurs and officials, and it bolstered an Indian market of production, consumption, and speculation that developed a life of its own, one not easily molded by the preferences of the colonial state, American elites, or the European world-system.[55] The colonizers' schemes to beat back share arrangements and to control or even eliminate independent Indian marketing yielded at most fleeting victories, partly because the resistance to such attempts was so unyielding and the risks of a concerted drive against customary practices so unsettling.[56]

To set the case of Potosí in context, consider its significance within the silver economy of Spanish America as a whole. I have already pointed out its position as the leading center of silver production in the early colonial period. Two further observations are in order. First, because Potosí's riches drew high priority, it constitutes, among the range of major silver centers, the example most likely to corroborate Wallerstein's analysis. Potosí and Huancavelica (Peru), whose mines provided an American source of mercury for amalgamation, received preferential treatment in the organization of rotating draft labor. In these centers, the state was least disposed to place trust in the vagaries of voluntary labor. Elsewhere, labor systems in the mines moved more rapidly toward private arrangements unassisted by corvée labor. Oruro (Bolivia), for example, a major silver-producing center early in the seventeenth century, drew some

10,000 laborers by 1617–1618, and this competition apparently made labor more scarce in Potosí. Yet it rarely received any *mita* quotas from the state, and such allotments as it received (550 *mitayos*) were insignificant.[57] In Mexico, most of whose best silver mines were situated north of the densely populated Indian heartland, corvée labor played a minor role in silver production. In the northern mines, "coerced cash-crop labor" almost always took the form of Indian or African slavery and accounted for very small shares of the labor force. The overwhelming majority of laborers were hired Indians (*naborías*).[58]

Second, the drive by laborers to establish customary share arrangements appeared not only in Potosí but in virtually every major silver center of Mexico and Peru-Bolivia. The Mexican case is particularly well documented, and scholars agree that, for most of the colonial period, the laborers' shares (known in Mexico as *pepenas* or *partidos,* depending on time, place, and the particular rules of ore division) in the ores they produced constituted a far more important reward than fixed money wages. In Mexico, as in Potosí, the share system developed in the context of a notoriously unruly labor force whose appropriations of ore and general independence lowered the profits of mineowners. In Mexico, as in Potosí, petty refiners diverted particularly rich ores to their crude smelting ovens and probably benefited from the independent ore trade facilitated by the share system. In much of Mexico, apparently in contrast to Potosí, mineowners and the state eventually rolled back the laborers' customary share rights. Beginning in 1766, a strong, repressive campaign, backed by military force, curtailed and in some mines eliminated the shares of the workers. The labor system moved in the direction of "forced paid labor" (for instance, round-ups of "vagrants" and "idle" laborers) or combinations of forced and wage labor.[59] David Brading's (1971) meticulous study of the mining economy argues that the silver boom of the late eighteenth century derived in part from this successful campaign to discipline labor.[60] Before the 1760s, however, in the major mines of Mexico as well as in Potosí, share relations proved stubbornly difficult to resist. Mineowners might control the damage but could rarely muster the political will needed to establish an enduring alternative.

The more closely the case of silver is examined, the more limited is the world-system's power to explain either the history of labor or the division of surplus between laborer and employer. This is not to argue for the irrelevance of the world-system. After all, Europe did establish an enormous silver production sector in America on terms that provided the world-system a colonial surplus, and this accomplishment rightfully constitutes an important chapter in the history of European capitalism. To slight the world-system, or the impact of capitalism on Spanish America, is to ignore the obvious. The point is, however, that the world-system constituted only one of several great "motor forces" that shaped patterns of labor and economy in the periphery; it did not always constitute the decisive causal force even in sectors of high priority;

and the various limitations on the world-system's power help to explain the chasm, on a descriptive level, between the world-system model and the reality it purports to illuminate. In the case of silver, any adequate explanation of the shifting labor system, or the division of the economic pie, would have to grant independent causal weight not only to the world-system and its needs but also to the laborers' resistance and assertion of "rights," and to the rise in America of regional and interregional markets and elites whose "logic" and interests did not always coincide with those of the world-system.[61] We have, then, three great motors—the world-system, popular strategies of resistance and survival within the periphery, and the mercantile and elite interests joined to an American "center of gravity." Observe, in addition, that Western Europe's own internal divisions and competitions affected the political coherence and will of the "world-system," and that, within Spanish America, colonial elites and authorities pursued multiple goals and interests that sometimes divided them against themselves despite their shared general interest in silver production.[62]

Under these circumstances, historical explanation that reduces patterns of labor and economy in the periphery to a reflection of the capitalist world-system is one-dimensional and misleading—even for silver, the early world-system's most valued American treasure.

Test Cases (II): Sugar

For reasons of space and logic, my examination of the sugar plantation sector will spare the reader the degree of detail presented for silver. The case of silver alone, given its stature in the early modern world-system, is sufficient to establish that the fundamentals of Wallerstein's interpretation are severely flawed when viewed from the American periphery. From the narrow point of view of merely "affirming" or "discrediting" Wallerstein, the analysis of silver makes a detailed review of sugar unnecessary—or, more precisely, redundant. From a larger point of view, however, the case of sugar merits some discussion. It would be illuminating to know whether sugar represents a more felicitous example of the validity of Wallerstein's interpretation, or whether it also raises major problems for the world-system paradigm. Sugar, moreover, offers an indisputably "sympathetic" test of the paradigm. As mentioned earlier, the greater Caribbean region includes some examples of a nearly "pure" periphery—islands of slave plantations ruthlessly molded to serve the interests of absentee capitalist rulers, colonial outposts utterly dependent on fresh infusions of African slaves and unable otherwise to function or reproduce themselves as societies in their own right. What better example could one hope to find of a capitalist world-system whose global impact undermines the validity of local units of analysis and whose characteristic pattern combines, in a single, interlocked structure, free labor in the core and forced labor in the periphery?

Let us grant from the outset that the descriptive side of Wallerstein's paradigm applies better to the labor systems that eventually emerged in major sugar regions than to those associated with silver. In the main, African slave labor produced the sugar that sweetened diets and profits in Europe. There still remains, however, the question of explanation. *Why* did African slave labor come to play this role in sugar production? Does a line of explanation derived from the world-system provide a sufficient answer to this question? The issue becomes all the more complex when we note that colonizers actually tried out several labor strategies in the sugar zones and that African slave labor was not at the outset a foregone conclusion.[63] Wallerstein's scheme may apply better to the outcomes that characterized labor in the sugar zones than to the processes leading to and explaining such outcomes.

Recognition of the early diversity in sugar labor requires the suspension, at least temporarily, of two entrenched notions: that African slavery was from the start the preferred, optimal, or only labor relation adaptable to large-scale sugar production; and that patterns in the Atlantic sugar islands colonized by Portugal and Spain in the fifteenth century predetermined the labor model (African slavery) the Iberians would later apply to sugar production in America. Recent scholarship on the Atlantic sugar islands is producing a somewhat more differentiated picture of labor. If it is true that slave labor predominated on Portuguese Madeira, it is also true that on the Spanish Canaries, European sharecroppers, especially Portuguese, appear to have constituted the bulk of the labor force in sugar.[64] In the Spanish Caribbean as well as Portuguese Brazil, colonizers and Crown attempted to establish thriving sugar-producing zones, and in both cases African slave labor at first constituted only one of several significant labor strategies.

The ascent of sugar in the sixteenth-century Spanish Caribbean is a story less well known (perhaps because the boom aborted precipitously in the 1580s) than that of Brazil, but by the 1560s the island of Española supported several dozen sugar plantations, the larger ones staffed by several hundred slave laborers each.[65] By then, African slavery constituted the nearly exclusive source of nonmanagerial labor. But earlier, mixed labor relations and strategies were important. In the early 1500s, Indians as well as blacks worked in the primitive sugar mills (*trapiches*), and in 1512, the collapse of the Indian population led one official of the Council of the Indies to propose that the sharecropping system of the Canaries be transferred to Española.[66] The recommendation meshed well with the critique of Spanish-Amerindian relations by Bartolomé de Las Casas, among others, and the Crown did experiment somewhat with European-based labor in America. But this strategy proved unrealistic, and the Indian population continued its downward plunge.[67] Even so, the importation of African slave labor occurred slowly and fitfully, hampered by vagaries of price, supply, and royal policy. As late as 1520, when the new governor, Rodrigo de Figueroa, supervised a major expansion of the sugar sector, his reports to the Crown underscored the continuing significance of Indian labor. At a time when African slaves were in short supply, Figueroa used Indian labor grants as well as generous credit to commit colonizers to constructing forty new, substantial sugar mills (*ingenios*). One of Figueroa's most intriguing comments referred to Indians who had "come from outside of this island" and worked as *naborías,* an ambiguous category (in the context of the early Caribbean) of native individuals who were separated from their original communities and who presumably received a wage.[68] The role of imported Indian labor (whether free *naborías,* slaves, or theoretically free *naborías* subjected to slavery in practice) is a topic on which useful research and statistics are unavailable. But it is suggestive to recall that slave raiding was common in the greater Caribbean region, that Amerindian slave exports occasionally reached as far as the Canaries, and that a massive Indian slave trade took hold in Nicaragua and Honduras in the 1520s and 1530s.[69]

Historians still know far too little about early labor in the Spanish Caribbean. But we know enough to suggest that the inability to subject European colonizers to sharecropping or other peasant-based labor systems and the comparative advantages and disadvantages of imported Indian labor must loom large in the explanation of nearly complete reliance on African slavery—a form of labor replete with its own disadvantages, including heavy initial outlays, continuing losses due to flight, and the fear of revolt by an African majority population.[70] And to explain the relative disadvantages and eventual failure of European and Indian labor invariably returns the discussion to local conditions—among them, geography, disease, power, and conflict—that molded the options, constraints, and opportunities faced by the "world-system."[71]

It is for the case of Portuguese Brazil that we enjoy the best analysis of these issues. In a fascinating and meticulous study, Stuart B. Schwartz (1978, cf. 1985) charted the shifting pattern of labor in the early sugar colony.[72] Three findings are especially pertinent. First, for better than a half-century after their turn to sugar in the 1530s, the Portuguese experimented seriously with five labor strategies. Four focused on Indian labor: barter relations to acquire native labor; outright enslavement of Indians; "peasantization," whereby Indians who were settled in villages run by Jesuits could provide labor outside the villages; and wage labor. Not until the 1580s did the labor strategy of the Portuguese sugar planters shift decisively toward African slavery. Second, Schwartz pointed out that, even after the 1580s, Indian labor played a far more important continuing role than once suspected. On the Engenho Sergipe, for example, Indian slaves outnumbered Africans by two to one in 1591, and the baptismal record listed 50 percent more Indian mothers than Afro-Brazilian mothers during 1595–1608.[73] For Bahia as a whole, Schwartz estimated that Indian slaves outnumbered Africans by three to one on the sugar plantations in the 1590s. Village Indians, some of them presumably available to supplement the work force on the plantations, outnumbered slave Indians by two to one. In Pernambuco, the other main sugar region, Indian slaves outnumbered their African counterparts by two to one in the mid-1580s. The overwhelmingly Afro-Brazilian labor force usually associated with the sugar plantations of Brazil's Northeast did not appear until around the 1630s (Schwartz 1985: 70–71, 1984: 437). Third, the strong preference for African slave labor took shape in response to a crisis of Indian labor in the 1560s and 1570s. Epidemic disease struck hard in 1562–1563, and a general Indian rebellion rocked Bahia in 1567. These local conditions, in turn, aggravated political disputes about Indian slavery within the Portuguese world (a conflict that sometimes aligned Jesuits and Crown against planters). The Indians' decline in numbers, and their emphatic and even violent resistance, raised questions about the political and economic viability of Indian labor and, in any event, widened the gap between the expected benefits of Indian and African labor. The wider the gap, the more justified the comparatively heavy investments required to purchase Africans. To be sure, the world-system and its markets also played an important role in such calculations, since high prices for sugar on the international market in the early 1600s increased still further the disparity between the expected returns on African versus Indian labor. But it was the earlier conjuncture of disease, violent resistance, and political conflict that threw into doubt the continuing practicality of Indian labor on a large scale and transformed African slavery into *the* optimal strategy for those looking into the future. As Schwartz remarked, "The system of labor and the nature of the labor force were determined not only in the court at Lisbon or in the countinghouses of Amsterdam and London but also in the forests and canefields of America" (1985: 72).[74]

The conclusion is inescapable. Hindsight—the knowledge that Brazil's great sugar plantations ended up depending mainly on African slave labor—has led us to assume a more rapid and complete transition to African slavery than is justified by the historical record. Not until the 1620s or 1630s, nearly a hundred years after the Portuguese set out to establish sugar as the mainstay of Brazil, can researchers justifiably expect to find that sugar plantation slaves were overwhelmingly African or Afro-Brazilian. Most important, the world-system's needs and theoretically optimal labor pattern, while important, do not suffice to explain the outcome of the labor system in the sugar plantation periphery. At the heart of the labor question were conditions that made local Indian and European populations insufficiently exploitable, compared to African slave populations, for the purpose of sugar plantation production. In the interplay between these local conditions of production and the interests and opportunities derived from the international market lies a more powerful explanation of the rise of socioeconomic structures overwhelmingly dependent on African slavery.

This argument is consistent with what historians know about the early history of slave plantation societies in British America. From sugar in Jamaica and Barbados, to rice in South Carolina, to tobacco in Virginia, colonizers at first relied on indentured servant labor to produce commodities for the international market or on a mixed labor strategy that sometimes blurred the distinction between white servant and black slave. On the mainland, Indian labor was in some instances also significant. But, eventually, the European and Indian populations proved insufficiently exploitable, compared to African slaves imported from afar, to serve as the foundation for plantation production. The reasons for this turn the analysis once more to local conditions that shaped the productivity of labor and the limits of social control. Such conditions included not only patterns of health and mortality but also the real and feared effects of popular resistance and the refuge given to such resistance by poorly controlled frontier zones. Given these local conditions, and attractive commodity prices on the international market, elites came to center their strategies on African slave labor. But this outcome occurred only over time, through the trials and tribulations created by life in America, and at first seemed neither obvious nor especially optimal or desirable.[75]

One might object that roughly similar outcomes in the plantation tropics of Spanish, Portuguese, and British America demonstrate the overriding force of macro-level causes, in this case the world-system. But such an argument violates historical accuracy and commits a logical fallacy. The argument is inaccurate because outcomes were only "roughly" similar, and obsessions with eventual outcomes may obscure vast differences along the way. The labor relations and techniques of control in Brazil in 1580—where Indian slaves and recently constituted peasants supplied the bulk of the labor force, and where a good deal of production relied on share arrangements between large planters and small cane growers (*lavradores de cana*) who owned a few slaves—differed enormously from the organization of sugar production and labor by its main American competitor, Española. Española had moved more quickly to the classic Afro-American slave plantation model. The argument is also logically flawed, since one may just as easily explain roughly similar outcomes in terms of roughly similar local variables (patterns of indigenous culture, population and health trends, indigenous and European resistance to plantation labor, the proximity of frontiers) as by determination on an international level. My point here is one of method and logic. It is not to argue for the irrelevance of the international market or of the needs of a European world-system either capitalist or in transition to capitalism. The prices for specific commodities on the international market, and the efforts by European imperial states and merchants to organize and benefit from international trade in prized commodities, including Africans, had an important hand in defining local incentives and the expected returns on African slave labor. An explanation that ignores the world-system is as limited and reductionist as one derived from the world-system.

For the case of sugar, as for silver, the more closely we scrutinize the problem of explanation, the more unavoidable is the conclusion that the logic and necessities of the capitalist world-system, while important, fail to account for the evolution of labor. In both cases, the emerging world-system remains important as a concept explaining America's subjugation to mercantile exploitation. But its power to reduce the periphery to a functionally optimal role serving the core of international capitalism proves more contingent—more constrained, buffeted, and driven by the force of independent causal "motors" and by internal contradictions—than is suggested by Wallerstein's theoretical framework. Ironically, in his specific historical analysis of sugar and labor in volume 2, Wallerstein demonstrated his awareness of and agreement with much that has been said. But he avoided serious analysis of the *implications* of such findings for the overarching framework proposed in volume 1.[76]

Even on the level of description, for which the case of sugar fits Wallerstein's scheme better than silver, appearances from afar may be somewhat deceiving. The term "slavery" has limited descriptive value, since it has been used to describe a wide variety of social and economic relations. It arouses debate even as an abstract and theoretical category.[77] To evaluate the descriptive validity of the world-system framework for the case of sugar therefore requires a closer look at the specific social relations and customs that defined the meaning of African "slavery" on American sugar plantations. For, as Sidney Mintz has argued so eloquently and persistently, the slaves often carved out, even under extreme and dehumanizing conditions, a sphere of activities and customary rights that in certain respects made them "proto-peasants." Often, slaves in the Caribbean not only grew their own food (a concession that served the interests of planters so long as it was narrowly constrained) but also sold food to the free population, invaded the sphere of petty marketing by the thousands, and controlled as much as 20 percent of the coin in regional circulation. Similar patterns were known, although perhaps less frequent or pronounced, in the sugar regions of Brazil. In both areas, the slaves asserted rights of possession in plantation lands and in the fruits of their labors in ways that bore some resemblance to peasant adaptations and that implicitly challenged their formal condition as chattel property. It is this "proto-peasant" dimension that enabled plantation slaves to metamorphose quickly into a "reconstituted peasantry" (to use Mintz's apt term) after emancipation.[78] The descriptive and theoretical issues merge in the following question: how wide a "breach" in their condition as slaves need Afro-Americans have opened, how much like peasants and petty commodity producers need they have become, before it becomes misleading to describe plantation slavery as a capitalist labor design by, for, and of the world-system?[79]

The descriptive gap between Wallerstein's international division of labor on the one hand and the history of labor and surplus extraction on the other is less easily discerned in the case of sugar than in that of silver. This is especially true as one moves past the early years in the formation of labor strategies. But the gap is nonetheless significant, a symptom of the limits of the world-system as an explanatory concept or organizing principle. The explanatory prism of the world-system (like all such prisms) may blind the eye to the significance of certain kinds of descriptive data. In the cases of sugar and silver, unfortunately, the consequences of such blind spots are serious. Even for labor, a topic central to the whole framework, the world-system paradigm takes as its point of departure a description that is at best somewhat misleading, at worst thoroughly inaccurate.

Back to the Drawing Board

The foregoing analyses of silver and sugar imply that we must return to the academic drawing board. The state of affairs is even more dismal than may be apparent thus far. The failure of Wallerstein's Europe-centered paradigm does not necessarily mean that established lines of criticism and alternative models fare better upon application to America. As we shall see, the standard line of criticism from within a Europe-centered framework runs into curiously similar descriptive and theoretical difficulties in Latin America and the Caribbean. Just as serious, and not unrelated, the standard critiques fail to rescue and reinterpret some of Wallerstein's genuine insights about the limits of our inherited categories, among them "feudalism" and "capitalism," in colonized America. My purpose in this and the concluding section is twofold: to explain more fully why historians must go back to the drawing board and question our most basic organizing precepts, and to sketch the outlines of a new model. Along the way, I will have occasion to single out significant insights in Wallerstein's work but to situate them in a new context.

Let us begin by reviewing and drawing out briefly three main deficiencies of Wallerstein's model for Latin America and the Caribbean. First, the paradigm failed to describe and to explain reasonably well its two most important historical "test cases," those of silver and sugar, even though critical analysis in this essay has tested the model on its own terms by focusing on labor patterns, a topic rightfully central in Wallerstein's own presentation. Second, these two test cases hint at major theoretical problems. The analyses of silver and sugar provided above establish that local conditions of production, broadly conceived, had central importance in defining the choices and constraints faced by entrepreneurs. The specific technologies, social relations, and subsistence possibilities that shaped the production process, and the shifting capacity of laboring populations to resist greater subjugation, set contours of power and struggle that limited social control and recast what was desirable or even possible from the point of view of capital accumulation. In this perspective, assigning theoretical priority to the rise of a capitalist world market that spawned varied but functionally desirable versions of capitalism in the periphery is fundamentally misleading. This criticism meshes well with the Marxist emphasis on the theoretical importance of the mode of production—the dynamic combination of technologies and social relationships that distinguish one kind of productive system from another—rather than profit-oriented exchange relations as a distinguishing feature of capitalism. A further theoretical problem arises when we look more closely at the character of the "world market." In Spanish America especially, the mining booms and the urban centers gave rise to America-centered market interests and incentives whose weight rivaled or even dwarfed those linked to the international market. The problem of reconciling these diverse and sometimes competing centers of gravity in the world marketplace with the picture of a single world-economy directed from the European core raises thorny theoretical issues as yet unresolved in Wallerstein's paradigm.

Third, the interpretation of early colonial America as a mere variant of world capitalism becomes historically misleading if one adopts a perspective that looks ahead to the nineteenth and twentieth centuries. Two anomalies or paradoxes from the later period would require explanation. One of these I have already mentioned. The classic picture of transitions to capitalism, wherein earlier subsistence strategies and coercive labor strategies are replaced by wage labor and growing internal markets for basic subsistence goods, is recognizable in various regions of Latin America in the late nineteenth and twentieth centuries. Conceptualizing colonial Latin America as "capitalist" masks the rupture and strife provoked by this great transformation.[80] A second paradox derives from the apparent "involution" or "regression" of some agrarian regions earlier in the nineteenth century into feudalism.[81] Regions commercially dynamic in colonial times—characterized by considerable commodity production on haciendas and *obrajes* (primitive textile factories), by investment and reinvestment of liquid wealth in agrarian enterprise, and by faltering subsistence economies allowing for infusions of temporary wage labor into a diversified ensemble of labor relations—turned toward greater insulation from market forces, deterioration and decapitalization of haciendas, fuller dependence on rent and forced labor by resident hacienda peons. However we conceptualize the colonial economy, and whatever respects we pay to its dynamic profit-oriented aspects and its capacity to reduce human beings to mere repositories of exploited labor-power, a theoretically valid conceptualization must incorporate the historical potential of dynamic regional economies to "regress" into a pattern more closely resembling feudalism.[82] Neither Wallerstein nor his critics conceptualize capitalism as a kind of economic system or organization that responds to crisis by lapsing into feudalism. Layoffs, strikes, bankruptcies and reorganization, technological innovation, political turmoil, welfare measures, attempts at self-employment, and underground economies—all these we associate with cyclical or secular crises in a capitalist economy. Reversions to feudalism we do not. To do so would make capitalism a concept so elastic as to border on meaninglessness.

If Wallerstein's world-system runs aground on issues of substance and theory, however, so do the standard alternatives. The most prominent critical alternatives dispute the notion that integration of diverse territories into an international and profit-driven commercial system constitutes a sufficient basis for conceptualizing the economy of such territories as "capitalist." [83] The criticism is valid, but the alternative theses proposed or implied in such critiques are not—at least not necessarily. The problem arises because we remain too dependent on theoretical concepts derived from the experience of Western Europe. In this experience, feudalism preceded capitalism. The natural alternative to the thesis of capitalism becomes the thesis of feudalism (or alternatively, slavery, the other key mode of production that preceded capitalism in the European experience). The attractive theoretical critique of emphasis on "commercial capitalism" draws on Marx to argue first that transformations in the sphere of production account far more successfully than commercial changes for the historically distinctive features of capitalism, and also that merchant capital is inherently conservative insofar as the mode of production is concerned. Merchant capital, in this argument, exploits already existing modes of production by manipulating terms of trade and harnessing them to the world-economy, but it has no interest in the dynamic transformation and modernization of archaic productive systems.[84] The key intellectual innovation that accounts for the paradox that archaic technologies and social relations of production were harnessed to European capitalism argues that capitalism, as a system, articulated archaic modes of production (mainly feudalism or slavery) in America with a capitalist mode of production in Europe. In this argument, the integration of heterogeneous "parts" (modes of production) into a systemic "whole" dominated by capitalism does not imply that the internal structure and laws of each and every "part" were themselves capitalist.

The Europe-centered alternative to Wallerstein, then, leads almost "naturally" to the following four alternative theses: first, the colonized American periphery was feudal, precapitalist, or archaic rather than capitalist; second, social relations of production matter more than markets or the profit principle for establishing the capitalist or noncapitalist laws, or internal dynamics, of the economy; third, merchant capital was both profoundly conservative and parasitic because it characteristically limited itself to siphoning off a surplus from relatively backward and static modes of production; and fourth, the most perceptive theoretical way to interpret the colonial economy in its international context is through the concept of articulation between archaic and capitalist modes of production.

In my view, only the second of these four theses holds up under scrutiny, and problems with the other three point to particular insights that may be rescued from Wallerstein despite the failure of his paradigm as a whole. At bottom, Europe-centered theory critical of Wallerstein's conceptualization of capitalism does not resolve any better the paradoxical features of the colonial economy discussed earlier (see pages 30–32). That earlier discussion pointed to several patterns central to colonial economic life yet difficult to reconcile with the feudal thesis: the pervasive power of mercantile interests and the profit-investment principle to transform regional economies, that is, to restructure the technologies, social relations, and outputs that defined production; the destructive, partly proletarianizing impact of mercantile exploitation on small producers and their subsistence economies; the tendency of dynamic economic sectors to reduce human beings to short-term, exchangeable repositories of labor-power; and the rise of urban and mining camp regions characterized by significant internal markets and somewhat freer forms of labor, including relations resembling wage labor.

To these general points may now be added a further "anomaly." The technologies and work patterns associated with silver and sugar production often gave these leading sectors a precociously "industrial" character. Independently of one another, the most distinguished students of silver and sugar all seem struck by the emphatically "industrial" aspects of production: the massive scale of investments in machinery and engineering works, the complexity of the division of labor and the alienation of laborers from the production process, the intensely regimented and time-conscious work rhythms normally associated with nineteenth-century factories.[85] The "industrial" aspects of the silver and sugar sectors would matter little if these constituted secondary appendages to the colonial economy at large or if they constituted "enclaves" sharply demarcated from the rest of the economy. Alas, history is not so cooperative. Silver and sugar were central to the organization of regional and supraregional economic spaces, and silver, especially, exerted profound secondary consequences even in distant agrarian hinterlands.[86]

In short, critical alternatives wedded to the rise of feudalism or other archaic modes of production in colonial America are grossly misleading, and they gloss over "anomalies" central to colonial economic life as a whole. The notion of articulation of heterogeneous modes of production in a wider economic system remains theoretically promising but is weakened if the dominant "mode" in America is assumed to be "feudalism." [87]

In the end, Wallerstein homed in on two specific insights worth underscoring despite the problems with the general interpretation. First, under colonial conditions, which allied merchant capital with imperial political power in the fluid environment of a frontier or "outpost," merchant capital could exert an aggressive, organizing, and transformative impact on technologies and social relations of production. This historical possibility in the colonized periphery is at odds with "classic" Marxian views of the conservatism of merchant capital. It cautions us not to assume too rigidly, under colonial conditions, that local social relations of production constitute *the* point of departure for analyzing the trajectory of merchant capital or its impact on methods of production. Second, the colonial problem exposes the limited historical applicability of our Europe-centered categories, especially "feudalism" and "capitalism." Wallerstein was right to reject "feudalism" as a meaningful category for understanding peripheries drawn into the radically transformed world of the sixteenth century. He was less illuminating when he responded to our limited conceptual choices by revising "capitalism" into a concept so elastic and omnipotent that the results simply add to the theoretical confusion and fail to describe or explain success-fully the history of labor in the periphery. But at least he understood the nature of the conceptual dilemma.

A third insight, though one not intended by Wallerstein, may be derived from his insistence that the underlying logic of an economy may be rooted precisely in its tendency to combine diverse relations of production into an opti-mal package. In Wallerstein's vision, this is a defining feature of the capitalist world-economy as a whole and explains why forced labor in the periphery, intermediate arrangements in the semiperiphery, and free labor in the core are unified in the single logic of capitalism. We have already seen that the scheme breaks down in the American periphery. The irony, however, is that the prin-ciple ascribed by Wallerstein to the world-economy as a whole comes closer to defining economic patterns *within* the American periphery. Repeatedly in colonial Latin America and the Caribbean, one encounters a shifting combi-nation of heterogeneous relations of production in a pragmatic package. This heterogeneity of labor relations occurred within single units of production and applied to the bulk of low-status physical laborers (not merely to the more obvious and commonplace distinctions between supervisory employees and skilled experts on the one hand and "unskilled" physical laborers on the other). Again and again, scholars of the mines, haciendas, plantations, and *obrajes* of colonial America find that entrepreneurs fused a diverse array of labor rela-tions, including approximations of wage labor, complicated tenancy, share and debt-credit arrangements, and forced labor drafts and slavery, into a single productive process.[88] One might go so far as to assert that what is distinctive about the economic logic of colonial and neocolonial situations is precisely the entrepreneurial tendency to combine variegated labor strategies—considered somewhat more antithetical, mutually exclusive, and sequential in a Europe-centered context—into a unified package.[89] The material motivations inspiring such a strategy were threefold: to maximize profits, to insure against setbacks in the supply or benefits of labor derived from any particular labor strategy, and perhaps also to facilitate social control through a structure of "divide and rule" within the labor force. This "law of diversity" may speak not only to the material uncertainties, opportunities, and contradictions particular to colonial life but also to distinctions in morality, ethos, and political culture that differentiated colony from metropolis. In any event, it adds yet another "anomaly" to those that make questionable the standard Europe-centered alternatives to Wallerstein.

Challenge and Renewal

The great challenge historians face is to construct a new model, or at the least a new perspective, sufficiently penetrating to render meaningful and explicable the apparent paradoxes and anomalies of colonial economic life. This new approach needs to incorporate the genuine insights of currently contending models and interpretations, but it must also succeed in incorporating the idiosyncracies neglected or trivialized by a Europe-centered straitjacket yet central to the socioeconomic history of colonized America. This daunting task is beyond the scope of this essay and the current competence of its author. At this juncture, I can only propose some starting points. On the level of specific historical analysis, we will need to take seriously all three "motors" identified earlier—the European world-system, popular strategies of resistance and survival within the periphery, and the mercantile and elite interests joined to American "centers of gravity." It is in the contradictory interplay between these three grand motors, and in the divisions and contradictions internal to each of them, that we will find keys to a deeper understanding of the structures, changes, and driving forces of colonial economic life.[90] On the level of theory and basic categories, we would do well to examine carefully the earlier innovations, largely neglected in the United States, of our Latin American colleagues. Particularly significant are two of their proposals: first, that we consider seriously a theory of colonial modes of production and, second, that we consider seriously the possibility that the foundation of the colonial economy was the dominance of commercial capital over production and the corresponding absence of a consolidated mode of production in the usual sense.[91] In the encounter between history and theory, our Latin American colleagues have in this instance led the way. We should engage their work and, to put it another way, move the intellectuals of the periphery into the core of our discussion.

Notes

This essay was originally published in *American Historical Review* 93:4 (Oct. 1988):829–72. It is reprinted here as originally published, except for changes in citation and reference style to conform to the style of this book, and minor editorial changes. The *AHR* version was accompanied by a debate between the author and Immanuel Wallerstein on pp. 873–97 of the same journal, and was developed from a paper originally presented at the American Historical Association Convention in Chicago,

December 27–30, 1986. The author wishes to thank various people for helpful and stimulating comments: members of the panel and audience at the original session, especially Immanuel Wallerstein; participants at the History and Society Seminar of the University of Minnesota, where the paper was presented in February 1987; colleagues Roger Bartra, Allen Hunter, Gerda Lerner, Florencia Mallon, and Thomas Skidmore; and three anonymous reviewers of the manuscript for the *AHR*. The author also thanks David Weber for inviting him to write the original paper, John Coatsworth for gracious encouragement, and the University of Wisconsin Graduate Research Committee for assistance that facilitated completion of the essay.

1 A streamlined "text edition" of Wallerstein 1974 (which deleted the notes and bibliographical list but added a special preface and brief bibliographical essay) was published in 1976. Readers should note that all citations given in arabic numerals are from the 1974 edition; all citations in roman numerals are from the 1976 preface.

2 See esp. Wallerstein 1980, where he asserted "the essential *continuity* between the long sixteenth and seventeenth centuries, with the one great difference [being cyclical expansion and contraction]" (7–8).

3 On the periphery in Wallerstein 1980, see 129–75. In general, vol. 2 of *The Modern World-System* series is more cognizant of phenomena in the periphery—social conflicts, local geography, a diversity of labor arrangements—that *could* be taken to complicate the thesis sketched in vol. 1, but it avoids following through on their possible implications. The result is that the basic model set forth in vol. 1 remains unaltered. For Wallerstein's treatment of labor in Mexico in general, and in its silver mines in particular, see 1980:147–55, esp. n. 130. For recognition of social conflict in the periphery but a method of explanation that subsumes the causes, outcomes, and impacts of such events under the needs of the world-system, or of American elites responding to the world-system, see 130–31, 137, 139–40, 144–45, 154–55 (incl. n. 130), 167–74 (esp. 172–74 and n. 219).

4 Wallerstein is a prolific scholar who has published numerous other works on the world-system. Particularly helpful for rounding out one's sense of Wallerstein's views on a variety of issues related to the world-system, and for appreciation of his diverse and sometimes penetrating insights, are the essays available in Wallerstein 1979, 1983 (an especially perceptive work to this reader), 1984. This article will focus, however, on the paradigm as developed in *The Modern World-System*, vol. 1 (1974) and applied in vol. 2 (1980), both because these are Wallerstein's most systematic and thoroughly researched historical analyses and because his subsequent essays have not, to my knowledge, changed the essentials of his historical interpretation. With good reason, the books of *The Modern World-System* series are Wallerstein's most influential scholarship. [Note: Since the original publication of this essay, Wallerstein has published a third volume in the *World-System* series, but its contents do not affect the argument of this essay. See Wallerstein 1989.]

5 Important discussions from a mainly European perspective include Brenner 1977; DuPlessis 1977; Kriedte 1983 (orig. 1980); Sella 1977; Skocpol 1977. The fuller European literature is ably reviewed in DuPlessis 1987; see also Brenner 1976, and the debate and commentary in subsequent issues of *Past and Present*. These important essays may also be consulted in Aston and Philpin 1985.

6 Mariátegui 1928; Simpson 1929, significantly revised in a 1950 edition; Chávez Orozco 1938; Freyre 1933 (4th "definitive" ed. in 2 vols., 1943); McBride 1936; Puiggrós 1943; Zavala 1944; Borah 1951; Chevalier 1963 (orig. 1952); Lambert 1967 (orig. 1963). It should be noted that the interpretation of Latin American societies as feudal or neofeudal was not always among the central preoccupations of these works, but all nonetheless contributed to a feudal-like image. Gilberto Freyre, for example, was more concerned with the roots of Brazilian culture and national character than with feudalism, but his interpretation emphasized the bonds of dependence and patriarchalism that suffused the relation of aristocratic masters and their slave-servant populations on great landed estates, and he readily admitted the resemblance to feudalism. Compare the works by Morse 1954, 1964; O. Paz 1950 (rev. ed. 1959); and Tannenbaum 1946. For the intellectual context of writings by U.S. scholars, see the excellent essay by Keen 1985.

7 Miranda was part of the community of exiled Spanish intellectuals who resided in Mexico and helped launch El Colegio de México, a leading center of research and higher learning. (I thank my Mexican colleague Roger Bartra for this information.) Marchant resided in the United States but had been born in Rio de Janeiro, visited fairly regularly, and was a visible and involved figure in Brazil. See Russell-Wood 1985:694–95, and the obituary in *Hispanic American Historical Review* 62 (August 1982):459.

8 The connection of this recasting of colonial history and the emerging critique of the West is illuminated in the interviews held with James in 1975 and 1982, and reprinted in MARHO 1984:266–77.

9 See CEPAL 1949, 1951, 1969. See also the sources cited in note 11 below. Prebisch wrote CEPAL 1949 and was named CEPAL's executive secretary in 1950. More recent examples of CEPAL thinking, including that of Prebisch, may be followed in *CEPAL Review* (1976–).

10 This is to some extent a simplification because a number of people crossed the boundaries of these categories, thereby blurring, for example, the distinction between "in-house" and "external" criticism of CEPAL ideas. The various axes of debate sometimes intersected, intellectuals of diverse views knew and influenced one another, and CEPAL was sufficiently dynamic and inclusive to pull diverse figures under its institutional umbrella at one point or another. Andre Gunder Frank, for example, notwithstanding his polemics against moderate developmentalists, originally wrote one of his celebrated essays as a report for CEPAL. See Frank 1969a (rev. ed.; orig. ed. 1967):xii. My knowledge of the intellectual history of this period was greatly enhanced by the sources cited in note 11 below. A revealing warning against retrospective simplifications of this intellectual history is made by F. H. Cardoso (1977a:7–12).

11 Very helpful retrospectives by leading Latin American intellectuals on the origins and evolving response to the CEPAL and dependency ideas include F. H. Cardoso 1977a, 1977b; Halperín-Donghi 1982. Cardoso's essays cited above and several other illuminating articles on the history of CEPAL and dependency ideas are reprinted in F. H. Cardoso 1980. Also useful are Kahl 1976:14–17, 129–94; Hirschman 1971:85–89, 279–311; Love 1980. It is also worth noting that, despite the

growing conservatism of the West, especially in the United States, by the start of the 1950s, the intellectual critiques of the West and of advanced capitalism by Latin Americans did not occur in hermetically sealed intellectual isolation. The North Atlantic World also generated important critiques, among the most important of which were Polanyi 1944 (rpt. ed. 1957); Myrdal 1956, slightly revised in the better known Myrdal 1957; Baran 1957.

12 For a sampling of major works in three diverse countries, see the following: *for Brazil,* Bastide and Fernandes 1955 (2d rev. ed. 1959); F. H. Cardoso 1962, 1964; Fernandes 1965; Furtado 1959; Viotti da Costa 1966 (2d rev. ed. 1982); *for Mexico,* González Casanova 1965; Stavenhagen 1963; cf. Marroquín 1957, Fuentes 1962; *for Peru,* Bravo Bresani 1967; Malpica 1964 (3d rev. ed. 1968); Matos Mar et al., 1969 and the subsequent volumes in the *Perú—Problema* series organized by the Instituto de Estudios Peruanos; Quijano Obregón 1968, 1971. Among the works of the 1940s mentioned in the text, the books by Bagú (1949) and Prado (1942) circulated in new editions in the 1960s, and Miranda's essay (1941–46) was republished in pamphlet form by the Universidad Nacional Autónoma de México in 1965.

Naturally many of these works focused on topics particular to the countries in question: in Brazil, the myth of racial democracy and the legacy of slavery; in Mexico, the political order created by the Mexican Revolution and the continuing subordination of poor people and regions; in Peru, the split of the "nation" between Indian highlands and creole coast, and the dominance of coastal society by oligarchs and foreign capitalists. Nonetheless, the works and authors cited also formed part of a more general conjuncture of criticism in Latin America that blended into the critique of the feudalism thesis begun in the 1940s, and some authors had influence well beyond particular countries. (The fact that a number of critical intellectuals suffered exile in the 1960s facilitated this process.) Other works of more general influence and circulation included Stavenhagen 1968; Vitale 1968, 1969 (3d ed. 1972); dos Santos 1967. Stavenhagen 1968 is an expanded version of an article that first appeared in the Mexican newspaper *El Día* in June 1965; Vitale 1968 first appeared in the Chilean magazine *Estrategia* 5 (July 1966), according to Vitale 1969:19 n. 11.

13 For orientations to the literature from a variety of viewpoints and for further bibliographical references, see the following, in addition to the citations in note 11 above: Assadourian et al. 1973 (9th ed. 1982); Bartra et al. 1975 (rpt. in Lima, 1976); Chiaramonte 1984:89–95; Chilcote and Edelstein 1974; Chilcote 1983; Cooper 1981; Foster-Carter 1978; Klarén and Bossert 1986: esp. the essays by Klarén on 3–33 and by Bossert on 303–34; *LAP* 1974, 1981; Larson 1983; Palma 1978; Roseberry 1983:59–70; Taylor 1985.

14 A revised English-language version of Cardoso and Faletto's book was published in 1979 by the Univ. of California Press.

15 It should be noted that, notwithstanding the resonance of his 1969 work with dependency ideas, Halperín-Donghi has also strongly criticized the reductionism in much of the dependency literature (see 1982).

16 See especially the following textbooks: Burns 1972; Keen and Wasserman 1980; Skidmore and Smith 1984; cf. the popular interdisciplinary text by Wolf and Hansen 1972. These texts and Stein and Stein 1970 each sold well enough to justify reprints

or new editions and remained in print as of 1986. (My copy of Wolf and Hansen 1972 indicates that it was in its third printing by 1973.) One important new textbook that bears little imprint of dependency ideas is Lockhart and Schwartz 1983. Another textbook author treats dependency ideas with reserve but considers them too influential to ignore: see McAlister 1984:387–90.

17 The flexibility and evolution of Cardoso and Faletto is indicated by the changes introduced in the subsequent editions of their celebrated book and in an important article by F. H. Cardoso (1973). On the changes in various editions of Cardoso and Faletto's book, Packenham 1982 is somewhat useful although marred by the author's tendentious hostility to Cardoso and Faletto and by a narrow view of the oral and printed means by which ideas circulated in Santiago and elsewhere in Latin America. Reference to the translations of Frank 1969a (orig. 1967) may be found in the preface to the revised 1969 edition, p. xx. An enormously perceptive account of the reception of Frank's work in Latin America and in the United States is Halperín-Donghi 1982; cf. F. H. Cardoso 1977a.

18 As the prior discussion and notes 10 and 13 make clear, Frank's celebrated work (1969a) was not an isolated breakthrough but a part of a wider stream of revisionism undertaken by Latin Americans. In this regard, see esp. Stavenhagen 1968, 1963; González Casanova 1965. Frank wrote and continues to write a large number of books and articles, but it is his early work—mainly amplifications or extensions of the key ideas of his 1969a (orig. 1967) work—that is most important for the purposes of this essay. Other important early books were Frank 1969b, 1972. On the modifications introduced in the latter book, see Brenner 1977:83–86. A later publication on colonial Mexican agriculture was actually researched and written in 1965–66 and reflects his early views: see Frank 1979:vii–xii.

19 See the collection of articles, most of them first published in *Science and Society* in the 1950s, reprinted in Hilton et al. 1976; and Dobb 1947 (rev. ed. 1963). On the renewed interest in this debate in Latin America, see the citations in Assadourian et al. 1973; Bartra et al. 1975.

20 The most forceful proponents of this view were Dobb and Takahashi, in Hilton et al. 1976. Cf. Hobsbawm 1967.

21 See the sources cited in note 5 above.

22 On the weight of mining and mercantile exploitation in the structure and organization of economic life, the work of Carlos Sempat Assadourian is fundamental: 1973, 1982 (which reprints essays originally written in the 1960s and 1970s), and 1979; cf. Stern 1985. See also Bakewell 1971; Brading and Cross 1972; and the still useful classic by Wolf 1959:176–87.

23 See the discussion of silver mining below and the sources cited in notes 53, 59, and 60.

24 For examples, see Duncan and Rutledge 1977; Kay 1980; Mallon 1983; Womack, Jr. 1969:esp. 41–54. Cf. Bauer 1979.

25 For a comparison of Marxist and non-Marxist conceptualizations of capitalism, see Dobb 1947 (rev. ed. 1963):1–32; cf. Marx 1969, 1964.

26 It is by now a commonplace to observe that work and health conditions meant that the African slave populations of Brazil and the Caribbean were replaced by fresh imports from Africa rather than through biological replacement in America.

Planters commonly made estimates of life expectancy requiring that the short-term exchange-value of commodities produced by slaves be sufficient to ensure profitability despite high mortality and low net fertility rates. (By "net" fertility rates, I mean the rate of live births after subtracting out the rate of death in infancy.) In Bahia, Brazil, in the mid-eighteenth century, it appears that sugar planters recovered the cost of purchase and maintenance of a slave after only three and a half years. Contemporary estimates had it that a slave's life expectancy was in the range of seven to fifteen years, a revealing calculation despite the adjustments that must be made for infant and child mortality. See Schwartz 1985:226, but for context and caution about such calculations, see also 346–78; see also Klein 1986:154–61. On the commodification of forced labor in the mines of Spanish America, see Stern 1982:84–89, 148–57; Tandeter 1981a; Bakewell 1984: passim; and the discussion of silver mining later in this essay.

27 This is rather obvious to anyone familiar with the scholarship of Latin Americans in the period and is quite evident in Assadourian et al. 1973; and Bartra et al. 1975. By "Marxian," I refer both to scholarship self-defined as "Marxist" and scholarship strongly influenced by or engaged with the Marxist tradition but not necessarily self-identified with that tradition. U.S. readers should note, however, that Latin American intellectuals were often less timid than their U.S. counterparts about identifying their work as "Marxist" and that, given the variety of "Marxist" perspectives and debates that flourished from the 1960s on, such self-identifications implied little about intellectual orthodoxy or creativity. Finally, I should also mention the obvious: the creativity and originality of the period does not deny that it also witnessed a plethora of cruder Marxian publications. Every perspective generates its share of pedestrian work, and the Marxian corner was no exception.

28 See esp. C. F. S. Cardoso 1973a, 1973b, 1975. The third essay was originally presented at a panel on modes of production at the International Congress of Americanists held in Mexico City in September 1974 (all three essays, therefore, antedated circulation of Wallerstein 1974). Cf. Gorender 1978; Mata 1975 (orig. 1972). For the influence of such concepts in other "Third World" areas in the early 1970s, see Banaji 1972. For the subsequent evolution of Ciro F. S. Cardoso's ideas on slavery and colonial production, see Cardoso and Pérez Brignoli 1979, vol. 1; C. F. S. Cardoso 1979, 1984.

29 See Macera 1971; Semo 1973; cf. Bartra 1975; Carmagnani 1976. More recent publications along these lines include Morin 1979; Romano 1984; Villanueva 1985. Some of the key ideas on haciendas expounded in this literature—especially on the great estate's resilient capacity to blend servile labor with production for the market—were anticipated in pioneering studies by Wolf and Mintz 1957; Wolf 1959:202–11; Góngora 1960; Gibson 1964:326–34. The best studies of hacienda profit mechanisms over the course of fluctuating market cycles are Florescano 1969; Larson 1980. A pioneering and influential contribution to the articulation concept was Rey 1973; an overview and rigorous theoretical critique is presented in Wolpe 1980:1–43.

30 See Assadourian 1973, 1982; Chiaramonte 1975; Garavaglia 1973a, 1973b. For subsequent work on this issue by these authors, see Assadourian 1979, n.d.; Chiaramonte 1984; Garavaglia 1983.

31 I have in mind here especially Assadourian, "Integración y desintegración regional en el espacio colonial: un enfoque histórico," orig. pub. in the Chilean journal *EURE: Revista Latinoamericana de Estudios Urbanos Regionales* in 1972 and well known in South America in xerox and mimeograph form before its reprinting in Lima in Assadourian 1982:109–34; Assadourian et al. 1973, orig. pub. in Argentina in 1973, and in its ninth printing by Siglo Veintiuno (Mexico City, Buenos Aires, Madrid) as of 1982; Bartra et al. 1975, orig. pub. in Mexico in 1975 and republished in a Peruvian ed. in 1976; and Semo 1973, orig. pub. in 1973 in Mexico, where it had reached its twelfth printing as of 1983, and also published in a Cuban edition by Casa de las Américas in 1979. The important essays by Ciro F. S. Cardoso included in Assadourian et al. 1973 were also published in Brazil (Santiago 1975:61–143). It is not an exaggeration to say that only Ernesto Laclau's celebrated article (1971) circulated widely in both the United States and Latin America.

32 Palerm 1980:65–88 (see also 89–145); cf. Novais 1974, which has much in common with Williams 1944; Glausser R. 1974. Palerm's thoughtful critique of theory and relative receptivity to discussions of colonial capitalism bear comparison with two important essays by Sidney W. Mintz (1977, 1978; cf. 1985b).

33 See Halperín-Donghi 1982:129, whose argument on this point is in certain respects similar to mine.

34 For explicit engagement by students of Latin American or Caribbean history of key ideas formulated in Wallerstein 1974 (as distinct from, say, engagement of Andre Gunder Frank or various branches of the dependency literature), see Cardoso and Pérez 1979:1:152–58; Chapa 1981; Garavaglia 1983:22–24; Hall 1984, Mintz 1979, 1978; Palerm 1976; Roseberry 1983:59–66; Schwartz 1978; Wolf 1982:21–23, 297–98; Zeitlin 1984:220–37. For engagement of Wallerstein by students of the Spanish Borderlands, see Almaguer 1981; Weber 1986:81 n. 71. This list is not the product of a systematic, exhaustive investigation, but I believe that it reflects well the state of responses to Wallerstein. Three points stand out. First, very few of the respondents are Latin Americans. Second, the response was rather delayed; not until the 1980s does one even begin to identify a clustering of commentary, especially by Latin Americans. Third, and just as important, is a qualitative matter. The comments by Latin Americans on Wallerstein lack the intensity—as measured either by the heat of polemics or by the pursuit of a systematic appraisal—that were common in the response to Andre Gunder Frank in the late 1960s and early 1970s.

35 See García Márquez 1976:187–88, 208, 225, 229. The genius of García Márquez's humor, to a Latin American eye, lies in the way it is not all that far-fetched; this episode is no exception. After all, colonizers in Spanish America dug out, processed, and shipped off the insides of great silver mountains to turn the wheels of economic life and obsessions in Europe. I am grateful to my colleague in Spanish American literature, Professor Jill Netchinsky, Tufts University, for drawing my attention to García Márquez's use of the Columbus passages.

36 See in this regard the instructive comments of Zeitlin (1984:227–28 n. 15) on Wallerstein 1974; cf. my comments on Wallerstein 1980 in note 3 above.

37 Several discussions by Sidney W. Mintz are fundamental to considerations of capitalism and noncapitalism in the Caribbean context: see Mintz 1977, 1978; 1985b:55–61, 65–66, 180–86, et passim; 1961. On early Jamaica as a "pseudo-society," see

Patterson 1979; cf. Dunn 1972; James 1938; and the sophisticated discussion of settlement colonies and exploitation colonies in Knight 1978:56–66. The danger of the "pseudo-society" concept, of course, is that it might encourage one to slight the ways even the most extreme plantation islands witnessed the eventual development of a social and cultural life that made them more than deformed outposts of Europe (Patterson himself avoided this danger). On the slaves as culture builders from the earliest moments of their enslavement, see the seminal essay by Mintz and Price 1976.

38 Cf. Fox-Genovese and Genovese 1983:22–23.

39 Genovese 1969:part 1. In part 2 of the same book, Genovese argued that, precisely because of his extremism as an ideologue, George Fitzhugh is an illuminating example of the sometimes obscure philosophical direction in which the master class of the antebellum South was heading.

40 See the contrasts drawn between the western Paulista planters and those of the Paraíba Valley in Viotti da Costa 1966:passim; 1985:152–53, 157–59, 168–69, 222–23, 227–28.

41 For important early contributions to the history of *mita* labor in Potosí, see Basadre 1939; Crespo Rodas 1955–56; Helmer 1959:124–43; Kubler 1946:371–73; Rowe 1957:172–76; cf. Villarán 1964:101–45; Wiedner 1960:357–83. On the prevalence of the "classic" picture as of the early 1970s, see the comments of Brading and Cross 1972:557–60; cf. Padden 1975:xvii–xxiii; Villamarín and Villamarín 1975:2, 17, 19–20, 74–79. On the technical aspects and scale of production, see Brading and Cross 1972:547–56, 568–79; Bakewell 1984:8–32, 137–51; Bakewell 1975, 1977. Older works still useful are Bargalló 1969; 1955:esp. 107–66; Cobb 1947.

42 For recent research on social relations in Potosí during the early years, see Assadourian 1979; Bakewell 1984:14–19, 33–60; Barnadas 1973b. For the overall context of early colonization in Bolivia, see Barnadas 1973a. On the fragility of early nativewhite relations and the limits this imposed on European power, see Stern 1981. A major research effort to revamp our understanding of the history of mining has been undertaken by the Instituto de Estudios Peruanos and is described in Assadourian et al. 1980.

43 Matienzo 1567:132–33, 162–64; cf. Assadourian 1979:231–32.

44 See esp. Bakewell 1984:17–18, 65–120; Bakewell 1975; cf. Cole 1985:1–19. For the interconnected and in certain respects parallel case of the Huancavelica mercury mines, see Stern 1982:81–89, 106–09.

45 See Assadourian 1979:253–56; Bakewell 1984:127–28; cf. Tandeter 1981a:101.

46 See Bakewell 1984:123–31, 134–35, 161; Cole 1985:32–44, 56–57, et passim; Sánchez-Albornoz 1978:69–149; Tandeter 1981a:102–03. Tandeter (1981a:98–136) performed an economic analysis of *mita* rent for the late eighteenth century and demonstrated convincingly that it was central to profitability in this period. For comparison with the fate of the *mita* and the evolution of labor in Huancavelica, see Stern 1982:116–31, 140–57; cf. Basto Girón 1954:5–6, 10–13; Lohmann Villena 1949:103, 107, 120, 144–45, 160–61, 178, 185–86, 222, 242–43, 251–60, 266, 284–85, 285 n. 31.

47 See Bakewell 1984:36, 43–59; cf. Stern 1982:71–79; Lohmann Villena 1965.

48 Capoche 1585:166–67; Assadourian 1979:268–71; Bakewell 1984:79, 75.

49 Capoche 1585:109, 150–67, 174; Barnadas 1973b:16–70; Assadourian 1979:269–70; Bakewell 1984:123, 140–41. For the continuation of smelting in *guayras* in the seventeenth century, see the famous work by the Potosí priest Alonso Barba 1637:130–31, 139–41 (Book 4, chaps. 1, 6).

50 Capoche's treatise (1585:69–189) is one of the most highly regarded and frequently used documents on early Potosí.

51 Capoche 1585:173–74; cf. Ayans 1596:39–40, 66; Bakewell 1984:121–22; Cole 1985:62–63. On the preference for the *mita* drafts over other forms of labor, from a narrow economic point of view, in another Andean mining region, see Stern 1982:192, 260 n. 10.

52 Note that even when employers initially conceded a single piece of good ore per unit of work as part of the "wage," employers held an interest in defining the ore concession as a "wage," a fixed standard of payment according to work performed, rather than a "share," a right of fractional appropriation in the *product* of the work performed. Thus the issue is complex, since the distinction between "wage" and "share" is not, strictly speaking, identical to that between payment in silver coin or unprocessed ore. The *mingas* essentially transformed ore conceded as part of a "wage" into customary rights of appropriation and even possession in the mine and its product.

53 See Tandeter 1981b:43–65 (production figures are on 51); Tandeter 1981a. In 1778, Miguel Feijoó de Sosa's report to Viceroy Guirior calculated that *kajcheo* ores accounted for 53 percent of the refined silver recorded in Potosí's Banco de Rescates (official silver-purchasing bank) during the period 1773–77. Feijoó de Sosa to Guirior, Lima, September 10, 1778, printed in Paz 1786:2:350–51.

54 This statement is more certain for the mines than the refineries, about which information is more sparse. But the refineries hardly corroborate Wallerstein's picture either, since the question, for the case of the refineries, is whether "wage" or "share" relations were more dominant.

55 The most innovative work in Andean economic history has emphasized the rise of internal American markets, especially interregional markets, into a force with a logic of its own, sometimes more important in commercial terms than the international flow of trade. See Assadourian 1979, 1982 (esp. 109–34, 277–321); cf. Stern 1985:134–39, 142–43; Garavaglia 1983.

56 The strongest and most politically organized effort to deal with the issue came during 1579–84 and is presented in Barnadas 1973b; Capoche 1585:150–67; cf. Assadourian 1979:254–55, 268–70. It is obvious from the sources, however, that Indian share arrangements and ore marketing constituted a problematic issue that festered before and after this period, and that colonizers tried a variety of means to limit the damage—by curtailing the customary rights and independence of voluntary workers or by intensifying forced labor in the mines. For helpful discussions, see Bakewell 1984:46–54, 84; Cole 1985:23–25, 52–53; Tandeter 1981a:104–05; cf. Matienzo 1567:16–20, 134–35; Stern 1982:74–75.

57 Bakewell 1984:113–14. The importance of ore shares in the private labor system that developed in Oruro is underscored in a fine study that appeared after this article was drafted: Zulawski 1987:405–30, esp. 411–20.

58 See Bakewell 1984:182–83; Bakewell 1971; Florescano 1980:72–74; Chapa 1981.

For the eighteenth century, see Brading 1971; Morin 1979:92–101. One of the most original and significant points in Bakewell's study of Potosí is that the conventional contrast between free labor in the Mexican mines and forced labor in the Andean mines is greatly overdrawn. See Bakewell 1984:179–86.

59 See Bakewell 1971:121–29, 145–46, 189, 193, 199–201, 209–10; Brading 1971:147–49, 157, 197, 233–38, 274–78, 282, 284–91; and Chapa 1981:523–28. Luís Chávez Orozco has published several collections of documents illuminating the important labor conflict at Real de Monte in 1766: see Chávez Orozco 1935, 1960a, 1960b; cf. Arellano Z. 1976; and the comments on Ladd 1988 in note 60 below.

60 See Brading 1971:156–58, 274–78, 284–91. Ladd 1988, a fine book, appeared after this essay was drafted. In her splendid analysis of labor conflicts over share rights, Ladd argues convincingly that the workers of Real del Monte successfully defended their *partidos* (although new rules of ore mixing reduced the quality of *partido* ores claimed by the workers). Brading's more comprehensive study (1971) demonstrates that Ladd erred, however, when she implied (92, 96–97, 120, 124) that customary share rights continued to prevail in Mexico's other silver mines. Especially in Guanajuato, the most important silver-mining zone in the late eighteenth century, attacks against laborers' customary rights were more ruthlessly and successfully enforced than at Real del Monte.

61 The focus of this article's assessment of Wallerstein's world-system is on labor, and an extended analysis of American markets and elite interests whose own logic sometimes diverged from that of Europe is out of place here. But a rapidly expanding secondary literature exists on this point. For the logic of the American marketplace in Andean South America, see the sources cited in note 55 and the following: Andrien 1985: esp. chap. 2; Assadourian n.d.; Larson 1980, 1988; Harris, Larson, and Tandeter 1987; cf. Stern 1982. For works that illuminate the internal divisions and the Americanization of bureaucracy that constrained metropolitan power in Habsburg South America during the sixteenth and seventeenth centuries, see Phelan 1967; Andrien 1985; Cole 1985; Lohmann Villena 1957; Parry 1953; Stern 1982:93–102, 115–32; cf. Schwartz 1970; Lynch 1973: chap. 1; Phelan 1978. The wider imperial context for much of this literature is the decline of Spain; for stimulating debate on the subject and orientation to its historiography, see Kamen 1978 (and the debate cited in the bibliographical reference below). For further clarification of context and issues, see Elliott 1984, 1986; Israel 1982; Phillips 1987.

62 Wallerstein himself (1974, 1980) did a masterful job of demonstrating internal rivalries within Europe and saw hegemony within the core of the capitalist world-economy as relatively rare (1980:38 et passim; cf. 1984:37–46). What this may imply for the validity of his conceptual framework is not thoroughly scrutinized, in my judgment. On Spain and Portugal's dependence on rival European powers, see the classic essay by Stein and Stein 1970; cf. the emphasis on Malthusian limits in Phillips 1987. For a specific example of the way multiple narrow goals and interests could serve, within Spanish America, to divide elites against themselves in ways that thwarted realization of the general interest uniting them, see Stern 1982: chap. 5. Compare the sources on bureaucracy cited in note 61 above.

63 The most careful and nuanced discussion of the variety of labor relations linked to sugar production in the Caribbean is made by Sidney W. Mintz, to whom I am considerably indebted in the following discussion. See Mintz 1977:256–57, 260–61; 1978:85–90; 1985b:52–54.

64 Fernández-Armesto 1982:84–86, 202. Cf. the sugar-related contracts in Marrero Rodríguez 1974: esp. Contracts 13, 14, 61, 107, 114, 127, 185, 186, 237, 255. If read carefully, the intensively researched study of slavery on the Canaries by Lobo Cabrera 1982 confirms the impression that African slavery was of modest consequence in production on the islands before the 1520s and perhaps after. It also underscores the importance of the early Canaries mainly as a way station, or import-export market, for slaves destined for Europe and America. See 141–65, 205–13, 232–37. The evidence in Lobo Cabrera's work also suggests the possibility, however, that labor on sugar plantations in this period may have often relied on a mix of European sharecropper labor with small numbers of slaves borrowed, loaned, rented, or owned by the sharecroppers.

65 See Echagoian 1568:441–61, esp. 446; Mintz 1985:32–35, esp. 34; Deive 1980:1:51–102; Ratekin 1954. For a good overview of the early Spanish Caribbean, see Sauer 1966.

66 See Saco 1938:1:204; Fernández-Armesto 1982:85 n. 81.

67 For the political and ideological context of experiments with European colonizers as agriculturalists, see Hanke 1949: esp. 54–71; Sauer 1966:203–06. On the related issue of European images of Indians, see Pagden 1982.

68 Figueroa to Carlos I, November 14, 1520, in Wright 1916:773, 772 (quotation). Cf. Deive 1980:1:71; Sauer 1966:201–02, 212; Tolentino Dipp 1974:160–61; Moya Pons 1976:72.

69 Sauer 1966: passim; Fernández-Armesto 1982:173–74; Lobo Cabrera 1982:141; Radell 1976:67–76; cf. MacLeod 1973:50–52; Sherman 1979:20–82.

70 On the fear of revolt, see Deive 1980:2:437–41, 602–04. The first important slave revolt on the island occurred in 1522.

71 For an especially careful and perceptive discussion along these lines from which, as usual, I have benefitted substantially, see Mintz 1977:253–70, esp. 255–57, 267–68 n. 11.

72 The argument is presented succinctly in Schwartz 1978, and in revised and fuller form in Schwartz 1985:15–72. The pioneering work on Indian labor and the transition to African slave labor was Marchant 1942b. For Portuguese-Indian relations as a whole, see Hemming 1978.

73 Schwartz 1985:67 (Table 3–5), 61 (Table 3–3). My calculation of mothers deletes the category of "Negro/crioulo" given in Table 3–3, because Schwartz (1985:516 n. 31) indicated this term was applied to Indians as well as Africans on the chapel register.

74 Equally critical, albeit from a different theoretical perspective, of the explanatory value of the world-system for the colonial Brazilian case is Hall 1984.

75 The literature on early British America and the servant-slave mix is voluminous, but the best work on early labor strategies and the local conditions, including social conflict, that led to increased reliance on African slaves is Morgan 1975. For Bar-

bados, Jamaica, and South Carolina (the most "Caribbean" of the colonies on the British American mainland), I have found the following especially useful: Dunn 1972: esp. 59–74, 212–23; Craton and Walvin 1970: esp. 20–21, 32, 51–52; Wood 1974. For a recent overview, see Beckles 1985; cf. the pioneering and controversial early statement by Handlin and Handlin 1950. On the sometimes underestimated significance of Indian slavery in British America, and for general context, see G. Nash 1974:111–14, 145–53.

76 See Wallerstein 1980:171–75. For more detailed references, see note 3 above; cf. Cooper 1981:10, 59–60 n. 36.

77 Recent episodes in the scholarly debate about the fundamental meaning of "slavery" include Kopytoff and Miers 1977; Patterson 1982; cf. Cooper 1979; Lerner 1986:76–100. David Brion Davis has illuminated the changing meanings, symbolism, and implications of the slavery concept, especially in the context of Western civilization, in several important books: 1966, 1975, 1984. A sense for the variety of slave experiences in Latin America and the Caribbean may be gained from the recent overview by Klein 1986, and its excellent bibliographical essay.

78 These themes run throughout Mintz's work on the Caribbean. See Mintz 1979, 1985a, 1974 (part 2), 1978:91–96. The estimate that 20 percent of the coin in circulation was controlled by slaves is from Jamaica in the late eighteenth century (cited in Mintz 1978:95). Cf. Gaspar 1985:145–49; Schwartz 1985:157, 159, 252–53, 458 (but for a contrasting view of Brazil's sugar zones, see Gorender 1978:241–67).

79 For a provocative statement on the "breach" and its limits, see C. F. S. Cardoso 1979:133–54.

80 It is significant that the bitter conflict over mine labor in Mexico in the eighteenth century stemmed from attempts of entrepreneurs to convert share relations into straightforward wage labor. Given the laborers' capacity and determination to resist the new scheme, but their inability to defeat labor reforms altogether, the outcome increased the role of forced paid labor in the mines. On this specific case, see the sources in note 59 above; for a more theoretical discussion of the limits of free wage labor in a colonial context, and the structural contradictions that forced entrepreneurs to pursue free and coercive labor strategies simultaneously, see Stern 1982:138–57, esp. 155–57.

81 The phenomenon is quite well known to students of southern Andean regions. For Cuzco, see Glave and Remy 1983:291, 341–87 (esp. 369, 371), 402–03, 455–97 (esp. 488–89), 515–22. For Ayacucho, see Huertas Vallejos 1974; 1977:52–53; Díaz Martínez 1969; cf. Stern 1982. For Cochabamba, see Larson 1988. Cf. the more general comments in Assadourian et al. 1980:15–16; Halperín-Donghi 1969:134–59, esp. 142–43; Bonilla 1987:220–21. Wolf and Mintz's classic essay on "Haciendas and Plantations" (1957) pointed precisely to the distinctive characteristics of haciendas (as compared to capitalist plantations) that enabled them to survive through involution during depressed times and to open outward in more dynamic ways during prosperous times.

82 Note that I refer here to economic patterns corresponding more to "feudalism" by Wallerstein's own definition of the contrast between the "serfdom" associated with

feudalism and the "coerced cash-crop labor" associated with capitalism. Wallerstein 1974:91, 126–27.

83 The alternative approach can be traced back at least as far as the Dobb-Sweezy debate and the classic essay by Hobsbawm cited in notes 19 and 20 above. Within the more recent cycle of such discussion, particularly outstanding works include (in chronological order) Genovese 1969; Laclau 1971; Brenner 1976, 1977; and Fox-Genovese and Genovese 1983. An extremely significant work that uses the mode of production concept seriously, yet steps creatively outside standard Europe-centered categories, is Wolf 1982.

84 As should be clear from my earlier analysis, I agree with the first part of the twofold argument drawn from Marx. The second part is in my view more problematic and reductionist both as a historical tool of analysis and as an interpretation of Marx. Marx's discussion of commercial capital in *Capital*, like the entire discussion of capitalism, slides back and forth between two levels of analysis: a theoretical level designed to show that the inner "secret" of capital accumulation rests not on commercial exchange and gouging as such but on the distinctive social relations and forces of production that enable entrepreneurs to accumulate profits even if they pay a "fair" market price for labor-power; and a historical level of analysis that looks at capitalism as it actually emerged and existed and that acknowledges more readily the historical importance of markets, merchant capital, and colonialism in the creation and expansion of capitalism. Those who draw on Marx to stress the inherent conservatism of merchant capital seem to me to have conflated these two levels of analysis and to have sidestepped Marx's own unresolved ambiguities.

85 See Bakewell 1984:13, 137–40, 152–54; Brading and Cross 1972:549–51; Mintz 1985b:46–52; Schwartz 1985:142–45, 152–55.

86 See Assadourian 1982:109–221, 277–321; Stern 1985:134–40; 1982:47–50, 74–75, 80–113, 138–61, 185–86; cf. Schwartz 1985:239–41; and the comment in note 87 below.

87 It is quite instructive that scholars who stress the predominance of feudalism in colonial Spanish America but are simultaneously aware of the complicating "capitalist" features evident in the silver mines handle the contradiction by seeing the mines as a kind of economic appendage or enclave whose secondary effects were minor in an overwhelmingly agrarian society. For a prominent early example from Mexico, see Chávez Orozco 1938. Modernized into a theoretical statement on the articulation of modes of production, the same approach leads to the conclusion that capitalism was "embryonic," joined to and stifled by a dominant feudal mode of production. A prominent and sophisticated example is Semo 1973.

88 This characteristic is so familiar empirically that almost any colonial scholar who has researched the documents of particular enterprises will recognize it. Especially valuable on this point is Macera 1971:171–204. For a fuller sampling of research on Mexico and Peru demonstrating varied labor relations even on agrarian enterprises whose labor regimes might seem less internally heterogeneous from afar, see the following: Brading 1978:31–38, 75–76, 95–114; Cushner 1980:81–86, 89–91; Florescano 1975: passim; Glave and Remy 1983:133–38, 341–69; Konrad 1980:222–

36, 246–54, 318–23, 326–30; Martin 1985:121–53; Morin 1979:257–83; Polo y la Borda G. 1976:50–69; Stern 1982:141–46, 155–57, 191; Tutino 1975; Van Young 1981:236–64; cf. Van Young 1983:23–24. The literature on labor has also established that Charles Gibson's criticisms of the classic image of debt peonage were correct. See Gibson 1964:252–56; Bauer 1979.

89 See Stern 1982:155–57; cf. Velasco Avila 1985. One important exception is the tendency of sugar plantations to rely mainly on African slavery during boom periods. But such cases were rarer than often assumed, and the contrast may be one of degree. See Mintz 1977:260–61. It is also possible, of course, that the conventional reading of labor in European history is misleading and that, during a "long" early modern period, variegated labor patterns of the kind discussed here were far more prevalent in Western Europe than usually assumed. The literature on "protoindustrialization" in Europe perhaps points in this direction and resonates interestingly with the colonial Latin American experience, but a theoretically informed and systematic comparison of the findings of the protoindustrialization literature with research on labor and economy in colonial Latin America lies beyond the scope of this essay. I hope to take up the matter in a future essay. On "protoindustrialization," see Mendels 1972; Medick 1976; Kriedte, Medick, and Schlumbohm 1981; Kriedte 1983; and DuPlessis 1987:23–26.

90 Beyond a certain point, such a method calls on the historian to merge the perspectives of social history and political economy. To arrive at a deep understanding, for example, of "popular strategies of resistance and survival" in a colonial context may require a well-rounded consideration of social relations and cultural ideals, raising topics such as ethnicity, gender, or religion that are more commonly assigned to "social history." Consider, for instance, the pertinent unanswered questions about the role of gender relations and household strategies in the structure and evolution of the Potosí silver economy suggested by the earlier observation (p. 40 above) that women labored as the smelters and vendors of ores appropriated by male *minga* laborers in share arrangements. For more contemporary examples illustrating this methodological point for the case of the Bolivian tin mines, which replaced silver in preeminence in twentieth-century Bolivia, see J. Nash 1979; Barrios de Chungara 1978; Delgado P. 1985.

91 A third innovation, the proposal that we conceptualize the colonial economy as a complex and historically specific articulation of various modes of production into a unique "whole," is more well known. But it too has largely escaped the rigorous critical engagement needed to test, refine, and draw out its promise or limitations.

I am well aware that, by the late 1970s and early 1980s, a certain disillusionment with the mode of production concept set in among some intellectuals on the left, including Latin Americans, who had once used the concept more readily. Indeed, I would argue that, in part *because* the concept passed out of scholarly fashion, theoretical innovations on colonial Latin America proposed in the early 1970s generally escaped the sustained critical and empirical appraisal they deserved. The shift of the intellectual winds was linked to a broader disquiet about general theory and about Marxism derived from dissatisfaction both with classical orthodoxy and with the theoretical schemes and categories that proliferated in the 1960s and 1970s. The old universal theories were replaced not by conceptual breakthroughs commanding broad assent but by a plethora of theoretical schemes and political agendas whose rapid multiplication and varied quality reinforced a sense of intellectual fragmentation and limited comprehension. In my view, the perceived "crisis of theory" was a kind of mirror image of the perceived "explosion of theory," and it affected non-Marxist as well as Marxist scholarship. Among intellectuals on the left, Ernesto Laclau himself has contributed importantly to this sobering rethinking of theory. See Laclau 1977; Laclau and Mouffe 1985.

References

The following abbreviations are used: CEPAL for Comisión Económica para América Latina; *LAP* for *Latin American Perspectives*.

Almaguer, Tomás. 1981. "Interpreting Chicano History: The World-System Approach to Nineteenth-Century California." *Review* 4 (Winter):459–507.
Alonso Barba, Álvaro. 1637. *Arte de los metales, en que se enseña el verdadero beneficio de los de oro, y plata* . . . Facs. rpt. of 1770 ed., 1925. Mexico City: Compañía Fundidora de Fierro y Acero de Monterrey.
Andrien, Kenneth J. 1985. *Crisis and Decline: The Viceroyalty of Peru in the Seventeenth Century*. Albuquerque: Univ. of New Mexico Press.
Arellano Z., Manuel, ed. 1976. *Primera huelga minera en Real de Monte, 1766*. Mexico City: PRI, Comisión Nacional Editorial.
Assadourian, Carlos Sempat. 1973. "Modos de producción, capitalismo y subdesarrollo en América Latina." In Assadourian et al. 1973:47–81.
Assadourian, Carlos Sempat. 1979. "La producción de la mercancía dinero en la formación del mercado interno colonial: el caso del espacio peruano, siglo XVI." In Florescano 1979:223–92.
Assadourian, Carlos Sempat. 1982. *El sistema de la economía colonial: mercado interno, regiones y espacio económico*. Lima: Instituto de Estudios Peruanos.
Assadourian, Carlos Sempat. n.d. *Análisis sobre la formación del sistema colonial*. Mexico City: Grijalbo.
Assadourian, Carlos Sempat, et al. 1973. *Modos de producción en América Latina*. 9th ed., 1982. Mexico City: Siglo Veintiuno Editores.
Assadourian, Carlos Sempat, et al. 1980. *Minería y espacio económico en los Andes, siglos XVI–XX*. Lima: Instituto de Estudios Peruanos.
Aston, Trevor, ed. 1967. *Crisis in Europe, 1560–1660*. Garden City, N.Y.: Anchor.
Aston, T. H., and C. H. E. Philpin, eds. 1985. *The Brenner Debate: Agrarian Class Structure and Economic Development in Pre-Industrial Europe*. New York: Cambridge Univ. Press.
Ayans, Antonio de. 1596. "Breve relación de los agravios que reciben los indios que ay desde cerca del Cuzco hasta Potosí . . ." In Ruben Vargas Ugarte, ed., *Pareceres jurídicos en asuntos de Indias* (Lima: Compañía de Impresiones y Publicidad, 1951).
Bagú, Sergio. 1949. *Economía de la sociedad colonial: ensayo de historia comparada de América Latina*. Buenos Aires: Ateneo.

Bakewell, Peter J. 1971. *Silver Mining and Society in Colonial Mexico: Zacatecas, 1546–1700*. Cambridge: Cambridge Univ. Press.

Bakewell, Peter J. 1975. "Registered Silver Production in the Potosí District, 1550–1735." *Jahrbuch für Geschichte von Staat, Wirtschaft und Gesellschaft Lateinamerikas* 12:67–103.

Bakewell, Peter J. 1977. "Technological Change in Potosí: The Silver Boom of the 1570s." *Ibid.* 14:60–77.

Bakewell, Peter J. 1984. *Miners of the Red Mountain: Indian Labor in Potosí, 1545–1650*. Albuquerque: Univ. of New Mexico Press.

Banaji, Jairus. 1972. "For a Theory of Colonial Modes of Production." *Economic and Political Weekly* (Bombay) 7:2498–502.

Baran, Paul A. 1957. *The Political Economy of Growth*. New York: Monthly Review Press.

Bargalló, Modesto. 1955. *La minería y la metalurgía en la América española durante la época colonial*. Mexico City: Fondo de Cultura Económica.

Bargalló, Modesto. 1969. *La amalgamación de los minerales de plata*. Mexico City: Compañía Fundidora de Fierro y Acero de Monterrey.

Barnadas, Josep M. 1973a. *Charcas: orígenes históricos de una sociedad colonial*. La Paz: Centro de Investigación y Promoción del Campesinado.

Barnadas, Josep M. 1973b. "Una polémica colonial: Potosí, 1579–1584." *Jahrbuch für Geschichte von Staat, Wirtschaft und Gesellschaft Lateinamerikas* 10:16–70.

Barrios de Chungara, Domitila, with Moemma Viezzer. 1978. *Let Me Speak! Testimony of Domitila, A Woman of the Bolivian Mines*. Trans. Victoria Ortíz. New York: Monthly Review Press.

Bartra, Roger. 1975. "Sobre la articulación de modos de producción en América Latina." In Bartra et al. 1975:5–19.

Bartra, Roger, et al. 1975. *Modos de producción en América Latina*. Reprint ed. 1976. Lima: Delva Editores.

Basadre, Jorge. 1939. "El régimen de la mita." In Valega 1939:187–203.

Bastide, Roger, and Florestan Fernandes. 1955. *Brancos e negros em São Paulo*. 2d rev. ed., 1959. São Paulo: Companhia Editora Nacional.

Basto Girón, Luis J. 1954. *Las mitas de Huamanga y Huancavelica*. Lima: Editora Médica Peruana.

Bauer, Arnold J. 1979. "Rural Workers in Spanish America: Problems of Peonage and Oppression." *Hispanic American Historical Review* 59 (Feb.):34–63.

Bazant, Jan. 1950. "Feudalismo y capitalismo en la historia de México." *El Trimestre económico* 17:81–98.

Beckles, Hilary McD. 1985. "Plantation Production and White Proto-Slavery: White Indentured Servants and the Colonization of the English West Indies, 1624–1645." *Americas* 41 (Jan.):21–45.

Bonilla, Heraclio. 1987. "The Indian Peasantry and 'Peru' during the War with Chile." In Stern 1987:219–31.

Borah, Woodrow. 1951. *New Spain's Century of Depression*. Berkeley: Univ. of California Press.

Brading, David. 1971. *Miners and Merchants in Bourbon Mexico, 1736–1810*. Cambridge: Cambridge Univ. Press.

Brading, David. 1978. *Haciendas and Ranchos in the Mexican Bajío: León, 1700–1860*. New York: Cambridge Univ. Press.

Brading, David, and Harry E. Cross. 1972. "Colonial Silver Mining: Mexico and Peru." *Hispanic American Historical Review* 52 (Nov.):545–79.

Bravo Bresani, Jorge. 1967. *Desarrollo y subdesarrollo: de la economía del hambre a la economía del hombre*. Lima: F. Moncloa.

Brenner, Robert. 1976. "Agrarian Class Structure and Economic Development in Pre-Industrial Europe." *Past and Present* 70 (Feb.):30–75.

Brenner, Robert. 1977. "The Origins of Capitalist Development: A Critique of Neo-Smithian Marxism." *New Left Review* 104 (July–Aug.):25–92.

Burns, Bradford E. 1972. *Latin America: A Concise Interpretive History*. Englewood Cliffs, N.J.: Prentice Hall.

Capoche, Luis. 1585. "Relación general del asiento y Villa Imperial de Potosí . . ." Reprinted in *Biblioteca de Autores Españoles*, 122 (Madrid: Ediciones Atlas. 1959), 69–189.

Cardoso, Ciro F. S. 1973a. "El modo de producción esclavista colonial en América." In Assadourian et al. 1973:193–242.

Cardoso, Ciro F. S. 1973b. "Sobre los modos de producción coloniales de América." In Assadourian et al. 1973:135–59.

Cardoso, Ciro F. S. 1975. "Los modos de producción coloniales: estado de la cuestión y perspectiva teórica." In Bartra et al. 1975:90–106.

Cardoso, Ciro F. S. 1979. *Agricultura, escravidão e capitalismo*. Petrópolis: Editora Vozes.

Cardoso, Ciro F. S. 1984. *Economía e sociedade em áreas colonais periféricas: Guiana Francesa e Pará (1750–1817)*. Rio de Janeiro: Graal.

Cardoso, Ciro F. S., and Hector Pérez Brignoli. 1979. *Historia económica de América Latina*. 2 vols. Barcelona: Crítica.

Cardoso, Fernando Henrique. 1962. *Capitalismo e escravidão no Brasil meridional*. São Paulo: Difusão Europeia do Livro.

Cardoso, Fernando Henrique. 1964. *Empresário industrial e desenvolvimento econômico no Brasil*. São Paulo: Difusão Europeia do Livro.

Cardoso, Fernando Henrique. 1973. "Associated-Dependent Development: Theoretical and Practical Implications." In Stepan 1973:142–78.

Cardoso, Fernando Henrique. 1977a. "The Consumption of Dependency Theory in the United States." *Latin American Research Review* 12:7–12.

Cardoso, Fernando Henrique. 1977b. "The Originality of a Copy: CEPAL and the Idea of Development." *CEPAL Review*: Second Half 1977 Volume:7–40.

Cardoso, Fernando Henrique. 1980. *As idéias e seu lugar: ensaios sobre as teorias do desenvolvimento*. Petrópolis: Editora Vozes.

Cardoso, Fernando Henrique, and Enzo Faletto. 1969. *Dependencia y desarrollo en América Latina*. Mexico City. Rev. English ed. 1979: *Dependency and Development in Latin America*. Trans. Marjory Mattingly Urquidi. Berkeley: Univ. of California Press.

Carmagnani, Marcello. 1976. *Formación y crisis de un sistema feudal*. Mexico City: Siglo Veintiuno Editores.

CEPAL (Comisión Económica para América Latina). 1949. *The Economic Develop-*

ment of Latin America and Its Principal Problems. English reprint of orig. Spanish ed., 1950. New York: United Nations Department of Economic Affairs.

CEPAL. 1951. *Economic Survey of Latin America, 1949*. New York: United Nations Department of Economic Affairs.

CEPAL. 1969. *El pensamiento de la CEPAL*. Santiago de Chile: Editorial Universitaria.

Chapa, Jorge. 1981. "Wage Labor in the Periphery: Silver Mining in Colonial Mexico." *Review* 4 (Winter):509–34.

Chávez Orozco, Luís. 1935. *La situación del minero asalariado en la Nueva España a fines del siglo XVIII*. 2d ed., 1978. Mexico City: Centro de Estudios Históricos del Movimiento Obrero Mexicano.

Chávez Orozco, Luís. 1938. *Historia económica y social de México: ensayo de interpretación*. Mexico City: Ediciones Bota.

Chávez Orozco, Luís. 1960a. *Conflicto de trabajo con los mineros de Real de Monte, Año de 1766*. Mexico City: Talleres Gráficos de la Nación.

Chávez Orozco, Luís. 1960b. *Los salarios y el trabajo en México durante el siglo XVIII*. 2d ed., 1978. Mexico City: Centro de Estudios Históricos del Movimiento Obrero Mexicano.

Chevalier, François. 1963. *Land and Society in Colonial Mexico: The Great Hacienda*. Trans. Alvin Eustis (orig. French ed. 1952). Berkeley: Univ. of California Press.

Chiaramonte, José Carlos. 1975. "El problema del tipo histórico de sociedad: crítica de sus supuestos." In Bartra et al. 1975:107–25.

Chiaramonte, José Carlos. 1984. *Formas de sociedad y economía en hispanoamérica*. Mexico City: Grijalbo.

Chilcote, Ronald H. 1983. "Dependency or Mode of Production? Theoretical Issues." In Chilcote and Johnson 1983:9–30.

Chilcote, Ronald H., and Joel C. Edelstein. 1974. "Introduction: Alternative Perspectives of Development and Underdevelopment in Latin America." In Chilcote and Edelstein, eds., *Latin America: The Struggle with Dependency and Beyond*. New York: Halsted Press, 1–87.

Chilcote, Ronald H., and Dale L. Johnson, eds. 1983. *Theories of Development: Mode of Production or Dependency?* Beverly Hills, Calif.: Sage Publications.

Cobb, Gwendoline Ballantine. 1947. "Potosí and Huancavelica: Economic Bases of Peru, 1545 to 1640." Ph.D. diss., Univ. of California, Berkeley.

Cole, Jeffrey A. 1985. *The Potosí Mita, 1573–1700: Compulsory Indian Labor in the Andes*. Stanford: Stanford Univ. Press.

Cooper, Frederick. 1979. "The Problem of Slavery in African Studies." *Journal of African History* 20:103–25.

Cooper, Frederick. 1981. "Africa and the World Economy." *African Studies Review* 24 (June–Sept.):1–86.

Craton, Michael, ed. 1979. *Roots and Branches: Current Directions in Slave Studies*. Toronto: Pergamon Press.

Craton, Michael, and James Walvin. 1970. *A Jamaican Plantation: The History of Worthy Park, 1670–1970*. Toronto: Univ. of Toronto Press.

Crespo Rodas, Alberto. 1955–56. "La 'mita' de Potosí." *Revista histórica* (Lima) 22:169–82.

Cushner, Nicolas P. 1980. *Lords of the Land: Sugar, Wine, and Jesuit Estates of Coastal Peru, 1600–1767*. Albany: State Univ. of New York Press.

Davis, David Brion. 1966. *The Problem of Slavery in Western Culture*. Ithaca, N.Y.: Cornell Univ. Press.

Davis, David Brion. 1975. *The Problem of Slavery in the Age of Revolution, 1770–1823*. Ithaca, N.Y.: Cornell Univ. Press.

Davis, David Brion. 1984. *Slavery and Human Progress*. New York: Oxford Univ. Press.

Deive, Carlos Esteban. 1980. *La esclavitud del negro en Santo Domingo (1492–1844)*. 2 vols. Santo Domingo: Museo del Hombre Dominicano.

Delgado P., Guillermo. 1985. "Industrial Stagnation and Women's Strategies for Survival at the Siglo XX and Uncía Mines." In Greaves and Culver 1985:162–70.

Denevan, William M., ed. 1976. *The Native Population of the Americas in 1492*. Madison: Univ. of Wisconsin Press.

Díaz Martínez, Antonio. 1969. *Ayacucho: hambre y esperanza*. Ayacucho: Ediciones Waman.

Dobb, Maurice. 1947. *Studies in the Development of Capitalism*. Rev. ed., 1963. New York: International Publishers.

Dos Santos, Theotonio. 1967. "El nuevo carácter de la dependencia (gran empresa y capital extranjero)." *Cuadernos del Centro de Estudios Socioeconómicos* 6:9–50.

Duncan, Kenneth, and Ian Rutledge, eds. 1977. *Land and Labour in Latin America: Essays on the Development of Agrarian Capitalism in the Nineteenth and Twentieth Centuries*. Cambridge: Cambridge Univ. Press.

Dunn, Richard S. 1972. *Sugar and Slaves: The Rise of the Planter Class in the English West Indies, 1624–1713*. Chapel Hill: Univ. of North Carolina Press.

DuPlessis, Robert S. 1977. "From Demesne to World-System: A Critical Review of the Literature on the Transition from Feudalism to Capitalism." *Radical History Review* 4 (Winter):3–41.

DuPlessis, Robert S. 1987. "The Partial Transition to World-Systems Analysis in Early Modern History." *Radical History Review* 39:11–27.

Echagoian, Juan de. 1568. "Relación de la isla Española . . ." Pub. in *Boletín del Archivo General de la Nación* (Trujillo, Dominican Republic) 4 (Dec. 1941):441–61.

Elliott, J. H. 1984. *Richelieu and Olivares*. New York: Cambridge Univ. Press.

Elliott, J. H. 1986. *The Count-Duke of Olivares: The Statesman in an Age of Decline*. New Haven: Yale Univ. Press.

Fernandes, Florestan. 1965. *A integração do negro na sociedade de clases*. 2 vols. São Paulo: Dominus Editora.

Fernández-Armesto, Felipe. 1982. *The Canary Islands After the Conquest: The Making of a Colonial Society in the Early Sixteenth Century*. New York: Oxford Univ. Press.

Florescano, Enrique. 1969. *Precios del maíz y crisis agrícolas en México (1708–1810)*. Mexico City: El Colegio de México.

Florescano, Enrique, ed. 1975. *Haciendas, latifundios y plantaciones en América Latina*. Mexico City: Siglo Veintiuno Editores.

Florescano, Enrique, ed. 1979. *Ensayos sobre el desarrollo económico de México y América Latina (1500–1975)*. Mexico City: Fondo de Cultura Económica.

Florescano, Enrique. 1980. "La formación de los trabajadores en la época colonial,

1521–1700." In Pablo González Casanova, ed., *La clase obrera en la historia de México, Tomo 1: De la colonia al imperío*. Mexico City: Siglo Veintiuno Editores, 9–124.

Foster-Carter, Aidan. 1978. "The Modes of Production Controversy." *New Left Review* 107:47–77.

Fox-Genovese, Elizabeth, and Eugene D. Genovese. 1983. *Fruits of Merchant Capital: Slavery and Bourgeois Property in the Rise and Expansion of Capitalism*. New York: Oxford Univ. Press.

Frank, Andre Gunder. 1969a. *Capitalism and Underdevelopment in Latin America: Historical Studies of Chile and Brazil*. Rev. ed. (orig. 1967). New York: Monthly Review Press.

Frank, Andre Gunder. 1969b. *Latin America: Underdevelopment or Revolution?* New York: Monthly Review Press.

Frank, Andre Gunder. 1972. *Lumpenbourgeoisie: Lumpendevelopment: Dependence, Class, and Politics in Latin America*. New York: Monthly Review Press.

Frank, Andre Gunder. 1979. *Mexican Agriculture, 1521–1630: Transformation of the Mode of Production*. New York and Paris: Cambridge Univ. Press.

Freyre, Gilberto. 1933. *Casa-grande e senzala*. 4th "definitive" ed. in 2 vols., 1943. Rio de Janeiro: J. Olympio.

Fuentes, Carlos. 1962. *La muerte de Artemio Cruz*. Mexico City: Fondo de Cultura Económica.

Furtado, Celso. 1959. *Formaçao econômica do Brasil*. Rio de Janeiro: Editora Fondo de Cultura.

Garavaglia, Juan Carlos. 1973a. "Introducción." In Assadourian et al. 1973:7–21.

Garavaglia, Juan Carlos. 1973b. "Un modo de producción subsidiario: la organización económica de las comunidades guaranizadas durante los siglos XVII–XVIII en la formación regional altoperuana-rioplatense." In Assadourian et al. 1973:161–91.

Garavaglia, Juan Carlos. 1983. *Mercado interno y economía colonial (Tres siglos de historia de la yerba mate)*. Mexico City: Grijalbo.

García Márquez, Gabriel. 1976. *The Autumn of the Patriarch*. Trans. Gregory Rabassa. New York: Harper & Row.

Garner, Richard L. 1988. "Long-Term Silver Mining Trends in Spanish America: A Comparative Analysis of Peru and Mexico." *American Historical Review* 93 (Oct.):898–935.

Gaspar, David Barry. 1985. *Bondmen and Rebels: A Study of Master-Slave Relations in Antigua, with Implications for Colonial British America*. Baltimore: Johns Hopkins Univ. Press.

Genovese, Eugene D. 1969. *The World the Slaveholders Made: Two Essays in Interpretation*. New York: Pantheon.

Gibson, Charles. 1964. *The Aztecs under Spanish Rule: A History of the Indians of the Valley of Mexico, 1519–1810*. Stanford: Stanford University Press.

Glausser R., Kalki. 1974. "Orígenes del régimen de producción vigente en Chile." In Glausser R. and Vitale 1974:5–158.

Glausser R., Kalki, and Luis Vitale. 1974. *Acerca del modo de producción colonial en América Latina*. Medellín: Ediciones Tiempo Crítico.

Glave, Luis Miguel, and María Isabel Remy. 1983. *Estructura agraria y vida rural andina: Ollantaytambo entre los siglos XVI y XIX*. Cuzco: Centro de Estudios Rurales Andinos "Bartolomé de las Casas."

Góngora, Mario. 1960. *Origen de los inquilinos de Chile central*. Santiago de Chile: Universidad de Chile Seminario de Historia Colonial.

González Casanova, Pablo. 1965. *La democracia en México*. Mexico City: Ediciones Era.

Gorender, Jacob. 1978. *O escravismo colonial*. São Paulo: Editora Atica.

Greaves, Thomas, and William Culver, eds. 1985. *Miners and Mining in the Americas*. Manchester: Manchester Univ. Press.

Hall, John R. 1984. "World-System Holism and Colonial Brazilian Agriculture: A Critical Case Analysis." *Latin American Research Review* 19:43–69.

Halperín-Donghi, Tulio. 1969. *Historia contemporánea de América Latina*. Madrid: Alianza Editorial.

Halperín-Donghi, Tulio. 1982. " 'Dependency Theory' and Latin American Historiography." *Latin American Research Review* 17:115–30.

Handlin, Oscar, and Mary F. Handlin. 1950. "Origins of the Southern Labor System." *William and Mary Quarterly* (3d ser.) 7:199–222.

Hanke, Lewis. 1949. *The Spanish Struggle for Justice in the Conquest of America*. Reprint Ed., 1965. Boston: Little, Brown.

Harris, Olivia, Brooke Larson, and Enrique Tandeter, eds. 1987. *Participación indígena en los mercados surandinos: estrategias y reproducción social, siglos XVI a XX*. La Paz: Centro de Estudios de la Realidad Económica y Social.

Hartz, Louis, et al. 1964. *The Founding of New Societies*. New York: Harcourt, Brace and World.

Helmer, Marie. 1959. "Notas sobre la encomienda peruana en el siglo XVI." *Revista del Instituto de Historia del Derecho* 10:124–43.

Hemming, John. 1978. *Red Gold: The Conquest of the Brazilian Indians, 1500–1760*. Cambridge, Mass.: Harvard Univ. Press.

Hilton, Rodney et al. 1976. *The Transition from Feudalism to Capitalism*. London: Verso.

Hirschman, Albert O. 1971. *A Bias for Hope: Essays on Development and Latin America*. New Haven: Yale Univ. Press.

Hobsbawm, E. J. 1967. "The Crisis of the Seventeenth Century" (orig. 1954). In Aston 1967:5–62.

Huertas Vallejos, Lorenzo. 1974. "Historia de las luchas sociales de Ayacucho, 1700–1940." Unpublished manuscript.

Huertas Vallejos, Lorenzo. 1977. "Prólogo." *Revista del Archivo Departamental de Ayacucho* 1:52–53.

Israel, Jonathan I. 1982. *The Dutch Republic and the Hispanic World, 1606–1661*. Oxford: Clarendon Press.

James, C. L. R. 1938. *The Black Jacobins: Toussaint L'Ouverture and the San Domingo Revolution*. Rev. ed., 1963. New York: Vintage.

Kahl, Joseph A. 1976. *Modernization, Exploitation, and Dependency in Latin America: Germani, González Casanova, and Cardoso*. New Brunswick, N.J.: Transaction Books.

Kamen, Henry. 1978. "The Decline of Spain: A Historical Myth?" *Past and Present* 81 (Nov.):24–50.

Kay, Cristóbal. 1980. *El sistema señorial europeo y la hacienda latinoamericana.* Mexico City: Ediciones Era.

Keen, Benjamin. 1985. "Main Currents in United States Writings on Colonial Spanish America, 1884–1948." *Hispanic American Historical Review* 65 (Nov.):657–82.

Keen, Benjamin, and Mark Wasserman. 1980. *A Short History of Latin America.* Boston: Houghton Mifflin.

Klarén, Peter F., and Thomas J. Bossert, eds. 1986. *Promise of Development: Theories of Change in Latin America.* Boulder, Colo.: Westview Press.

Klein, Herbert S. 1986. *African Slavery in Latin America and the Caribbean.* New York: Oxford Univ. Press.

Knight, Franklin W. 1978. *The Caribbean: The Genesis of a Fragmented Nationalism.* New York: Oxford Univ. Press.

Konrad, Herman W. 1980. *A Jesuit Hacienda in Colonial Mexico: Santa Lucía, 1576–1767.* Stanford: Stanford Univ. Press.

Kopytoff, Igor, and Suzanne Miers. 1977. "African 'Slavery' as an Institution of Marginality." In Miers and Kopytoff 1977:3–81.

Kriedte, Peter. 1983. *Peasants, Landlords, and Merchant Capitalists: Europe and the World-Economy, 1500–1800.* Orig. Gern ed., 1980. Leamington Spa: Berg Pub.

Kriedte, Peter, Hans Medick, and Jürgen Schlumbohm. 1981. *Industrialization before Industrialization: Rural Industry in the Genesis of Capitalism.* New York and Paris: Cambridge Univ. Press.

Kubler, George. 1946. "The Quechua in the Colonial World." In Steward 1946–59, vol. 2.

Laclau, Ernesto. 1971. "Feudalism and Capitalism in Latin America." *New Left Review* 67 (May–June):19–38.

Laclau, Ernesto. 1977. *Politics and Ideology in Marxist Theory.* London: N.L.B.

Laclau, Ernesto, and Chantal Mouffe. 1985. *Hegemony and Socialist Strategy: Towards a Radical Democratic Politics.* London: Verso.

Ladd, Doris. 1988. *The Making of a Strike: Mexican Silver Workers' Struggles in Real del Monte, 1766–1775.* Lincoln: Univ. of Nebraska Press.

Lambert, Jacques. 1967. *Latin America: Social Structure and Political Institutions.* Trans. Helen Katel. Orig. French ed., 1963. Berkeley: Univ. of California Press.

LAP. 1974. *Latin American Perspectives* 1:1 (thematic issue on dependency).

LAP. 1981. *Latin American Perspectives* 8:3–4 (thematic issue on dependency).

Larson, Brooke. 1980. "Rural Rhythms of Class Conflict in Eighteenth-Century Cochabamba." *Hispanic American Historical Review* 60 (Aug.):407–30.

Larson, Brooke. 1983. "Shifting Views of Colonialism and Resistance." *Radical History Review* 27:3–20.

Larson, Brooke. 1988. *Colonialism and Agrarian Transformation in Bolivia: Cochabamba, 1550–1900.* Princeton: Princeton Univ. Press.

Lerner, Gerda. 1986. *The Creation of Patriarchy.* New York: Oxford Univ. Press.

Lobo Cabrera, Manuel. 1982. *La esclavitud en las canarias orientales en el siglo XVI (negros, moros y moriscos).* Tenerife: Excmo. Cabildo Insular de Gran Canaria.

Lockhart, James, and Stuart B. Schwartz. 1983. *Early Latin America: A History of Colonial Spanish America and Brazil*. New York: Cambridge Univ. Press.

Lohmann Villena, Guillermo. 1949. *Las minas de Huancavelica en los siglos XVI y XVII*. Seville: Escuela de Estudios Hispano-Americanos de Sevilla.

Lohmann Villena, Guillermo. 1957. *El corregidor de indios en el Perú bajo los Austrias*. Madrid: Ediciones Cultura Hispánica.

Lohmann Villena, Guillermo. 1965. "Juan de Matienzo, autor del 'Gobierno del Perú' (su personalidad y su obra)." *Anuario de Estudios Americanos* 22:767–886.

Love, Joseph. 1980. "Raúl Prebisch and the Origins of the Doctrine of Unequal Exchange." *Latin American Research Review* 15:46–60.

Lynch, John. 1973. *The Spanish-American Revolutions, 1808–1826*. New York: Norton.

McAlister, Lyle N. 1984. *Spain and Portugal in the New World, 1492–1700*. Minneapolis: Univ. of Minnesota Press.

McBride, George. 1936. *Chile: Land and Society*. New York: American Geographical Society.

Macera, Pablo. 1971. "Feudalismo colonial americano: el caso de las haciendas peruanas." Orig. pub. in *Acta Histórica*. Rpt. in Macera 1977, 3:139–227.

Macera, Pablo. 1977. *Trabajos de historia*. 4 vols. Lima: Instituto Nacional de Cultura.

MacLeod, Murdo J. 1973. *Spanish Central America: A Socioeconomic History, 1520–1720*. Berkeley: Univ. of California Press.

Mallon, Florencia E. 1983. *The Defense of Community in Peru's Central Highlands: Peasant Struggle and Capitalist Transition, 1860–1940*. Princeton: Princeton Univ. Press.

Malpica, Carlos. 1964. *Los dueños del Perú*. 3d rev. ed., 1968. Lima: Ediciones Ensayos Sociales.

Marchant, Alexander. 1942a. "Feudal and Capitalistic Elements in the Portuguese Settlement of Brazil." *Hispanic American Historical Review* 22 (Aug.):493–512.

Marchant, Alexander. 1942b. *From Barter to Slavery: The Economic Relations of Portuguese and Indians in the Settlement of Brazil, 1500–1580*. Baltimore, Md.: Johns Hopkins Press.

MARHO (Mid-Atlantic Radical Historians Organization). 1984. *Visions of History*. New York: Pantheon.

Mariátegui, José Carlos. 1928. *7 ensayos de interpretación de la realidad peruana*. Lima: Biblioteca Amauta.

Marrero Rodríguez, Manuela, ed. 1974. *Extractos del protocolo de Juan Ruiz de Berlanga, 1507–1508*. La Laguna de Tenerife: Consejo Superior de Investigaciones Científicas.

Marroquín, Alejandro. 1957. *La ciudad mercado (Tlaxiaco)*. Mexico City: Imprenta Universitaria.

Martin, Cheryl English. 1985. *Rural Society in Colonial Morelos*. Albuquerque: Univ. of New Mexico Press.

Marx, Karl. 1964. *Pre-Capitalist Economic Formations*. Ed. E. J. Hobsbawm. New York: International Publishers.

Marx, Karl. 1969. *Capital*. 3 vols. New York: International Publishers.

Mata, Héctor Malavé. 1975. "Reflexões sobre o modo de produção colonial latino-americano." Orig. 1972. Rpt. in Santiago 1975:144–80.

Matienzo, Juan de. 1567. *Gobierno del Perú*. Rpt. in Guillermo Lohmann Villena, ed., *Travaux de l'Institut Français d'Etudes Andines* 11 (Paris, 1967).

Matos Mar, José, et al. 1969. *Perú—Problema*. 2d ed. Lima: Moncloa-Campodonico.

Medick, Hans. 1976. "The Proto-Industrial Family Economy: The Structural Function of Household and Family during the Transition from Peasant Society to Industrial Capitalism." *Social History* 3 (Oct.):291–315.

Mendels, Franklin. 1972. "Proto-Industrialization: The First Phase of the Industrialization Process." *Journal of Economic History* 32:241–61.

Miers, Suzanne, and Igor Kopytoff, eds. 1977. *Slavery in Africa: Historical and Anthropological Perspectives*. Madison: Univ. of Wisconsin Press.

Mintz, Sidney W. 1961. Review of Stanley M. Elkins's *Slavery*. *American Anthropologist* 63 (June):579–87.

Mintz, Sidney W. 1974. *Caribbean Transformations*. Chicago: Aldine Pub. Co.

Mintz, Sidney W. 1977. "The So-Called World-System: Local Initiative and Local Response." *Dialectical Anthropology* 2 (Nov.):253–70.

Mintz, Sidney W. 1978. "Was the Plantation Slave a Proletarian?" *Review* 2 (Summer):81–98.

Mintz, Sidney W. 1979. "Slavery and the Rise of Peasantries." In Craton 1979:213–42.

Mintz, Sidney W. 1985a. "From Plantation to Peasantries in the Caribbean." In Mintz and S. Price 1985:127–53.

Mintz, Sidney W. 1985b. *Sweetness and Power: The Place of Sugar in Modern History*. New York: Penguin.

Mintz, Sidney W., and Richard Price. 1976. *An Anthropological Approach to the Afro-American Past: A Caribbean Perspective*. Philadelphia: Institute for the Study of Human Issues.

Mintz, Sidney W., and Sally Price, eds. 1985. *Caribbean Contours*. Baltimore: Johns Hopkins Univ. Press.

Miranda, José. 1941–46. "La función económica del encomendero en los orígenes del régimen colonial de Nueva España (1525–1531)." *Anales del Instituto Nacional de Antropología e Historia* 2:421–62.

Morgan, Edmund S. 1975. *American Slavery, American Freedom: The Ordeal of Colonial Virginia*. New York: Norton.

Morin, Claude. 1979. *Michoacán en la Nueva España del siglo XVIII: crecimiento y desigualdad en una economía colonial*. Mexico City: Fondo de Cultura Económica.

Morse, Richard M. 1954. "Toward a Theory of Spanish American Government." *Journal of the History of Ideas* 15:71–93.

Morse, Richard M. 1964. "The Heritage of Latin America." In Hartz et al. 1964:123–77.

Moya Pons, Frank. 1976. *Historia colonial de Santo Domingo*. 2nd ed. Santiago, Dominican Republic: UCMM.

Myrdal, Gunnar. 1956. *Development and Under-Development: A Note on the Mechanism of National and International Inequality*. Cairo: National Bank of Egypt.

Myrdal, Gunnar. 1957. *Rich Lands and Poor: The Road to World Prosperity*. New York: Harper.

Nash, Gary B. 1974. *Red, White, and Black: The Peoples of Early America.* Englewood Cliffs, N.J.: Prentice Hall.

Nash, June. 1979. *We Eat the Mines and the Mines Eat Us: Dependency and Exploitation in Bolivian Tin Mines.* New York: Columbia Univ. Press.

Novais, Fernando A. 1974. *Estrutura e dinâmica do antigo sistema colonial (séculos XVI–XVIII).* São Paulo: Centro Brasileiro de Análise e Planejamento.

Ortíz, Fernando. 1940. *Contrapunteo cubano del tabaco y el azúcar . . .* Havana: J. Montero.

Packenham, Robert A. 1982. "Plus ça change . . . : The English Edition of Cardoso and Faletto's *Dependencia y desarrollo en América Latina.*" *Latin American Research Review* 17:131–51.

Padden, R. C. 1975. "Editor's Introduction." In Bartolomé Arzáns de Orsúa y Vela, *Tales of Potosí.* Ed. Padden, trans. Frances M. López-Morillas. Providence, R.I.: Brown Univ. Press.

Pagden, Anthony. 1982. *The Fall of Natural Man: The American Indian and the Origins of Comparative Ethnology.* New York: Cambridge Univ. Press.

Palerm, Angel. 1976. "La formación colonial mexicana y el primer sistema económico mundial." Rpt. in Palerm 1980:89–124.

Palerm, Angel. 1980. *Antropología y marxismo.* Mexico City: Editorial Nueva Imagen.

Palma, Gabriel. 1978. "Dependency: A Formal Theory of Underdevelopment or a Methodology for the Analysis of Concrete Situations of Underdevelopment?" *World Development* 6:881–924.

Parry, J. H. 1953. *The Sale of Public Office in the Spanish Indies Under the Hapsburgs.* Berkeley: Univ. of California Press.

Patterson, Orlando. 1979. "Slavery and Slave Revolts: A Sociohistorical Analysis of the First Maroon War, 1665–1740." In Price 1979: 246–92.

Patterson, Orlando. 1982. *Slavery and Social Death: A Comparative Study.* Cambridge, Mass: Harvard Univ. Press.

Paz, Melchor de. 1786. "Diálogo sobre los Sucesos varios acaecidos en este Reyno del Perú." Rpt. in Luis Antonio Eguiguren, ed., *Guerra separatista.* Vol. 2. Lima, 1952: Librería e Imprenta Gil.

Paz, Octavio. 1950. *El laberinto de la soledad.* Rev. ed., 1959. Mexico City: Fondo de Cultura Económica.

Petras, James, and Maurice Zeitlin, eds. 1968. *Latin America: Reform or Revolution?* Greenwich, Conn.: Fawcett Publications.

Phelan, John Leddy. 1967. *The Kingdom of Quito in the Seventeenth Century: Bureaucratic Politics in the Spanish Empire.* Madison: Univ. of Wisconsin Press.

Phelan, John Leddy. 1978. *The People and the King: The Comunero Revolution in Colombia, 1781.* Madison: Univ. of Wisconsin Press.

Phillips, Carla Rahn. 1987. "Time and Duration: A Model for the Economy of Early Modern Spain." *American Historical Review* 92 (June):531–62.

Polanyi, Karl. 1944. *The Great Transformation: The Political and Economic Origins of Our Time.* Rpt. ed., 1957. Boston: Beacon Press.

Polo y la Borda G., Jorge. 1976. *La Hacienda Pachachaca: autobastecimiento y comercialización (segunda mitad del siglo XVIII).* Lima: Biblioteca Peruana de Historia, Economía y Sociedad.

Prado, Caio, Jr. 1942. *Formação do Brasil contemporâneo: Colônia*. São Paulo: Livraria Martins Editora.

Price, Richard, ed. 1979. *Maroon Societies: Rebel Slave Communities in the Americas*. 2d ed. Baltimore: Johns Hopkins Univ. Press.

Puiggrós, Rodolfo. 1943. *De la colonia a la revolución*. 2d ed. (orig. 1940). Buenos Aires: Editorial Lautaro.

Quijano Obregón, Aníbal. 1968. "Tendencies in Peruvian Development and in the Class Structure." In Petras and Zeitlin 1968: 289–328.

Quijano Obregón, Aníbal. 1971. *Nacionalismo, neoimperialismo y militarismo en el Perú*. Buenos Aires: Ediciones Periferia.

Radell, David R. 1976. "The Indian Slave Trade and Population of Nicaragua during the Sixteenth Century." In Denevan 1976:67–76.

Ratekin, Mervyn. 1954. "The Early Sugar Industry in Española." *Hispanic American Historical Review* 34 (Feb.):1–19.

Rey, Pierre-Philippe. 1973. *Les Alliances des classes*. Paris: F. Maspero.

Romano, Ruggiero. 1984. "American Feudalism." *Hispanic American Historical Review* 64 (Feb.):121–34.

Roseberry, William. 1983. *Coffee and Capitalism in the Venezuelan Andes*. Austin: Univ. of Texas Press.

Rowe, John H. 1957. "The Incas under Spanish Colonial Institutions." *Hispanic American Historical Review* 37 (May):155–99.

Russell-Wood, A. J. R. 1985. "United States Scholarly Contributions to the Historiography of Colonial Brazil." *Hispanic American Historical Review* 65 (Nov.):683–723.

Saco, José Antonio. 1938. *Historia de la esclavitud de la raza africana en el Nuevo Mundo. . .* 4 vols. Havana: Cultural.

Sánchez-Albornoz, Nicolás. 1978. *Indios y tributos en el Alto Perú*. Lima: Instituto de Estudios Peruanos.

Santiago, Théo, ed. 1975. *América colonial*. Rio de Janeiro: Pallas.

Sauer, Carl O. 1966. *The Early Spanish Main*. Berkeley: Univ. of California Press.

Schwartz, Stuart B. 1970. "Magistracy and Society in Colonial Brazil." *Hispanic American Historical Review* 50 (Nov.):715–30.

Schwartz, Stuart B. 1978. "Indian Labor and New World Plantations: European Demands and Indian Responses in Northeastern Brazil." *American Historical Review* 83 (Feb.):43–79.

Schwartz, Stuart B. 1984. "Colonial Brazil, c. 1580–c. 1750: Plantations and Peripheries." In Leslie Bethell, ed., *The Cambridge History of Latin America*. Vol. 2. New York: Cambridge Univ. Press.

Schwartz, Stuart B. 1985. *Sugar Plantations in the Formation of Brazilian Society: Bahia, 1550–1835*. New York: Cambridge Univ. Press.

Sella, Domenico. 1977. "The World-System and Its Dangers." *Peasant Studies* 6 (Jan.):29–32.

Semo, Enrique. 1973. *Historia del capitalismo en México: los orígenes, 1521–1763*. Mexico City: Ediciones Era.

Sherman, William L. 1979. *Forced Native Labor in Sixteenth-Century Central America*. Lincoln: Univ. of Nebraska Press.

Simpson, Lesley B. 1929. *The Encomienda in New Spain: Forced Native Labor in the Spanish Colonies, 1492–1550*. Significantly revised in a 1950 ed. Berkeley: Univ. of California Press.

Skidmore, Thomas E., and Peter H. Smith. 1984. *Modern Latin America*. New York: Oxford Univ. Press.

Skocpol, Theda. 1977. "Wallerstein's World Capitalist System: A Theoretical and Historical Critique." *American Journal of Sociology* 82:1075–90.

Stavenhagen, Rodolfo. 1963. "Clases, colonialismo y aculturación: ensayo sobre un sistema de relaciones interétnicas en Mesoamérica." *América Latina* (Rio de Janeiro) 6 (Oct.–Dec.):63–103.

Stavenhagen, Rodolfo. 1968. "Seven Fallacies about Latin America." In Petras and Zeitlin 1968:13–31.

Stein, Stanley J., and Barbara H. Stein. 1970. *The Colonial Heritage of Latin America: Essays on Economic Dependence in Perspective*. New York: Oxford Univ. Press.

Stepan, Alfred, ed. 1973. *Authoritarian Brazil*. New Haven, Conn.: Yale Univ. Press.

Stern, Steve J. 1981. "The Rise and Fall of Indian-White Alliances: A Regional View of 'Conquest' History." *Hispanic American Historical Review* 61 (Aug.):461–91.

Stern, Steve J. 1982. *Peru's Indian Peoples and the Challenge of Spanish Conquest: Huamanga to 1640*. Madison: Univ. of Wisconsin Press.

Stern, Steve J. 1985. "New Directions in Andean Economic History: A Critical Dialogue with Carlos Sempat Assadourian." *Latin American Perspectives* 12 (Winter):133–48.

Stern, Steve J., ed. 1987. *Resistance, Rebellion, and Consciousness in the Andean Peasant World, 18th to 20th Centuries*. Madison: Univ. of Wisconsin Press.

Steward, Julian, ed. 1946–59. *Handbook of South American Indians*. 7 vols. Washington, D.C.: Government Printing Office.

Tandeter, Enrique. 1981a. "Forced and Free Labour in Late Colonial Potosí." *Past and Present* 93 (Nov.): 98–136.

Tandeter, Enrique. 1981b. "La producción como actividad popular: 'ladrones de minas' en Potosí." *Nova Americana* 4:43–65.

Tannenbaum, Frank. 1946. *Slave and Citizen: The Negro in the Americas*. New York: Vintage.

Taylor, William B. 1985. "Between Global Process and Local Knowledge: An Inquiry into Early Latin American Social History, 1500–1900." In Zunz 1985:115–90.

Tolentino Dipp, Hugo. 1974. *Raza e historia en Santo Domingo: los orígenes del prejuicio racial en América*. Santo Domingo: Editora de la Universidad Autónoma de Santo Domingo.

Tutino, John. 1975. "Hacienda Social Relations in Mexico: The Chalco Region in the Era of Independence." *Hispanic American Historical Review* 55 (Aug.):496–528.

Valega, José Manuel, ed. 1939. *El virreinato del Perú*. Lima: Editorial Cultura Ecléctica.

Van Young, Eric. 1981. *Hacienda and Market in Eighteenth-Century Mexico: The Rural Economy of the Guadalajara Region, 1675–1820*. Berkeley: Univ. of California Press.

Van Young, Eric. 1983. "Mexican Rural History Since Chevalier: The Historiography of the Colonial Hacienda." *Latin American Research Review* 18:5–62.

Velasco Ávila, Cuahtémoc. 1985. "Labour Relations in Mining: Real de Monte and Pachuca, 1824–74." In Greaves and Culver 1985:47–67.

Villamarín, Juan, and Judith Villamarín. 1975. *Indian Labor in Mainland Colonial Spanish America*. Newark: Univ. of Delaware, Latin American Studies Program.

Villanueva, Margaret. 1985. "From Calpixqui to Corregidor: Appropriation of Women's Cotton Textile Production in Early Colonial Mexico." *Latin American Perspectives* 12 (Winter): 17–40.

Villarán, Manuel Vicente. 1964. *Apuntes sobre la realidad social de los indígenas ante las leyes de Indias*. Lima: Talleres Gráficos P. L. Villanueva.

Viotti da Costa, Emília. 1966. *Da senzala à colônia*. 2d rev. ed., 1982. São Paulo: Livraria Editora Ciências Humanas.

Viotti da Costa, Emília. 1985. *The Brazilian Empire: Myths and Histories*. Chicago: Univ. of Chicago.

Vitale, Luis. 1968. "Latin America: Feudal or Capitalist?" In Petras and Zeitlin 1968:32–43.

Vitale, Luis. 1969. *Interpretación marxista de la historia de Chile II: la colonia y la revolución de 1810*. 3d ed., 1972. Santiago de Chile: Prensa Latinoamericana.

Wallerstein, Immanuel. 1974. *The Modern World-System: Capitalist Agriculture and the Origins of the European World-Economy in the Sixteenth Century*. (See note 1 on the preface to the 1976 ed.) New York: Academic Press.

Wallerstein, Immanuel. 1979. *The Capitalist World-Economy*. New York and Paris: Cambridge Univ. Press.

Wallerstein, Immanuel. 1980. *The Modern World-System II: Mercantilism and the Consolidation of the European World-Economy, 1600–1750*. New York: Academic Press.

Wallerstein, Immanuel. 1983. *Historical Capitalism*. London: Verso.

Wallerstein, Immanuel. 1984. *The Politics of the World-Economy: The States, the Movements, and the Civilizations*. New York and Paris: Cambridge Univ. Press.

Wallerstein, Immanuel. 1989. *The Modern World-System III: The Second Era of Great Expansion of the Capitalist World-Economy, 1730–1840s*. New York: Academic Press.

Weber, David J. 1986. "Turner, the Boltonians, and the Borderlands." *American Historical Review* 91 (Feb.):66–81.

Wiedner, David L. 1960. "Forced Labor in Colonial Peru." *Americas* 16 (April):357–83.

Williams, Eric. 1944. *Capitalism and Slavery*. Chapel Hill: Univ. of North Carolina Press.

Wolf, Eric R. 1959. *Sons of the Shaking Earth: The People of Mexico and Guatemala—Their Land, History, and Culture*. Chicago: Univ. of Chicago Press.

Wolf, Eric R. 1982. *Europe and the People Without History*. Berkeley: Univ. of California Press.

Wolf, Eric R., and Edward C. Hansen. 1972. *The Human Condition in Latin America*. New York: Oxford Univ. Press.

Wolf, Eric R., and Sidney Mintz. 1957. "Haciendas and Plantations in Middle America and the Antilles." *Social and Economic Studies* 6:380–412.

Wolpe, Harold, ed. 1980. *The Articulation of Modes of Production: Essays from Economy and Society.* London and Boston: Routledge and K. Paul

Womack, John, Jr. 1969. *Zapata and the Mexican Revolution.* New York: Knopf.

Wood, Peter H. 1974. *Black Majority: Negroes in Colonial South Carolina from 1670 Through the Stono Rebellion.* New York: Knopf.

Wright, Irene, ed. 1916. "The Commencement of the Cane Sugar Industry in America, 1519–1538 (1563)." *American Historical Review* 21 (July):755–780.

Zavala, Silvio. 1944. "Orígenes coloniales del peonaje en México." *El trimestre económico* 10:711–48.

Zeitlin, Maurice. 1984. *The Civil Wars in Chile (or the Bourgeois Revolutions that Never Were).* Princeton: Princeton Univ. Press.

Zulawski, Ann. 1987. "Wages, Ore Sharing, and Peasant Agriculture: Labor in Oruro's Silver Mines, 1607–1720." *Hispanic American Historical Review* 67 (Aug.):405–30.

Zunz, Olivier, ed. 1985. *Reliving the Past: The Worlds of Social History.* Chapel Hill: Univ. of North Carolina Press.

3 *Frederick Cooper*

Africa and the World Economy

Africa's involvement in the changing world economy has been a long one, and its effects on the lives of Africans have been profound. Samir Amin and W. W. Rostow, Felix Houphouet-Boigny and Samora Machel would hardly dispute such a statement. But the question of whether this involvement has led Africans along a road toward material and social progress or into a dead end is very much in dispute.

The title of this paper is the same as that of the introductory section of S. Herbert Frankel's classic study of 1938, *Capital Investment in Africa*. Becoming part of the world economy, for Frankel (1938:1–3, 7), entailed the diffusion of Europe's capital, technology, ideas, and "civilized" form of government to closed, static, and undifferentiated economies. Now, writers such as André Gunder Frank (1967), Samir Amin (1974a, 1976), Walter Rodney (1972), and Immanuel Wallerstein (1979) stress instead the inexorable logic of a capitalist world system, whose effects on Africa are stifling instead of liberating. Both views share a unitary conception of the world economy, the first through a smug assumption that existing economic structures are part of civilization, and the second through an argument that sees change in Africa as a reflection of the growth of capitalism in Europe. The first conception of a world economy defined Africa's role as little more than holding back progress on a predetermined road; the second implied that Africa's influence on the world economy was not nearly so great.

In the 1960s, scholars of Africa reversed such biases for a time. Especially among historians, an Africanist perspective emphasized "African activity, African adaptations, African choice, African initiative" (Ranger 1968:xxi). Some scholars rejected explanations of economic change that stressed foreign trade, implying that the true mission of the Africanist was to uncover the underlying essence and internal dynamics of African society.[1] The strength of Africanist scholarship lay in its stress on methods to recover African voices from the past and the seriousness with which it examined the specificity of African social structures. But Africanists proved their point too easily: that Africans had their own points of view and their own history was revealing only to people who had believed they did not. A new generation of students took that point for granted and found that Africanists offered no particular set of questions and theoretical issues. There was never a crisis in African historical scholarship, but scholars began a wider search for perspectives that would explain just what Africa's place in the world was, now that they were freed of the need merely to assert that it had one.[2]

In two seminal contributions appearing in 1973, A. G. Hopkins and E. A. Alpers reasserted, in opposite ways, the importance of world markets: the former argued that African smallholders' effective response to markets was the great success story of African economic history, the latter that Africa's incorporation into such markets had fatally curtailed the possibility of autonomous and balanced development.[3]

But the Africanist concern with specificity should not be forgotten. It is not that variations and complexity need be trumpeted for their own sake or that we should restart the quest for the purified essence of a "Yoruba economy" or an "African economy." We should remember what the most fundamental questions are. Whether one accepts the most Pollyannaish conception of economic take-off or the starkest view of underdevelopment, one is talking about the degree to which productive systems increase their output, efficiency, and interdependence. These are questions that scholars too often talk around. Neoclassical development economists are too apt to treat growth as a self-propelling process and to underplay the social basis of production. Dependency theory regards the organization of production as a derivative of a society's place in the world economy; locating Africa in the periphery defines the way goods are produced, and the future as well. Marxism, in theory, should reverse these directions of analysis, making the forces and relations of production the starting point, but many Marxists treat capitalism as an implacable entity redefining social structures through its own requirements. They fail to penetrate very far into the encounter of capitalism with Africans.

Once that door is opened, the significance of particular struggles and distinct processes of change becomes hard to avoid. Did the systems of production in Africa generate their own dynamics, their own internal conflicts, and their own blockages to further development? Did the dynamics of these systems affect the way they were transformed in the process of capitalist expansion? Was the nature of production in capitalist plantations, mines, and industries shaped by the people who did the producing and by the dynamics and tensions generated within the confrontation itself? It may well be that the contrary directions generated within Africa prove as significant as overall patterns of development or exploitation.

Very few areas of inquiry are not germane to these concerns. I have tried to hinge a discussion of theory and an interpretation of historical processes around a single point—the connection of world economy and African production.[4] The internal structure of households, demography, ecology, disease, the ways Africans and Europeans thought about economic questions, the organization of international trade and finance, and the nature of state power all impinge on that point. Scholars have made considerable progress in analyzing such topics, and each deserves careful consideration. To a significant extent, conflicting perspectives similar to those discussed here affect other such issues, and even a thorough analysis of any aspect of economic life leads back to the men and women in the fields, factories, and dockyards.

Theories

The healthiest development in African studies since the 1960s has been the shattering of any illusions of theoretical consensus. At first, it seemed as if western scholars could help Africans to understand their past and their future without questioning the notions that the role of western institutions in Africa was progressive and that advice and analysis were purely scientific and objective. An obsession with methodology and technique in several disciplines substituted for a more far-reaching questioning of assumptions and theories, and more searching critiques—like Paul Baran's writings (1957)—seemed isolated on the fringe. Things have since become more polarized, as much because the recent history of Africa has made smug progressivism appear implausible as because of any greater insight within the ivory tower. Instead of each field offering its wisdom, each academic discipline now has its debates, or rather its version of the same debates.

Nevertheless, the lines of argument are not as simple as left and right.[5] A radical stance toward the existing economic order does not necessarily imply any one theoretical position, and orthodoxy in terms of basic theory does not always lead to shared practical programs or predictions. The most orthodox of development economists share with their most vocal critics, the dependency theorists, a focus on exchange, even if one sees world trade as progressive and the other as quite the contrary. Dependency theory shares with Marxism a radical rejection of the status quo, but it undertakes economic analysis from a different angle. Approaches to the study of Africa and the world economy can be grouped in three categories, although disputes within each can be important and occasionally illuminating: neoclassical economics and its offshoots (including Keynesian economics)—what one practitioner (Elkan 1976: 691) calls "textbook economics"; dependency theory and its variants, also known as the development of underdevelopment or world system theory; and Marxist analyses of the distinctive nature and interaction of modes of production.

Neo-Classical Economics, Development, and Economic History

In terms of praxis and prognosis, development economics appears to be in a healthy state of ferment. Some experts recommend industrialization, others agricultural development; some encourage commercial farmers to increase the scale of their operations, while others favor peasants; some look to the growth of a modern sector that draws resources from backward sectors, while others stress rural self-sufficiency or else the value of an urban informal sector; and still others have stripped away all accretions to the market model of the economy which is the underlying basis of this school, arguing that Africans will do best if the market is left alone (Killick 1980). Yet the most purist and the most reformist variants share a vision of what economic development should be that is equally pristine, utopian, and abstracted from the social and political reality of economic change. If the ferment in the field has produced a number of concrete, sensible plans, it has done little to question its own assumptions. Above all, such approaches leave a great and misleading gap between their two basic units of analysis: the individual economic actor, making individual transactions, and the economy, which in practice means the national economy.

What development is all about, Bruce Johnston and Peter Kilby (1975:3–34) assert, is the movement of "individual productive units" from "meager self-sufficiency" to "prosperous interdependence as producers . . . integrated into a national network of markets, information flows, and social institutions."[6] In some abstract sense, differentiation, specialization, and integration may be good things, but the seeming universality of this movement should not obscure the questions of through whose efforts, for whose benefit, and at whose expense did differentiation take place, and why did it take certain forms and not others? Individual productive units may be part of collectivities that exclude others from access to resources and exercise power over others. National economic policies may reflect particular interests within the nation and be deeply affected by forces from outside, something that is too often taken as a mere fact which African states can only take as it is. Neoclassical economics is unable to treat power as an intrinsic part of economic life or to analyze the importance of economic interests to the exercise of power. Hence, many economists call on detached and disembodied governments to make decisions about "the economy" for the benefit of "the society."[7]

In recent years, the myth of the rational, profit-maximizing, autonomous smallholder has replaced the myth of the backward communal cultivator (e.g. Anthony et al. 1979:18). This focus turns away from one of the most basic dimensions of economic change—the efforts of some people to make others' decisions for them. The stress on the model smallholder points away from asking if the largest holders or those with access to state power might profit most from keeping resources away from others and from asking if the smallest holders—with equal rationality—might try to avoid too much dependence on markets that they feel are rigged against them. Strategies on both ends of the spectrum might have different implications for expanding production than the notion of the model smallholder. The concept of economic rationality does not get us very far; we need to understand different, if not opposed, rationalities.[8]

Economists' stress on export-led growth dates from the early 1950s. A growing capitalist sector, using modern techniques and wage labor, would attract manpower and resources away from a subsistence sector. W. A. Lewis (1954; 1958) is best remembered for the arresting directness of this theory, but he might be better remembered for his wise awareness of the complications of the process, above all that vested economic interests (such as large plantation owners) and governments created inequalities that ultimately went against the growth process. Economic growth was thus a self-propelling engine, but one that had to be carefully maintained and steered clear of obstacles in its path. Thus Lewis (1970:38) warned of "artificial discouragement" to growth caused by the power of landowners. But why is their behavior artificial and export-led growth natural?

Two decades later, an influential report from the World Bank made a startling admission: "It is now clear that more than a decade of rapid growth in underdeveloped countries has been of little or no benefit to perhaps a third of their population."[9] The idea that economic growth should be good for people was proving elusive, even as growth itself was proving difficult to sustain. "Redistribution with Growth" became the new slogan of the World Bank, while the International Labour Office (1976) coined a more modest but related phrase, "Basic Needs."[10] Such approaches were interventionist; the invisible hand needed to be guided. However worthy the specific proposals of the organizations, the premise of the development economics of the 1970s was politically naive. The very people who benefited from inequality were politely asked to redistribute their gains. The state became a *deus ex machina* solution to the shortcomings of the growth model. Such a view fails to penetrate the connection of economic and political power, substituting a pious hope that considerations of long-term stability would triumph over self-interest. To Lewis's belief that the state could promote economic growth was added a stronger measure of modernization theory: a view that fundamental social processes—the strengthening of the state, the expansion of economic output, and the integration of new peoples as full and useful participants in the institutional, social, political, and cultural patterns of the modern world—were inherently desirable, progressive, and self-propelling. Thus the World Bank defined the problem as poverty, avoided asking if subordination and exploitation were intrinsic parts of certain forms of economic growth, and implied that "the problem" could be solved without disturbing the power of capital. Without a deeper analysis of the social basis of wealth and poverty, the new development economics of the 1970s became what Dudley Seers (1979b) called "Development Economics Plus"—a dram of equity and a grain of redistribution had been tacked onto the old theories of growth without rethinking basic assumptions.[11]

The most important opponents of the interventionists seemingly reversed this belief in the state and planned progress: the market must be left pure. Yet the purists' belief that the market can be separated from the state and social structure is as naive as the interventionists' belief in the detached state acting on behalf of progress and society. The purists defend the unguided invisible hand, insisting that government manipulations, marketing boards, and foreign aid have only distorted its workings. Such a view implies—and P. T. Bauer (1971:41) has not shied away from saying it—that people get from the market what they deserve. Poor resources, poor skills, and lack of initiative make poor people. Of course, the only way of deciding whether everyone gets a proper reward is to define what the market provides as just. It is harder to say whether the owner of land or a factory gets an appropriate reward for performing necessary economic functions, or whether he is able to make certain functions necessary so that they will be rewarded (Marglin 1974).

Both extremes of development economics share a common abstraction from the social basis of economic life. The conservative P. T. Bauer would elicit little disagreement from Marxists by arguing that West African marketing boards contribute greatly to the self-aggrandizement of government officials and little to the country as a whole, but Bauer's pristine conception of what an economy should be leaves him no way of explaining the structures out of which marketing boards emerged and were retained, and he leaves farmers as faceless followers of price changes.[12] It is well to say—as does Walter Elkan (1976:692) in defending "textbook economics"—that economic theory can point to the importance of market imperfections. But if the market model treats the most important problems as exogenous factors to be invoked to explain why things do not work out correctly, perhaps the model and the exogenous factors should change places.

The desirability of growth is not at issue; nor is the fact that external trade can stimulate growth. Whether such growth will spread throughout the economy and whether an enduring pattern of innovation and rising productivity will ensue is as complex a question as who will benefit. Gerald M. Meier (1975:452–53), trying to explain why the best example of export-stimulated growth in early colonial Africa—cocoa farming in the Gold Coast—left such a meager legacy to future generations, wrote, "the functions of the price system were poorly articulated during the colonial period, when markets remained localized, subsistence production continued to account for a substantial proportion of national product, and traditional rules and customary obligations prevailed."[13] This is not an explanation at all, but something to be explained. It is doubtful we can explain why market stimulus proved to have so narrow an effect without analyzing the interests of specific social groups—producers, merchant capital (internal and foreign), and politicians—as well as their ability to mobilize resources and control labor.

It is hard for a noneconomist to read very much development economics without being struck by the self-image that lies behind the writing, the image of a shirt-sleeved, no-nonsense advisor getting down to the brass tacks of producing more food or raising more credit, providing technical expertise while somewhat distastefully keeping a distance from African politics. Like any theory, development economics deserves both to be evaluated on its merits and to be understood as part of history. It evolved at a time when the frank cultural arrogance and racism implicit in the ideologies and spirit of colonial rule were losing their political viability. Like other liberal social sciences, development economics subsumed the operations of particular groups within particular structures under the notions of universal and scientific laws. In the circumstances of the move toward decolonization in the 1950s, it continued to stress the importance of state action while defining the terms of action by general principles rather than the superiority of particular people. Most important, it was a concept that appealed as much to local elites as to intellectuals and leaders overseas, emphasizing the progressive and national value of their own self-interested actions, and providing a basis of shared concepts and values between the developed and developing worlds. All this was reinforced by the international nature of economics education, the world-wide community of scholars, and international agencies. Development, more than any other idea, helped to provide an intellectual basis for a transnational class in an era of political nationalism and economic connectedness.[14] It helped to shape, as well as to articulate, a view that harmonized a world order whose basic nature was taken as given with the idea of autonomous development within it. What development economics explored the least was the relationship between domestic exploitation in African countries and the international system. An intellectual and social history of development economics would be most interesting.

What kind of economic history can be written using models that stress the market and external trade as an engine of growth? A. G. Hopkins' study of West Africa, written in 1973, marks a watershed in this approach. The very conventionality of Hopkins's economic theory was what made the book so innovative. He showed that the economic behavior of Africans could be explained as adequately by market responsiveness as could the behavior of anyone else. Given the simplistic view of "traditional" agriculture that many development economists use as a baseline for studying change (e.g., Fei and Ranis 1964:3; Schultz, 1964:4), this simple task was a valuable one. Criticisms of Hopkins on the grounds that his theories apply only to the Western world are unpersuasive (Dalton 1976, and Hopkins' reply, 1976c). The more serious question is how much they apply to advanced capitalist countries as well. While Hopkins advances intriguing explanations for a wide range of phenomena— from the slave trade to recent politics—through such concepts as changes in terms of trade, transportation costs, staple theory, and vent-for-surplus, he gives a less convincing and less historical portrait of structures in both precolonial and colonial Africa. He is right to say that African kinship systems were no obstacle to economic development, but fails to ask if particular kinship or community structures shaped particular *forms* of economic development. His argument that African societies chose slave over wage labor through a kind of cost-benefit analysis bears no relationships to historical alternatives, and misses—through Hopkins's artificial universalism—the crucial point that it is only in particular circumstances that labor power becomes a commodity independent of the laborer (Cooper 1979:108–9). Hopkins is at his best when he transcends his own market model to argue that the slave trade created aristocracies whose power was based on the need for coordinated military operations and so were threatened by the growth of cash-crop production, which gave aristocracies no such advantage. Hopkins links this process (discussed below) to the crisis that led to the partition of Africa, but he then loses the value of this emphasis on the specificity of social structure in a portrayal of colonial states as little more than facilitators and "umpires." [15] This argument, eight years after Hopkins's important book, has held up less well than his others (see below). The weight of explanation for change in the early colonial era falls on one of neoclassical theory's weaker propositions, mainly the vent-for-surplus theory (Hopkins 1973:231–35; also, Hogendorn 1975).

Criticisms of this theory have not arisen solely out of theoretical arguments— although those have been made too—but also out of detailed local studies, notably by Berry (1975:2–6), Tosh (1980), and M. Johnson (1974).[16] Vent-for-surplus theory is an attempt to explain the rapid expansion of cash-crop production before 1913 and to make the entire process appear painless. With land and labor to spare, African cultivators need only a "vent" for the surplus which the already available land and labor could provide, and colonial governments provided the cheap transport and other facilitating measures to create the vent, while the increased availability of manufactured goods and the spread of exchange made using the vent ever more desirable. The mobilization of idle resources is in fact important, although the argument is more persuasive when one can focus on specific groups, as Sara Berry does in connecting Ibadan warriors, who had lost their role but not their ambitions, to cocoa planting.[17]

But the theory is typical of the asocial bias of much neoclassical economic history. Vent-for-surplus theory ignores the actual nature of agrarian systems, the interplay of different crops and seasonal tasks, and the fact that adding crops did force very real sacrifices and important transformations in food-crop production as well as in nonagricultural activities. It ignores the specificity of precolonial social structures and the possibility that subsequent activities did not reflect a homogeneous response of individual cultivators but instead reflected either the continued coercive capacity of old regimes or the ability of ex-slaves or peasants to escape their overlords; both cases, and especially the latter, could amount to a profound social transformation. Even the process of capital formation within kinship groups had a great impact on the structure of those groups and on relations between people who controlled land, the planters, and the planters' laborers.[18] Perhaps most important, the examples of cash-crop expansion that most scholars dwell on have to be set against the equally important examples of resistance to cash-crop production, and we need some explanation for which pattern prevailed. Then too, this theory makes it hard to understand why all colonial governments were obsessed with the need to make producers' choices for them—via cultivation quotas, taxes payable in money, forced labor, or the manipulation of the power of local elites to make others produce exportable surpluses (see below). The theory makes no claim to explain the wider impact of export growth on the economy as a whole and on the colonial era as a period, and so Hopkins turns to the concept of the open economy. This is an accurate description of many features of colonial economies, but it is not an explanation of why the traits he lists go together or appear under particular circumstances; in fact, both the description and the lack of explanation are shared by Hopkins's rivals, the dependency theorists.[19] Without a thorough consideration of the structure of colonial states or a social analysis of production more specific than the notion of autonomous households, we are left with weak tools to distinguish the possibility of ever-wider development through export growth and multiplier effects from the possibility of involution, domination, and stagnation.

In terms of empirical research, the achievements of this variety of economic history remain impressive, especially in providing a sense of the extent of change in precolonial Africa and in examining trade.[20] Its greatest strength is exemplified by Philip Curtin's (1975) impressive chapter on foreign trade in his study of economic change in the Senegambia region. Yet Curtin's book also reveals much about the implicit priorities of a form of economic history. Social structure, farming patterns, slavery, and political systems are all discussed as background, not as part of history. His chapter on production says more about products than about the way they were produced. Thus, Curtin's ability to tease subtle and long-term changes in trading patterns out of elusive evidence is not followed up with a complete analysis of how those changes affected the nature of economic power or led to structural change in local societies.

There are, however, scholars who work within a similar framework of economic history but arrive at a very different assessment of, for example, colonial economies. Stephen Baier (1980), a student of Curtin, carefully portrays the breakdown of an older commercial system in the desert-edge of West Africa and gives an assessment of French economic action quite at variance with Hopkins's view of the colonial state as an enabling agent. By close analysis of the structures of commercial organizations and the structures of the colonial economy—monopoly buying firms, currency manipulations by the state, tax policy, the erection of borders and the collection of duties, and pacification—Baier explains the erosion of old mechanisms of coping with drought and the narrowing of economic roles. None of this threatens neoclassical theory: one can argue that the French did not play by the rules of a market economy and accordingly made a mess of things. The issue, however, is not whether markets are good or bad but whether the market mechanism explains very much of what actually happened in Africa, at the hands of European states or corporations as much as African peasants.

Dependency, Underdevelopment, and the Capitalist World Economy

Some development economists in Latin America had been taking an increasingly pessimistic view of the relationship of developed and underdeveloped economies even when their Africanist brethren were joyfully adding up cocoa shipments. From the late 1940s, Raúl Prebisch emphasized the distinction between center and periphery in the world economy, and he argued that there was a tendency for terms of trade to go against the latter. He also examined structural obstacles to capital accumulation and industrialization in the periphery. Although he saw no inherent tendency in international trade to develop the periphery, he saw the problems of underdevelopment as being curable, through national planning and international trade agreements, and he acquired great influence as Secretary General of the United Nations Commission on Trade and Development.[21]

But a break was made from the limits of the debate among "structuralist" development economists in the 1960s, when Andre Gunder Frank (1967) forcefully argued that the relationship of center and periphery was not simply a difficult problem but the very essence of capitalism. Frank denied that the poverty of the periphery was a prior state out of which each nation or region had to struggle or a consequence of "feudal" economies in Latin America. Such regions were part of a single capitalist economy in which the poverty, distortions, and stagnation of the periphery were an intrinsic part of the dynamism and wealth of the center. Similar arguments have been elaborated with important variations by such scholars as Samir Amin, Walter Rodney, and Immanuel Wallerstein (reviewed in Roxborough 1979).

Trade does not develop peripheral economies; it drains them of surplus. This inversion of the dogma of the developmentalists, like most inversions, actually goes right back to the most basic assumption of the opposition. Both neoclassical economists and Marxists have noted that the ancestors of Frank, Amin, and Wallerstein are in many ways closer to Smith and Ricardo than to Marx and Lenin, a pedigree which the dependency theorists do not claim (Hopkins 1976a; Laclau 1971; Brenner 1977) Developmentalists and underdevelopmentalists share, above all, a deterministic view of exchange.

Crucial to such analyses is the concept of unequal exchange. Anyone would acknowledge that a product made in one part of the world with, say, ten hours of labor, is frequently exchanged for another item, which under labor conditions elsewhere took fifteen hours to make. Exchange—item by item—is most often unequal, but unequal exchange—on a social level—is exchange that stays unequal, a self-perpetuating relationship of center and periphery. Arghiri Emmanuel (1972) assumes perfect competition in international trade, international mobility of capital but not of labor, lower wages in the periphery (which he takes as a given), production through wage labor in both center and periphery, plus several other restrictive assumptions. The lower wages, he argues, will not result in higher profits from peripheral production, for an equilibrium will develop at the lower cost level. The differences resulting from the fact that a given quantity of labor produces less exchange value at the periphery constitutes unequal exchange and benefits the users of raw materials or consumer products in the center, while draining the periphery of much of the social value of its labor. A Ricardian would reply that the periphery may indeed get less than the center from exchange, but more than it would have got from no trade at all; trade is not a zero-sum game (Hopkins 1976:40–41). Samir Amin, unlike Emmanuel, argues (1974a:63) that unequal exchange results from wage differentials greater than differentials in productivity. Then why wouldn't investors flock to such places and thus drive up the wage rate? This "cannot be explained without bringing in the policy . . . followed by the capital that dominates in the periphery, as regards organization of the surplus of labor power. How capital organizes proletarianization in the periphery, how the specializations that it imposes there give rise to a permanent and growing surplus of labor power in relation to demand—these are the real problems that have to be solved if the fact in question is to be accounted for" (Amin 1974a:63).[22] Amin gives an example of the organization of proletarianization. Yet the very specificity of the one case he discusses suggests that the actions of capital are essential, which presumably would mean that the actions of local rulers, local landowning classes, peasants, or slaves might affect the outcome

as well. Amin's discussion (1974a) of "peripheral social formations" suggests
that the social organization of the periphery is itself a consequence of its peripheral position; but if social structure causes the drainage of surplus from the
periphery, and if social structure is determined by being in the periphery, we
have come full circle. The attempt to make a drainage theory of international
exchange universal—independent of the struggles that take place in specific
parts of the world—has made it tautological.[23]

Wallerstein transforms theories of underdevelopment into Parsonianism on
a world scale. He posits a single world system based on the division into core
and periphery—with semiperiphery in between—in which a unique pattern of
labor usage characterizes each area: "Free labor is the form of labor control
used for skilled work in core countries whereas coerced labor is used for less
skilled work in peripheral areas. The combination thereof is the essence of
capitalism. When labor is everywhere free, we shall have socialism" (Wallerstein 1974:127). Forms of labor are thus nothing more than a mechanical
reflection of market-optimizing strategies of dominant classes, without reference to the dominated or to the contradictions and dynamics of labor systems
within core and periphery (Skocpol 1977:1079; Brenner 1977:54–57). System
maintenance or jockeying for position within the system become the crucial
processes of history. Internal struggles are merely quests for semiperipheral or
core status. Functionality substitutes for analysis of historical processes: "The
semiperiphery is then assigned as it were a specific economic role" (Wallerstein 1979:23). But Wallerstein's model does not explain why some peripheral
countries are promoted and some are not.[24]

Wallerstein's view of historical processes are as reductionist as his conception of labor and conflict: "The process of incorporation may be thought of as
a transformation that normally takes at least fifty years to complete" (Wallerstein and Martin 1979:193). Incorporation is thus a singular process—a local
economy is either in the world system or out of it; it is a passive process, as far
as those being incorporated are concerned; and it follows a universally determined schedule, rarely delayed and never stopped by obstacles to making the
organization of production conform to the demands of world markets. Africa,
of course, was assigned its specific role in the periphery. By making peripheralization into the basic historical process that affected Africa, Wallerstein can
treat the difference between family labor on a coffee farm and wage labor in a
gold mine—or between the structures of South Africa and Nigeria—as little
more than variations on a theme.[25]

As Africanists were jumping on the bandwagon of underdevelopment and
world-system theories, many Latin Americanists were getting off, taking the
plunge into the specific to look at the responses of particular classes to changes
in world markets and to examine particular mechanisms for extracting commodities and labor as well as resistance to them (Duncan and Rutledge 1977;

A. Bauer 1979; Katz 1974; Martinez-Alier 1977). Much of post-Frank dependency theory in Latin America has moved away from a rigid view of the
permanent dichotomy of periphery and core and toward a greater emphasis
on internal dynamics and internal class structure, still within a framework that
focuses on the constraints on capitalist development arising from the economic
power of industrialized nations and multinational corporations (Cardoso and
Falleto 1979; Sunkel 1973; Evans 1979; Girvan 1973).[26] From a more classically
Marxist theoretical standpoint, Ernest Mandel has attempted to conceptualize
the complexity and interrelationship of economic change not through a drainage theory applying to a dichotomized world, but through a concept of uneven
development—a "specific combination of pre-capitalist, semi-capitalist and
capitalist relations of production" (Mandel 1975:365; see also Kay 1975:107–
19). The spread of capitalism spawned wage-labor factories in Massachusetts,
haciendas in Brazil, mines using migrant labor with subsistence wages in South
Africa, and peasants in Uganda: explaining what evolved where entails asking
both what capital did and what it encountered, a question which will be pursued
below. Unequal exchange—and other characteristics of core-periphery relations—are thus not explanations, but consequences of the uneven pattern of
capitalist development.

What difference does it make whether profits within a worldwide system
of exchange come from the exploitation of wage laborers or of slaves or of
peasants? As Robert Brenner (1977) argues, many kinds of economic systems
entailed extensive trade. But why did one of them—the capitalist system—lead
to continual growth in productivity and increasing ability to affect the course
of change in other regions? The answer, Brenner insists, lies in the production
process itself.[27]

The alienation of workers from the means of production—free labor—gives
workers little choice but to work and capitalists little choice but to employ
workers more efficiently than their competitors. The slaveowner can respond
to incentives by forcing more work out of slaves or to contraction by relying
on the inward-looking nature of the plantation; the peasant can shield himself
from the market by his own subsistence production; but the capitalist cannot
hide, nor can the landless worker. Important as the expansion of world trade
in early-modern Europe was, the process of destroying the complex rights in
land that English tenants had and the polarization of society into the landed and
the landless were essential to creating the dynamic of inescapable competition.
Brenner is less clear on the question of why some dominant classes pressed their
power to the alienation of peasants' land, while others failed, and he has taken
the English model of agricultural capitalism too far—important variations exist
in the development of European capitalism. Nonetheless, his approach begins
to suggest why some trading partners developed internally while others did
not, and above all it emphasizes the need to take a more dynamic view of

what happens in the periphery. One is forced to ask why particular systems of production and different struggles for control of land and labor—in the context of a growing system of exchange but not as a mere reflection of it—led to structures with different potentials for continual growth.[28]

If dependency and world-system theories fail to penetrate the most basic processes which shaped the past, they approach the future from a perspective so radical that it is conservative. Since the only true analysis is on the world level and the basic contradiction is between core and periphery, local class conflict and political struggles are beside the point. For Wallerstein, even the successful revolutions of this century accomplished little more than "mercantilist semi-withdrawal" or an advance to a better position within the world capitalist system. Fortunately, we are assured that "secular developments in the structure of the capitalist world-system" will cause it to self-destruct in the "twenty-first or twenty-second century." It is certainly a good idea to warn against thinking that every ujamaa village constitutes a mortal blow to capitalism, but the insistence that analysis take place on a world level and no other as well as the functionalist nature of the theory has reduced action to triviality. Even Amin's fuller analysis of the mechanisms by which the center operates and his recognition of the relationship between those mechanisms and social formations in the periphery stops short of dissecting the nature of class within peripheral societies; it is unclear whether ruling classes within Africa are part of the problem or part of the solution. Amin combines the notion of "autocentric development"—which begins to sound like autarchy—with the idea that a transition to socialism is vital and can only take place at the level of the entire world. Whatever the intent of the various contributors to dependency theory, such approaches lend themselves to a superficial "Third Worldism," in which the most self-interested of local exploiting classes can join their more progressive fellow peripheralists in denouncing the exploitation of the periphery by the core (Wallerstein 1979:33, 67; Amin 1976:382–83).[29]

A growing number of empirical studies in many disciplines have been influenced by the concepts of underdevelopment and center-periphery relations, while valuable evidence of the power of European capital in commerce has come from scholars outside this persuasion.[30] Most lacking is a quantitative sense of the surplus-draining operation; Amin (1974a:57–59) comes up with a number, but he makes such simplified assumptions that it might as well come from out of his hat. The methodological problems are severe, not least of which is developing a counter-factual proposition for comparison—equal exchange? autarchy? More modestly, attempts to test such propositions as whether the drainage of capital from the periphery via the slave trade helped to bring about the industrial revolution in the center confirm the need for skepticism (Anstey 1975a; Engerman 1975).[31]

Where theory and research should illuminate each other is in studies of the

relationship of local economies and world trade. A notable attempt to address
such questions explicitly through dependency theory is E. A. Alpers's study
(1975) of East-Central Africa. It is a thoroughly researched book, and Alpers
analyzes brilliantly how changes in trading patterns in one part of the vast
and interconnected region—linked since the fifteenth century to European and
Asiatic mercantile systems—had ramifications elsewhere. But his argument is
least convincing just where the theory is weakest, above all in leaping from
external trade to underdevelopment without a thorough analysis of production
and power. Alpers portrays "healthy" systems of exchange geared to local production becoming "distorted" through the growth of trade in ivory and slaves,
which did not provide "fair" or "equal" compensation for the labor power lost
in the slave trade. But Alpers's view of healthy precontact economies is based
entirely on ex post facto reconstruction, and he makes little attempt to assess
the possibilities and limitation of change within such structures. Hence his view
of underdevelopment leaves the question of under what?—does Alpers have
an implicit counterfactual model of autonomous local development, perhaps
an industrial revolution manqué on the shores of Lake Malawi? Or merely a
romanticized stasis? A fuller analysis of how goods were produced and power
exercised is needed to demonstrate the distorting effects of trade. Alpers's
book—for all the richness of its analysis of commercial networks—suffers
from a vagueness of conceptualization and a missing level of analysis characteristic of the theoretical work of Frank, Amin, and Wallerstein. He is thus left
contrasting emotive adjectives—"healthy" versus "distorted" economies—
without an analytical basis for distinguishing the dependency theorists' distortion from the neoclassical economists' comparative advantage (1975:29, 31,
201–3, 252).[32]

When all this is said, however, it is still hard to avoid the conclusion that the
focus on the world as a whole is indispensable. The problem is that dissecting complex problems with concepts like underdevelopment, incorporation,
unequal exchange, and core-periphery relations is rather like performing brain
surgery with an ax: the concepts cut, but messily. What is needed is a fuller
discussion of what is systematic about the world system, and that means more
sensitive theoretical and empirical examinations of distinct types of capital,
their development, and interrelation; of the flow of credit and investment—
from the trust system of the slave trade to the International Monetary Fund
and multinational corporations; of the control and diffusion of technology; of
commercial organizations; of states; and of the often contradictory ways that
specific classes react and adapt to changing opportunities and constraints in
world markets.

Marxism and Modes of Production

If a focus on exchange proves incapable in itself of separating development from underdevelopment, the focus must shift to production. Marx called production the "hidden abode" (1967:176), deeply concealed by layers of mystification in orthodox economics. But production in noncapitalist economies is an abode that Marx himself only glimpsed, and which his followers still find difficult to uncover.

Some non-Marxists have also taken the specificity of African systems of production seriously. Polly Hill pioneered what is now a large body of detailed studies of agricultural systems (Hill 1963, 1970, 1972).[33] On a loftier theoretical plain, Karl Polanyi has sought to draw a sharp line between modern economies and others, labeled primitive and archaic. In the primitive economies of Africa, material transactions were nested in the social matrix, so that rules of reciprocity or redistribution—not supply and demand—shaped exchange. But the debates between Polanyi's "substantivists" and Hopkins's "formalists" have been tedious, adding up to little more than a conclusion that neither market behavior nor the particular structures in which it takes place (in "modern" as much as in "primitive" economies) can be ignored (Polanyi 1944, 1966; Dalton 1968, 1976).

The most important attempt to transcend this false dichotomy has come from Marxists in France, and it has made the specificity of modes of production the starting point. The work of the anthropologists Claude Meillassoux (1960), Maurice Godelier (1972, 1977), Emmanuel Terray (1972), and Pierre-Philippe Rey (1971, 1973), as well as of Jean Suret-Canale (1964) and Catherine Coquery-Vidrovitch (1969), has led to major breakthroughs. It has entered the English language through the work of, among others, Barry Hindess and Paul Hirst (1975) as well as John Taylor (1979; see also Seldon 1978; Kahn and Llobera, 1980). Kinship, these anthropologists would argue, is not rooted in a peculiarly African love of kinsmen but rather in the conditions of arable agriculture. Its basis lies in the vulnerability of a new generation as they must acquire seeds, ritual and technical knowledge, and food to get through the growing season, all of which provide elders with a basis of control over social reproduction, over the ability of a new generation to replicate the structure of the old. Elders' control is extended through control of access to women. While this approach stresses the exercise of power of elders over junior men and all women, it also suggests that younger men acquire a future stake in the system's reproduction—for they one day will be elders—and hence in ideologies and religious systems that stress age and descent. Meillassoux and others thus seek to explain in materialist terms the pervasiveness of kinship, which other anthropologists take for granted,[34] and to differentiate this pattern of control and ideology from other situations—as in hunting and gathering societies—

where the requirements of reproduction do not foster the elaboration of descent systems or bridewealth (Meillassoux 1960; Godelier 1975). One can also see the possibility that external trade or opportunities to serve an outside power might give younger men a chance to found their own households outside of the elders' sphere of control, thereby undermining elders' control of reproduction (Beinart 1982). Then, too, the acquisition of slaves or the collection of tribute by a single kinship group within a society may begin to define another mode of production, with its own ideology and social relations. Such considerations have informed a growing and important body of local studies (Meillassoux 1964, 1975a; Rey 1971; Pollet and Winter 1968).

If at this point the concept of a mode of production begins to suggest the complex intertwining of technology, the social organization of production, and ideology, it also begins to skirt the dangers of excessive abstraction and reification characteristic of the Marxism of Louis Althusser, which has greatly influenced the French anthropologists. Modes of production become actors, and the seemingly necessary requirements for their reproduction become causes. The leap from structure into process, above all, has alarmed historians like E. P. Thompson (1978).[35] The very attempt to make the mode of production a comprehensive concept leads Althusserians into the same tendency to explain everything in terms of functional necessity that Marxists criticized in earlier schools (but see Cohen 1978:249–98).

Precapitalist modes of production are very difficult to specify. If every way of catching an antelope or growing a banana defines a mode of production, the concept blends into the empiricism that Marxists scorn (Terray 1972). The lineage mode of production is being applied to Africa just as non-Marxist anthropologists have cast doubt on the category of lineage. The subordination of women is explained as necessary to the reproduction of the lineage mode of production, but this does not explain how or why women acquiesced to their roles, while much evidence suggests that their actual roles in both production and reproduction were far more complex than the dichotomy between the two implies (Guyer 1981; O'Laughlin 1977; Edholm et al. 1977; Mackintosh 1977). A slave mode of production is a more dubious proposition: the forced importation of detached outsiders can strengthen kinship groups against kings or kings against kinship groups, and the use of slaves as producers cannot be explained at all without reference to wider systems of exchange.[36] On the other hand, attempts to define modes of production at a comprehensive level—such as a colonial mode of production or Coquery-Vidrovitch's African mode of production (Alavi 1975; Coquery-Vidrovitch 1969)—get so far away from the point of production that they merely shift the question of determination to another sphere: Why should a political process, colonialism, determine production, or why should trade?[37]

The thorniest problem of all is how to go from the systemic and self-reinforcing nature of a mode of production to an understanding of how they transform themselves, how they are transformed from outside, or how they are preserved in the face of outside pressure. The specific problem recent Marxist analysts have posed themselves is not the classic transition of feudalism to capitalism, but its opposite: How does capitalism become dominant in regions such as Africa without replicating itself in each instance? The starting point for studies of "articulation" is Marx's famous statement that capital always takes labor as it finds it. The question is what it does with labor. To explain that, Althusserians note that the logic of each mode of production unfolds on an abstract level and that the articulation of these modes produces a social formation. In some arguments, one mode of production is necessarily dominant in any social formation, for its requirements of reproduction subordinate the others.[38]

But what does dominance mean? Theorists are concerned to avoid the sin of voluntarism, to insist that dominance has to do with the logic of the capitalist mode of production and not the will of capitalists. So we have dominance and articulation, without dominators or articulators. This is a perfectly valid theoretical procedure, but the historian is apt to wonder if things actually happen merely because they must. The very mechanisms that transform the logical necessity that capital act in certain ways in order to reproduce itself into historical reality may generate their own contradictions and produce a reality that falls short of necessity.

This reasoning from "capital logic" poses especially serious problems in the version of articulation put forward by Claude Meillassoux and Harold Wolpe. They argue that capital conserves precapitalist modes of production at precisely the point where the food they produce covers part but not all of subsistence costs; this atrophied sector pays the costs of reproduction of the labor force— raising children, maintaining women, and caring for the elderly—allowing capitalists to pay males lower wages and to earn "superprofits." Such an argument defines away all possibility of incomplete domination, of resistance to capitalism, or of African societies being ordered in any way except to maximize the advantage of capital. But how is one to tell whether cultivators' continued access to the soil represents their resistance to the work rhythms and powerlessness of wage labor rather than a perfectly functional part of a superexploitative system? This is Marxism without a class struggle: wage rates and the structure of migration are reduced to derivatives of capital's requirements, and the most difficult question of all—why workers acquiesced—is explained in an ad hoc, atheoretical fashion, while the struggles of workers to shape the timing and conditions of labor and cultivation are ignored. Once again, function becomes cause, and we are ill-equipped to understand how migratory labor was obtained, the complexity of the relationship between the spheres of production and reproduction, the problems of disciplining and socializing workers, or the instability and tension that beset migratory labor systems (Meillassoux 1975b; Wolpe 1972).[39] These are questions to which we shall return.

The concept of articulation at least helps to specify a basic problem: expanding capitalism encountered not merely cultivators, but social formations with their own coherence and forms of exploitation. Pierre-Philippe Rey emphasizes the specificity of these formations. Feudalism in Europe was conducive to the nurturing of early capitalism in ways that other modes of production were not, above all because of the development of property in land and agricultural rent.[40] Outside of Europe, articulation was a multistaged process, entailing an alliance of capital with dominant classes in existing precapitalist modes of production. As these allies produced more raw materials for the benefit of capital, precapitalist forms of exploitation were intensified. This process did not cause capitalism to "take root." A new stage allowing for the creation of capitalist production, using free labor, and the expanded reproduction of capitalism required the violence of colonization—the subordination of locally dominant classes and the implantation of capitalist institutions, in marketing systems, transport, and plantations. Even then, exploitation within the still incompletely dominated structures of African social formations generated resistance. The "freeing" of labor for capitalist mines, industries, and plantations thus represented the exodus of men seeking to escape the class struggle at home. Rey sees a final stage—still in the future—when such social formations are no longer necessary and wage labor has become generalized.

If Rey's substitute class struggle is possible, then why not a genuine class struggle, one that undermines the power of precapitalist ruling classes? Migration—whether in search of a job or a new place to farm—has in some cases contributed to the destruction of dominant classes and to the weakening of the power of elders within households (Cooper 1980: chapter 5; Beinart 1982). Rey's argument depends on problematic factors—alliances with specific classes, struggles, violence—without assessing the importance of different outcomes. The colonization of Africa "freed" labor in a different sense from that which, in Marx's analysis, led to the development of capitalism—freeing labor both *to* enter a market in labor power and *from* any alternative means of survival. If market incentives increased incentives for local rulers to exploit their subjects, colonization often undermined their means to do so. The individual's need for protection became less of a restraint on mobility. So Africans could increasingly be "free" of the paternalism and tyranny of kings or slave-owners without being "free" of land; the accumulation of agricultural capital by a dominant class became more difficult rather than less; and workers came forth in larger number; but—with continued ability to return to the land or to seek new land—they resisted being pushed into a committed, disciplined working class. We are back to the question of what dominance means.

Much of the thrust behind the recent trends in Marxist scholarship—and in dependency theory as well—stems from attempts to come to grips with the evident domination of capitalism in a situation where the essence of capitalism, the alienation of means of production and wage labor, is only sometimes relevant. But perhaps the search for alternative ways of conceiving capitalist domination can give a wooden and ahistorical perspective upon a process that involved a complex and conflict-ridden encounter with Africans. The limited extent of primitive accumulation, the lack of generalized wage labor, and the continuation of extensive nonmarket production may not have been mere aspects of a profit-maximizing mechanism for a somewhat vaguely defined capitalist system, but important constraints on the dynamism of capitalism.

Geoffrey Kay (1975:54–55) and Ernest Mandel (1975:44–74) face this problem explicitly: a well-paid worker, in a well-capitalized factory in the developed world produces more and generates a higher rate of surplus value than a low-paid, poorly productive worker. But why wouldn't all capital rush to make investments that raise productivity, leading to the extension of capitalist development throughout the world, a process which some Marxists, notably Bill Warren (1980), insist is happening? Kay claims it is not, and insists that a distinction between merchant and industrial capital explains why. The former gets its profit from exchange and so can only exist in conjunction with productive capital. The rise of industrial capitalism in Europe reduced merchant capital to subordinate status there, but elsewhere merchant capital was left free to bring back raw materials and create markets on behalf of industrial capital. Production could be carried out by noncapitalist producers or by plantations and mines that—because they paid below subsistence wages—were not fully constrained by the competitive laws of industrial capitalism. Low wages discouraged mechanization. Only in the long run—Kay looks at the 1930s—did merchant capital's limited control over the production process catch up with it. Then it moved into production and turned to capital-intensive methods. Only by that time the structures of underdevelopment—above all a marginalized work force willing to work for low wages—were already entrenched, and capital-intensive production coincided with unemployment.

Something like this has happened. But Kay tries to make an argument about specific historical processes into a general characteristic of what he calls underdevelopment, and he places great weight on an historical relationship between merchant and industrial capital and on production processes in underdeveloped economies that he does not fully explain.[41] Access to the world market (or merchant capital itself) may foster the development of powerful classes that use tenants, slaves, or low-wage workers to produce, and those classes may block further development; the restraining powers of hacienda owners in South America or concessionary companies in Mozambique—and the massive numbers of underemployed and unemployed people they spawned—are clear. Yet all these forms of exploitation involved a confrontation with workers; how profits could be extracted depended on how they could be controlled. And while merchant capital's dealings with peasants might soften them up for later exploitation as marginalized workers, neither Kay nor others have argued very carefully why this should necessarily be so; a peasant with a few cocoa bushes may well be better able to resist subsequent pressures than a cultivator with no way of earning cash.[42] On the other hand, the classic Marxist drive toward capitalism has also happened in once underdeveloped areas, as in the United States.

Mandel, however, suggests a reason why the process of capital accumulation and the development of the forces of production may have gone furthest in the countries that made the transformation to wage labor at the earliest time. Transport costs before the development of steamships and railways allowed each ruling class a certain leeway to get on with its business of expropriating peasants. But the transport revolution—maturing just as Africa was becoming seriously involved in producing export crops—made it possible for a new wave of people to be quickly brought into a system of exchange and for value to be realized through the processing of the raw materials they produced by industrial capital. This created vested interests on the part of capital in Europe, colonial states, merchant capital, and productive capital in Africa to maintain cheap labor systems and low producer prices for peasants, a process which created underemployment and discouraged the drive toward higher capitalization and productivity. In other words, outside capital—interested in raw materials and exchange—got to African cultivators before African ruling classes, whose profit would come from production, could get to them. This is an important argument, but it still requires attention to the dynamics and limitations of production within Africa (Mandel 1975:51–59).

Uneven development is thus a more textured phenomenon than the idea of an underdeveloped periphery. Capitalism has tendencies both to revolutionize production and to make it stagnate. The essence of capitalism—the accumulation of surplus value—is necessarily expansionist and revolutionary, but the very process of accumulation is directed by specific classes with specific needs. Those classes' efforts to secure cheap raw materials or to avoid competition may stand in the way of the capitalist system's drive toward increasing the rate and size of surplus value accumulation.[43] The direction that is taken depends on complex patterns in world markets, in capital flows, on struggles in the workplace, and on the exercise of class power. All this suggests that a much closer scrutiny of production is needed than the new-fangled concepts of articulation, dependency, and underdevelopment allow. Perhaps a return to those central but neglected aspects of the old Marxism—primitive accumulation, the labor process, and class struggle—might be salutary.

Primitive accumulation is not the mere amassing of productive resources; it is the exclusion from access to the means of production of an entire class. It implies not merely the acquisition of titles to land, but the effective denial of access: it thus requires both the systematic exercise of force and its legitimation, hence it requires the exercise of state power (Brenner 1977; Thompson 1975; Hay et al. 1975). Accumulation is thus a process that one class must do to another and one that will be resisted. It is an historical phenomenon. In Europe, the specific nature of the classes that led the transformation to capitalism led to distinct patterns of capitalist development (Moore 1966).[44]

By focusing on accumulation in Africa, one might understand the limits of responses to market expansion from the early nineteenth century onward as much as its extent. Through consideration of how a relatively small group of whites in South Africa gained control of land and the subsequent transformation of the collection of rent into the control of labor, one might begin to distinguish the course of capitalist development in South Africa from Nigeria or Zambia. It is necessary not just to stress the exclusionary nature of primitive accumulation but also to examine the dynamics, implications, and limitations of other forms of accumulation, something students of agrarian history have in fact begun to do (Berry 1975; Cooper 1980; Parkin 1972; Kitching 1980). For example, the growth of cocoa exports in West Africa entailed the accumulation of often large holdings of trees without a sharp and growing dichotomy of an owning class and a propertyless class. The original holders of rights in land shared those rights with immigrants who planted trees, and the very limitations of the marketability of land fostered such arrangements by making production the only source of value in land.[45] Planters mobilized kinship and client labor and hired workers as well, but many workers could aspire to accumulate enough resources to plant trees themselves. Perhaps such a process can become exclusionary and rigid when cocoa land runs out, but in some cases cocoa accumulators made a leap to the national level, investing not in further accumulation in the countryside but in education and politics. Access to the national center seemed to offer better prospects for a new generation (Berry 1975; Berry 1984; Chauveau and Richard 1977).

Colin Leys (1978) argues that both the dynamics and the blockages of economic change must be understood by analyzing specific processes of accumulation. One must carry such an analysis from the point of production to its intersection with the world system. The limited alternatives of world commodity markets and the great power of multinational corporations do indeed constrain the scope of local capitalists, but one must still ask the extent to which local capitalists command local resources and, above all, labor power. A debate is raging among students of Kenya about the extent to which a class of Kenyans, beginning in the colonial era, acquired land and labor and has since extended its control to large-scale agriculture using wage labor and then to industry and services (Leys 1978; Kaplinsky et al. 1980; Kitching 1980; Swainson 1980; Beckman 1980). Hence it is very much an open question whether an indigenous capitalist class is limited to a comprador role, may be the weaker partner in an alliance with transnational capital, or may itself come to dominate such an alliance. It is a further question, which will be taken up later, whether national or transnational capital will prosper more by increasing productivity or by preventing anyone else from doing so. If such an examination requires a full understanding of the relationship of different capitals and of all factors—international and national—affecting the creation, realization, and reproduction of surplus value, a focus on the accumulation processes themselves is crucial.

The relationship of rural accumulation and alienation to the growth of wage-labor forces is turning out to be very complex. Scholars have spent most of their time discussing what made workers go to work, a process which goes under the excessively general concept of proletarianization. Equally important to understand are the labor processes by which capital turned the workers' time into output. The specificity of capitalist labor processes should be the starting point: compared with, for example, slave labor, the motivations of workers, the nature of discipline, and the cultural meaning of work were different. But a growing literature on England and America has drawn attention to the distinctive forms of the labor process under capitalism. The direct supervision of the boss—armed above all with the "sanction of the sack"—was later supplemented or replaced by a new emphasis on the setting of work rhythms by machines, and later still by the use of bureaucratic and psychological techniques of control. These forms of control arose at particular points in capitalist development, and each engendered particular forms of resistance, hence new cycles of control and resistance. Such changes never eclipsed the cruder forms of labor control in certain categories of work, and industrial countries developed "segmented labor markets" that channeled different kinds of workers into different kinds of jobs (Edwards 1979; Braverman 1974; Burawoy 1978; Elbaum et al. 1979; Piore 1979).

This literature has much to offer students of labor in Africa, but Charles van Onselen is one of few historians who has examined work itself in any detail. He shows (1976b) that gold miners in Rhodesia who had been recruited in different ways were often shuttled into distinct roles in the mines and housed in different parts of the compound, for forced laborers, understandably, had to be watched more carefully for desertion. Van Onselen analyzes the multifaceted nature of control in the totalitarian system of the mining compound, and he shows that even as the role of direct coercion in recruiting labor diminished, the coercive nature of labor control within the mine did not. Even van Onselen spends more time in the compound than in the mine shaft, and we get an incomplete picture of the relationship between technology and labor control.[46] While the compound was a powerful instrument of coercion, urban labor in general was volatile, and—as argued later—the difficulties of disciplining, socializing, and motivating a rapidly circulating labor force led to a crisis in the aftermath of the

Great Depression, and to consideration among colonial authorities of whether the nature of the labor process had to change. By examining the exact ways that workers made commodities, and the wider ramifications of particular labor processes, a fuller sense of the tensions and dynamics of labor can be obtained.

Then there is the elusive question of class. The origins of the struggle of the bourgeoisie and proletariat in Marxist theory is in the process of primitive accumulation. There is nothing particularly Marxist to go fishing for classes in every situation, and the weakness of class formation may be as essential to stress as its importance. More generally, a dominant class can be defined by the total range of resources at its command and by its ability to exploit those who lack such command over resources (Kitching 1980; Joseph 1980; Sklar 1979). Class, E. P. Thompson (1963:11) reminds us, is an historical concept: frozen in time, there are only isolated individuals and isolated actions (but see Cohen 1978:73–79). It makes sense to investigate warrior classes in pre-colonial kingdoms, whose collective control of military might enabled them to accumulate goods from outside (by catching slaves and buying imports) and to exercise power over cultivators within the kingdom. It is equally important to look at how kings might try to break the collective nature of warrior's status; one can cite both cases where royal despotism overrode class, and where a warrior class dispensed with a king altogether.[47] It is also interesting to analyze, as does Ivor Wilks (1975), the development of class conflict between a ruling class and a merchant class, but the analysis can only be historical, for the mere existence of merchants does not make them a class, nor does the mere existence of slaveowners make them a class (Cooper 1979:123–24).

Much of the class struggle in England that Thompson (1963) so brilliantly describes was a struggle not to be a working class, not to be reduced to so much interchangeable labor power, but to preserve the autonomy of the artisan, the skills and collective identity of skilled workers, and the rights of tenants on the land. The shared experiences of this phase of struggle in turn shaped the consciousness and patterns of action of the English working class once that phase of the battle was lost. Or as Adam Przeworsky (1977:372) put it, "political class struggle is a struggle about class before it is a struggle among classes." [48]

Such considerations have been lost in much Marxist writing on class formation in colonial and postcolonial Africa. Thus Charles Perrings (1979) insists that the light of copper miners' class consciousness can only lie at the end of a tunnel of proletarianization. Certainly, the workers' village connection will affect the nature of workers' struggles, but their position as workers will not be defined in a purely objective manner, independent of the ongoing social processes and conflicts (Przeworsky 1977:367). More satisfactory is van Onselen's discussion (1976b) of how quickly central African workers came to grips with the organization of labor recruitment and industry, both resisting and manipulating it through individual action and social networks that cross the overemphasized divide between rural and urban spheres.[49] This makes class formation no less of a complex and elusive process, but it is one that must be assessed over time and in reference to the entire system that workers faced.

Most controversial of all has been the relevance of class to post-colonial societies. Besides those who dismiss the relevance of class altogether are scholars who stress the absence of any role for a dominant African class in production: they are an auxiliary bourgeoisie, a bourgeoisie of the civil service, a political class, or a petty bourgeoisie. The frequent stress on the state and its personnel as intermediaries between international capital and local producers is the political concomitant of underdevelopment theory (Lonsdale 1981). But if accumulation by a national class is not foreclosed, if the state's control of re-sources—even given the power of multinationals—is the source of substantial autonomy, and if rulers must come to grips with the difficult task of controlling workers and peasants and containing the effects of accumulation, the nature of that class needs a more careful and more dynamic examination. Richard Joseph (1980:27) makes good sense in suggesting that a dominant class in Nigeria or Kenya may be better defined by their "project" than by their current situation. Such classes are committed to furthering their own role in a capitalist econ-omy and in mobilizing all possible resources on their own behalf; they were not the first class in world history to use the state to such an effect.[50] Their class nature emerges above all in their quest to control and extract surplus from workers and peasants; indeed, the manipulations of produce-buying and wages have been among the most volatile issues in many independent African coun-tries. The closing off of opportunities for mobility marks a new phase in class formation (relevant case studies are Beckman 1976; Jeffries 1978; Schatzberg 1980). But it is not a project that has been altogether successful, and the very difficulties of transforming privileged access to resources into accumulation of productive capital have often fostered the tendency of this class project to take the easier forms of urban real estate speculation and compradorism. The class basis of state action has been compromised by the particularistic power base of its members and the high stakes of state control. Problems of analysis arise not because a national bourgeoisie's control of production is irrelevant to their position but because the importance of this issue makes it the center of conflict and uncertainty.[51]

If the impetus behind the recent spurt of Marxist scholarship on Africa includes dissatisfaction with the functionalism and particularism of the con-ventional wisdom—tendencies which are worth reacting against—the results have probably gone too strongly against particularism and not strongly enough against functionalism.[52] Marxist scholarship has done less well in painting in Africa on a great picture of production and reproduction than in developing the paints and the brushes, with basic but complex concepts such as accumulation, labor control, and class struggle. Marxists have helped to stress the fact that precolonial kings, colonial states, and postcolonial rulers have all had to grapple with the problems of controlling resources, transforming that control into productive labor, and containing or avoiding the threat from below. By stressing the give and take of these processes, both Marxists and others have slowly begun to draw a picture of change and the limits of change that transcends images of mechanical responses to markets or implacable domination.

Conflict and Convergence

Neoclassical economics, dependency theory, and Marxist analyses constitute various ways of looking at the connection between Africa and the world economy. They do not, however, constitute a set of niches to which each thinker must be assigned. They help instead to illuminate basic assumptions which often go unspecified. The split between neoclassical economists and Marxists is fundamental, dividing an attempt to make all factors comparable and interchangeable through the market and a notion that such a conception is a "fetishism" masking the social basis of production. Yet, it is possible to tug dependency theory in both directions. What is most original and most daring about it is also the most dubious: its emphasis on the world economy as a single system of extraction. Dependency theory fundamentally is a theory of exchange—treating production as a derivative—and so a perceptive orthodox economist like Hopkins (1976a) finds it easy to accept much of what it has to offer and to discard the rest. The overlap of dependency theory with the structuralist branch of development economics is even clearer (Godfrey 1980:1–2; Pinto and Knakal 1973; Girvan 1973). On the other hand, if Samir Amin's title, *Accumulation on a World Scale*, were fully followed through in his book, much of his theories could be assimilated to Marxism; but it is accumulation—a class phenomenon—which dependency theory treats most inadequately. Marxists should, however, combine their emphasis on accumulation within the sphere of production and on the tensions, contradictions, and dynamism within labor processes with a fuller consideration of issues that dependency theorists stress— the movement of capital and of surplus, the changing international division of labor, and uneven development. Still, however basic the theoretical divisions, each can learn from the others, and research done within one framework has already illuminated the others.

Eras and Issues

Periodization: A Caveat

The relationship of Africa and the world economy was a changing one. How is one to distinguish periods and transitions in basic structures? The problem is that all of Africa did not always jump in unison. To divide into periods the history of a continent this large and complex is to assume that the outside world is not only important, but determinant.[53] My aim here is more modest. It is important to examine breaks and transitions, but they may be in local systems of production and class control, in regional commercial networks, or in the entire nature of relationship of Africa with Europe. By focusing on the latter, one can identify crises where basic structures could be changed systematically or not at all. The following pages are organized on the basis of transformations, stressing not only the extent of change, but its limitations, wherein lay the seeds of further transformation. I have not attempted local or regional chronologies but look instead at basic processes through which distinct patterns of change may be analyzed.

From Gold to Slaves

Africa was the western world's principal source of slaves from the fifteenth to the nineteenth centuries. Now, Africans can be found sweeping the streets of Paris, part of a quite different but important system of labor movement. In between, Europeans lamented the shortage of labor in Africa, and Chinese and Indians were transported to labor in the West Indies and even to build railroads in East Africa and harvest sugar in Natal. The next-best alternative to slave labor in early English colonies had come from the very core of the world economy—English indentured servants—while in the twentieth century, Africans from the most peripheral parts of the periphery, for example Mali, joined people from the edges of the core—Portugal, southern Italy, and similar regions—in the demeaning conditions of migratory labor. The flows of labor across space and time were complex.

Why did Africa play such a big part in a specific period in the worldwide division of labor? Wallerstein has a simple answer: African slaves were attractive not because slave labor is intrinsically cheap but because they had no opportunity costs. Workers within the world system who produce sugar do not produce something else, but the loss from external workers falls outside the world system and is thus irrelevant to it. Similarly, the slave trade was abolished because its very growth had gradually brought Africa from a position external to the world economy into its periphery, and by the time of abolition—1807 in the case of Great Britain—the desire for commodities that slaves might have produced in Africa meant that the world system had begun to absorb the true cost of enslavement (Wallerstein 1976:32–36; 1974:87–90; 1973:7–9).

The dichotomy of external and peripheral, however, is too simplistic to fit the rise of the slave trade and too muddled to explain its fall.[54] Wallerstein provides no specific analysis of labor costs.[55] The external arena's trade is distinguished from that of the periphery by the nonessential nature of the items involved. Yet during the period when slave exports were rising at a roughly exponential rate (1626–1700), West Africa's gold exports—as crucial an item as any in the world economy at that time—were worth more than its exports of slaves. Even the Royal Africa Company got 40 percent of its income from the sale of African products other than slaves. Indeed, the Gold Coast, during the fifteenth and sixteenth centuries and even later, imported labor from Benin, via Portuguese traders.[56] Then, too, recent studies of imports to Africa suggest that they were far more varied, far more subject to the complexities of supply and demand and the skill of African traders than the luxury trade model which Wallerstein posits (Richardson 1978:303–30). Curtin (1975:312, 326–27) shows that capital goods—iron bars that saved substantial labor in the production of tools—were particularly important in the early days of the Senegambian slave trade. And most important, Wallerstein's argument—even if it were not wrong—would explain why planters sought slaves in Africa, not why Africans wanted to supply them.

The trouble with Wallerstein's interpretation of the end of the slave trade is that the British abolished their slaving in 1807, when ground-nut and palm oil exports were a mere trickle, but slave-produced sugar was still a flood (Drescher 1977; Anstey 1975b; Hopkins 1973; Northrup 1976; Brooks 1975). Even later—and in such differently organized economic systems as the Niger Delta and Dahomey—continued slave exports and rising palm oil exports proved compatible for some time (Northrup 1976; Law 1977a). All that remains from this line of argument is that Africa's involvement in the world economy intensified in the era of the slave trade. We knew that.

What we know least is the nature of the social structures that responded to the demand for slaves. John Fage (1969, 1980)—a decade after the great debate with Walter Rodney (1966) over the relationship of the slave trade and Africa slavery—belabors the point that servile status in some West African societies antedated the Atlantic trade, but he only underscores how little we can tell about what those structures were. The models of the slave trade economy that several neoclassical economists have proposed leave those structures blank, and the authors conclude that the models in fact do not explain why slaves were sold.[57] Curtin (1975:156–68; 1978:224) creates an artificial dichotomy between political and economic motivations for slaving, thus making it difficult to see the way in which the economic position of decision-makers shaped their politics.[58]

Recent studies have picked away at deterministic arguments linking trade and political forms. Trading has been correlated with statebuilding, weapons systems with political systems, and warrior aristocracies with slave-based production. All such direct linkages now seem dubious.[59] Instead, historians are focusing on connections, tensions, and contradictions among groups and classes, and the way that they were played out over time. Any aspiring ruling class faced a double problem: how to extract surplus—which meant control of labor—and how to realize the surplus—which meant exchange. The latter problem raised the potentially fruitful but potentially competitive relationship of localized rulers with merchant networks, as well as with the outside world. Even if a class could choose between selling produce and selling people— as occurred with Sahelian grain or coastal palm oil at particular times—they faced the other side: how to control labor. Much of the desirability of the use of slaves in growing food for palaces and crops for export lay in the difficulty of checking both the entrenched social power of local kinship groups and their potential mobility. At the same time, recent literature on slavery in Africa (Cooper 1979; Meillassoux 1975a) has stressed the limitations of slaveowners' power, above all the danger that slaves might themselves become entrenched and conscious of their collective identity, and of the slaveowners' consequent reliance on new waves of imports to reproduce the labor force. The interplay of external and internal uses of slaves thus shaped not only the possibilities for realizing a surplus but the nature of labor control as well: the external outlet for adult male slaves could complement the local use of younger and female slaves (Manning 1981). The ending of such an outlet could raise the question of controlling a growing body of slave descendants while still bringing in new slaves.

In a fascinating if tentative look at the origins of Asante society, Ivor Wilks hints that any attempt to explain state formation, such as that made by Emmanuel Terray, by the imperatives of gold production and slave-gathering aristocracies might be backwards. Gold production may well have been the province of very small productive units, and early attempts by states to control production only killed it off. But money from gold gave its Akan producers— whose subsistence hitherto came from hunting and gathering—a chance to import labor to undertake the difficult task of clearing the forest. The absorption of these slaves—who otherwise would have formed a threatening slave caste— helped to shape the Asante matriclans, institutions not found among otherwise similar groups beyond the difficult forest environment (Wilks 1978; see also Kea 1986; Dumett 1979:45–46; Wilks 1979:28; Meillassoux 1978:122). The recognition of how thorny an issue labor could be raises questions of interrelations of trade and power in somewhat modified form. If the import of slaves produced matriclans, did their export strengthen the subsequent emergence of the state? And did the decline of their export—raising anew the problem of control over labor—herald a new conflict between the ruling class and other social groups, both kinship-based producers and merchants who profited from the renewed trend toward decentralized production?

Slaving is a very special sort of economic enterprise. Slaving is essentially stealing, but it is a social act—requiring military organization to work on a significant scale (Curtin 1979:15–16). Slave catchers range widely, but they do not stay around; slaving is not linked to a specific point of production. And above all the realization of surplus through selling—a single transaction that takes the slave out of the hair of the slaver—contrasts sharply to the continuous process of supervision or extraction characteristic of most agricultural or industrial endeavors. There is no labor process. But for warriors to exist as such, there must be war, there must be slaving. Otherwise surplus can only come from a labor process, and warriors may or may not control it. Richard Roberts (1980) thus argues that the warriors' need to ensure their own social reproduction led to the continuation and extension of slaving.[60] And the very widespread but discontinuous nature of the process caused its effects to be spread extremely far.

The nature of slaving created its own limits: widespread violence and insecurity led people to come together in defensive settlements, to move into isolated areas, or to set aside their resistance to authority in the face of their dire need for protection. Such efforts could cause warriors to fail at the very endeavor on which they depended to remain dominant at home. Some slaving powers that lost their ability to direct exploitation outward became self-consuming, selling their own people.[61] At the same time, slaving could not be isolated from the otherwise complex and varied dimensions of social organization. Warriors needed merchants to realize the profits of their wars and raids. Curtin suggests that as much as 85 to 90 percent of the f.o.b. cost of a slave in Saint Louis might go to various middlemen in the Senegambia to pay for transport, holding, and above all protection. At the same time, armies had to be fed, slave ships and caravans to be supplied, and cultivators might go on cultivating, and exchanging products, even as their rulers sold slaves. It is thus essential to examine the political economy of protection, transport, agriculture, and local marketing as much as of slave catching, and above all to analyze the potentially ambivalent relationship between warrior states and merchants. The ability of the latter to extend their networks—without which they could not serve warrior states— gave them a potentially dangerous autonomy. The long development of trading systems, of new social relationships that grew out of them, and of the Islamic ideologies that gave a coherence and deeper meaning to such social structures were to have revolutionary implications.[62]

Meillassoux (1978) argues—although this question needs much more analysis—that the gold trade and the merchants of the early Sudanic states were important but did not determine the kind of state that arose. The character of that state derived above all from the power of armies to raid beyond the sphere of political control and the ability of military rulers to erect an apparatus of state—using slaves and other mechanisms—independent of local production and social organization. The warriors needed the trans-Saharan slave trade for their continued reproduction, but as readily raided populations diminished and resistance increased, this form of reproduction undermined itself, while the incorporation of slaves—women and children—into the region of continuous control began to create a different sort of economy, with more emphasis on slave production and with a correspondingly greater role for merchants. The military state lost its unique role in social reproduction and its decline went along with a long era of important economic, social, and religious developments in the Sudanic region. Then when the Atlantic slave trade created new outlets for slaves, warrior states like Segu Bambara rose again, but they now had to come to grips with merchant communities that were both more effective and more powerful.[63]

As soon as one takes into account the conflicting social groups and contrary tendencies within interconnected regions, the differing internal dynamics of slave-exporting economies take on increased importance. Robin Law notes (1977b:303–12) that Benin—strong before the slave trade became intense—kept that trade at a distance, while Dahomey, Oyo, and Asante did not. For internal control, Oyo relied most on slave retainers, thereby failing to cut across and undermine kinship groups, while the other kingdoms built around the state's crucial role in slave acquisition to coopt free people (sometimes playing them off against slaves) and thus to penetrate more deeply into social structure. Centralized kingdoms did not spring automatically from the slave trade, and kings had to exercise continual vigilance against merchant groups and alternative sources of power, not always successfully. At the same time, the example of southeastern Nigeria stands out as a warning that even this shaky connection may not be a necessary one.[64] David Northrup (1978) portrays a region that actually fits neoclassical conceptions of economic development. The growth of trading networks, diverse and competing pathways of commerce, institutions (notably the canoe house) that could adapt to competitive and militarized trading, interdependence between areas that supplied captives, grew provisions for the slave ships, and handled the actual export created a regional economic system not so specifically linked to the peculiarities of slaving. Lest one take too sanguine a view of decentralization in a slave-trading economy, the example of much of east-central Africa suggests that in a much larger area, with a more spread-out population in a delicate ecosystem, and alternative routes for slave caravans, competitive slaving could undermine small-scale polities, force people into protective settlements too dense for the environment, and lead to social disintegration (Alpers 1975; Iliffe 1979; and Wright 1975).

All this is to suggest how much recent research has moved back into Africa, and raises issues about the dialectic of internal and external change. The slave trade is one instance where empirical research—following in Curtin's footsteps—has focused on a worldwide system, and it has in fact paved the way toward a more inward examination.[65] Connecting that research to the considerable work in local and regional African history is not easy, however, as the facile developmentalism of Fage and the doubtful utility of neoclassical models suggests. The comparative advantage of slaves in the seventeenth and eighteenth centuries, the fragmentation of African polities, and the density, distribution, and mobility of population were important: all made slaving possible (but not necessary) and alternative forms of surplus appropriation difficult (but not impossible). The wide distribution of Africa's population in the eighteenth century made it easier to catch people but hard to keep them working, whereas in India both population density and the power of dominant classes made it easier for rulers to exploit labor and harder for them to steal men away from other protector-exploiters. But as landlessness in India has accelerated faster than the ability of its colonial and indigenous powers to employ labor, the export of "free" indentured labor became feasible, while Africa's role as laborer supplier was tied to the mechanism of slaving (see Tinker 1974). Yet, population density and distribution should not be treated as autonomous and determining causes of economic processes.[66] Population distribution was as much a consequence of class power as a cause. Jack Goody (1978) argues that in the Voltaic region the development of states that lived off booty and slaves led large numbers of people to flee to defensible areas, so that places near the center of the kingdom came to have a low population density, while remote and not necessarily very fertile places had dense populations in decentralized polities. Population density may affect a ruling class's options and ability to extract surplus in certain ways, but the existence of such a class and the structures through which it operates must be explained in their own right. A dialectic view of the relationship of population, political power, and economic change is most revealing (Manning 1981; J. Thornton 1980).

The enslavement process was based, above all, on exploitation at a distance. In some areas, the threat of sale overseas and, more important, the acute need to belong to a social order that conflict generated gave rulers a powerful means of keeping the slaves they retained under control and at work, but the very opportunity which the outlet for slaves presented made it unnecessary for rulers to undertake the more daunting challenge of acquiring exclusive control over domestic resources and labor—in short, to begin a process of primitive accumulation. When the slave trade waned, the incentives for ruling classes to make people produce grew, but the means of controlling production remained tenuous.

From Slaves to Peanuts

If the concept of incorporation is inadequate to explain why Europe turned against the slave trade and slavery, it becomes necessary to penetrate more deeply into the logic of capitalism, not simply as a system of exchange but as a mode of production. To be sure, capitalism has long profited handsomely from various forms of labor, entailing various degrees of coercion, but just as surely opposition has sprung up within the governing classes to labor systems—from slavery to the South African pass system—that violate notions of a free market in labor power. David Brion Davis (1975) has cut through the false opposition of economic and humanitarian explanations of the antislavery movement to argue that antislavery was an ideological consequence of the development of capitalist production in Europe. By defining slavery as both archaic and barbarous, free labor ideologues made a point that was by no means obvious to the hard-pressed workers and expropriated rural tenants of late eighteenth- and early nineteenth-century England: that wage labor was economically and morally superior to any other form. Both violence and paternalism had ultimately to fall before the demands for a labor force obtained through the market and disciplined through fear of the sack and internalization of the work ethic. Measures against the slave trade were applied when slavery was still profitable and before alternative production in Africa had become important, but increasing experience with the difficulties of actually transforming slave labor caused all the European powers to act cautiously before extending abolition into Africa (Cooper 1980:24–46).

The importance and the tensions of the post-slave-trade era lie in the fact that expanding commodity trade did not determine the structure of production in Africa. On this subject, Hopkins (1973:139–48) makes his most ambitious excursion beyond his market model, arguing that slave trading created military aristocracies that tried to outlive the economic circumstances that had spawned them, leading to a period of conflict. Although Hopkins relies too much on the concept of technical economies of scale (few planter classes have depended on the inherent advantages of large operations), he correctly points to the opposition of military aristocracies, whose unique advantages pertain to slave trading, and cash crop producers, whose strength lay in their small farms, the increasing complexity of trading systems, and the decreasing cost of European consumer goods.[67] The point is not that the first gave way to the second, but that patterns of struggle were altered. States still tried to control bulking, transportation, and protection. In Asante, Dahomey, and Yorubaland, kings tried to control merchants who were themselves trying to extend their connections to European traders and small-scale producers. In the Senegambia, peanut cultivation gave peasants money that could be used to oppose warriors, but only through the development of an organization and an ideology through the Islamic brotherhoods could peasants be protected. The brotherhoods in turn developed what was for the peanut-growers a more predictable and less devastating form of exploitation. The process of labor migration (including that of slaves who deserted their masters), becoming religious disciples, and entrance into an expanding community of cultivators thus entailed a new form of social organization built around a complex and differentiated productive process and political structure.[68]

The social transformations of the Senegambia are one of several processes that suggest how much is concealed in the notion of expanding production by households, smallholders, or peasants. Slave production was also rising, and large, centrally supervised units developed in forest kingdoms of West Africa, in Islamic states in the Western and Central Sudan, and in the commercial empire of the East African coast. Slave production, as suggested earlier, posed the problem of controlling slaves in the production process itself. The transformed basis of wealth brought new fears, particularly of the male slaves who had once been shipped off.[69] Equally important, royal plantations brought rulers no nearer to exclusive control of productive resources; in a sense, they represented yet another way around the difficulties of primitive accumulation. Production by households or other social groups grew in response to the same market incentives that ruling classes enjoyed, and those groups often purchased slaves themselves.

Interestingly, plantation development was taken the furthest by the least militaristic of slaveholding aristocracies, the Arabs and Swahili of the East African coast. Both the efficacy of their commercial system and its narrowness—geographically concentrated at Zanzibar and economically dominated by a few Indian firms closely linked to leading planter families—concentrated access to credit, slaves, and markets in a few hands. Even they feared the consequence of letting a slave class build up over generations and reproduced the labor force by continued importation rather than by natural growth. But if the military states of West Africa could subtly shift their surplus appropriation to collecting tribute or taxes from people who had passed through slavery, the coastal planters stuck to what they controlled best, market-based reproduction of a plantation labor force, and used ex-slaves as plantation overseers, traders, or loosely bound clients, or let them drift to the fringes of the fertile, well-located land which they owned and their slaves kept cultivated. Their economic power, however, was inseparable from a specific form of reproduction—the slave trade.[70] For ruling classes throughout Africa, expansion of cash-crop exports brought forth conflicting forms of production and reproduction, the control of which posed a volatile problem.

Even within households, relations of production and patterns of control were varied and changing. Roberts (1984) shows how the expansion of market production and the availability of slave labor within households eroded women's sphere of production and expanded patriarchal control among the Maraka. But in the early colonial era, the exodus of slaves led to increased pressure by patriarchs on their sons, who eventually began to leave as well (see also Guyer 1980, 1981; Etienne 1977; Pollet and Winter 1968). So the household, like the slave plantation, could be an arena of internal conflict shaped by external changes.

The social basis of trade in the nineteenth century has been analyzed much more fully than the social basis of production. We have a good idea of the development and extension of trading networks based on ties of ethnicity, kinship, and clientage. We realize that trading required tight control over people—such as trading slaves of canoe houses in the Niger Delta—as well as solidarity to confront producers, buyers, kings, toll collectors, and bandits. We know of the interdependent yet conflictual relationship of traders and rulers, and that trading networks—reinforced by and reinforcing Islamic ideologies—could contribute to events, such as the Dyula revolutions, which recast the nature of power and production as well as trade itself. We have an idea of the importance of exchange within and between regions of foodstuffs and locally manufactured goods.[71] Complex as the intersecting patterns of local, regional, and external trade were, the trend toward generalized and integrated markets—where anybody could exchange any commodity for any other through the medium of money—was far from dominant, as much because of continued violence, enslavement, and conflict as because of limitations in the division of labor and the range of goods valuable enough to cover transport costs. Trade had to be a social act, but social structures could be a consequence of economic change as much as market structure reflected social organization.[72]

The indigenous pioneers of West African trade were to undergo a striking reversal of fortune in the next phase in the relationship of Europe and Africa. Those most closely tied to external trade—who often had cultural and religious affinities to Europe as well—in the Gold Coast, Senegal, Sierra Leone, and elsewhere lost their autonomy and importance in the early colonial era (Kaplow 1977; Amin 1971; Priestley 1969:158–81). Internal marketers did better, although their sphere of operations was often narrowed, and new traders sprang up in areas that European merchant houses ignored.[73] The fate of the merchants is indicative of the vulnerability of merchant capital, in Europe as much as in Africa. While some scholars argue that merchant capital is the first wave of an assault on independent producers, merchants are in fact dependent on their relationship to producers. Unless merchant capital—as giant firms often do—moves toward vertical integration and enters production, it can only attempt to move closer to the point of production, to avoid sharing the limited difference between buying cheap and selling dear and to narrow the alternatives of producers (Kay 1975; Mandel 1975). The history of commerce is largely a history of vigorous competition and vigorous efforts to limit competition, of symbiosis and conflict between producer and merchant. European merchant capital in the nineteenth century benefited from the quick response of African rulers and peasants to changing markets, but it was in no position to enter the sphere of production itself, to maintain the predictability of commodity flows, to raise productivity and lower production costs, or to stop the struggles over conflicting forms of production that its own success had unleashed. It was limited to competing for a larger share of the middle ground between producer and consumer, and African merchant capital was caught in the same terrain. But the European merchants could draw on the resources of powerful states and sophisticated economies to attempt a systematic clearing of the ground between it and the point of production, as well as to begin a more difficult assault on the abode of production itself, while the African merchants could not.

Imperialism

As much energy has been consumed by the artificial opposition of political and economic explanations of imperialism as by the conflict between humanitarian and economic analyses of abolitionism. But now the debate seems calmer, and the divergent schools overlap more on the question of explaining the burst of colonization in the late nineteenth century than on most issues (Owen and Sutcliffe 1972; Barratt Brown 1974; Hyam 1976; Cain and Hopkins 1980). Most Marxists would admit that the Leninist explanation of imperialism has its weaknesses. Rather than capitalism having become overripe and in desperate need of overseas outlets for investment that could not be made at home, investments in new colonies, in independent countries overseas, in old dominions, and at home grew together (Warren 1980; Barrett Brown 1974). Most would also admit the relevance of political and diplomatic arguments— only by looking at the interaction of states can the rapidity and the process of partition be understood—but they would insist that underlying economic interests made these dimensions relevant.[74] On the other hand, the most severe critics of Hobson and Lenin can concede the importance of trade. Some studies have shown as well that perceptions of economic gain—especially in the case of France—can be more relevant to understanding what happened than the realities (Fieldhouse 1973; Newbury and Kanya-Forstner 1969; Hynes 1979). And Ronald Robinson's recasting of arguments about the breakdown of older collaborative mechanisms between Europeans and Africans is compatible with Marxist arguments that stress why European demands escalated in the late nineteenth century (Robinson 1972; Weiskel 1980:239–40).

There have been two major breakthroughs in the 1970s toward a closer examination of imperialism. One is Hopkins's synthesis of the connection of cash-crop production, rapid improvements in transportation, increasing competition among European traders, among African traders, and between both peoples, and economic changes and crises within Europe. Hopkins's emphasis on economic evolution and business cycles in Europe is by no means incompatible with Marxist stress on structural change: the increasing scale of industrial investment in Europe and increasing danger of working-class disorder required not only that industry's supplies of raw materials and markets be large, but that they be predictable. The disruption of cotton supplies during the American Civil War and again during the boll weevil epidemic unleashed an obsession with cotton that preoccupied the British Empire for decades (Hopkins 1973:124–66; Semmel 1960; Ulrich-Wehler 1972; Warren 1980; Barratt Brown 1974). The growth of industry throughout Western Europe brought to the fore the contradictory imperatives of capitalism: competition and regularity, the anarchy of private competition and the social character of production. Free trade, as Hopkins argues, had never been an absolute standard, only the logical stance of the premier trading nation, but heightened competition caused by the challenges of French and above all German industrialization and by cheapening transport helped to lead key commercial interests to pressure the state to stake out exclusive rights to territory, a process that would secure access to some areas even if it would undermine opportunities for competing for all of them.[75] The other side of the picture was painted in Africa. The peasants, slaves, and rulers who grew the new crops also produced conflict that jeopardized the predictability of commerce. In East Africa as well, the welcome flow of commodities from slave plantations was inseparable from the violence and depredation necessary to reproduce the labor force. If the divisibility of the new exports of Africa and the new consumer goods and the small scale of potential producing units lowered the entry costs of traders and producers alike, kings, theocratic rulers, warriors, and planters only fought harder to preserve specific kinds of economic structures. It was precisely because changes in the world market did not redefine the organization of labor and commerce in Africa that disruptive conflict was extended; hence, a new obsession with law and order. European merchants in coastal West Africa feared fighting would cut off supplies from the interior and worried about the security of property within the ports themselves.[76] Less than a century before, disorder had been the basis of profit.

The other breakthrough in studies of imperialism has been made by South African historians, notably Shula Marks, Anthony Atmore, and Stanley Trapido.[77] Their stress is on labor, above all the fact that labor recruitment is not simply a matter of individual decisions but a question of control across social divisions and a wide geographical area. If an export-oriented economy in the mid-nineteenth century was still compatible with the existence of Afrikaaner republics, of hemmed-in but independent African kingdoms, and of cash-crop growers who farmed on their own even if they had lost political power, the development of a mass labor force was not.[78] The British made some efforts to systematize labor control in the Cape earlier in the century, and rising demands for plantation labor in Natal led to a new emphasis on political unity in the 1870s (Etherington 1979). But the mineral revolution required a very particular notion of "good government"—one systematic and powerful enough to recruit laborers and trace deserters over a wide area, and "honest" enough to channel them (and other resources) to the most deserving employers. By 1879 Natal could no longer tolerate the Zulu kingdom, and by the 1890s, certain gold-mining interests were intriguing against the seemingly incompetent and corrupt Afrikaaner republics, until the British moved decisively to destroy the republics and begin the process of "reconstruction" of the mining industry (Marks and Trapido 1979; Guy 1979). The striking fact about South Africa was the extent to which these visions were carried through.

Although Hopkins stresses commerce and Marks and the other South African historians labor, both emphasize the importance of change within the European economy and the systematic breaks that were needed to transcend the limitations and contradictions of earlier structures. If industrial capitalism in the early nineteenth century had forged links to a vast number of Africans who produced for it and consumed its products, it also made the consequences of the competition and conflict which it generated unbearable.

Less well thought out but equally fascinating is the ideological dimension of the imperialist thrust. Serious as the national rivalries for trade and territory were, the imperial powers still saw it necessary to meet and to articulate, at the Berlin and Brussels Conferences, standards of imperial morality (Miers 1975). The standards themselves went to the heart of the image of disorder: European states should stamp out the trade in slaves, arms, and liquor. If one remembers the long struggle in England to restrain the unruly and antiwork culture of the Irish and English working class, one might see the generalization of class biases to an entire continent and to an entire race, but if one looks more closely, it is the lowest orders within Africa—above all slaves—that were singled out as the laziest and most obstreperous of all (Cooper 1980:28–40; Derman 1973:49; Weiskel 1979:216). The violence of the slavers and the culture of the slaves—both vastly exaggerated—came to be important symbols of Europe's redefined stance toward Africa. Political fragmentation and conflict were now incompatible with an expanding capitalist economy. But order and profit had always been conflicting imperatives, and African rulers had long stumbled on the problem of systematically controlling the productive activities of their subjects. The new rulers would find these problems no less difficult.

Agriculture and the Colonial State

If Hopkins (1973) called attention to basic problems of economic structure as the causes of imperialism, these concerns suddenly disappear in his analysis of its consequences. The intervening states intervened little, and favorable terms of trade before World War I stimulated a self-propelling process of vent-for-surplus and multiplier effects, in which colonial states were little more than "Great White Umpires." For Wallerstein (1976:41–42), as well, colonial states followed a path of least resistance and encouraged cash crop production. On the other hand, scholars such as Jean Suret-Canale (1971), E. A. Brett (1973), and Richard Wolff (1974) picture a crushingly powerful colonial state stifling

African autonomy and redefining economic structures in the interests of the extraction of surplus by the metropole. But if states tried to intervene much more decisively than Hopkins suggests, they did so far less effectively than Suret-Canale would have it.

All colonial powers would have rejoiced if commodities came in with no trouble or expense on their part, beyond providing infrastructure. Important as are the instances when something like this happened, historians have allowed a modest number of examples to define the basic character of pre–World War I Africa.[79] Equally important are the frustrations of colonial officials at low volumes of produce that came into ports and railroads, the inconsistency of production—for example with the transitory phase of African rubber collection[80]—and the deeply held belief in late nineteenth century ideology that work had to be directed from above and working classes vigilantly watched. The desire for raw materials and revenue could not be separated from the question of *how* goods were going to be produced.[81] Economic decisions were too important to be left to the peasant or to the itinerant trader.

Getting Africans to grow useful crops might mean bringing in new landlords and managers—such as the Kenyan settlers—or making old aristocracies into landlords and managers, shorn of the violence that had earlier disrupted things; or relying on direct administrative compulsion; or else accepting that goods could be reliably produced without any landowners or managers at all. The last may seem wisest in retrospect, but it needs to be examined historically.

The colonial state was not a machine to pump surplus into the pot of capital. As John Lonsdale and Bruce Berman argue, any state must cope with contradictions, and a colonial state in particular comes between the metropolitan interests, the bureaucrats or settlers which it needs in the field, the African leaders whose assistance is required to extend control, and the African population who must somehow be induced to do the work without destroying the entire operation. The state, above all, had to confront the social consequences of changing structures of production (Lonsdale and Berman, 1979). Its tendency to make its control systematic conflicted with its tendency to cut costs, while capital's tendency to build structures that would insure long-term returns on investment conflicted with its tendency to grab what was to be grabbed. What emerged depended not only on the ups and downs of world trade or on abstracted notions of the requirements of the capitalist mode of production but on the encounter with Africans as well.

Contradictions emerged quickly. In Northern Nigeria, Lord Lugard wished to transform a powerful, slaveraiding, slaveholding, tribute-collecting aristocracy into a class of landlords; he wished to modify their means of controlling labor without reducing its extent. At the same time, he wanted to rationalize tax collection and administration through that same class. But the desire for a productive ruling class cut across the basis of that class's power, and what

Lugard got was "extortion, plunder and administrative chaos." Fearing revolts, the British backed off and ended their attempt to create a landholding class. In coastal East Africa, the British also saw the transformation of slaveowners into capitalist farmers and slaves into an agricultural proletariat as the only way to maintain production. They sought to redefine the cultural norms of slaves into a Victorian work culture. The attempt failed before the increasing mobility of the ex-slaves and the fact that landowners had to accede to their demands for access to land if they were to salvage anything at all from their estates.[82] In French West Africa, the French saw a large potential labor force that backward and militaristic local rulers were not using effectively, but they were at a loss how to make use of them. In Mali, French demands for grain led first to expansion of production by slaveowners but then to a mass exodus of slaves. The French also created *villages de liberté,* where they tried to set slaves to work themselves (Roberts and Klein 1980; Bouche 1968; Derman 1973). These were only a few of the attempts by European powers to convert African rulers into the controllers of labor, attempts which most often proved the fundamental difficulty of controlling a labor force. Colonial pacification made it easier for ex-slaves and others to seek empty land, jobs in town, or new patrons. So African rulers frequently found primitive accumulation and labor control more elusive objectives than ever; often, their economic power disintegrated altogether.

White planters also had their difficulties in French West Africa and the Belgian Congo, even with forced labor; they remained an enclave in Tanganyika and faded in Uganda; they persisted in Angola and Mozambique by dint of much forced labor and the deliberate elimination of alternatives.[83] Only in South Africa and (to a lesser extent) Rhodesia can one speak of a capitalist transformation in agriculture before World War II, of wage labor becoming both dominant and generalized within agriculture.

This often unsuccessful effort by colonial states to develop an agrarian class structure and division of labor that would make production more systematic coexisted with the "freebooting" tendency of the early colonial years (Hopkins 1976b:280). The first white man on the scene stood to gain windfall profits and usually paused little to consider long-range implications. On a vast scale, King Leopold's Congo was the epitome of the economy of grabbing—based on the gathering of rubber in a manner that destroyed the plants as well as people. Yet if this was one side of imperialism, it caused great ambivalence among imperialists. Even when rubber and profits were coming forth, such systems cast a pall of violence over a vast area, making the generalization of commercial relations and the reproduction of the system impossible. Leopold, and the Portuguese in Angola, were attacked in Europe for deviating from the principles of a free market and imperial order.[84] Yet one cannot dismiss the Congo concessions too quickly; such operations persisted in a more sanitized but equally brutal form in French territory north of the Congo River and similar policies influenced Belgian policy for decades after Leopold. As Jean-Philippe Peemans argues (1975), powerful and interlocking concessions, state monopolies, and compulsory cultivation of food for the mines and cotton for exports helped to build an effective infrastructure to consolidate the power of particular corporations (see also Jewsiewicki 1977; Coquery-Vidrovitch 1972).

The history of compulsion in colonial Africa turns out to be a long one, and cannot be dismissed as short-lived and short-sighted policies that are not more than an unpleasant aside to the true history of market expansion or a dose of force necessary to "incorporate" African societies into the world economy (as in Wallerstein and Martin 1979). The imposition of production quotas on households or villages, the fixing of prices by the state, and the reliance on administrative sanctions to make sure crops were grown extends from German cotton schemes in Tanganyika in 1905 to Portuguese cotton cultivation from 1936 until 1961 to French food projects in the 1940s in the Cameroons to British food-production schemes in Zanzibar in the 1940s to agricultural policy in Zaire from Leopold to Mobutu (Iliffe 1979:168–69; Vail and White 1978; Guyer 1978; F. Wilson 1944; Gran 1979; and Schatzberg 1980:75–82). The French did not abolish the indigénat until 1946. Compulson often bred resistance (Isaacman et al. 1980; Iliffe 1979:168–202; Schatzberg 1980:79–80).

More mundane but most general was colonial tax policy, which officials sometimes admitted was intended less to collect revenues than to require each household to make a minimum contribution to the cash economy. Nevertheless, the impact of tax may have been overstated. Hut taxes still left Africans to choose how they would earn the cash, and colonial economies were not monolithic enough to eliminate alternatives such as selling cattle, petty trade, or— most common—marketing crops that the state did not care about. If set too high, taxes were more likely to cause mass migration than increased production—something that had important consequences in Portuguese and French Africa. So the concomitant of tax policy was an attempt to exercise "closer administration," to get Africans to stay in villages or in locations.[85] Once again controlling mobility was a crucial issue, and an expensive and difficult problem. The colonial state's effort to control African cultivators was to escalate sharply in the 1940s, to a large extent because its control had not been secured in the early colonial era.

African peasants, it would seem, were not dependent enough. If a dominant class could not control land and labor, the pressures of the market and the interventions of the state circled around the peasant farm without entering it directly. A household that grew its own food might respond vigorously to market incentives and be hurt grievously by depression, but it still had a significant ability to hold the market at arm's length (Friedmann 1980). Markets per se do not lock in peasants. As Sidney Mintz emphasizes, markets can provide alternatives, and the demands of the state and the pressures toward wage labor could be fended off by those who could make use of alternatives. The question was not *the* market, but specific markets. Too little marketing—whether the result of deliberate policy or of poor transport—could narrow the alternatives of African cultivators far more than too much involvement in markets,[86] and the effectiveness of state intervention—direct or on behalf of landlords—required a bureaucratic presence. That was not only expensive, but dangerous, and the history of rural protests and revolts against the demands of the state is as long as the history of compulsion. Examples of colonial states' backing off in the face of African opposition are becoming increasingly apparent.[87]

Peasants, by definition, are partially involved in markets, partially subordinated to ruling classes or the state, and partially autonomous within the production unit, growing food and mobilizing labor in the household. But too often scholars imply that once a peasant has been identified, the way he farms, his ideas, his politics, and even his future have been specified.[88] The peasant's partial subordination might take the form of taxes or else of the daily confrontation with a landlord whose power of eviction and control of credit affected every decision he made. The notion of a peasant household does not suggest how the head of a household actually controls family labor or point to the efforts of women and young men to redefine their economic roles. Nor does it specify the class structure of which the peasant is a part.[89] If we are going to have any sense of process in African agricultural history, we are going to have to look both more inwardly and outwardly than the concept of a peasantry suggests.

Studies of rural Africa are developing an increasingly complex picture of the directions of change. On one extreme, impoverishment has become very serious both in areas with long involvement in world markets (the Transkei, Senegal) and in areas where market systems are poorly developed or have collapsed (Western Tanzania, Southern Angola, the Sahel). When declining self-sufficiency led to labor migration, the loss of labor for clearing bush could lead to the upsetting of a delicate ecological balance, a build-up of disease carrying tsetse flies, loss of productive capacity, and further migration. When cash crops were grown in marginal savanna areas and when competing labor demands of cash crops encouraged replacement of diverse food crops with soil-depleting maize, soil erosion and decreasing yields led to a need for more cash, more emphasis on cash crops, and more soil erosion and malnutrition (Ford 1971; Tosh 1980; Iliffe 1979; Palmer and Parsons 1977; Vail 1976; Cliffe and Moorsom 1979).

In contrast, there are the accumulating cultivators: the cocoa farmers of Western Nigeria, the Ivory Coast and Ghana, the coffee planters of Kilimanjaro and Central Kenya, and the copra producers of the hinterland of the Kenyan coast. The wealthiest relied heavily on wage labor and specialized cash-crop production, sometimes buying food from other farmers. Yet one has to be careful about looking for a kulak behind every cocoa bush. The complementarity of migratory "colonization" and migratory labor in cocoa fields muted the contradiction of labor and ownership; labor could be a step toward accumulation of cocoa trees. Such mobility obviously could not go on forever, but it remains a question whether this would lead to the consolidation of control by a class of planters. That question involves the totality of resources that can be mobilized and opportunities in a national economy as well as relations of production. While there is evidence as far back as the Gold Coast cocoa holdups of 1930–31 and 1937–38 of contradictions between big cocoa planters and small planters and hired workers, such potential conflict can be masked or lessened by the performance of brokerage and patronage services by large planters, who may prefer to "invest" in political power at the center instead of the consolidation of agrarian power.[90]

Finally, there are the ornery peasants, the figures that bothered colonial officials the most and still bedevil their successors. These were the peasants who would produce a little but not a lot, who resisted what extension agents regarded as improved techniques, and who rejected cash crops that the state encouraged (Tosh 1980; Cooper 1980: chaps. 6, 7). The peanut growers of the Senegambia are often invoked as a class of people who became so enmeshed in cash-crop cultivation that they had stopped growing food. Yet they surprised their government in the early 1970s by a massive drop in peanut production and a switch to food crops. The Islamic brotherhoods—hitherto cooperative first with the French and later with conservative Senegalese politicians—began to act like trade unions and forced a reversal of government pricing policy. Similar switches to food production have occurred among other of Africa's most famous cash croppers, the cocoa farmers of Ghana (Cruise O'Brien 1979:223; Beckman 1976:219). Nonproduction remains the ultimate defense of the peasant.

The Great Depression revealed that if the market could be held at arm's length, it could not be avoided. Taxes had to be paid, and some items now had to be bought. Responses varied: some switched to new crops; others continued at the same pace investments they had begun in the 1920s or before; many increased their "self-exploitation," so that a minimum level of income could be attained at the lower prices; some resisted the increasing or more painful exactions of chiefs or officials, sometimes successfully; and the most highly capitalized of cash-crop producers, the big cocoa planters of the Gold Coast, acted very much like a farmer class facing hard times and predatory merchants, organizing collectives to force prices up and restructure the marketing system.[91] From the point of view of colonial states, the depression revealed the great virtue of partial commercialization in agriculture: peasants' minimum cash needs would keep them producing cheap commodities, but their subsistence production would take care of their social security. Even colonial regimes like Kenya's undertook projects to facilitate marketing peasant crops, but they typically confronted the increased importance of peasant production with measures to force peasants into patterns of resource use and management that the states deemed best. Meanwhile, commercial and financial systems were restructured to harness this peasant effort to the interests of struggling metropolitan economies (Coquery-Vidrovitch 1977; Munro 1975:189–246; Brett 1973; Baier 1980).

Peasants served colonial economies well in the depression, but the true challenge came with the imperatives for increased production during the period of recovery, the war, and the postwar commodities boom. Peasants responded to increased prices. Yet—unlike the capitalist farmer inalterably bound to markets in food and labor—the peasant did not necessarily have to maximize his effort or relentlessly innovate in the face of competition (Brenner 1977; Friedmann 1980). However much African behavior in the 1940s and 1950s can be explained by responses to rising prices, the behavior of colonial governments cannot. The 1940s was the era of what Low and Lonsdale (1976:12) call "the second colonial occupation" of Africa, a massive assault on the partial autonomy of the cultivator. The agricultural extension agent replaced the district officer as the embodiment of colonial authoritarianism. New regulations about seeds, contouring, cattle dipping, and marketing went along with massive efforts to get Africans to produce more. A British official in Tanganyika captured the spirit of new direction in 1945 very well: "the African must be compelled to help himself" (Iliffe 1979:473). The madness of the effort for direct control is often seen in the Groundnut Scheme in Tanganyika, but it is madness of a very characteristic sort, growing out of a belief that centralized direction is more productive and predictable than peasant production. These ideas shaped a wide range of large-scale projects in the late colonial and postcolonial eras.[92]

But what form would control take? M. P. Cowen (1980) discusses a disagreement in the postwar British government between those who wished to manage workers and those who favored the exercise of administrative power over peasants. Reflecting complex social forces in the Labour Government, the bureaucracy, and British capital, as well as the desire to minimize investment in plant and equipment that might drain extremely scarce foreign exchange— a consideration that also strongly influenced French policy at this time— smallholder schemes were interventionist, but had ambiguous implications for rural accumulation. The Colonial Development Corporation's tea project in Kenya, for example, entailed close supervision of smallholder planting, strict quality control, and fixed producer prices. But if agricultural administration narrowed household autonomy, it also "permitted households to survive as economic units of production . . . and belittled the scale and rate at which land could be accumulated and a reserve army of labour formed for the extraction of surplus value by the indigenous class of capital" (Cowen 1980; also Leys 1978:249). Yet late-colonial schemes were frequently directed not at the amorphous peasantry that had once satisfied colonial officials, but toward "progressive farmers," who were aided by extension services and linked to bureaucracies by increasingly influential cooperative schemes. Their accumulation was often assisted by land registration and consolidation programs, as in Kenya's Swynnerton plan. Support of progressive farmers would promote a class with a vested interest in production for the market and in stability, even if the logical extension of such class differentiation might produce a landless peasantry, which colonial regimes and their successors feared as a source of instability (Sorrenson 1967; Cruise O'Brien 1971a). At independence, Kenya's new rulers were building on their earlier efforts at accumulation by stepping into settlers' shoes, but they were constrained by their own political relations with smallholders and by the volatility of the land question, as well as by the interests of international capital in the existing structure production. In contrast, Ghana's ruling class sought to undermine farm-based accumulation, and move from the bureaucracy and state-marketing mechanisms to establish their own class power in rural areas. Smallholders in Africa—those who actually were small—have variously sought to join the accumulators, to make demands for patronage or brokerage services upon them, to retain their autonomy by balancing different kinds of economic activities, and to curtail—by means varying from witchcraft accusations against the rich to riots to political action—both rural accumulators and interventionist bureaucrats (Cowen 1980; Beckman 1976; Samoff 1980; van Hekken and van Velzen 1972; Berry 1980; Beer and Williams 1975; Lamb 1974).

Thus conflict and uncertainty over rural class formation has coexisted with a statist orientation. Independent states have followed colonial regimes in what Frances Hill (1977) calls the "quest for control." Ghana's rulers tried to create a rural proletariat without a bourgeoisie on state farms; Nigeria's sought a rural bourgeoisie without a proletariat on heavily mechanized farms; Tanzania wanted direct bureaucratic control over peasants. None of these schemes—nor any of numerous others—has had much success. Caught in the contradiction of the desirability, difficulty, and dangers of capitalist production, states have pestered peasants and sought to control access to land, labor, credit, markets, and other resources, without necessarily bringing about a basic transformation in the social basis of agriculture. There still remains in much of Africa, in Goran Hyden's words (1980), an "uncaptured peasantry." [93]

South Africa, in contrast, emphasizes the meaning of a capitalist transformation of agriculture—both the extraordinary difficulty it entails and the degree of control that results. The basis of such a transformation lies in the accumulation of land and the daily task of supervising labor. It required not an abstract category of capital but concrete mechanisms to exclude cultivators from rights to land and to manage them as laborers. Its roots in South Africa lie in the expansion of whites into the countryside and their retention of a distinct identity as well as links to the centers of commerce and the state. That in itself did not constitute a capitalist transformation: white landowners before the 1890s still lived off largely autonomous black farmers on their lands. What Stanley Trapido calls the "second alienation"—gaining control of Africans' time as well as their land—was made desirable by the expansion of maize markets in the 1890s, but it was made possible by the *prior* development of a distinct landowning class. The problem of capitalist transformation was on the one hand a class problem: it had to be effected systematically, for otherwise renters and squatters would drift to the least demanding landlords, which they in fact did their best to do. But its basis also lay in the minute events that took place on each farm: the assertion of direct supervision by the landowner of farm tasks, the curtailing of rights to plant crops and graze cattle, the expulsion of white tenants, and the undermining of the security of black tenants. These were coercive acts, involving action by individual farmers, farmers acting together, and by the state; and they were revolutionary acts as well.[94]

If the literature on South Africa has emphasized the distinctiveness of capitalist agriculture, it has also recognized its complexity. Within the farm, owners supervised production, but for decades had to concede to their laborers some access to land (Morris 1976). The relationship of white farms to African reserves has always been more complex than the simple opposition of capitalist production and precapitalist reproduction, but that relationship has also been not so much an abstract relationship of modes of production as the focus of state control on the movement of people. A large "Bantu Administration" and capitalist control within each farm has been necessary to transform South African agriculture, but its result has been a vast intensification of production and the parallel growth of agriculture and industry. The process has not been without conflict among whites, but it has also been carried out with a great deal of pragmatism and flexibility (Greenberg 1980; Trapido 1971; Cooper 1981).

If the arena of production is the scene of a struggle for control, so too is commerce. Even the most trade-oriented of nations, Great Britain, had an aversion to traders, above all the nasty, competitive but often efficient world of the small trader. What colonial regimes preferred was the orderly world of the giant merchant house or the trading monopoly (Ehrlich 1973; Brett 1973). The first great thrust of colonial economic policy—railway construction—was in regions where trade was already developed, an attempt to get nearer the point of production and to bypass middlemen. The siting of railways was a political act and can best be understood as an attempt to specify the parameters of a marketing system. Such decisions often determined who would be cultivators and who would be wage laborers; they redefined cost structures that producers faced; and, probably more than anything, they laid out an infrastructure that undermined earlier systems of exchange and delicate patterns of regional com-plimentarity, pushing even cultivators who retained considerable autonomy as producers in the direction of what Amin calls "extraverted" accumulation. The financial consequences of such investment could confront states with con-straints that shaped the boundaries of decision-making by future generations of policy makers.[95]

European merchant capital also sought to get as close to the point of produc-tion as possible, pushing away once powerful and effective African traders. In the Gold Coast, the large cocoa-buying firms extended their power ever closer to the cocoa growers. In 1937–38, they pushed too hard, driving the middle-men they were displacing and the farmers into an alliance in an effective cocoa hold-up. The firms were sufficiently well integrated to reverse course and take their profits at another point between the cocoa bush and the chocolate bar, and the government—in the wake of the turmoil—turned to an equally cen-tralized mechanism of crop purchasing, the marketing board. Economists have ever since argued that this institution is less efficient than a free market, but their quite sound arguments have had little influence on colonial and postcolo-nial regimes, as state monopoly purchasing boards spread throughout Africa (Southall 1978; Beckman 1976; P. T. Bauer 1971).

Hopkins (1976b:274–75) suggests that a second partition of Africa both pre-ceded and followed the first, the division of territory by large and powerful firms. Organizational strength, capitalization, and planning for predictable but unspectacular profits was the basis of the new commercial order; governments cracked down on itinerant traders and urban hawkers, and favored concentra-tion in trading centers, extensive licensing, and monopoly power for cotton ginners and other processers of crops (Brett 1973; 237–65). The power and strategies of firms like S.C.O.A., C.F.A.O., and Unilever have begun to attract attention, and deserve more. As is the case of production, existing evidence hints that the extension of commercial networks or efforts at vertical integra-tion by such firms were not without difficulties and limitations, and the story of European firms in Africa is neither a saga of the triumph of superior organi-zation nor a tale of ever-growing monsters sweeping the innocent before them (Coquery-Vidrovitch 1975; Pedler 1974; Fieldhouse 1978).

Paradoxically, the functioning of African, Indian, and Lebanese social net-works in the control of commerce is better understood than the operations of the European giants. This work underscores the importance of clientage, kinship, and ethnicity in controlling the flow of credit, merchandise, and information. In some cases, trade became highly specialized and controlled by landlords and brokers in a small number of regional centers. In others, as with the Indi-ans of East Africa, the small incomes of spread-out producer-consumers made generalization essential, and since the trader could only survive by combining produce buying, retailing, and the extension of credit, the need for close ties to wholesalers and creditors in major cities fostered a social structure of commerce that was very difficult for outsiders to penetrate. In Uganda, for example, British regulations combined with Indian economic structures to entrench a "rigidly controlled framework of commerce" (Ehrlich 1965: 469; Zarwan 1976; A. Cohen 1969; Baier 1980).

Equally important is consumption. Giovanni Arrighi (1973) and dependency theorists have argued that new patterns of consumption—often stimulated in an early period of favorable conditions for smallholder production—hooked Africans into irreversible participation in the world economy. Yet the problem has received much less investigation than it deserves. Some studies have shown the decline of traditional crafts and growing dependence on imports. But studies of West African cloth suggest that local producers could resist the classic product of the industrial revolution. More recently, Posnansky's visit to Ghanaian villages revealed that craft production could be revived when import markets failed.[96] It is hard to distinguish without more theoretical precision and evidence between "dependency" and "comparative advantage"—obtaining better goods at lower cost in labor. And the most interesting aspect of Arrighi's argument, the growing need of Africans to keep up a cash income in order to pay for their childrens' education, takes us into another dimension of the problem: households strive not merely for physical survival, but to get by or push ahead in a developing class system. That class system in turn reflects not merely markets and the local structure of production but also a national system of production, distribution, and power, and changing cultural definitions of status (Berry 1984).

Labor and the Changing Structure of Capitalism

Each mode of production, Marxists would argue, has its own logic, its own way of unfolding over time. But the logic of capitalism unfolds not simply at the level of the world economy as a whole, but within islands of wage labor. The most advanced forms of capitalist organization appear within the most backward economies. This tendency results not only from the technological and organization sophistication of firms—all the lessons of history do not need to be relearned—but in the confrontation of labor and management in mines, dockyards, plantations, and railway yards. If migratory labor minimized costs, the laborers still had to be controlled on the job. Management could raise production or counteract labor unrest by doing more of the same— more systematic exercise of coercion, reliance on ever larger armies of grudging workers—or it could seek new forms of the labor process analogous to the bureaucratic and technological forms of labor control and the efforts to stabilize the social position of laboring classes in Europe. The contradictory logics of capitalism came into question in particular historical circumstances and produced divergent responses.

Such considerations require going beyond the overly linear way in which both neoclassical economists and many of their radical critics have discussed the growth of wage labor in Africa. The former take off from W. A. Lewis's (1954) dualist model: people leave areas of surplus labor, where the marginal product of labor is zero, for areas where capital investment leads to a marginal product, and hence wages, that are high enough to overcome the migrants' inertia and the costs of migration. Productivity differentials were so high between the two sectors that such wages were consistent with acceptable profits, and so labor supplies would be unlimited until the surplus labor of the subsistence sector had been drawn in. Lewis's theory is a kind of vent-for-surplus model of labor. It has since been elaborated, notably by John Harris and Michael Todaro (1970), who take into account that the marginal productivity in rural areas is not zero and that the chances of getting a job, as well as wage differentials, affect migration rates.[97]

Such economic explanations of why people migrate make far more sense than the "bright lights" theory, and they have stimulated valuable studies (Sabot 1979; Eicher and Byerlee 1972) of the flow of people and responses to wage rates and unemployment. However mathematically sophisticated, such models reflect a deep but largely unstated ordering of priorities: structures that migrants leave and the ones they enter are taken as givens, and it is the individual act of movement between the two that the migrationists seek to explain. Yet, "traditional" economies were themselves shaped historically, and were affected by the very forces that created the capitalist sector.[98]

Giovanni Arrighi (1973) insists that it is the givens of such models that demand explanation, and only an historical analysis can explain why, contrary to Lewis, labor was at first scarce and then plentiful. He argues that the undermining of production in the peasant sector and the development of wage labor in the capitalist were two sides of the same process; dualism is a misleading and ahistorical notion. The creation of new wants was relevant to the process, but African producers could respond to them in their own ways. In Rhodesia—his focus—an entire range of coordinated action by mining capital, settlers, and the state made peasants into workers: requiring taxes in money, pushing Africans into inadequate reserves, locating railways away from African areas, fixing wage rates, using state agencies to recruit and discipline labor. By the 1920s, what Arrighi calls political means of recruitment could give way to economic: the rules of the labor market were followed only after the game was over. At that point, Africans had to work, and their rates of participation in the labor market kept rising, whether real wages were falling, rising, or static.[99]

The attack on dualism has been elaborated within the structuralist-Marxist perspective: the preservation of subsistence agriculture, as much as the destruction of its autonomy and productive capacity, becomes the basic element of colonial capitalism, reducing the wages that capitalists must pay to keep the work force alive. I have already argued that such formulations are theoretically inadequate. Nor can they get at the unfolding of African labor history. They miss how difficult it was to get Africans off the land, how hard Africans fought to maintain their agricultural cycle and to manipulate new markets as much as to avoid total commitment to them, and hence how little alternative capital had to some form of migratory labor.[100] The separation of capitalist production and precapitalist reproduction is too neat to explain the use of resident labor on settler farms in South Africa, Rhodesia, and Kenya, where both functions took place within the same estate.[101] The argument that wage rates and conditions of employment were set by the reproductive requirements of capitalism misses the complexity of workers' efforts to redefine those conditions themselves, using their own social networks to find alternatives that provided slightly better wages, less dangerous work, less oppressive employers, or workplaces that allowed access to land or a chance to live as a family (van Onselen 1976b; Perrings 1979; Vail and White 1980; Penvenne 1979).

The encounter of workers and employers did not await the crystalization of a proletariat, and in the daily confrontation of the workplace lay the instability of migratory labor systems. As with peasant production, the period when migrant laborers came forth fairly smoothly, did enough work, and did not create too much turmoil was relatively brief in regions where the labor force was substantial and concentrated—in Southern and Central Africa as a whole and in port cities, railways, and mines throughout the continent. The system worked best when cheapness was more important than output, mainly in the Depression. In Zambia and Katanga, the copper mines moved toward a long-term work force shortly after they opened, reversed course in the Depression, and moved again toward stabilization once production picked up again. Zambian mines encouraged miners to bring their wives, hoping that the locus of reproduction, like that of production, would remain under their eyes, although they and the male miners found that the women became far more independent than they were supposed to be. After the war, the mines faced the consequences— which the state hoped it could avoid—that stabilization meant a fully urbanized population (Perrings 1979; Heisler 1974; Parpart 1983; Chauncey 1981).

If capital seized the initiative toward stabilization in the copperbelt, labor thrust it upon capital in many other parts of Africa. The years between 1935 and 1950 were the time of the greatest urban labor turmoil Africa has known, before or since. Mombasa and Dar es Salaam witnessed major strikes in 1939 and 1947 and unrest in between; there was a general strike in Nigeria in 1945, in the Gold Coast in 1950; urban riots struck the Cameroons and the Gold Coast; a major strike hit the railways of French West Africa in 1947; the docks of Durban were in turmoil throughout the war, and the greatest mine strike in

South African history occurred in 1946. Unrest affected relatively long-term workers, as in the copperbelt strike of 1940, and the most rapidly circulating of casual workers, as in Mombasa in 1939 and 1947. Whether wage labor was the only source of cash or not, it was an essential one, and workers struggled over its conditions.[102] The unrest reflected not merely wartime inflation, but the trend toward the intensification of labor and inflation—in part a consequence of intensification—that began as early as 1935 and persisted into the 1950s.

The crisis of intensified production and resistance exposed the deep structural problems of colonial labor systems. Capital and the state had not created a reserve army of the unemployed, but a guerrilla army of the underemployed. Employers fought to establish control with restrictive contracts, pass laws, compounds, and oppressive supervision; workers fought back with desertion, slowdowns, and efforts to shape their own work rhythms and social structures.[103] From the point of view of capital, the disadvantages of such a labor system became most acute when production rose, the work force became concentrated, and the labor process became increasingly complex. With rapidly circulating workers, the sanction of the sack threatened only a period of work, not a lifetime job; a good worker could not be separated from a poor one; skills had to be taught to a pool vastly larger than the actual workforce; and even the unskilled or semiskilled could not be socialized and nurtured into a "respectable working class" clearly distinguished from the dangerous masses (Cooper 1987). Meanwhile, strikes and riots were forcing firms to raise wages anyway.

Most strikingly in British Africa, labor departments began to move towards decasualizing and stabilizing labor forces in key sectors. They were often opposed by rural administrators who feared the loss of control by traditional authorities. Employers, especially in agriculture, feared that paying stabilized workers enough to support their families would ruin the labor market for all; and most employers only grudgingly conceded the higher wages, more effective industrial relations machinery, and better channels for promotion that their own interest in stability implied. The changes involved restructuring how people worked as well as how long, and as states took up questions of welfare and pensions in the 1950s, it slowly became clear that the issue of shaping a working life had become as central as controlling the working day.[104]

The South African government, in the aftermath of the 1946 mine strike, considered following a similar course.[105] Manufacturing industry, above all, wanted more and longer-term urbanization. But such pressures threatened farmers and less capitalized industry. The conflict between two tendencies of capitalism—to make the most of cheap labor and to generalize and develop wage labor production—was critical in the 1948 election. In choosing the former, South Africa's voters opted for a system whose maintenance required an increasingly brutal apparatus—above all escalation in the pass law system—that could control migrants in all phases of their lives.[106]

The demands and conflicts generated within capitalist labor processes can thus lead to sophisticated forms of labor control, greater emphasis on labor-reducing machinery, and higher wages within key areas of production without a wider transformation of conditions of low wages, low productivity, and low demand. Solutions to the postdepression problems of creating an orderly and productive work force helped to cause the current problems of urban explosion and the widening of the gap between the potential of an urban job and the opportunities for getting one. The manifest defects of the labor aristocracy thesis should not stand in the way of a more dynamic examination of differentiation in the labor force.[107] In Kenya, for example, higher wages and altered work organization in docks, railways, and the civil service in the mid-1950s and the subsequent Africanization of supervisory personnel gave a one-time-only push upward to a segment of the work force. Meanwhile, in agriculture squatters were displaced and wages remained low, accentuating the segmentation of the labor force. On the other hand, in Ghana and Nigeria in the 1960s, trends toward losses in real income and tendencies to compress wage differentials had the reverse effect, pushing the segments together. If the former process fostered classic trade unionism, the latter encouraged a kind of populism, the hostility of a broad group of have-nots—workers, petty traders, job seekers, and riff-raff—toward the haves. This tendency was particularly strong in general strikes in Ghana in 1961 and 1971 and in Nigeria in 1964 (Weeks 1971a; Stichter 1976–77; Sandbrook 1977; Jeffries 1978; Peace 1979).

For the poor, "straddling" has been a crucial strategy, an attempt to use social networks and relationships to bridge the segments. The fluid relationship of people with jobs in the formal and informal sectors and between city and countryside has muted somewhat the dichotomy of the unemployed and the working class that seemed to follow logically from stabilization. But for such a process to diffuse class conflict, the strategy of straddling has to work. Populist rumblings suggest that it may not always do so (Berry 1980; Cowen and Kinyanjui 1976; Hart 1976; Gutkind 1967).

Closer study of historical questions such as these has shifted the emphasis of many students of labor from the juxtaposition of structures—for which labels like traditional, subsistence, precapitalist, modern or capitalist often substitute for an analysis of their nature and contradictions—toward analysis of social action. It is not enough to study the role of coercion and market forces in bringing forth workers, but it helps to examine how capital and the state attempted to redefine social structures and cultural values that shaped workers' choices on and off the job. Institutions like compounds and urban locations are being studied in conjunction with health regulations, urban planning, and criminal law to get a picture of the totality of control over time and space in the lives of workers. And Charles van Onselen, most notably, has looked into the nooks and crannies of urban society to discover how workers sought to redefine those structures and norms, resisting or manipulating even the most repressive labor systems (van Onselen 1976b, 1982; Worger 1983; Swanson 1977; Sadler 1979; Wilkinson 1981). The relationship of distinct forms of labor control and of resistance, as well as the connection between the work place and the wider society remain among the most important areas of study.

Meanwhile, we are beginning to get a much fuller picture of the connection of agriculture and industry than either the model of spontaneous movement to areas of high productivity or the model of rural decay leading to proletarianization suggests. The kinds of jobs migrants sought, their ability to bargain, and the kinds of social ties they could develop reflected regional differentiation, migrants' places in the life cycle, family structure, income, and rural conflicts. William Beinart (1982) found that in Pondoland up to the 1930s, increasing migration to the gold mines went along with increasing agricultural production. Wage labor enabled young men to buy cattle, found their own homesteads, and slowly accumulate productive capital independently of the patriarchal control of elders, who themselves were trying to harness young men's earnings to their own accumulation.[108] Such patterns seem to have had an even more lasting effect in Kenya. Kitching (1980) suggests that rural accumulation and urban differentiation form part of a single but complex process of struggle for access to all possible resources. At one extreme would be a poorly paid urban worker, whose remittances fail to cover the subsistence of a wife living on an inadequate plot, who therefore seeks wage labor on a nearby farm. At the other extreme is a well-paid skilled worker or civil servant, able to invest in land on which his wife can grow and market crops, in turn hiring laborers such as the poor woman described above. Such a process resembles classic capitalist accumulation: wage labor is generated as rural differentiation marginalizes or excludes a portion of the population. Yet both at the top and the bottom of the heap, people engage in straddling between economic activities (Cowen and Kinyanjui 1976; Hay 1976).

Straddling implies that parts of production processes lie outside the market and that forms of struggle take place not simply through direct confrontation in workplace or plantation but by the balancing of alternative types of resources. This does not necessarily mean that conflicts over land or wages were any less acute. In fact, striking workers could stay out longer if they could draw on their own or relatives' food supplies; disgruntled ex-slaves and tenants have ruined landlords by desertion; and rural capitalism has often been thwarted by the inability to keep laborers on the farm (Moorsom 1977: 81–86; Cooper 1980). That peasantries and proletariats can be differentiated and overlapping presents no *a priori* reasons why they should be quiescent or militant, but it does imply that any analysis of class formation and class action will have to transcend static and homogeneous categories and explore a single, complex, and changing social field.

If wage labor is far from a uniform category, so too is capital. The Firestone tire factory in Nairobi, a nearby farm, and a small machine shop may be involved with markets and labor in different ways. Followers of Nicos Poulantzas stress fractions of capital, all sharing opposition to labor but with distinct interests. Settler capital, national capital, transnational capital, mining capital, and so on can all be considered fractions. There is much in the attempt at specificity, but the Poulantzian conceptions on the one hand risk reifying somewhat fuzzy categories (e.g., national capital) into concrete entities capable of acting coherently, and on the other hand merge into the notions of interest-group politics in bourgeois social science.[109]

A more modest distinction, applying to all these categories of capital, may be a first step toward understanding the tensions that need to be examined. Marx separates "absolute surplus value"—what a capitalist gets by making workers put in more hours than needed to pay the costs of their subsistence—from "relative surplus value"—extension of accumulation by increasing productivity. Of course, any capitalist would like to do both, but the social conditions for maintaining the two entail contradictions. The accumulation of absolute surplus value depends above all on the elimination of alternatives for workers; the accumulation of relative surplus value creates alternatives. This is exactly what many political disputes in settler economies have been about: settlers who cannot or will not raise productivity fight to keep their labor from those who can.[110] The epitome of a system based on exclusive access to labor was the chartered companies of Mozambique, each given rights to recruit and exploit labor in a particular region. Thus the Sena Sugar Company made its money not by producing sugar efficiently but by having exclusive rights to coerced male labor, and when the Salazar government, in the interests of Portuguese self-sufficiency, demanded rice and cotton in addition to sugar, the company's response was to squeeze labor out of another category of workers, in this case women (Vail and White 1978, 1980).

The intensification of production through the extraction of more absolute surplus value has been a stimulus to rebellion, as in the Portuguese territories in a time of economic expansion in the 1960s.[111] Even small urban working classes in the midst of apparent labor surpluses, as in the post-war years, have resisted intensified production or decreased consumption. But instead of pushing harder, employers can substitute capital for labor and possibly diffuse conflict with higher wages. So the conflict between different forms of capital is also a dispute over social order. Still, investment and labor reform can create new kinds of resistance while diffusing others. An assembly line, unlike a plantation, can be shut down at a single point by organized workers. The Durban strikes of 1973—heralding a still-ongoing period of labor unrest—show the potential for far-reaching conflict in manufacturing industry even without formal labor organization.[112]

The question of development, Colin Leys argues, is whether the entrenched extractors of absolute surplus value can be supplanted by classes capable of developing the forces of production and accumulating relative surplus value. The question involves not simply the relationship of capital to labor, but the structure of marketing and investment as well. A settler who sells tobacco overseas may favor minimizing wages without concern for the small size of the local market, while the settler who sells maize might benefit from industrialization and increased demand. A multinational corporation might favor capital-intensive production and a stable, well-paid work force. At the same time, it might insist on a monopoly agreement on its import substitution products, which would raise costs and dampen the developmental effects of competition; in Kenya, the large majority of multinational manufacturers have insisted on such protection.[113]

Increasing the accumulation of relative surplus value, however, may only in some circumstances spread through the economy as a whole. As John Weeks (1977) shows in a stimulating study of industry in Peru, the relationship of pre-capitalist, technologically backward agriculture within a country to advanced capitalism outside gives a special meaning to a high-productivity sector. By definition, increasing relative surplus value means that a smaller proportion of the working day is devoted to meeting workers' subsistence needs; increasing productivity in the case of goods workers consume is what raises the rate of surplus value extraction in the system as a whole. The most intractable obstacle to decreasing the cost of such goods is backwardness of agriculture or of other consumer-goods sectors. But in an interconnected world, capital has alternatives: it can import cheap food produced by capitalist agriculture— something that has recently become significant in Africa—or it can substitute machinery for human labor power. Such strategies tend to strengthen the hand of foreign capital, with its close integration into international markets, or to make national capital act the same way as foreign—with consequent drains on foreign exchange, greater dependence on existing export items, and eventually a crisis of investment. Gavin Kitching makes a related point about export agriculture in Kenya: any effort by the dominant class within the state to increase its own accumulation runs into the fact that labor in agriculture is not fully commoditized and could react to a higher rate of extraction (via price manipulation or taxation) by a retreat instead of by increased production. In either case, a ruling class has an alternative to reliance on external capitalism's greater productivity: to expropriate peasants more rapidly, transforming the social basis of agriculture, or to cut down the level of consumption of workers. Hence the critical importance of rural and urban resistance and of the ineffectiveness of most African governments' efforts at repression. The point is not that the existence of advanced capitalist countries and powerful corporations makes domestic accumulation impossible—the alternative paths are crucial, for example, in Brazil and South Africa—but that it presents choices to a ruling class which allow it to accumulate much wealth and some capital without a direct assault on the autonomy of cultivators.[114]

Thus the question of developing productive forces within African countries is not the same as the question of the autonomy of a national bourgeoisie. A ruling class, for example Rhodesian settlers in the 1960s, may rally to economic nationalism because they believed heavy-handed exploitation (absolute surplus value extraction) was vital for them, but optional for capital-intensive multinationals; an African ruling class may be eager to attract multinationals not only because it lacks capital and technology, but to avoid the consequences of heavy-handed exploitation. On the other hand, the tremendous growth of the large corporation with worldwide connections has changed the context in which new resources are developed, and some would argue for the worse: multinationals, according to their critics, raise more capital locally than they bring in, while draining away profits; they push product lines standardized to the needs of other markets; they make local economies increasingly dependent on technology, expertise, and semiprocessed materials monopolized by the giant concerns; they use technology that makes ineffective use of local resources and labor and thus makes the national economy less interconnected rather than more; and they extract a high price for their investments in the form of agreements that block competition from other multinationals and local entrepreneurs. The corporations' defenders can acknowledge many such criticisms and still insist that weak local linkages are better than none at all—any assessment of foreign capital requires an implicit counterfactual model of what a national bourgeoisie might do. Hence, although national and international capital do make decisions in different ways and with different implications, the underlying issue is still the general process of capital accumulation and its limitations.[115]

The debate on the effects of the international economy is often set forth in terms of an abstract concept of national interest, but the opportunities and constraints that foreign capital poses for domestic ruling classes may be a more realistic basis for assessing the basis on which decisions about foreign investment are actually made. Steven Langdon (1979) argues that ruling classes have a symbiotic relationship to multinationals, a matter both of mutual interest and an overlapping of class boundaries of corporate and national managers (Sklar 1976). But this concept does not tell us where symbiosis may lead both partners. The conservative nature of multinational investment may provide government revenues, sinecures or distributorships for politicians, and other benefits without the dangers of primitive accumulation, but their limited scope and limited linkages within the national economy constrain the ruling class's project of self-aggrandizement combined with enough redistribution to maintain its tenuous and vital hold on the state. A ruling class, as Leys (1978) and Nicola Swainson (1980) insist is happening in Kenya, can aggressively move into productive and distributional investments that multinationals ignore, push multinationals out of other areas, and form joint ventures uniting state capital, private national capital, and multinational capital. At the other extreme, a ruling class, as Bonnie Campbell (1978) argues is happening in the Ivory Coast, can avoid the risk of creating autonomous class forces at home by leaving a wide field to foreign investment (see also Langdon and Mytelka 1979). In South Africa in the late 1920s and 1930s, a white government led a massive shift in patterns of accumulation, using revenues from gold to realize the distinctly national goals of building up capital goods industries and state enterprises. Even there, symbiosis remained. The creation of a black working class could not have taken place without both forms of capital, and the continued expansion of national markets provided a larger pie for all forms of capital even if shares were in dispute. In South Africa and Rhodesia under UDI—and in a very different way in Zambia—multinationals have been able to accommodate to ruling class policies that they did not necessarily like (Bozzoli 1978, 1981; Greenberg 1980; Baylies 1980; Sklar 1975). While multinational corporations are entities unto themselves, it is necessary to analyze the entire structure of capital, with its subcategories that remain far from neat and far from independent of each other yet which do pull in different directions. Richard Sklar (1976:87) is probably correct to suggest that the fate of the bourgeoisie in managing both corporations and states "will probably be determined by domestic struggles, not by anti-imperialist struggles that pit insurgent nations against foreign powers."

Even to say that is to emphasize that the global nature of capitalism is changing. Ernest Mandel (1975:62) distinguishes the era of "classic imperialism" from that of "late capitalism," a change that involves the structure of corporations, the international division of labor and the altered but in many ways increased role of the state. Of crucial importance to Africa, in Mandel's analysis, were the limitations on productivity intrinsic to the structure of low-wage labor in the colonies. As labor productivity rose in the industrialized countries, but not in the colonies, the relative price of raw materials began to rise. In the 1940s, as in the early colonial era, the need for commodities could not be separated from the social processes that produced them. This time, the transformation that took place did not simply entail the imposition of capitalist work discipline, which itself had not often gone very far, but large-scale investment in raw-materials production and a "fundamental upheaval in technology, organization of labour and relations of production," in short a widespread shift toward the production of relative surplus value. The effects of this process were uneven, for its costs encouraged substitutions of synthetics, above all in textiles and rubber, and it cut some areas out of their old niches in the world economy, generating more surplus labor and in so doing encouraging some local production of finished products.

It is important to understand the global nature of postwar change. But it was more complicated than that. More could be extracted in terms of absolute surplus value, and it was in South African gold mines, in Kenyan settler farms in the late 1940s, in Portuguese Africa in the 1960s, or in Rhodesia after UDI. It is thus critically important to analyze unrest and strikes, the long-term conflicts generated in the above instances, and the turmoil of the period 1935–50. Then, too, structural imperatives for change do not mean that the changes actually took place. Particular class interests could limit the drive toward the production of relative surplus value, and the fragility of capital's control of production, above all in agriculture, could create frustrating blockages to numerous plans for raising productivity. Even as Africa's exports rose 526 percent by value between 1945 and 1960—eclipsing the rises of the previous period of transformation (growth of 164 percent from 1897 to 1913)—some mineral industries folded in the midst of transforming the organization of labor, industry grew to a limited extent, and structural change in agriculture—except where a capitalist transformation had already occurred—often proved disappointing and impermanent.[116]

Paradoxically, the transformation of the postwar era subjected the worker to greater control on the shop floor, while in the same period control over the state devolved to people who were not only Africans but who hardly at that point constituted a capitalist class. The economics of decolonization remain to be explained. Yet the paradox is central to unraveling what happened, for the extension of control to ground level had always been the great obstacle to colonial states' plans for capitalist development. The new focus on economic change and on state investment brought with it a rapid search for the progressive African, whose role remained highly ambiguous but who fitted into developmentalist visions far better than the once-favored chiefs (Cell 1980; Lee 1967; Suret-Canale 1972). Nevertheless, even enterprises that were leading the process of restructuring the workplace—the Zambian copper mines or the East African Railways—believed that changes required, if anything, closer supervision, and they were far slower to Africanize supervisory posts than to raise wages and recognize unions. When pressures for the Africanization of middle management became insurmountable, the need for top-down control, as Michael Burawoy (1972) argues, became greater still (see also Grillo 1974:53–73).

The trouble was that it was very difficult to keep the lid on such changes. However important it is to emphasize the global factors that fostered decolonization—the ideological climate of the postwar era, the opposition of the United States to neomercantilist colonial policies, and the growing confidence of corporations that they could bring pressure on any kind of government—independence was not given but won, and it was won much sooner than the architects of imperial devolution expected. The progressive African farmer or

businessman proved quick to resent continued restrictions and eager to use the
state for his own benefit. Most important in the crucial years of the late 1940s
was the threat from below. The fear that urban masses might unite under an
Nkrumah, an Azikiwe, or a Kenyatta was very strong in the Colonial Office and
not unrealistic (Hargreaves 1979:44; Hopkins 1973). Such politicians proved
adept during the 1950s in articulating the grievances of diverse rural and urban
protesters while presenting themselves to the colonial state as the only alternative to the revolt of the masses. It was thus the class character of postwar
changes—that it pushed forth both more self-conscious workers and entrepreneurs—which set in motion forces very difficult to contain. Colonial powers
spent much of their energy insuring that power would be devolved to people
they could live with, and the thorny case of Kenya proved to be a model in
their quest to maintain continuity in the principles of an economic system even
as its personnel changed.[117]

The comprador, or neocolonial, model of regimes that emerged from this
process is a vast oversimplification, underestimating the importance of the state
in modern economies and the different relationships with foreign capital for
which ruling classes or factions within them press (Langdon 1979:230–31;
Sklar 1979; Joseph 1980; Leys 1978; and Williams and Turner 1978). Why a
particular ruling class may acquire a higher degree of autonomy requires analysis not only of structures but of processes. In the case of Kenya, Leys argues, the
fact that white settlers had undermined peasants' ability to produce cash crops
without destroying their autonomy altogether was crucial. International merchant capital was unable to establish a direct link to peasant production. Even
as Great Britain and much of international capital came to regard the settlers as
expensive and dangerous, a class of Kenyan accumulators had already developed its roots in the Kenyan highlands. Its origins lay in the colonial era, but
after independence it used the state and Britain's desire to maintain the sanc-
tity of private property and continuity of economic structures to step further
into the settlers' position as capitalist producers. Unlike other African political
classes, it inherited from the settlers the most difficult aspect of developing
capitalist agriculture, the creation of landless workers. As this class extended
its control over agriculture, it began to move into manufacturing as well, both
cooperating with and pushing away multinationals. But other scholars insist
that the Kenyan ruling class still has a weak position in production, above all in
industry, and that the state has narrow options in its relations with international
capital (Leys 1978; Kaplinsky 1980; Langdon 1977). Another set of limitations faces a national capitalist class: the pressures of the landless for land, of
workers for higher wages, and of peasants for more of the fruits of agricultural
production have proved difficult for even the most aggressive of bourgeoisies
to ignore. The largest number of the poor still engage in straddling between
inadequate farms and inadequate jobs, avoiding total subjection to wage labor,
and those at the top engage in straddling between government positions, com-

mercial endeavors, and investment in production. The control of labor remains a difficult task for a relatively wealthy and powerful African ruling class, as it was for colonial regimes and African kings before.

Trends

The present [this was written in 1981] is necessarily a turning point of sorts: it divides alternatives that might still happen from those that did not. Whether the present decade will turn out to be any more interesting than any other ten years in Africa's long history remains to be seen. Instead of discussing the myriad and complex economic issues that affect Africa, I intend only to make a few observations that derive from the historical interpretation developed in these pages.

The present era does not suggest that parts of the world labeled *periphery*, or the Third World, are heading toward a common future. Africa itself is heading in different directions. Parts of it are becoming detached from the world economy. In one of the great stalwarts of smallholder production, Ghana, cocoa harvests have dropped, and many farmers have turned to growing food for sale or for their own use, a phenomenon that goes back to 1965. Village crafts have revived as connections with world markets have declined, part of a process of social involution made possible by the fact that even market expansion had not destroyed redistributive social mechanisms in villages.[118] Smuggling and migration preserve links to stronger export economies, and there is no denying how painful the process of market withdrawal can be for a country like Ghana, but the fact remains that the seemingly unidirectional advance of the market can reverse itself. Equally important is the lack of action by international agencies and capital to keep Ghana a full participant in the world economy. And if the I.M.F. can make Ghana pass an austerity budget, it is not clear that it, any more than the state, can make cocoa growers produce. Nor did international capital or western nations line up upon the fall of Idi Amin to bring back to the fold that other jewel of the British Empire, Uganda. In Zaire, the all-embracing labor system within the copper mines and the wealth it produces have not led to greater integration or interdependence in all parts of the country. Much of it has now withdrawn from commercial relations further than at any time in its recent history into an economy of subsistence and state-run pillage, while the French orchestrate precise military operations to preserve access to the one point that matters.[119]

At the same time, wealthy and self-conscious dominant classes have emerged in several African countries and in some cases have pressed forward in agriculture and industry. If Kenya's elite has been concerned with the political dangers of pushing too hard, they have still bought plantations and factories and used the state to obtain privileged access to resources. But in a country often compared to Kenya, the Ivory Coast, a ruling class's ability to strike deals with foreign enterprise (as well as the French state) has allowed it to amass wealth while sticking to limited roles in agriculture and government, restraining the autonomy and growth of forces within the bourgeoisie itself and avoiding dangers of too much accumulation (Campbell 1978). And Nigeria has had the extraordinary luck to acquire great wealth without needing to exploit labor. But to translate that wealth into capital accumulation would mean losing the advantages of painless enrichment, requiring either the payment of noncompetitive wages (compared to suppliers or potential rivals who lack oil) or the risk of the periodic confrontations with workers and peasants that bedeviled the pre-oil days. Instead, the political class invests in the politics of patronage, in highly visible projects—especially schools and roads—and in safer investments, such as urban real estate, construction, and distribution. Industrialization is slow compared to the possibilities of domestic capital formation, and Nigeria's once-flourishing export agriculture is in danger, while food is imported. Thus Nigeria exhibits another variation in economic change: the expansion of the market, a flowering of entrepreneurial talent, the amassing of wealth, but not capitalist accumulation (Berry 1984; Biersteker 1978; Schatz 1977).

Unlike the other large and mineral-rich countries of Africa, South Africa has experienced a capitalist transformation of production. Its work force is almost entirely separated from the land—the homelands are a dumping ground, not a mode of production—and its industries produce capital goods as well as consumer items. South Africa is also a reminder that there is no one rationality to capitalism—the seemingly irrational divisions of race and the risks of confrontation can lead to a sophisticated economic structure. But try as South Africa's ruling class does to avoid the fact that it has created a working class, it has. The question of restructuring the labor system that rose in the 1940s was brought home again in the 1970s, as waves of unrest among urban workers and youth revealed the limits of labor control, while industry itself tried to bend, very carefully, its patterns of labor use to obtain more skilled workers and more flexibility. The government's choice is no longer, as some would have it, between evolution and revolution. It may well have both. Unprecedented wage increases in the mid-1970s and cautious labor reforms have already led to more unrest rather than less.[120]

How can one explain this parting of the ways? Not without close analysis of class power, accumulation, and labor control. South Africa's economic growth and the nature of the challenges to its structures are both as much the consequences of capitalism as of repression. That the ruling class in Kenya has done as much as it has reflects the colonial roots of its own accumulating drive and its ability to take advantage of the prior existence of large farms, landless workers, and infrastructure and services to serve a national class's interests rather than simply to link peasants and markets. But even in Kenya, and to a greater extent in the Ivory Coast, Uganda, Ghana, and Nigeria, varying degrees and forms of accumulation and structures that provide access to resources in highly unequal ways have not meant the exclusion of the majority of the people from access to land. On a society-wide basis, primitive accumulation, in Marx's sense of the term, has not gone very far. In Ghana and the Ivory Coast, much agricultural labor has come from outside the country. Poor as Sahelian migrants are, they remain hard to pin down and discipline. Their suffering has not been translated into the power of a class of rural capitalists over a class of laborers.[121]

Where primitive accumulation is so limited, there is a considerable degree of indeterminacy between the structure of producing units and the structure and operations of the national economy. In Ghana, a ruling class developed in the 1950s out of a broad but shallow social base and tried to foster state-centered accumulation by taking on the cocoa planters, trying to foster investment at the expense of workers' wages, and challenging international capital. Nkrumah's regime instead drove cocoa farmers to reduce production and workers to engage in crippling strikes, while amassing debts to foreign interests. In the Ivory Coast, crops are produced in a similar way, but the planter origins of the ruling class, its neocolonial relationship with France, and its circumspect policy of domestic accumulation have allowed that class to prosper without either disaster or major structural change. In Nigeria, oil—because it is produced without much labor—allows for a far higher degree of enrichment, redistribution, and infrastructural development without getting any closer to capitalist development. This relative autonomy of the state has been the strength of African rulers: the power of the state itself gave them instant power to bargain with international capital and to influence the distribution of domestic resources. It was also their weakness, for they had fragile power bases, other than the state itself, from which to consolidate control. How particular ruling classes fared had much to do with the historical processes that got them there: with the groups that supported them, with the regional, cultural, and religious divisions of the country and the degree to which such divisions represented rival power bases, with the ability of other individuals to develop clienteles, with the adequacy of resources to distribute, and with challenges from workers or peasants. Why a state (and not just a particular regime) loses its capacity to act effectively, as in Ghana, or remains stable, as in the Ivory Coast, can only be explained in a multicausal and historical fashion.[122] How strongly even a stable state can push toward capitalist development is a matter of contention, but it is clear that a state's disintegration is likely to lead to the collapse of economic institutions and to social involution.

Over the long period which this paper has covered, not only the international division of labor but also the nature of labor processes within each region have changed considerably. Masses of workers are no longer moved between continents to undertake principal roles in production, but large numbers now move themselves, often to fill jobs in secondary labor markets in African cities and in Europe and America (Piore 1979; Portes 1978; Fröbel et al. 1980; Friedman 1978). Much manufacturing has been exported from the industrial nations, so that economic power, while as concentrated in a limited number of corporate hands as ever, is not as spatially confined. Multinational corporations have considerable power, above all, to choose the kind of state they need to cooperate with and the kind of labor force they will have. They cannot avoid the actual confrontation with workers, and they depend on the state to contain it, but they do exercise some choice over the battleground. Africa's guerrilla army of the underemployed may well appear less attractive than the more disciplined battalions of South Korea, Taiwan, and Hong Kong, or even the foot soldiers of Brazil or South Africa, who are anything but footloose. Whether Africa plays a significant role in the shift in manufacturing for markets in Europe and North America is doubtful, and within Africa concentration is likely in a very limited number of places, such as Zimbabwe and South Africa, where effective state services and a labor force that is well socialized and dependable as well as cheap are available.[123]

Capital has not invariably won the battles it fought during the first and second occupations of Africa—to make production predictable and orderly throughout the continent—but it has altered the spatial structure of production so that winning everywhere is less important. Capital's greater intensity and mobility allow it greater selectivity in concentrating on islands of production or on basic raw materials, while the extent of Africa's integration into commodity markets and labor flows that has already taken place makes further penetration desirable but not the goal that it was in the 1890s or 1940s. So Ghana and Uganda can be forgotten if the state cannot function or cultivators resist growing cash crops, and most of Zaire can be left to Mobutu's predators as long as the copper mines keep running. If Nigeria's population does nothing but consume and stay out of the way of oil production, the loss of a once important agricultural producer is acceptable. This too is doubtlessly a phase—the very concentration of workers in centers of production will create challenges that raise costs and threaten continuity—and all that potential labor power that is not being used effectively may become increasingly important. Yet the march of Africans into the world economy does not appear to follow a straight line.

The resistance of African cultivators to domination in labor and produce markets—through mobility and social involution—is not new in African history. African kings found it difficult, but not always impossible, to transform the power to inflict violence into the power to produce, even when the growing markets of the nineteenth century gave them every incentive to do so. They—like their modern-day counterparts—found that external relationships can be easier to develop than internal control and that those relationships can bring in wealth even if they provide little basis for continual growth or security.[124] Colonial regimes discovered that African cultivators were hard to subdue. The cultivators used new opportunities for movement and new sources of income to get rid of old oppressors without necessarily becoming tied down to new ones. The process of keeping a labor force at work had to be systematic. Where this has occurred, it has led to class structures, racial divisions, and ideologies which allowed for economic expansion but left little way out of the polarization and confrontation on which they were based.

It would be pure historicism to suggest that future generations of Africans would have been better off had their ancestors stopped moving, stopped resisting kings or colonizers, and let the historical forces of capitalism get on with it. It is also unclear whose descendants would have benefited, or how things would have turned out were Africa the paradise of peasants that some scholars believe it to be. As things happened, Africans had much to resist. The stockaded villages of communities trying to ward off slave traders, the defensive farming strategies of squatters, or migrants' use of earnings to start small farms have in fact impeded the consolidation of economic power by kings, landlords, and businesses, but such structures offered fewer possibilities for changes that would protect the next generation against new onslaughts and new pressures. Such resistance has at times been fatal to would-be agrarian capitalists, of indigenous or immigrant origin. But for a colonial state or a multinational corporation, the meaning of the constraints on primitive accumulation are different: Africa yields profits, but the mass of surplus value that can be generated is limited. The laments of international organizations and development economists about the intractable backwardness of Africa is not a conspiratorial attempt to conceal the pillage of Africa, but a reflection of the fact—although they would not put it this way—that Africa is an underexploited continent.[125]

What are the forces for radical change? To an extent, the very indeterminacy of many African states in relation to the structure of production has given some leaders a chance to pursue radical social philosophies in countries not that different from those presided over by conservative rulers. The experience of Guinea and Tanzania—the longest-surviving of such governments—is not a hopeful one. The options of such countries in world markets, as Amin and Wallerstein have pointed out, do not amount to much. Equally important is the domestic question of what they have to socialize. Little capital formation can come from a peasantry that is both poor and uncaptured, and too often socialist states, notably Tanzania, have cajoled and ordered around peasants in the manner of the colonial state.[126] Whether a rural population, as in Mozambique, that has gone through the radicalizing experience of fighting for its independence will present possibilities for agrarian reorganization unlike the bureaucratized approach of Tanzania remains to be seen.[127] But the most hopeful opportunities are presented in Zimbabwe, where there is something to socialize. Robert Mugabe is far from being unprogressive by not immediately redistributing all land despite the obvious pressures of the landless; such a move might take a productive agricultural system back to square one. Whether relatively well-developed forces of production can be harnessed to meet the needs of a majority of the people and subjected to some kind of truly democratic control, or whether a Kenyan solution, with more at stake than in Kenya itself, will prove too tempting, is another question.

The social processes that underlie challenges to both white and black regimes are more complex than most analyses of them. Radical scholars have tried too hard to identify their favorite revolutionary class: the proletariat, the peasantry, the lumpenproletariat, or to denigrate rival favorites, not to mention kulaks, labor aristocracies, or the petty bourgeoisie (Fanon 1965). But static categories will not help to unravel dynamic political processes. Whether such entities are distinct or not and whether they are driven together or apart depends on particular patterns of economic and social change. Migrants may have split allegiances, but if a high degree of rural-urban interaction exists and if both areas share one fortune, a much wider field of action is brought in. In central Kenya in the 1950s, rural squatters and the urban lumpenproletariat were involved in insurrection together, but the nature of urban social control enabled the state to keep such groups as railwaymen isolated. In Zanzibar in the 1950s an ethnically diverse population including urban laborers, migrant agricultural workers, squatters, and indigenous peasants were gradually driven together by the rigidities of the plantation system and the efforts of the planter class to use the state more decisively on its own behalf. Within cities themselves, the fluidity of social relations may lead the most impoverished to believe that their best strategy is an individualistic one—to find a patron—but such thinking may change if patrons cannot deliver. Straddling between urban and rural areas may also be an individualistic way of minimizing risk and finding opportunities, but only if alternatives actually exist. And segmentation in the labor force may generate distinct interests and economistic trade unionism, but either declining real wages (as in Ghana in the 1960s) or structural obstacles to improvement (as in South Africa) may lead to more unified working-class action (Furedi 1973; Cooper 1980; Sandbrook 1977; Jeffries 1978). How strong such a class challenge may be depends as much on the nature of social networks and community structures as on the policies of state and capital.

The biggest leap is from the short-lived uprising or the general strike to a political movement. As Theda Skocpol (1979) points out, it is easier to explain why peasants might want to rebel than how they might succeed. Urban and rural disturbances have in fact administered severe shocks to African regimes, but they have most often remained on the level of inchoate populism that reflects the diversity of the people involved. This has helped to bring some regimes down, but has most commonly led to an even vaguer military populism. Urban concentration—especially in certain kinds of communities, like Sekondi, Ghana—has led to traditions of militancy that in turn politicizes a national labor movement (Jeffries 1978), but by now conditions in Africa are so divergent that there has not been a continent-wide wave of labor unrest such as that which shocked colonial powers in the 1940s. In South Africa, the concentration and complexity of industry, the maintenance of a brutally repressive labor system, and the oppression that overrides differentiation in the black labor force has made urban workers (and, as in Soweto, future workers) the central threat to the regime. Strong as the South African state is, the sense that workers have already made it yield adds a dynamic element to the situation, while the government's own techniques of repression—dumping people in impoverished homelands—spreads the urban ferment to rural areas. South Africa's structure, however, suggests that current patterns of resistance represent a different process from the remarkably successful rural-based social movements that developed in northern Mozambique and Rhodesia in times of intensified production and repression. Notably in northern Mozambique, the confrontation itself led to a complex network in villages that began to shape a counter-state even before the collapse of the Portuguese regime.

We know enough about the actions of African workers and peasants, and about revolutionary movements as well, to realize that social conflict does not await the attainment of capitalist development. African cultivators have never been able to separate their involvement in world markets from the social context of production and exchange. Who was to control economic life, who was to benefit, and what was to be lost were inescapable questions. They hardly needed to wait for their own crystalization and self-awareness as a peasantry or a proletariat in order to engage in social action; they hardly had to think of themselves as being engaged in a confrontation with capitalism; but they have been frustrating and difficult people to fit into a dominated world. The quest for an alternative world is more elusive still.

Notes to Original Essay

Comments and advice from Peter Anyang-Nyongo, Ralph Austen, Sara Berry, Naomi Chazan, Philip Curtin, Steven Feierman, William Freund, Martha Gephart, Jane Guyer, Steven Langdon, Michael Lofchie, John Lonsdale, and Patrick Manning have been of great assistance in the preparation of this paper. First published in *African Studies Review* 24 (June/Sept. 1981):1–86.

1 See, for example, the attack on A. G. Hopkins's argument that structural tensions induced by the ending of the overseas slave trade led to the Yoruba wars of the nineteenth century, by J. F. A. Ajayi and R. A. Austen (1972), with a rejoinder by Hopkins (1972). The offending article by Hopkins is "Economic Imperialism in West Africa: Lagos, 1880–92" (1968).

2 For an account of the passing of Africanist hegemony which takes a more dramatic view of it than I do, see Ranger 1976.
3 Rodney (1972) also had great influence in the 1970s.
4 I deliberately use the term *world economy* loosely to avoid the prior imposition of conclusions about Africa's place in it. Neither the idea that the world economy is a mere aggregation of individual market transactions nor the functionalist and unitary conception advocated by Wallerstein is very powerful. The actual mechanisms of the economy—from the International Monetary Fund to trading houses—need close attention, as does the question of resistance to them. By concentrating on one point in a complex picture I hope to get beyond perspectives that either ignore structure or treat it deterministically.
5 Much too neat is the attempt of Timothy Shaw and Orobola Fasehun (1981) to separate an orthodox view—stressing autonomous processes within the national unit, predicting economic growth and political consensus, and favoring capitalism—from a radical view that stresses dependence within a global system, analyzes specific class interests, predicts underdevelopment and contradictions, and favors socialism.
6 So strongly do some economists believe in interdependence that they berate Africans for their primitive and irrational attachment to self-sufficiency. African women have come under particularly strong fire. See de Wilde 1967:53–56.
7 See, for example, Fei and Ranis 1964:152, and Meier 1975:466. For further criticism centered on the issue of power, see Nafziger 1976:18–34, Berry 1981:7–8, and Staniland 1981.
8 It was thus perfectly rational for the political class in Ghana to undermine the economic base of cocoa farmers, although it discouraged production; it is perfectly rational in different circumstances for well-connected Kenyans to buy large parcels of land and obtain favorable access to credit while attending to other sources of income, thus producing less efficiently than the holders of much smaller plots with minimal access to credit or services, but with nothing to do other than work hard on the farm; and it is rational for squatters in coastal Kenya to avoid growing relatively lucrative tree crops and grow subsistence crops instead for fear of being tied to one plot of land and one landowner. For a valuable discussion of the relationship of class tensions to development, see Berry 1980:401–24.
9 Chenery et al. 1974:xiii. Similar worries have led Meier (1976:6) to a strangely tentative definition of development: "the process whereby the real per capita income of a country increases over a long period of time—subject to the stipulations that the number below an 'absolute poverty line' does not increase, and that the distribution of income does not become more unequal." Meier will wet his toe, but not more, in equity and distribution, but only as an afterthought, and certainly not to include preexisting structure within the purview of the analysis.
10 A revealing insight into changing views comes from a paper by Seers (1979a) written in 1969 and republished in 1979 with a new postscript by the author. It should also be added that the concepts behind the Basic Needs approach are not so new, but resurrect ideas current among economists in the late 1930s and 1940s, before the era of decolonization and emphasis on growth. See Rimmer 1979:33–37.
11 Seers (1979b) rejected the tacking-on approach altogether, claiming that growth was not necessarily "even positively correlated" with a broader, human-oriented view

of development. Without that positive view of growth, Seers argued, the discipline of development economics was dead. For further analysis of the weaknesses and political naiveté of 1970s development economics, see Seers 1979a:27, Leys 1974, 1975, and Godfrey 1978. For an example of an approach to the politics of redistribution that is more hope than analysis—theoretical or empirical—of the connection between economic and political power, see Bell 1974.

12 One of Bauer's attacks on marketing boards from 1953 is reprinted in Bauer 1971:387–422.

13 It is, of course, possible for neoclassical economists to argue that their models can include virtually any factor by incorporating it into supply curves and production functions. Indeed, what Marxists call the class struggle may be nothing more than a cost of production. This is a valid argument, but it turns economics into lists of factors and can only be invoked in an ad hoc fashion. Nor does it get at collective behavior, except indirectly. The hard question is what should be the starting point and focus of analysis.

14 Transnational class formation may be as important to study as transnational corporations. See Sunkel 1973 and Sklar 1976. On development as ideology, see Caire 1974 and Campbell 1976.

15 Hopkins writes (1973:189): "In economic affairs the political officers merely acted as Great White Umpires, ensuring that the rules were observed, not that they were changed." He cited Lord Lugard as having had great influence in arguing that "colonial rule should be based on co-operation and mutual interests" but neglects to mention that Lugard, in Northern Nigeria, meant mutual interest with an aristocracy, whom he wished to convert into a landlord class capable of making peasants work. The rules regarding land were anything but traditional, and the state anything but a neutral umpire.

16 For a radical critique of vent-for-surplus theory, see Freund and Shenton 1977.

17 Berry (1975:51–52) also stresses the role of merchants and Christians, and uses a comparative approach to pinpoint who did and who did not take to cocoa at specific times. She thus puts much more stress on the mobilization of resources than their ready availability and on the extent of social change that the very process of mobilization entails.

18 Tosh (1980) stresses that in savanna areas adding cash crops put enormous strains on labor and forced reductions in the quality and variety of food crops. For example, cassava—which demands little labor but provides little protein—became a much more important staple as a consequence of cash cropping. In forest areas, the sacrifice may have been less.

19 Hopkins (1973:168–72) presents the model, based on work by Dudley Seers. It stresses the narrow range of agricultural and mineral products exported, the importance of expatriate interests, the influence of major industrial powers, and the fiscal conservatism of metropolitan powers. On such questions as the effects of monopoly power on external commerce and of imported goods on local manufacturing, Hopkins presents superficial arguments for a limited negative impact (1973:203); dependency theorists have by and large been equally superficial in arguing the opposite case.

20 Particularly useful for the explicitness with which it argues that trade diffused its

benefits and built long-lasting and adaptable structures within a specific situation is Northrup 1978. Important collections on trade include Gray and Birmingham 1970, and Meillassoux 1971. This is only a sample of what is now a large body of literature.

21 Raul Prebisch's views can be found in the reports of the Economic Commission for Latin America, which he headed, while the report of the UNCTAD Conference of 1964 is a fascinating and revealing document in the history of ideas toward economic development. See also Prebisch 1971 and, for a discussion of these important ideas, Pinto and Knakal 1973, and Petras (1978:22–32).

22 For a close critique of Emmanuel and Amin, see de Janvry and Kramer 1979.

23 In another book, Amin (1976:149) relies on the same example, Giovanni Arrighi's analysis of Rhodesia (which itself is atypical and incomplete, as I will discuss below). Coquery-Vidrovitch (1977) argues that exchange became unequal in the 1930s; to be so temporally specific, the concept must be bent rather a lot. Smith (1980) also stresses the tautologous logic of the theory of unequal exchange.

24 Wallerstein's assumptions and methods are spelled out most boldly in his essays (1979). An example of promotion from periphery to semiperiphery is developed by Peter Evans (1979) in the case of Brazil, but—influenced by the more class-oriented view of development mentioned below—he tries to explain how it happened. Accumulation can take place on the periphery, leading to a creation of a partially autonomous, wealthy, and politically powerful national bourgeoisie. In Brazil, such a pattern led to industrialization. Evans is correct to point to the possibility of an alliance between a national bourgeoisie, transnational capital, and the state, but he is less persuasive in trying to explain why industrialization along these lines remains dependent. Such factors as the importance of multinational corporations and foreign debt are shared by nondependent countries, and Evans seems to freeze Brazil in its current situation—compared to equally static developed countries—thus blurring the question of whether Brazil is on a specific path toward capitalist development whose outcome cannot so easily be confined within the bounds of dependency. The most distinguishing fact about Brazil is the extent of labor repression, and Evans— and to a much greater extent Amin and Wallerstein—fail to treat such problems in a specific and dynamic manner.

25 In a 1976 article, Wallerstein wrote that colonial powers' concern with getting commodities from the periphery led them to follow the path of least resistance in Africa, fostering peasant production. Faced with the problem that his model left the most dramatic instance of transformation in Africa—South Africa—as an exception that he could only explain by invoking an exogenous factor, the political power of white settlers, Wallerstein later recast his model (Wallerstein and Martin 1979). The creation of split households, divided between subsistence production and the creation of surplus for the capitalist world system, became the defining characteristics of production at the periphery, occupying the place of cash cropping in the earlier model. The new version equally trivialized the distinction between a family farm and a gold mine. For a more thorough evaluation of Wallerstein's work, see Freund 1979, Brenner 1977, Skocpol 1977, and Howe and Sica 1980:250–59.

26 Useful debates and further articles on dependency theory and capitalist develop-

ment may be found in *Latin American Perspectives* 1978, issues 5, 3, and 4; 1979, issues 6, 2, and 3. For another sympathetic reassessment of dependency theory—in the light of increasing evidence of forms of industrialization in the periphery as well as Marxist criticism of the theory—see Godfrey 1980 and Bienefeld 1980. The two authors conclude that dependency theory remains viable, but more as a set of essential questions than a tidy answer.

27 In a way, Brenner is saying that the defenders of capitalism have a point—capitalism unleashes a great deal of creative energy into the economy—but he insists that they are right for the wrong reasons. The free market has little to do with it, but accumulation and control of the production process do. Bill Warren (1980) takes Marx's progressive view of capitalism so far—insisting that it is dynamic, fosters liberal values, and tends to remake societies all over the world in its own image—that it is often hard to see what he, as a Marxist, has against it.

28 In reference to Africa, Colin Leys (1978:241–66) argues that transfer of surplus does not explain underdevelopment, but is itself caused by particular patterns of accumulation and class formation. For other ways in which Brenner's ideas can be applied to Africa, see Ranger 1978 and Cooper 1980.

29 For political criticisms of Frank, Amin, and Wallerstein from the left, see Warren 1980, who sketches the political history of underdevelopment theory; Freund 1979:177–78; Brenner 1977:90–92; and Olivier 1975.

30 See, for example, Baier's discussion (1980) of a hierarchy of credit extending from Europe to Tripoli to the desert traders of the Sahel. Baier appears more influenced by central place theory than by dependency, but his specific findings are congruent with the latter as well.

31 See also the severe critique of "dependency empiricism" by Howe and Sica 1980:259–79, and Patrick Manning's comments on the difficulties of formulating counterfactual models (1974:15–22).

32 Another book—again with considerable merit—that uses the concept of underdevelopment is Colin Bundy 1979. Problems that arise from Bundy's use of this theory are examined in detail in Cooper 1981.

33 Hill's analyses are weakened by a definition of capitalism so broad that it is hard for anyone who has ever bought a cow not to be a capitalist, and by failure to take class and economic power seriously.

34 Before dismissing British social anthropology's sensitivity to this point, one should read Keith Hart's reappraisal (1978) of Meyer Fortes's early work.

35 For other critiques, see Mouzelis 1980 and Goodfriend 1979. For two critiques by non-Marxists, see Firth 1975 and Sahlins 1976. A basic text is Althusser and Balabar 1970.

36 For criticisms of the concept of a slave mode of production, see Cooper 1979:116, and Patterson 1979:49–52. Meillassoux is rightly skeptical of the concept (1975a:24–25), but Terray (1975:389–454) defends it.

37 Several scholars have tried to rescue studies of states from empiricism through the "tributary mode of production," but they have not yet presented a better answer to the thorniest question—why people fork over goods to chiefs and kings. Nor does their own evidence make a necessary connection between particular ways of

producing a surplus, class structure, and state structure. For a theoretical discussion and attempts to use the concept, see Wolf 1981:49–52, and Crummey and Stewart 1981.

38 Terray (1975) argues that a slave mode of production was dominant in Gyaman because a ruling class of warriors lived off slave labor in gold mines, reproducing that labor force by its control of warfare. But it had to restrain its own exploitation of local kinship groups to insure their loyalty in war. The demands of reproducing the slave mode of production thus resulted in the dominance of that mode over tributary and lineage modes. The evidence, however, does not make it clear that slaves did mine the gold or that Gyaman—under Asante power for much of the time— had such an autonomous ruling class. In Asante itself, the concept of a dominant slave mode of production elucidates little of the manner in which a ruling class tried to manipulate and control diverse forms of surplus extraction. See Dumett 1979 and Wilks (1975). The connection of state and modes of production is perceptively discussed in Lonsdale 1981.

39 For a penetrating criticism of Meillassoux's theories, see O'Laughlin 1977. The assumption that a single class, capitalist or otherwise, gets its way evades what Levine and Wright (1980:58) call "the central problem for any adequate theory of history"—"the transformation of interests into practices."

40 For agricultural rent to become important, people had to be kept still long enough for it to be collected, so Rey's (1976:41–67) emphasis on the juridical meaning of land is complemented by Guy Standing's treatment of feudalism (1981) as a process of immobilization. These arguments apply not only to feudalism per se, but to other social formations, rooted in the same legal tradition and enforced by state institutions, that rigidified land rights and helped to shape a class that could expropriate peasants, most notably in nineteenth-century South Africa. On the other hand, Wolf's (1981) argument that feudalism was merely one variant on a tributary mode of production does not distinguish between the way the connection of class power to land in feudalism facilitated the transition to capitalism, while other kinds of tributary systems, as in most African kingdoms, did not.

41 On these points, I agree with Bernstein. But Bernstein (1976:58) would like to establish capitalism's dominance by "controlling the conditions of reproduction of the small farmer rather than by expropriating him." This was easier said than done.

42 Bundy (1979) makes the softening up argument, but much of his evidence suggests that peasants who marketed grain and accumulated cattle were the hardest to get into the labor market. See Cooper 1981:289–93.

43 A vivid example of the two tendencies—toward monopoly and stagnation and toward competition and growth—as played out over 150 years in Mozambique may be found in Vail and White 1980. Considerations such as these are a principal reason why the stress in some Marxist writing (most forceful in Warren 1980) on the progressive nature of capitalism needs to be examined very carefully. The countertendency should be set against the tendency.

44 Moore's book (1966) has influenced several interpretations of capitalist development in South Africa (e.g., Trapido 1971).

45 This contrasts with coastal Kenya, where the colonial government's registration of

land titles and willingness to enforce property laws from outside the local community led both to a market in land titles detached from conditions of production and to conflict that paralyzed investment. See Cooper 1980: chap. 5.

46 There is much valuable material on work and labor control in Johnstone 1976 and Perrings 1979. There is also some contemporary research on work in factories and on both European and African conceptions of work. See Peil 1972, Wallman 1979, and Fabian 1973.

47 Fallers (1973) shows in the case of Buganda how despotism triumphed over aristocracy, but he generalizes this into a distinction between inequality—a dyadic relationship—and stratification, without explaining the conditions in which the one is or is not the other. A case of a warrior class using its collective strength to dispense with a king is the *tyeddo* of the Senegambia (Klein 1968). See also Roberts 1980.

48 See also Hobsbawm 1964. If traditions formed in early struggles against capital continued to shape the labor movement, later phases also entailed the development of a "respectable working class" that no longer did cultural battle with the bourgeoisie. An important question to ask about labor in Africa before the 1950s is the extent to which the development of a respectable working class was precluded, and the laborers—in their entirety—resembled the residuum of casual workers and criminals that proved difficult to control and threatened to contaminate respectable workers in Victorian England (Stedman Jones 1973–74; 1971).

49 Migrant workers may protest differently from stabilized ones, but ranking them hierarchically on a scale of militancy does not help. An older tradition of copperbelt ethnography still helps to illuminate many aspects of mineworkers' lives (Epstein 1958).

50 Some scholars use the concept of a petty bourgeoisie to get around the inchoate state of dominant classes. That is to use a static category to describe a problem of becoming. Kitching (1980) uses it so broadly that it includes producers too large to be petty and too small to be bourgeois, and he fails to give any content—social, cultural, or political—to the class identity of the petty bourgeoisie.

51 See the discussion of these issues in Joseph 1980, Sklar 1979, Lonsdale 1981, and the large literature they cite. Peel (1980) notes that in a Yoruba community before colonization, ruling classes had external sources of wealth (from selling slaves), as they did after independence (from oil revenues, via the state), but that in both cases local elites needed local power bases and were subject to strong sanctions if they failed to fill redistributive norms. Class action, in the form of riots and in the name of community, had important effects.

52 For strong criticism of Althusserian functionalism, see Mouzelis 1980:372 and O'Laughlin 1977.

53 This problem particularly affects dependency theorists, although their efforts have raised useful points. See Amin 1972, Wallerstein 1976, and Coquery-Vidrovitch 1976. Hrbek (1968:48) provides an intelligent critique of these problems, then periodizes African history by coincidence, noting that "many far-reaching events" took place between 1805 and 1820, which although unrelated constitute a landmark.

54 Wallerstein's reasoning (especially in 1973:7–8) depends almost entirely on discussing consequences of different patterns of trade, for example, whether they strengthen

or weaken states. Wallerstein himself notes that his reasoning may appear circular, and his defense relies not on a theoretical or logical argument but on an empirical one. His empiricism, as indicated here, is doubtful.

55 These sweeping assertions of relative costs of different forms of labor within the world system substitute for specific evidence, but more careful studies show that slavery can be cheap and efficient, but is not necessarily so. The other side of the cost question is the fact that slave owners could put women and children to work far more readily than could other labor users, and that the worker does not decide at what point to exchange income for leisure. In some cases, abolition led to large reductions in labor time, without necessarily reducing subsistence costs for workers. See Patterson 1979:61; Fogel and Engerman 1974; and Ransom and Sutch 1978.

56 Only for a brief period at the peak of the slave trade (late eighteenth century) did the Gold Coast's annual slave exports attain a value equal to the gold trade at its peak (seventeenth century). See Bean 1974:354, 355; Curtin 1969:266; Rodney 1969:13–21; and Wilks 1978:521. Curtin, in his commentary on an earlier draft of this paper, argued that the gold trade did not decline because of the slave trade or changes in the world price but because of a rise in the real value of gold (in goods) within West Africa, for reasons that are not well understood.

57 Robert Thomas and Richard Bean's comparison (1974) of slaving to highseas fisheries—based on the fact that slavers paid for the operation but not for the resource they were catching and depleting—is dubious. Fish do not fight back; they do not create social structures that affect the outcome of the process and force fishermen to adjust the scale or techniques of their operation. And Thomas and Bean not only assume an equilibrium among competing slavers, but assume that the equilibrium was continuous, allowing no chance for structures arising at a particular moment to become entrenched. They underplay entry costs precisely because they do not consider the social basis of slaving. They even note (p. 909) that their fishermen could be an army or a lone kidnapper without it making any difference to their model. Henry Gemery and Jan Hogendorn (1974, 1979) likewise treat societies involved in slaving as an economic and social blank: they do not distinguish between the economic behavior of individuals, states, and traders; they assume that African economies before the slave trade were as they were after it—theirs is an asocial vent-for-surplus model. They also discuss the gains and losses for West Africa without distinguishing between slavers and the enslaved. In this discussion, they assume that the only alternative to slaving was that the would-be slaves engage in subsistence cultivation, and hence their assumptions already eliminate any possibility of qualitative change. If Africans did nothing but eat, economic history would indeed be simplified. In the end, they are struck by the fact that Africa as a whole gained little, and probably lost, from the slave trade, as far as their model goes. But is a process akin to theft even supposed to maximize total utility for perpetrator and victim combined? Having explained that utility-maximizing models—for Africa as a whole, and with slaving left as an unstructured process of people selling each other—do not explain why West Africa engaged in the slave trade, they conclude (as do Thomas and Bean) that political fragmentation and private gain must be the

explanation. The long voyage through implausible assumptions gets us to where we began.

58 Curtin, however, is careful to note the limitations of his data and the ambiguity of the results. Elsewhere (Curtin et al. 1978:224) he suggests that political models may be more appropriate at an early phase, economic ones at a later one, at least in Dahomey or Biafra. The transition from one to another would be more interesting to explain, and there the intertwining of the political and the economic must be stressed. For a criticism of Curtin's distinctions, see Roberts 1980.

59 On trade and state-building, see Fage 1969 and Coquery-Vidrovitch 1969; on weapons and political organization, see Goody 1971; and on the slave mode of production and the state, see Terray 1974. Such views have been criticized by, among others, Wrigley (1971), Roberts (1980), and Dumett (1979).

60 The possibility of *realizing* the fruits of predation gave the external slave trade a crucial dimension, but predation—an act of surplus acquisition distinct from the labor process—was important to military and state power in such kingdoms as Buganda and the Zulu, and is discussed in a revealing article by Caulk (1978).

61 For two very different portraits of reactions to insecurity, see Cissoko 1969, and Wright 1975. Defensive submission to authority and autophagous slaving are both illustrated in Vail and White 1980.

62 Curtin, commentary on draft of this paper; Meillassoux 1971:55. For a case study, see Roberts 1980; the consequences of the networks are discussed in a voluminous literature on the Islamic revolutions.

63 For another attempt to come to grips with the connection of the slave trade, production, and slavery, see Klein and Lovejoy 1979.

64 Law (1977a, 1977b) argues that Oyo, distant from export ports, had more difficulty than more coastward states in controlling the flow of captives. Dahomey did better, but still merchant-chiefs, gaining their slaves by purchase rather than capture, were forces to be reckoned with. Equally important is how rulers confronted people who did manage to acquire substantial wealth. Meillassoux (1968) points to mechanisms to "sterilize" wealth, converting it into immediate display rather than letting it accumulate as capital that might lead to the creation of a class around that wealth. Wilks (1979) presents examples of the use of death duties and prestigious titles to achieve such goals in a potentially contentious situation in Asante.

65 Curtin's figures from *The Atlantic Slave Trade* (1969) have stood up well, and scholars have concentrated on adding new data and focusing more precisely on smaller exporting zones or finer breakdowns of the data. Other work has stressed the financing of the trade, the organization of voyages, mortality, and mechanisms of slave gathering in Africa. An idea of recent work may be glimpsed in Gemery and Hogendorn's collection (1979), while Joseph Miller's new book (1989) on the Angolan slave trade gives an indication of the substantial ground still being covered.

66 For a powerful criticism of demographic determinism, see Brenner 1976; see also Nell 1979. The much-discussed Nieboer hypothesis is of direct relevance to the slaving question, but it is neither precise nor sufficient. Nieboer argued that "closed resources"—limited access to land—provided no incentives for enslavement, but

that "open resources" forced elites to tie down their labor force. This does not explain why anyone would want slave labor, or how slaves could be obtained or, what is more difficult, how slaves could be kept. Those questions require a prior analysis of class and power. See Patterson 1977.

67 Such important plantation crops as cotton, coffee, and cloves entail few technical economies of scale, but sugar, tea, and sisal do.

68 Berry (1975:26–27) points out the ways in which Yoruba kings could contest the influence of smallholders. See also Law 1977a, and Wilks 1975. On the politics of peanuts, see Klein 1973; Cruise O'Brien 1971b, 1975; and Copans 1980.

69 The demographic implications of switching from selling males and retaining females to retaining both are discussed in Manning 1981; Law 1977a:573; Wilks 1975:177; and Northrup 1979:13–14.

70 Cooper 1977, and Sheriff 1987. Lovejoy (1979) extends the concept of a plantation economy to Northern Nigeria, a controversial point among specialists in that region. The question is not whether plantations existed there, but how can one analyze, over time, the relationship among the different forms of surplus extraction available to the ruling class and the different forms of resistance to them?

71 This literature is too vast to cite, but a good introduction is still Meillassoux 1971, while Abner Cohen 1971 greatly influenced consideration of the social organization of trade. Some recent studies include Lovejoy 1980; M. Johnson 1974; Roberts 1984; and Northrup 1978.

72 Thus the Hausa social mechanisms in the twentieth-century cattle trade were essentially new, not a derivative of being ethnically Hausa; indeed, the meaning of ethnicity was transformed in the process of organizing trade (A. Cohen 1969).

73 On the narrowing of a once complex and diversified trading system into one limited to a few items, notably cattle, see Baier 1980. The Indians of East Africa seem like an exception, since they were around in both the nineteenth and twentieth centuries. Yet it was very often different Indian groups; the great houses of the nineteenth century rarely survived, while groups like the Oshwals came in during the colonial period and prospered. The Indian role in the nineteenth century was linked to a small number of entrepôts, above all Zanzibar, and to financing a small number of large caravans and large planters. The key to the twentieth-century operations was spreading out and organizing the flow of goods, credit, and information for very spread-out, small operations. See Zarwan 1976.

74 One can readily concede much of Robinson and Gallagher's (1961) argument about the conservative nature of the British shift from informal to formal empire: what else would one expect of what had been the predominant industrial and commercial power?

75 See Hopkins 1973:157. On the other end of the spectrum, the weakest of European powers had no choice but to tighten its political control over territory once the others moved, and in a sense Portugal was the most economic of imperialists (Clarence-Smith 1979).

76 As trade became more specialized and competitive, socially defined credit relationships had to give way to credit backed up by property, and the protection of property

rights thus became a new issue for European traders in West African ports. See Hopkins 1980. On law and order, see Lloyd 1972.

77 See, for example, Atmore and Marks 1979; Marks and Trapido 1979. This discussion builds on a long debate over the connection of mining capital to imperialism, including the work of G. A. Blainey, Donald Denoon, Alan Jeeves, and others. For a recent installment, see Mendelsohn 1980, and Denoon 1980. For another point of view, see Kubicek 1979.

78 Stanley Trapido (1980a) notes the association of South African liberalism in the nineteenth century with merchants who did business with Africans and who saw the need for a political community embracing men of property of all races. As the development and control of a mass labor force eclipsed trade with Africans as an economic issue, such a viewpoint first lost its influence and then subtly changed. Liberals thought of building a respectable, decently treated work force.

79 The market responsiveness of the idealized smallholder is stressed in Hopkins 1973 and Hogendorn 1975. Of Hogendorn's examples of successful cash cropping in the early colonial era, none led to anything close to autonomous development for future generations, and several collapsed even as cash-crop production.

80 Weiskel (1980) convincingly shows how the initial ability of the French in the Ivory Coast to live off African produce failed to last, and they soon became convinced that the problem of harnessing labor had to be solved, leading to a direct and violent confrontation with the Baule. Something similar happened with the Anyi, and the trade-loving British in Benin—even though the local people were supplying rubber and palm products—began to exercise "autocratic powers" over planting and concessions. West Africa is, of course, the best case for colonial umpires, and the deliberately antipeasant policies of southern, central, and parts of eastern Africa are familiar. See also Groff 1980; Igbafe 1979:343–44; Palmer and Parsons 1977; Vail and White 1980.

81 I have tried to show (Cooper 1980) how deeply such assumptions were built into British thinking on East Africa at the turn of the century, so much so that any balanced consideration of alternative systems of production was impossible. On the class baggage of Victorian imperialists, see Stedman Jones 1971; Semmel 1960; and A. W. Thornton 1959.

82 See Watts 1987, and Cooper 1980. In Uganda—often cited as an example of pro-peasant British policy—the colonial authorities first tried to create a system of landlordism, dominated by the old chiefs. But the power of the chiefs was hard to turn into power over their subjects' labor, and peasant production, with wage labor coming from outside Buganda, came to the fore. See Mamdani 1976:41–49; West 1972; and Wrigley 1959.

83 In Katanga, the Belgians tried to use whites as capitalist farmers, then blacks; when that failed, they turned to state-administered compulsory cultivation. See Jewsiewicki 1977; Suret-Canale 1971; Brett 1973; and Vail and White 1980.

84 The British Foreign office paused long enough in its attack on "slave" labor in Angola to sign a treaty with Mozambique for the supply of labor to the gold mines of South Africa. Mine labor, ideologically, was free. But now the South African

system is attacked in liberal circles as a deviation from ideas of a free economy. The meaning of free labor changes, but the importance of liberal criticisms of profitable but "unfree" forms of capital accumulation reveals great continuity, from slavery to apartheid. On the predatory and coerced labor of the early colonial era, see Anstey 1966; Harms 1975; and Duffy 1967.

85 The importance of mass migration to escape tax and of forced labor to the history of French West Africa is stressed in Asiwaju 1976; see also Vail and White 1980. Attempts at villageization, which usually did more to disrupt agriculture than to stimulate it, run from early colonial era to *ujamaa* villages to today. For one example, see Vail 1976:136.

86 See Mintz 1974:180–224. One might compare parts of western Tanganyika in the early colonial era, where nearby markets for grain gave people the choice of working or not working for plantations, with eastern Tanganyika, where isolation made labor the only source of cash (Iliffe 1979:151–63, 311–17).

87 For example, the British launched an all-out assault on Giriama autonomy, provoked a rebellion, repressed it, and then let the Giriama squatters whom they had forced into the Reserve drift back onto the better coastal lands, where they took up squatting again. The British were too shaken by the revolt and its aftermath to stop them. See Cooper 1980:219–24; see also Lonsdale and Berman 1979; Isaacman 1976; Iliffe 1979; Beer and Williams 1975; Newbury 1980; Amselle 1978; and Vail and White 1980.

88 We would all be better off without concepts like "peasantization." See Post 1972, and Klein 1980:9–44.

89 For more on this point, see Friedmann 1980; Cooper 1981; and Ennew et al. 1977. Shanin (1979) has a more positive view of the concept.

90 Parkin notes that accumulators whose rights in productive property depend on sanction from within the community must be careful to cultivate relations within that community, while their ability to bring in outside sanctions—above all government agencies—can lead to conflict within the community. On the other hand, conflict between accumulators and the state, as between Ghana's cocoa farmers and Nkrumah's government, can lead the latter to develop rural organizations to undercut the former. See Parkin 1972; Beckman 1976; Rhodie 1968; Southall 1978; Chauveau and Richard 1977; and Berry 1984. For a comparative discussion of the class cleavages and alliances in rural politics, see Samoff 1980.

91 Coquery-Vidrovitch (1977) presents a wealth of information on prices and outputs during the depression, and draws on case studies published in a special issue of *Revue Française d'Histoire d'Outre-Mer* 63 (1976). See also Guyer 1979; Berry 1975; Rhodie 1968; and Southall 1978.

92 For a recent review of how bad the economics of a scheme so dear to the heart of the Colonial Office could be, see Hogendorn and Scott 1983. The model project for much of the colonial era, the Gezira Scheme in the Sudan, was successful in its centralizing effects, through control of irrigation, technology, and a hierarchy of tenancies. See Barnett 1977; for a review of numerous schemes of the colonial and independence eras, see Voll 1980.

93 See also Frances Hill 1977, and Oculi 1987. Christopher Leo (1978) shows that

despite the strong class biases of an ambitious development scheme, "progressive" farmers performed no better with their favored access to resources than those who were scarcely helped at all. The richer farmers were engaged in a wide range of commercial and political activities and regarded land as something to collect; the poorer farmers had nothing to do but farm.

94 See Bundy 1979; Trapido 1978; Keegan 1979; Slater 1980; and Trapido 1980b. On the importance of changes in land control preceding market incentives to rationalize production, see the theoretical discussion above.

95 When neoclassical economists interpret the behavior of peasants (or of states) in terms of response to prices, they sometimes treat as a given the most interesting aspect of the question—how the structures that determined prices were established. This definition of what is relevant mars, for example, Bates 1976. For a sharp contemporary analysis of the politics of railway routes, see Ross's (1968, orig. publ. 1927) criticism of the Kenyan Government's plans for the Uasin Gishu line in *Kenya from Within*. The effects of railway policy are discussed in several articles in Palmer and Parsons 1977, especially Vail 1977:365–95, and in Iliffe 1979:135–51. See also Katzenellenbogen 1973 and Amin 1976:202–14.

96 Baier (1980:213) and Beinart (1982:69–73) note the decline of craft production, but Johnson (1974) and Roberts (1984) note the continuation of textile industries.

97 See also Todaro 1976, and Fei and Ranis 1964. Berg (1965) recognizes the importance of coercion before the 1930s, but his analysis loses force through its assumption of a stable cultural and economic equilibrium in village life. His explanation for why Africans continued to seek work comes down to a single factor: the creation of new wants. The nature of opportunities for meeting those wants is taken as a given. With assumptions like that, migration is good for migrants by definition.

98 Weeks (1971b) points out that the Lewis-Fei-Ranis model pretends to be value-free, but a key assumption—that rural wage rates remain constant even while urban migration takes place—requires mechanisms to keep wages from rising; that is, the model presumes a repressive class structure and argues that this is desirable in the name of promoting a capitalist sector. Other valuable criticisms of the neoclassical models include Portes 1978; Arrighi 1973; van Onselen 1975; Amin 1974a:65–124; and Meilink 1978.

99 Although Arrighi's conclusions are opposed to Lewis's, his methods are essentially neoclassical. His central concept is that of the effort price, or opportunity cost, and he neatly separates the economic from the political. Political means were used to drive the effort price of agricultural labor above that of wage labor, when economic means became sufficient.

100 In the case of Zanzibar, the British explicitly tried to make slaves into a fully committed agricultural proletariat. They were unable to do so and began to manipulate the partial involvement of different peoples in aspects of plantation work (Cooper 1980). For case studies written within structuralist frameworks, see Amselle 1976, and Rey 1976.

101 Morris (1976) stresses that the insistence of Africans on access to land as part of remuneration for labor was a crucial reason that labor tenancy persisted so long. See also Rennie 1978, and Furedi 1975.

102 The literature on labor unrest includes Stichter 1978; Iliffe 1975; Oyemakinde 1975; Jeffries 1978; Joseph 1974; Suret-Canale 1978; Hemson 1977; and O'Meara 1975. This only scratches the surface.

103 See van Onselen 1976b. Although in theory the cheap reproduction of labor should be fostered by African brewing and prostitution, authorities had a very ambivalent attitude toward them, as well as toward the illegal but cheap housing settlements that workers so often founded themselves. They feared exactly what made workers prefer the more permissive settlements to oppressive locations and compounds, a chance to structure income-earning and daily life without direct control. See van Onselen 1976a; Proctor 1979; Lodge 1981; and White 1990.

104 Official ambivalence is discussed in Heisler 1974. Changes in the structure of work have not been adequately discussed yet, but are taken up in my work on Mombasa (1987) and in Crisp (1983). See also Parpart 1983; Burawoy 1972; and Clayton and Savage 1974.

105 The crisis had earlier roots, which themselves had similar causes. The growth of manufacturing on the Rand after World War I led the state to ignore its own segregationist rules when convenient and allow African settlements to grow, which were not as tightly controlled as locations. But even miners, housed in compounds, had contacts there on days off, and participated in rising ferment in the Transvaal working class. The 1920 African mineworkers' strike reflected this ferment, and the oppressive conditions that hit the miners above all. The mineowners, as many capitalists were to do later, thought they might prevent future action by splitting the black work force and letting the most frustrated and skilled workers achieve higher pay and status. Bonner (1979) speculates that this response to black unrest from the most urbanized and stable segment of a migratory work force may have led to a white counterreaction and the 1922 white mineworkers' strike.

106 See O'Meara 1975, and Greenberg 1980. In Bulawayo, Rhodesia, employers stabilized carefully chosen jobs, and retained migrant labor in others. See S. Thornton 1978.

107 There is a great deal of discussion of this thesis in Sandbrook and Cohen 1975. As originally formulated by Giovanni Arrighi and John Saul, the labor aristocracy thesis stated that an upper stratum of workers had become sufficiently privileged that they had little in common with the lower stratum, and the peasantry and could be expected to behave conservatively. Opponents have argued that a closer look at income differentials and trends suggests that the real cleavage is between managers and high-level bureaucrats and all workers, while analysis of social networks suggests a close and interdependent relationship of all strata of the proletariat. There is much in this, but as Saul himself says (1975:308), what needs to be examined above all are processes.

108 Wolpe (1972) argued that the symbiosis of capitalist production and precapitalist reproduction was stable until the reserves degenerated so badly in the 1930s and 1940s that they could no longer perform their function, leading to a crisis that the Nationalist government took up. But Simkins (1981) argues that total production in the reserves was stable from 1918 to 1965 and met a constant proportion of requirements from 1918 to 1955. So their decline was a consequence of Nationalist policies rather than a cause. For valuable insight into the complexities of rural production

and labor migration, see Mayer 1980; Beinart 1982; Webster 1978; Murray 1978; and Cliffe 1978.

109 For a Poulantzian analysis of South Africa and a criticism of it, see Davies et al. 1976, and Bozzoli 1978. See also Davies 1979, and Yudelman 1975.

110 Marx 1967:508–19. On the struggle for the accumulation of absolute surplus value in Kenya and South Africa, see Berman and Lonsdale 1980, and Greenberg 1980.

111 There is a useful but somewhat mechanical discussion of this issue in Paige 1975.

112 Edwards (1979) connects forms of labor control with forms of resistance. On the origins of the current labor turmoil in South Africa, see Institute for Industrial Education 1974.

113 Leys 1978; Baylies 1980; Langdon 1979:229. In the colonial era, policies of deliberate nonindustrialization were also important (Brett 1973:267–75).

114 See Weeks 1977, and Kitching 1980:418–30. The fragile ruling classes in Kenya and Nigeria, for example, were taken aback by peasant unrest and populist agitation as well as by more subtle pressures on politicians from their home bases. See Beer and Williams 1975; Leys 1974; and Lamb 1974.

115 Bjorn Beckman (1980) suggests that both sides in the ongoing debate on Kenya put too much emphasis on whether capital is foreign or local, and not enough on whether that question affects the prospects for the generalization of capitalist relations of production. The importance of counterfactual models is stressed by Biersteker (1978). For examples of differing perspectives on multinational corporations, see Barnet and Müller 1974, and Vernon 1977.

116 Munro 1976:178. For two cases of failure in the midst of labor transformation, see Freund 1981, and Crisp 1983. For a skeptical view of recent economic change in Africa, see Langdon and Mytelka 1979.

117 The most important principle involved was that of private property. See Wasserman 1976, and Njonjo 1977.

118 See Beckman 1976:291; Kraus 1980:16; Posnansky 1980; and Rathbone 1978:34. My perception of trends contrasts with that of Wallerstein (1976:48–50), who envisions the completion of the process of incorporation, the end of subsistence production, and the flowering of agribusiness in the Sahel. By stressing commodities and forgetting the process by which they are produced, he predicts a common course for South Africa, Nigeria, and Zaire into the semiperiphery.

119 Schatzberg 1980. Gran (1979) argues that the disasters of the Zairois economy can be traced to its connection with the world economy. There is much in this argument, but the world economy is getting very little out of the collapse of production in rural Zaire. If the Zairois political class owes its existence to outside forces, it has taken off on its own internal mission.

120 See the perceptive article by Yudelman (1975). On current (c. 1980) labor turmoil, see Wilson 1980; Bonner 1980; Horner and Kooy 1980; and current issues of the *South African Labour Bulletin*.

121 Cocoa farmers in Ghana and Nigeria experienced severe losses of labor; in the Ivory Coast, the promise of access to land and the chance, however small, of moving into the ranks of cocoa planters, is necessary to induce migrant laborers to come to work for planters. See Kraus 1980; Berry 1984; and Chauveau and Richard 1977.

122 The unformed nature of a ruling class may help to explain why certain states are

fragile, but not why some break down and others do not. See the controversy between Saul (1976) and Williams (1976).

123 Langdon and Mytelka (1979) are rightly skeptical about new investment in manufacturing in Africa. In Kenya, for example, export manufacturing declined after efforts to build it up. See Langdon 1987:45.

124 The word that Yoruba use for development today has its origins in the concept used in precolonial days that stressed the importance to royal power of controlling external forces (Peel 1978).

125 This way of putting the problem owes much to Kay (1975:55). But Kay's next line, that capitalism therefore created underdevelopment, has something of the magical about it.

126 See R. Johnson 1978; Freyhold 1979; Hyden 1980; and Mansasu and Pratt 1979; see also Rosberg and Callaghy 1979, and Thomas 1974.

127 A reason for skepticism about the socialist transformation of peasant agriculture was expressed well in what a Mozambican peasant found to praise in the new government: "FRELIMO is letting us rest." Quoted in Vail and White 1980. For another view, see Isaacman 1978.

References for Original Essay

Ajayi, J. F. A., and R. A. Austen. 1972. "Hopkins on Economic Imperialism in West Africa." *Economic History Review* 25:303–6.

Alavi, Hamza. 1975. "India and the Colonial Mode of Production." *The Socialist Register*:160–97.

Alpers, E. A. 1973. "Re-Thinking African Economic History." *Kenya Historical Review* 2:163–88.

Alpers, E. A. 1975. *Ivory and Slaves in East Central Africa*. Berkeley: Univ. of California Press.

Althusser, Louis, and Etienne Balabar. 1970. *Reading Capital*. Trans. by Ben Brewster. London; New Left Books.

Amin, Samir. 1971. "La politique coloniale française à l'égard de la bourgeoisie commerçante sénégalaise (1820–1960)." In Claude Meillassoux, ed., *Development of Indigenous Trade and Markets in West Africa*. London: Oxford Univ. Press, 361–76.

Amin, Samir. 1972. "Underdevelopment and Dependence in Black Africa: Origins and Contemporary Forms." *Journal of Modern African Studies* 10:503–24.

Amin, Samir. 1974a. *Accumulation on a World Scale: A Critique of the Theory of Development*. Trans. Brian Pearce. New York: Monthly Review Press.

Amin, Samir. 1974b. "Introduction." In *Modern Migrations in Western Africa*. London: Oxford Univ. Press, 65–124.

Amin, Samir. 1976. *Unequal Development: An Essay on the Social Formations of Peripheral Capitalism*. Trans. Brian Pearce. New York: Monthly Review Press.

Amselle, Jean-Loup, ed. 1976. *Les Migrations Africaines*. Paris: Maspero.

Amselle, Jean-Loup. 1978. "La conscience paysanne: la revolte de Ouolosseboujou (juin, 1968, Mali)." *Canadian Journal of African Studies* 12:339–55.

Anstey, Roger. 1966. *King Leopold's Legacy*. London: Oxford Univ. Press.

Anstey, Roger. 1975a. "The Volume and Profitability of the British Slave Trade, 1761–

1807." In Stanley L. Engerman and Eugene D. Genovese, eds., *Race and Slavery in the Western Hemisphere: Quantitative Studies*. Princeton: Princeton Univ. Press, 33–50.

Anstey, Roger. 1975b. *The Atlantic Slave Trade and British Abolition*. Atlantic Highlands, New Jersey: Humanities Press.

Anthony, Kenneth R. M., Bruce F. Johnson, William O. Jones, and Victor C. Uchendu, eds. 1979. *Agricultural Change in Tropical Africa*. Ithaca, New York: Cornell Univ. Press.

Arrighi, Giovanni. 1973. "Labour Supplies in Historical Perspective: A Study of the Proletarianization of the African Peasantry in Rhodesia." In Giovanni Arrighi and John Saul, eds., *Essays on the Political Economy of Africa*. New York: Monthly Review Press, 180–234.

Asiwaju, A. I. 1976. "Migration as Revolt: The Example of the Ivory Coast and Upper Volta Before 1945." *Journal of African History* 17:577–94.

Atmore, A., and S. Marks. 1979. "The Imperial Factor in South Africa in the Nineteenth Century: Towards a Reassessment." *Journal of Imperial and Commonwealth History* 3:105–39.

Baier, Stephen. 1980. *An Economic History of Central Niger*. Oxford: Oxford Univ. Press.

Baran, Paul. 1957. *The Political Economy of Growth*. New York: Monthly Review Press.

Barnett, Tony. 1977. *The Gezira Scheme: An Illusion of Development*. London: Cass.

Barnet, Richard, and Ronald Müller. 1974. *Global Reach: The Power of Multinational Corporations*. New York: Simon and Schuster.

Barratt Brown, Michael. 1974. *The Economics of Imperialism*. Harmondsworth, England: Penguin.

Bates, Robert H. 1976. *Rural Responses to Industrialization: A Study of Village Zambia*. New Haven, Connecticut: Yale Univ. Press.

Bauer, Arnold. 1979. "Rural Workers in Spanish America: Problems of Peonage and Oppression." *Hispanic American Historical Review* 59:34–63.

Bauer, P. T. 1971. *Dissent on Development*. London: Weidenfeld and Nicholson.

Baylies, Carolyn. 1980. "Imperialism and Settler Capital: Friends or Foes?" *Review of African Political Economy* 18:116–26.

Bean, Richard. 1974. "A Note on the Relative Importance of Slaves and Gold in West African Exports." *Journal of African History* 15:351–56.

Beckman, Bjorn. 1976. *Organizing the Farmers: Cocoa Politics and National Development in Ghana*. Uppsala; Scandanavian Institute of African Studies.

Beckman, Bjorn. 1980. "Imperialism and Capitalist Transformation: Critique of a Kenyan Debate." *Review of African Political Economy* 19:48–62.

Beer, Christopher E. P., and Gavin Williams. 1975. "The Politics of the Ibadan Peasantry." *African Review* 5:235–56.

Beinart, William. 1982. *The Political Economy of Pondoland, 1860–1930*. Cambridge: Cambridge Univ. Press.

Bell, C. L. G. 1974. "The Political Framework." In Hollis Chenery, Montek S. Ahluwalia, C. L. G. Bell, John H. Dudley, and Richard Jolly, *Redistribution with Growth*. London: World Bank, 52–72.

Berg, Elliot. 1965. "The Development of a Labor Force in Sub-Saharan Africa." *Economic Development and Cultural Change* 13:394–412.

Berman, B. J., and J. M. Lonsdale. 1980. "Crises of Accumulation, Coercion, and the Colonial State: The Development of the Labor Control System in Kenya, 1919–1929." *Canadian Journal of African Studies* 14:37–54.

Berry, Sara. 1975. *Cocoa, Custom and Socio-Economic Change in Rural Western Nigeria*. Oxford; Oxford Univ. Press.

Berry, Sara. 1980. "Rural Class Formation in West Africa." In Robert H. Bates and Michael F. Lofchie, eds., *Agricultural Development in Africa: Issues of Public Policy*. New York: Praeger, 401–24.

Berry, Sara. 1981. "Capitalism and Underdevelopment in Africa: A Critical Essay." African Studies Center Working Paper, Boston University.

Berry, Sara. 1984. *Fathers Work for Their Sons: Accumulation, Mobility, and Class Formation in an Extended Yoruba Community*. Berkeley: Univ. of California Press.

Bernstein, Henry. 1976. "Underdevelopment and the Law of Value: A Critique of Kay." *Review of African Political Economy* 6:51–64.

Bienefeld, Manfred. 1980. "Dependency in the Eighties." *IDS Bulletin* 12, no. 1:5–10.

Biersteker, Thomas J. 1978. *Distortion or Development? Contending Perspectives on the Multinational Corporation*. Cambridge, Mass.: MIT Press.

Bonner, Philip. 1979. "The 1920 Black Mineworkers' Strike: A Preliminary Account." In Belinda Bozzoli, ed., *Labour Townships and Protest: Studies in the Social History of the Witwatersrand*. Johannesburg: Ravan, 273–97.

Bonner, Philip. 1980. "Black Trade Unions in South Africa Since World War II." In Robert M. Price and Carl G. Rosberg, eds., *The Apartheid Regime: Political Power and Racial Domination*. Berkeley: Univ. of California Press, 174–93.

Bouche, Denise. 1968. *Les villages de liberté en Afrique noire française 1887–1910*. The Hague: Mouton.

Bozzoli, Belinda. 1978. "Capital and the State in South Africa." *Review of African Political Economy* 11:40–50.

Bozzoli, Belinda. 1981. *The Political Nature of a Ruling Class: Capital and Ideology in South Africa, 1890–1933*. London: Routledge.

Braverman, Harry. 1974. *Labor and Monopoly Capital: The Degradation of Work in the Twentieth Century*. New York: Monthly Review Press.

Brenner, Robert. 1976. "Agrarian Class Structure and Economic Development in Pre-Industrial Europe." *Past and Present* 70:30–75.

Brenner, Robert. 1977. "The Origins of Capitalist Development: A Critique of Neo-Smithian Marxism." *New Left Review* 104:25–92.

Brett, E. A. 1973. *Colonialism and Underdevelopment in East Africa: The Politics of Economic Change, 1919–1939*. London: Heinemann.

Brooks, George. 1975. "Peanuts and Colonialism: Consequences of the Commercialization of Peanuts in West Africa, 1830–70." *Journal of African History* 16:29–54.

Bundy, Colin. 1979. *The Rise and Fall of the South African Peasantry*. London: Heinemann.

Burawoy, Michael. 1972. *The Colour of Class on the Copper Mines: From African*

Advancement to Zambianization. Manchester: Manchester Univ. Press.

Burawoy, Michael. 1978. "Toward a Marxist Theory of the Labor Process: Braverman and Beyond." *Politics and Society* 8:247–312.

Cain, P. J., and A. G. Hopkins. 1980. "The Political Economy of British Expansion Overseas, 1750–1914." *Economic History Review*, 2d series, 33:463–90.

Caire, Guy. 1974. "Idéologies du développement et développement de l'idéologie." *Tiers Monde* 15:5–30.

Campbell, Bonnie. 1976. "L'Idéeologie de la croissance: une analyse du Plan Quinquennal de Développement 1971–1975 de la Côte d'Ivoire." *Canadian Journal of African Studies* 10:211–33.

Campbell, Bonnie. 1978. "Ivory Coast." In John Dunn, ed., *West African States: Failure and Promise*. Cambridge: Cambridge Univ. Press, 66–116.

Cardoso, Fernando Henrique, and Enzo Falleto. 1979. *Dependency and Development in Latin America*. Trans. Marjory Mattingly Urquidi. Berkeley: Univ. of California Press. (Originally published in 1971.)

Caulk, R. A. 1978. "Armies as Predators: Soldiers and Peasants in Ethiopia c. 1850–1935." *International Journal of African Historical Studies* 11:457–93.

Cell, John W. 1980. "On the Eve of Decolonization: The Colonial Office's Plans for the Transfer of Power in Africa, 1947." *Journal of Imperial and Commonwealth History* 8:235.

Chauncey, George Jr. 1981. "The Locus of Reproduction: Women's Labour in the Zambian Copperbelt, 1927–1953." *Journal of Southern African Studies* 7:135–64.

Chauveau, Jean-Pierre, and Jacques Richard. 1977. "Une peripherie recentrée: à propos d'un système local d'économie de plantation en Côte d'Ivoire." *Cahiers d'Etudes Africaines* 17:485–523.

Chenery, Hollis, Montek S. Ahluwalia, C. L. G. Bell, John H. Dudley, and Richard Jolly. 1974. *Redistribution with Growth*. London: World Bank.

Cissoko, Sekene Mody. 1969. "Traits fondamentaux des sociétés du Soudan occidental du XVII au début du XIX' siècle." *Bulletin de l'Institut Fondamental d'Afrique Noire* 31, serie B:1–30.

Clarence-Smith, W. G. 1979. "The Myth of Uneconomic Imperialism: The Portuguese in Angola, 1836–1926." *Journal of Southern African Studies* 5:165–80.

Clayton, Anthony, and Donald Savage. 1974. *Government and Labour in Kenya, 1895–1963*. London: Cass.

Cliffe, Lionel. 1978. "Labour Migration and Peasant Differentiation: Zambian Experiences." *Journal of Peasant Studies* 5:326–46.

Cliffe, Lionel, and Richard Moorsom. 1979. "Rural Class Formation and Ecological Collapse in Botswana." *Review of African Political Economy* 15/16:35–52.

Cohen, Abner. 1969. *Custom and Politics in Urban Africa: A Study of Hausa Migrants in Yoruba Towns*. Berkeley: Univ. of California Press.

Cohen, Abner. 1971. "Cultural Strategies in the Organization of Trading Diasporas." In Claude Meillassoux, ed., *Development of Indigenous Trade and Markets in West Africa*. London: Oxford Univ. Press, 266–84.

Cohen, G. A. 1978. *Karl Marx's Theory of History*. Princeton: Princeton Univ. Press.

Cooper, Frederick. 1977. *Plantation Slavery on the East Coast of Africa*. New Haven: Yale Univ. Press.

Cooper, Frederick. 1979. "The Problem of Slavery in African Studies." *Journal of African History* 20:103–25.

Cooper, Frederick. 1980. *From Slaves to Squatters: Plantation Labor and Agriculture in Zanzibar and Coastal Kenya, 1890–1925*. New Haven: Yale Univ. Press.

Cooper, Frederick. 1981. "Peasants, Capitalists, and Historians: A Review Article." *Journal of Southern African Studies* 7:284–314.

Cooper, Frederick. 1987. *On the African Waterfront: Urban Disorder and the Transformation of Work in Colonial Mambasa*. New Haven: Yale Univ. Press.

Copans, Jean. 1980. *Les Marabouts de l'arachide*. Paris: Le Sycamore.

Coquery-Vidrovitch, Catherine. 1969. "Recherches sur un mode de production africain." *La Pensée* 144:61–78.

Coquery-Vidrovitch, Catherine. 1972. *Le Congo au temps des grandes compagnies concessionnaires, 1898–1930*. Paris: Mouton.

Coquery-Vidrovitch, Catherine. 1975. "L'Impact des intérets coloniaux: S.C.O.A. et C.F.A.O. dans l'Ouest Africain, 1910–1965." *Journal of African History* 16:595–621.

Coquery-Vidrovitch, Catherine. 1976. "La mise en dépendance de l'Afrique noire: essai de périodisation, 1800–1970." *Cahiers d'Etudes Africaines* 16:5–58.

Coquery-Vidrovitch, Catherine. 1977. "Mutation de l'imperialisme français dans les années 30." *African Economic History* 4:103–52.

Cowen, M. P. 1980. "The British State, State Enterprise, and an Indigenous Bourgeoisie in Kenya after 1945." Conference on the African Bourgeoisie. Dakar.

Cowen, M. P., and Kabiru Kinyanjui. 1976. "Some Problems of Class Formation in Kenya." Nairobi: Institute of Development Studies.

Crisp, Jeff. 1983. "Productivity and Protest: Scientific Management in the Ghanaian Gold Mines, 1947–1956." In Frederick Cooper, ed., *Struggle for the City: Migrant Labor Capital and the State in Urban Africa*. Beverly Hills: Sage, 91–130.

Cruise O'Brien, Donal. 1971a. "Cooperators and Bureaucrats: Class Formation in a Senegalese Peasant Society." *Africa* 41:263–77.

Cruise O'Brien, Donal. 1971b. *The Mourides of Senegal*. Oxford: Oxford Univ. Press.

Cruise O'Brien, Donal. 1975. *Saints and Politicians*. Cambridge: Cambridge Univ. Press.

Cruise O'Brien, Donal. 1979. "Ruling Class and Peasantry in Senegal, 1960–1976: The Politics of a Monocrop Economy." In Rita Cruise O'Brien, ed., *The Political Economy of Underdevelopment: Dependence in Senegal*. Beverly Hills: Sage, 209–27.

Crummey, Donald, and C. C. Stewart, eds. 1981. *Modes of Production in Africa: The Precolonial Era*. Beverly Hills: Sage.

Curtin, Philip D. 1969. *The Atlantic Slave Trade: A Census*. Madison: Univ. of Wisconsin Press.

Curtin, Philip D. 1975. *Economic Change in Precolonial Africa: Senegambia in the Era of the Slave Trade*. Madison: Univ. of Wisconsin Press.

Curtin, Philip D. 1979. "The African Diaspora." *Historical Reflections* 6:1–17.

Curtin, Philip D., Steven Feierman, Leonard Thompson, and Jan Vansina. 1978. *African History*. Boston: Little, Brown.

Dalton, George, ed. 1968. *Primitive Archaic and Modern Economies: Essays of Karl Polanyi*. Garden City, N.J.: Anchor.

Dalton, George. 1976. "Review of A. G. Hopkins, An Economic History of West Africa." *African Economic History* 1:51–101.

Davies, Robert H. 1979. *Capital, State, and White Labour in South Africa, 1900–1960*. Brighton, England: Harvester Press.

Davies, Robert, David Kaplan, Mike Morris, and Dan O'Meara. 1976. "Class Struggle and the Periodisation of the State in South Africa." *Review of African Political Economy* 7:430.

Davis, David Brion. 1975. *The Problem of Slavery in the Age of Revolution, 1770–1823*. Ithaca, N.Y.: Cornell Univ. Press.

De Janvry, Alain, and Frank Kramer. 1979. "The Limits of Unequal Exchange." *Review of Radical Political Economics 11*, no. 4:3–15.

Derman, William. 1973. *Serfs, Peasants, and Socialists: A Former Serf Village in the Republic of Guinea*. Berkeley: Univ. of California Press.

Denoon, Donald. 1980. "Capital and Capitalists in the Transvaal in the 1890s and 1900s." *The Historical Journal* 23:111–32.

De Wilde, John. 1967. *Experiences with Agricultural Development in Tropical Africa*. Vol. 1. *The Synthesis*. Baltimore: Johns Hopkins Univ. Press.

Drescher, Seymour. 1977. *Econocide: British Slavery in the Era of Abolition*. Pittsburgh, Pa.: Univ. of Pittsburgh Press.

Duffy, James. 1967. *A Question of Slavery: Labour Policies in Portuguese Africa and the British Protest, 1850–1920*. Cambridge, Mass.: Harvard Univ. Press.

Dumett, Raymond. 1979. "Precolonial Gold Mining and the State in the Akan Region: With a Critique of the Terray Hypothesis." *Research in Economic Anthropology* 2:37–68.

Duncan, Kenneth, and Ian Rutledge, eds. 1977. *Land and Labour in Latin America: Essays in the Development of Agrarian Capitalism in the Nineteenth and Twentieth Centuries*. Cambridge: Cambridge Univ. Press.

Edholm, Felicity, Olivia Haris, and Kate Young. 1977. "Conceptualizing Women." *Critique of Anthropology 3*, nos. 9–10:101–30.

Edwards, Richard. 1979. *Contested Terrain: The Transformation of the Workplace in the Twentieth Century*. New York: Basic Books.

Ehrlich, Cyril. 1965. "The Uganda Economy, 1903–1945." In Vincent Harlow and E. M. Chilver, eds., *History of East Africa*. Vol. 2. Oxford: Oxford Univ. Press, 395–475.

Ehrlich, Cyril. 1973. "Building and Caretaking: Economic Policy in British Tropical Africa." *Economic History Review* 26:649–67.

Eicher, Carl, and Derek Byerlee. 1972. "Rural Employment, Migration, and Economic Development: Theoretical Issues and Empirical Evidence from Africa." African Rural Employment Paper No. 1. Michigan State Univ.

Elbaum, Bernard, William Lazonick, Frank Wilkinson, and Jonathan Zeitlin. 1979.

"Symposium: The Labour Process, Market Structure, and Marxist Theory." *Cambridge Journal of Economics* 3:227–303.

Elkan, Walter. 1976. "Concepts in the Description of African Economies." *Journal of Modern African Studies* 14:691–95.

Emmanuel, Arghiri. 1972. *Unequal Exchange: A Study of the Imperialism of Trade*. Trans. Brian Pearce. New York: Monthly Review Press.

Engerman, Stanley L. 1975. "Comments on Richardson and Boulle and the 'Williams Thesis'." *Revue française d'histoire d'outre-mer* 62:331–36.

Ennew, Judith, Paul Hirst, and Keith Tribe. 1977. "Peasantry as an Economic Category." *Journal of Peasant Studies* 4:295–322.

Epstein, A. L. 1958. *Politics in an Urban African Community*. Manchester: Manchester Univ. Press.

Etherington, Norman. 1979. "Labour Supply and the Genesis of the South African Confederation in the 1870s." *Journal of African History* 20:235–53.

Etienne, Mona. 1977. "Women and Men, Cloth and Colonization: The Transformation of Production-Distribution Relations among the Baule (Ivory Coast)." *Cahiers d'Etudes Africaines* 17:41–63.

Evans, Peter. 1979. *Dependent Development: The Alliance of Multinational State and Local Capital in Brazil*. Princeton: Princeton Univ. Press.

Fabian, Johannes. 1973. "*Kazi*: Conceptualizations of Labor in a Charismatic Movement among Swahili-speaking Workers." *Cahiers d'Etudes Africaines* 13:293–325.

Fage, J. D. 1969. "Slavery and the Slave Trade in the Context of West African History." *Journal of African History* 10:393–404.

Fage, J. D. 1980. "Slaves and Society in Western Africa, c. 1445–c. 1700." *Journal of African History* 21:289–310.

Fallers, Lloyd. 1973. *Inequality: Social Stratification Reconsidered*. Chicago: Univ. of Chicago Press.

Fanon, Franz. 1965. *The Wretched of the Earth*. Trans. by Constance Farrington. New York: Grove Press.

Fei, J. D. H., and Gustav Ranis. 1964. *Development of the Labor Surplus Economy: Theory and Policy*. Homewood, Ill.: R. D. Irwin.

Fetter, Bruce. 1973. "L'Union Minière du Haut Katanga, 1920–1940: la naissance d'une sous culture totalitaire." *Cahiers de CEDAF* 6:1–40.

Fieldhouse, D. H. 1973. *Economics and Empire, 1830–1914*. London: Weidenfeld and Nicolson.

Fieldhouse, D. H. 1978. *Unilever Overseas: The Anatomy of a Multinational, 1895–1965*. London: Croom Helm.

Firth, Raymond. 1975. "The Skeptical Anthropologist: Social Anthropology and Marxist Views on Society." In Maurice Bloch, ed., *Marxist Analyses and Social Anthropology*. London: Malaby Press, 29–60.

Fogel, Robert, and Stanley Engerman. 1974. *Time on the Cross*. Boston: Little, Brown.

Ford, John. 1971. *The Role of Trypanosomiasis in African Ecology: A Study of the Tsetse Fly Problem*. Oxford: Oxford Univ. Press.

Frank, Andre Gunder. 1967. *Capitalism and Underdevelopment in Latin America*. New York: Monthly Review Press.

Frankel, S. Herbert. 1938. *Capital Investment in Africa: Its Course and Effects*. Oxford: Oxford Univ. Press.

Freund, William. 1979. "Review of Immanuel Wallerstein, *The Capitalist World Economy*" *Race and Class* 21:173–78.

Freund, William. 1981. *Capital and Labour in the Nigerian Tin Mines*. London: Longman.

Freund, William, and Robert Shenton. 1977. "Vent-for-Surplus Theory and the Economic History of West Africa." *Savanna* 6:191–96.

Freyhold, Michaella Von. 1979. *Ujamaa Villages in Tanzania*. New York: Monthly Review Press.

Friedman, Jonathan. 1978. "Crises in Theory and Transformations of the World Economy." *Review* 2:131–46.

Friedmann, Harriet. 1980. "Household Production and the National Economy: Concepts for the Analysis of Agrarian Formations." *Journal of Peasant Studies* 7:158–84.

Fröbel, Folker, Jürgen Heinrichs, and Otto Kreye. 1980. *The New International Division of Labour: Structural Unemployment in Industrialized Countries and Industrialization in Developing Countries*. Cambridge: Cambridge Univ. Press.

Furedi, Frank. 1973. "The African Crowd in Nairobi." *Journal of African History* 14:275–90.

Furedi, Frank. 1975. "The Kikuyu Squatters in the Rift Valley, 1918–29." In B. A. Ogot, ed., *Hadith 5* Nairobi: East African Literature Bureau, 177–94.

Gemery, Henry, and Jan Hogendorn. 1974. "The Atlantic Slave Trade: A Tentative Economic Model." *Journal of African History* 15:223 46.

Gemery, Henry, and Jan Hogendorn. 1979. "The Economic Costs of West African Participation in the Atlantic Slave Trade: A Preliminary Sampling for the Eighteenth Century." In Henry Gemery and Jan Hogendorn, eds., *The Uncommon Market: Essays in the Economic History of the Atlantic Slave Trade*. New York: Academic Press, 143–61.

Girvan, Norman. 1973. "The Development of Dependency Economics in the Caribbean and Latin America: Review and Comparison." *Social and Economic Studies* 22:1–33.

Godelier, Maurice. 1972. *Rationality and Irrationality in Economics*. Trans. Brian Pearce. New York: Monthly Review Press.

Godelier, Maurice. 1975. "Modes of Production, Kinship, and Demographic Structures." In Maurice Bloch, ed., *Marxist Analyses and Social Anthropology*. London: Malaby Press, 3–28.

Godelier, Maurice. 1977. *Perspectives in Marxist Anthropology*. Trans. Robert Brain. Cambridge: Cambridge Univ. Press.

Godfrey, Martin. 1978. "Prospects for a Basic Needs Strategy: The Case of Kenya." *IDS Bulletin* 9:41–44.

Godfrey, Martin. 1980. "Editorial: Is Dependency Dead?" *IDS Bulletin 12*, no. 1:1–4.

Goodfriend, Douglas E. 1979. "*Plus ça change, plus c'est la même chose*: The Dilemma of the French Structural Marxists." In Stanley Diamond, ed., *Toward a Marxist Anthropology: Problems and Perspectives*. The Hague: Mouton, 93–124.

Goody, Jack. 1971. *Technology, Tradition, and the State in Africa*. London: Oxford Univ. Press.

Goody, Jack. 1978. "Population and Polity in the Voltaic Region." In J. Friedman and M. J. Rowlands, eds., *The Evolution of Social Systems*. Pittsburgh: Univ. of Pittsburgh Press, 417–29.

Gran, Guy, ed. 1979. *Zaire: The Political Economy of Underdevelopment*. New York: Praeger.

Gray, Richard, and David Birmingham, eds. 1970. *Precolonial African Trade*. Oxford: Oxford Univ. Press.

Greenberg, Stanley. 1980. *Race and State in Capitalist Development*. New Haven, Conn.: Yale Univ. Press.

Grillo, R. D. 1974. *Race, Class, and Militancy: An African Trade Union, 1939–1965*. New York: Chandler.

Groff, David. 1980. "The Development of Capitalism in the Ivory Coast: The Case of Assikasso, 1880–1940." Ph.D. diss. Stanford Univ.

Gutkind, Peter C. W. 1967. "The Energy of Despair: Social Organization of the Unemployed in Two African Cities." *Civilizations* 17:186–211, 380–402.

Guy, Jeff. 1979. *The Destruction of the Zulu Kingdom*. London: Longman.

Guyer, Jane. 1978. "The Food Economy and French Colonial Rule in Central Cameroun." *Journal of African History* 19:577–97.

Guyer, Jane. 1979. "The Depression and the Administration in South-Central Cameroun." Paper for American Historical Association.

Guyer, Jane. 1980. "Food, Cocoa, and the Division of Labour by Sex in Two West African Societies." *Comparative Studies in Society and History* 22:355–73.

Guyer, Jane. 1981. "Household and Community." *African Studies Review* 24, nos. 2–3:87–138.

Hargreaves, John. 1979. *The End of Colonial Rule in West Africa*. London: Macmillan.

Harms, Robert. 1975. "The End of Red Rubber: A Reassessment." *Journal of African History* 16:73–88.

Harris, John, and Michael P. Todaro. 1970. "Migration, Unemployment, and Development: A Two-Sector Analysis." *American Economic Review* 60:126–42.

Hart, Keith. 1976. "The Politics of Unemployment in Ghana." *African Affairs* 75:488–97.

Hart, Keith. 1978. "The Economic Basis of Tallensi Social History in the Early Twentieth Century." *Research in Economic Anthropology* 1:185–216.

Hay, Douglas, Peter Linebaugh, John Rule, E. P. Thompson, and Cal Winslow. 1975. *Albion's Fatal Tree*. New York: Pantheon.

Hay, Margaret Jean. 1976. "Luo Women and Economic Change During the Colonial Period." In Nancy Hafkin and Edna Bay, eds., *Women in Africa*. Stanford, Calif.: Stanford Univ. Press, 87–110.

Heisler, Helmuth. 1974. *Urbanization and the Government of Migration: The Inter-Relation of Urban and Rural Life in Zambia*. New York: St. Martin's Press.

Hemson, David. 1977. "Dock Workers, Labour Circulation, and Class Struggles in Durban, 1940–59." *Journal of Southern African Studies* 4:88–124.

Hill, Frances. 1977. "Experiments with a Public Sector Peasantry: Agricultural Schemes and Class Formation in Africa." *African Studies Review* 20:25–42.

Hill, Polly. 1963. *Migrant Cocoa Farmers of Southern Ghana*. Cambridge: Cambridge Univ. Press.

Hill, Polly. 1970. *Studies in Rural Capitalism in West Africa*. Cambridge: Cambridge Univ. Press.

Hill, Polly. 1972. *A Village and a Setting*. Cambridge: Cambridge Univ. Press.

Hindess, Barry, and Paul Q. Hirst. 1975. *Pre-Capitalist Modes of Production*. London: Routledge.

Hobsbawm, Eric. 1964. *Labouring Men*. London: Weidenfeld and Nicolson.

Hogendorn, J. S. 1975. "Economic Initiative and African Cash Farming: Pre-Colonial Origins and Early Colonial Developments." In Peter Duignan and L. H. Gann, eds., *Colonialism in Africa, 1870–1960*. Vol. 4. *The Economics of Colonialism*. Cambridge: Cambridge Univ. Press, 283–328.

Hogendorn, J. S., and K. M. Scott. 1983. "The Economics of the East African Groundnut Scheme." In Robert Rotberg, ed., *Imperialism, Colonialism, and Hunger*. Lexington, Mass.: Lexington Books, 167–98.

Hopkins, A. G. 1968. "Economic Imperialism in West Africa: Lagos, 1880–92." *Economic History Review* 21:580–600.

Hopkins, A. G. 1972. "Rejoinder to J. F. A. Ajayi and R. A. Austen." *Economic History Review* 25:307–12.

Hopkins, A. G. 1973. *An Economic History of West Africa*. London: Longman.

Hopkins, A. G. 1976a. "Clio-Antics: A Horoscope for African Economic History." In Christopher Fyfe, ed., *African Studies Since 1945: A Tribute to Basil Davidson*. London: Longman, 31–47.

Hopkins, A. G. 1976b. "Imperial Business in Africa. Part II: Interpretations." *Journal of African History* 17:267–90.

Hopkins, A. G. 1976c. "Reply to George Dalton." *African Economic History* 2:81–83.

Hopkins, A. G. 1980. "Property Rights and Empire Building: Britain's Annexation of Lagos, 1861." *Journal of Economic History* 40:777–98.

Horner, Dudley, and Alide Kooy. 1980. "Conflict on South African Mines, 1972–1979." Univ. of Cape Town, Southern Africa Labour and Development Research Unit Working Paper No. 29.

Howe, Gary N., and Alan M. Sica. 1980. "Political Economy, Imperialism, and the Problem of World-System Theory." *Current Perspectives in Social Theory* 1:235–86.

Hrbek, Ivan. 1968. "Towards a Periodisation of African History." In T. O. Ranger, ed., *Emerging Themes in African History*. Nairobi: East African Literature Bureau, 35–52.

Hyam, Ronald. 1976. *Britain's Imperial Century, 1815–1914: A Study of Empire and Expansion*. London: Batsford.

Hyden, Goran. 1980. *Beyond Ujamaa in Tanzania: Underdevelopment and an Uncaptured Peasantry*. Berkeley: Univ. of California Press.

Hynes, William G. 1979. *The Economics of Empire: Britain, Africa, and the New Imperialism, 1870–95*. London: Longman.

Igbafe, Philip Aigbona. 1979. *Benin Under British Administration*. Atlantic Highlands, N.J.: Humanities Press.

Iliffe, John. 1975. "The Creation of Group Consciousness: A History of the Dockworker of Dar es Salaam." In Richard Sandbrook and Robin Cohen, eds., *The Development of an African Working Class*. London: Longman, 49–72.

Iliffe, John. 1979. *A Modern History of Tanganyika*. Cambridge: Cambridge Univ. Press.

Institute for Industrial Education. 1974. *The Durban Strikes, 1973*. Durban: Institute for Industrial Education.

International Labour Office. 1976. *Employment Growth and Basic Needs: A One-World Problem. Report of the Director-General of the International Labour Office*. Geneva: International Labour Office.

Isaacman, Allen. 1976. *The Tradition of Resistance in Mozambique*. Berkeley: Univ. of California Press.

Isaacman, Allen. 1978. "Transforming Mozambique's Rural Economy." *Issue* 8, no. 1:17–24.

Isaacman, Allen, et al. 1980. " 'Cotton is the Mother of Poverty': Peasant Resistance Against Forced Cotton Cultivation in Mozambique, 1938–1961." *International Journal of African Historical Studies* 13:581–615.

Jeffries, Richard. 1978. *Class, Power, and Ideology in Ghana: The Railwaymen of Sekondi*. Cambridge: Cambridge Univ. Press.

Jewsiewicki, Bogumil. 1977. "Unequal Development: Capitalism and the Katanga Economy, 1919–40." In Robin Palmer and Neil Parsons, eds., *The Roots of Rural Poverty in Central and Southern Africa*. London: Heinemann, 317–45.

Johnson, Marion. 1974. "Cotton Imperialism in West Africa." *African Affairs* 73:178–87.

Johnson, R. W. 1978. "Guinea." In John Dunn, ed., *West African States: Failure and Promise*. Cambridge: Cambridge Univ. Press, 37–65.

Johnston, Bruce, and Peter Kilby. 1975. *Agriculture and Structural Transformation: Economic Strategies in Late-Developing Countries*. New York: Oxford Univ. Press.

Johnstone, Frederick. 1976. *Class, Race, and Gold*. London: Routledge.

Joseph, Richard A. 1974. "Settlers, Strikers, and Sans-Travail: The Douala Riots on September 1945." *Journal of African History* 15:669–87.

Joseph, Richard A. 1980. "Theories of the African Bourgeoisie: An Exploration." Conference on the African Bourgeoisie. Dakar.

Kahn, Joel S., and Josep R. Llobera. 1980. "French Marxist Anthropology: Twenty Years After." *Journal of Peasant Studies* 8:81–100.

Kaplinsky, Rafael. 1980. "Capitalist Accumulation in the Periphery—The Kenyan Case Re-Examined." *Review of African Political Economy* 17:83–105.

Kaplinsky, Rafael, J. S. Henley, and Colin Leys. 1980. "Debates." *Review of African Political Economy* 17:83–113.

Kaplow, Susan B. 1977. "The Mudfish and the Crocodile: Underdevelopment of a West African Bourgeoisie." *Science and Society* 41:317–33.

Katz, Freidrich. 1974. "Labor Conditions on Haciendas in Porfirian Mexico: Some Trends and Tendencies." *Hispanic American Historical Review* 54:1–47.

Katzenellenbogen, S. E. 1973. *Railways and the Copper Mines of Katanga*. Oxford: Oxford Univ. Press.

Kay, Geoffrey. 1975. *Development and Underdevelopment: A Marxist Analysis*. London: Macmillan.

Kea, Ray. 1986. "The 'Laboring Classes' in 17th- and 18th-Century Gold Coast States:

A Note on the Political Economy of Pre-Capitalist Social Labor." In Donald Crummey, ed., *Banditry, Rebellion, and Social Protest in Africa*. London: James Currey.

Keegan, Tim. 1979. "The Restructuring of Agrarian Class Relations in a Colonial Economy: The Orange River Colony, 1902–1910." *Journal of Southern African Studies* 5:234–54.

Killick, Tony. 1980. "Trends in Development Economics and Their Relevance to Africa." *Journal of Modern African Studies* 18:367–86.

Kitching, Gavin. 1980. *Class and Economic Change in Kenya: The Making of an African Petite-Bourgeoisie*. New Haven, Conn.: Yale Univ. Press.

Klein, Martin A. 1968. *Islam and Imperialism in Senegal: Sine-Saloum, 1847–1914*. Stanford, Calif.: Stanford Univ. Press.

Klein, Martin A. 1973. "Social and Economic Factors in the Muslim Revolution in Senegambia." *Journal of African History* 13:419–41.

Klein, Martin A., ed. 1980. *Peasants in Africa*. Beverly Hills: Sage.

Klein, Martin A., and Paul E. Lovejoy. 1979. "Slavery in West Africa." In Henry Gemery and Jan Hogendorn, eds., *The Uncommon Market: Essays in the Economic History of the Atlantic Slave Trade*. New York: Academic Press, 181–235.

Kraus, Jon. 1980. "The Political Economy of Conflict in Ghana." *Africa Report* 25 (March–April):9–16.

Kubicek, Robert V. 1979. *Economic Imperialism in Theory and Practice: The Case of South African Gold Mining Finance, 1886–1914*. Durham, N.C.: Duke Univ. Press.

Laclau, Ernesto. 1971. "Feudalism and Capitalism in Latin America." *New Left Review* 67:19 38.

Lamb, Geoff. 1974. *Peasant Politics*. Lewes, England: Julian Friedmann.

Langdon, Steven. 1977. "The State and Capitalism in Kenya." *Review of African Political Economy* 8:90–98.

Langdon, Steven. 1979. "Multinational Corporations and the State in Africa." In Jose J. Villamil, ed., *Transnational Capital and National Development*. Hassocks, England: Harvester, 223–40.

Langdon, Steven. 1987. "Industry and Capitalism in Kenya: Contributions to a Debate." In Paul Lubeck, ed., *The African Bourgeoisie*. Boulder, Colo.: L. Rienner, 343–82.

Langdon, Steven, and Lynn T. Mytelka. 1979. "Africa in the Changing World Economy." In Colin Legum, William Zartman, Steven Langdon, and Lynn Mytelka, *Africa in the 1980s: A Continent in Crisis*. New York: McGraw Hill, 165–91.

Latin American Perspectives. 1978. Nos. 5, 3 & 4.

Latin American Perspectives. 1979. Nos. 6, 2 & 3.

Law, Robin. 1977a. "Royal Monopoly and Private enterprise in the Atlantic Trade: The Case of Dahomey." *Journal of African History* 18:555–77.

Law, Robin. 1977b. *The Oyo Empire c. 1600–c. 1836*. Oxford: Oxford Univ. Press.

Lee, J. M. 1967. *Colonial Development and Good Government: A Study of the Ideas Expressed by the British Official Classes in Planning Decolonization, 1939–1964*. Oxford: Oxford Univ. Press.

Lele, Uma. 1975. *The Design of Rural Development: Lessons from Africa*. Baltimore: Johns Hopkins Univ. Press.

Leo, Christopher. 1978. "The Failure of the 'Progressive Farmer' in Kenya's Million-Acre Settlement Scheme." *Journal of Modern African Studies* 16:619–38.

Levine, Andrew, and Erik Olin Wright. 1980. "Rationality and Class Struggle." *New Left Review* 123:47–68.

Lewis, W. Arthur. 1954. "Economic Development with Unlimited Supplies of Labour." *The Manchester School* 22:139–91.

Lewis, W. Arthur. 1958. "Unlimited Labour: Further Notes." *The Manchester School* 26:1–32.

Lewis, W. Arthur. 1970. "The Export Stimulus." In W. Arthur Lewis, ed., *Tropical Development, 1880–1913: Studies in Economic Progress*. London: Allen & Unwin, 13–45.

Leys, Colin. 1974. *Underdevelopment in Kenya: The Political Economy of Neo-Colonialism*. Berkeley: Univ. of California Press.

Leys, Colin. 1975. "The Politics of Redistribution with Growth: The 'Target Group' Approach." *IDS Bulletin* 7, no. 2:48.

Leys, Colin. 1978. "Capital Accumulation, Class Formation, and Dependency—The Significance of the Kenyan Case." In Ralph Miliband and John Seville, eds., *The Socialist Register, 1978*. London: Monthly Review Press, 241–66.

Lloyd, Trevor. 1972. "Africa and Hobson's Imperialism." *Past and Present* 55:130–53.

Lodge, Tom. 1981. "The Destruction of Sophiatown." *Journal of Modern African Studies* 18:107–32.

Lonsdale, John. 1981. "State and Social Processes in Africa: A Historiographical Survey." *African Studies Review* 24, nos. 2–3:132–226.

Lonsdale, John, and Bruce Berman. 1979. "Coping with the Contradictions: The Development of the Colonial State in Kenya." *Journal of African History* 20:487–506.

Lovejoy, Paul E. 1979. "The Characteristics of Plantations in the Nineteenth-Century Sokoto Caliphate (Islamic West Africa)." *American Historical Review* 84:1267–92.

Lovejoy, Paul E. 1980. "Kola in the History of West Africa." *Cahiers d'Etudes Africaines* 20:97–134.

Low, D. A., and John Lonsdale. 1976. "Introduction." In *The Oxford History of East Africa*. Vol. 3. Oxford: Oxford Univ. Press, 1–64.

Mackintosh, M. 1977. "Reproduction and Patriarchy: A Critique of Meillassoux, *Femmes, Greniers, et Capitaux*." *Capital and Class* 2:119–27.

Mamdani, Mahmood. 1976. *Politics and Class Formation in Uganda*. New York: Monthly Review Press.

Mandel, Ernest. 1975. *Late Capitalism*. Trans. Joris De Bres. London: New Left Books.

Manning, Patrick. 1974. "Analyzing the Costs and Benefits of Colonialism." *African Economic History Review* 1, no. 2:15–22.

Manning, Patrick. 1981. "The Enslavement of Africans: A Demographic Model." *Canadian Journal of African Studies* 15:449–526.

Mansasu, Bismarck U., and Cranford Pratt. 1979. *Toward Socialism in Tanzania*. Toronto: Univ. of Toronto Press.

Marglin, Stephen. 1974. "What Do Bosses Do? The Origins and Functions of Hierarchy in Capitalist Production." *Review of Radical Political Economy* 6, no. 2:33–60.

Marks, Shula, and Stanley Trapido. 1979. "Lord Milner and the South African State." *History Workshop Journal* 8:50–80.

Martinez-Alier, Juan. 1977. *Haciendas, Plantations, and Collective Farms*. London: Cass.

Marx, Karl. 1967. *Capital*. Vol. 1. Trans. Samuel Moore and Edward Aveling. New York: International Publishers.

Mayer, Philip, ed. 1980. *Black Villagers in an Industrial Society: Anthropological Perspectives on Labour Migration in South Africa*. Cape Town: Oxford Univ. Press.

Meier, Gerald M. 1975. "External Trade and Internal Development." In Peter Duignan and L. H. Gann, eds., *Colonialism in Africa, 1870–1960*. Vol. 4. *The Economics of Colonialism*. Cambridge: Cambridge Univ. Press, 427–69.

Meier, Gerald M. 1976. *Leading Issues in Economic Development*. 3d ed. New York: Oxford Univ. Press.

Meilink, H. A. 1978. "Some Economic Interpretations of Migration." *African Perspectives* 1:51–66.

Mcillassoux, Claude. 1960. "Essai d'interpretation du phenomène économique dans les sociétés traditionelles d'autosubsistence." *Cahiers d'Etudes Africaines* 4:38–67.

Meillassoux, Claude. 1964. *Anthropologie économique des Gouro de Côte d'Ivoire*. Paris: Mouton.

Meillassoux, Claude. 1968. "Ostentation, destruction, reproduction." *Economies et Sociétés* 2:460–72.

Meillassoux, Claude, ed. 1971. *The Development of Indigenous Trade and Markets in West Africa*. London: Oxford Univ. Press.

Meillassoux, Claude, ed. 1975a. *L'Esclavage en Afrique pré-coloniale*. Paris: Maspero.

Meillassoux, Claude. 1975b. *Femmes, greniers, et capitaux*. Paris: Maspero.

Meillassoux, Claude. 1978. "Role de l'esclavage dans l'histoire de l'Afrique occidentale." *Anthropologie et Sociétés* 2:117–48.

Mendelsohn, Richard. 1980. "Blainey and the Jameson Raid: The Debate Renewed." *Journal of Southern African Studies* 6:157–70.

Miers, Suzanne. 1975. *Britain and the Ending of the Slave Trade*. New York: Holmes and Meier.

Miller, Joseph C. 1989. *Way of Death: Merchant Capitalism and the Angolan Slave Trade, 1730–1830*. Madison: Univ. of Wisconsin Press.

Mintz, Sidney. 1974. *Caribbean Transformations*. Chicago: Univ. of Chicago Press.

Moore, Barrington, Jr. 1966. *The Social Origins of Dictatorship and Democracy: Lord and Peasant in the Making of the Modern World*. Boston: Beacon.

Moorsom, Richard. 1977. "Underdevelopment, Contract Labour, and Worker Consciousness in Namibia, 1915–72." *Journal of Southern African Studies* 4:52–87.

Morris, M. L. 1976. "The Development of Capitalism in South African Agriculture: Class Struggle in the Countryside." *Economy and Society* 5:292–343.

Mouzelis, Nicos. 1980. "Modernization, Underdevelopment, Uneven Development: Prospects for a Theory of Third World Formations." *Journal of Peasant Studies* 7:353–74.

Munro, J. Forbes. 1975. *Colonial Rule and the Kamba: Social Change in the Kenya Highlands, 1889–1939*. Oxford: Oxford Univ. Press.

Munro, J. Forbes. 1976. *Africa and the International Economy, 1800–1960*. London: J. M. Dent.

Murray, Colin. 1978. "Migration, Differentiation, and the Developmental Cycle in Lesotho." *African Perspectives* 1:127–44.

Nafziger, Wayne E. 1976. "A Critique of Development Economics in the U.S." *Journal of Development Studies* 13:18–34.

Nell, Edward J. 1979. "Population Pressure and Methods of Cultivation: A Critique of Classless Theory." In Stanley Diamond, ed., *Toward a Marxist Anthropology: Problems and Perspectives*. The Hague: Mouton, 457–68.

Newbury, C. W., and A. S. Kanya-Forstner. 1969. "French Policy and the Origins of the Scramble for West Africa." *Journal of African History* 10:260–75.

Newbury, M. Catherine. 1980. "Ubureetua and Thangata: Catalysts to Peasant Political Consciousness in Rwanda and Malawi." *Canadian Journal of African Studies* 14:97–111.

Njonjo, Apolo. 1977. "The Africanization of the White Highlands." Ph.D. diss. Princeton Univ.

Northrup, David. 1976. "The Compatibility of the Slave and Palm Oil Trades in the Bight of Biafra." *Journal of African History* 17:353–64.

Northrup, David. 1978. *Trade Without Rulers: Pre-Colonial Economic Development in Southern-Eastern Nigeria*. Oxford: Oxford Univ. Press.

Northrup, David. 1979. "Nineteenth-Century Patterns of Slavery and Economic Growth in Nigeria." *International Journal of African Historical Studies* 17:1–16.

Oculi, Okello. 1987. "Green Capitalism in Nigeria." In Paul Lubeck, *The African Bourgeoisie*. Boulder, Colo.: L. Rienner, 167–89.

O'Laughlin, Bridget. 1977. "Production and Reproduction: Meillassoux's *Femmes, Greniers et Capitaux*." *Critique of Anthropology* 2, no. 8:3–33.

Olivier, Jean-Pierre. 1975. "Afrique: Qui exploite qui?" *Les Temps Modernes* 346:1506–51; 347:1744–75.

O'Meara, Dan. 1975. "The 1946 African Mine Workers' Strike and the Political Economy of South Africa." *Journal of Commonwealth and Comparative Politics* 13:146–73.

Owen, Roger, and Robert Sutcliffe, eds. 1972. *Studies in the Theory of Imperialism*. London: Longman.

Oyemakinde, Wale. 1975. "The Nigerian General Strike of 1945." *Journal of the Historical Society of Nigeria* 7:693–710.

Paige, Jeffrey. 1975. *Agrarian Revolution: Social Movements and Export Agriculture in the Underdeveloped World*. New York: Free Press.

Palmer, Robin, and Neil Parsons, eds. 1977. *The Roots of Rural Poverty in Central and Southern Africa*. London: Heinemann.

Parkin, David. 1972. *Palms, Wine, and Witnesses*. London: Intertext.

Parpart, Jane. 1983. *Labour and Capital on the African Copperbelt*. Philadelphia: Temple Univ. Press.

Patterson, Orlando. 1977. "The Structural Origins of Slavery: A Critique of the Nieboer-Domar Hypothesis from a Comparative Perspective." In Vera Rubin and

Arthur Tuden, eds., *Comparative Perspectives on Slavery in New World Plantation Societies*. New York: New York Academy of Sciences, 12–34.

Patterson, Orlando. 1979. "On Slavery and Slave Formations." *New Left Review* 117:31–68.

Peace, Adrian. 1979. *Choice, Class, and Conflict: A Study of Nigerian Factory Workers*. Brighton, England: Harvester Press.

Pedler, Frederick. 1974. *The Lion and the Unicorn in Africa: A History of the Origins of the UAC, 1787–1931*. London: Heinemann.

Peel, J. D. Y. 1978. "*Olaju*: A Yoruba Concept of Development." *Journal of Development Studies* 14:139–65.

Peel, J. D. Y. 1980. "Inequality and Action: The Forms of Ijesha Social Conflict." *Canadian Journal of African Studies* 14:473–502.

Peemans, Jean-Philippe. 1975. "Capital Accumulation in the Congo Under Colonialism: The Role of the State." In Peter Duignan and L. H. Gann, eds., *Colonialism in Africa: 1870–1960*. Vol. 4. *The Economics of Colonialism*. Cambridge: Cambridge Univ. Press, 165–212.

Peil, Margaret. 1972. *The Ghanaian Factory Worker: Industrial Man in Africa*. Cambridge: Cambridge Univ. Press.

Penvenne, Jeanne. 1979. "The Streetcorner Press: Worker Intelligence Networks in Lourenco Marques, 1900–1902." Boston Univ. African Studies Center Working Paper No. 26. Boston.

Perrings, Charles. 1979. *Black Mineworkers in Central Africa: Industrial Strategies and the Evolution of an African Proletariat in the Copperbelt, 1911–41*. London: Heinemann.

Petras, James. 1978. *Critical Perspectives on Imperialism and Social Class in the Third World*. New York: Monthly Review Press.

Pinto, Anibal, and Jan Knakal. 1973. "The Centre-Periphery System Twenty Years Later." *Social and Economic Studies* 22:34–95.

Piore, Michael J. 1979. *Birds of Passage: Migrant Labor and Industrial Societies*. Cambridge: Cambridge Univ. Press.

Polanyi, Karl. 1944. *The Great Transformation*. New York: Rinehart.

Polanyi, Karl. 1966. *Dahomey and the Slave Trade*. Seattle: Univ. of Washington Press.

Pollet, Eric, and Grace Winter. 1968. "L'organisation sociale du travail agricole chez les Sonninke (Diahuru, Mali)." *Cahiers d'Etudes Africaines* 8:509–34.

Portes, Alejandro. 1978. "Migration and Underdevelopment." *Politics and Society* 8:1–48.

Posnansky, Merrick. 1980. "Necessity Is the Mother of Invention in Ghana." African Studies Association paper.

Post, Ken. 1972. " 'Peasantization' and Rural, Political Movements in Western Africa." *Archives Européenes de Sociologie* 13:223–54.

Prebisch, Raul. 1971. *Change and Development in Latin America: The Great Task*. New York: Praeger.

Priestley, Margaret. 1969. *West African Trade and Coast Society: A Family Study*. London: Oxford Univ. Press.

Proctor, André. 1979. "Class Struggle, Segregation, and the City: A History of Sophia-town, 1905–40." In Belinda Bozzoli, ed., *Labour, Townships, and Protest: Studies in the Social History of the Witwatersrand*. Johannesburg: Ravan, 49–89.

Przeworsky, Adam. 1977. "Proletariat into a Class: The Process of Class Formation from Karl Kautsky's *The Class Struggle* to Recent Controversies." *Politics and Society* 7:343–401.

Ranger, T. O., ed. 1968. *Emerging Themes in African History*. Nairobi: East African Literature Bureau.

Ranger, T. O. 1976. "Towards a Usable African Past." In Christopher Fyfe, ed., *African Studies Since 1945: A Tribute to Basil Davidson*. London: Longman, 17–30.

Ranger, T. O. 1978. "Growing from the Roots: Reflections on Peasant Research in Central and Southern Africa." *Journal of South African Studies* 5:99–133.

Ransom, Roger, and Richard Sutch. 1978. *One Kind of Freedom: The Economics of Emancipation*. Cambridge: Cambridge Univ. Press.

Rathbone, Richard. 1978. "Ghana." In John Dunn, ed., *West African States: Failure and Promise*. Cambridge: Cambridge Univ. Press, 22–35.

Rennie, J. K. 1978. "White Farmers, Black Tenants, and Landlord Legislation: Southern Rhodesia, 1890–1930." *Journal of Southern African Studies* 5:86–98.

Revue Francaise d'Histoire d'Outre-Mer 1976. Vol. 63.

Rey, Pierre-Philippe. 1971. *Colonialisme, néo-colonialisme, et transition au capitalisme*. Paris: Maspero.

Rey, Pierre-Philippe. 1973. *Les alliances de classes*. Paris: Maspero.

Rey, Pierre-Philippe. 1976. "Introduction théorique." In Pierre-Philippe Rey, ed., *Capitalisme négrier: la marche des paysans vers le prolétariat*. Paris: Maspero, 41–67.

Rhodie, Sam. 1968. "The Gold Coast Cocoa Hold-up of 1930–31." *Transactions of the Historical Society of Ghana* 9:105–18.

Richardson, David. 1978. "West African Consumption Patterns and Their Influence on the Eighteenth-Century English Slave Trade." In Henry Gemery and Jan Hogendorn, eds., *The Uncommon Market: Essays in the Economic History of the Atlantic Slave Trade*. New York: Academic Press, 303–30.

Rimmer, Douglas. 1979. "Some Origins of Development Economics." *IDS Bulletin* 10, no. 4:33–37.

Roberts, Richard. 1980. "Production and Reproduction in Warrior States: Segu Bambara and Segu Tokolor, c. 1712–1890." *International Journal of African Historical Studies* 13:389–419.

Roberts, Richard. 1984. "Women's Work, and Women's Property: Household Social Relations in the Maraka Textile Industry in the Nineteenth Century." *Comparative Studies in Society and History* 26:229–50.

Roberts, Richard, and Martin A. Klein. 1980. "The Banamba Slave Exodus of 1905 and the Decline of Slavery in the Western Sudan." *Journal of African History* 21:375–94.

Robinson, Ronald. 1972. "Non-European Foundations of European Imperialism: Sketch for a Theory of Collaboration." In Roger Owen and Robert Sutcliffe, eds., *Studies in the Theory of Imperialism*. London: Longman, 117–42.

Robinson, Ronald, and John Gallagher. 1961. *Africa and the Victorians*. New York: St. Martin's Press.

Rodney, Walter. 1966. "African Slavery and Other Forms of Social Oppression on the Upper Guinea Coast in the Context of the Atlantic Slave Trade." *Journal of African History* 7:431–43.

Rodney, Walter. 1969. "Gold and Slaves on the Gold Coast." *Transactions of the Historical Society of Ghana* 10:13–28.

Rodney, Walter. 1972. *How Europe Underdeveloped Africa*. London: Bogle-L'Ouverture.

Rosberg, Carl G., and Thomas M. Callaghy, eds., 1979. *Socialism in Sub-Saharan Africa: A New Assessment*. Berkeley: Univ. of California Press.

Ross, William McGregor. 1968. *Kenya from Within*. London: Cass (orig. pub. 1927).

Roxborough, Ian. 1979. *Theories of Underdevelopment*. London: Macmillan.

Sabot, R. H. 1979. *Economic Development and Urban Migration: Tanzania, 1900–1971*. Oxford: Oxford Univ. Press.

Sadler, A. W. 1979. "Birds in the Cornfield: Squatter Movements in Johannesburg, 1944–1947." *Journal of Southern African Studies* 6:92–123.

Sahlins, Marshall. 1976. *Culture and Practical Reason*. Chicago: Univ. of Chicago Press.

Samoff, Joel. 1980. "Underdevelopment and Its Grass Roots in Africa." *Canadian Journal of African Studies* 14:5–36.

Sandbrook, Richard. 1977. "The Political Potential of African Urban Workers." *Canadian Journal of African Studies* 11:411–33.

Sandbrook, Richard, and Robin Cohen, eds., 1975. *The Development of an African Working Class*. London: Longman.

Saul, John. 1975. "The 'Labour Aristocracy' Thesis Reconsidered." In Richard Sandbrook and Robin Cohen, eds., *The Development of an African Working Class*. London: Longman, 303–10.

Saul, John. 1976. "The Unsteady State: Uganda, Obote, and General Amin." *Review of African Political Economy* 5:12–38.

Schatz, Sayre. 1977. *Nigerian Capitalism*. Berkeley: Univ. of California Press.

Schatzberg, Michael G. 1980. *Politics and Class in Zaire: Bureaucracy, Business, and Beer in Lisala*. New York: Africana.

Schultz, Theodore W. 1964. *Transforming Traditional Agriculture*. New Haven, Conn.: Yale Univ. Press.

Seddon, David, ed. 1978. *Relations of Production: Marxist Approaches to Economic Anthropology*. Trans. Helen Lackner. London: Cass.

Seers, Dudley. 1979a. "The Meaning of Development." In David Lehmann, ed., *Development Theory: Four Critical Case Studies*. London: Cass, 9–30.

Seers, Dudley. 1979b. "The Birth, Life, and Death of Development Economics." *Development and Change* 10:707–19.

Semmel, Bernard. 1960. *Imperialism and Social Reform*. Cambridge, Mass.: Harvard Univ. Press.

Shanin, Theodor. 1979. "Defining Peasants: Conceptualizations and Deconceptualizations Old and New in a Marxist Debate." *Peasant Studies* 8:38–60.

Shaw, Timothy, and Orbola Fasehun. 1981. "Nigeria in the World System: Alternative Approaches, Explanations, and Projections." *Journal of Modern African Studies* 18:551–74.

Sheriff, Abdul M. H. 1987. *Slaves, Spies, and Ivory in Zanzibar*. London: James Currey.

Simkins, Charles. 1981. "Agricultural Production in the African Reserves." *Journal of Southern African Studies* 7:256–83.

Sklar, Richard. 1975. *Corporate Power in an African State*. Berkeley: Univ. of California Press.

Sklar, Richard. 1976. "Postimperialism: A Class Analysis of Multinational Corporate Expansion." *Comparative Politics* 9:75–92.

Sklar, Richard. 1979. "The Nature of Class Domination in Africa." *Journal of Modern African Studies* 17:531–52.

Skocpol, Theda. 1977. "Wallerstein's World Capitalist System: A Theoretical and Historical Critique." *American Journal of Sociology* 82:1075–90.

Skocpol, Theda. 1979. *States and Social Revolutions*. Cambridge: Cambridge Univ. Press.

Slater, Henry. 1980. "The Changing Pattern of Economic Relationships in Rural Natal, 1838–1914." In Shula Marks and Anthony Atmore, eds., *Economy and Society in Pre-Industrial South Africa*. London: Longman, 148–70.

Smith, Sheila. 1980. "The Ideas of Samir Amin: Theory or Tautology?" *Journal of Development Studies* 17:5–21.

Sorrenson, M. P. K. 1967. *Land Reform in Kikuyu Country*. Nairobi: Oxford Univ. Press.

Southall, Roger J. 1978. "Farmers, Traders, and Brokers in the Gold Coast Coco Economy." *Canadian Journal of African Studies* 12:185–211.

Standing, Guy. 1981. "Migration and Modes of Exploitation: Social Origins of Immobility and Mobility." *Journal of Peasant Studies* 8:173–211.

Staniland, Martin. 1981. "The Underdevelopment of Political Economy." Center for International Affairs, Working Paper No. 32. Los Angeles: Univ. of California—Los Angeles.

Stedman-Jones, Gareth. 1971. *Outcast London: A Study of the Relationship between Classes in Victorian Society*. Oxford: Oxford Univ. Press.

Stedman-Jones, Gareth. 1973–74. "Working-Class Culture and Working-Class Politics in London, 1870–1900: Notes on the Remaking of a Working Class." *Journal of Social History* 7:460–508.

Stichter, Sharon. 1976–77. "Imperialism and the Rise of a 'Labor Aristocracy' in Kenya, 1945–1970." *Berkeley Journal of Sociology* 21:157–78.

Stichter, Sharon. 1978. "Trade Unionism in Kenya, 1947–1952: The Militant Phase." In Peter C. W. Gutkind, Robin Cohen, and Jean Copans, eds., *African Labor History*. Beverly Hills: Sage, 155–74.

Sunkel, Oswaldo. 1973. "Transnational Capitalism and National Disintegration in Latin America." *Social and Economic Studies* 22:132–76.

Suret-Canale, Jean. 1964. "Les sociétés traditionelles en Afrique noire et le concept du mode de production asiatique." *La Pensée* 177:19–22.

Suret-Canale, Jean. 1971. *French Colonialism in Tropical Africa, 1900–1945*. Trans. Till Goltheiner. London: Hurst.

Suret-Canale, Jean. 1972. *Afrique Noire: De la colonisation aux indépendances, 1945–1960*. Paris: Editions Sociales.

Suret-Canale, Jean. 1978. "The French West African Railway Workers' Strike, 1947–48." In Peter C. W. Gutkind, Robin Cohen, and Jean Copans, eds., *African Labor History*. Beverly Hills: Sage, 129–54.

Swainson, Nicola. 1980. *The Development of Corporate Capitalism in Kenya, 1918–1977*. Berkeley: Univ. of California Press.

Swanson, Maynard. 1977. "The Sanitation Syndrome: Bubonic Plague and Urban Native Policy in the Cape Colony, 1900–1909." *Journal of African History* 18:387–410.

Taylor, John G. 1979. *From Modernization to Modes of Production: A Critique of the Sociologies of Development and Underdevelopment*. London: Macmillan.

Terray, Emmanuel. 1972. *Marxism and "Primitive" Societies: Two Studies*. Trans. Mary Klopper. New York: Monthly Review Press.

Terray, Emmanuel. 1974. "Long Distance Exchange and the Formation of the State: The Case of the Abron Kingdom of Gyaman." *Economy and Society* 3:315–45.

Terray, Emmanuel. 1975. "La captivité dans le royaume abron du Gyaman." In Claude Meillassoux, ed., 1975a.

Thomas, Clive. 1974. *Dependence and Transformation: The Economics of the Transition to Socialism*. New York: Monthly Review Press.

Thomas, Robert, and Richard Bean. 1974. "The Fishers of Men: The Profits of the Slave Trade." *Journal of Economic History* 34:885–914.

Thompson, E. P. 1963. *The Making of the English Working Class*. New York: Vintage.

Thompson, E. P. 1975. *Whigs and Hunters: The Origins of the Black Act*. New York: Pantheon.

Thompson, E. P. 1978. *The Poverty of Theory and Other Essays*. New York: Monthly Review Press.

Thornton, A. W. 1959. *The Imperial Idea and Its Enemies*. London: Macmillan.

Thornton, John. 1980. "The Slave Trade in Eighteenth Century Angola: Effects on Demographic Structure." *Canadian Journal of African Studies* 14:417–29.

Thornton, Stephen. 1978. "European Entrepreneurs and the Exploitation of African Labour in Bulawayo, 1935–1953." Paper for African Studies Association of the United Kingdom Conference.

Tinker, Hugh. 1974. *A New System of Slavery: The Export of Indian Labour Overseas, 1830–1920*. London: Oxford Univ. Press.

Todaro, Michael P. 1976. *Internal Migration in Developing Countries*. Geneva: International Labour Office.

Tosh, John. 1980. "The Cash-Crop Revolution in Tropical Africa: An Agricultural Reappraisal." *African Affairs* 79:79–94.

Trapido, Stanley. 1971. "South Africa in a Comparative Study of Industrialization." *Journal of Development Studies* 7:309–20.

Trapido, Stanley. 1978. "Landlord and Tenant in a Colonial Economy: The Transvaal, 1880–1910." *Journal of Southern African Studies* 5:26–58.

Trapido, Stanley. 1980a. " 'The Friends of the Natives': Merchants, Peasants, and the Political and Ideological Structure of Liberalism in the Cape, 1854–1910." In Shula

Marks and Anthony Atmore, eds., *Economy and Society in Pre-Industrial South Africa*. London: Longman, 247–74.

Trapido, Stanley. 1980b. "Reflections on Land, Office, and Wealth in the South African Republic, 1850–1900." In Shula Marks and Anthony Atmore, eds., *Economy and Society in Pre-Industrial South Africa*. London: Longman, 350–68.

Ulrich-Wehler, Hans. 1972. "Industrial Growth and Early German Imperialism." In Roger Owen and Robert Sutcliffe (eds.) *Studies in the Theory of Imperialism*. London: Longman, 71–92.

Vail, Leroy. 1976. "Ecology and History: The Example of Eastern Zambia." *Journal of Southern African Studies* 3:129–55.

Vail, Leroy. 1977. "Railway Development and Colonial Underdevelopment: The Nyasaland Case." In Robin Palmer and Neil Parsons, eds., 1977.

Vail, Leroy, and Lendeg White. 1978. "Tawani, Machambero!: Forced Cotton and Rice Growing on the Zambezi." *Journal of African History* 19:239–63.

Vail, Leroy, and Leudeg White. 1980. *Capitalism and Colonialism in Mozambique: A Study of Quelimane District*. Minneapolis: Univ. of Minnesota Press.

Van Hekken, P. M., and H. U. E. Thoden Van Velzen. 1972. *Land Scarcity and Rural Inequality in Tanzania*. The Hague: Mouton.

Van Onselen, Charles. 1975. "Black Workers in Central African Industry: A Critical Essay on the Historiography and Sociology of Rhodesia." *Journal of Southern African Studies* 1:228–46.

Van Onselen, Charles. 1976a. "Randlords and Rotgut, 1886–1903: An Essay on the Role of Alcohol in the Development of European Imperialism and Southern African Capitalism." *History Workshop Journal* 2:33–89.

Van Onselen, Charles. 1976b. *Chibaro: African Mine Labor in Southern Rhodesia, 1900–1933*. London: Pluto.

Van Onselen, Charles. 1982. *Studies in the Social and Economic History of the Witwatersrand 1886–1914*. London: Longman.

Vernon, Raymond. 1977. *Storm over the Multinationals: The Real Issues*. Cambridge, Mass.: Harvard Univ. Press.

Voll, Sarah Potts. 1980. *A Plough in Field Arable: Western Agribusiness in Third World Agriculture*. Hanover, N.H.: Univ. Press of New England.

Wallerstein, Immanuel. 1973. "Africa in a Capitalist World." *Issue 3*, no. 3:1–11.

Wallerstein, Immanuel. 1974. *The Modern World System*. Vol. 1. New York: Academic Press.

Wallerstein, Immanuel. 1976. "The Three Stages of African Involvement in the World-Economy." In Peter C. W. Gutkind and Immanuel Wallerstein, eds., *The Political Economy of Contemporary Africa*. Beverly Hills: Sage, 30–57.

Wallerstein, Immanuel. 1979. *The Capitalist World Economy*. Cambridge: Cambridge Univ. Press.

Wallerstein, Immanuel, and William G. Martin. 1979. "Peripheralization of Southern Africa II: Changes in Household Structure and Labor Force Formation." *Review* 3:193–207.

Wallman, Sandra, ed. 1979. *Social Anthropology of Work*. London: Academic Press.

Warren, Bill. 1980. *Imperialism: Pioneer of Capitalism*. London: New Left Books.

Wasserman, Gary. 1976. *Politics of Decolonization: Kenya Europeans and the Land Issue, 1960 65*. Cambridge: Cambridge Univ. Press.

Watts, Michael. 1987. "Peasantry, Merchant Capital, and the Colonial State: Class in Northern Nigeria, 1900–1945." In Paul Lubeck (ed.), *The African Bourgeoisie*. Boulder, Colo.: L. Rienner, 59–96.

Webster, David. 1978. "Migrant Labour, Social Formations, and the Proletarianization of the Chopi of Southern Mozambique." *African Perspectives* 1:157–76.

Weeks, John. 1971a. "Wage Policy and the Colonial Legacy—A Comparative Study." *Journal of Modern African Studies* 9:361–97.

Weeks, John. 1971b. "The Political Economy of Labor Transfer." *Science and Society* 35:463–80.

Weeks, John. 1977. "Backwardness, Foreign Capital, and Accumulation in the Manufacturing Sector of Peru, 1954–1975." *Latin American Perspectives* 4:124–45.

Weiskel, Timothy. 1979. "Labor in the Emergent Periphery: From Slavery to Migrant Labor Among the Baule Peoples, 1880–1925." In Walter Goldfrank, ed., *The World-System of Capitalism: Past and Present*. Beverly Hills: Sage, 207–33.

Weiskel, Timothy. 1980. *French Colonial Rule and the Baule Peoples: Resistance and Collaboration, 1889–1911*. Oxford: Oxford Univ. Press.

West, Henry W. 1972. *Land Policy in Buganda*. Cambridge: Cambridge Univ. Press.

White, Luise. 1990. *The Comforts of Home: Prostitution in Colonial Nairobi*. Chicago: Univ. of Chicago Press.

Wilkinson, Peter. 1981. "A Place to Live: The Resolution of the African Housing Crisis in Johannesburg, 1944–1954." University of Witwatersrand, African Studies Seminar Paper, 27 July 1981. Johannesburg.

Wilks, Ivor. 1975. *Asante in the Nineteenth Century*. Cambridge: Cambridge Univ. Press.

Wilks, Ivor. 1978. "Land, Labour, Capital, and the Forest Kingdom of Asante: A Model of Early Change," pp. 487–534 in J. Friedman and M. J. Rowlands (eds.) *The Evolution of Social Systems*. Pittsburgh, Penn.: Univ. of Pittsburgh Press.

Wilks, Ivor. 1979. "The Golden Stool and the Elephant Tail: An Essay on Wealth in Asante." *Research in Economic Anthropology* 2:1–36.

Williams, Gavin. 1976. "There Is No Theory of Petit-Bourgeois Politics." *Review of African Political Economy* 6:84–89.

Williams, Gavin, and Terisa Turner. 1978. "Nigeria." In John Dunn, ed., *West African States: Failure and Promise*. Cambridge: Cambridge Univ. Press, 132–72.

Wilson, F. B. 1944. "Emergency Food Production in Zanzibar." *East Africa Agricultural Journal* 10:93–100.

Wilson, Francis. 1980. "Current Labor Issues in South Africa." In Robert M. Price and Carl G. Rosberg, eds., *The Apartheid Regime: Political Power and Racial Domination*. Berkeley: Univ. of California Press, 152–73.

Wolf, Eric R. 1981. "The Mills of Inequality: A Marxian Approach." In Gerald D. Berreman, ed., *Social Inequality: Comparative and Developmental Approaches*. New York: Academic Press, 41–57.

Wolff, Richard. 1974. *The Economics of Colonialism: Britain and Kenya, 1870–1930*. New Haven, Conn.: Yale Univ. Press.

Wolpe, Harold. 1972. "Capitalism and Cheap Labour Power in South Africa: From Segregation to Apartheid." *Economy and Society* 1:425–56.

Worger, William. 1983. "Workers as Criminals: The Rule of Law in Early Kimberley." In Frederick Cooper, ed., *Struggle for the City: Migrant Labor, Capital, and the State in Urban Africa*. Beverly Hills: Sage, 51–90.

Wright, Marcia. 1975. "Women in Peril: A Commentary on the Life Stories of Captives in Nineteenth-Century East-Central Africa." *African Social Research* 20:800–19.

Wrigley, C. C. 1959. *Crops and Wealth in Uganda*. Kampala: East African Institute of Social Research.

Wrigley, C. C. 1971. "Historicism in Africa: Slavery and State Formation." *African Affairs* 70:113–24.

Yudelman, David. 1975. "Industrialization, Race Relations, and Change in South Africa." *African Affairs* 74:82–96.

Yudelman, David. 1983. *The Emergence of Modern South Africa*. Westport, Conn.: Greenwood Press.

Zarwan, John. 1976. "Indian Businessmen in Kenya: A Case Study." Ph.D. diss. Yale University.

Postscript: Africa and the World Economy

The preceding paper was written a decade ago—it is the earliest of the essays collected here—and it stands as part of its times. Like the studies of the 1960s and 1970s on the agrarian question in Latin America, my essay reflects on and itself reflects a phase in the evolution of scholarship on Africa. Not incidentally, in volume alone the output of the years stressed in my essay represents a significant fraction of all Africanist scholarship that has ever been published. Those were the years not only of intense excitement in Africanist scholarship, but of going beyond sheer fascination with the dynamics of a newly independent group of nations towards a focus on critical and thorny problems of analysis.

Those two decades began with determined efforts by Africanist and African scholars to assert that Africa had a history, social forms, and political patterns that deserved to be taken seriously in their own right; they ended with a trend toward incorporating Africa into global discussions. The 1970s was a time when Africanists were thinking a lot about grand theory, and were focusing particularly on structuralist approaches. This was the honeymoon period in the marriage of French structuralism and Marxism, and concepts such as the articulation of modes of production opened up a fruitful way in which local pictures could be incorporated into global tableaux. This was a welcome trend when it opened up the question of local-regional-continental-global connections. But when that question was treated as an answer—when evocation of a "peripheral social formation" defined the nature of a social process—these approaches could lead to a sterile determinism. That certainly was a tendency, although far from the only one, in Marxist scholarship at the time, while the insistence of some researchers working within the world-system or dependency frameworks that the only relevant level of analysis was the global one lent itself to endless recasting of highly abstract formulations rather than to serious work on bits of the puzzle. On the other hand, the claim of neoclassical economists that Africans' behavior could be explained simply by the assumption that they were responding rationally to market incentives seemed radical in the early 1970s—vis-à-vis widely held assumptions that Africans had "culture" while westerners had "incentives"—but seemed rather simplistic by the end, as the multiple meanings of rationality and the multiple structures that mediated between individuals and markets proved as revealing as the market model itself.

What stands out in the scholarship of the 1970s, however, is how much the global claims forced place-centered social scientists to think, at least, about broader contexts, and how the explosion of local-level research made possible a serious engagement with theory on a variety of fronts. Researchers did not have to get stuck at any one level of analysis.

Claims to exclusive control of theoretical high ground were being made then, and they still are: neoclassical economists still make claims to the universality of their models, and rational-choice theorists have extended these models into other domains of social life, while at the same time postmodernists (at least some of them) deny the validity of any claims to universality at all, and see the world as a kaleidoscope of shifting discourses. These two viewpoints, in their pure forms, deserve each other. The continual crossing of levels—engagement with the nitty-gritty of experience and the sharp edge of theory—has not outlived its usefulness.

What has another decade of experience, research, and debate signified? Too much has happened to answer that question in a thorough way.[1] What follows is personal and impressionistic, but does serve to make a basic point: that analyses of political economy are themselves part of the world. The categories which social analysts impose on the world create their own realities, as much as theoretical fashions reflect the shifting terms in which power is contested in and among states.

The most important changes occurred not in academia but in Africa. The 1980s were a period of crisis, at its most extreme in massive starvation in places like the Sudan and Mozambique, but extending to pervasive failures of infrastructure, of industrial and commercial enterprises, and of agricultural output for both internal and export markets, while many states have accumulated vast external debts without increasing political and economic capacities. Many African countries have had negative real growth rates during the 1980s, and these have lasted far too long to be considered anything less than a major structural problem. Still, the nature of the problem or problems is not uncontroversial. Sara Berry (1984) has pointed out that the global diagnoses rely on official statistics which, whatever their claims, in practice reflect *marketed* production, or more specifically production marketed through formal channels. As Janet MacGaffey (1987) has shown in relation to Zaire, the "second" economy of an African state may well be larger and more vital than the first, and the use of official statistics for diagnostic or remedial purposes may bear (for better or worse) only a limited connection to realities experienced by most citizens. When one of the most fundamental questions is precisely the relationship of local-level economic activity to the formal structures of state or major private enterprises, methods of measurement may themselves define the problem which international agencies set out to solve. No one, however, denies the reality of famine in, for example, the Sudan, nor should anyone try to romanticize a reincarnated economy of subsistence production and local exchange networks hidden from state scrutiny. But if one is to understand *how* as well as to what extent African producers are failing to advance production, one cannot assume that the world of state statistics and formal markets is coterminous with the world of African farmers.

Then comes the question of explanation. All too many commentators on Africa, particularly but not exclusively journalists, have taken to what might be called "Africa bashing." The focus is most often on African governments. They stand accused of corruption, incompetence, and an urge to self-aggrandizement that stifles any initiative not directly controlled by the state. Implicit in much Africa bashing is a comparison with Asia—particularly with South Korea, Singapore, Taiwan, Hong Kong, Malaysia, and Thailand. Without a coherent explanation for what about Africa gives rise to the syndrome of oppressiveness and economic mismanagement, Africa bashing sometimes sounds like the resurrection of the myth of the backward African of an older era.[2]

The experience of the 1980s in fact offers few positive models for any theoretical school. The self-styled socialist regimes of Africa do not exactly provide an antidote to the disillusioning collapse of socialist regimes in Europe. The impoverishment of, for example, Mozambique is admittedly overdetermined—by externally sponsored guerilla movements even more than by the state of the world economy—but in the final analysis such regimes have not demonstrated that a form of economic organization can be found which simultaneously produces enough of a surplus for the projects of a socialist state and is perceived by the cultivators as nonexploitative.

On the other hand, the two nations whose profarmer, proexport market policies have been most enthusiastically applauded by the free marketeers have lost much of their luster in recent years. The Ivory Coast "miracle" now appears quite unmiraculous—based on temporarily favorable export markets, the sale of nonrenewable resources like hardwoods, and on the same ponderous alliances of state and multinational enterprises that have elsewhere fostered spurts of economic growth without creating a web of internal linkages capable of sustaining and deepening that growth. The depression in the ivorien economy recently led to civil unrest that underscores the thin veneer of stable political and economic structures in an export-oriented regime. The case for Kenyan "exceptionalism" has also weakened, not so much because of any dramatic crisis in production as because of the political side of political economy: the increasingly exposed fragility of the state, which like other governments has not been able to follow a consistent "liberal" strategy of fostering economic initiative, but allocates productive resources to build up political friends and prevent the emergence of rivals, while repressing any debate over the nature and consequences of this allocative process. Robert Bates, a leading critic of antifarmer policies in many African states for whom Kenya was a crucial counterexample, has himself pointed to the convergence of Kenya's political economy with that of its neighbors (1989:149).

The experiences of the past decade thus pose serious and still contested problems of analysis, and each school of thought discussed in the original paper has had a divergence of responses, without any one of them abandoning its home territory. Perhaps the most dramatic development of the period has been the resurgence of what I referred to as *purism of the market,* to a large extent at the expense of more interventionist variants of orthodox development economics. The process is not just of academic interest. The World Bank's Structural Adjustment Program and the International Monetary Fund's conditions for lending money to African governments unable to pay their foreign-exchange bills have been exercises of international economic power that have given many African governments little choice but to surrender many of the key tenets of an approach to economic development which stressed planning and state intervention. The Bank and especially the I.M.F. have insisted that governments who wished to use their facilities should drastically reduce the size of their bureaucracies, scale back social programs—often including health and education—loosen currency controls, privatize state enterprises, and strip away government policies intended to privilege national investors and restrict foreign economic penetration. Behind such imposed policies is the contention that if African governments pull back and allow market signals to "get prices right," the invisible hand will do a far better job of allocating resources for development than has the visible and heavy hand of state bureaucrats. The record of the last decades lends this argument considerable plausibility, at least from the negative side, and market purism has had impressive intellectual and financial power behind it.

Making such arguments, at least at this level of generality, also requires unlearning some of the most valuable lessons of research in recent decades. The market purists are in effect comparing African governments as they actually are—with all their corruptions and incompetences—with the market as an abstraction. But African cultivators never have made and never will make their decisions in the face of "the market"—they confront markets. These markets are themselves historically and socially constructed, and an enormous amount of research on rural Africa has shown how deeply rooted in complex social processes both innovations and limitations in processes of production and commercialization have been. The African cultivator is not an acultural responder to price signals, but exists within social structures as well as normative systems. How productive resources are allocated in an agricultural community— particularly when the commodization of land and labor is not a given but a contested issue—cannot be taken for granted, and people's access to subsistence and other consumption goods is allocated as well through a variety of social mechanisms. Changing them, as was the case in the development of capitalism in Europe, entails the redefinition of moral community and moral obligations. And power over people and resources is not exerted by state bureaucrats alone.

In various parts of the world, groups gaining control over resources like land do not just prosper by mobilizing productive resources, but by restricting the access of others to them.[3]

In addition, capitalist development, as experienced in England or South Korea, has always been a complex social and institutional process in which states have played vital roles, and in this sense a Structural Adjustment Policy could have a negative effect on the process it is intended to promote. Dismantling educational and health programs that promote productivity and stability among workers is not obviously of positive benefit to capitalist development, and the conditions that gave rise to a more socially aware conception of development under late colonial rule in the 1940s have not necessarily become irrelevant now. These comments neither defend the status quo in most African states nor deny the possibility that new entrepreneurial energies could in fact be liberated in much of Africa, but they do emphasize that the debate over such issues should focus on concrete social and economic processes in Africa and not center on the false opposition of sullied states and pristine markets.[4]

It should not be assumed that development economics has been taken over entirely by the purists. The development industry remains a vast one, applying varied approaches and theories, and much of it remains highly interventionist. The World Bank—having swung through redistribution with growth, accelerated development, and structural adjustment since the early 1970s—moved its 1990 report toward a variant on human capital approaches, pronouncing in favor of supporting basic services, such as health, that would sustain, at least minimally, and make more readily useful in the world economy Africa's most painfully obvious resource: cheap labor. Then in 1991 it pronounced in favor of a "market-friendly" approach in which market-dominated economy appeared as the ultimate end but not the only means (World Bank 1990, 1991). Meanwhile, some market-minded scholars have been trying to convince their even more market-minded fellows that institutions, historically determined, shape the nature of markets; this work leads at times to interesting convergences with the radical branch of political economy.[5]

The increasing misery of much of Africa would come as no surprise to a dependency theorist: such is the fate of the periphery in the world economy, and piecemeal attempts to break out of this structural position are doomed to failure. Nor would the tendency of African governments to safeguard their prerogatives as gatekeepers between producers and the world economy—trying to hold off the I.M.F.'s assault but ultimately capitulating rather than breaking with the outside forces on which the elite depends—be inconsistent with dependency theory. As such, dependency theory seems to offer the kind of systemic explanation of African governments' "errors" that the market purists could not. Dependency theory's difficulties have come elsewhere in the "periphery," in Asia most notably. Without a set of prior criteria that would indicate why one part of the periphery can escape and another cannot, the power of dependency theory's predictions may come from the unfailing accuracy of circular reasoning.[6] It is not clear that the kind of self-critical and creative theoretical work within (and beyond) dependency theory that has gone on in Latin America (and which is alluded to by Steve Stern in this volume) has taken place in Africa, or at least produced new theoretical breakthroughs.[7] Perhaps a return to the roots of dependency theory in the structural economics of post–World War II Latin America, and its more recent developments, might be particularly salutary, allowing a focus on the dynamic relationship between local and regional structures and global patterns of capital flow, on the structures of multinational corporations and international institutions, and on the blockages—as well as the openings—within the system of global exchange in an era of rapid movement of finance and information. Certainly, the global dimension remains understudied empirically: we know more about rituals of power among the Ndembu than we do about the way in which an organization like the World Bank articulates its hegemony and maintains coherence among its own personnel.

What has become hardest to defend about dependency and related theories is the contention that the poverty of the periphery can be explained by its functionality to the world system as a whole. It is even less clear in 1990 than it was in 1980 that Africa's poverty serves any useful function to global capitalism: Africa could be a far more reliable source of raw materials and a source of a larger mass of surplus value than it is. Africa's poverty and the nature of its labor systems may keep the costs of labor and of peasant-grown commodities down, but it means that a vast potential of productive power, on a world level, goes untapped. As I argued earlier, the frustrations of would-be exploiters, local and overseas, with the difficulties of tapping Africa's labor power runs through its history. As kings, colonialists, and multinational corporations have learned, Africa's spaces and Africa's social structures have offered powerful means of resistance to control over labor, and the external orientation of African economies is as much a consequence as a cause of the standoffs that repeatedly have taken place in the struggles over the control of work inside Africa. But the significance of the labor of Africa (or any other part of the world) to capitalist development is historically variable, and over the long run Africans have had to face the consequence of how hard they have been to exploit. Ralph Austen has recently written (1987) an interpretation of African economic history hinged around the irony that as Africa has become more and more involved in and responsive to global economic trends, its labor and its products have become decreasingly important to the world economy.

If one does not accept the simple argument that Africa is poor because world capitalism requires it to be poor, one confronts the question Paul Richards draws out of an argument like mine about the elusiveness of African labor power. African populations, he contends, are poor and isolated, but relatively self-reliant; colonial and postcolonial development policies were frustrated by the self-reliance as much as the poverty. But, Richards asks (1985:16), could not "inventive self-reliance" be turned into a resource for economic growth rather than an obstacle to economic control? Dependency theorists on the international level, analysts from Bates (1983) to Bayart (1989) on the state level, have explained why neither local elites nor external aid agencies see things that way. But Africa's own inventiveness—the energy devoted to making something out of very little, to finding new uses and new meanings for local resources and imported goods and practices—remains the least-tried approach to economic advance. The theorists have not proven that it is an impossible one.

Marxists these days—with good reason—are probably more likely than most to admit that new theoretical departures are in order. Whether such a process will be creative or paralyzing remains to be seen. Some scholars now identify themselves as post-Marxists, both in the sense of having moved on and in the sense of having moved via the Marxist texts. This is part of a still wider trend among critical schools toward "post-something" scholarship: we have the post-structuralists and the postmodernists as well as the post-Marxists. Some of this is posturing: such a self-designation turns confusion into a claim to have gone beyond the major intellectual currents of our time. But these "posts" do retain a connection with the old Marxism that is valuable and which distinguishes itself from the more certain orthodoxies of neoclassical economics and dependency theory, namely a conviction that the basic categories for analyzing economic life (the market, the commodity) are themselves historically and socially constructed. This is true of class and capital as well, and problematizing those categories—stripping them of their universalistic and mechanistic properties—is both threatening and revealing to Marxist analysis. Indeed, this development in theoretical debate takes back to Europe a set of arguments that had been going on in regard to Africa: the extent to which categories like class or processes like proletarianization impose an external and misleading framework on the divisions and dynamics of African societies. The issue now appears less as another version of the thesis that Africa is an exotic place where Western rules do not apply than as a more general one of whether the privileging of, say, the category of class over the category of gender, in European history as much as in African, is a fruitful starting assumption at all (see for example Laclau and Mouffe 1985; Scott 1988). Some might think that once such sacred premises are questioned, the entire Marxist theoretical edifice—or indeed any overarching theoretical construction—will fall. Nonetheless, the development of capitalism is an historical phenomenon that has to be confronted, and the consequences of the commoditization of land and labor need to be worked out theoretically and historically. This territory may need to be remapped, but the problem which Marx made his life's work is not about to go away.

The opening up of such questions has had a significant, and salutary, effect on research. This is too vast an area to review here, but one basic issue illustrates the importance of asking different sorts of questions: gender. At the time of my original paper, feminist critics of structuralist Marxism were pointing out that assuming, for example, the existence a lineage mode of production under patriarchal control naturalized male domination and failed to probe how gender was constituted and how identity and power were defined and contested. Gender was a basic category of analysis in some of the ground-level studies of farming systems and household structure in rural Africa that were characteristic of the 1970s (reviewed in Guyer 1981), and in a few pioneering works on urban Africa (Strobel 1979). Since then, a number of scholars have been showing that thinking in terms of gender does not simply add one more story to an otherwise unchanged narrative but forces a rethinking of basic social questions. As simple an observation as the fact that most slaves exported from Africa were male and most retained within Africa were female affects the way we should write about slavery, about demography, about the changing meanings of maleness and femaleness in social relations (Robertson and Klein 1983). Studies such as those of Elias Mandala (1990) and Elizabeth Schmidt (1992) show the importance of struggles between men and women over access to resources and the fruits of labor both before and after colonization. Mandala, for example, locates female subordination not in some kind of aboriginal patriarchy but in the differential vulnerability of women in the era of the slave trade; many women later regained better control over the production process and its fruits in a period of cash-crop production; and they become increasingly vulnerable in new ways when crop production and marketing faltered and male labor migration became a vital support for households. Meanwhile, Luise White (1990) shows how women helped to shape the social order of colonial cities. Prostitutes helped to provide sexual and other services to an overwhelmingly male migrant labor force, and some pioneered house ownership among Africans. At crucial moments, their ambiguous presence set off debates among colonial officials and African males about the nature of property, respectability, and class. In the capital city—from which male political authority cast its gaze outward—lay a physical and symbolic space which officials convinced themselves they had to reconquer (see also Stoler 1989).

To a significant extent, the 1970s fashion for studies in political economy has not so much been replaced but broadened to include an analysis of power in a different sense. Quite a few scholars on the left have jumped from Marx to Foucault, from commoditization to texts, from political economy to literary criticism. There is new interest in seeing how, for example, colonial regimes, symbolically and discursively, imposed a grid of power over Africa—putting Africans into boxes in census forms and categories in ethnographic surveys, thereby defining the African "Other" and simultaneously the modernism of the colonial enterprise itself (Mudimbe 1988; Cooper and Stoler 1989; Rabinow 1989). There have been polemics of late between the Foucauldians and the Marxists, some of theoretical interest, most turning complementary perspectives into hegemonic claims and counterclaims. But is there anything in this trend toward cultural and linguistic analysis that is relevant to the "dismal science" which was the subject of this essay?

Let me answer that by an illustration concerning the most basic political and economic issue of the 1980s and 1990s: development. James Ferguson's recent study (1990) of development projects in Lesotho ties together the political and symbolic effects of the worldwide development effort with the limitations of its economic effects on the ground. Development agencies, he shows, define the object of their intervention as aboriginal poverty, as bringing Africans "virtually untouched by modern economic development" (Ferguson 1990:25) into commercial relations and providing for them the materiel and knowledge needed to participate in a market economy. Applied to Lesotho—surrounded by South Africa—the argument is absurd: its poverty is anything but aboriginal, its people anything but inexperienced in a monetized economy but trapped for the last century in South Africa's version of economic development. But even if the developers know better, they cannot say so, for their access to such countries depends on defining themselves as apolitical technocrats, doing a job that no fair-minded person could legitimately oppose. The effects of defining the problem this way were not limited to the prefaces of development plans: the concrete projects were designed to integrate farmers and cattle-raisers into commercial circuits, not to find ways in which returned labor migrants could save their remittances more effectively or to find how women, who generally did not migrate, could gain more secure access to resources. Solving a problem which existed in their own world but not in the world of Lesotho, the projects predictably failed. But their very failure reinforced the idea that Lesotho's people were backward and hapless, all the more in need of intervention from wise outsiders. In Lesotho, the foreign technocrats and the bureaucrats of the national government often had divergent interests, but they could find an area of overlap in which defining development problems as technical and amenable to action by reenforcing state institutions. The development process, then, did not alleviate poverty, as was its stated goal, or make Africans more exploitable within the world economy, as some critics allege. Nationally and internationally, however, it deepened the disempowerment of the large majority of the African population, defining them politically and ideologically as people whom someone else needed to develop.

This kind of analysis (see also Feierman 1990) does not, unlike much work in the postmodernist mold, leave discourses interacting only with other discourses, but simultaneously studies discourse and the exercise of economic and political power, at international, national, and regional levels. Nor does it claim that power is everywhere, as Foucault tends to do, but sees power in quite particular sites. Ferguson analyzes a set of institutions and ideologies which are unable to accomplish goals they themselves defined, but which nonetheless reinforce a political structure.

Perhaps in the 1990s the study of the development of development—examining the origins and multiple meanings of this elusive and critical concept—will get the kind of attention which the development of underdevelopment received in the 1970s. The study of underdevelopment—from its critics as well as its advocates—had in its very choice of vocabulary a tendency to give an aura of normality to the pattern of development which Africa supposedly fell *under*. The process of defining development as the ultimate goal on a political agenda—within an African state or at an international level—lends an aura of power to certain models of the future and excludes others from consideration.[8]

The historian cannot help but react to the current controversies over development policies with a sense of *déja vu,* and to see such recent approaches as Structural Adjustment less as new solutions than as a phase in an alternation between planned interventions intended to get at the social bases of poverty and more laissez-faire policies, each of whose failures and contradictions leads to the next cycle. Development became an explicit policy of colonial regimes a half-century ago, at a time when imperial powers were anxious to convince themselves and the rest of the world—including the West Indian and African workers whose strikes and riots in the 1930s and 1940s had shaken imperial self-confidence—that colonialism was a force for positive economic and social change in the postwar era. The failure of developmentalist intervention by African states so often invoked in the 1980s is not new either: my reading in British and French archives in the early and mid-1950s suggests that officials were admitting to themselves the failure of their ambitious and highly touted development drives of the late 1940s. They ran up simultaneously against the complexity of transforming African systems of production to align them with European conceptions of science and rationality (cf. Adas 1989) and against the failure of European and American private investment to follow public investment, as planners expected it would.[9] By the early 1950s, colonial regimes were retrenching on plans that had come nowhere close to being fulfilled and distancing themselves politically from the consequences of failure. They in effect bequeathed to their African successors a set of problems—and a set of expectations—whose consequences they themselves could not face.

Those failures of the 1950s followed in turn from the failure—explicitly and repeatedly acknowledged in England and France by the 1940s—of economic policies that relied on European and African entrepreneurs and markets to turn the "imperial estates" of the colonial powers into predictably productive parts of empire. After the strike wave of the late 1930s and 1940s, officials in Great Britain and later in France, admitted that market-centered approaches had not provided a basis for meeting Africans' material needs, but nonetheless had dangerous social consequences within the narrow channels of communication and the islands of production, which was what they had to show for the previous half century of rule. Colonial officials despaired that the ragtag army of the partially employed would ever constitute the productive and orderly cultivators and workers the postwar world needed. They thought that the way in which labor-power—in wage labor or smallholder agriculture—was reproduced affected the way it produced and the kinds of political problems it raised.

African leaders of the 1960s had little reason to think that a return to the conditions of the prewar era would be a step toward progress (Cooper 1987). However self-serving the economic policies of postcolonial governments, it is not apparent that on this basic point they were wrong. Nor in today's painful economic and social circumstances is it obviously helpful for debates over possible policies to take the form of one side which cries "urban bias" and advocates government withdrawal from influencing wages and food prices, and another which assumes that any move against current entitlements constitutes class warfare of the rich against the poor. It would be more constructive to analyze actual conditions of production and reproduction in the concrete conditions in which people live and production takes place.[10]

Whether a market-centered strategy, or any other development strategy, will have more consistently beneficial effects on output and welfare than past attempts remains to be seen. Many advocates of "getting prices right" are far from optimistic about the net effect this will have.[11] A cold analysis of possibilities in the world market for African commodities would not necessarily have much hope to offer, and meanwhile the effect of decimating government services is not obviously going to be to promote the institutional basis for capitalist development. As in the interventionist branches of the development industry, however, the purists of the market are engaged in a moral discourse. They turn around an international discussion in which critical voices claimed the moral high ground and in which multinational corporations and developed states— or, more abstractly, the very structure of a capitalist world economy—stood accused of impoverishing Africa, and place the blame squarely on African governments, on socialist ideals run amok, and on misconceived interventionist policies of Western liberals. They hold Africa to a universal standard: the optimizing effects of the market. And should it become possible within these terms to claim plausibly that world markets are reasonably open, the poverty of Burkina Faso or Uganda becomes an unfortunate fact but not an injustice.[12]

In these pages I have emphasized the ideological and political meanings of economic action: the devising, implementation, and failure of development plans have as much effect on relations of power and moral discourse as on investment levels, exchange rates, and debt rescheduling. Ten years ago I put more emphasis on the other side of the coin, on the political determinants of economic action: the African producer makes choices in regard to planting crops, investing, and consumption in social world and a world of power, within a local community, within a region, within a nation, and within global structures, all affecting each other. In both regards, the most fundamental questions remain open and contested. We are now in an era when disillusionment with the results of decolonization is a commonplace, when the well-known models for economic progress offer meager hope to Africa, and when the very terms in which moving Africa out of its current morass is discussed seem to reproduce its powerlessness. We need, in this situation, to regain a sense of the specificity in which change takes place and the variety of paths to the future which Africans imagine for themselves. We also need to understand how powerful are the constraints within the world as it exists today, not only on economic behavior, but on the range of ideas which enter the arena of political debate.

Notes to Postscript

I am grateful to Carol Heim, Florencia Mallon, and Steve Stern for comments on an earlier draft of this postscript.

1 I have updated the paper itself in only one way: changing references to unpublished or forthcoming work that has since come forth. I have also cut a number of notes for the sake of simplification. I have refrained from referring to new research even when it better illustrates, or contradicts, points made in the original essay.

2 In some regards, the indictments of African governments coming from the right coincide with those coming from the left, notably corruption and a tendency to devote resources to promoting narrow class interests rather than using them for more socially constructive ones. The left (in its various guises) tends to posit that such tendencies follow directly from the junction of an underdeveloped country with a capitalist world economy; the right sees them as errors stemming logically from an interventionist approach to economic problems, that is, from listening to the bad advice of socialists or liberals. The former explanation tends to the mechanical; the latter leaves unanswered the question of why African governments didn't listen to the readily available wisdom of the other side. And if the two poles can often agree on what constitutes the failures of African governments, it is much less apparent what constitutes the success of Asian economies. It is certainly not the absence of government intervention into economic affairs, or the absence of repression.

3 The political analogue of the market vs. state dichotomy is the ongoing discussion over the civil society vs. state dichotomy, which similarly fails to see how much the two interpenetrate each other. For an idea of the vigor of this debate, see the commentary by Mahmood Mamdani and the rejoinders to it in *CODESRIA Bulletin* 2 (1990):7–11, and 3 (1990):10–13, 16.

4 The complexity of African states and their relationships to social and economic processes have been the subjects of considerable theoretical and empirical work in the past decade. Bayart 1989 is a particularly rich example.

5 See Bates (1983, 1989), who is quite explicit about convergences and differences between "rational choice theory" and Marxism, although in my opinion he has trouble with the problem of analyzing collective action, which Marxists also stumble on once they discard their *a priori* notion that classes are necessarily the primary units of action. Perhaps the most curious convergence occurs in the work of Goran Hyden (1983). His is an argument for a market-centered approach, but one whose logic parallels that of a kind of fundamentalist Marxism. He at least advances a reason why African economies have failed to invest productively and why African governments make so many "bad" decisions. Hyden's so-called economy of affection puts the onus on the embeddedness of Africans in relations of kinship and clientage, which keep them from being captured either by state power or (the point of his most recent book) by market relations. But the notion of an economy of affection is a vague and vacuous one, incapable of distinguishing between the supposedly burdensome African pattern of kinship and clientage and the kinds of social relationships which have fed the transformation of other kinds of economic structures. Hyden does go a step further, arguing that it is kinship groups' access to land which protects them from the disciplining effect of markets. Here he reaches a point beyond which he does not want to go: the logical implication of his argument is that the one way out of Africa's impasse is for its governments, presumably with international assistance, to dispossess Africans of their land, forcing them to return to work for a small class of landowners who will insure that discipline of the labor market is maintained and the economy of affection banished. There are more than a few Marxists who would be sympathetic to such an argument, but Hyden does not make it. He leaves his argument dangling, along with the question of whether such an assault on cultivators' alleged autonomy would bring them any of the benefits of capitalist development or merely its pain.

6 Such predictions are hazardous. Wallerstein predicted (1976:49), largely on the basis of size, that Nigeria and Zaire were Africa's likeliest candidates for promotion to the semiperiphery. Even oil didn't get Nigeria there, and Zaire is, if anything, moving in the opposite direction.

7 As Florencia Mallon will explain in her afterword, innovation flowed in the opposite direction in the case of structuralist Marxism, which was pioneered by Africanists and picked up and adapted by Latin Americanists. Mallon also points out that the most influential text of the dependency school in the African context was by a scholar from Guyana, Walter Rodney (1972).

8 Twenty-five years ago, Aristide Zolberg (1966) argued that by positing national development as the fundamental goal of policy, African governments denied that there was any legitimate basis for opposition. One could not be against development. Similar questions need to be asked about the uses of this concept among international agencies.

9 See also Marseille 1984; Fitzgerald 1988; and Morgan 1980:vol. 3, 7–15.

10 The "urban bias" charge against African governments is at the very least a rough and potentially misleading proxy for the fundamental inequalities of wealth and power that do exist. The urban domain is not neatly separable from the rural, and this way

of dividing things groups together certain elites—city-based bureaucrats, genuinely wealthy and powerful, but who also have a power base and a rural network of clients and supporters—with wage workers, whose much lower earnings and relationships have become part of rural and urban networks. While it is true that some urban labor unions have made themselves political forces to be reckoned with, it is also true that since 1960 many such unions have fallen victim to repression and cooptation, and the idea that a consistently powerful urban political movement can make itself felt to an extent that farmers cannot is at best a questionable generalization.

11 When I first presented this paper to the African Studies Association meeting in 1980, Michael Lofchie's commentary on it—while arguing that pursuing policies of comparative advantage in particular crops was the best African governments could do—was phrased in such a carefully qualified way (and quite responsibly so) that, in my reply, I labeled it the *theory of comparative disadvantage*.

12 What often gets left out of such discussions within the market framework, as Bates (1983:136) points out, is how restrictive are the assumptions under which market allocations produce ethically justified allocations of resources.

References for Postscript

Adas, Michael. 1989. *Machines as the Measure of Men: Science, Technology, and Ideologies of Western Dominance*. Ithaca, N.Y.: Cornell Univ. Press.

Austen, Ralph. 1987. *African Economic History*. London: James Currey.

Bates, Robert. 1983. *Essays on the Political Economy of Rural Africa*. Cambridge.

Bates, Robert. 1989. *Beyond the Miracle of the Market: The Political Economy of Agrarian Development in Kenya*. Cambridge: Cambridge Univ. Press.

Bayart, Jean-François. 1989. *L'état en Afrique: la politique du ventre*. Paris: Fayard.

Berry, Sara. 1984. "The Food Crisis and Agrarian Change in Africa: A Review Essay." *African Studies Review* 27:59–112.

Cooper, Frederick. 1987. *On the African Waterfront: Urban Disorder and the Transformation of Work in Colonial Mombasa*. New Haven, Conn.: Yale Univ. Press.

Cooper, Frederick, and Ann Stoler. 1989. "Tensions of Empire: Colonial Control and Visions of Rule." Introduction to a special section of *American Ethnologist* 16:609–21.

Feierman, Steven. 1990. *Peasant Intellectuals: Anthropology and History in Tanzania*. Madison: Univ. of Wisconsin Press.

Ferguson, James. 1990. *The Anti-Politics Machine: "Development," Depoliticization, and Bureaucratic Power in Lesotho*. Cambridge: Cambridge Univ. Press.

Fitzgerald, Edward Peter. 1988. "Did France's Colonial Empire Make Economic Sense? A Perspective from the Postwar Decade, 1946–1956." *Journal of Economic History* 48:373–85.

Guyer, Jane. 1981. "Household and Community in African Studies." *African Studies Review* 24:87–138.

Hyden, Goran. 1983. *No Shortcuts to Progress: African Development Management in Perspective*. London: Heinemann.

Laclau, Ernesto, and Chantal Mouffe. 1985. *Hegemony and Socialist Strategy: Towards a Radical Democratic Politics*. London: Verso.

MacGaffey, Janet. 1987. *Entrepreneurs and Parasites: The Struggle for Indigenous Capitalism in Zaire*. Cambridge: Cambridge Univ. Press.

Mandala, Elias. 1990. *Work and Control in a Peasant Economy: A History of the Lower Tchiri Valley in Malawi, 1859–1960*. Madison: Univ. of Wisconsin Press.

Marseille, Jacques. 1984. *Empire colonial et capitalisme français: histoire d' un divorce*. Paris: Albin Michel.

Morgan, D. J. 1980. *The Official History of Colonial Development*. London: Macmillan.

Mudimbe, V. Y. 1988. *The Invention of Africa*. Bloomington, Ind.: Univ. of Indiana Press.

Rabinow, Paul. 1989. *French Modern: Norms and Forms of the Social Environment*. Cambridge, Mass.: MIT Press.

Richards, Paul. 1985. *Indigenous Agricultural Revolution*. Boulder, Colo.: Westview.

Robertson, Claire, and Martin Klein, eds. 1983. *Women and Slavery in Africa*. Madison: Univ. of Wisconsin Press.

Rodney, Walter. 1972. *How Europe Underdeveloped Africa*. London: Bogle-L'Ouverture.

Schmidt, Elizabeth. 1992. *Peasants, Traders, and Wives: Women in the History of Zimbabwe 1890–1939*. Portsmouth, N.H.: Heineman.

Scott, Joan W. 1988. *Gender and the Politics of History*. New York: Columbia Univ. Press.

Stoler, Ann. 1989. "Making Empire Respectable: The Politics of Race and Sexual Morality in 20th-Century Colonial Cultures." *American Ethnologist* 16:634–60.

Strobel, Margaret. 1979. *Muslim Women in Mombasa, 1890–1975*. New Haven, Conn.: Yale Univ. Press.

Wallerstein, Immanuel. 1976. "The Three Stages of African Involvement in the World-Economy." In Peter C. W. Gutkind and Immanuel Wallerstein, eds., *The Political Economy of Contemporary Africa*. Beverly Hills: Sage, 30–57.

White, Luise. 1990. *The Comforts of Home: Prostitution in Colonial Nairobi*. Chicago: Univ. of Chicago Press.

World Bank, 1990. *World Development Report 1990*. New York: Oxford Univ. Press.

World Bank. 1991. *World Development Report 1991*. New York: Oxford Univ. Press.

Zolberg, Aristide. 1966. *Creating Political Order: The Party-States of West Africa*. Chicago: Rand McNally.

PART 2
Rethinking Peasants

4 *Allen F. Isaacman*

Peasants and Rural Social Protest in Africa

Peasants are an ambiguous social category. They are difficult to define, and their political behavior defies most generalizations. Nevertheless, social scientists, many working outside of Africa, have produced a voluminous literature debating both the critical characteristics and the analytical utility of the term *peasant*.

Some take the view that peasants have been defined so broadly and contradictorily as to render the concept virtually useless and that the notion should either be discarded or referred to only by negation (Dalton 1972; Hill 1963; M. Moore 1972; Ennew, Hirst, and Tribe 1977; Friedmann 1980). Other scholars obviously disagree, having advanced definitions of the *essence* of peasants and varieties of agrarian change. Culturalists such as Kroeber (1948) and Redfield (1956) highlighted the peasants' folk version of a higher culture. Chayanov (1966) emphasized the demographic cycle of the peasant household, exhibiting a natural pattern of growth and change. Wolf (1966) and Godelier (1973) shifted the focus to the historically derived relationships of domination in which peasants were subsumed. Shanin defined peasants "as a kind of arrangement of humanity" (1973:76) in which their partial involvement in the market and their partial subordination to the state or appropriating class were their most salient characteristics.

These debates were reproduced within African Studies. Those skeptical that the concept had any analytical value initially prevailed. This position was defended most vigorously in a theoretical essay by Fallers (1961) and in Hill's (1963) masterful work on agrarian change in southern Ghana. As late as 1972, Post noted that "most writers either evade this issue or display analytical uncertainty or forthrightly reject the term [peasant]" (1972:223). A small group of political economists argued that peasants existed as an exploited class, but not until the colonial period (Atieno-Odhiambo 1974; Bundy 1972; Leys 1975; Post 1972; Saul and Woods 1971). By the end of the 1970s this broad political-economy approach to peasants predominated. According to Klein, editor of the widely read study *Peasants in Africa* (1980), most Africanists agreed that *peasants* referred to agriculturalists who control the land they work either as tenants or smallholders, are organized largely in households that meet most of their subsistence needs, and are ruled by other classes, who extract a surplus either directly or through control of state power.

This consensus, however, did not obviate the inherent problem of capturing the diverse range of peasant relationships and experiences within a single construct. Therefore, some scholars retained a healthy skepticism of the term, while others preferred to use *peasant* as shorthand rather than as a precise analytical category (Cooper 1981b; Beinart and Bundy 1987). Africanists have also attempted to resolve this dilemma by grappling with the idea of the development of *peasantries,* analyzing such broader processes as the uneven capitalist penetration of the countryside, the growth of commodity production, the restructuring of gender and household relations, and the development of oscillating peasant workers. These analyses, I will argue, have moved us far beyond the notion of a homogeneous peasantry (see pp. 219–21). In the process they have also deepened our understanding of the complexities of agrarian change, linking them to local, national, and transnational factors.

For all their insights, however, these studies have paid relatively little attention to the organization of work. Work was critical in structuring the rhythm of peasants' daily lives, their relationship to the natural order, the way different groups organized production and consumption and long-term social reproduction strategies and the timing of important social events and religious ceremonies.[1] In short, work, or more precisely the varied forms of the labor process (Isaacman 1989; Trouillot 1988; Watts 1988), had a profound impact on the material as well as the cultural universe of peasants. The cultural dimension needs to be stressed as part of a more integrated understanding of material and cultural processes. Production and control of scarce resources are integrally bound up with a cultural understanding of how work is defined and valued. In rural societies as different as the Hausa of northern Nigeria (Hill 1972; Watts 1983b) and the Tshidi of South Africa (Comaroff and Comaroff 1987), peasants experienced a deep sense of shame when they were forced to sell their labor rather than work their own land. Other peasant communities reinvented tradition to cope with household labor crises.[2]

The labor process provides a framework for exploring the multiple ways in which work was organized in different peasant societies. In order to understand the forms of the labor process among peasantries, we must examine (1) the composition and organization of the peasant labor force; the degree to which (2) necessary and surplus labor are separate in both time and space; (3) peasants are able to set in motion the instruments of production independently of the landlord, state, or ruling class; (4) peasant labor is supervised by outside agents, and work obligations are secured through political institutions; and (5) peasants assume the risks of production. By focusing on the way different peasantries negotiate their positions in relation to the labor process, we highlight the fact that peasants exist only as part of a larger social order, in which ruling-class agendas, state politics, and international markets impinge on their daily lives and subsume a portion of their labor. But the labor process also provides a way to explore the varied opportunities available to peasants willing to take risks in order to structure their workday and the composition of their work force and to decide what to produce and for whom. It also raises the possibility that women and men, and young and old within a particular community were engaged in quite different patterns of work. For example, it enables us to incorporate into our analysis critical domestic chores such as cooking, carrying firewood, and caring for infants, which are themselves a source of potential conflict and cannot be ignored. This allocation of work is culturally constructed, linked to notions of the labor ethic, gender ideologies, the "conjugal contract," normative obligations based on family, kinship and ancestor worship, and the struggle over meaning (see Comaroff and Comaroff 1987; Donham 1985, 1989; Feeley-Harnik 1984, 1987; Guyer 1984c, 1988; Mandala 1990; Watts 1989). The labor process thus offers a strategic entry into the fundamental question of how power was negotiated and exercised in the countryside and what the potential was for peasants to dissent.

In reality, a study of peasants and rural social protest cannot be separated from a study of rural life in its fullest expression. To provide coherence to this essay, I have focused my discussion of peasant protest on the connection between the partial autonomy of peasants and the types of struggles in which they were engaged. The uniqueness of peasants is the degree of autonomy they had in relation to the colonial state and the appropriating classes. This autonomy was inextricably linked to their ability to mobilize their own labor power through the household and their access to land, which, together, gave them command over subsistence. That state power was mediated through local and political institutions and that peasants generally retained their own language, historical memories, and forms of expressive culture reinforced the autonomy derived from the labor process by limiting the degree to which an authoritative colonial discourse could penetrate rural societies.

By focusing on historically specific forms of the labor process, we see that peasants enjoyed much greater autonomy than did rural or urban workers. However tenuous the access of labor-tenants and sharecroppers to land, they were not divorced from the means of production, nor were they subject to the same degree of surveillance and labor control as their worker counterparts. Even under the most controlled systems of forced cultivation, neither the state nor its merchant allies had the manpower to oversee the daily labor of all peasant households legally under their domain (Dampierre 1960; Guyer 1978; Iliffe 1967; Isaacman 1985; McCarthy 1982; Nayenga 1979; Zwanenberg 1974). Peasants also had the option, within varying externally imposed constraints, to produce when and what they wanted, and they were subordinated to capital primarily through the exigencies of the market.

In short, the peasant labor process enabled them to shield critical resources and to implement individual remedies to combat state and ruling-class oppression. It is this partial autonomy as well as the realization of their limited power which helps explain why peasants were prone to engage in localized or hidden forms of resistance rather than in broader social movements. Just as peasants were reluctant to become involved in confrontation, so neither the state nor the appropriating classes were usually interested in destroying the peasantry, but only in controlling it more effectively. South Africa stands as the most notable exception. Thus, I would contend that for both oppressor and oppressed, jockeying and negotiating to reshape this partial autonomy represented the principal terrain of struggle.

Sometimes peasants found it necessary to join broader insurgency movements to maintain or expand their degree of autonomy. Colonial history provides many examples of collective opposition to forced cultivation, labor-intensive antierosion schemes, and the expropriation of rural lands. In all these cases, state or capitalist intervention at the point of production created volatile conditions in the countryside. Similar struggles over control of and access to critical resources took place within rural communities and peasant households, revealing intraclass and interclass conflict as well as gender and generational conflict. We are only beginning to understand how peasants have continuously engaged their political universe, challenging the notion that peasants are passive, invisible victims who recede from history except in times of crisis (Stern 1987:9–10).

The body of the paper is divided into four major sections. The first very briefly reviews the literature before 1980, which tended to ignore peasants as political actors. The second examines the shape of the post-1980 agrarian historiography and the critical role accorded peasants in it. The third discusses the methodological and substantive problems posed by inserting agrarian studies and peasant protest into the history of precolonial Africa. The fourth highlights major themes in the study of peasants in colonial Africa—the hidden forms of struggle, the social basis of conflict within peasant communities, and the interrelationship between social movements and ideology.

Because of the scope of the subject and the desired length of the essay, I have had to limit its temporal and spatial dimensions. I will not examine the literature on the relationship between peasants and the postcolonial state, an important issue in contemporary Africa, which raises a broad range of theoretical and comparative questions and merits its own review paper. Similarly, the essay focuses exclusively on sub-Saharan Africa, although it does refer to Valensis' pioneering study of Tunisian peasants and, of course, to Fanon's theory of revolution. Throughout the paper I have consciously avoided getting mired in the semantic debate surrounding the term *peasant*. Instead, I have focused on the relatively unexplored political effects of the partial autonomy of different peasantries inextricably linked to the nature of the labor process. The paper is essentially about social conflict, exploitation, and rural protest defined in the broadest terms. As such, this essay highlights the material basis of intraclass as well as interclass struggle while stressing the need for scholars studying agrarian politics to pay greater attention to gender relations and the construction of insurgent ideologies from below. Many other features of peasant life remain on the sidelines. Art, literature, philosophical speculation, among other things, fall outside the scope of this paper, while religion is treated in a fairly cursory way to avoid repeating material covered in previous SSRC-commissioned essays (MacGaffey 1981; Ranger 1986a). And because this is not a study of agrarian labor or rural struggle per se, I have alluded to the literature on slaves or rural workers only when it was relevant to the debate on peasants. These omissions and the way I have framed the issues make this essay a personal and provisional reading of a complex and controversial body of literature.

Peasant Politics Passed Over, 1930–1980: A Historiographical Overview

That peasants are inherently tricky to deal with conceptually helps to explain why they were often rendered invisible in the literature. But the issue is broader than one of definition. Until the past decade or so, scholars encapsulated rural societies in a series of paradigms—structural-functionalism, African agency, modernization theory, underdevelopment theory, and modes of production analysis—which most often ignored or marginalized peasants as political actors. Even a cursory review of this literature suggests how the choice of analytical categories closed off sustained discussion of peasant initiatives and resourcefulness in resisting colonial domination. Many of these issues have been addressed in a variety of complex ways in earlier SSRC papers (Berry 1984b; Cooper 1981a; Feierman 1985; Freund 1984a; Guyer 1981b; Jewsiewicki 1987; Lonsdale 1981; Ranger 1986a) and can only be summarized in a somewhat terse and schematic fashion as a backdrop to this review. Such a review necessarily obscures variations within each school of thought just as an emphasis on paradigmatic oppositions often conceals substantive similarities between them.

Structural-functionalism, as the theoretical basis for anthropological writing about Africa, dominated the literature from the 1930s to the 1950s, the heyday of colonialism. A core assumption shared by most structural-functionalist ethnographers was that each African society was a bounded system with its own internal logic and coherence. Radcliffe-Brown, using a biological metaphor, even compared each individual *tribe* to a separate organism (1952: chap. 9). Ethnographers working in this tradition tried to understand the systematic character of each society. By *system* they meant relations among elements of social structure studied synchronically, at one moment in time. The structural-functionalist emphasis on synchrony—the rejection of history—was in part a reaction against the speculative and often unsubstantiated reasoning of earlier evolutionary and diffusionist approaches (Harris 1968).

The ethnographic practice of anthropologists working in the tradition of either Radcliffe-Brown or Malinowski reinforced the sense that these bounded societies were the most appropriate units of study. The ethnographers placed a high value on mastery of local languages and on long periods of field research. In many cases their research yielded sophisticated insights about the complexities of local African culture, as in Victor Turner's (1957) descriptions of Ndembu ritual. But the emphasis on local languages tended to reinforce the assumption that *tribes* were self-enclosed systems.[3]

Because the structural-functionalist ethnographers rejected hypothetical history and put the greatest emphasis on personal observation, the ethnographer's time as well as place was privileged. Historical records seemed pallid by comparison to the rich first-hand experience of field research. Oral narratives were known to have rich social content, and in some cases to have been structured to meet social needs rather than to report history accurately (Bohannan 1954b; Radcliffe-Brown 1952). Because of the general emphasis on synchronic analysis and on the social embeddedness of narrative, few anthropologists worked at creating critical methods for historical reconstruction based on oral tradition. As a result, structural-functionalists often framed their work in an ahistorical fashion in which *tribes* were reified in a timeless ethnographic present cut off from history (Alavi 1973; Asad 1973; Comaroff 1984; Feierman 1990; Harris 1968; Mintz 1982; Vansina 1969). As John Comaroff (1984:573) notes, "the problem was not that these ethnographers were unaware of the contemporary historical context: it was, rather, the dualism according to which they came to treat 'traditional' societies, in the heuristic present, as closed systems, and then (in different studies, or in final chapters of monographs) to examine 'social change' as a discrete issue." Other critics contended that the ahistorical bias reflected the underlying agenda of structural-functionalists to provide a scientific rationalization of the status quo and to manipulate *traditional* political institutions and religious institutions to promote social control (Asad 1973; Gregg and Williams 1948; Strauder 1974).[4]

The structural-functional framework had far-reaching implications for the study of peasant politics. *Traditional* society was presumed to be ordered by a coherent set of principles in which the division of labor and the social roles that individuals played were reciprocally and collectively functional. It was not that structural-functionalists were unaware of conflict. They saw dispute and violence as a necessary adjustment to reproduce the social order rather than as a force for systemic change (Fortes and Evans-Pritchard 1940; Fortes 1945; Gluckman 1940; Harris 1968; Worsley 1961). A coherent system of symbols, mnemonics, and rules gave conflict a predictable social form, processes of prosecution, and a set of possible outcomes. *Peasants* as an economically and politically dominated social category were conspicuously absent from the literature. Ethnographers favored such descriptive terms as *tribal, lineage members, subsistence producer, and traditional agriculturalists,* all devoid of potential political or class meaning. Rarely questioned was the traditional rulers' economic and ideological legitimacy over their subjects. "Where kingdoms existed," Lonsdale notes, functional anthropologists assumed that "there was only one theory of government; the constitution was a sacred value system" (Lonsdale 1981:171). And even "rituals of rebellion" (Gluckman 1954) were portrayed as structural safety valves in which hostilities toward the rulers were acted out by their subjects in a way that preserved the social order. Similarly, the emphasis anthropologists placed on kinship principles and their theoretical distinction between domestic and public spheres tended to preclude a political analysis of domestic relations (Guyer and Peters 1987).

The question of colonial domination and the ways in which rural societies coped with and struggled against foreign rule fell outside the scope of most ethnographic studies. Ethnographers alluded to what Balandier (1966) called the "colonial situation," but they never really studied it as part of the social system (for exceptions, see Epstein 1958; Wilson 1936). When ethnographers did write about issues of race or of labor, as Hilda Kuper did in her book on *The Uniform of Colour* (1974), and as Max Gluckman did in "Analysis of a Social Situation in Modern Zululand" (1940), these studies were kept analytically separate from the main body of African ethnography, rarely penetrating the systematic study of tribes.[5] And, unlike the work of their urban counterparts, who studied the politics of trade unions or dance groups (Epstein 1958; Mitchell 1956), rural ethnographers rarely commented on how new organizations and formations in the countryside might have served as a basis of political or cultural insurgency.

The attempts to break spatial and temporal boundaries became more intense in the 1950s, when most anthropologists were taking part in a discussion of the importance of history (Eggan 1954; Firth 1954). By the late colonial period the concept of tribe as the most appropriate unit of analysis also came into question. Out of these debates, theorists began to posit more than one intellectual model of social relation in every social context and began to see change, conflict, and symbolic manipulation as absolutely intrinsic to social and cultural life in the precolonial (Bradbury 1964; Cunnison 1959; Fallers 1956; Gluckman 1956; Smith 1960; Stenning 1959) and colonial (Barnes 1954; Bohannan 1959; A. Richards 1954; Watson 1958; Wilson 1951, 1957) countryside. However, peasants as a social category and as political actors making their own history remained all but invisible (Dalton 1972; Fallers 1961).

If structural-functionalists rendered peasants invisible, modernization theorists acknowledged their existence but sought to transform them into *innovative* capitalist farmers. Writing in the 1950s and 1960s, the era of *economic take-off,* they expressed unbridled faith in technology and capitalism (Lerner 1958; McClelland 1961; Rostow 1960; Weiner 1966). This discourse on development was particularly appealing to agricultural economists and local extension officers, who had to formulate rural policies designed to promote "progressive farmers," "rational economic men," and political stability (Chipungu 1987; Cooper 1981a) in an era of labor crises which accompanied accelerated efforts at development following the Second World War.

But structural-functionalists left an indelible mark on Africanist literature, and modernization theory did not, in part because these theorists gave a low priority to sub-Saharan Africa as opposed to Japan, Turkey, India, and Latin America. For many students of modernization, the social and economic barriers standing in the way of *take-off* in Africa were formidable (Dalton 1967; Fogg 1971; Herskovits and Harwitz 1964; Hunter 1969). Peasant opposition to a variety of *betterment schemes* confirmed these suspicions. The principal contribution of modernization theorists to peasant historiography was to reinforce the notion that rural Africans, particularly peasant women, were generally resistant to innovation (Staudt 1987).

The 1960s also witnessed the birth of African Studies as a field of scholarly inquiry coinciding with and shaped by the nationalist campaigns sweeping the continent. Most Africanist research attacked the racially and culturally arrogant myths about *unchanging* African societies and stressed African autonomy, authenticity and agency.[6] Scholars demonstrated African initiative through meticulously researched studies of precolonial state formation (Akinjobin 1967; D. Cohen 1972; Feierman 1974; Miller 1976; A. Roberts 1973; Vansina 1966), complex long-distance trading systems (Curtin 1975; Dike 1957; Gray and Birmingham 1970), the emergence of rural capitalist farmers (Berry 1974; Hill 1963; Hopkins 1973), and the process of cultural change (Balandier 1968; Herskovits 1962; Isaacman 1972). But the issue of African resistance to colonialism and its connection to modern nationalist movements dominated this literature.[7]

Although a review of the nationalist historiography falls outside the scope of this paper (see M. Young 1986), it is useful to summarize where peasants fit in this literature. In many respects, Hodgkin's (1957) pioneering study, *Nationalism in Colonial Africa*, set the terms of the debate. For all its wonderful insights and attention to economic grievances, Hodgkin's organizing concept of anticolonial protest did not leave sufficient space to incorporate rural protest except as precursor to nationalism. A number of prominent scholars initially adopted a similar line of reasoning (Davidson 1969; Ranger 1968a; M. Young 1965). With independence impending, scholars shifted their emphasis from protest to parties and from struggle to national integration. Nationalist parties, in their many forms, were seen as the essential terrain of politics and were invested with the mandate of popular mobilization (Coleman 1958; Apter 1963; Sklar 1963; Weiss 1967; Zolberg 1964). Peasants had to be organized and led. Fourteen years after Hodgkin's pioneering study, Rotberg and Mazrui edited a 1,400-page tome, *Protest and Power in Black Africa* (1970), with only two references to peasants in its elaborate index.[8]

Thus, in this world of African agency, peasants remained largely invisible. Precolonial historiography paid little attention to the organization of rural agricultural production and the ways in which surplus extraction may have caused malnutrition, disease, differentiation, and class conflict. Discussions of social class and peasant initiative were also conspicuously absent from most of the resistance literature. Peasants were subsumed under such vague categories as the "people," "rural ethnic groups," "the rural masses" or "rural radicals" (Lemarchand 1970; Lovens 1975; Weiss 1967). To the extent that peasants explicitly figured in the discussion of rural protest, they were often treated as an undifferentiated bloc following indigenous authorities or latter-day nationalists. Iliffe's (1967) work on the Maji-Maji rebellion in Tanganyika, Furedi's 1974 essay on the Mau-Mau, Joseph's (1977) research on radicalism in the Cameroon and Lonsdale's (1968:146) important insight that a rural-based nationalism was "coordinated rather than instigated by the educated elite" stand out as exceptions. Peasants also found a powerful, although not unambiguous, voice in Frantz Fanon (1963; see also Perinbaum 1973).[9]

The failure of the new independent African nations to resolve their economic and political problems in the 1970s caused many Africanists to shift their attention from the roots of nationalism to the roots of underdevelopment. Underdevelopment, or dependency theory, borrowed from Latin Americanists, explained Third World impoverishment in terms of the world capitalist system's success in extracting surplus through unequal exchange with the periphery. In the hands of scholars like Alpers (1973), Amin (1972), Leys (1975), Rodney (1972), and Wallerstein (1976), it represented a powerful critique of the modernization studies while providing a plausible explanation for Africa's continued impoverishment.

Underdevelopment theory, however, offered little analytical space for peasants to emerge as a source of sustained historical change.[10] To be sure, peasants could have their moment in the sun. Bundy's highly influential article (1972), followed by his monograph *The Rise and Fall of the South African Peasantry* (1979), served as a model for a number of studies on the ways in which innovative peasants were invariably strangled by the forces of colonial capitalism (Palmer and Parsons 1977; Phimister 1974). This strangulation thesis, although a corrective to prior depictions of peasants as "uneconomic men," was not entirely satisfactory. It tended to collapse a complex process of rural transformation into a single trajectory, and it viewed local communities, their distorted structures and contemporary problems, simply as the product of exogenous historical forces.[11]

Modes-of-production analyses sought to address these very issues. Rather than focusing on unequal exchange, modes-of-production theorists emphasized the organization of labor and control of production, thus holding out the possibility of making an important breakthrough in peasant studies. Taking advantage of a favorable political and intellectual climate in the 1960s (Coquery-Vidrovitch 1976b; Godelier 1977; Jewsiewicki and Letourneau 1985), French Marxists, such as Meillassoux (1964, 1972, 1973, 1975), Rey (1973, 1974), Terray (1972, 1974), Godelier (1973, 1975, 1977), and Coquery-Vidrovitch (1972b, 1976b) offered insightful, if controversial (Comaroff 1980b; Hindess and Hirst 1975; O'Laughlin 1977) ways of conceptualizing kinship, class, labor, and ideology in African agrarian societies. Their provocative essays inspired anglophonic scholars, particularly Wolpe (1972) and Bernstein (1979), to focus on the ways in which capitalism distorted precapitalist agrarian societies.[12]

For all this promise, modes-of-production analysts have as yet not added substantially to our understanding of peasant politics. To be sure, the works of Meillassoux (1981), Henn (1984), Kimble (1982, 1985), Rey (1975), and Wolpe (1980) have provided important theoretical insights into the class-based notion of the differentiated household. And the studies of Cordell (1985), Bazin and Terray (1982), Shenton (1986), and Terray (1985a) have effectively linked production, exchange, and rural oppression. But much of the literature has focused on class analysis without class struggle, and a great deal of time has been spent identifying and labeling precapitalist assemblages as "slave," "lineage," "tributary," "fishing," "peasant," as well as more conventional "feudal," "Asiatic" modes (Crummey and Stewart 1981; Jewsiewicki 1987; Jewsiewicki and Letourneau 1985; N'daou 1988). At the same time, many scholars underplayed the critical issue of social reproduction and have not paid sufficient attention to technical and ecological factors and how they have changed over time (Mandala 1990; Seddons 1978). To the extent that peasants figured as an analytical category, they tended to be reified as distorted vestiges of a mode of production on the verge of extinction. Not surprisingly, peasant protest generally fell outside the scope of this literature.

Thus, in sharp contrast to the rich historiography on agrarian change and rural conflict in Europe and other parts of the Third World,[13] peasant studies in Africa through the 1970s remained in a state of relative infancy. During this period there was a deepening of the agrarian literature (Berry 1975; Hill 1970, 1977; Hogendorn 1978). Important research was conducted on local differentiation set within a larger regional and world perspective (A. Cohen 1969; Karp 1978; Parkin 1972), and the beginnings of a discussion on peasants (Bernstein 1977, 1979; Hay 1979; Post 1977; Ranger 1978; G. Williams 1976; Wilson 1969), but rarely on peasant politics emerged (Lamb 1974; Post 1972). This emphasis changed rapidly as Africanists were influenced by a wider body of literature in which peasants and agrarian conflict figured prominently.[14] Rural-based struggles in Angola, Guinea-Bissau, Mozambique, and Zimbabwe reinforced interest in peasant politics.

Peasant Agrarian Studies and Rural Protest: An Emerging Literature, ca. 1980–1988

The seemingly intractable agrarian crisis in Africa has propelled peasant studies to new prominence.[15] A decade of droughts, famines, declining agricultural production, and increased food imports all demanded agendas for thought as well as agendas for action. Although scholars agreed that these problems had to be addressed, they disagreed on their underlying causes. The appalling conditions on the continent precipitated vigorous theoretical, methodological, and ideological debates. The failure of African socialism (Amselle 1984; Cournanel 1984; Gibbon and Neocosmos 1984; von Freyhold 1979) and the intensifying conflict within South Africa highlighted how little we know about the countryside as a terrain of struggle—both past and present. Only by asking the questions about resistance, about accommodation and collaboration and cooperation, about gender relations and how social reproduction is organized have scholars been able to raise questions of how rural communities survive. These issues loom particularly large in the struggle to transform South Africa (Beinart and Bundy 1987; Beinart, Delius, and Trapido 1986; Bozzoli 1983b, 1987; Bradford 1987; Keegan 1986, 1988; Lodge 1983; van Onselen 1990).

Just as Africa experienced an economic crisis, so Africanists experienced an intellectual crisis precipitated, in part, by the failure of their prior interpretations of the countryside to explain declining productivity and acute poverty.[16] Africanist research agendas came under increasing criticism from a wide range of scholars, including many who, like Bernstein (1985), Beinart and Bundy (1987), and Ranger (1986b), had helped to construct the prior paradigms. For all their differences, the three authors discarded or radically altered earlier formulations in favor of those that give greater prominence to peasants as historical actors.[17] Rural class struggle and peasants, who are more complex and differentiated, moved to the center of their analyses.

Much of the critical rethinking came from diverse sets of scholars, many of whom had remained outside the prior debates. Feminist scholars, for example, argued persuasively that what the literature portrayed as the *peasant reality* was, in fact, an undifferentiated *male reality,* shaped in turn by rarefied structural-functionalist assumptions about kinship and the sexual division of labor. Consequently, there was little possibility to conceptualize such issues as the social construction of gender, patriarchy, and the household as a potential terrain of struggle (Bozzoli 1983a; Mandala 1982; Mbilinyi 1982; Strobel 1982; Staudt 1986). Students of ecology complained that most researchers had detached peasants from their habitat and ignored critical environmental issues, such as soil types, plant diseases, and rainfall (Chipungu 1986, P. Richards 1983; Tosh 1980). Radical populists and neo-Marxists sought to create analytical space where scholarship on work and everyday life could flourish (Bozzoli 1983b; Mandala 1990; Marks and Trapido 1987). Scholars exploring the interrelationship between the material and cultural world stressed that rural communities were capable of creating an alternative oppositional culture and were not necessarily victims of false consciousness and ruling-class hegemony (Barber 1986; Jean Comaroff 1985; Comaroff and Comaroff 1989; Coplan 1987; Fields 1985). Out of this intellectual ferment a new agrarian scholarship began to emerge in which peasants became a central, though not exclusive, focus of analysis.[18]

Apart from an emphasis on peasants, the most salient feature of this literature is the absence of a dominant paradigm or school of thought. This is not to imply that the new literature is shapeless, but that it confronts the heavy structuralism of both underdevelopment theory and modes-of-production analysis, and offers an alternative approach examining the relationship between social action and social structure over time. (For a theoretical discussion, see Abrams 1982; Bourdieu 1977; Giddens 1979, 1981; Karp 1986.) It also seeks to move beyond old dualisms—such as global political economy and ethnography and culture and materialism—to expand the scope of scholarly inquiry.[19] Although often at odds with each other, Marxists, populists, feminists, and culturalists all posed the problem of the countryside in a new language. Scholars examined questions of power, justice, struggle, social identity, and class not simply as abstractions but as issues deeply rooted in the daily practices and experiences of different peasantries and rural workers. This more open conceptualization has helped to stimulate serious discussion of a number of critical issues which heretofore have been ignored or examined only superficially.

For example, in the past decade, scholars have begun to pay greater attention to ecology and the complex ways in which peasants interacted with their environment.[20] Thornton and Wilks discuss how soil types, rainfall patterns, and population density combined to structure production in the precolonial Kongo and Asante, respectively (McCaskie 1980; Thornton 1983; Wilks 1976). Dias and Miller stress the pivotal role of environmental changes, disease, and famine in the history of precolonial Angola (Dias 1981; Miller 1982). Mandala explains how the changing water levels of the Tchiri River affected commodity production and class, gender, and generational relations in southern Malawi during the first half of this century (Mandala 1982, 1984). And, in a recent dissertation, Delehanty argues that the combination of land degradation and scarcity as well as class tensions and a frontier ideology drove many peasants from colonial Niger to relocate on the harsh desert fringe (Delehanty 1988). Other scholars emphasize the critical role of plant, animal, and human diseases in the social reproduction of agrarian societies (Ballard 1986; Feierman 1985; Ford 1971; Ohadike 1981; Packard 1984; Vail 1977).

Africanists have also challenged the assumption that peasants were incapable of generating scientific and technological innovations (Berry 1974; Chipungu 1987; S. Martin 1984; P. Richards 1983). In much the same vein, scholars of quite different intellectual persuasions[21] have begun to question the ahistorical assumptions and undocumented generalizations about rural property rights and land tenure systems (Chanock 1982, 1985; Comaroff 1980b; Crummey 1978; Depelchin 1979; Downs and Reyna 1988; Hay 1982; McCaskie 1980; S. Moore 1986). Increased and critical attention to ecology, demography, technology, and tenure have become essential elements of a more nuanced and complex agrarian formulation.

Scholars have also criticized prior formulations which were not sufficiently attentive to historical change. In an important review of the field, Ranger (1986b) notes that underdevelopment theorists and modes-of-production analysts often accord peasants too small a place on the African historical landscape. They tend to link the emergence of peasants to colonialism, to rely on such ahistorical abstractions as *natural economy* in describing precolonial Africa, and to consign peasants to extinction prematurely. In fact, most peasant communities were quite resilient, and when they did undergo a transformation it was often only partial. Strangled Mozambican and Zairois peasants were often resurrected as forced cotton cultivators (Isaacman et al. 1980; Jewsiewicki 1980b; Vail and White 1978), and landless Malawians survived as *thangata* labor tenants (McCracken 1983; Newbury 1980; Page 1978). The emergence of sharecroppers from Gambia to Lesotho (C. Murray 1981; A. F. Robertson 1987) as well as a variety of oscillating peasant workers testify to the complexity of this process.

The realization that most peasantries were not doomed to extinction stimulated scholars to try to determine when as well as why these partial transformations occurred. Some researchers, whose perspective was national rather than local, examined the ways in which shifting colonial labor policies narrowed or expanded the range of peasant options at particular times (Jewsiewicki 1980a; Raikes 1978). Other scholars mapped out the patterns of change which a particular peasantry experienced during the colonial period (Guyer 1984a; Mandala 1990). Africanists have also begun to focus on those transforming moments that precipitated a rupture in the economy of the countryside. The impact of World War I (Killingray 1978; Page 1978; Rathbone 1978), the far-reaching consequences of the Great Depression (Austen 1986; Munro 1976), and increased state intervention in rural production after World War II have received particular attention (Lonsdale 1968; Throup 1987).

This new scholarship has also begun to free the study of peasants and rural agricultural workers from an artificially imposed national framework. It makes little sense to speak of Kenyan, Ghanian, or Mozambican peasants as if they were homogeneous categories (Howard 1976; Kanogo 1987; Kitching 1980; Wuyts 1978). Variations in ecology, labor systems, and the effects of commodity production within and between regions of the same country render such an approach useless. Local as well as transnational factors also helped to structure the daily lives of rural women and men (Kitching 1980).

In formulating this new agrarian historiography, Africanists have looked beyond their own restricted intellectual community on an unprecedented scale. They have drawn on the rich intellectual tradition of European social and agrarian historians both of the Annales school and of a variety of Marxist traditions.[22] They have learned from the scholarship on slave resistance,[23] agrarian change, social movements in the Third World,[24] and gender and household relations.[25] They have also benefited from both Marxist and neo-Marxist recognition of culture and consciousness as a terrain of struggle (Gramsci 1971; Hunt 1989; Stedman-Jones 1983; Williams 1980).

However, the most important characteristic of this new agrarian scholarship is that it has cut across the traditional disciplinary boundaries that have stifled creativity. Studies as different as Olivier de Sardan's social history of nineteenth- and twentieth-century Songhay-Zarma, Feierman's analysis of the interaction of peasant intellectuals and nationalists in Tanzania, and Jean Comaroff's discussion of the material and cultural encounter in the South African countryside demonstrate the fruitfulness of melding anthropology and history (Jean Comaroff 1985; Feierman 1990; Olivier de Sardan 1984). Similarly, Mandala's work on Malawi (1982, 1984, 1990) and Guyer's analysis of peasant commodity production in the Cameroons (1980b, 1984a) combine the theoretical concerns of ecologists and feminists with detailed historical investigation (Guyer 1984a; Mandala 1984).

Placing peasants at the center of the analysis raises a number of conceptual and methodological issues that had previously been understated or overlooked. How can we think about peasants without reducing them to a homogeneous block? What sources must scholars consult to reconstruct and understand the ambiguities and complexities of peasant societies? In what ways does social conflict, rather than just the logic of capitalism, shape the political, economic, and ideological contours of the countryside?

Rethinking the Definition of Peasants

The analytical difficulty of capturing the diverse range of relationships and experiences within a single construct motivated a number of Africanists to try to unpack the term. They emphasized instead the development of historically specific peasantries. Some scholars have linked the emergence of different peasantries to regional variations in the political economy of colonial Africa. They have pointed to the distinction between impoverished squatters and share-croppers in Southern Africa, where the presence of European planters restricted their opportunities, and those in West Africa, where, in the absence of settlers, they were encouraged by the colonial government to grow cash crops, and they prospered (Amin 1972; Austen 1986; Berry 1984b). While this distinction has some merit, recent studies of the uneven capitalist impact in both regions call into question such sweeping regional generalizations and highlight the need to periodize agrarian transitions more precisely (Beinart and Bundy 1987; Bozzoli 1983b; A. F. Robertson 1987).

Other researchers have emphasized the decisive role that commodity production played in the process of rural differentiation. Disruption in the cycle of household production with an attendant decline in food production, increased vulnerability to the vagaries of the world market, and rural impoverishment have all been attributed to both state and transnational requirements that peasants produce and sell specified crops under unfavorable conditions (Bernstein 1979; Cooper 1981b; Watts 1983b). The effects of commodification, however, were not uniform on the continent or within any given society. Shenton and Lennihan (1981) argue, for example, that in northern Nigeria during the first two decades of this century, merchant capital used its control of credit to bifurcate the peasantry into impoverished and wealthy, exploited and exploiters. Howard (1980) documents a somewhat similar process of rural differentiation in neighboring Ghana. Even in the harsh forced cotton-production schemes in Mozambique, Angola, Zaire, and Chad, chiefs and favored male peasants accumulated substantial amounts of capital, while other members of their communities starved (Buijtenhuijs 1978; Isaacman 1985; Likaka 1991; R. Pelissier 1978; Sturzinger 1983).

Commodity production yielded more than just impoverished and accumulating peasantries. It also yielded defiant and ornery ones (Cooper 1981b). Because neither the colonial state nor merchant interests could effectively oversee peasant production or completely lock them into the market, peasants enjoyed varying degrees of autonomy. When confronted with food shortages, excessive labor demands, or unfavorable market conditions, peasants reduced commodity production or even withdrew entirely from the market (Bunker 1982; Howard 1980; Isaacman et al. 1980; Jewsiewicki 1980a; McCracken 1983). Hyden (1980:18) takes this argument one step further in his controversial formulation of the "uncaptured peasant." [26] He suggests that "African peasants are less integrated into the cash economy than peasants elsewhere" and as a result "enjoy considerable autonomy with respect to outside institutions such as the market and the state."

Feminist scholars, rejecting assumptions about the complementarity of men's and women's work, have argued that commodity production further bifurcated rural societies along gender and generational lines. They stress that the organization of labor, the control of critical resources, the process of social reproduction, and the forms of peasant struggle are all inexorably related to gender. Bradford (1987), for example, has documented the very different history of male and female labor tenants and the power of patriarchy in rural South Africa. Schmidt's (1987) doctoral dissertation on rural Zimbabwe confirms Ranger's (1986b) "peasant option" thesis with the caveat that "the thriving peasant agriculture that threatened the profitability of white settler farming was, for the most part, the work of women" (Schmidt 1987:53). Thus, neither the forms of oppression women experienced nor their coping and accumulating strategies can be subsumed under a generalized notion of peasantry that disregards gender.

Finally, anthropologists and historians have linked peasant diversity to labor migration and the growth of an urban working class. They focus on oscillating peasant workers who played a critical role in the colonial history of eastern and southern Africa. One group of scholars argues that they *straddled* the boundary between rural and urban, and, therefore, represent a distinct and important social force as a partial peasantry in the countryside (First 1983; Kitching 1980; Parkin 1975; Stichter 1982). They see straddling as an effective coping strategy to ensure the social reproduction of the peasant household. Others disagree. They contend that the concept of a peasant worker is too blunt an instrument and that these oscillating migrants were proletarianized workers with a rural residence and a patch of land (Cliffe 1978; C. Murray 1981). [27] This debate carries important implications for the study of peasant politics since it raises the question of how rurally based migrants actually perceived their own social identities.

I would suggest that the notion of the labor process, when combined with an analysis of property relations, [28] offers a way to sharpen still further the distinction between different peasantries in time and space. Petty commodity producers, forced commodity cultivators, independent household producers, sharecroppers, labor tenants (squatters), and oscillating peasant workers were each enmeshed in different labor processes and property arrangements which varied additionally by gender and generation. Petty commodity producers, who controlled their own labor and means of production but rarely the terms of exchange (Bernstein 1988; Friedmann 1980; Gibbon and Neocosmos 1984), stand in sharp contrast both to those peasants forced to grow specific crops under a highly regulated labor and marketing system (Dampierre 1960; Isaacman et al. 1980; Jewsiewicki 1980b; Little 1987; R. Pelissier 1978; Sturzinger 1983) and to independent household producers who sought to resist or minimize commodity production in favor of production for use (Bryceson 1982b; Olivier de Sardan 1984). These peasantries, in turn, experienced a different reality from labor tenants or squatters who had only conditional access to the land acquired by giving up control of a portion of their labor (Crush 1987; Kanogo 1987; Keegan 1986, 1988; J. O'Brien 1983; Trapido 1978, 1986). Sharecroppers, on the other hand, jealously guarded their labor and instead yielded a percentage of their crops to get temporary access to land (Groff 1980; Keegan 1982; A. F. Robertson 1987). Peasant households in which members periodically worked in towns or on estates were involved in a distinctly different labor process and property relations from the domestic unit that remained intact. Thus, in addition to sharpening the distinctions between different peasantries, detailed empirical research of the labor process may reveal the type of partial autonomy different peasantries retained as well as the interests motivating, and capacities underpinning, their potential for dissent.

Listening to Peasant Voices

The ways in which scholars conceptualized peasantries are inextricably tied to the types of data they used. It is not by chance that the literature of the 1960s and 1970s, which had rendered peasants invisible or had reduced them to the status of hapless victims, was also excessively and uncritically dependent on written sources. Although consulting the colonial archives was far easier than going to the field and talking to peasants,[29] the nature of this material inevitably biased the research. Studies dependent on colonial documents necessarily argued that colonialism precipitated the process of peasantization. But the problem is even more fundamental. Embedded in this documentation was a subtle colonial discourse that masked and distorted social realities, touching on every facet of peasant life.[30] Archival data also tended to emphasize exchange relations over production and production over social reproduction, thereby ignoring critical dimensions of peasant village and household life. And the data obscured the hidden forms of peasant protest which succeeded only if they remained clandestine. When, for example, colonial officials discovered actions such as feigning illness, illegal intercropping, and sabotage, they almost invariably depicted them as yet another indication of the "lazy and uneconomic nature of the African" (Isaacman et al. 1980; Watts 1988).

Until the 1980s, however, most scholars working on rural agrarian issues continued to rely on colonial records, and they overlooked or underused oral material. Many assumed they could tease out critical data on labor, household production, social reproduction, and rural protest exclusively from archival material (Chretien 1972; O'Toole 1984; Roche 1976; Weiskel 1980).[31] A few went so far as to interview European officials and educated Africans, while ignoring peasants entirely (Lovens 1975; Tronchon 1974). Clarence-Smith, in his study *Slaves, Peasants and Capitalists in Southern Angola*, rather cavalierly notes that he only consulted archival or published sources "partly because of growing doubts as to the value of oral traditions for this historian" (1979b:viii).[32] Bradford's (1987:xiv) observation is particularly appropriate on this point: "much of the testimony of blacks who lived through the 1920s is as reliable as the words of whites now enshrined in archives or publications" which almost inevitably "are crusted over with racial and class prejudices; almost inevitably they ignore or partially distort the resistance of the rural poor drawn from a subject race."

To note the limits of colonial or missionary records is not to negate the possibility that a careful reading of these texts can yield important analyses of the countryside. Clearly, it can. Much of the best work on the social history of rural South Africa is derived entirely from written sources, especially those that were not in the public domain (Beinart and Bundy 1987; Comaroff and Comaroff 1989; Crush 1985; Trapido 1978). Similarly, recent publications by Chanock (1985), S. Moore (1986), and Wright (1982) demonstrate how differing peasant perspectives on such critical issues as land tenure, taxation, property rights, and gender relations can be extracted from court records. Nevertheless, even the richest of these documents is a colonial artifact in which peasants' words, ideas, and ideologies have been mediated through the eyes and ears of non-peasant chroniclers whose agendas are shaped by their own race, class, and gender.

That Africanists are beginning to pay greater attention to the voices of peasants—old and young, women and men, sharecroppers and prospering commodity producers—as well as their descendants is a mark of the field's growing maturity. All these voices need to be listened to critically and carefully, precisely because there is no *authentic voice* or transcending unity that structured the diverse experiences of African peasantries and because these oral documents are social texts with hidden and often multiple meanings.

For all the difficulties oral testimonies pose (Hamilton 1987; Henige 1982; Miller 1980; Schoffeleers 1985; Vansina 1985), carefully collected and rigorously analyzed, they can provide important material for a new social history of the countryside. Botte (1974), Newbury (1988), and Vidal (1974), for example, used Rwandan oral data to move beyond elite history and to dismantle the notion of plural societies. Delehanty (1988) and Watts (1983b), working in Niger and northern Nigeria respectively, extracted valuable information on crop-management systems and famine strategies.

Above all else, oral testimonies provide researchers with the possibility of understanding the complexities of rural life by getting at peasants' self-perceptions and trying to decipher what they might mean. While there is obviously not a perfect correlation between what peasants thought and the social realities in which they lived, their understanding of what they saw and understood is as important to consider as the social structures that limited their choices and options. It was Kanogo's (1987) willingness to listen to Kenyan squatters' voices which enabled her to begin to penetrate their inner world and reconstruct their notions of justice, property, community, and Mau-Mau oathing in ways that Throup's (1987) carefully researched archival study could not do. Similarly, allowing peasants to speak for themselves enabled Bradford (1987) to present a nuanced view of rural Transvaal. These accounts contain not only invaluable first-hand experiences but also the critical subjective elements that historians often find so difficult to capture. It also enables scholars to experiment with narrative style to capture the wide range of rural experiences (J. Berger 1979; Cohen and Atienho-Odhiambo 1989; Comaroff and Comaroff 1987; Landeg White 1987).

A number of researchers groping with the impulse to write history from the *bottom up* (Berry 1985; Geiger 1986, 1987; Isaacman 1988; Marks 1987; Mbilinyi 1988; Romero 1988; van Onselen 1990) have turned increasingly to life histories. To date, much of the most interesting work has been done by feminist scholars analyzing the intersection of race, class, and gender primarily, but not exclusively, in urban areas (Bozzoli 1991; Cock 1984; Geiger 1986; Marks 1987). Oral autobiographies of peasants offer an obvious opportunity to incorporate their voices into our scholarship. There have been some promising starts. The University of Witwatersrand's African Studies Institute has embarked on major life story projects on sharecroppers and tenants in the countryside. Keegan's (1988) portrait of the life stories of four rural South Africans not only captures the richness and varieties of their experiences, but through the reminiscences of these individuals provides new insights about the forces of social change in the countryside (see also Wright 1984). Published fragments of Kas Maine's oral autobiography powerfully document his successful struggle against proletarianization and capitalist labor discipline and the opportunities to retain some degree of autonomy which sharecropping offered:

Boers who practice sharecropping didn't follow and push sharecroppers around. They did not say hurry, hurry. No! You worked independently. You didn't eat their food. There was the land only. They were concerned only about sharing the produce. (Nkadimeng and Reilly 1984)

Van Onselen's (forthcoming) life history of Kas Maine penetrates the material and ideological universe of a sharecropping family and outlines the complex process of cultural osmosis that permeated class and racial boundaries in the rural Transvaal, while suggesting that oral evidence garnered from landlords, when treated critically, can also help to fill in critical gaps in our knowledge. And despite the difficult military and economic situations in Mozambique, the Centro de Estudos Africanos has launched a number of projects in which the life histories of peasants and rural workers figured prominently.[33] The best known of these is *Black Gold: The Mozambican Miner, Proletarian and Peasant* (First 1983).

In addition to the individual voices of African peasants, scholars have begun to examine their collective voices captured in songs, proverbs, festivals, theater, and nonverbal forms of popular culture such as dance. These sources offer a unique, although not always easily accessible, view of the complexities of everyday life. Submerged in many of these cultural forms is "a hidden transcript of the oppressed" (James Scott 1985). A careful decoding of these texts often provides an opportunity for researchers to uncover and understand the thoughts and actions of peasants. To refer to these songs and other cultural artifacts as *hidden,* however, runs the risk of viewing them exclusively from an external perspective—since the performers and audience were well aware of their meaning even if the colonial authorities and capitalists were not. These songs, proverbs, and dances passed on vital information, values, and social commentary. In this sense, there was nothing hidden about them. They survived precisely because they were intelligible, authentic, and particularly powerful—precisely because they could not be easily read from outside.

Vail and White's (1978) pioneering study of peasant songs in colonial Mozambique provides insights into local definitions of power and justice and demonstrates how forced cotton and rice producers were able to mock and dehumanize their oppressors. In neighboring Malawi, Vaughan (1987) uses similar songs to document how the 1949 famines heightened gender conflicts within peasant communities. And Presley (1986) finds rich social commentaries critical of collaborating chiefs, missionaries, forced labor, and the indigenous practice of female circumcision in the songs of Kikuyu women. Similarly proverbs from Burundi (Rodegem 1974), Hausaland (Freund 1984b; Watts 1983b), the Gold Coast (Kea 1982), and Ethiopia (Crummey 1986) reveal deeply embedded contradictions and class tensions between peasants and their overlords.

By privileging peasant voices, students of agrarian change have broken significant new economic, political, and cultural ground, while at the same time opening up a difficult set of methodological and substantive tissues. The interpretation of peasant statements and actions often depends on nuanced understandings of the local conception which defines causality, of human misfortunes, and of the world. Scholars who listen to these peasant voices vary greatly in their mastery of local language and culture. The possibilities of misinterpretation are especially clear when actions of peasant resistance are tied up with forms of authority or of ritual expressions inherited from the precolonial period. The problem of translation and language, in their broadest sense, presents a constant challenge for scholars (Hunt 1989; Karp 1988; Joan Scott 1987). Vail and White's work, for example, has been criticized both because they made errors of translation and because they were not sufficiently attentive to the sociolinguistic dimensions of language (Mandala 1983; Watts 1987a). Moreover, how people say things can be as important as what they actually say (Karp 1988). Humor and irony, for example, are often subtle and powerful means of expression through which peasants may articulate their concerns and hidden political agendas (Karp 1988). Understanding the way different peasantries construct their own reality thus provides a strategic entry to understanding their efforts to maintain a measure of control over their changing world. A number of recent studies which emphasize the symbolic as well as the material content of rural protest (Comaroff and Comaroff 1989; Feierman 1990; Fields 1985; Lan 1985; Mandala 1990; MacGaffey 1983; Packard 1980; Van Binsbergen 1981) suggest the importance of such cognitive interpretations.

The issue of meaning is inextricably linked to how researchers listen to peasant voices. Understanding discourse is, after all, a process of give and take, and the purposes of the sender of the messages and those of the receiver are not necessarily coterminus. Students of agrarian change have to guard against the tendency to prefigure the interviews to evoke from their informants what they want to hear. The challenge is to be attentive when these peasant voices do not provide material that fits neatly into our preexisting analytical categories or, even worse, when they call them into question. To listen carefully is both to loosen our control over the interview process and to empower our informants. Such an approach also recognizes that peasants have multiple identities and are not merely producers of commodities.

Finally, even if researchers attentive to the conventions of culture are able to capture the meaning or meanings embedded in oral presentations, they can never be certain that they can capture anything more than the meaning at the moment. In the final analysis, each interview and each performance represents a unique interaction located in a historically specific setting (Barber 1986; Scheub 1985). Knowledge is situational and partial, and peasant voices are often polyvocal. Each encounter in the field is an act of construction rather than merely a reproduction of historical fact (Thelen 1989). In each encounter peasants reshape, combine, reorganize, and omit detail from the past in both an active and subjective way. Figuring out ways of listening for silence is a particularly challenging task.[34]

These difficulties notwithstanding, the challenge of interpretation is vital. Although there is no *authentic* peasant voice, taken as a whole these oral testimonies and performances provide the last best hope to reconstruct the diverse experiences of African peasantries. As Barber reminds us, "for the majority of African peoples," they "were the only channel of public communications" (1987).

Conceptualizing Agrarian Protest

Thinking about peasantries rather than peasants and listening to their many voices have far-reaching implications for the study of agrarian protest. At a minimum, they require a critical reevaluation of those theories that tend to universalize peasant behavior and communities. One consequence of adopting as primal fact either the classical interpretation that peasants possessed a low class consciousness[35] (Alavi 1973; Hobsbawm 1973; Marx 1926) or the contrary view of them as true revolutionaries uncorrupted by urban bourgeois society (Fanon 1963) is to close off, or at best narrow the terms of debate. A similar criticism can be leveled at some of the most influential recent literature which assumes that all peasants are essentially "risk minimizing" (James Scott 1976b), "profit maximizing" (Popkin 1979), or "uncaptured" (Hyden 1980). These propositions leave little space for more open-ended definitions of social conflict and contradictions that do not fit within some preconceived notion of a peasant *mentalité,* and they foreclose the possibility of exploring and understanding the very notion of power and politics held by differing peasantries in their specificity. Bernstein (1988), for example, emphasizes the contradictory class positions of peasants as petty commodity producers and the quite divergent politics they are likely to pursue.

The study of peasant struggle also requires that Africanists address the issue of resistance against whom and toward what. Is resistance only the organized, systematic, and collective action that seeks to negate the basis of oppression? A number of scholars argue that only insurrections represented political action and that everyday struggles do not ultimately qualify as resistance since they did not directly challenge the system (Genovese 1974; Mullin 1972). James Scott (1985) advances a broader formulation. "Class resistance," he argues, "includes any act by a member of a subordinate class intended either to mitigate or deny claims by the superordinate class or to advance its own claims vis-à-vis those superordinate classes" (James Scott 1985: 290).

The principal deficiency of Scott's formulation is that it overemphasizes the struggles of peasantries against the state, landowners, and merchants, and pays insufficient attention to the complex issues of dissent and division within rural communities. Such struggles over power and the control of scarce resources often contained intraclass, as well as interclass, dimensions. Gender and generational conflicts within the domestic unit or community fall into this latter category. The colonial state's policy of squeezing peasants off the land, which often precipitated fierce competition between landless peasants, poor peasants seeking to hold onto the little bit they still owned, and prosperous commodity producers for those parcels that remained in the African domain, contain aspects of both dimensions (Kanogo 1987; Ranger 1985).

Several advantages are derived by expanding Scott's definition to include intraclass conflict. It serves as a corrective to the previous literature, which overemphasized peasant rebellions even though they occurred relatively infrequently and were typically crushed.[36] It also allows scholars to examine in a more systematic way a wide range of localized, often hidden, forms of protest, which are the critical "weapons of the weak" (Adas 1981, 1986; Isaacman et al. 1980; James Scott 1985; Watts 1988). Feigning illness, sabotage, social banditry, and flight rarely challenged the system of oppression directly—although the *challenge* may exist in a legacy upon which later generations drew. In this respect these protests should not be idealized. Yet they did enable different embattled peasantries to maintain or even expand their autonomy against a dominant class and its state allies who had the opposite objective. Most interesting for the purposes of this paper are the variety of strategies used by different peasantries, possessing different resources and enmeshed in different labor processes, to pursue their own agendas.

Finally, this conceptualization of resistance incorporates insurgent thought as well as action. The symbols, norms, and ideological forms that different peasantries constructed shaped not only their self-identities and consciousness but their political behavior. Not all peasants fatalistically accepted the social order and the state's definition of justice. Some, concerned about the crises of social reproduction, health, and fertility, sought to ritually reconstruct their societies. Antiwitchcraft cults often represented efforts to combat the social disruption generated by colonial economic and political policies (Bohannan 1958; Fields 1985; Packard 1980). Others forged coherent insurgent ideologies. The construction of a viable political language drawing on long-standing cultural values to address contemporary social realities was itself contested by the colonial state and its allies who sought to colonize peasant consciousness (Comaroff and Comaroff 1989). Colonial efforts notwithstanding, rural communities often played a critical role in organizing larger social movements. The hidden forms of struggle, the social basis of conflict within peasant communities, the construction of insurgent ideologies, and the ambiguous relationship of different peasantries to larger social movements both in precolonial and colonial Africa will be the focus of the remainder of this study.

Injecting Peasantries into Precolonial Agrarian History

The organization and control of rural labor are as important for the agrarian history of precolonial Africa as they are for the later period. Yet, Africanists have generally ignored the ways in which different peasant labor regimes helped to shape the agrarian history of precolonial Africa.[37] We know very little about the variability in the systems of production. It matters a great deal if peasants were spending 40 percent of their labor time farming and the rest of their time gathering, hunting, and cattle-keeping or 80 percent of their time in agriculture. It also matters which members of the peasant communities were engaged in which activities. In short, we need to learn much more about the peasant labor process in different parts of precolonial Africa. Peasantry means something different when referring to the Senegal River Valley, the equatorial forest, central Zimbabwe, highland Ethiopia, and the oasis on the Sahara. And it may mean something different when referring to quite different labor processes even within the same area, as in the case of the Central Sudan.[38]

It is difficult to reconstruct, or hypothesize, how agricultural production was organized, labor controlled, and land distributed during the precolonial era because data are fragmentary, at best, for much of this period. Inadequate documentation also makes it hard to specify those precise mechanisms used to control, threaten, and exploit peasants. Without a prior and simultaneous study of the forms of rural domination, it is quite difficult to study the nature of resistance and the range of conflicts between the state, the local elite, peasant households, and individuals within these households.

Precolonial agrarian historiography suffers, for example, from a thin archaeological record and a reluctance to tease out material on differentiation, nutrition, labor, and commoditization, and to link the findings to theory.[39] (For exceptions see.Connah 1987; Garlake 1978; Hall 1987a, 1987b; Wilmsen 1983, forthcoming). This lacuna contrasts sharply to the rich pre-Columbian Mexican and Peruvian data (Adam 1977; Keatinge 1988; Schele and Miller 1986; Wauchope 1967–76) which have enabled Latin Americanists to analyze ancient agrarian regimes and the social basis of rural conflict. Oral traditions, the other major corpus of early historical material which might provide insights on rural societies, pose different problems. Not only do they lack temporal specificity, but they are often the social and ideological charter of the ruling class or strata. Thus, they tend to emphasize the political and religious history of the elite rather than the daily lives of the ordinary subject population.[40] Reconstructing agrarian history is further complicated by the paucity of written records. Without such documents, it is impossible to determine population size, patterns of land distribution, variations in landholdings and surface area cultivated, volume of agricultural produce, and the actual taxes peasants paid.[41] Where written records have survived, they tend to be fragmentary and almost invariably exhibit an external bias.[42]

Regardless of the thinness of data, scholars have suggested that local conditions may have actually retarded or inhibited the widespread development of precolonial peasantries. In a pathbreaking study of West Africa, Goody (1971) argued that the absence of the plow, draught animals, and the wheel meant that though there was more land in Africa than in other parts of the world, it was less productive and therefore required a substantial amount of labor. Because land was readily available, labor had to be immobilized; hence, in many areas, slaves captured through aristocrat-sponsored warfare became the dominant labor form. Other scholars explain the lack of a significant precolonial peasantry in terms of a weak market system, harsh environmental conditions, a conservative production strategy, and state systems that lacked the power to organize and appropriate rural production (Austen 1987; Bates 1987a; Harms n.d.).

Whatever their line of reasoning, many Africanists presumed two points: that captives were the primary producers of agricultural commodities, and, conversely, that peasants were inconsequential, if present at all, on the precolonial landscape.[43]

These points did not go uncontested. In a provocative essay, Hay (1974) argued that peasant communities were a regular feature of Africa's precolonial political economy. The critical issue was not timing but the process by which peasants came into being. Although from a different theoretical orientation than Hay, and not necessarily agreeing among themselves, Copans (1980), Coquery-Vidrovitch (1976b), Guy (1982), and Slater (1977) all came to a similar conclusion about the existence of precolonial peasants.

Scholarship in the 1980s, although limited, confirms that peasants were an integral part of the economic and social landscape of precolonial Africa. Consider the case of nineteenth-century northern Nigeria. Using extensive oral data, Hausa and Arabic documents, and nineteenth-century journals, diaries, and travelogues, Mahadi (1982), Usman (1981), and Watts (1983b) highlight the dual role peasants played as commodity producers and as a force for radical political change. Watts documents how corvée labor, wage labor, slavery, and peasant household labor existed side by side in the Sokoto Caliphate. He asserts that peasant, rather than slave, labor predominated.[44] Although Mahadi and Usman often interchange the term *peasant* with *commoner* and *farmer,* both also provide a detailed discussion of how the aristocracy appropriated peasant surplus. Usman and Watts also document the struggles of the downtrodden to limit state extraction and increase food security. These three monographs, the unusually rich historiography on slave labor (Hill 1972; Hogendorn 1977; Lovejoy 1978, 1979, 1983; Smith 1954), and a recent paper in which Hill[45] stresses that most slaves were owned by peasant households suggests the complexity of precolonial agrarian labor regimes in northern Nigeria.

Building upon a rich, although diverse, body of research on the Amhara society (Gamst 1970; Hoben 1973; Levine 1965; Pankhurst 1967), scholars have also begun to examine rural class relations in nineteenth-century Ethiopia (Aregay 1984; Crummey 1978, 1984, 1986; Fernyhough 1986; McCann 1985, 1987; Quirin 1977). Crummey argues that the Amharic core was essentially a feudal society in which "the rulers supported themselves by means of exactions from the peasants, primarily in the form of tribute rather than rent" (1980:135). Sharecropping figured prominently as a secondary mode of extraction. Although historically the nobility had successfully manipulated patron-client relations to contain class conflict, increased taxes, which exacerbated food shortages, precipitated a number of peasant insurrections during the second half of the nineteenth century (Crummey 1986; Fernyhough 1986). In the Gondar region to the northwest, Falasha peasants struggled against the central authority's invasion and natural calamities to ensure their economic and cultural survival (Quirin 1977), while in neighboring Wallo peasants joined with local aristocrats to blunt the imperial advances of the Ethiopian state (McCann 1987).

Peasants also figured prominently in the early history of Mozambique, where the *prazo* system rested largely on the appropriation of their surplus (Isaacman 1972; Newitt 1973). From the seventeenth through the nineteenth centuries, Afro-Portuguese estate-holders, backed by their slave armies, collected an annual tribute in peasant produce. These commodities supported the estate-owner and his slave army, and were used to outfit slave and ivory-trading expeditions into the interior. To a large measure, the history of the *prazos* is a history of struggle between the peasants, slaves, and estate-holders over the expropriation of this surplus and the *prazeiros'* demands for labor.

The irrigated rice system which underpinned the nineteenth-century Madagascar kingdom of Merina also depended upon intensive peasant labor (Berg 1981; Campbell 1988; P. Larson 1985). Peasants were forced to pay in eight separate taxes an appreciable portion of what they produced. The aristocracy used these resources to maintain a powerful state apparatus and to trade with neighboring interior peoples. Although the peasants were legally free, the distinction between peasants and slaves was often blurred. The state forcibly conscripted some peasants into the army and made others work on public-works projects. In reaction to the harsh labor and tax requirements, an estimated 100,000 peasants and slaves fled to peripheral areas outside the control of the kingdom during the nineteenth century (P. Larson 1985).

A discussion of peasants in precolonial Africa would be incomplete without reference to Kea's *Settlements, Trade and Politics in the Seventeenth-Century Gold Coast* (1982) and Thornton's *The Kingdom of Kongo* (1983). Although neither book focuses on peasants and both rest entirely on written documentation, they make an important contribution to agrarian history. Kea links the development of a peasantry to the twin processes of land privatization and urbanization, both of which predated the arrival of European merchants. He analyzes the development of the class structure based on landlord extraction from peasants of agricultural surplus in the form of land rent. By the seventeenth century, peasants were forced to cultivate twice as much land as they needed for subsistence just to meet the rent. The result was increased impoverishment, riots, insurrections, and banditry. Unlike the Gold Coast, the major locus of struggle in the seventeenth-century Kongo was between the urban-based senior aristocracy and the tax paying peasantry. A well-developed ideological structure which legitimated the hegemony of the aristocracy, backed by the threat of force,[46] was not sufficient to contain peasant opposition to forced taxes. By the end of the century, these interclass conflicts and the intraclass struggle between nobles, which peasants often manipulated, had led to the decentralization of the kingdom (see also Vansina 1966).

Three conclusions flow from this cursory review of the literature. First, in many parts of precolonial Africa peasants were neither marginal nor invisible. While precolonial states rarely, if ever, organized peasant production, the extraction of surplus through rent, taxes, and tribute was widespread. To the examples previously cited, the literature further suggests that peasants may have figured prominently in the agricultural and political history of Rwanda (Vidal 1974), Kuba (Vansina 1978), Burundi (Botte 1974), the Nuba (Ewald forthcoming), and the Duma of Zimbabwe (Mtetwa 1976), as well as in the slave-based economies of Sinnar (Spaulding 1982), and Songhay-Zarma (Olivier de Sardan 1984). Although there are indications that peasantries were more widespread than previously thought, the diverse ways peasants came into being and the social reproduction of peasant communities requires detailed investigation. This involves an analysis of the reorganization of the labor process, the nature of rent, the extension of market relations, changing gender relations, and the imposition of new forms of domination, especially in larger states. This peasant transition, moreover, was not irreversible. Many peasants withdrew from market relations, escaped from the effective reach of the state, or were captured and enslaved. Meillassoux (1986) has demonstrated how common this pattern of enslavement was throughout the nineteenth century.

Second, precolonial peasant regimes were far more varied than has previously been assumed. Because the state was usually unable to organize production, land was relatively abundant, and markets often weak, a consensus has emerged in the literature that the principal incentive to produce commodities was to satisfy tribute, taxes, or rent obligations. Apart from these payments, the bulk of peasant labor went into production for use, suggesting that most precolonial peasants were essentially independent household producers. Other peasants, however, especially those in West Africa, used their access to land and control of labor to profit from the nineteenth-century *commercial revolution*. Sparked by increasing European demand for peanuts, palm oil, and other cash crops, many rural communities restructured production and in the process transformed themselves into fairly prosperous petty commodity producers (Austen 1987; Bowman 1987; Brooks 1975; Hopkins 1973).

In stark contrast to these successful commodity producers stood precolonial peasantries who were denied access to land and had no alternative but to exchange a portion of their household labor for conditional access to farms. Sharecropping and labor-tenancy systems seem to have developed where good quality soil was scarce, demographic pressures great, or land politicized. Although the documentation is fragmentary, there is evidence of sharecropping in such diverse societies as Asante (Arhin 1983; Wilks 1976), Wolof of Senegambia (Searing 1988), Ethiopia (Crummey 1980; Quirin 1977), and along the Sahelian fringe (Iliffe 1987; Monod 1972). Labor-tenancy, or the exchange of a fixed amount of peasant labor for land, is reported in both precolonial Rwanda and Burundi (Botte 1974; Iliffe 1987; Vidal 1974). However, the analytical distinction between labor-tenancy and sharecropping was often blurred. In the Gambia, a mixed labor-tenancy sharecropping system flourished after the 1848 groundnut boom (Swindell 1984).

Similarly, several scholars note that the distinction between impoverished peasantries and slaves, in the fluid context of late nineteenth-century West Africa, was not always clear. In the Saharan saltworks, free peasants "were kept in economic and political conditions of servitude that were not very different from slavery" (Lovejoy 1983). Conversely, there is evidence primarily from West Africa to support the hypothesis of a "peasant breach" in the slave system. First advanced by Caribbeanists (Cardoso 1979; Mintz 1979), it posits that many slaves actually lived as part-time peasants producing for the market and accumulating a certain amount of wealth.[47] Roberts and Klein find a similar phenomenon in the nineteenth-century Western Sudan. "Slaves had the right to free time and a plot of land" which enabled them "to accumulate property and to sell their produce in the market" (Roberts and Klein 1980:380). In his *African Economic History*, Austen (1987) confirms the existence of this phenomenon in parts of precolonial West Africa.[48]

The crucial issues that emerge from this discussion are the control of labor and the varied transitions from slave to freedmen. Both involved an ongoing process of negotiations, struggle, and adjustment to the development of a *proto-peasantry* under slavery, an inherently contradictory development which often served the short-term goals of slaves and masters (Mintz 1979). It allowed these proto-peasants to feed themselves, accumulate and bequeath wealth, and increase their autonomy, all within the constraints of a bounded slave system. In the long run, these contradictory tendencies could only be resolved through jockeying and struggling over power. This contest between slaves, slaveowners, and the state resulted in a wide range of different and changing labor and social arrangements, including the emergence of ex-slaves as tenant farmers, sharecroppers, household producers, and prosperous commodity producers (Roberts and Miers 1988).

Thus, rather than a single precolonial prototype, several quite distinct peasantries engaged in different labor processes figured prominently in the political economy of sub-Saharan Africa. In some societies, such as the Wolof, independent household producers, sharecroppers, tenants, and slaves lived side-by-side, and in the course of a lifetime, an individual may have moved through two or more social categories (Searing 1988). The impact of slavery and slave ideology on relations between peasants and the appropriating classes is a subject that merits additional investigation, as does the complex and varied transition from slaves to peasants.[49]

Finally, we need to incorporate the notions of contradiction and social conflict into the analysis of precolonial agrarian societies. For far too long, scholars have assumed a type of pristine harmony and peasant quietism which neither logic nor the historical record sustains. To call for this new direction in research is not to deny that in precolonial Africa there were powerful ideological forces and historical practices that acted to inhibit, deflect, or contain peasant unrest. Most African states developed elaborate ritual and ideological systems that sought to legitimate the basis of rule in consent rather than coercion (Feierman 1990; Freund 1984b; Vansina 1962, 1978). Kingship ideology that inextricably linked the fertility of peasants and of their land to the personal health and well-being of the king was a powerful mechanism of social control. Vertical ties of kinship connecting peasants to the aristocracy as well as an internalized belief in one's ethnic superiority further mediated against social unrest (Clarence-Smith 1979a; Crummey 1980; McCann 1987; Vansina 1978).

But to assume that ruling-class ideology was never contested or that peasants were unaware that reciprocity masked deep inequalities is to accept the assumptions and self-perceptions of the rulers. The literature suggests that peasants challenged the presumed hegemony of the aristocracy. As in the colonial period, there is ample evidence of peasants moving beyond the reach of the state or relocating on the land of a competing chief who required less. The weakness of most states and the availability of arable land facilitated peasant flight (Vansina 1966). At other times they dissented more discreetly. In a study of political discourse among the Shambaa, Feierman (1990) emphasizes the tension between the king and commoners articulated at the coronation of a new ruler. Similarly, ritual conflicts between newly appointed aristocrats and their peasant subjects in the Kongo (Thornton 1983), and proverbs and oral poetry depicting exploitation in Ethiopia and the Gold Coast (Crummey 1980; Kea 1982; McCann 1987) suggest that peasants were able to produce a culture of opposition. It also appears that peasants used the state religion, whether Islam[50] in northern Nigeria or Christianity in the Kongo, to attack despotic rulers and ineffective governments, even if they did not challenge the structure of society itself (Last 1970; Thornton 1983; Vansina 1966; Watts 1983b).

But even more to the point, the relatively scanty literature on precolonial agrarian history contains examples of different peasantries struggling against exploitive practices that did not conform to the ideals articulated in the dominant ideology and threatened their partial autonomy. As in preindustrial Europe, excessive taxes, which often triggered subsistence crises, seem to have been the most common grievance. Tax revolts are documented in such disparate regions as the Kongo, Ethiopia, the Gold Coast, the Kuba kingdom, the Shambaa state, and on the Mozambique *prazos* (Crummey 1980, 1984; Isaacman 1972; Newitt 1973; Thornton 1983; Vansina 1978).[51] Similarly, the Ethiopian government's demand that peasants billet state troops during a nineteenth-century famine produced a violent reaction (Crummey 1984). Conflict over land, although less well documented, erupted in Rwanda and Burundi (Botte 1974; Iliffe 1987; Vidal 1974), the Sokoto Caliphate (Watts 1983b, 1988), and the Tuareg-controlled Sahelian fringe (Iliffe 1987). And where the state or landlords attempted to organize production, as in Madagascar and the Sokoto Caliphate, there is evidence of wide-scale opposition from both peasants and slaves (P. Larson 1985; Lovejoy 1986a). In other instances, peasants, lacking the power to stand up to the state, engaged in hidden or less visible forms of protest to shelter their produce against demands that they considered unreasonable or that threatened their food security (Kea 1982; Thornton 1983; Watts 1983b).

I would also suggest that we need to reexamine the social basis of the succession and secession crises themes which have figured so prominently in the historiography of precolonial Africa. Rather than assuming that an undifferentiated rural population blindly followed a particular pretender to the throne or aided an outlying governor or local land chief, it makes more sense to consider such alliances transitory. Instead of presuming unity, we should try to ascertain how peasants might have taken advantage of these intraclass conflicts to promote their own interests, as in nineteenth-century Wolof society (Searing 1988) and in northern Ethiopia (McCann 1987). In the classic political history *Kingdoms of the Savanna*, written two decades ago, Vansina (1966) pointed to numerous examples of "popular opposition" to despotic rulers and predatory chiefs. Shortly thereafter, Wrigley (1971) challenged the statist biases dominating the precolonial literature. It is time to take up this challenge.

Similarly, Africanists cannot continue to overlook the related issues of dissent and division within precolonial rural communities. Conspicuously absent from the material cited are any sustained discussions of the social tensions created by patriarchy and gender exploitation. Indeed, only a handful of studies address these issues. Berger's monograph *Religion and Resistance* (1981) emphasizes how the Kubandina spirit-possession cult was a predominantly democratic female organization which articulated a sense of women's opposition to male-dominated social systems. In a provocative, if somewhat speculative, essay on the Shambaa, Mbilinyi (1982) argues that the extensive production and reproduction obligations accompanying the marriage contract were necessary because women were neither pliant nor passive but struggled against the efforts of husbands, elders, and the ruling aristocracy to control their labor. Kinsman (1983) links gender exploitation in early nineteenth-century Tswana society to increased commoditization.[52] She contends that as the demand for grain rose, men, who controlled the land, seized the surplus their wives and sisters had produced and had previously retained. This assault "supported the growth of a male-dominated peasantry on the one hand, and an increasingly wealthy, agricultural based aristocracy on the other" (Kinsman 1983:40). Rural women reacted in a variety of ways: some successfully resisted this assault, others submitted, while still others turned to Christianity, which held out the promise of gender equality.

Several new works, based on detailed field research, promise to extend the discussion of social tension and internal dissent within nineteenth-century agrarian societies. Schmidt's work (1992) on ideology and gender among the Shona suggests that patriarchy was both widespread and a source of social conflict throughout much of precolonial Zimbabwe. Mandala (1990) demonstrates how Manganja elders manipulated male prepuberty schools to control the labor of the young. And in a fascinating variation on the common pattern of patriarchy and class oppression, Ewald (forthcoming) emphasizes how the resistance of Nuba peasants compelled the ruling class to turn inward and impose harsh production requirements on their own household members. The Nuba aristocracy was forced to adopt this strategy to feed their slave armies upon whom the maintenance of their class and state power rested.

Peasantries and Rural Struggle in a Colonial Capitalist Context: Emerging Themes

The lives of peasants—women and men, old and young—were dramatically transformed under colonial capitalism. Commodity production, however incomplete, penetrated all but the remotest corners of the continent, deleteriously affecting most households and communities. Alien and increasingly powerful colonial states sought to organize and control labor, and consequently to reduce peasant autonomy. To achieve this objective and simultaneously maintain social control, the colonial states imposed a new legal and judiciary system, redefined property relations, and co-opted or removed indigenous authorities.

The pace of change and level of rural social conflict varied between and within territories. Nevertheless, throughout the colonial period the material and cultural worlds of peasants were relentlessly attacked. These attacks did not go unanswered. Recently, scholars have begun to examine the ways in which peasants have coped with and struggled against both the claims on their labor and produce and the denigration of their cultural heritage. Three issues have received increasing attention in the literature and have expanded the boundaries of African peasant studies: the everyday or hidden forms of peasant resistance; the inter- and intraclass conflicts within peasant communities; and the interrelationship between peasant ideology and insurgent action. While the focus of this paper is on peasant protest, it is well to remember that their actions had a constant impact on the colonists, their politics, culture, values, and consciousness.

Peasants and Everyday Struggle

The ongoing, if prosaic, struggle between peasants and those who sought to extract from them their labor, rent, food, and taxes is a critical chapter in the social and political history of colonial Africa. The concept of *everyday* or *hidden* forms of resistance, derived from American slave and European agrarian historiography (Bauer and Bauer 1942; Blassingame 1972; Blok 1972; Genovese 1974; Mullin 1972; Tilly 1982), offered Africanists a strategic entry into the less visible ways in which rural men and women helped to make their own history (Beinart and Bundy 1987; Bradford 1987; Isaacman and Isaacman 1977; Isaacman et al. 1980; Last 1970; Ranger 1986b; Watts 1988; see also R. Cohen 1980, concerning urban workers). Work slowdowns, pilfering, sabotage, dissimulation, flight, and the other weapons of the weak were more than just a nuisance to the powerful. The sum total of these otherwise insignificant acts could and sometimes did have far-reaching consequences. It is important to stress, however, that the concept of everyday resistance can be quite problematic. Used crudely or taken out of context, it can distort or render meaningless the notion of resistance itself.

At the level of description, the term *everyday resistance,* often interchanged in the literature with *hidden, normal, routine* forms of resistance, is somewhat misleading (James Scott 1985). Although intercropping, work slowdowns, pilfering, and dissimulation may have occurred daily, clearly flight and sabotage did not. The other descriptive terms suffer from a similar lack of precision. To call these actions *hidden* is to view them from the top down. Peasants who engaged in such protests understood the risks and benefits of their actions. The terms *normal* and *routine* presuppose that all peasant struggles followed a particular trajectory or, at least, could be reduced to a specific ensemble of actions.

Compounding this problem of semantics is the tendency in the literature to lump together many actions with different intentions and outcomes. Feigning illness, sabotage, flight, and banditry are quite different oppositional forms with divergent intended consequences (Adas 1986; Isaacman et al. 1980; Tilly 1982).

In the final analysis, what these daily or hidden protests are presumed to share is that they were *not* rebellions, revolutions, or other broad-based social movements—the very acts that our scholarly tradition privileges in ways that might distort the historical record. Instead, they tended to be individual, localized forms of insurgency (Adas 1986; Hobsbawm 1969; Isaacman et al. 1980; Joan Scott 1986; Watts 1988). Yet, arguments by negation are often problematic and distinctions based on scale are not always accurate. In colonial Africa there are examples of work slowdowns, crop sabotage, and flight involving hundreds of peasants and sometimes more (Asiwaju 1976; Cordell and Gregory 1982; Feierman 1990; Gahama 1983; Isaacman et al. 1980; Jewsiewicki 1980b; Mulambu-Mvuluya 1974; Olivier de Sardan 1984; Swai 1982). To the perpetrators these actions embodied at least some vague notion of collective identity and possessed an internal structure and logic even if it is not easily discernible to scholars.

That these insurgent acts were often clandestine poses the additional problem of intent. Many such acts went unrecorded; and even if we can document that a particular act occurred, unless we are able to listen critically to the voices of the actors, it is extremely difficult to determine their intentions. In some cases motivation may be inferred from the act itself. Clearly, labor tenants who sabotaged the equipment of European landlords in the Kenyan highlands or in the South African veld were making a political statement (Bradford 1987; Kanogo 1987). So, too, were cotton producers in Zaire, Ubangi-Share, Malawi, Tanganyika, and Mozambique who cooked their seeds before planting them (Isaacman et al. 1980; Jewsiewicki 1980a; Vaughan 1982). But such relatively unambiguous cases tend to be the exceptions.[53]

More often than not, I suggest, intent may have been polyvalent. Ethiopian, Angolan, Zimbabwean, and Mozambican *bandits* who robbed tax collectors, for example, may have had several motives (Clarence-Smith 1979b; Crummey 1986; Fernyhough 1986; Isaacman 1977). Plundering may have been a way of resisting surplus extraction, of feeding an undernourished family, and of accumulating a small amount of capital. Peasants covertly withholding taxes or fleeing coercive labor regimes were often driven by similar concerns. Although the question of multiple motives creates a certain analytical ambiguity, in real life people act ambiguously. For our discussion of what *counts* as resistance, it seems sufficient to demonstrate that one intent of the insurgents was to block or undercut the claims of the state or appropriating class.

That these *daily* forms of resistance may have served as safety valves perpetuating the system of exploitation raises additional doubts about the concept's utility. If rice sharecroppers in Gambia surreptitiously withheld a portion of their crop (Watts 1988) and subsequently defined their act as *cheating*, were they not legitimating existing property and class relations? And when state officials or representatives of the ruling class disregarded foot-dragging, small-scale pilfering, and illegal squatting, did they not do so, in part, because these acts locked peasants into the status quo? Thus, some authors argue that these acts encouraged peasants to work the system to their maximum advantage while, in effect, precluding the possibility of dismantling it (Hobsbawm 1973; Stoler 1986; C. White 1986).

Despite the problems inherent in the concept of everyday resistance, to ignore the weapons of the weak is to ignore the peasants' principal arsenal. Precisely because of the nature of the labor process, peasants enjoyed much greater autonomy than did rural or urban workers. This partial autonomy was more conducive to hidden forms of resistance than to broader social movements. Such actions rarely made headlines, but they made perfect sense and were the most pervasive form of rural protest.

Several qualifications are necessary, however, to extend and deepen the discussion of everyday rural struggle. Although peasants seemed to have a proclivity for these covert acts, clandestine resistance was not a knee-jerk reaction but often the result of carefully considered decisions which carried potentially serious consequences. Many peasants remained intimidated, others passively indignant. Moreover, the actions peasants pursued were often related to the structural constraints imposed by the specific labor processes in which they were enmeshed. Peasantries incorporated in different labor processes negotiated and struggled from different positions of relative strength. There is ample evidence throughout colonial Africa that impoverished labor tenants with little stake in the system struck back at their landlords by withholding their labor or through acts of sabotage (Bradford 1987; Cooper 1980; Crush 1987; Kanogo 1987; Throup 1987). For sharecroppers, who had somewhat greater control over the means of production and the final output, such tactics would obviously have been counterproductive.

The concept of everyday resistance also needs to be disaggregated to capture the diverse intentions of the actors as well as the consequences of their actions. The overwhelming majority of these everyday conflicts centered around three critical issues: the control of peasant labor, withholding peasant production, and the politics of retribution. These social struggles drew upon deeply held values of justice, kinship obligations, and work which were embedded in historical memories and expressive cultures that peasants retained and remade as part of their partial autonomy.

The Struggle over Labor

Flight seems to have been most commonly used by peasants to maintain control over their own labor. Especially in the first third of this century, porous colonial boundaries and the availability of large unoccupied tracts of arable land facilitated the flight of millions of disgruntled peasants. Many fled to neighboring colonies. Others, reluctant to break all ties to their families and historic homeland, clandestinely fled to sparsely populated areas where they reconstructed refugee communities beyond the effective control of the colonial regime. A variety of forced labor and tax policies, which threatened the food security and viability of peasant households, precipitated much of this (Coquery-Vidrovitch 1985; Cordell and Gregory 1982; Guyer 1978; Isaacman et al. 1980; Jewsiewicki 1980a; Latour-Dejean 1980).

Although some scholars contend that equating flight with resistance does "violence to language" (Vail and White 1983:919), Asiwaju was right to emphasize "that migration as protest proved far less costly to Africans and had much the same effect on the colonial authorities as did the other more militant forms of protest" (1976:593–94; see also Coquery-Vidrovitch 1985; Cordell and Gregory 1982; Crush 1987; Isaacman et al. 1980; Kopytoff 1987; Musambachime 1988; Ranger 1985; Watts 1988). *Fugitives* are quite explicit about their political motivation. Listen to the words of several northern Mozambican peasants who fled the repressive forced cotton regime:

On the prearranged night we brought our knives and clubs and our wives and children who were carrying food. We moved cautiously in the dark to avoid the *sepais* [African police] who we had been informed were located at Nachidoro. We agreed to fight to the last drop of blood to avoid capture (Isaacman et al. 1980:597).

West African colonial officials also acknowledged the political intent behind these acts (Cordell and Gregory 1982:220). In the post–World War II era, more effective transportation and communication systems reduced the viability of this tactic except in the most backwater regions (Isaacman et al. 1980; McClellan 1984; R. Pelissier 1984).

Labor flight took on an entirely different meaning for tenant farmers and sharecroppers located primarily in settler colonies. Flight was only an option when accessible land was abundant (Bradford 1983; Crush 1985; Kanogo 1987; Keegan 1982; McCracken 1983; Palmer 1986; Throup 1987; Trapido 1978). Since the settlers had appropriated most of the arable land, the peasants' options were to live on overcrowded reserves or be subject to capitalist labor discipline, or to become involved in sharecropping or tenant farming. Given the unattractive alternative, sharecroppers and, to a lesser degree, tenants were often reluctant to flee the system. Instead, they sought to exercise leverage over their living and working conditions by skipping to less harsh landlords or by threatening to do so. In South Africa, this practice was known as "jumping the fence" and occurred with great regularity during the first two decades of the century. Clever sharecroppers were able to negotiate control over a larger percentage of the crop and to obtain increased land to farm, while shrewd tenants received production bonuses and protection against tax collectors (Keegan 1982; Nkadimeng and Reilly 1984; Trapido 1978). A similar phenomenon occurred in Swaziland, where the weak settler community, fearing a large-scale insurrection, made a number of concessions to attract and keep tenants (Crush 1985, 1987). To the north, in the highland regions of Kenya, peasants fled from those estates whose owners opposed squatters owning livestock to those who tolerated it (Kanogo 1987). In the end, the leverage that flight offered tenants and sharecroppers proved transitory. As settlers in southern and eastern Africa turned to mechanization and as they, and indigenous capitalist farmers, were able to secure new sources of labor, the bargaining power of tenants and sharecroppers declined precipitously (Austen 1987; J. O'Brien 1983).

For many peasants, particularly women, covertly withholding a portion of their daily labor from commodity production was less risky than flight and increased the possibility of meeting household food requirements. This strategy was more viable in remote areas, where the colonial state remained relatively weak and capitalist penetration was limited. As late as the 1950s in frontier regions as diverse as the Niger desert fringe (Delehanty 1988; Olivier de Sardan 1984), southern Ethiopia (McClellan 1984), the Bagamoyo hinterland of Tanzania (Bryceson 1982b), and the northern tip of Mozambique (Isaacman et al. 1980), peasants resisted government and merchant pressure to promote cash-crop production on an appreciable scale.

Covert labor struggle was most intense where the colonial state sought to impose new labor demands on an already overburdened population. Widespread rural opposition to antierosion schemes as well as to forced cotton production are cases in point.

Although forced cotton production varied from one colony to another,[54] it produced a similar set of grievances and widespread covert opposition. Because cotton was labor-intensive, requiring several weedings per year, and because its agricultural cycle often coincided with the principal food crops, its imposition caused a production bottleneck and threatened food supplies.[55] This was particularly true where the state prohibited intercropping (Bassett 1988; Isaacman et al. 1980; Jewsiewicki 1980b). Since the price paid for cotton was artificially depressed, peasants could not hope to purchase the grains they were unable to produce. Thus, they could only feed their families by extending their workday substantially. Predictably, food shortages, famines, and rural impoverishment plagued the forced cotton regimes of Africa (Dampierre 1960; Isaacman et al. 1980; Jewsiewicki 1980b; O'Laughlin 1973; Vaughan 1982).

Faced with this attack on their households, peasants fought back in quiet, but effective, ways. There are numerous examples of peasants of Tanzania, Kenya, Uganda, Malawi, Cameroon, Zaire, Chad, and Mozambique who, despite harsh penalties, cultivated less than the required amounts, planted their cotton after the designated dates, weeded fewer times and later than required, covertly abandoned their cotton fields to work their gardens, illegally intercropped, or allowed their cotton to rot (Dampierre 1960; Isaacman et al. 1980; Jewsiewicki 1980b; Likaka 1991; Little 1987; McCarthy 1982; Mulambu-Mvuluya 1974; O'Laughlin 1973; Vaughan 1982). Many also refused to burn the plants after the harvest, increasing the likelihood of pest infestation.[56] In Zaire, Malawi, and Mozambique there is evidence that peasants boiled seeds either as an act of protest or, perhaps, to deceive colonial officials into believing that their land was ill-suited for cotton production (Isaacman et al. 1980; Jewsiewicki 1980b; Vaughan 1987). Such acts of defiance convinced British officials to abandon coercion in the 1920s and 1930s, a decade before their French counterparts and more than a quarter of a century before their Belgian and Portuguese allies.

The British were not nearly so flexible about the post–World War II antierosion schemes which pitted poorer peasants, primarily women, against chiefs, wealthier peasants, and colonial officials. Although such projects might have been originally designed to promote food production, the colonial regime imposed these improvements primarily to increase commercial production and enhance their domination of the countryside. Women opposed the antierosion programs because by eliminating marginal terrain, often the only land available to them, it reduced the amount of accessible farmed land and because laboring long hours building ridges on their hillside farms was an intolerable burden which reduced the time to work in the fields. In 1947 Kenyan women living in the highlands failed to appear for the compulsory communal terracing campaign, leaving the task to a handful of elderly men. They sustained this boycott for two years (Throup 1987). At the same time, poor peasant women in the Usambara region of Tanzania first refused to participate in antierosion projects and then came to work carrying tiny weeding hoes totally inadequate for the task (Cliffe et al. 1975; Feierman 1990). They also covertly destroyed seedlings for the reforestation program (Feierman 1990; Swai 1982). Antierosion projects evoked a similar reaction in the Tchiri Valley of Malawi (Mandala 1990), in neighboring Zambia (Chipungu 1987), and South Africa (Beinart 1989; McAllister 1989). A decade later, women in the Kom region of western Cameroon defied agricultural officers who insisted that they ridge their mountain slopes horizontally which would have made their system of cooperative farming on vertically oriented fields unworkable. For three years they refused to comply, enduring harassment and heavy fines by colonial officials (Ardener 1975; Rogers 1980).

Just as opponents of the antierosion schemes faced harsh retribution if they were caught, so throughout this century tenants faced the prospect of losing access to farmland if they failed to satisfy their work obligations. Yet cooperating often meant perpetuating the cycle of impoverishment and vulnerability. The ways in which they sought to resolve this dilemma reflected their perceived bargaining power. Where they were in a relatively weak position, as in South Africa, labor tenants covertly manipulated work agreements. It was common practice to send the youngest and least productive family members to work on the landlords' farms, so that the physically stronger and most experienced workers could produce for the household (Nkadimeng and Reilly 1984; Trapido 1978). By contrast, in early twentieth-century Swaziland settlers' fears of unrest enabled many tenants, who were already farming the land, either to delay or to avoid signing binding contracts (Crush 1985, 1987). And in Kenya, in the heady pre–Mau Mau days, squatters adopted an even more aggressive posture, defying work rules, disregarding limits on the size of their land and herds, and even refusing to abandon the land when ordered to do so (Throup 1987).

Withholding Peasant Production

Peasants, whatever their role in the labor process, also pursued a variety of evasive tactics to minimize surplus extraction. For most, the colonial state was the principal predator. At least until World War I, peasants were able to protect much of their surplus through concealment, collusion, and under-reporting. Thus, for example, the Sahoue and Holli of Dahomey impeded the access of revenue collectors by planting thick bushes around their villages or by attacking road crews (Coquery-Vidrovitch 1985; Garcia 1970). Hausa peasants repeatedly cut telegraph lines to prevent the understaffed British colonial administration from controlling the Sokoto hinterland (Last 1970). Other rural communities gave false information to revenue officials and census collectors. Colonial ledgers and the annual reports of administrations are littered with references to peasants who *forgot* local ordinances, hid cattle, disguised granaries, and falsified the ages and marital status of family members (Isaacman and Isaacman 1983; Spittler 1979; Watts 1988). One British official stationed in northern Nigeria during World War I wrote in his memoirs that "the art of lying . . . has reached a very high state of perfection among the natives of the northern provinces" (Watts 1988:137). When deception failed, rural communities occasionally resorted to ambushing tax collectors (Gahama 1983; Garcia 1970, Latour-Dejean 1980; R. Pelissier 1978, 1984).[57]

Peasants also contested colonial policies they believed would reduce their assets. When French colonial officials introduced a famine reserve program in Niger, the rural population refused to participate, assuming that the millet would end up in the hands of state officials (Latour-Dejean 1980). Similarly, thousands of male peasants from Tanzania to South Africa refused to comply with dipping requirements to combat stock diseases, fearing that they would lose a measure of control over one of their few remaining assets, while in some areas women protested because they had to keep the dip tanks filled, even though the cattle belonged to the men (Beinart and Bundy 1980, 1987; Ranger 1985; Swai 1982).

Peasants also struck back at rural merchants who engaged in price-gouging, rigged their scales, and charged exorbitant interest on loans. The historical record is replete with examples of peasants destroying crops, adulterating products, bypassing prescribed markets, and organizing boycotts (Beinart and Bundy 1987; Bunker 1986; Isaacman et al. 1980; Jewsiewicki 1980b; Lennihan 1982; Likaka 1991; McCracken 1983; Watts 1988). While these actions were ostensibly about withholding production, they suggest that we need to pay greater attention to peasant struggles for improved terms of inclusion within mercantile capitalism.

Getting Even: The Politics of Retribution
The politics of retribution differed from the other forms of everyday struggle in intent and strategy. Peasants, rather than withholding resources, lashed out at the most immediate structures and symbols of their oppression. Because open confrontation would have been suicidal, retribution was most often covert. Sabotage, arson, ambushes, and banditry were used against landlords, merchants, collaborating chiefs, and African police. When successfully carried out, they rarely left a paper trail for historians.

Sabotage is reported most commonly in labor regimes that were particularly repressive and in which peasants had the least stake. While it made little sense for commodity producers to destroy their own crops or machinery, labor tenants working for the landlord and peasants forced to cultivate cash crops from which they in no way benefited were hardly bound by such constraints. Although it is difficult to know with what frequency sabotage occurred, the fact that the eastern and southern African countryside was underpoliced certainly left isolated European settlers vulnerable. In the boldest acts of defiance, labor tenants occasionally attempted to poison or kill brutal farmers (Bradford 1987). These attacks were not directed solely against Europeans, however. Hutu peasants engaged in similar covert actions against Tutsi landlords, while in cotton regimes stretching from Uganda to Chad and from the Ivory Coast to Zaire, African labor overseers, police, and chiefs also felt the wrath of the impoverished subject population (Bassett 1988; Dampierre 1960; Isaacman 1985; Sturzinger 1983; Tosh 1978).

Peasants also attacked rural merchants—often the most visible and immediate symbols of oppression. Smoldering resentment periodically erupted in looting, sabotage, and the destruction of shops (Beinart and Bundy 1987; Caulk 1984; Isaacman et al. 1980; Likaka 1991; Watts 1988; Weiskel 1980). These acts raise the vexing problem of distinguishing between crime and social protest. Within the context of African agrarian historiography, scholars have been engaged in a spirited debate around the question of social banditry.

One school of thought (Clarence-Smith 1979b; Coquery-Vidrovitch 1985; Isaacman 1977; Keller 1973; Kea 1986; Ranger 1985; Roche 1976; Seleti 1987) rejects the penchant of colonial regimes for dismissing most forms of rural protest as deviant criminal behavior. Drawing inspiration from Hobsbawm

(1965, 1969), they insist that a distinction be made between social bandits who attacked the institutions that oppressed the rural populace and those outlaws and brigands who indiscriminately preyed upon all sectors of society. These scholars contend that the concept of social banditry provides an alternative view of social conflict in rural societies experiencing the disruptive impact of colonial capitalism. Proponents of this thesis point to examples of social banditry in Tanzania (Feierman 1990), Ethiopia (Caulk 1984), southern Angola (Clarence-Smith 1979b; Seleti 1987), the Shaba province of Zaire (Coquery-Vidrovitch 1985), the Mozambican-Zimbabwean border (Isaacman 1977), southern Zimbabwe (Ranger 1985), and South Africa (Bradford 1987). In the final analysis, social bandits sought to redress grievances, but they rarely sought to create broader social movements with a more radical political agenda.

Hobsbawm's original formulation has come under attack among scholars working outside of Africa (Blok 1972; Lewin 1979; O'Mally 1979), and a number of Africanists have voiced skepticism about its analytical utility. Some see the study of social banditry as one more example of the "glorification of the inconsequential." [58] The most explicit criticism of the social banditry thesis advanced by Crummey in *Banditry, Rebellion and Social Protest in Africa* (1986) argues that the concept is ambiguous and that much of the brigandage in colonial Africa was without class meaning.[59] This debate demonstrates the difficulty of abstracting analytical categories from their specific historical context. The distinction that Hobsbawm posed was certainly true at the extremes, although it is probably true that on the ground the differences were often blurred. Some social bandits had more than just a noble agenda. But several articles in *Banditry, Rebellion and Social Protest* reveal that acts of banditry sometimes evolved as social practice of the oppressed and thus "became entangled in a more general pattern of social protest" (Freund 1986:60). And in the final analysis, the myth of social banditry may be as important in the historical and political perception of peasant communities as the actual intentions of the actors.

The interaction between rural protest, social banditry, and common banditry in Africa clearly merits further investigation. In the interim, I would argue that there is ample documentation (see, for example, Coquery-Vidrovitch 1988) that social bandits existed, at least as a transitional category operating on the margins of two worlds. As their space for action narrowed, they had to opt for either the *social* or the *bandit* part of their self-definition. Those who selected the former joined rural social movements. Those opting for the latter became brigands trying to survive beyond the reach of the law or mercenaries selling their martial skills to the highest bidder.

This discussion of everyday resistance would be incomplete without reference to popular culture produced and performed regularly in the countryside. Peasants' songs, proverbs, jokes, dance, and the plastic arts were the only uncensored media of public discourse during the colonial period. As such, they were a forum for ridicule as well as criticism (Kanogo 1987; Page 1978; Vail and White 1983; Vaughan 1987). Class tensions are also quite explicit in the voices of Wallo peasants reciting their oral poetry.[60] The values, norms, sense of justice, and anger inscribed in these performances often helped to shape a culture of insurgency. So, too, did the caricatures of European officials and settlers carved by northern Mozambican peasant artists (Alpers 1988).[61]

The creation of an oppositional culture is itself a political act. By singing, acting, or speaking their own histories peasants taught each other new ways of thinking about themselves and their world. Defiance of the dominant culture was an act of empowerment and often heightened peasant opposition which, in turn, influenced their consciousness. Similarly, successful acts of defiance provided heroic episodes from which it was possible to construct an oppositional ideology. Thus, there existed a profound interrelationship between dissident thought and action.

In the final analysis, these recurring and localized actions were not merely gestures of peasant frustration. They produced a number of partial if, at times, only momentary victories. At the turn of the century in South Africa, rural opposition to the Glen Grey Act, which raised taxes and challenged the indigenous land-tenure system, compelled state officials to slow down the process of land privatization and to abandon the proposed labor tax (Beinart and Bundy 1987). In Ghana labor boycotts and work slowdowns enabled migrant workers to gain a measure of protection through sharecropping arrangements (Austen 1987). Opposition to tenancy in Malawi's Tchiri Valley was the critical factor in the collapse of the settler estate economy during the 1920s (Mandala 1990). The tactics of forced cotton cultivators in Zaire and Mozambique also significantly reduced output (Isaacman et al. 1980; Likaka 1991), and the threat of Bugisu peasants to destroy their coffee trees forced rural merchants to raise prices (Bunker 1986).

It must be reiterated that none of these actions, although pervasive, attacked the structures of class, racial, and gender oppression. In this respect, they have been characterized as *weak* forms of resistance. Yet to varying degrees they did enable embattled peasantries to protect a measure of autonomy, and they reduced the level of oppression, however marginally. Africanists also need to pay greater attention to the ways in which these acts of defiance helped to shape an insurgent ideology and supported the development of larger social movements.

Internal Dissent: The Conflict Within Peasant Communities

Just as Africanists have begun to shift their attention from the highly visible though sporadic insurrections to less dramatic forms of protest, so, too, they have begun to focus on the less visible conflicts within peasant communities and households. This interest stems, in part, from an increasing appreciation of the uneven impact of commodity production. The incorporation of Africa into the modern capitalist world economy accentuated rivalries and divisions between chiefs and their subjects, wealthier and poorer peasants, creditors and debtors, women and men, young and old. These conflicts at both the community and domestic level were based on intraclass as well as interclass tensions which often antedated the colonial period.

At the community level, the most pronounced and best-documented conflicts were between loyalist chiefs and their subject populations.[62] Throughout colonial Africa, chiefs were placed in a contradictory position vis-à-vis both the colonial state and the peasantry, requiring them to mediate between the oppressor and the oppressed. Few were able to do so. Their ambiguous roles as paid state functionaries and as guardians of community resources accentuated these tensions. Because the colonial state, being relatively weak, was initially unable to play a decisive role in restructuring rural production, this unpopular task fell to the chiefs. They served as labor recruiters (Guyer 1978; Killingray 1978; Lonsdale and Berman 1979; Page 1978; Sutton 1983), tax collectors, and supervisors of forced agricultural production (Austen and Headrick 1983; Bassett 1988; Dampierre 1960; Guyer 1978; Isaacman 1985; Nayenga 1981; Sturzinger 1983; Tosh 1978; Vaughan 1987). To the extent that chiefs opted for collaboration, their actions intruded on the peasant labor process and the partial autonomy of their subjects.

Even where the colonial administration used strong hereditary chiefs, these historic authorities had little room to negotiate. As a result, their ability to command mass loyalty and to govern by consensus declined. Chiefs had to make a judicious calculation of when to enforce colonial policies and when to speak out in opposition to the state. Each had obvious costs. However much they may have wished to straddle, most chiefs usually opted to be loyalists.

This should not come as a great surprise. The colonial regimes eliminated or replaced indigenous authorities who openly opposed them, and the chiefs had substantial privileges and power to protect for themselves and their heirs. Access to women (Isaacman 1985; Mandala 1982; Mbilinyi 1988; C. Murray 1981), control of the best land (C. Murray 1981; Olivier de Sardan 1984), use of unpaid labor to work their fields (Guyer 1978; Isaacman 1985; Tosh 1978; Vincent 1981), financial and technical support from the extension service (Chipungu 1986), and preferential treatment at the market (Isaacman 1985; Bassett 1988) were all dependent on their continued collaboration. For many chiefs, their conditional access to power and scarce resources enabled them to escape the peasant labor process and to become part of the nascent class of *modernizing* capitalist farmers, while privatization and politicization of land, labor, and other critical resources were making their subjects increasingly impoverished.

Tensions surfaced first in those areas where the state-appointed chiefs lacked historical legitimacy. In places as diverse as the Yansi region of the Congo

(Smith 1976) and the Kombo area of Casamance (Roche 1976), peasants demanded that colonial authorities replace illegitimate rulers. Popular opposition quickly surfaced against the new *saurata* class in northern Nigeria who were perceived as substitutes for the deposed *emirs* (Watts 1987b). And in Tanzania, Shambaa peasants disobeyed loyalist chiefs who lacked reputations as rainmakers and hence were unable to "heal the land" (Feierman 1990).

Royal descendants who were perceived as closely allied with the colonial system also risked creating considerable hostility. At the outset of the 1914 revolt in Upper Volta, peasants specifically earmarked for assassination "chiefs and other people devoted to the whites" (Hebert 1970:6). In Malawi, angry villagers attacked land chiefs and headmen who participated in the forced recruitment of porters and soldiers during World War I (Page 1978). And in neighboring Zambia militant Watchtower converts subverted the authority of chiefs (Fields 1985). Forty years later in Rwanda the first target of the Hutu insurrection were the Tutsi chiefs who had reaped the most benefits from the colonial regime (Newbury 1983, 1988), while Tiv insurgents organized antiwitchcraft cults to attack colonial chiefs (Bohannan 1958).

Violent eruptions (see also Killingray 1978; Mandala 1990; Weiskel 1980) were the exception. With the consolidation of state power, confrontation became more dangerous, and disaffected peasants increasingly resorted to covert action. Work slowdowns reduced production on the chiefs' lands, just as withheld payments and sabotage directly challenged the chiefs' prerogatives (Bradford 1987; Guyer 1978; Isaacman 1985; Thomas 1983; Watts 1988). Covert peasant activity against the colonial capitalist system also reduced the capacity of chiefs to accumulate capital. Flight, for example, denied them tax revenues, gifts, and tributary labor. But most important, sustained peasant intransigence led the state to remove ineffective chiefs, thereby entirely depriving them of their power, privilege, and prestige.

The opposition of impoverished peasants to accumulating chiefs is only a part, albeit an important one, of the story of rural politics. Not all chiefs collaborated, and not all peasants opposed their local authorities. Sometimes chiefs and peasants worked closely together to minimize the disruptive colonial impact (see Crowder 1988). While most chiefs and headmen dutifully collected taxes in Malawi, many joined peasants in resisting both tenancy and wage labor in defense of the food economy (Mandala 1990). On other occasions, they even joined in open opposition to colonial policies that collided with both their interests and those of at least some segment of the rural population. Examples are the 1912 alliance between Ndunqutze, a Tutsi claimant to the throne, and Hutu peasants in northern Rwanda against German forced labor policies (Maquet 1961); the union of Baule chiefs and their subjects in the Ivory Coast when colonial labor demands threatened rural production (Weiskel 1980); and the peasant-driven, but chief-directed, 1917 Zambesi rebellion in Mozambique

(Isaacman 1976). These insurrections suggest that the power and authority embedded in the institution of chieftaincy should not be underestimated and should be differentiated from the personal standing and ability to command of any particular ruler. Backed by historical tradition, notions of order, and religious authority, chieftaincy could be transformed into an insurgent institution in the contest to control the countryside. At the same time chiefs often vied for power with local merchants, modernizing capitalist farmers, and mission-educated elites for control over the countryside (Austin 1988; Beinart and Bundy 1987; Jean Comaroff 1985; Lonsdale 1968; Saul 1973, 1975; Vincent 1981). Both the complexity and intensity of these struggles suggest that we need to pay greater attention to the social basis of rural conflict and recognize the multiple and often contending identities—ethnic, religious, regional as well as class—that shaped rural politics.

That internal conflicts over critical resources not only pit impoverished Africans against wealthier Africans, but also occasionally against each other, highlights the complexity of rural politics. The situation was particularly volatile where land was scarce and peasants faced the threat of extinction. In the 1920s conflicts periodically broke out between South African labor-tenants competing for the same tracts of land (Bradford 1987). The colonial Zimbabwean policy of squeezing peasants off the land also precipitated fierce competition among peasants and among them and capitalist farmers, black plough hirers, and rural traders for those parcels that remained in the African domain (Ranger 1985). At the same time, in the Gezira scheme local tenants competed with Hausa migrant tenants for access to irrigated land (O'Brien 1983). In 1940 wealthy Malawian farmers living in the fertile Tchiri Valley allowed their cattle to destroy the unfenced gardens of poorer peasants, primarily women, and then appropriated their land (Mandala 1984, 1990), while the struggle over land in Rwanda erupted into open warfare in the late 1950s between Hutu peasants and their Tutsi landowning overlords.[63]

Because commodity production transformed the labor process, property rights, and income relations between male and female peasants and between generations, the household often became a terrain of conflict. At stake was who would control and distribute these critical resources. This was especially true during periods of famine, when the allocation of food within the community and within the family often "highlight[ed] the tensions and struggles which in normal times lie under the formal structure of social relations" (Vaughan 1987:121).

Although students of agrarian history have come to recognize how the organization of labor by sex and relations of power are two different dimensions of the production process (Guyer 1984c; Meillassoux 1981; H. Moore 1988; Staudt 1987), they disagree on how to conceptualize gender differentiation and domestic oppression. Basically, there are three overlapping approaches (Bozzoli 1983a; Comaroff 1987; Guyer 1988; Robertson and Berger 1986). Materialist explanations for gender oppression tend to emphasize the functionality of female subordination for capitalism (Bozzoli 1983a; Meillassoux 1972; Robertson and Berger 1986; Wolpe 1972). Meillassoux (1972) argues that male wages below the family cost-of-living characterized peripheral capitalism, which depended on female subsistence activities for the social reproduction of the rural household. Other scholars, most notably Wolpe (1972), stress that the logic of capitalist accumulation requires this division of labor and created it when it did not exist, as in the case of rural South Africa. In the process, rural women were impoverished and oppressed.

Several feminist scholars focusing on economic development take issue with this emphasis. They argue that peasant women were important agents of change as well as victims of oppression (Boserup 1970; Cloud 1986; Creevey 1986; Lancaster 1976). They contend that the contribution of rural women has been grossly undervalued, both by male members of their societies and by male scholars.[64] Thus, for example, the work of African women in the agricultural sector carries lower social value than the work of men, which, in turn, reflects male attitudes of superiority (Boserup 1970; Lancaster 1976). While insisting correctly on the centrality of women's labor, by defining the conflict in gendered terms, many of these authors tend to underplay the class basis of female peasant oppression and the fact that there was differentiation among women as well. This tendency is especially true among feminist scholars who remain closely tied to modernization and developmental theories (Cloud 1986; Creevey 1986).

In an effort to move beyond these narrowly constructed materialist and developmentalist approaches, a number of Africanists examine how gender and class intersect in specific social systems (Bozzoli 1983a; Geiger 1982; Mandala 1982; Mbilinyi 1985; Muntemba 1980; Robertson and Berger 1986; Stichter 1985; Schmidt 1988; Staudt 1986; Vaughan 1987). Gender assumes an analytical status of its own, which is essential for explaining politics generally as well as recurring inequities between women and men (H. Moore 1988; Joan Scott 1986). In terms of the countryside, such an approach focuses on how changing power relations in the household may correlate with changing relations of peasants to capitalism (Robertson and Berger 1986).

At the center of such an analysis is the unequal relationship of power between men and women as well as between generations. The roots of this relationship often antedated the colonial period but were transformed in significant ways by the colonial capitalist system. African elders, missionaries, and representatives of the colonial state often combined in an effort to try and forge a new social order in which chosen men "were public actors, both economic and political, and women the private apolitical guardians of the household" (Staudt 1987: 29; see also Comaroff and Comaroff 1989; Mbilinyi 1988; Schmidt 1992).

The tendency of the colonial state to select specific males as modernizing agents and principal cash crop producers not only reinforced unequal power relations between men and women of the same age but intensified them across generational and gender lines. To enhance commodity production, the state offered them a number of critical resources rarely made available to rural women or to younger male kin. Such men gained access to and control over hybrid seeds, new technology and, most important, unused or communally owned land.[65] This combination of resources enabled them to consolidate their power and reinforce their control over the labor process (Boserup 1970; Delehanty 1988; Etienne 1980; Hay 1976; Mandala 1990; Martin 1984; Muntemba 1980; Schmidt 1991; Staudt 1987; Strobel 1982). Reinterpreted *customary law* also reinforced gender and generational differentiation, as did redefined rights of inheritance (Chanock 1982, 1985; Mbilinyi 1988; Staudt 1987).

Colonial policies generally enabled male heads of households to organize and control family labor and agricultural output more effectively.[66] However, throughout the continent there were substantial variations in the ways that senior men sought to exercise this power. In some regions, primarily in West Africa, women were often relegated to the production of food crops and were denied access to highly profitable cash crops (Bukh 1979; Dorward 1987; Guyer 1984b; Martin 1984). Among the Baule of the Ivory Coast (Etienne 1980) female peasants were even excluded from cultivating crops that they had historically grown. In other parts of the continent, male heads of households accumulated capital by reallocating family labor time as well as controlling the marketable surplus. In parts of Zambia (Wright 1983b), for example, the introduction of the plow provided the incentive for male household heads to pressure women, who had historically done the bulk of the agriculture, to increase their labor output. While wives assumed most of the agricultural and domestic chores, their husbands controlled most of the surplus. This enabled powerful elders to obtain additional land and wives, which heightened gender and class differentiation in the countryside. But even as household heads were increasing their power, new demands for labor and commodities created opportunities for some dependents to break the bonds of patriarchy (Berry 1985; Guyer and Peters 1987; Mandala 1990; Schmidt 1991; Watts 1988).

The general decline in women's power and the tension it generated were not restricted to peasant households where men were present to organize and control commodity production. There is a substantial literature on the frustration, pain, and anguish of female-headed households in areas such as southern Mozambique, Lesotho, Botswana, and parts of Malawi, which became dependent on the cash incomes of oscillating peasant workers to supplement food production (First 1983; Izzard 1985; Murray 1976, 1977, 1980, 1981; Peters 1983; Vaughan 1987). According to Murray, "in the southern African periphery women very often assume the onus of managing the rural economy but have very little control over the resources with which to manage it effectively . . . and as a result this . . . disjunction between power and responsibility is the source of much bitterness, frustration and marital disharmony" (1981:167). Put somewhat differently, the resources over which peasant women had most access, land and food production, were becoming less significant, leaving them in an increasingly tenuous domestic position (Hay 1976; Schmidt 1992; Vaughan 1987). Malawian women, dependent on agriculturally related activities and disconnected from wage economies, were particularly vulnerable to famine, for example, and as a group they experienced appreciably more hardship than men (Vaughan 1987).[67] Without minimizing the suffering, it is also important to note that the absence of men often reinforced female solidarity and agricultural cooperation, which enabled some rural households to cope and survive, however tenuously (McCann 1987; Vickery 1986).

Male household heads extended their patriarchal power over younger male kin as well, while simultaneously expanding their ability to accumulate capital by expanding, transforming, and constructing new bride wealth and bride-service obligations. In Malawi, for example, the cotton boom precipitated a labor shortage which elders resolved, in part, by increasing bride-service in the cotton fields (Mandala 1990). Similarly, Eggon elders of Nigeria dramatically increased bride-price demands to immobilize young men who would otherwise have fled to the adjacent hills, which were being opened up for farming (Dorward 1987). Bride-service and bride-price, in turn, provided the material and ideological basis for the future oppression of women by their husbands. In the words of one South African tenant farmer, "I must work for the baas, but not my wife . . . I buy a woman to work for me" (Bradford 1987:37). Buying wives through bride-price or bride-service set in motion a process by which these women and their offspring often became the principal agricultural laborers and their husbands the principal beneficiaries. In some regions the social significance of bride wealth, marriage, and women was completely transformed.[68]

Although the tendency has been to emphasize the dependency and vulnerability of women and junior male kinsmen, the capacity of male household heads to direct and control family labor should not be taken for granted (Carney 1988a, 1988b; Folbre 1986; Guyer 1984b; Guyer and Peters 1987; Watts 1988). Their power was often linked to the specific labor regimes in which their households were enmeshed. Male tenant farmers, for example, often found themselves in the ambiguous position of recruiting family members to work for their landlord. For very different reasons, neither forced cultivators nor oscillating peasant-workers could exercise such authority. In one very dramatic example, Bashu migrant laborers in eastern Zaire attacked women as witches to try to regain control of their lives, which had been disrupted by the penetration of capitalist relations of production in the countryside (Packard 1980).

While gender and generational inequality linked to class exploitation has been stressed in the literature, Africanists need to pay closer attention to the power sources of women and younger males, and the conditions under which they were able to exercise power.[69] Fragmentary evidence suggests that many peasant women and alienated youths were able to shield some portion of their labor and produce from expropriation by male household heads. The strategies they adopted were strikingly similar to those employed against the colonial capitalist system. Even within relatively confined rural communities, the peasant labor process provided space for the direct producers to pursue such tactics. The weapons of the weak could be successfully turned inward.

There is ample evidence of both women and young men fleeing the intensified pressures within the rural household (Mbilinyi 1985, 1938; Schmidt 1992; Stichter 1985). However, for runaway women the options were relatively limited. They could seek refuge at missionary stations, flee with a lover who might ultimately become a new husband, or clandestinely migrate to the cities. Rural women liberated from their households often found their new settings to be as precarious as their old. Nevertheless, throughout the colonial period they continued to flee. It is important to remember, however, that a number of women who migrated to towns did so to help their own impoverished peasant households (C. White 1986). For young men, opportunities in the cities and mines were somewhat better. That the extent of this flight was extensive is reflected in the fierce opposition it aroused among male elders and state officials, who often acted in unison to contain it (Hay 1982; Henn 1984; Lonsdale and Berman 1979; Mbilinyi 1985, 1988; Schmidt 1992; Luise White 1983).

A number of scholars argue that for the majority of rural women living under conditions of inequality, there was little incentive to work harder or for longer hours (Mandala 1982; Muntemba 1982; Staudt 1987). Overburdened, they often resisted efforts to restructure the labor process in ways that would increase their workloads, reduce their access to critical resources, and intensify food shortages. They, more than any segment of the rural population, understood the precarious balance between household production and commodity production. Ultimately, their principal weapon was their control over their labor power. Muntemba tells us that along the railway region of Zambia, "some women expressed their discontent by withdrawing their labor from household fields, particularly at peak labor periods" and that "local men labeled the women's reaction 'laziness' and 'insubordination' " (Muntemba 1982:100). In South Africa during the years preceding World War II, the state encouraged sharecroppers to increase the production of sunflowers to meet the growing demand for margarine. Male heads of household were quick to respond to this opportunity. Their wives and daughters, however, resisted this development since the proceeds from the nonedible sunflowers went into male pockets, and all they received for their labor were painful blisters. On a number of occasions they sabotaged sunflower crops, conscious of the fact that by doing so they were also marginally reducing household income.[70] Three decades later among Mandinka households, women challenged patriarchal property control by clearing unclaimed tidal swamp and establishing individual ownership of these rich rice lands. In doing so, they reclaimed a portion of their labor from household control (Carney 1988a, 1988b; Watts 1988).

The evidence suggests that throughout Africa rural women were probably the principal opponents of expanded agricultural demands, forced cultivation, antierosion schemes, and the introduction of new labor intensive technology, all of which narrowed their economic and social space in the local arena. This type of reactive power, though difficult to document and measure, had important consequences for the political economy of colonialism. Had this not been true, agronomists and extension officers would not have attacked the *backwardness* of rural women so vigorously, despite the fact that in specific times and places women took to commercial agriculture with great alacrity.[71]

There is also a tantalizing connection between dissent in the domestic sphere and the collective protests of women against colonial oppression which requires additional investigation. To the extent that women struggled within the household, it can be argued that their acts of defiance were empowering and enhanced their confidence in the power of collective action. When colonial policies precipitated major crises over access to and control of critical resources, many peasant women were prepared to do battle against them just as they had confronted elders and spouses. Thus, for example, women transformed methods used to curb male excesses, such as obscenity and wild behavior, into instruments of collective action against the colonial state (Rogers 1980). Their confrontations with the colonial regime occurred most frequently during periods of economic hardship. The 1929 women's war in Nigeria (Ifeka-Moller 1975; Van Allen 1976), the tax revolt of Pare women in Tanzania sixteen years later (Feierman 1990), the public refusal of a large number of pregnant women in central Mozambique to cultivate cotton in the face of food shortages (Isaacman et al. 1980), and the violent reaction of Kom women in the Cameroun to antierosion schemes (Rogers 1980) all demonstrate the militancy of peasant women. We need to move beyond the particular movements of confrontation to examine whether there have been persistent themes in these struggles at either the politico-material or cultural levels, so that these movements are not treated as isolated eruptions. Such an approach requires both careful comparison and detailed analysis of specific gendered struggles for political space over the *longue duree*.

Peasant-Based Social Movements and Insurgent Ideologies

The inherited wisdom about peasant parochialism and predictability has been challenged by a small, but growing, number of scholars who argue that peasants were capable of constructing a culture of opposition and linking it to insurgent action. They contend that peasants were able to organize protest movements and that to do so required the development of a shared oppositional language and insurgent ideology. By combining a review of the literature on social movements and ideologies it is possible to outline the complex and varied interrelationship between peasant thought and action.[72] Obviously, not all rural social movements were peasant-inspired. Many were connected to urban struggles in complex and diverse ways (Bradford 1987; Coquery-Vidrovitch 1988, 1989; Kanogo 1987). But there is sufficient evidence to challenge the commonly held position that rural movements were inevitably inspired from outside or from above. Nowhere has this assumption been more deeply rooted than in the literature on nationalism.

Until the past decade, scholars viewed rural protest primarily through the prism of nationalism. They defined all significant rural movements as nationalist, protonationalist, or linked to nationalism (Hodgkin 1957; Ranger 1968a; Young 1965). They presumed that educated nationalist leaders were able to construct a political language which both penetrated and resonated throughout nonliterate rural communities, winning the hearts and minds of rural folk. Moreover, because of their nationalist preoccupation they paid scant attention to rural protests designed to safeguard critical household resources but not to capture the colonial state.

More recent scholarship advances at least two scenarios radically different from the conventional nationalist interpretation. The first envisions the possibility of opposition inspired, organized, and directed by peasants. The second posits the existence of broad-based radical movements, primarily nationalist in nature, in which peasants played an essential, if not a determinant, role. Such movements, of course, contained ambiguities and contradictions, and were often themselves terrains of struggle. In both scenarios, peasants are understood to be "continual initiators" (Stern 1987) engaged in political relations among themselves and with nonpeasants. Rural social movements are not just momentary aberrations, but are often part of a long oppositional history which over time took many shapes and forms, part of a larger engagement in the political world.

The literature on colonial Africa suggests that peasant-organized social movements occurred primarily under two conditions: where hidden forms of protest no longer proved possible, and where colonial capitalist practices threatened peasant autonomy in unprecedented ways.

It is one of the central propositions of this paper that both the structural position of peasants and the ensemble of societal power predisposed them to pursue localized covert forms of protest. However, such strategies were not always feasible. In the face of growing pressure, peasant communities often found it necessary to marshal their collective resources to confront colonial oppression. Two examples will suffice. The 1914–16 Holli peasant revolt in Dahomey took place after twenty years of tax evasion, flight, manipulation of census data, and clandestine cross-border sales of agricultural produce had failed to alleviate French pressure (Almeida-Topor 1980). A similar pattern of localized defiance preceding a major insurrection took place in the Zambesi Valley of Mozambique, where new demands for conscript labor to serve as porters in the East African military campaign and the imposition of a forced cotton regime sparked a rebellion from 1917 to 1921 (Isaacman 1976).[73]

Exploitive labor policies, excessive taxation, and pillaging through the market, each threatening the subsistence of peasants and violating their sense of justice, triggered numerous collective protests from below. The flurry of rural tax revolts accompanying the imposition of colonial rule and a second wave of revolts during World War I are cases in point.

State intervention at the point of production posed the most direct challenge to the peasantry and, predictably, unleashed widespread social unrest. Witness the wave of revolts against forced cash-crop cultivation in the Congo, Upper Volta, Zaire, Angola, Tanzania, and Madagascar (Jewsiewicki 1980b; Iliffe 1967; Pelissier 1977; Tronchon 1974), and the widespread protests against cattle dipping and antierosion schemes. Settler appropriation of choice rural lands, threatening the survival of peasant communities, precipitated squatter movements throughout eastern and southern Africa (Beinart and Bundy 1987; Kanogo 1987; Lodge 1983; Mbeki 1984; Throup 1987). Finally, the efforts of merchant capital to impose superexploitive terms of trade fueled a number of boycotts and a spate of rural marketing cooperatives, varying substantially in social composition and class agenda.[74]

While the recent literature offers ample evidence of peasant-organized social movements, most of the accounts are fragmentary and largely descriptive. The tendency to treat these movements in a cursory way is hardly surprising, given their relatively small scale and short duration, and the fact that many political theorists perceive power to be one-dimensional. Those with the most power and knowledge act upon those who lack it. Viewed from such a perspective, illiterate peasants are the ultimate victims. Thus, most of this literature merely highlights the specific grievances that precipitated peasant uprisings, outlines the most dramatic moments of confrontation, and details the ultimate demise of the rural insurgents.

Rarely do we get a view inside the movements themselves or an understanding of how power, contested in practice, transformed the insurgents. Such an interior perspective requires an expanded frame of reference and a sharper focus of analysis. One must consider how these localized movements might be part of a longer tradition of resistance to authority. In taking this longer view we need to develop modes of analysis attentive to enduring cultural continuities without overlooking critical ruptures in rural societies. Notions of justice, vengeance, and legitimacy are historically derived and, with symbols of past resistance, are a powerful vehicle to mobilize peasant protest.

We also must sharpen in three important ways our analysis of how power is contested at the grassroots level. First, if we reject the notion that peasant movements must inevitably be led from above or outside, we have to be able to explain how rural communities with limited resources organized themselves.[75] By resources I mean not only tangibles such as arms and labor, but also organizational skills and experience to construct a vocabulary and a program capable of tapping powerful historical memories as well as deeply felt peasant anger while overcoming their fear of oppression.

Second, we need to pay greater attention to differentiation within peasant societies and the movements they spawn. The greater the differentiation, the more difficult it will probably be to forge autonomous movements and the greater the likelihood that such movements will be unable to maintain unity. Throughout this paper I have cited examples of peasant communities wracked by class divisions as well as by gender, religious, and ethnic tensions. These studies have shown how such divisive tendencies fragmented, undercut, and aborted collective action. Such divisions, of course, may be deflected, confronted, or even transformed by the very practice of shared struggle.

Finally, we need to examine how and under what conditions autonomous rural movements might have shifted their ideas, language, and strategies to confront changing relations of power. This requires that we begin to periodize peasant actions within and across regions. For example, the initial reactions of peasants to colonial control were often to try to protect resources and preserve local values. By the post–World War II period, peasants had embarked upon protests that questioned the colonial system. They began to envision, however vaguely, some notion of a new political order. We need to explore how this shift in emphasis occurred. In doing so, the complex and often ambiguous role of peasants in nationalist movements must come to the fore.

Within the past decade Africanists have returned to this issue, and they have done so in the context of agrarian history and rural class struggle.[76] Their work shows that the encounter between nationalist leaders and rural insurgents was far more complex, variable, and ambiguous than suggested in the earlier interpretations. Not surprisingly, they have focused on radical nationalist movements. The rich and diverse Mau-Mau literature offers the most extensive discussion of the relationship between peasants and nationalists. It is instructive to examine the evolution of this literature and the infusion of class, gender, and generational factors into the nationalist debate.[77]

The standard nationalist interpretation, Rosberg and Nottingham's *The Myth of 'Mau-Mau': Nationalism in Kenya* (1966), was very much a product of its times. The authors criticized the official European view that Mau-Mau was a reversion to savagery precipitated by traumatic social change. Instead, they argued that it was a rational political movement and, in fact, represented the militant wing of a modern nationalist organization directed from Nairobi. According to this account, Africans were divided by region and tribe rather than by class position. The aggrieved and aggressive Kikuyu played the dominant insurgent role. Peasants first come into this literature in Barnett and Njama's radical nationalist critique, *Mau-Mau from Within* (1966). The authors as well as Kinyatti (1983) and Ng'ang'a (1977) conclude that Mau-Mau was an authentic peasant movement betrayed from above by an educated nationalist elite which feared rural radicalism.

By contrast, much of the more recent literature on Mau-Mau hinges on the fierce competition for land and labor that left rural Kikuyu communities reeling, badly divided, and prone to act. There is, however, no consensus on where the critical struggles were fought or who fought them. Furedi (1974) and Kanogo (1987) identify the white highlands as the principal terrain of conflict. Throup (1985, 1987) emphasizes the overcrowded Kikuyu reserves,[78] while Bates (1987b) stresses both regions as key foci of the rebellion. As for the social composition of the insurgents, Furedi argues that the more privileged squatters, in combination with a group of relatively privileged petty traders, farm foremen, and dairy clerks, were the driving force in Mau-Mau. Kanogo argues instead that the leadership came from the grassroots and that the social base of Mau-Mau was the most impoverished squatters including those who had already lost their land. Both authors agree that the squatter resistance movements were at the core of Mau-Mau and that these rural radicals had a very different strategy and class agenda from the conservative Kenyan nationalists who ultimately sold them out. Throup, on the other hand, contends that the willingness of the chiefs to enforce the heavy-handed antierosion policies of the colonial state brought them into conflict with the mass of peasants. These internal conflicts created a rural constituency ready to be mobilized.

In a pathbreaking unpublished essay, Lonsdale (1988) locates Mau-Mau within a broader historical and ideological legacy. He suggests that well before the colonial period the Kikuyu had constructed a labor theory of value that justified private wealth and property gained through labor as an inalienable right of all Kikuyu. As land became increasingly inaccessible, in both the highlands and reserves, and as labor was expropriated to meet the different demands of settlers and the state, the historic connection between labor and property was broken. Lonsdale notes that it was not only the settlers, chiefs, and lineage heads, but also the elder statesmen of the Kikuyu Central Association who acquired land, thereby separating poorer peasants from their property. Mau-Mau represented a challenge to both the KCA leadership, which purported to speak for the "people," and to the colonial capitalist system represented by a younger generation of men, who faced the prospect of being without property and thus having reduced possibilities of marriage.

Just as Lonsdale's essay introduces the question of generational conflict, Presley (1986), Kanogo (1987), and Luise White (1990) inject gendered politics into the Mau-Mau debate. Presley confronts the tendency in both the

Mau-Mau and nationalist literature in general to ignore African women as conscious political actors. Through extensive oral interviews, she gained access to peasant women's views of their own lives and experiences and documented their critical role in the struggle. She concludes that women enjoyed "a far greater degree of sexual parity within the movement than previous scholarship of the subject had indicated" (1986:54). Kanogo also stresses the important contribution that women made, but emphasizes the intense struggle they had to wage within Mau-Mau to overcome sexual discrimination, especially within the guerrilla army.[79] In a provocative essay, Luise White (1990) argues that gender was at the very heart of the Mau-Mau struggle. From practice replayed daily in the forest, a new definition of gender, at least among Mau-Mau leaders, was constructed. The definition rooted in notions of equality and companionate marriage, confronted colonial social engineers who had quite different ideas about the rights of husbands to control wives, about labor stabilization, and about the domestication of women. The colonial regime could recapture the definitional terrain, White argues, only by brutally smashing Mau-Mau.

From these contending interpretations of Mau-Mau, each offering a partial view of social reality, emerge many of the critical elements from which new interpretations of nationalism in rural Africa might be constructed. The ambiguous and variable relationships between nationalist leaders and peasant communities, themselves internally differentiated in a variety of ways, provide the building blocks from which to reconceptualize the struggle for power during the waning years of the colonial period. At minimum, such an approach should enable us to move beyond the one-dimensional notion that all-powerful nationalist movements spoke for and led the illiterate peasant masses or at least some subset who were particularly prone to revolutionary action.

Recent scholarship on Zimbabwe offers another example of how the nationalist literature has evolved. Ranger's *Peasant Consciousness* (1985), Lan's (1985) book on the interrelationship between guerrillas, spirit mediums, and peasants, and Kriger's (1988) recent essay stand at the center of this new historiography. Ranger attacks the presumption that peasants were victims of false consciousness and were only able to transcend narrow parochial concerns under the modernizing nationalist leadership of ZANU. He argues instead that intensified state intervention from the 1930s onward unified rural communities and created a sense of common oppression and class consciousness which enabled them to make a substantial contribution to the ideology and program of ZANU. Lan extends Ranger's analysis by carefully reconstructing the critical role that spirit mediums played by transforming ZANU guerrillas into the legitimate owners of the land and by mobilizing peasant support behind them. In reconstructing the dynamics of this alliance, Lan pays particular attention to the power of historical memory and the peasants' own interpretation of the relationship between land, ancestor worship, and political legitimacy. Kriger, on the other hand, argues that there were sharp interclass as well as intraclass conflicts dividing Shona communities, complicating ZANU efforts to mobilize peasants. She stresses the tensions between poor peasants and the rural petty bourgeoisie, between rural immigrants and foreign immigrants, and between younger women and village elders, which at times diverted attention from the war. And she concludes that "mobilization was achieved though coercion rather than guerrilla ideology" (1988:312). For Kriger, peasants were thus caught between the violence perpetrated by the guerrillas and that of state security.[80]

Other important dimensions of the peasant-nationalist encounter in Africa have also been studied, although in much less detail. Geiger (1982, 1987), Feierman (1990), and Iliffe (1979), for example, emphasize the critical role women played in mobilizing support for TANU in the countryside at a time when men were often intimidated by loyalist chiefs. The Mozambican material suggests that FRELIMO's difficulty in mobilizing skeptical peasants could not be overcome until the movement was able to protect them, improve their lives, and develop a new revolutionary practice in the liberated zones (Henriksen 1983; Isaacman and Isaacman 1983; Mondlane 1969; Munslow 1983; Saul 1979). Even after FRELIMO gained a broad base of rural support, class, ethnic and gender conflicts complicated the independence struggle (Henriksen 1983; Isaacman and Isaacman 1983; Munslow 1983; Saul 1979). Although a history of rural struggle in South Africa has yet to be written, the evidence suggests that social, ideological, and organizational barriers between peasants and the nationalist-democratic forces on the one hand and socialist revolutionary forces on the other complicated the construction of broad-based alliances (Bundy 1984; Lodge 1983; Mbeki 1984). The momentary successes of the ICU in the 1920s (Bradford 1987), the All African Convention, the ANC, and the Congress Alliance a few decades later are significant precisely because they were unique (Lodge 1983). Only through careful empirical research will we be able to determine how rural radicalism culminating in the rash of revolts in Witzieshoek, the Transkei, Pondoland, and the Natal reserves between the 1940s and the early 1960s might have been part of a larger political campaign that extended beyond these specific locales (Lodge 1983, 1984, 1986). Delius (n.d.) argues quite convincingly that Sebatakgomo, a migrant organization, drawing on a past history of Pedi migrant associations, not only served as an effective bridge between the ANC, the South African Communist Party, and the countryside, but helped to sustain the Sekhukhuneland revolt of 1957–1961.[81] Finally, a discussion of peasant nationalist encounters creates analytical space to reexamine the complex and varied ways in which rural struggles may have been tied to urban conflicts. Such an analysis is critical if we are to get a better understanding of the social base, internal dynamics, and underlying objectives of the movements themselves.

The existence of peasant-inspired social movements and their prominence in nationalist campaigns suggest that peasants could construct an oppositional culture. We need, therefore, to reconsider the vast literature which saw peasants either as inherently conservative and bound to ingrained habits or as inevitable victims of false consciousness or ruling-class hegemony.[82] And we need to analyze how peasant communities developed the insights and knowledge to forge an insurgent ideology.

Influenced by the writing of Gramsci[83] (1971), Rudé (1964), Scott (1985), and Williams (1980), among others, Africanists have begun to grapple with this issue. It is not by chance that the debate is most intense in the literature of South Africa, where the contemporary situation makes the stakes so high.

In a pioneering essay on South Africa, Bozzoli (1983b) rejects the proposition that ideology is disseminated in some uncontested way by the state apparatus, mystifying and subordinating the lower classes. The view from below, whether it be from rural homelands or urban ghettoes, does not sustain the contention of such a unitary ideological configuration. Instead, Bozzoli emphasizes, there are many different cultures in South Africa, each of which has its own shape and history, and not all of which are functional to capitalism or apartheid. Beinart and Bundy (1987) make a similar point with reference to peasants in the Transkei, where peasants have multiple identities—class, ethnic, gender, religious—and are therefore potentially receptive to multiple appeals.

In the world of rural politics the language of religion has often been transformed into the language of protest.[84] Mandala (1990) notes that a number of the custodians of the Mbona ancestral cult played a critical ideological and organizational role in opposition to colonial antierosion schemes.[85] Fernandez's 1982 study of Fang origin myths suggests that embedded in these accounts is the claim that they have the power to shape their own destiny and a rejection, at least implicit, of a sense of powerlessness which often accompanies colonial subjugation.[86] Jean Comaroff (1985) demonstrates the critical role that Zionist churches played as instruments of cultural resistance—the principal weapon available to the impoverished and displaced Tshidi peasant workers residing along the South African-Botswana border. Tshidi Zionism, she argues, represented an important expression of subversive bricolage[87] fought against an intrusive colonial capitalist order. Fields argues convincingly that Watchtower adherents opposed and then overthrew a number of state-sponsored customary rulers "by using the ritual idioms that pervaded everyday political discourse" (1985:160) which were more likely to be religious than secular. And Coquery-Vidrovitch (1988) and Olivier de Sardan (1984) have stressed that the language of Islam often provided atomized and ethnically divided peasants with a basis of unity as well as an alternative vision to oppose the modernizing Christian ideology of the colonial administration.

The partial autonomy of peasantries, I would contend, placed them in a unique position to remake their traditions and formulate a critique of colonial capitalism. Who more than peasants laboring long hours only to be separated from their hard-earned produce have experienced and understood the meaning of exploitation? If cotton was the "mother of poverty" (Isaacman et al. 1980), it was also the "mother of rural radicalism" (Mulambu-Mvuluya 1974; Jewsiewicki 1980b).

Although Africanists are beginning to recognize that struggles were taking place at the level of peasant ideology as well as in the more visible and political domain, agreement ends here. There is no consensus on whether the act of constructing an oppositional culture constitutes resistance per se (Comaroff 1985; Scott 1985; Watts 1988) or whether it merely represents the creation of a context for subsequent acts of insurgency (Bozzoli 1983b). Moreover, scholars are only now beginning to investigate the ways in which peasant communities forged this oppositional culture. It is one thing to claim, or even to demonstrate, the existence of a culture of insurgency and quite another to analyze how and by whom this ideology was constructed.

The recent literature on the southern African countryside, with its emphasis on dialogue between peasants and radical activists, offers a promising start. Beinart and Bundy (1987) and Bradford (1987) argue that insurgent cultures were constructed in South Africa as a result of complex and often contested encounters between different combinations of activists, migrant workers, rural religious leaders, teachers, and peasantries. The outcome of this struggle for the hearts and minds of the oppressed varied considerably. Bradford examines the complex dialogue between urban nationalist-oriented ICU activists and the rural tenants who had nurtured their own oppositional culture and ideas of justice. She observes that one of the strengths of these organic leaders, especially in Natal, was that they quickly learned how to listen and to follow as well as to shape the movement from above. In the end, "the illiterate underclass both spread the message and imposed their views on educated activists, so there were radical changes in the content of ICU ideas on the land question" (1987:18). In many respects, the works of Ranger (1985) and Lan (1985) come to a similar conclusion.

In their different ways, these studies provide an analysis of the dialogue, contradictions, and cross-fertilization that took place between radical activists and local peasant communities, and they also recognize that peasants had nurtured oppositional notions before this encounter. But they are able to outline this process only in the most general sense. None of these studies seeks to locate these insurgent tendencies within a longer historical or cultural perspective, admittedly a difficult task.

Feierman's remarkable book, *Peasant Intellectuals: Anthropology and History in Tanzania* (1990) confronts this task with subtlety and skill.[88] In it he challenges the image of peasants passively receiving external ideologies or, at best, reacting to external initiatives. Instead, his is a history of peasant political discourse and of the peasant intellectuals who create and transmit it. When peasants organize political movements, or when they reflect on collective experience, they speak about how politics can be ordered to bring life rather than death, to bring prosperity rather than hunger, and to bring justice rather than inequity. The means for achieving these are defined by peasants themselves. It is peasants who draw upon a rich variety of past forms of political language; it is peasants who create new political discourse (1990:3).

Feierman thus dramatically alters the angle of vision through which the question of rural politics can be viewed. His analysis rests on two fundamental propositions: first, that these peasant intellectuals are engaged in socially recognized organizational, directive, educative or expressive activities; second, that the central terms of this discourse, "healing and harming the land," have endured over the past century or longer. As cultural creators, the peasant intellectuals can shape the inherited language to explain current problems and to offer possible solutions.

During the nineteenth century when the Shambaa state was intact, *traditional* intellectuals came primarily from the ranks of the renowned rainmakers, many of whom were land chiefs. The British colonial regime captured many of the traditional intellectuals by designating them as state-appointed chiefs, thereby undermining their legitimacy. Peasants who had participated as low-level functionaries and had returned to farming filled the intellectual void. Ex-clerks had some experience beyond the village world, yet unlike chiefs and African bureaucrats at the higher level, they were capable of formulating dissenting discourse without suffering economic consequences. Here, again, the partial autonomy of peasants had its rewards.

When the colonial government sought to impose erosion-control schemes, these peasant intellectuals vociferously opposed them. Their authoritative voices inspired collective peasant opposition throughout the Shambaa territory. "Healing the land" still occupied the central place in their discourse and in village debates. But the peasant intellectuals created new forms of political discourse, raising the issue of democracy, the role of chiefs, the meaning of freedom and slavery, and the nature of gender relations. The peasant intellectuals subsequently became the first generation of TANU activists and, therefore, these local debates informed TANU and were, in turn, informed by the larger debate as they evolved within TANU. Thus, while emphasizing the critical role of peasant intellectuals, Feierman's research reveals a complex and interconnected terrain which linked peasants and cadres, villages and cities.

Feierman's study is the richest analysis of peasant intellectuals and the construction of a dissenting ideology. It is by no means unique. In their coauthored book on the Transkei, Beinart and Bundy emphasize that rural societies were able to represent themselves, especially in moments of crises. "The local struggles," they note, "constantly threw up intellectuals: individuals . . . [who] although they embodied elements of a 'derived' and 'structured' ideology, were firmly rooted in their own local communities and also deployed 'traditional' or 'inherent ideology' " (1987:32). Comaroff (1985) and Fields (1985) demonstrate how Tshidi and Bemba peasants, increasingly subject to proletarianization and subordination, forged an oppositional discourse expressed through religious idioms. And Mandala (1990) stresses the alliances between Mbona raincallers and militant peasants. These pioneering studies are exemplary because they explore how peasants thought and acted rather than accepting an *a priori* formula of how peasants were supposed to think and act. Many more such studies are needed.

Final Comments

During the past decade or so, Africanists have begun to focus on peasants as historical actors enmeshed in a complex and often contradictory array of class, community, and household relationships. They have posed new ways of thinking about the construction of social identities, the battle over ideologies, and, above all else, the struggle for power in the countryside. The advantage of this shift from earlier patterns of thinking about rural politics is that it can convey some of the elements of ambiguity, contradiction, and conflict that peasants experienced in their daily lives. This new focus recognizes peasants as political actors helping to make their own history. The uniqueness of peasants is the degree of relative autonomy they had vis-à-vis the state and the appropriating classes. It was this partial autonomy, linked to the labor process, that helps to explain why peasants were prone to engage in subterranean protests rather than in broader social movements. Since the state and the appropriating classes sought to control rather than to destroy the peasantry, the principal form of struggle was over the extent of this partial autonomy. Detailed and historically specific research on the labor process is likely to reveal the types of partial autonomy different peasantries retained as well as their potential for dissent at the national, community, and household levels. It is important, however, not to claim too much for these insurgent acts. At best, they produced partial victories which safeguarded or expanded their relative autonomy but which rarely challenged the system of oppression. Rural social movements often held such objectives. What we need to explore is the social base of these movements, the historically specific role that different peasantries played, and the complex ways in which the struggles of peasants and migrant workers, villagers and urban dwellers, rural intellectuals and nationalist leaders may have been interconnected.

To deepen and expand the analysis of rural politics, scholars must also pay critical and careful attention to the many peasant voices waiting to be heard.

These oral documents, with their multiple and often hidden meanings, offer an internal view of rural life with all its ambiguities and contradictions. While there is not a perfect correspondence between what peasants thought, or even what they think they thought, and the social realities in which they lived, their understanding of this reality is as important as the structures of oppression that limited their choices and constrained their actions. The richness and variety of the reminiscences will broaden the ways in which Africanists think about agrarian change and rural social protest.

Notes

This essay first appeared in *African Studies Review* 33, no. 2 (Sept. 1990): 1–120. Support for this project came from generous grants from the Graduate School of the University of Minnesota and from the American Council of Learned Societies. I am deeply indebted to a number of scholars and friends for detailed comments, suggestions, and bibliographical assistance. I want to thank Michael Adas, Ralph Austen, William Beinart, John Comaroff, Fred Cooper, Catherine Coquery-Vidrovitch, Steven Feierman, Karen Fields, Jane Guyer, Jean Hay, Bogumil Jewsiewicki, Ivan Karp, Tom Lodge, Paul Lovejoy, Pier Larson, Elias Mandala, Florencia Mallon, Donald Moore, Randy Packard, James Quirin, Terence Ranger, Richard Roberts, Elizabeth Schmidt, Steve Stern, Charles van Onselen, Jan Vansina, and Michael Watts for their criticisms and support. I learned a great deal from a number of my colleagues at the university who encouraged me throughout this project and read one or more drafts of the study: Ron Aminzade, Harry Boyte, Susan Geiger, James Johnson, Barbara Laslett, Bruce Lincoln, M. J. Maynes, Charles Pike, John Stuart, and Luise White were always there when I needed them. I have also benefited from the comments of graduate students at the University of Chicago, Northwestern University, Stanford University, and the University of California, as well as students at the University of Minnesota who introduced me to a wide body of theoretical and comparative material. George Roberts offered valuable stylistic comments, as did Helena Pohlandt-McCormick. Finally, I owe a special debt of gratitude to Barbara Isaacman, who was not only my harshest critic but a source of constant emotional support.

1 By *social reproduction,* I mean those activities, responsibilities, and relationships that are critical for the maintenance of the daily as well as the intergenerational life of peasants. Because of their partial autonomy, peasants had a greater range of choices regarding how they could organize the work of production, which was often the work of social reproduction. Shifting demands of reproduction necessarily changed how production was organized and vice versa. In short, each shaped and was shaped by the other, and both need to be incorporated into an analysis of the peasant labor process. For a theoretical discussion of social reproduction, see Laslett and Brenner 1989. For a penetrating analysis of the labor process, see Burawoy 1979.

2 Sotho heads of sharecropping families with few sons, for example, attempted to overcome the labor shortage by administering herbs to women. "Working the women," as this practice became known, removed the historical prohibition on their

using oxen to plough the fields (personal communication, Charles van Onselen, April 4, 1989).

3 In *Schism and Continuity* (1957), for example, Turner acknowledged that some men and women went off to the copperbelt and to white-owned farms, and others left local villages to take up commercial agriculture on their own, but his analysis treated any connection between Ndembu and the wider world as extraneous. The central dynamics of the social system were defined in terms of synchronic relationships within the *tribal* unit, more specifically, the Ndembu village.

The notion of *tribe* cannot be treated as a primal fact or totally disregarded as a colonial construction. An analysis of the historical creation of tribalism, or ethnic consciousness, as an ideological statement must be linked to concrete social, economic, and political transformations taking place on the ground. For a recent discussion of different scholarly interpretations of tribalism, see Vail 1989.

4 The extent to which an alliance between the colonial administration and anthropologists had solidified has generated a contentious, often polemical debate, which falls beyond the scope of this paper. It is clear, however, that there were at least moments of rapprochement based on shared assumptions about the centrality of the term *tribe*. Several leading anthropologists, such as Malinowski (1929), did argue that anthropologists could and should provide greater service to Africa's colonial regimes. On the other hand, in his study *The Rise of Anthropological Theory* (1968:535), Harris rejects the blanket critique of ethnographers engaged in a colonial endeavor, noting that "most of the British social anthropologists would probably pass muster as left-wing liberals or socialists."

5 One can read Kuper's major ethnographic work, *An African Aristocracy*, with little sense that the Swazi about whom she wrote were also at the same time living in the world she described in *The Uniform of Colour*.

6 The literature on precolonial Ethiopia tends to be an exception. It includes a number of accounts analyzing state-peasant relations; see Kobishchanov (originally published in the Soviet Union in 1966 and translated and published in English in 1979), Gamst 1970, and Tamrat 1972. I want to thank Jim Quirin for sharing his rich knowledge of Ethiopian historiography with me.

7 See Apter 1963, Coleman 1958, Hodgkin 1957, Ranger 1968a, and Young 1965.

8 One of the ironies of the nationalist historiography is that even as it demanded that all rural movements worth studying be linked to independence struggles, it often obliterated peasants from history. In part, this paradox can be explained by the fact that nationalism as a field of inquiry emerged "in intimate symbiosis" with the rise of independence movements that claimed to speak for all the people, especially the inarticulate rural masses (Young 1986). Moreover, as an ideological proposition premised on a common past and a shared future for all citizens, nationalism invariably obliterated the importance of class (Poulantzas 1978). An urban modernizing bias among both scholars and most nationalist leaders reinforced the tendency to render peasants invisible. For an incisive auto-critique of this nationalist position, see Basil Davidson 1977.

9 At a more general theoretical level, dissenting voices objected to the uncritical cele-

bration of ambiguous terms such as *local initiative* and argued that there was ample evidence of differentiation and exploitation within African societies (Bernstein and Depelchin 1978–79; Copans 1978; Wrigley 1971).

10 As Leys, a leading underdevelopment theorist, noted, "in one critical respect, underdevelopment theory tends to resemble development theory—it concentrated on what happens to the underdeveloped countries, rather than on the total historical process involved, including the various forms of struggle against imperialism and colonialism which grow out of the condition of underdevelopment" (1975:20).

11 The limits of the strangulation theory stem from flaws embedded in underdevelopment theory. As Cooper (1981b:289) observes, underdevelopment theory "substitutes a grand teleology for analysis of causation and process; it gives the market a deterministic role in the world economy and either ignores production processes or treats them as mechanical derivatives of world market structure." See Brenner's (1977) critique as well.

12 Surrounding the modes-of-production debate were a good deal of polemics and exaggerated claims by both proponents and detractors. In 1981 the editors of a collection of essays entitled *Modes of Production in Africa* (Crummey and Stewart 1981:15) dismissed much prior Africanist research as "sloppy and boring," and proclaimed that they and their colleagues had "begun to explore fundamental questions concerning the social history of Africa." Four years later, Clarence-Smith (1985:19) boldly pronounced, "Thou shalt not articulate modes of production." He called for a restricted use of the concept to the level of theory, warning that the "cutting edge of a fine intellectual razor has progressively been transformed into a monstrous blunt instrument" (22).

13 Rural-based revolutions in Algeria, China, Cuba, and Vietnam heightened interest in the study of peasant politics. The defeat of the United States in Vietnam accelerated this process.

14 The literature on Southeast Asia and the lively debates it generated were particularly influential (see Popkin 1979; Scott 1976b).

15 For an excellent discussion of the theoretical, ideological, and political consequences of the agrarian crises, see Berry 1984b; see also Bernstein's (1985) provocative essay.

16 Neither modes-of-production analysis nor underdevelopment theory seemed to yield new insights into these problems or to provide a strategic entry into the larger issue of rural transformation. African agency proponents confronted a similar dilemma, while modernization and developmental theorists could hardly make a credible case on the heels of two developmental decades.

17 In an important redefinition of the resistance debate, Ranger (1986b) has shifted his attention from nationalism to agrarian protest and from undifferentiated African agency to rural class struggle and peasant insurgency. Similarly, Bundy has moved away from the underdevelopment paradigm, which underpinned his highly influential "strangulation thesis." In *Hidden Struggles* (1987:4), Bundy and his co-author Beinart state that "our ultimate purpose is to claim a larger weight or place for the history of rural peoples in South Africa." In a somewhat different vein, Bernstein (1985) shifts his view of peasants from one that sees them trapped in the

crisis of reproduction to one that emphasizes their ambiguous class position as petty commodity producers.

18 This emphasis recognizes both the demographic realities of the continent and the impossibility of separating peasants from the larger society of which they are a part and which shapes their very being as peasants. This new literature also recognizes that in many societies peasants were and are now a permanent social category.

19 Such an approach, of course, runs the risk of constructing a history without a vantage point or theoretical grounding. For an elaboration of this position from a Marxist perspective, see Morris (1987) and M. Murray (1988a).

20 Much more research is still needed in this area. Scholars need to pay greater attention to the natural world which shaped and was in turn shaped by peasant production. For all the renewed interest in ecology, few studies have begun to approach the meticulous and sophisticated analysis which makes Lee's (1979) monograph on the Kung San so powerful. *The Journal of Southern African Studies* (1989) has recently devoted an entire issue to conservation and ecology.

21 Compare Depelchin's (1979) discussion on land tenure with that of McCaskie (1980). Crummey's (1978) research challenges the notion that land in Amhara could not be sold, and promises to open up a whole new area of research.

22 See Bloch 1966; Braudel 1972, 1973; Brenner 1977, 1986; R. H. Hilton 1973, 1975; Hobsbawm 1965, 1969, 1980; Shanin 1971b, 1972; and Tilly 1978, 1982.

23 See Blassingame 1972 and Genovese 1974.

24 See Chaliand 1969; Deal 1975; Desai 1979; Hobsbawm 1973; Paige 1975; Popkin 1979; and Scott 1976b, 1985.

25 See Boserup 1970 and Joan Scott 1986.

26 Bunker (1982) extends Hyden's thesis, arguing that when these ornery peasants, such as the coffee cultivators of Bagisu, produced highly valued cash crops that represented a substantial portion of foreign exports, they enjoyed substantial leverage. For a critique of Hyden's theoretical approach, see Mamdani (1985) and Staudt (1987).

27 There is also no consensus on whether these peasant migrants have impoverished rural households and communities by depriving them of labor or have provided new opportunities for capital accumulation through technology, thereby compensating the households for the loss of their labor (First 1983; Guyer 1981b; Murray 1981).

28 By *property relations,* I mean the ownership or the degree of control that direct producers had over the means of production and the product of their labor. The nature of property relations was a major source of contestation between the direct producers, on the one hand, and the appropriating classes and the state, on the other. As a result of these struggles, property relations varied substantially over time and space (Brenner 1986:23–53).

29 There were some notable exceptions. See, for example, the extremely rich unpublished dissertations of Rogers (Geiger) 1973, and Hay 1972, both of which were based on extensive fieldwork.

30 Interpreting this documentation poses several methodological problems, including determining the interrelationship between text, meaning, and power, and the "construction of the other" (Clifford 1987).

31 "To get the story straight with only warped sources is not a simple task; but it is not impossible," noted Weiskel. "African history can be written even from the most partial sources if an analytical perspective is kept in mind" (1980:xviii).

32 Clarence-Smith's skepticism was part of a larger reaction to the privileged status that oral traditions had been given during the 1960s and 1970s.

33 In introducing the first issue of *Nao Vamos Esquecer!* (*We Won't Forget!*), the editorial collective declared the need to formulate a "popular revolutionary problematic" which recognized that "the living history resides in the bosom of the people and it is they who are the principal source of its inspiration and production" (1983:5).

34 For a preliminary but fascinating discussion of the methodological, ethical, and political problems which groping with these silences presents, see Moore and Roberts et al. 1989.

35 There is a tendency in the literature to read Marx (1926) as antipeasants. Proponents of this position most often refer to his reference in the *Eighteenth Brumaire* to peasants as "a sack of potatoes." In the same discussion, however, he distinguishes between conservative peasants and revolutionary peasants who want to overthrow the old order.

36 This is true not only in Africa and the Third World, but also of peasant struggles in Europe (Bloch 1966).

37 To date, the most detailed analysis of precolonial labor history has focused on slavery (Cooper 1977; Lovejoy 1983, 1986a; Meillassoux 1986; Miller 1988; Roberts 1987; Sheriff 1987; Spaulding 1982; Terray 1985a; Vansina 1978).

38 I am grateful to Paul Lovejoy and Jan Vansina for stressing this point in criticism of an earlier draft of this paper. For a provocative theoretical essay, see Guyer 1988.

39 The lack of funding for major research projects on the scale of those that have been undertaken in Latin America has certainly contributed to the paucity of archaeological data for most parts of Africa.

40 For a detailed discussion of the limits of oral data, see Hamilton 1987; Henige 1982; Miller, ed. 1980; Schoffeleers 1985; and Vansina 1985.

41 Embedded in the earliest colonial records are accounts of traditions from the late nineteenth century that refer to population size and taxation. Although these figures are, no doubt, inflated, they may provide some baselines from which to reconstruct the period just before the European conquest.

42 The accounts of European missionaries, travelers, and officials offer important insights into the process of production and extraction in places as diverse as the Kongo and Madagascar (P. Larson 1985; Thornton 1983). None of these studies, however, even begins to approach the depth of detail of Valensi's (1985) meticulously documented reconstruction of eighteenth- and nineteenth-century Tunisian peasant societies. Based on extensive Arabic and European records, his work is both a tour de force and a sober reminder of the limits of our own data.

43 To quote Klein (1980:13), "slaves rather than peasants were the primary source of surplus and the most important form of investment in those societies more involved in market relations." Whether this generalization can be sustained outside of West Africa is still an open question.

44 Lovejoy comes to the exactly opposite conclusion. He argues that nineteenth-

century northern Nigeria had one of the largest slave-based plantation systems in the world. He acknowledges that peasants were an important, although secondary, source of agricultural production (Lovejoy 1978, 1979).

45 Personal communication from Terence Ranger, April 10, 1989.

46 There is some evidence that peasants, alienated by excessive taxation, formed the bulk of Jaga troops. Personal communication from Jan Vansina, February 2, 1989.

47 Mason (1973) has advanced this thesis in his study of Nupe. He points to the existence of relatively autonomous slave villages, with slave headmen who farmed for a master to whom they gave a portion of the crop. Lovejoy has suggested, however, that this "peasant breach" was actually a phenomenon of the early twentieth century and was transposed by colonial officials and scholars back to the earlier period. Personal communication from Paul Lovejoy, February 9, 1989.

48 Austen (1987:48) concludes that "slaves devoted all or most of their time to family plots and were only required to turn over a specified portion of each year's production to their masters. Agricultural slavery could, for the individual who experienced it, eventually evolve into a status little different from the tributary obligations of nominally 'free peasants.' Village slaves in well-situated areas often sold enough crops and handicrafts on their own accounts to be considered relatively prosperous."

49 Searing (1988) argues for a fierce ideology of freedom among Wolof peasants derived by contrast to slavery. In a recent paper Hill suggests that in Kano the use of male slaves by peasant families meant that peasant wives and daughters were not used, explaining the later spread of Islamic seclusion (personal communication from Terence Ranger, April 10, 1989). On the transition from slavery, see Cooper 1980, and Roberts and Miers 1988. Lovejoy and Hogendorn are currently completing a major study on this subject.

50 There does not appear to be a substantial body of research on the social basis of the nineteenth-century *jihads*. Last (1974), Rodney (1972), and Watts (1983b) all raise major theoretical issues but only treat them in passing. Similarly, Robinson's (1985) important monograph focuses on political and theological struggles. This is obviously an important gap which merits serious investigation.

51 That many of these revolts took place in frontier areas populated by different ethnic groups suggests that we should pay much greater attention to the social basis of secession crises. We need to try to tease out the complex ways in which class, ethnic, and religious loyalties may have become interconnected during these struggles. The frequency of such conflicts also suggests the relative weakness of most precolonial states or, stated somewhat differently, that peasants enjoyed a substantial degree of autonomy.

52 John Comaroff's research suggests that the tendency to seize agricultural surplus preceded this period. Male appropriation of surplus to provide for expanding households often became the basis of their political power (personal communication with John Comaroff, March 24, 1989). For a somewhat different analysis of internal conflict than either that of Kinsman or Comaroff, see Okihiro 1984 and Wilmsen, forthcoming.

53 Even in these cases, which appear unambiguous in terms of the ultimate objective, the specific motivation is not always clear. Peasants might have cooked the seeds

to strike out at the system, to avoid intense labor demands, to get African chiefs in trouble, to defy male elders who controlled the produce, or some combination of the above.

54 The colonial state used a variety of coercive strategies to stimulate cotton production, ranging from the organization of communal plots supervised by chiefs (Fearn 1961; Tetzlaff 1970; Wrigley 1959) to forced household production (Bassett 1988; Dampierre 1960; Isaacman et al. 1980; Jewsiewicki 1980b; O'Laughlin 1973; Vail and White 1978). Not all cotton production, however, was forced. In regions with well-developed precolonial textile industries, such as in northern Nigeria, and in regions where climatic conditions were favorable or where natural irrigation permitted two planting seasons, as in the Tchiri Valley of Malawi, peasants voluntarily cultivated cotton (Mandala 1982, 1984; Shenton and Lennihan 1981). In the Lake Victoria area, two rainy seasons facilitated the integration of cotton with food crops. But even under such conditions, administrative pressure in the form of taxation and labor requirements was initially necessary to stimulate Lanqi cotton production (Tosh 1978).

55 Peasants employed a variety of strategies to try to overcome this production bottleneck. In Sukumaland peasants practiced phased cultivation of both food crops and cotton. This entailed extending the work over several months to ensure an adequate supply of food. It resulted, however, in a reduced cotton yield (Rotenhan 1968). Among the Teso, where land and labor were relatively abundant, peasant households got around the labor bottleneck with the adoption of plough cultivation in the later half of the 1920s (Vail 1972).

56 On the basis of my fieldwork in Mozambique, it is clear that peasants were aware that burning the cotton plant would improve the quantity and quality of their cotton, but they were also aware that the time spent could more productively be used growing food and more profitable cash crops.

57 Armed attacks against tax collectors are well documented in such diverse places as Niger, Dahomey, Burundi, and Angola (Gahama 1983; Garcia 1970; Latour-Dejean 1980; R. Pelissier 1978).

58 To quote Swai, "Of late the debate on resistance movements has been extended to an investigation of the phenomenon of social banditry [Isaacman, Ranger, Freund]. But, as has been said of American 'radical historiography' . . . it is a kind of history which is too busy celebrating successful tactics and militant actions, too busy attempting to give 'radicals' their own history—which is to say a false sense of accomplishment and therefore a pious satisfaction with the past" (1982:153–54).

59 Austen (1986:102), who contributed to this volume, finds "that the most fruitful Western model for African heroic criminality is the colonial era *picaro,* an individual relatively isolated from African society, yet not integrated into the European-dominated state."

60 See McCann 1987:89 for a particularly powerful class critique found in Wallo oral poetry.

61 The best examples of this art produced by Makonde and Makua sculptors, many of whom were also peasants subjected to forced cotton cultivation, can be found in the Museum in Nampula. For a discussion of this art, see Alpers 1988.

62 The ambiguous and often contradictory role of colonial chiefs attracted the attention of a number of prominent anthropologists (Fallers 1956; Fortes and Evans-Pritchard 1940; Gluckman 1940, 1942; Richards 1939; Turner 1957).

63 Newbury's (1988) analysis of the 1958–59 insurrection rests on the proposition that the "tribal" categories "Tutsi" and "Hutu" were actually class-based constructs shaped largely during the colonial period. These ethnic terms actually distinguished landlord-chiefs from impoverished clients.

64 Creevey (1986:1–2) begins her edited collection with the following:

> There is a pervasive bias . . . against the technology and needs of rural women. . . . The pro-male and anti-female bias applies in other spheres, too. Ploughing, mainly carried out by men, has received more attention than weeding or transplanting, mainly carried out by women. Cash crops, from which the male heads of household benefit disproportionately, have received more attention than subsistence crops which are more of a concern for women . . . it is rare indeed to find substantial changes in perception, attitude or behavior among the male majority of professionals.

65 Even where women had access to land, as in Ghana and Nigeria, it was often restricted (Afonja 1986; Vellenga 1986), and they faced acute labor shortages (Guyer 1984a; Roberts 1987; Whitehead 1981).

66 In the domestic sphere, as in others, colonial policies often produced contradictory and unintended consequences. While the position of senior males was often strengthened, this was not necessarily the case. Even as household heads were increasing their power, new demands for labor and commodities created new opportunities for dependents to escape. In many places young men entered the wage-labor market, and women ran away to towns. Moreover, there is evidence that struggles and accommodation over labor, land, and other scarce resources may have been shaped by seasonality (Schroeder 1989).

67 Vaughan notes that young men sent foraging during the famines also experienced a high mortality rate.

68 In the Rungwe region of Tanzania, according to Mbilinyi, "bridewealth had become a commodity, women had become objects of purchase and sale, and marriage and adultery had become moments of commodity circulation and accumulation." The term which was used to signify the act of payment of bridewealth was *kulipa* (to pay). The same term was used for market transactions (Mbilinyi 1988).

69 This requires careful investigation of their motives, resources, and strategies to determine the extent to which rural women enjoyed more options than conventional theorists have assumed.

70 Personal communication with Charles van Onselen, April 4, 1989.

71 The colonial vision was often an evolutionary one in which female farming was by definition backward. Given the emerging state of the literature, there is probably no way of knowing yet the relative importance of such diverse factors as agricultural knowledge among women, their commitment to preserve their partial autonomy, and their opposition to colonialism and European culture in structuring insurgent actions (personal communication with Jane Guyer, April 20, 1989).

72 By a *social movement,* I mean a configuration of individuals or groups willing to

come together and engage in a series of direct political actions to achieve their collective goals. In the case of peasants, this minimal definition raises a number of questions that fall outside the scope of this review essay but merit serious consideration. Under what conditions do peasants decide to act politically? How do they come together? Where do they get the resources? How do they overcome their disorganization and gain the knowledge to use the resources at their disposal? In short, we need both a theory of political situations as well as more extensive analysis of resource mobilization. For a review of the social movement literature, see McAdam, McCarthy, and Zald 1988; Tarrow 1988; Traugott 1978.

73 Although essentially an insurrection from below, more militant elements within the disposed royal family, under pressure from peasants and spirit mediums, agreed to lead the insurrection. The role of spirit mediums as *traditional* intellectuals needs careful investigation in Mozambique, similar to the type of research conducted by Lan (1985) in neighboring Zimbabwe.

74 The decision of the rural underclass to organize boycotts of shops in Dahomey or South Africa (Almeida-Topor 1980; Beinart and Bundy 1987), to withhold cash-advance-system debt in northern Nigeria (Shenton and Lennihan 1981; Watts 1983b), or to destroy underpriced commodities in Malawi and Zaire (McCracken 1983; Likaka, 1991) was quite a different phenomenon from the Ghanian cocoa hold-ups (Austin 1988) and the actions of the Zambian African Farmers Association (Chipungu 1982). The latter were designed to promote the interests of prosperous chiefs or of a nascent class of capitalist farmers often at the expense of poorer peasants.

75 The question of internal organization is both critical and understudied. Bradford's (1987) work on the ICU in South Africa and Migdal's (1974) and Popkin's (1979) comparative studies are important exceptions. Skocpol (1979, 1982), on the other hand, argues that peasant revolution occurred when states experienced a crisis of leadership and authority, and could no longer exercise control over the countryside—in short, when peasant autonomy was greatest.

76 By the early 1970s, a small, but increasingly significant, group of scholars had integrated peasants into the nationalist literature. They also had begun to treat problematically the nature of the encounters between peasants and nationalist leaders (Furedi 1974). But it was precisely at this moment, when nationalism was being redefined in more contingent terms, that the subject fell into eclipse. The political and economic crises in Africa undermined both the power of nationalist discourse and the claim that it was a compelling mode of analysis. "As nationalist thought was assimilated into state ideology," Young (1986:436) argues convincingly, "it suffered the de-legitimacy of the state itself."

77 My discussion of Mau-Mau benefited from the knowledge and insights of Luise White.

78 Sorrenson (1967) also identified the Kikuyu reserve as the principal terrain of struggle. He argues that increasing land shortages pitted senior lineage heads against junior clients who challenged their right to control land.

79 Ultimately, Kanogo argues, they prevailed. In the process they transformed them-

selves and their male comrades. "There was no man or woman leader for gender was immaterial" (1987:146).

80 Ironically, Kriger leaves us with the somewhat familiar view of peasants as victims, even as she portrays them as engaged in vigorous internal struggle. Phimister (1987) also argues that from 1976 onward the relations between ZANU guerrillas and peasants in some areas were becoming strained. In the first instance, there was a marked decline in guerrilla discipline, and increasing demands made by them of the peasants. While he stresses the variability in relations from one region to another, he emphasizes that ZANU's program was increasingly at odds with the aspirations of poor peasants.

81 The Sekhukhuneland insurrection as well as the 1959–65 Poqo movement suggest the power of rural ideology among migrant workers who maintained strong cultural and material ties to the countryside (Delius n.d.; Lodge 1984).

82 Such an approach confronts a long and rich intellectual tradition. These assumptions about peasants can be found in the writings of Marx and Weber as well as in those of their intellectual descendants.

As Watts noted, until relatively recently, one of the few terrains on which Marxist and conventional social science thinking actually met in an amicable symbiosis was that of peasant politics. The Marxian legacy of an individuated peasant livelihood and consciousness—"potatoes in a sack" as Marx himself described the French peasantry—profoundly inseparable from the "barbarian" and "vegetable" conditions of rural idiocy, dovetailed perfectly with the "peasants as generic type" literature so fashionable in the 1950s and 1960s. If the *Eighteenth Brumaire* cast the conservative peasant in "stupefied bondage to the old order," the essentialism of Redfield, Foster, Banfield, and Lewis raised the peasant *mentalité* to a personality type: passive, distrustful, fatalistic, incapable of innovation, shackled with an antediluvian outlook and, in what must have seemed a massive affront to a generation of capitalist development theoreticians, thoroughly unable to defer gratification. It is, of course, true that Marx himself anticipated the most revolutionary of all circumstances when landed classes were in the throes of dispossession as market forces developed, but he could hardly have predicted the astonishing peasant mobilizations in the major revolutionary movements of the twentieth century (Watts 1988:117).

83 At a theoretical level, Gramsci's attention to the cultural and ideological dimension of domination has had a profound impact on scholarly analysis of the subordinated classes, including peasants. At the same time, scholars have read Gramsci's discussion on peasants in many different ways. In part, the contending interpretations reflect the difficulty of unraveling key portions of *Prison Notebooks* and teasing out a consistent theory from his work. It also reflects the fact that Gramsci's thinking about peasants as political actors changed over time (Arnold 1984; Davidson 1984). Scott (1985:317) rejects the notion of hegemony, suggesting that Gramsci and his successors have "substituted a kind of ideological determinism for the material determinism they sought to avoid." He argues that peasants were able to demystify the prevailing ideology and develop a counter-hegemonic view. Arnold and a number of Indian scholars associated with *Subaltern Studies* interpret Gramsci quite differently.

Arnold (1984:160, 162) contends that Gramsci did not reduce peasants to mere victims of false consciousness but recognized that subaltern society was engaged in a continuing dialectical tussle within itself, between its active and its passive voice, between acceptance and resistance, between isolation and collectivity and between disunity and cohesion. Subalterns might receive the substance of their culture from the hegemonic classes but make it their own by impregnating it with nonhegemonic values or by selecting some aspects and rejecting others.

84 Religious movements covered the entire spectrum from accommodation and quietism to insurgency. A number of syncretistic movements, such as Harrism, preached an ideology of resignation or of social advancement. Separatist churches in southern Africa tended to adopt a more militant character, although this was not always the case. The role of Islam in colonial Africa was particularly ambiguous. In some cases, such as northern Nigeria and Zanzibar, Islam served as a means for chiefs to enter into alliance with colonial authorities. In other parts of the continent, such as Mauritania, Niger, and the Sudan, Islam provided the ideological basis for anticolonial uprisings (Coquery-Vidrovitch 1988; Ranger 1986a).

85 Custodians of the Mbona cult not only advanced the traditional argument that the ridges would impede Mbona, the provider of rain, from visiting the land, but they also challenged the assumed technical superiority of British experts (Mandala 1990).

86 I want to thank Randy Packard for calling my attention to the Fang origin myths and the various ways the myths can be read. Personal communication, January 27, 1988.

87 Jean Comaroff (1985:11) notes that "although the church continued to serve as an accessible source of signs and organizational forms, these became the elements of a syncretistic bricolage deployed to carry a message of protest and resistance, and to address the exigencies of a runaway world."

88 Feierman's study is very much a book that transcends older dualisms; a book that integrates thick description and historical change; a book that integrates the study of political discourse and political economy.

References

Abrams, Philip. 1982. *Historical Sociology*. Ithaca: Cornell Univ. Press.

Achebe, Chinua. 1959. *Things Fall Apart*. Greenwich, Conn.: Fawcett Crest.

Adam, Richard. 1977. *Pre-Historic Meso-America*. Boston: Little, Brown.

Adas, M. 1980. " 'Moral Economy' or 'Contest State'? Elite Demands and the Origins of Peasant Protest in Southeast Asia." *Journal of Social History* 13:521–46.

Adas, M. 1981. "From Avoidance to Confrontation: Peasant Protest in Pre-Colonial and Colonial Southeast Asia." *Comparative Studies in Society and History* 23:217–47.

Adas, M. 1986. "From Footdragging to Flight: The Evasive History of Peasant Avoidance Protest in South and Southeast Asia." *Journal of Peasant Studies* 13, no. 2:64–86.

Afonja, Simi. 1986. "Land Control: A Critical Factor in Yoruba Gender Stratification." In Robertson and Berger 1986:78–81.

Ake, Claude. 1981. *A Political Economy of Africa*. London: Longman.

Akinjobin. 1967. *Dahomey and Its Neighbors*. Cambridge: Cambridge Univ. Press.

Alavi, Hamza. 1973. "Peasant Classes and Primordial Loyalties." *Journal of Peasant Studies* 1:23–62.

Alexandrov, Y. G. 1974. "The Peasant Movements of Developing Countries in Asia and North Africa After the Second World War." In Landsberger 1974: 351–77.

Allen, William. 1965. *The African Husbandman*. New York: Barnes and Noble.

Almeida-Topor, Hélène d'. 1980. "Une société paysanne devant la colonisation: La Résistance des Holli du Dahomey (1894–1923)." In Catherine Coquery-Vidrovitch, ed., *Sociétés paysannes du Tiers Monde*. Lille: Presses Universitaires de Lille, 81–89.

Almeida-Topor, Hélène d'. 1981. "From Avoidance to Confrontation: Peasant Protest in Pre-Colonial and Colonial Southeast Asia." *Comparative Studies in Society and History* 23:217–47.

Alpers, Edward. 1973. "Rethinking African Economic History." *Ufuhamu* 3, no. 3:97–129.

Alpers, Edward. 1975. *Ivory and Slaves: Changing Patterns of International Trade in East Central Africa to the Later Nineteenth Century*. Berkeley: Univ. of California Press.

Alpers, Edward. 1988. "Representation and Historical Consciousness in the Art of Modern Mozambique." *Canadian Journal of African Studies* 22:73–94.

AlRoy, Gil Carl. 1966. *The Involvement of Peasants in Internal Wars*. Princeton: Princeton Univ. Press.

AlRoy, Gil Carl. 1967. "The Peasantry in the Cuban Revolution," *Review of Politics* 29:87–99.

Amin, S. 1972. "Underdevelopment and Dependence in Black Africa—Origins and Contemporary Forms," *Journal of Modern African Studies* 10, no. 4:503–24.

Amselle, J. L. 1978. "La conscience paysanne: la révolte de Ouolosse-bougou (Juin 1968, Mali)." *Canadian Journal of African Studies* 12, no. 3:339–55.

Amselle, J. L. 1984. "Socialisme capitalisme et précapitalisme au Mali (1960–1982)." In Henry Bernstein and Bonnie K. Campbell, eds., *Contradictions of Accumulation in Africa: Studies in Economy and State*. Beverly Hills: Sage, 249–66.

Anderson, David, and David Throup. 1985. "Africans and Agricultural Production in Colonial Kenya: The Myth of the War as a Watershed." *Journal of African History* 26:327–46.

Apter, David E. 1963. *Ghana in Transition*. New York: Atheneum.

Ardener, E. 1975. "Belief and the Problem of Women." In S. Ardeuer, ed., *Perceiving Women*. New York: Wiley, 1–17.

Aregay, Merid. 1984. "Millenarian Traditions and Peasant Movements in Ethiopia, 1500–1855." In Sven Rubenson, ed., *Proceedings of the Seventh International Conference of Ethiopian Studies*. Addis Ababa, East Lansing, and Uppsala: Michigan State Univ., 257–62.

Arhin, Kwame. 1983. "Peasants in Nineteenth-Century Asante." *Current Anthropology* 24 no. 4:471–80.

Armah, Ay Kwei. 1979. *Two Thousand Seasons*. Chicago: Third World Press.

Arnold, David. 1984. "Gramsci and Peasant Subalternity in India," *Journal of Peasant Studies* 11, no. 4:155–77.

Arrighi, G. 1970. "Labor Supplies in Historical Perspective: A Study of the Proletarianization of the African Peasantry in Rhodesia." *Journal of Development Studies* 6:197–235.

Asad, Talal, ed. 1973. *Anthropology and the Colonial Encounter*. Atlantic Highlands: Humanities.

Asiwaju, A. I. 1976. "Migrations as Revolt: The Example of the Ivory Coast and the Upper Volta Before 1945." *Journal of African History* 17:577–94.

Atieno-Odhiambo, E. S. 1972. "The Rise and Decline of the Kenyan Peasant, 1880–1992." *East African Journal* 9:11–15.

Atieno-Odhiambo, E. S. 1974. "The Rise and Decline of the Kenyan Peasant, 1888–1892." In E. S. Atieno-Odhiambo, ed., *The Paradox of Collaboration and Other Essays*. Nairobi: East African Literature Bureau, 90–102.

Austen, Ralph. 1986. "Social Bandits and Other Heroic Criminals: Western Models of Resistance and Their Relevance to Africa." In Crummey 1986:89–108.

Austen, Ralph. 1987. *African Economic History: Internal Development and External Dependency*. Portsmouth: Heinemann.

Austen, Ralph, and Rita Headrick. 1983. "Equatorial Africa Under Colonial Rule." In David Birmingham and Phyllis Martin, eds., *History of Central Africa*. London: Longman, 27–94.

Austin, Gareth. 1988. "Capitalists and Chiefs in the Cocoa Hold-Ups in South Asante, 1927–1938." *International Journal of African Historical Studies* 21, no. 1:63–95.

Ayrout, Henry Habib. 1963. *The Egyptian Peasant*. Boston: Beacon Press.

Balandier, Georges. 1965. *Sociologie actuelle de l'Afrique Noire*. Paris: Presses Universitaires de France.

Balandier, Georges. 1966. "The Colonial Situation: A Theoretical Approach." In Immanuel M. Wallerstein, ed., *Social Change: The Colonial Situation*. New York: Wiley, 34–62.

Balandier, Georges. 1968. *Daily Life in the Kingdom of the Kongo: From the Sixteenth to the Eighteenth Century*. London: Allen & Unwin.

Ballard, Charles. 1986. "The Repercussions of Rinderpest: Cattle Plague and Peasant Decline in Colonial Natal." *International Journal of African Historical Studies* 19, no. 3:421–50.

Barber, Karin. 1986. "The Popular Arts in Africa." Paper commissioned by ACLS-SSRC Africa Committee and presented at African Studies Association Meeting, Madison, Wisconsin.

Barber, Karin. 1987. "Popular Arts in Africa," *African Studies Review* 30, no. 3:1–78.

Barnes, J. A. 1954. *Politics in a Changing Society*. London: Oxford Univ. Press.

Barnett, Don. 1973. *Peasant Types and Revolutionary Potential in Colonial Africa*. Richmond: LSM Press.

Barnett, Don, and Karari Njama. 1966. *Mau Mau from Within*. New York: Monthly Review Press.

Bassett, Thomas. 1988. "The Development of Cotton in Northern Ivory Coast, 1910–1965," *Journal of African History* 29, no. 1:267–84.

Bates, Robert H. 1987a. *Essays on the Political Economy of Rural Africa*. Berkeley: Univ. of California Press.

Bates, Robert H. 1987b. "The Agrarian Origins of Mau-Mau: A Structural Account." *Agricultural History* 61, no. 1:1–28.

Bauer, Raymond, and Alice Bauer. 1942. "Day to Day Resistance to Slavery," *Journal of Negro History* 27, no. 4:388–419.

Bazin, J., and E. Terray, eds. 1982. *Guerres de lignages et guerres d'états en Afrique.* Paris: Editions des Archives Contemporaines.

Beer, C. E. F. 1976. *The Politics of Peasant Groups in Western Nigeria.* Ibadan: Ibadan Univ. Press.

Beer, C. E. F., and G. Williams. 1975. "The Politics of the Ibadan Peasantry." *African Review* 5, no. 3:235–56.

Beinart, William. 1980. "Production and the Material Basis of Chieftainship: Pondoland, c. 1830–1880." In Marks and Atmore 1980:120–46.

Beinart, William. 1981. "Conflict in Qumbu: Rural Consciousness, Ethnicity and Violence in the Colonial Transkei, 1880–1913." *Journal of Southern African Studies* 8:94–122.

Beinart, William. 1982. *The Political Economy of Pondoland, 1860–1930.* Cambridge: Cambridge Univ. Press.

Beinart, William. 1989. "Introduction: The Politics of Colonial Conservation." *Journal of Southern African Studies* 15:145–62.

Beinart, William, and Colin Bundy. 1980. "State Intervention and Rural Resistance: The Transkei, 1900–1965." In Klein 1980:271–316.

Beinart, William, and Colin Bundy. 1987. *Hidden Struggles in Rural South Africa.* Berkeley: Univ. of California Press.

Beinart, William, Peter Delius, and Stanley Trapido, eds. 1986. *Putting a Plough to the Ground.* Johannesburg: Ravan Press.

Beqiraj, Mehmet. 1966. *Peasantry in Revolution.* Ithaca: Center for International Studies, Cornell Univ.

Berg, Gerald. 1981. "Riziculture and the Founding of Monarchy in Imerina." *Journal of African History* 22, no. 3:289–308.

Berger, Iris. 1981. *Religion and Resistance: East African Kingdoms in the Pre-Colonial Period.* Tervuren: Musée Royale de l'Afrique Centrale.

Berger, John. 1979. *Pig Earth.* New York: Pantheon.

Berman, B., and Lonsdale, J. 1980. "Crises of Accumulation, Coercion, and the Colonial State: The Development of the Labor Control System in Kenya, 1919–1929." *Canadian Journal of African Studies* 14, no. 1:37–54.

Bernstein, Henry. 1977. "Notes on Capital and Peasantry." *Review of African Political Economy* 10:60–73.

Bernstein, Henry. 1979. "African Peasantries: A Theoretical Framework." *Journal of Peasant Studies* 6, no. 4:421–43.

Bernstein, Henry. 1985. "Agrarian Crises in Africa and Neo-Classical Populism." Univ. of London: Postgraduate Seminar on Peasants, paper presented.

Bernstein, Henry. 1988. "Capitalism and Petty-Bourgeois Production: Class Relations and Divisions of Labour," *Journal of Peasant Studies* 15, no. 2:258–71.

Bernstein, Henry, and J. Depelchin. 1978–1979. "The Object of African History: A

Materialist Perspective." *History in Africa* 5:1–19, 6:17–43.

Berry, Sara S. 1974. "The Concept of Innovation and the History of Cocoa Farming in Western Nigeria," *Journal of African History* 15, no. 1:83–95.

Berry, Sara. 1975. *Cocoa, Custom and Socio-Economic Change in Rural Western Nigeria*. London: Oxford Univ. Press.

Berry, Sara. 1984a. "Oil and the Disappearing Peasantry: Accumulation, Differentiation, and Underdevelopment in Western Nigeria." *African Economic History* 13:1–22.

Berry, Sara. 1984b. "The Food Crisis and Agrarian Change in Africa: A Review Essay." *African Studies Review* 27, no. 2:59–112.

Berry, Sara. 1985. *Fathers Work for Their Sons: Accumulation, Mobility, and Class Formation in an Extended Yoruba Community*. Berkeley: Univ. of California Press.

Bessant, Leslie. n.d. "History of Peasants and History by Peasants: The Chiweshe Reserve, Colonial Zimbabwe, 1935–1965." Unpublished manuscript.

Biebuyck, Daniel, ed. 1963. *African Agrarian Systems*. London: Oxford Univ. Press.

Birmingham, David. 1978. "The Coffee Barons of Cazengo." *Journal of African History* 19, no. 4:523–38.

Blackey, Robert H. 1974. "Fanon and Cabral: A Contrast in Theories of Revolution for Africa." *Journal of Modern African Studies* 12, no. 2:191–209.

Blassingame, John. 1972. The Slave Community: Plantation Life in the Antebellum South. New York: Oxford Univ. Press.

Blickle, Peter. 1981. *The Revolution of 1525: The German Peasants' War from a New Perspective*. Baltimore: Johns Hopkins Univ. Press.

Bloch, Marc L. 1966. *French Rural History*. London: Routledge and Kegan Paul.

Blok, Anton. 1969. "Mafia and Peasant Rebellion as Contrasting Factors in Sicilian Latifundism." *European Journal of Sociology* 10:95–116.

Blok, Anton. 1972. "The Peasant and the Brigand: Social Banditry Reconsidered." *Comparative Studies in Society and History* 14:494–503.

Boahen, A., ed. 1985. *UNESCO History of Africa*. Vol. 7. Berkeley: Univ. of California.

Boeder, Robert B. 1973. "The Effects of Labor Migration in Rural Life in Malawi." *Rural Africana* 20:37–46.

Boesen, Jannik. 1979. "On Peasantry and the 'Modes of Production' Debate." *Review of African Political Economy* 15, no. 16:154–61.

Boesen, Laura. 1953. *The Tiv of Central Nigeria*. London: International African Institute.

Bohannan, Paul. 1954a. *The Farm and Settlement*. London: H.M.S.O.

Bohannan, Paul. 1954b. "The Migration and Expansion of the Tiv." *Africa* 24, no. 1:2–16.

Bohannan, Paul. 1958. "Extra-Processual Events in Two Political Institutions." *American Anthropologist* 60:1–12.

Bohannan, Paul. 1959. "The Impact of Money on an African Subsistence Economy." *Journal of Economic History* 19:491–503.

Bonner, Philip. 1977. "Classes, the Mode of Production, and the State in Pre-Colonial Swaziland." Manchester History Seminar: unpublished paper.

Bonner, Philip. 1983. *Kings, Commoners, and Concessionaires: The Evolution and*

Dissolution of the Nineteenth-Century Swazi State. Johannesburg: Ravan Press.

Boserup, E. 1965. *The Conditions of Agricultural Growth: The Economics of Agrarian Change Under Population Pressure*. Chicago: Aldine.

Boserup, E. 1970. *Woman's Role in Economic Development*. London: Allen & Unwin.

Botte, Roger. 1974. "Processus de formation d'une classe sociale dans une société africaine précapitaliste," *Cahiers d'Études Africaines* 14, no. 1:605–26.

Bourdieu, P. 1977. *Outline of a Theory of Practice*. Cambridge: Cambridge Univ. Press.

Bowman, Joye. 1987. " 'Legitimate Commerce' and Peanut Production in Portuguese Guinea, 1840s–1880s." *Journal of African History* 28, no. 1:87–106.

Boyte, Harry. 1989. *Commonwealth: A Return to Citizen Politics*. New York: Free Press.

Bozzoli, Belinda. 1983a. "Marxism, Feminism and South African Studies," *Journal of Southern African Studies* 9/2: 139–71.

Bozzoli, Belinda. 1983b. *Town and Countryside in the Transvaal*. Johannesburg: Ravan Press.

Bozzoli, Belinda. 1987. *Class, Community and Conflict*. Johannesburg: Ravan Press.

Bozzoli, Belinda. 1991. *Women of Phokeng: Consciousness, Life Strategy, and Migrancy in South Africa, 1900–1983*. Portsmouth: Heinemann.

Bradbury, R. E. 1964. "The Historical Uses of Comparative Ethnography with Special Reference to Benin and Yoruba." In Jan Vansina et al., eds., *The Historian in Tropical Africa*. London: Oxford Univ. Press, 145–64.

Bradford, Helen. 1983. "A Taste of Freedom: Capitalist Development and Response to the ICU in the Transvaal Countryside." In Bozzoli 1983b:128–50.

Bradford, Helen. 1987. *A Taste of Freedom: The ICU in Rural South Africa, 1926–1930*. New Haven: Yale Univ. Press.

Bragança, Aquino de, and Immanuel Wallerstein, eds. 1982. *The African Liberation Reader*. Vol. 2. *The National Liberation Movements*. London: Zed Press.

Brantley, Cynthia. 1981. *The Giriama and Colonial Resistance in Kenya, 1800–1920*. Berkeley: Univ. of California Press.

Braudel, Fernand. 1972. *The Mediterranean and the Mediterranean World in the Age of Philip II*. 2 vols. New York: Harper & Row.

Braudel, Fernand. 1973. *Capitalism and Material Life, 1400–1800*. New York: Harper & Row.

Brenner, Robert. 1977. "The Origins of Capitalist Development: A Critique of Neo-Smithian Marxism." *New Left Review* 104:25–92.

Brenner, Robert. 1986. "The Social Basis of Economic Development." In John Roemer, ed., *Analytical Marxism*. Cambridge: Cambridge Univ. Press, 25–53.

Brett, E. A. 1973. *Colonialism and Underdevelopment in East Africa*. London: Heinemann.

Brooks, George E. 1975. "Peanuts and Colonialism: Consequences of the Commercialization of Peanuts in West Africa, 1830–1870," *Journal of African History* 16, no. 1:29–54.

Brunschwig, H. 1974. "De la Resistance Africaine à l'imperialisme européen," *Journal of African History* 15, no. 1:47–64.

Bryceson, Deborah Fahy. 1980a. "The Proletarianization of Women in Tanzania."

Review of African Political Economy 17:4–27.

Bryceson, Deborah Fahy. 1980b. "Changes in Peasant Food Production and Food Supply in Relation to the Historical Development of Commodity Production in Pre-Colonial and Colonial Tanganyika." *Journal of Peasant Studies* 7, no. 3:281–311.

Bryceson, Deborah Fahy. 1982a. "Peasant Commodity Production in Post-Colonial Tanzania." *African Affairs* 81:547–67.

Bryceson, Deborah Fahy. 1982b. " 'The Tepid Backwater': Bagamoyo District and Its Marginal Commodity Production Within the Tanganyika Colonial Economy, 1919–1961," *Transafrican Journal of History* 11:1–25.

Bryceson, Deborah Fahy, and Marjorie Mbilinyi. 1978. "The Changing Role of Tanzanian Women in Production: From Peasants to Proletarians," Bralup Service Paper. Univ. of Dar-es-Salaam.

Buch-Hansen, Mogens, and Henrick Secher Marcussen. 1982. "Contract Farming and the Peasantry: Cases From Western Kenya." *Review of African Political Economy* 23:9–36.

Buijtenhuijs, Robert. 1971. *Le mouvement "Mau-Mau" : Une révolte paysanne et anti-coloniale en Afrique Noire*. The Hague: Mouton.

Buijtenhuijs, Robert. 1978. *Le Fronlinat et les révoltes populaires du Tchad, 1965–1976*. The Hague: Mouton.

Bukh, J. 1979. *The Village Women in Ghana*. Uppsala: Scandinavian Institute of African Studies.

Bullock, R. A. 1974. "Subsistence to Cash: Economic Change in Rural Kiambu," *Cahiers d'Études Africaines* 56:699–714.

Bundy, Colin. 1972. "The Emergence and Decline of a South African Peasantry." *African Affairs* 71:369–88.

Bundy, Colin. 1977. "The Transkei Peasantry, c. 1890–1914: 'Passing Through a Period of Stress.' " In Palmer and Parsons, eds., *The Roots of Rural Poverty in Central and Southern Africa*. Berkeley: Univ. of California Press, 201–20.

Bundy, Colin. 1979. *The Rise and Fall of the South African Peasantry*. Los Angeles: Univ. of California Press.

Bundy, Colin. 1984. "Land and Liberation: The South African National Liberation Movements and the Agrarian Question, 1920s–1960s." *Review of African Political Economy* 29:14–29.

Bunker, Stephen. 1982. "Property, Protest, and Politics in Bugisu, Uganda." Paper presented at Symposium on Rebellion and Social Protest, Univ. of Illinois, Urbana.

Bunker, Stephen. 1986. "Property, Protest and Politics in Bugisu, Uganda." In Crummey 1986:271–91.

Burawoy, Michael. 1979. *Manufacturing Consent: Changes in the Labor Process Under Monopoly Capitalism*. Chicago: Univ. of Chicago Press.

Burawoy, Michael. 1985. *The Politics of Production: Factory Regimes Under Capitalism and Socialism*. London: Verso.

Burnham, Philip, and Thomas Christensen. 1983. "Karnu's Message and the 'War of the Hoe Handle': Interpreting a Central African Resistance Movement." *Africa* 53, no. 4:3–22.

Cabral, Amilcar. 1974a. *Return to the Source: Selected Speeches*. New York: Monthly Review Press.

Cabral, Amilcar. 1974b. *Revolution in Guinea: An African People's Struggle*. London: Stage 1.

Cabral, Amilcar. 1980. *Unity and Struggle: Speeches and Writings*. London: Heinemann.

Campbell, Gwyn. 1988. "Slavery and Fanompoana: The Structure of Forced Labour in Imerina (Madascar), 1790–1861," *Journal of African History* 29, no. 3:463–86.

Cardoso, Ciro. 1979. "A Brecha Camponesa no Sistema Escravita." *Agricultura, Escrividao e Capitalismo*. Petropolis: Editora Vozes.

Carlsen, John. 1980. *Economic and Social Transformation in Rural Kenya*. Uppsala: Scandinavian Institute of African Studies.

Carney, Judith. 1988a. "Struggles Over Land and Crops in an Irrigated Rice Scheme." In Jean Davison, ed., *Agriculture, Women and Land: The African Experience*. Boulder, Colo.: Westview Press, 59–78.

Carney, Judith. 1988b. "Struggles Over Crop Rights and Labour Within Contract Farming Households in a Gambian Irrigated Rice Project," *Journal of Peasant Studies* 15, no. 3:334–49.

Caulk, Richard. 1984. "Bad Men of the Borders: Shum and Shefta in Northern Ethiopia in the Nineteenth Century." *International Journal of African Historical Studies* 17:201–27.

Centro de Estudos Africanos, Oficina de Historia. 1983. "Editorial." *Nao Vamos Esquercer* 1:3–5.

Chabal, Patrick. 1983. *Amilcar Cabral: Revolutionary Leadership and People's War*. New York: Cambridge Univ. Press.

Chaliand, Gerard. 1969. *Armed Struggle in Africa*. New York: Monthly Review Press.

Chaliand, Gerard. 1978. *Revolution in the Third World: Myths and Prospects*. New York: Penguin.

Chanock, Martin. 1982. "Making Customary Law: Men, Women, and Courts in Northern Rhodesia." In Margaret Jean Hay and Marcia Wright, eds., *African Women and the Law*. Boston: Boston Univ. Press, 53–67.

Chanock, Martin. 1985. *Law, Custom and Social Order: The Colonial Experience in Malawi and Zambia*. Cambridge: Cambridge Univ. Press.

Chauveau, Jean-Pierre. 1980. "Agricultural Production and Social Formation: The Baule Region of Toumodi-Kakumbo in Historical Perspective." In Klein 1980:143–76.

Chayanov, A. V. 1966. *The Theory of Peasant Economy*. Homewood, Ill.: Irwin.

Chesneaux, Jean. 1973. *Peasant Revolts in China, 1940–1949*. London: Thames and Hudson.

Chilcote, Ronald, ed. 1972. *Protest and Resistance in Angola and Brazil*. Los Angeles: Univ. of California Press.

Chipungu, Samuel. 1981. "African Production in Mazabuka District: The Development of Subordination, 1900–1953." *Zambian Land and Labour Studies*, 32–43.

Chipungu, Samuel. 1982. "Class Formation and Class Struggle in Mazabuka District, Colonial Rule [sic]." Unpublished paper.

Chipungu, Samuel. 1986. "Locusts, Peasants, Settlers and the State in Northern Rhodesia (Zambia), 1929–1940," *Transafrican Journal of History* 15:54–80.

Chipungu, Samuel. 1987. "The State, Technology and Peasant Differentiation in Zambia," Ph.D. diss. Univ. of Minnesota.

Chodak, Szymon. 1969. *African Peasantry: A Sociological Concept*. Dar-es-Salaam: University College.

Chodak, Szymon. 1971. "The Birth of an African Peasantry." *Canadian Journal of African Studies* 5:327–47.

Chrétien, Jean Pierre. 1972. "La Révolte de Ndungutse (1912): forces traditionnelles et pression colôniale au Rwanda allemand." *Revue Française d'Histoire d'Outre-Mer* 59, no. 4:645–80.

Clarence-Smith, W. G. 1979a. "Slaves, Commoners and Landlords in Bulozi, c. 1875–1906." *Journal of African History* 20, no. 2:219–34.

Clarence-Smith, W. G. 1979b. *Slaves, Peasants, and Capitalists in Southern Angola, 1840–1926*. Cambridge: Cambridge Univ. Press.

Clarence-Smith, W. G. 1985. "Thou Shalt Not Articulate Modes of Production." In Jewsiewicki and J. Letourneau 1985:19–22.

Clarence-Smith, W. G., and Moorsom, R. 1975. "Underdevelopment and Class Formation in Ovamboland, 1845–1915." *Journal of African History* 16:365–81.

Clarke, Julian. 1980. "Peasantization and Landholding: A Nigerian Case Study." In Klein 1980:177–200.

Clarke, Julian. 1981. "Households and the Political Economy of Small-Scale Cash Crop Production in South-Western Nigeria." *Africa* 51, no. 3:807–23.

Cliffe, Lionel. 1972. "Nationalism and the Reaction of Enforced Agricultural Change in Tanganyika During the Colonial Period." In Lionel Cliffe and John Saul, eds., *Socialism in Tanzania*. Dar-es-Salaam: East African Printing House, 17–24.

Cliffe, Lionel. 1976. "Rural Political Economy of Africa." In P. Gutkind and I. Wallerstein, eds., *The Political Economy of Contemporary Africa*. Beverly Hills: Sage, 112–30.

Cliffe, Lionel. 1977. "Rural Class Formation in East Africa." *Journal of Peasant Studies* 4, no. 2:195–224.

Cliffe, Lionel. 1978. "Labour Migration and Peasant Differentiation: The Zambian Experiences." *Journal of Peasant Studies* 5:326–46.

Cliffe, Lionel, and Richard Moorsom. 1979. "Rural Class Formation and Ecological Collapse in Botswana." *Review of African Political Economy* 15, no. 16:35–52.

Cliffe, Lionel, W. L. Luttrell, and J. E. Moore. 1975. "The Development Crises in the Western Usambaras." In Lionel Cliffe et al., eds., *Rural Cooperation in Tanzania*. Dar-es-Salam: Tanzania Publishing House, 145–73.

Clifford, James. 1987. *The Predicament of Culture: Twentieth-Century Ethnography, Literature and Art*. Cambridge, Mass.: Harvard Univ. Press.

Cloud, Kathleen. 1986. "Sex Roles in Food Production and Distribution Systems in the Sahel." In Lucy Creevey 1986:19–51.

Coatsworth, J. n.d. "Patterns of Rural Rebellion in Latin America: Mexico in Comparative Perspective." Unpublished manuscript.

Cock, J. 1984. *Maids and Madams: A Study in the Politics of Exploitation*. Johannesburg: Ravan.

Cohen, Abner. 1969. *Custom and Politics in Urban Africa: A Study of Hausa Migrants in Yoruba Towns*. Berkeley: Univ. of California Press.

Cohen, David. 1972. *The Historical Tradition of Busoga, Mukatia and Kintu*. London: Oxford Univ. Press.

Cohen, David, and E. S. Atieno-Odhiambo. 1989. *Siaya: The Historical Anthropology of an African Landscape*. London: James Currey.

Cohen, John. 1974. "Ethiopia: A Survey on the Existence of a Feudal Peasantry," *Journal of Modern African Studies* 12, no. 4:665–72.

Cohen, John, and Dov Weintraub. 1975. *Land and Peasants in Imperial Ethiopia*. Assen: Van Gorcum.

Cohen, Robin. 1976. "From Peasants to Workers in Africa." In P. Gutkind and I. Wallerstein, eds., *The Political Economy of Contemporary Africa*. Beverly Hills: Sage, 155–68.

Cohen, Robin. 1980. "Resistance and Hidden Forms of Consciousness Among African Workers." *Review of African Political Economy* 19:8–22.

Coleman, James S. 1958. *Nigeria: Background to Nationalism*. Berkeley: Univ. of California Press.

Comaroff, Jean. 1985. *Body of Power, Spirit of Resistance: The Culture and History of a South African People*. Chicago: Univ. of Chicago Press.

Comaroff, John. 1978. "Rules and Rulers: Political Processes in a Tswana Chiefdom," *Man* 13, no. 1:1–20.

Comaroff, John, ed. 1980a. *Meaning of Marriage Payments*. New York: Academic Press.

Comaroff, John. 1980b. "Class and Culture in a Peasant Economy: The Transformation of Land Tenure in Barolong." *Journal of African Law* 24:85–113.

Comaroff, John. 1982. "Dialectical Systems, History and Anthropology: Units of Study and Questions of Theory." *Journal of African Studies* 8:143–72.

Comaroff, John. 1984. "The Closed Society and Its Critics: Historical Transformations in African Ethnography." *American Ethnologist* 11, no. 3:571–83.

Comaroff, John. 1987. "Sui Genderis: Feminism, Kinship Theory and Structural 'Domains.' " In J. Collier and S. Yanagisako, eds., *Gender and Kinship Theory*. Palo Alto, Calif.: Stanford Univ. Press, 53–85.

Comaroff, John, and Jean Comaroff. 1987. "The Madman and the Migrant: Work and Labor in the Historical Consciousness of a South African People." *American Ethnologist* 14, no. 2:191–209.

Comaroff, John, and Jean Comaroff. 1989. "The Colonization of Consciousness in South Africa." *Economy and Society* 18, no. 3:267–95.

Connah, Graham. 1987. *African Civilizations, Pre-Colonial Cities and States in Tropical Africa: An Archaeological Perspective*. Cambridge: Cambridge Univ. Press.

Cooper, Frederick. 1977. *Plantation Slavery on the East Coast of Africa*. New Haven, Conn.: Yale Univ. Press.

Cooper, Frederick. 1979. "The Problem of Slavery in African Studies." *Journal of African History* 20, no. 1:103–25.

Cooper, Frederick. 1980. *From Slaves to Squatters: Plantation Labor and Agriculture in Zanzibar and Coastal Kenya, 1890–1925*. New Haven: Yale Univ. Press.

Cooper, Frederick. 1981a. "Africa and the World Economy." *African Studies Review* 24, no. 3:1–86.
Cooper, Frederick. 1981b. "Peasants, Capitalists and Historians." *Journal of Southern African Studies* 7, no. 2:284–314.
Cooper, Frederick. 1988. "Mau-Mau and the Discourses of Decolonization." *Journal of African History* 29, no. 2:313–20.
Copans, Jean. 1978. "Paysannerie et politique au Sénégal." *Cahiers d'Études Africaines* 18:241–56.
Copans, Jean. 1980. "From Senegambia to Senegal: The Evolution of Peasantries." In Klein 1980:77–104.
Coplan, David. 1987. "Eloquent Knowledge: Lesotho Migrants' Songs and the Anthropology of Experience." *American Ethnologist* 14, no. 3:413–33.
Coquery-Vidrovitch, Catherine. 1972a. *Le Congo au temps des grandes compagnies concessionaires, 1898–1900*. Paris: Mouton and Co.
Coquery-Vidrovitch, Catherine. 1972b. "Research on an African Mode of Production." In M. Klein and G. Johnson, eds., *Perspectives on the African Past*. Boston: Little, Brown, 33–51.
Coquery-Vidrovitch, Catherine. 1976a. "Changes in African Historical Studies in France." In Christopher Fyfe, ed., *African Studies Since 1945*. London: Longman, 200–208.
Coquery-Vidrovitch, Catherine. 1976b. "The Political Economy of the African Peasantry and Modes of Production." In P. Gutkind and I. Wallerstein, ed., *The Political Economy of Contemporary Africa*. Beverly Hills: Sage, 90–111.
Coquery-Vidrovitch, Catherine. 1980a. "Les Paysans Africains: Permanences et Mutations." In Coquery-Vidrovitch 1980b:25–40.
Coquery-Vidrovitch, Catherine, ed. 1980b. *Sociétés Paysannes du Tiers Monde*. Lille: Presses Universitaires de Lille.
Coquery-Vidrovitch, Catherine. 1985. *Afrique Noire: Permanences et Ruptures*. Paris: Editions Payot.
Coquery-Vidrovitch, Catherine. 1988. *Africa: Endurance and Change South of the Sahara*. Berkeley: Univ. of California Press.
Coquery-Vidrovitch, Catherine. 1989. "Process of Urbanization in Africa." ACLS-SSRC commissioned paper presented at the 1989 African Studies Association, Atlanta.
Cordell, Dennis. 1985. *Dar al Kuti: Slave Raiding and the Last Years of the Trans-Saharan Slave Trade*. Madison: Univ. of Wisconsin Press.
Cordell, Dennis, and Joel Gregory. 1982. "Labour Reservoirs and Population: French Colonial Strategies in Koudougo, Upper Volta, 1914–1939." *Journal of African History* 23, no. 2:205–44.
Cournanel, Alain. 1984. "Economie Politique de la Guinea (1958–1981)." In Henry Bernstein and Bonnie K. Campbell, eds., *Contradictions of Accumulation in Africa*. Beverly Hills: Sage, 207–48.
Cowen, M. 1981. "Commodity Production in Kenya's Central Province." In J. Heyer, P. Roberts and G. Williams, eds., *Rural Development in Tropical Africa*. New York: St. Martin's Press, 121–42.

Cowen, M. 1982. "Some Recent East African Peasant Studies." *Journal of Peasant Studies* 9, no. 2:252–61.

Cowen, M. 1983. "The Commercialization of Food Production in Kenya After 1945." In R. Rotberg, ed., *Imperialism, Colonialism and Hunger: East and Central Africa*. Lexington: Lexington Books, 199–224.

Creevey, Lucy. 1986. *Women Farmers in Africa: Rural Development in Mali and the Sahel*. Syracuse: Syracuse Univ. Press.

Crehan, Kate. 1984. "Women and Development in North-Western Zambia: From Producer to Housewife." *Review of African Political Economy* 27, no. 28:51–66.

Crowder, M., ed. 1971. *West African Resistance: The Military Response to Colonial Occupation*. London: Hutchinson.

Crowder, M. 1988. *The Flogging of Phinehas MacIntosh: A Tale of Colonial Folly and Injustice, Bechuanaland, 1933*. New Haven: Yale Univ. Press.

Crummey, Donald. 1978. "Gondarine Rim Land Sales: An Introductory Description and Analysis." In Robert Hess, ed., *Proceedings of the Fifth International Conference on Ethiopian Studies*. Chicago, 469–79.

Crummey, Donald. 1980. "Abyssinian Feudalism." *Past and Present* 89:115–38.

Crummey, Donald. 1983. "Ethiopia Plow Agriculture in the Nineteenth Century." *Journal of Ethiopian Studies* 16:1–23.

Crummey, Donald. 1984. "Banditry and Resistance: Noble and Peasant in Nineteenth Century Ethiopia." In Sven Rubensen, ed., *Proceedings of the Seventh International Conference of Ethiopian Studies*. Addis Ababa, East Lansing, and Uppsala, 263–77.

Crummey, Donald, ed. 1986. *Banditry, Rebellion and Social Protest in Africa*. Portsmouth: Heinemann.

Crummey, Donald, and Charles Stewart, eds. 1981. *Modes of Production in Africa*. Beverly Hills: Sage.

Crush, Jonathan. 1985. "Landlords, Tenants and Colonial Social Engineers: The Farm Labour Question in Early Colonial Swaziland." *Journal of Southern African Studies* 11, no. 2:235–57.

Crush, Jonathan. 1987. *The Struggle for Swazi Labour, 1890–1920*. Kingston: McGill-Queen's Univ. Press.

Cunnison, Ian. 1959. *The Luapula Peoples of Northern Rhodesia*. Manchester: Manchester Univ. Press.

Curtin, Philip. 1975. *Economic Change in Pre-Colonial Africa: Senegambia in the Era of the Slave Trade*. Madison: Univ. of Wisconsin Press.

Dalton, G. 1964. "The Development of Subsistence and Peasant Economies in Africa." *International Social Sciences Journal* 16, no. 3:378–89.

Dalton, G., ed. 1967. *Tribal and Peasant Economies: Readings in Economic Anthropology*. New York: The National History Press.

Dalton, G. 1972. "Peasantries in Anthropology and History." *Current Anthropology* 13:385–415.

Dampierre, Eric de. 1960. "Coton noir, café blanc: Deux cultures du Haute-Oubangui à la veille de la Loi-Cadre." *Cahiers d'Études Africaines* 2:128–47.

Davidson, A. B. 1968. "African Resistance and Rebellion Against the Imposition of

Colonial Rule." In T. O. Ranger, ed., *Emerging Themes of African History*. Nairobi: East African Publishing House, 177–88.

Davidson, Basil. 1969. *The Liberation of Guinea: Aspects of an African Revolution*. Hammondsworth: Penguin.

Davidson, Basil. 1972. *In the Eye of the Storm: Angola's People*. Harmondsworth: Penguin.

Davidson, Basil. 1974. "African Peasants and Revolution." *Journal of Peasant Studies* 1, no. 3:269–90.

Davidson, Basil. 1977. "Nationalism Reconsidered." Paper presented at the African Studies Association Meeting, Denver.

Davidson, Basil. 1981a. *No Fist Is Big Enough to Hide the Sky: The Liberation of Guinea-Bissau and Cape Verde*. London: Zed Press.

Davidson, Basil. 1981b. *The People's Cause: A History of Guerrillas in Africa*. London: Longman.

Davidson, Basil. 1984. "Gramsci, the Peasantry and Popular Culture." *Journal of Peasant Studies* 11, no. 4:139–53.

Debray, Regis. 1970. *Strategy for Revolution*. New York: Monthly Review Press.

Deal, Douglas. 1975. "Peasant Revolts and Resistance in the Modern World: A Comparative View." *Journal of Contemporary Asia* 5, no. 4:414–45.

De Janvry, Alain. 1981. *The Agrarian Question and Reformism in Latin America*. Baltimore: Johns Hopkins Univ. Press.

Delehanty, James. 1988. "The Northward Expansion of the Farming Frontier in Twentieth Century Niger." Ph.D. diss. Univ. of Minnesota.

Delius, P. n.d. "Sebatakgomo: Migrant Organization, the A.N.C. and the Sekhukhuneland Revolt." Unpublished paper.

Delius, P. 1986. "Abel Erasmus: Power and Profit in the Eastern Transvaal." In William Beinart et al., eds., *Putting A Plough to the Ground*. Johannesburg: Ravan Press, 176–217.

Depelchin, J. 1976. "Toward a Problematic History of Africa." *Tanzania Zamani* 18:2–9.

Depelchin, J. 1979. "Toward a Reconstruction of Pre-Colonial Central African History." *Ufahamu* 9, no. 1:138–64.

Derman, William. 1972. "Peasants: The African Exception?" *American Anthropologist* 74, no. 3:779–82.

Derman, William. 1973. *Serfs, Peasants and Socialists: A Former Serf Village in the Republic of Guinea*. Los Angeles: Univ. of California Press.

Desai, A. R., ed. 1979. *Peasant Struggles in India*. Bombay: Oxford Univ. Press.

De Wilde, John C. 1967. *Experiences with Agricultural Development in Tropical Africa*. Vol. 1. *The Synthesis*. Baltimore: Johns Hopkins Univ. Press.

Diabate, Henriette. 1984. "Le Sannvin: Un royaume Akan de Côte d'Ivoire (1700–1901)." Thèse d'Etat, Université Paris, I.

Dias, Jill. 1981. "Famine and Disease in the History of Angola (1830–1930)." *Journal of African History* 22, no. 3:349–78.

Dike, K. O. 1957. *Trade and Politics in the Niger Delta*. Oxford: Oxford Univ. Press.

Dixon-Fyle, Mac. 1977. "Agricultural Improvement and Political Protest on the Tonga Plateau, Northern Rhodesia." *Journal of African History* 18, no. 4:579–96.

Donham, Donald. 1985. "History at One Point in Time: Working Together in Maale." *American Ethnologist* 12, no. 2:262–84.

Donham, Donald. 1989. *History, Power and Ideology: Essays on Marxism and Social Anthropology*. Cambridge: Cambridge Univ. Press.

Dorward, David. 1987. "The Impact of Colonialism on a Nigerian Hill-Farming Society: A Case Study of Innovation Among the Eggon." *International Journal of African Historical Studies* 20, no. 2:201–24.

Downs, R. G., and S. P. Reyna. 1988. *Land and Society in Contemporary Africa*. Hanover: Univ. of New Hampshire Press.

DuFour, Jean-Louis. 1975. "La révolte Touareg et le siège d'Agades." *Relations Internationales* 3:55–77.

Duggett, Michael. 1975. "Marx on Peasants." *Journal of Peasant Studies* 2, no. 2:159–82.

Dumont, René. 1957. *Types of Rural Economy: Studies in World Agriculture*. London: Methuen.

Eggan, F. 1954. "Social Anthropology and the Method of Controlled Comparison." *American Anthropologist* 56, no. 5:743–63.

Ennew, Judith, Paul Hirst, and Keith Tribe. 1977. " 'Peasantry' as an Economic Category." *Journal of Peasant Studies* 4, no. 4:295–322.

Epstein, A. L. 1958. *Politics in an Urban African Community*. Manchester: Manchester Univ. Press.

Etherington, N. 1978. *Preachers, Peasants, and Politics in Southeast Africa, 1835–1880*. London: Royal Historical Society.

Etherton, Michael. 1981. "Peasants and Intellectuals." *Africa* 51, no. 4:863–71.

Etienne, Mona. 1980. "Women and Men, Cloth and Colonization." In M. Etienne and E. Leacock, eds., *Women and Colonization: Anthropological Perspectives*. New York: Praeger, 214–33.

Evans-Pritchard, E. E. 1962. *Social Anthropology and Other Essays*. New York: Free Press.

Ewald, Janet. 1990. *Soldiers, Traders and Slaves: State Formation and Economic Transformation in the Greater Nile Valley, 1780–1898*. Madison: Univ. of Wisconsin Press.

Fallers, L. A. 1956. *Bantu Bureaucracy*. London: W. Hefer and Sons.

Fallers, L. A. 1961. "Are African Cultivators to be Called 'Peasants'?" *Current Anthropology* 2:108–10.

Fanon, Frantz. 1963. *The Wretched of the Earth*. New York: Grove Press.

Fanon, Frantz. 1969. *Toward the African Revolution: Political Essays*. New York: Grove Press.

Fearn, F. 1961. *An African Economy: A Study of the Development of the Nyanza Province of Kenya*. London.

Feder, Ernest. 1971. *The Rape of the Peasantry: Latin America's Land Holding System*. New York: Anchor.

Feeley-Harnik, Gillian. 1984. "The Political Economy of Death: Communication and

Change in Malagasy Colonial History." *American Ethnologist* 11, no. 1:1–19.

Feeley-Harnik, Gillian. 1987. "What Makes Work Worth Doing?" *American Ethnologist* 14, no. 4:737–51.

Feierman, Stephen. 1974. *A History of the Shambaa Kingdom*. Madison: Univ. of Wisconsin Press.

Feierman, Stephen. 1976. *The Shambaa Kingdom: A History*. Madison: Univ. of Wisconsin Press.

Feierman, Stephen. 1985. " 'Struggles for Control': The Social Roots of Health and Healing in Modern Africa." *African Studies Review* 28, no. 2–3:73–148.

Feierman, Stephen. 1988. "Peasant Intellectuals, Anthropology and History in Northern Tanzania." Unpublished manuscript.

Feierman, Stephen. 1990. *Peasant Intellectuals: Anthropology and History in Tanzania*. Madison: Univ. of Wisconsin Press.

Fernandez, J. 1978. "African Religious Movements." *Annual Review of Anthropology* 7:195–234.

Fernandez, J. 1982. *Bwiti: An Ethnography of the Religious Imagination in Africa*. Princeton: Princeton Univ. Press.

Fernyhough, Terry. 1986. "Social Mobility and Dissident Elites in Northern Ethiopia: The Role of Banditry." In Crummey 1986:151–72.

Fields, Karen. 1985. *Revival and Rebellion in Colonial Central Africa*. Princeton: Princeton Univ. Press.

First, Ruth. 1983. *Black Gold: The Mozambican Miner, Proletarian and Peasant*. New York: St. Martin's Press.

Firth, R. 1954. "Social Organization and Social Change," *Journal of the Royal Anthropological Institute* 84:1–20.

Fogg, C. Davis. 1971. "Smallholder Agriculture in Eastern Nigeria." In George Dalton, ed., *Economic Development and Social Change*. Garden City, N.Y.: Natural History Press, 575–96.

Folbre, Nancy. 1986. "Hearts and Spades: Paradigms of Household Economies." *World Development* 14, no. 2:245–56.

Ford, John. 1971. *The Role of Trypanosomiasis in African Ecology: A Study of the Tse Tse Fly Problem*. Oxford: Clarendon Press.

Forrest, Joshua B. 1982. "Defining African Peasants." *Peasant Studies* 9, no. 4:242–49.

Fortes, Meyer. 1945. *The Dynamics of Clanship Among the Tallensi*. London: Oxford Univ. Press.

Fortes, Meyer. 1953. "The Structure of Unilineal Descent Groups." *American Anthropologist* 55, no. 1:17–41.

Fortes, Meyer, and E. E. Evans-Pritchard. 1940. *African Political Systems*. London: Oxford Univ. Press.

Fox, Renée C., Willy de Craemer, and Jean-Marie Ribeaucurt. 1965. " 'The Second Independence': A Case Study of the Kwilu Rebellion in the Congo." *Comparative Studies in Society and History* 8, no. 1:78–110.

Freund, Bill. 1984a. "Labor and Labor History in Africa: A Review of the Literature." *African Studies Review* 27, no. 2:1–58.

Freund, Bill. 1984b. *The Making of Contemporary Africa*. Bloomington: Indiana Univ. Press.

Freund, Bill. 1986. "Theft and Social Protest Among Tin Miners of Northern Nigeria." In Crummey 1986:48–61.

Freund, Bill, and R. W. Shenton. 1977. " 'Vent-For-Surplus' Theory and the Economic History of West Africa." *Savanna* 6, no. 2:191–96.

Friedmann, Harriet. 1980. "Household Production and the National Economy: Concepts of the Analysis of Agrarian Formations." *Journal of Peasant Studies* 7, no. 2:158–84.

Fuglestad, Finn. 1983. *A History of Niger 1850–1960*. London: Cambridge Univ. Press.

Furedi, Frank. 1974. "The Social Composition of the Mau Mau Movement in the White Highlands." *Journal of Peasant Studies* 1, no. 4:486–505.

Gahama, Joseph. 1983. *Le Burundi sous l'administration Belge: La periode du Mandat*. Paris: Karathalag.

Gamst, F. C. 1970. "Peasantries and Elites Without Urbanism: The Civilization of Ethiopia." *Comparative Studies in Society and History* 12, no. 4:373–92.

Garcia, Luc. 1970. "Les Mouvements de Résistance au Dahomey (1914–1917)." *Cahiers d'Études Africaines* 37:144–78.

Garlake, Peter. 1978. "Pastoralism and Zimbabwe." *Journal of African History* 19, no. 4:479–93.

Geertz, C. 1963. *Agricultural Involution: The Process of Ecological Change in Indonesia*. Berkeley: Univ. of California Press.

Geiger, Susan. 1982. "Umoja Wa Wanawake Wa Tanzania and the Needs of the Rural Poor." *African Studies Review* 25, nos. 2, 3:45–65.

Geiger, Susan. 1986. "Women's Life Histories: Method and Content." *Signs* 11/2:334–51.

Geiger, Susan. 1987. "Women in Nationalist Struggles: TANU Activists in Dar-es-Salaam." *International Journal of African Historical Studies* 20, no. 1:1–26.

Genovese, Eugene. 1974. *Roll, Jordan, Roll*. New York: Vintage.

Gibbon, Peter, and Michael Neocosmos. 1984. "Some Problems in the Political Economy of 'African Socialism'." In H. Bernstein and B. Campbell, eds., *Contradictions of Accumulation in Africa*. Beverly Hills: Sage, 153–206.

Giddens, A. 1979. *Central Problems in Social Theory: Action Structure, and Contradiction in Social Analysis*. Berkeley: Univ. of California Press.

Giddens, A. 1981. *A Contemporary Critique of Historical Materialism*. 2 vols. Berkeley: Univ. of California Press.

Gluckman, Max. 1940. "Analysis of a Social Situation in Modern Zululand." *Bantu Studies* 14:1–30, 147–74.

Gluckman, Max. 1942. "Some Process of Social Change Illustrated from Zululand Data." *African Studies* 1, no. 4:243–60.

Gluckman, Max. 1954. *Rituals of Rebellion in Southeast Africa*. Manchester: Manchester Univ. Press.

Gluckman, Max. 1956. *Custom and Conflict in Africa*. Oxford: Basil Blackwell.

Godelier, M. 1973. "Structure and Contradiction in Capital." In R. Blackburn, ed., *Ideology and Social Science Reading in Critical Social Theory*. London: Fontana.

Godelier, M. 1975. "Modes of Production, Kinship and Demographic Structures." In *Marxist Analysis and Social Anthropology*, edited by Black, 3-28. London: Malay Press.

Godelier, M. 1977. *Perspectives in Marxist Anthropology*. Cambridge: Cambridge Univ. Press.

Goody, Jack. 1958. *The Developmental Cycle in Domestic Groups*. Cambridge: Cambridge Univ. Press.

Goody, Jack. 1971. *Technology, Tradition and the State in Africa*. Oxford: Oxford Univ. Press.

Gottlieb, M. 1972. "The Process of Differentiation in Tanzanian Agriculture and Rural Society." Economic Research Bureau, Univ. of Dar-es-Salaam.

Gourou, Pierre. 1975. *Man and Land in the Far East*. London: Longman.

Gramsci, A. 1971. *Selections from the Prison Notebooks*. Edited and translated by Quintin Hoare and Geoffrey Nowell Smith. New York: International Publishers.

Gray, Richard, and D. Birmingham. 1970. *Pre-Colonial African Trade*. Oxford: Oxford Univ. Press.

Gregg, D., and E. Williams. 1948. "The Dismal Science of Functionalism." *American Anthropologist* 50:594–611.

Gregory, Joel W., and Victor Piche. 1983. "African Return Migration: Past, Present, and Future," *Contemporary Marxism* 7:169–83.

Groff, David. 1980. "When the Knees Began Wearing the Hat: Commercial Agriculture and Social Transformation in Asikasso, Ivory Coast, ca. 1880–1940." Unpublished manuscript.

Gutto, S. B. O. 1981. "Law, Rangelands, Peasantry and Social Classes in Kenya." *Review of African Political Economy* 20:41–56.

Guy, Jeff. 1982. "The Destruction and Reconstruction of Zulu Society." In S. Marks and R. Rathbone, eds., *Industrialisation and Social Change in South Africa*. London: Longman, 167–94.

Guyer, Jane I. 1978. "Women's Work in the Food Economy of the Cocoa Belt: A Comparison." African Studies Working Paper No. 7. Boston Univ.

Guyer, Jane I. 1980a. "Female Farming and the Evolution of Food Production Patterns Amongst the Beti of South-Central Cameroon." *Africa* 50, no. 4:341–56.

Guyer, Jane I. 1980b. "Food, Cocoa and the Division of Labor by Sex in Two West African Societies." *Comparative Studies in Society and History* 22, no. 3:355–73.

Guyer, Jane I. 1981a. "The Raw, the Cooked and the Half-Baked: A Note on the Division of Labor by Sex." African Studies Center Working Paper No. 48, Boston Univ.

Guyer, Jane I. 1981b. "Household and Community in African Studies." *African Studies Review* 24, nos. 2, 3:87–137.

Guyer, Jane I. 1984a. *Family and Farm in Southern Cameroon*. Boston: African Studies Center, Boston Univ.

Guyer, Jane I. 1984b. "Women in the Rural Economy: Contemporary Variations." In Margaret Jean Hay and Sharon Stichter, eds., *African Women South of the Sahara*. London: Longman, 19–32.

Guyer, Jane I. 1984c. "Naturalism in Models of African Production." *Man* 19, no. 3:371–88.

Guyer, Jane I. 1988. "The Multiplication of Labor: Historical Methods in the Study of Gender and Agricultural Change in Modern Africa." *Current Anthropology* 29, no. 2:247–72.

Guyer, Jane I., and Pauline Peters, eds. 1987. "Introduction to Conceptualizing the Household: Issues of Theory and Policy in Africa." *Development and Change* 18, no. 2:197–213.

Hall, Martin. 1987a. "Archaeology and Modes of Production in Pre-Colonial Southern Africa." *Journal of Southern African Studies* 14, no. 1:1–17.

Hall, Martin. 1987b. *The Changing Past: Farmers, Kings and Traders in Southern Africa, 200–1860*. Capetown: David Philip.

Hamilton, C. A. 1987. "Ideology and Oral Traditions: Listening to the Voices 'From Below'." *History in Africa* 14:67–86.

Harms, Robert. n.d. "Production and Power in African History: African Peasants in Comparative Perspective." Unpublished manuscript.

Harries, Patrick. 1981. "Slavery, Social Incorporation and Surplus Extraction: the Nature of Free and Unfree Labor in South-East Africa." *Journal of African History* 22, no. 3:309–30.

Harris, Marvin. 1968. *The Rise of Anthropological Theory*. New York: Columbia Univ. Press.

Hart, Keith. 1982. *The Political Economy of West African Agriculture*. Cambridge: Cambridge Univ. Press.

Hay, Margaret Jean. 1972. "Economic Change in Luoland: Kowe, 1890–1945." Ph.D. diss. Univ. of Wisconsin.

Hay, Margaret Jean. 1974. "The Relevance of Peasant Analysis for African Economic History." Unpublished paper presented at summer seminar in African Economic History, Univ. of Wisconsin, Madison.

Hay, Margaret Jean. 1976. "Luo Women and Economic Change During the Colonial Period." In Nancy J. Hafkin and Edna G. Bay, eds., *Women in Africa*. Stanford: Stanford Univ. Press, 87–109.

Hay, Margaret Jean. 1979. " 'Peasants' in Modern East African Studies." *Peasant Studies* 8, no. 1:17–29.

Hay, Margaret Jean. 1982. "Women as Owners, Occupants and Managers of Property in Colonial Western Kenya." In Margaret Jean Hay and Marcia Wright, eds., *African Women and the Law: Historical Perspectives*. Boston: Boston Univ. Papers on Africa, no. 7, 110–24.

Hebert, Jean. 1970. "Révoltes en Haute-Volte de 1914 à 1918." *Notes et Documents Voltaiques* 3, no. 4:3–54.

Helleiner, G. 1966. *Peasant Agriculture, Government and Economic Growth in Nigeria*. New Haven: Yale Univ. Press.

Henige, David. 1982. *Oral Historiography*. London: Longman.

Henn, Jeanne K. 1984. "Women in the Rural Economy: Past, Present and Future." In Margaret Jean Hay and Sharon Stichter, eds., *African Women South of the Sahara*. London: Longman, 1–18.

Henriksen, Thomas. 1976. "People's War in Angola, Mozambique and Guinea-Bissau." *Journal of Modern African Studies* 14:377–99.

Henriksen, Thomas. 1983. *Revolution and Counterrevolution: Mozambique's War of Independence, 1964–1974.* Westport: Greenwood Press.

Herskovits, Melville. 1962. *The Human Factor in Changing Africa.* New York: Vintage.

Herskovits, Melville, and M. Harwitz, eds. 1964. *Economic Transition in Africa.* Evanston: Northwestern Univ. Press.

Heyer, J. 1972. "Peasant Farm Production Under Conditions of Uncertainty." *Journal of Agricultural Economics* 23:135–46.

Hill, Polly. 1963. *The Migrant Cocoa Farmers of Southern Ghana: A Study in Rural Capitalism.* Cambridge: Cambridge Univ. Press.

Hill, Polly. 1970. *Studies in Rural Capitalism in West Africa.* Cambridge: Cambridge Univ. Press.

Hill, Polly. 1972. *Rural Hausa: A Village and a Setting.* Cambridge: Cambridge Univ. Press.

Hill, Polly. 1976. "From Slavery to Freedom: The Case of Farm-Slavery in Nigerian Hausaland." *Comparative Studies in Society and History* 18, no. 3:395–426.

Hill, Polly. 1977. *Population. Prosperity and Poverty: Rural Kano, 1900–1970.* Cambridge: Cambridge Univ. Press.

Hilton, Anne. 1981. "The Jaga Reconsidered." *Journal of African History* 22, no. 2:191–202.

Hilton, Anne. 1985. *The Kingdom of Kongo.* Oxford: Clarendon Press.

Hilton, R. H. 1973. *Bond Men Made Free: Medieval Peasant Movements and the English Rising of 1381.* London: Temple Smith.

Hilton, R. H. 1974. "Peasant Society, Peasant Movements and Feudalism in Medieval Europe." In Landsberger 1974:67–94.

Hilton, R. H. 1975. *The English Peasantry in the Later Middle Ages.* London: Oxford Univ. Press.

Hindess, B., and P. Q. Hirst. 1975. *Pre-Capitalist Modes of Production.* London: Routledge and Kegan Paul.

Hirschmann, David, and Megan Vaughan. 1983. "Food Production and Income Generation in a Matrilineal Society: Rural Women in Zomba, Malawi," *Journal of Southern African Studies* 10, no. 1:86–99.

Hoben, Allan. 1970. "Social Stratification in Traditional Amhara Society." In Tuden and Plotnicov 1970.

Hoben, Allan. 1973. *Land Tenure Among the Amhara of Ethiopia: The Dynamics of Cognitive Descent.* Chicago: Univ. of Chicago Press.

Hobsbawm, E. J., ed. 1965. *Primitive Rebels.* New York: W. W. Norton.

Hobsbawm, E. J. 1969. *Bandits.* New York: Delacorte Press.

Hobsbawm, E. J. 1973. "Peasants and Politics." *Journal of Peasant Studies* 1, no. 1:3–22.

Hobsbawm, E. J. 1980. *Peasants in History: Essays in Honour of Daniel Thorner.* London: Oxford Univ. Press.

Hodgkin, Thomas L. 1957. *Nationalism in Colonial Africa.* New York: New York Univ. Press.

Hogendorn, J. S. 1976. "The Vent-for-Surplus Model and African Cash Agriculture to 1914." *Savanna* 5, no. 1:15–28.

Hogendorn, J. S. 1977. "The Economics of Slave Use on Two 'Plantations' in the Zaria Emirate of the Sokoto Caliphate." *International Journal of African Historical Studies* 10:369–83.

Hogendorn, J. S. 1978. *Nigerian Groundnut Exports: Origins and Early Development*. Zaria: Ahmadu Bello Univ. Press.

Hogendorn, J. S., and Paul Lovejoy. "Revolutionary Mahdism and Resistance to Colonial Rule in the Sokoto Caliphate." Forthcoming.

Holmquist, Frank. 1979. "Class Structure, Peasant Participation and Rural Self-Help." In Joel Barkan and John J. Okumu, eds., *Politics and Public Policy in Kenya and Tanzania*. New York: Praeger, 129–53.

Holmquist, Frank. 1980. "Defending Peasant Political Space in Independent Africa." *Canadian Journal of African Studies* 14, no. 1:157–67.

Holmquist, Frank. 1984. "Self-Help: The State and Peasant Leverage in Kenya." *Africa* 54, no. 3:72–91.

Hopkins, Anthony G. 1973. *An Economic History of West Africa*. New York: Columbia Univ. Press.

Howard, Rhoda. 1976. "Differential Class Participation in an African Protest Movement: The Ghana Cocoa Boycott of 1937–38." *Canadian Journal of African Studies* 10, no. 3:469–80.

Howard, Rhoda. 1980. "Formation and Stratification of the Peasantry in Colonial Ghana." *Journal of Peasant Studies* 8, no. 1:61–80.

Humbaraci, Arslan. 1966. *Algeria: A Revolution That Failed*. London: Pall Mall.

Hunt, Lynn. 1989. *The New Cultural History*. Berkeley: Univ. of California Press.

Hunter, Guy. 1969. *Modernising Peasant Societies: A Comparative Study in Asia and Africa*. London: Oxford Univ. Press.

Hutton, C., and R. Cohen. 1975. "African Peasants and Resistance to Change." In I. Oxaal, ed., *Beyond the Sociology of Development: Economy and Society in Latin America and Africa*. London: Routledge and Kegan Paul.

Hyden, Goran. 1980. *Beyond Ujamaa in Tanzania: Underdevelopment and an Uncaptured Peasantry*. Los Angeles: Univ. of California Press.

Ifeka-Moller, Caroline. 1975. "Female Militancy and Colonial Revolt: The Women's War of 1929, Eastern Nigeria." In Shirley Ardener, ed., *Perceiving Women*. New York: Wiley.

Iliffe, John. 1967. "The Organization of the Maji Maji Rebellion." *Journal of African History* 8, no. 3:495–512.

Iliffe, John. 1979. *A Modern History of Tanganyika*. Cambridge: Cambridge Univ. Press.

Iliffe, John. 1983. *Emergence of African Capitalism*. Minneapolis: Univ. of Minnesota Press.

Iliffe, John. 1987. *The African Poor: A History*. Cambridge: Cambridge Univ. Press.

Isaacman, Allen. 1972. *Mozambique: The Africanization of a European Institution. The Zambesi Prazos, 1750–1902*. Madison: Univ. of Wisconsin Press.

Isaacman, Allen. 1976. *The Tradition of Resistance in Mozambique: Anti-Colonial Activity in the Zambesi Valley, 1850–1921*. Berkeley: Univ. of California Press.

Isaacman, Allen. 1977. "Social Banditry in Zimbabwe (Rhodesia) and Mozambique,

1894–1907: An Expression of Early Peasant Protest." *Journal of Southern African Studies* 4:1–30.

Isaacman, Allen. 1982. "The Mozambican Cotton Cooperative: The Creation of a Grassroots Alternative to Forced Commodity Production." *African Studies Review* 25, nos. 2,3:5–25.

Isaacman, Allen. 1984. "The Role of Women in the Liberation of Mozambique," *Ufahamu* 13:128–85.

Isaacman, Allen. 1985. "Chiefs, Rural Differentiation and Peasant Protest: The Mozambican Forced Cotton Regime, 1938–1961," *African Economic History* 14:15–57.

Isaacman, Allen. 1988. "Colonial Mozambique, An Inside View: The Life History of Raul Honwana." *Cahiers d'Études Africaines* 109:59–88.

Isaacman, Allen. 1989. "Peasants, Social Protest and Africanists." *Journal of Social History* 22:745–66.

Isaacman, Allen, and Barbara Isaacman. 1977. "Resistance and Collaboration in Southern and Central Africa. ca. 1850–1920." *International Journal of African Historical Studies* 10, no. 1:31–62.

Isaacman, Allen, and Barbara Isaacman. 1983. *Mozambique: From Colonialism to Revolution, 1900–1982.* Boulder: Westview Press.

Isaacman, Allen, and Barbara Isaacman. 1984. "The Role of Women in the Liberation of Mozambique." *Ufahamu* 13, nos. 2,3:128–85.

Isaacman, Allen, and Barbara Isaacman. 1985. "Chiefs, Rural Differentiation and Peasant Protest: The Mozambican Forced Cotton Regime, 1938–1961," *African Economic History* 14:15–56.

Isaacman, Allen, and Barbara Isaacman. 1988. "Colonial Mozambique, an Inside View: The Life History of Raul Honwana." *Cahiers d'Études Africaines* 109:59–88.

Isaacman, Allen, Michael Stephen, Yussuf Adam, Maria Joao Homen, Eugenio Macamo, and Augustinho Pililao. 1980. "Cotton as the Mother of Poverty: Peasant Resistance to Forced Cotton Production in Mozambique, 1938–1961." *International Journal of African Historical Studies* 13:581–615.

Isaacman, Barbara, and J. Stephen. 1980. *Mozambique: Women, the Law and Agrarian Reform.* Addis Ababa: United Nations Economic Commission for Africa.

Izzard, Wendy. 1985. "Migrants and Mothers: Case Studies from Botswana." *Journal of Southern African Studies* 11:258–80.

Jacoby, Erich. 1961. *Agrarian Unrest in Southeast Asia.* 2d ed. London: Asia Publishing House.

Jewsiewicki, B. 1972. "Notes sur l'histoire socio-économique du Congo, 1880–1960," *Etudes d'Histoire Africaine* 3:200–41.

Jewsiewicki, B. 1980a. "Political Consciousness Among African Peasants in the Belgian Congo." *Review of African Political Economy* 19:23–32.

Jewsiewicki, B. 1980b. "African Peasants in the Totalitarian Colonial Society of the Belgian Congo." In Klein 1980: 45–76. Beverly Hills: Sage.

Jewsiewicki, B. 1981. "Lineage Mode of Production: Social Inequalities in Equatorial Central Africa." In Crummey and Stewart 1981: Beverly Hills: Sage, 93–114.

Jewsiewicki, B. 1983. "Modernisation ou destruction du village Africaine: L'économie politique de la 'Modernisation Agricole' au Congo Belge," *Les Cahiers du CEDAF* 5:1–86.

Jewsiewicki, B. 1987. "African Historical Studies as Academic Knowledge, Radical Scholarship and Usable Past." Paper commissioned by ACLS-SSRC Africa Committee, and presented at African Studies Association Meeting, Denver.

Jewsiewicki, B., and J. Letourneau. 1985. *Modes of Production: The Challenge of Africa*. Ste-Foy: SAFI.

Joseph, Richard A. 1977. *Radical Nationalism in Cameroun: Social Origins of the U.P.C. Rebellion*. London: Oxford Univ. Press.

Kandawire, J. A. K. 1977. "Thangata in Pre-Colonial and Colonial Systems of Land Tenure in Southern Malawi with Special Reference to Chingale." *Africa* 17, no. 2:185–91.

Kanogo, Tabitha. 1987. *Squatters and the Roots of Mau Mau*. Athens, Ohio: Ohio Univ. Press.

Karp, Ivan. 1978. *Fields of Change Among the Iteso of Kenya*. London: Routledge and Kegan Paul.

Karp, Ivan. 1986. "Agency and Social Theory: A Review of Three Books by Anthony Giddens." *American Ethnologist* 3:131–38.

Karp, Ivan. 1988. "Laughter at Marriage: Subversion in Performance." *Journal of Folklore Research* 25:35–52.

Kartodirdjo, Sartono. 1973. *Protest Movements in Rural Java: A Study of Agrarian Unrest in the Nineteenth and Early Twentieth Centuries*. Singapore: Oxford Univ. Press.

Katz, F. n.d. "Rural Uprisings in Mexico." Unpublished manuscript.

Kay, Geoffrey. 1975. *Development and Underdevelopment: A Marxist Analysis*. New York: St. Martin's Press.

Kea, R. 1982. *Settlements, Trade and Politics in the Seventeenth-Century Gold Coast*. Baltimore: Johns Hopkins Univ. Press.

Kea, R. 1986. "I Am Here to Plunder on the General Road: Bandits and Banditry in the Pre-Ninteenth Century Gold Coast." In Crummey 1986: 109–32.

Keatinge, Richard. 1988. *Peruvian Prehistory: An Overview of Pre-Inca and Inca Society*. Cambridge: Cambridge Univ. Press.

Keegan, Tim. 1979. "The Restructuring of Agrarian Class Relations in a Colonial Economy: The Orange River Colony, 1902–1910." *Journal of Southern African Studies* 5, no. 2:234–54.

Keegan, Tim. 1982. "The Sharecropping Economy, African Class Formation and the Natives Land Act of 1913 in the Highveld Maize Belt." In S. Marks and R. Rathbone, eds., *Industrialisation and Social Change in South Africa*. London: Longman, 195–211.

Keegan, Tim. 1983. "The Sharecropping Economy and the South African Highveld in the Early Twentieth Century." *Journal of Peasant Studies* 10, no. 2:201–26.

Keegan, Tim. 1986. "The Dynamics of Rural Accumulation in South Africa: Comparative and Historical Perspectives." *Comparative Studies in Society and History* 29:628 49.

Keegan, Tim. 1988. *Facing the Storm: Portraits of Black Lives in Rural South Africa.* Athens, Ohio: Ohio Univ. Press.

Keller, E. J. 1973. "A Twentieth-Century Model: The Mau-Mau Transformation From Social Banditry to Social Rebellion." *Kenyan Historical Review* 1:189–205.

Kielstra, Nico. 1978. "Was the Algerian Revolution a Peasant War?" *Peasant Studies* 7, no. 3:172–86.

Killingray, David. 1978. "Repercussions of World War I in the Gold Coast." *Journal of African History* 19, no. 1:39–59.

Kimble, J. 1982. "Labour Migration in Basutoland, c. 1870–1885." In S. Marks and R. Rathbone, eds., *Industrialization and Social Change in Southern Africa.* London: Longman, 119–41.

Kimble, J. 1985. "Clinging to the Chiefs: Some Contradictions of Colonial Rule in Basutoland, c. 1890–1930." In Henry Bernstein and Bonnie Campbell, eds., *Contradictions of Accumulation in Africa.* Beverly Hills: Sage, 25–69.

Kinsman, Margaret. 1983. " 'Beasts of Burden': The Subordination of Southern Tswana Women, ca. 1800–1840." *Journal of Southern African Studies* 10:39–54.

Kinyatti, Maina-Wa. 1983. "Mau Mau: The Peak of African Political Organization and Struggle for Liberation in Colonial Kenya." *Ufahamu* 12:90–123.

Kitching, Gavin. 1980. *Class and Economic Change in Kenya: The Making of an African Petite Bourgeoisie, 1905–1970.* New Haven: Yale Univ. Press.

Klein, Martin. 1980. *Peasants in Africa: Historical and Contemporary Perspectives.* Beverly Hills: Sage.

Knauss, Peter. 1978. "Algeria's 'Agrarian Revolution': Peasant Control or Control of Peasants." In Alan Smith and Claude Welch, eds., *Peasants in Africa.* Los Angeles: Crossroads Press, 65–78.

Kobishchanov, Yuri. 1979. *Axum.* University Park: Pennsylvania State Univ. Press.

Koehn, Peter. 1979. "Ethiopia: Famine, Food Production and Changes in the Legal Order." *African Studies Review* 22, no. 1:51–71.

Kofi, Tetteh A. 1978. "Peasants and Economic Development: Populist Lessons for Africa." In Alan Smith and Claude Welch, eds., *Peasants in Africa.* Los Angeles: Crossroads Press, 91–120.

Kopytoff, Igor. 1987. *The African Frontier: The Reproduction of Traditional African Societies.* Bloomington: Indiana Univ. Press.

Koslow, Jules. 1972. *The Despised and the Damned: The Russian Peasant Through the Ages.* London: Macmillan.

Kottak, Conrad Phillip. 1980. *The Past in the Present: History, Ecology and Cultural Variation in Highland Madagascar.* Ann Arbor: Univ. of Michigan Press.

Kriger, Norma. 1988. "The Zimbabwean War of Liberation: Struggles Within the Struggle." *Journal of Southern African Studies* 14:304–22.

Kroeber, Alfred Louis. 1948. *Anthropology.* New York: Harcourt, Brace.

Kuper, Hilda. 1961. *An African Aristocracy: Rank Among the Swazi.* Oxford: Oxford Univ. Press.

Kuper, Hilda. 1974. *The Uniform of Colour: A Study of White Black Relationships in Swaziland.* Johannesburg: Witwatersrand Univ. Press.

Kursany, Ibrahim. 1983. "Peasants of the Nuba Mountains Region." *Review of African Political Economy* 26:35–44.

La Guma, Alex. 1979. *Time of the Butcherbird*. London: Heinemann.

Labouret, H. 1941. *Paysans d'Afrique occidentale*. Paris: Gallimard.

Lamb, G. 1974. *Peasant Politics: Conflict and Development in Murang'a*. New York: St. Martin's Press.

Lan, David. 1985. *Guns and Rain: Guerrillas and Spirit Mediums in Zimbabwe*. Berkeley: Univ. of California Press.

Lancaster, Chet. 1976. "Women, Horticulture, and Society in Sub-Saharan Africa." *American Anthropologist* 78, no.3:539–64.

Landsberger, Henry, ed. 1969. *Latin American Peasant Movements*. Ithaca, N.Y.: Cornell Univ. Press.

Landsberger, Henry. 1974. *Rural Protest: Peasant Movements and Social Change*. London: Macmillan.

Larson, Brooke. 1983. "Shifting Views of Colonialism and Resistance." *Radical History Review* 27:3–20.

Larson, Pier. 1985. "Toward a Rural Social History of Imerina: The Nineteenth Century." M.A. thesis. Univ. of Wisconsin, Madison.

Laslett, Barbara, and Johanna Brenner. 1989. "Gender and Social Reproduction: Historical Perspectives." *Annual Review of Sociology* 15:381–404.

Last, Murray. 1970. "Aspects of Administration and Dissent in Hausaland, 1800–1968." *Africa* 40,no.4:345–57.

Last, Murray. 1974. "Reform in West Africa: The Jihad Movement of the Nineteenth Century." In J. F. Ade Ajayi and Michael Crowder, eds., *History of West Africa*. 2 vols. London: Longman, 2:129.

Latour-Dejean, Elaine de. 1980. "Shadows Nourished by the Sun: Rural Social Differentiation Among the Mwari of Niger." In Klein 1980: 55–102.

Launay, Michel. 1963. *Paysans Algériens: La terre. La viyne et les hommes*. Paris.

Lawson, Fred. 1981. "Rural Revolt and Provincial Society in Egypt, 1820–1824." *International Journal of Middle Eastern Studies* 13,no.2:131–51.

Lee, Richard. 1979. *The !Kung San: Men Women and Work in a Foraging Society*. Cambridge: Cambridge Univ. Press.

Lemarchand, René. 1962. *Political Awakening in the Belgian Congo*. Berkeley: Univ. of California Press.

Lemarchand, René. 1968. "Revolutionary Phenomena in Stratified Societies: Rwanda and Zanzibar." *Civilisations* 18:16–51.

Lemarchand, René. 1970. *Rwanda and Burundi*. New York: Praeger.

Lenin, V. I. 1960. *The Development of Capitalism in Russia: Collected Works*. Moscow: Progress Publishers.

Lennihan, Louise. 1982. "Rights in Men and Rights in Land: Slavery, Labor, and Smallholder Agriculture in Northern Nigeria." *Slavery and Abolition* 3,no.2:111–39.

Leo, Christopher. 1978. "The Failure of the 'Progressive Farmer' in Kenya's Million-Acre Settlement Scheme." *Journal of Modern African Studies* 16,no.4:619–38.

Lerner, Daniel. 1958. *The Passing of Traditional Society: Modernizing the Middle East*. Glencoe: Free Press.

LeRoy Ladurie, Emmanuel. 1974. *The Peasants of Languedoc*. Urbana: Univ. of Illinois Press.

LeRoy Ladurie, Emmanuel. 1987. *The French Peasantry, 1450–1660*. Berkeley: Univ. of California Press.

Levine, Donald. 1965. *Wax and Gold: Tradition and Innovation in Ethiopian Culture*. Chicago: Univ. of Chicago Press.

Levin, Michael D. 1980. "Export Crops and Peasantization: The Bakosi of Cameroun." In Klein 1980:221–42.

Levin, Richard, and Neocosmos, Michael. 1989. "The Agrarian Question and Class Contradictions in South Africa: Some Theoretical Considerations." *Journal of Peasant Studies* 16:230–59.

Lewin, L. 1979. "The Oligarchical Limitations of Social Banditry in Brazil: The Case of the 'Good' Thief, Antonio Silvino." *Past and Present* 82:116–46.

Lewis, Jack. 1984. "The Rise and Fall of the South African Peasantry: A Critique and Reassessment." *Journal of Southern African Studies* 11:1–24.

Lewis, John Wilson, ed. 1974. *Peasant Rebellion and Communist Revolution in Asia*. Stanford: Stanford Univ. Press.

Leys, Colin. 1971. "Politics in Kenya: The Development of Peasant Society." *British Journal of Political Science* 1,no.3:307–37.

Leys, Colin. 1975. *Underdevelopment in Kenya: The Political Economy of Neo-Colonialism, 1964–1971*. London: Heinemann.

Likaka, Osumaka. 1991. "Forced Cotton Cultivation in the Congo." Ph.D. diss. Univ. of Minnesota.

Lincoln, Bruce. 1987. "Ritual, Rebellion, Resistance: Once More the Swazi Ncwala." *Man* 22,no.1:132–56.

Little, Marilyn. 1987. "Natwe Development and Chronic Malnutrition in Sukumaland, Tanganyika, 1925–1945." Ph.D. diss. Univ. of Minnesota.

Lodge, Tom. 1983. *Black Politics in South Africa Since 1945*. Johannesburg: Ravan Press.

Lodge, Tom. 1984. "Insurrection in South Africa: The Pan-Africanist Congress and the Poqo Movement, 1939–1945." Ph.D. diss. Univ. of York.

Lodge, Tom. 1986. "The Poqo Insurrection, 1961–1968." In Tom Lodge, ed., *Resistance and Ideology in Settler Societies*. Johannesburg: Ravan Press, 179–222.

Lonsdale, John. 1968. "Some Origins of Nationalism in East Africa." *Journal of African History* 9,no.1:119–46.

Lonsdale, John. 1981. "State and Peasantry in Colonial Africa." In R. Samuel, ed., *People's History and Socialist Theory*. London: Routledge and Kegan Paul, 106–118.

Lonsdale, John. 1985. "States and Social Processes in Africa: A Historiographical Survey." *African Studies Review* 24,nos.2,3:139–225.

Lonsdale, John. 1988. "Wealth, Poverty and Civic Virtue in Kikuyu Political Thought." Unpublished paper presented at Stirling Commonwealth seminar, London.

Lonsdale, John, and Berman, Bruce. 1979. "Coping with the Contradictions: The Development of the Colonial State in Kenya, 1895–1914." *Journal of African History* 20,no.4:487–505.

Lovejoy, Paul. 1978. "Plantations in the Economy of the Sokoto Caliphate." *Journal of African History* 19,no.3:341–68.

Lovejoy, Paul. 1979. "The Characteristics of Plantations in the Nineteenth Century Sokoto Caliphate." *American Historical Review* 84,no.5:1267–92.

Lovejoy, Paul. 1983. *Transformations in Slavery: A History of Slavery in Africa.* Cambridge: Cambridge Univ. Press.

Lovejoy, Paul. 1986a. "Fugitive Slaves: Resistance to Slavery in the Sokoto Caliphate." In Gary Okihiro, ed., *Resistance: Studies in African, Caribbean, and Afro-American History.* Amherst: Univ. of Massachusetts Press, 71–95.

Lovejoy, Paul. 1986b. *Salt of the Desert Sun: A History of Salt Production and Trade in the Central Sudan.* Cambridge: Cambridge Univ. Press.

Lovens, Maurice. 1975. "La révolte de Masisi-Lubutu (Congo Belge Janvier-Mai 1944)." *Les Cahiers du CEDAF* 3–4.

McAdam, Doug, John McCarthy, and Myer Zald. 1988. "The Dynamics of Social Movements." In Neil Smelser, ed., *Handbook of Sociology.* Newbury Park: Sage, 695–738.

McAllister, P. A. 1989. "Resistance to 'Betterment' in the Transkei: A Case Study from Willowvale District." *Journal of Southern African Studies* 15:346–68.

McCann, James. 1985. "The Political Economy of Rural Rebellion in Ethiopia: Northern Resistance to Imperial Expansion, 1928–1935." *International Journal of African Historical Studies* 18,no.4:601–23.

McCann, James. 1987. *From Poverty to Famine in Northeast Ethiopia: A Rural History, 1900–1935.* Philadelphia: Univ. of Pennsylvania Press.

McCarthy, D. M. P. 1982. *Colonial Bureaucracy and Creating Underdevelopment: Tanganyika, 1919–1940.* Ames: Iowa State Univ. Press.

McCaskie, T. C. 1980. "Office, Land and Subjects in the History of the Manwere Fekuo of Kumase." *Journal of African History* 21,no.2:189–208.

McClellan, Charles. 1984. "State Transformation and Social Reconstitution in Ethiopia: The Allure of the South." *International Journal of African Historical Studies* 17,no.4:657–75.

McClelland, David Clarence. 1961. *The Achieving Society.* Princeton: Van Nostrand Company.

McCracken, John. 1983. "Planters, Peasants and the Colonial State: The Impact of the Native Tobacco Board in the Central Province of Malawi." *Journal of Southern African Studies* 9:179–92.

MacGaffey, W. 1977. "Cultural Roots of Kongo Prophetism." *History of Religion* 17,no.2:177–93.

MacGaffey, W. 1981. "African Ideology and Belief: A Survey." *African Studies Review* 24:227–73.

MacGaffey, W. 1983. *Modern Kongo Prophets: Religion in a Plural Society.* Bloomington: Indiana Univ. Press.

Mack, Beverly. 1988. "A Royal Hausa Woman." In Romero 1988:48–78.

Mahadi, Abdullah. 1982. "The State and the Economy: The Sarauta System and Its Roles in Shaping the Society and Economy of Kano, with Particular Reference to the Eighteenth and Nineteenth Centuries." Ph.D. diss. Ahmadu Bello Univ.

Mafeye, A. 1971a. "The Farmers: Economic and Social Differentiation." In Richards, Sturrock, and Fortt 1973: 198–231.

Mafeye, A. 1971b. "The Ideology of 'Tribalism'." *Journal of Modern African Studies* 9,no.2:253–61.

Malinowski, B. 1929. "Practical Anthropology." *Africa* 2:22–38.

Mamdani, Mahmood. 1982. "Karamoja: Colonial Roots of Famine in North-East Uganda." *Review of African Political Economy* 25:66–73.

Mamdani, Mahmood. 1985. "A Great Leap Backward: A Review of Goran Hyden's 'No Shortcut to Progress'." *Ufahamu* 14,no.2:178–94.

Mandala, Elias. 1982. "Peasant Cotton Agriculture, Gender and Inter-Generational Relationships: The Lower Tchiri (Shire) Valley of Malawi, 1906–1940." *African Studies* 25,nos.2,3:27–44.

Mandala, Elias. 1983. "Gold-Seekers, Prazo-Holders and Capitalists in Mozambique: A Review." *Canadian Journal of African Studies* 18:545–47.

Mandala, Elias. 1984. "Capitalism, Kinship and Gender in the Lower Tchiri (Shire) Valley of Malawi, 1850–1960: An Alternative Theoretical Framework." *African Economic History* 13:137–69.

Mandala, Elias. 1990. *Work and Control in a Peasant Economy: A History of the Lower Tchiri Valley in Malawi, 1859–1960*. Madison: Univ. of Wisconsin Press.

Maquet, Jacques J. P. 1961. *The Premise of Inequality in Rwanda: A Study of Political Relations in a Central African Kingdom*. London: Oxford Univ. Press.

Maquet, Jacques J. P. 1964. "La participation de la classe paysanne au mouvement d'indépendence du Rwanda." *Cahiers d'Études Africaines* 16:552–68.

Marcum, John. 1969, 1978. *The Angolan Revolution*. 2 vols. Cambridge: MIT Press.

Marks, Shula. 1970. *Reluctant Rebellion: The 1906–1908 Disturbances in Natal*. London: Oxford Univ. Press.

Marks, Shula. 1987. *Not Either an Experimental Doll: The Separate Worlds of Three South African Women*. Bloomington: Univ. of Indiana Press.

Marks, Shula, and Anthony Atmore. 1980. *Economy and Society in Pre-Industrial South Africa*. London: Longman.

Marks, Shula, and Stanley Trapido. 1987. *The Politics of Race, Class and Nationalism in Twentieth-Century South Africa*. London: Longman.

Martin, Jean. 1973. "Les débuts du Protectorat et la révolte servile de 1891 dans l'ile d'Anjouan." *Revue Française d'Outre Mer* 60,no.1:45–85.

Martin, Susan. 1984. "Gender and Innovation: Farming, Cooking, and Palm Processing in the Ngwa Region, South-Eastern Nigeria, 1900–1930." *Journal of African History* 25,no.4:411–27.

Marx, Karl. 1926. *The Eighteenth Brumaire of Louis Bonaparte*. New York: International Publishers.

Mason, Michael. 1973. "Captive and Client Labour and the Economy of the Bida Emirate, 1857–1901." *Journal of African History* 14,no.3:453–71.

Maxon, Robert. 1986. "A Kenya Petite Bourgeoisie Enters Local Politics: The Kisii

Union, 1945–1949." *International Journal of African Historical Studies* 19,no.3:451–62.

Mayer, Philip. 1980. *Black Villagers in an Industrial Society: Anthropological Perspectives on Labour Migration in South Africa*. Capetown: Oxford Univ. Press.

Mbeki, Govan. 1964. *South Africa: The Peasants' Revolt*. Baltimore: Penguin.

Mbeki, Govan. 1984. *South Africa: The Peasants' Revolt*. Penguin Africa Library.

Mbilinyi, Marjorie. 1977. "Women: Producers and Reproducers in Peasant Production." Economic Research Bureau Occasional Paper No. 77.3, Univ. of Dar-es-Salaam.

Mbilinyi, Marjorie. 1982. "Wife, Slave and Subject of the King: The Oppression of Women in the Shambala Kingdom." *Tanzania Notes and Records* 88–89:1–13.

Mbilinyi, Marjorie. 1985. " 'City and Countryside' in Colonial Tanganyika." *Economic and Political Weekly, Review of Women's Studies*: 88–96.

Mbilinyi, Marjorie. 1988. "Runaway Wives in Colonial Tanganyika: Forced Labour and Forced Marriage in Rungwe District, 1919–1961," *International Journal of Sociology of Law* 16:1–29.

Meillassoux, Claude. 1964. *Anthropologie économique des Gouro d'Ivoire*. Paris: Mouton.

Meillassoux, Claude. 1972. "From Reproduction to Production." *Economy and Society* 1,no.1:93–105.

Meillassoux, Claude. 1973. "The Social Organization of the Peasantry: The Economic Basis of Kinship." *Journal of Peasant Studies* 1,no.1:81–90.

Meillassoux, Claude. 1975. *L'esclavage en Afrique pré-coloniale*. Paris: Maspero.

Meillassoux, Claude. 1981. *Maidens, Meal and Money: Capitalism and the Domestic Community*. Cambridge: Cambridge Univ. Press.

Meillassoux, Claude. 1986. *Anthropologie de l'esclavage: le ventre de fer, et d'argent*. Paris: Presses Universitaires de France.

Miers, Suzanne, and Richard Roberts. 1988. *The End of Slavery in Africa*. Madison: Univ. of Wisconsin Press.

Migdal, Joseph. 1974. *Peasants, Politics and Revolution: Pressures towards Political and Social Change in the Third World*. Princeton: Princeton Univ. Press.

Miller, Joseph, ed. 1980. *The African Past Speaks: Essays on Oral Tradition and History*. Folkestone, England: Dawson.

Miller, Joseph. 1976. *Kings and Kinsmen: Early Mbundu States in Angola*. Oxford: Oxford Univ. Press.

Miller, Joseph. 1982. "The Significance of Drought, Disease and Famine in the Agriculturally Marginal Zones of West-Central Africa." *Journal of African History* 23,no.1:17–61.

Miller, Joseph C. 1988. *Way of Death: Merchant Capitalism and the Angolan Slave Trade, 1730–1830*. Madison: Univ. of Wisconsin Press.

Miller, Norman, and Roderick Aya. 1971. *National Liberation: Revolution in the Third World*. New York: Free Press.

Mintz, S. W. 1961. "The Question of Caribbean Peasantries: A Comment." *Caribbean Studies* 1,no.3:31–34.

Mintz, S. W. 1973. "A Note on the Definition of Peasantries." *Journal of Peasant Studies* 1,no.1:91–106.

Mintz, S. W. 1974. *Caribbean Transformation.* Chicago: University of Chicago Press.

Mintz, S. W. 1979. "Slavery and the Rise of Peasantries." *Historical Reflections* 6,no.1:213–53.

Mintz, S. W. 1982. "Afterword: Peasantries and the Rural Sector: Notes on Discovery." In Robert Weller and Scott Guggenheim, eds., *Power and Protest in the Countryside: Studies of Rural Unrest in Asia, Europe and Latin America.* Durham: Duke Univ. Press, 180–88.

Mitchell, J. C. 1956. *The Kalela Dance: Aspects of Social Relationships Among Urban Africans in Northern Rhodesia.* Rhodes-Livingstone Paper No. 27. Manchester: Manchester Univ. Press.

Momba, Jotham C. 1985. "Peasant Differentiation and Rural Party Politics in Colonial Zambia." *Journal of Southern African Studies* 11:281–94.

Mondlane, Eduardo. 1969. *The Struggle for Mozambique.* Baltimore: Penguin.

Monod, Theodore, ed. 1972. *Pastoralism in Tropical Africa.* Oxford: Oxford Univ. Press.

Moore, Barrington, Jr. 1966. *Social Origins of Dictatorship and Democracy: Lord and Peasant in the Making of the Modern World.* Boston: Beacon Press.

Moore, Don, and Richard Roberts et al. 1989. "Listen for Silences: What We Can Learn and What Is Not Knowable About African Social History." Roundtable paper presented at Joint Stanford-Berkeley African Studies Conference, April 22.

Moore, Henrietta. 1988. *Feminism and Anthropology.* Minneapolis: Univ. of Minnesota Press.

Moore, Mick. 1972. "On Not Defining Peasants." *Peasant Studies Newsletter* 1, no.1:156–58.

Moore, Sally Falk. 1986. *Social Facts and Fabrications: "Customary" Law on Kilimanjaro, 1880–1980.* Cambridge: Cambridge Univ. Press.

Morris, Mike. 1976. "The Development of Capitalism in South African Agriculture: Class Struggle in the Countryside." *Economy and Society* 5,no.5:292–343.

Morris, Mike. 1987. "Social History and the Transition to Capitalism in the South African Countryside." *African Perspective* 5–6:7–24.

Moscardi, E., and de Janvry, A. 1977. "Attitudes Toward Risk Among Peasants: An Econometric Approach." *American Journal of Agricultural Economics* 59,no.4:710–16.

Mousnier, Roland. 1970. *Peasant Uprisings in Seventeenth-Century France. Russia and China.* New York: Harper & Row.

Mtetwa, Richard. 1976. "The Political and Economic History of the Duma People of Southeastern Rhodesia from the Early Eighteenth Century to 1915." Ph.D. diss. Univ. of Rhodesia.

Mulambu-Mvuluya, Faustin. 1970. "Introduction à l'étude du rôle des paysans dans les changements politiques." *Cahiers Économiques et Sociaux* 8:435–50.

Mulambu-Mvuluya, Faustin. 1974. "Cultures obligatoires et colonisation dans l'ex-Congo Belge." *Les Cahiers du CEDAF* 6–7:1–99.

Mullin, Gerald. 1972. *Flight and Rebellion: Slave Resistance in Eighteenth-Century Virginia*. New York: Oxford Univ. Press.

Munro, J. Forbes. 1976. *Africa and the International Economy*. London: Aldine House.

Munslow, Barry. 1983. *Mozambique: The Revolution and Its Origins*. London: Longman.

Muntemba, Maud. 1978. "Expectations Unfulfilled: The Underdevelopment of Peasant Agriculture in Zambia: The Case of Kabwe Rural District, 1964–1970." *Journal of Southern African Studies* 5:59–85.

Muntemba, Maud. 1980. "Regional and Social Differentiation in Broken Hill Rural District, Northern Rhodesia, 1930–1964." In Klein 1980: 243–70.

Muntemba, Maud. 1982. "Women and Agricultural Change in the Railway Region of Zambia: Dispossession and Counterstrategies." In Edna Bay, ed., *Women and Work in Africa*. Boulder: Westview Press, 83–103.

Muriithi, J. Kiboi, and Peter Ndoria. 1971. *War in the Forest: The Autobiography of a Mau Mau Leader*. Nairobi: East African Publishing House.

Murray, Colin. 1976. "Marital Strategy in Lesotho: The Redistribution of Migrant Earnings." *African Studies* 35, no 2:99–122.

Murray, Colin. 1977. "High Bridewealth, Migrant Labour and the Position of Women in Lesotho." *Journal of African Law* 21:79–96.

Murray, Colin. 1980. "Migrant Labor and Changing Family Structure in the Rural Periphery of Southern Africa." *Journal of Southern African Studies* 6, no. 2:139–56.

Murray, Colin. 1981. *Families Divided: The Impact of Migrant Labour in Lesotho*. Cambridge: Cambridge Univ. Press.

Murray, Martin. 1988a. "The Triumph of Marxist Approaches in African Social and Labour History." *Journal of Asian and African Studies* 23:79–101.

Murray, Martin. 1988b. " 'Burning the Wheat Stacks': Land Clearance and Agrarian Unrest Along the Northern Middleburg Frontier, c. 1918–1926." *Journal of Southern African Studies* 15, no. 1:74–95.

Murray, Martin. 1989. "The Agrarian Question in South Africa." Unpublished manuscript.

Musambachime, M. C. 1988. "Protest Migrations in Mweru-Luapula, 1900–1940." *African Studies* 47, no. 1:19–34.

Nadel, S. F. 1942. *A Black Byzantium: The Kingdom of Nupe in Nigeria*. London: Oxford Univ. Press.

Nayenga, Peter. 1979. "Chiefs and the 'Land Question' in Busoga District, Uganda, 1895–1936." *International Journal of African Historical Studies* 12, no. 2:183–209.

Nayenga, Peter. 1981. "Commercial Cotton Growing in Busoga District, Uganda, 1905–1923." *African Economic History* 10:175–95.

N'daou, Mohamed Saidou. 1988. "French Marxist Theory and the Question of Social Differentiation in Sangalan Pre-Colonial Society." Unpublished paper.

Newbury, Catherine M. 1980. " 'Ubureetwa and Thangata': Catalysts to Peasant Political Consciousness in Rwanda and Malawi." *Canadian Journal of African Studies* 14, no. 1:97–111.

Newbury, Catherine M. 1983. "Colonialism, Ethnicity, and Rural Political Protest:

Rwanda and Zanzibar in Comparative Perspective." *Comparative Politics* 15, no. 3:253–80.

Newbury, Catherine M. 1988. *The Cohesion of Oppression: Clientship and Ethnicity in Colonial Kinyaga (Rwanda), 1860–1960*. New York: Columbia Univ. Press.

Newitt, M. D. D. 1973. *Portuguese Settlement on the Zambesi: Exploration, Land Tenure, and Colonial Rule in East Africa*. New York: Africana Publishing Corporation.

Newitt, M. D. D. 1988. "Drought in Mozambique, 1823–1831." *Journal of Southern African Studies* 15, no. 1:15–35.

Ng'ang'a, D. Mukaru. 1977. "Mau-Mau Loyalists and Politics in Murang'a." *Kenya Historical Review* 5, no. 2:365–84.

Ng'ang'a, D. Mukaru. 1981. "What Is Happening to the Kenyan Peasantry?" *Review of African Political Economy* 20:7–16.

Ngugi, Wa Thiong'o. 1967a. *A Grain of Wheat*. London: Heinemann.

Ngugi, Wa Thiong'o. 1967b. *Weep Not, Child*. London: Heinemann.

Ngugi, Wa Thiong'o. 1978. *Petals of Blood*. New York: Dutton.

Ngugi, Wa Thiong'o. 1982. *Devil on the Cross*. London: Heinemann.

Nkadimeng, Malete, and Reilly, Georgina. 1984. "Kas Maine: The Story of a Black South African Agriculturalist." In Bozzoli 1983b:90–127.

Nkemdirim, Bernard A. 1977. "Reflections on Political Conflict, Rebellion and Revolution in Africa." *Journal of Modern African Studies* 15, no. 1:75–90.

Nurse, G. T. 1975. "Seasonal Hunger Among the Ngoni and Ntumba of Central Malawi." *Africa* 45, no. 1:1–11.

Nzula, Albert, et al. 1979. *Forced Labour in Colonial Africa*. London: Zed Press.

O'Ballance, Edgar. 1967. *The Algerian Insurrection, 1954–1962*. London: Faber and Faber.

O'Brien, Donald Cruise. 1971. "Co-Operators and Bureaucrats: Class Formation in a Senegalese Peasant Society." *Africa* 41, no. 4:263–78.

O'Brien, Donald Cruise. 1979. "Ruling Class and Peasantry in Senegal, 1960–1976: The Politics of a Monocrop Economy." In Rita Cruise O'Brien, ed., *The Political Economy of Underdevelopment: Dependence in Senegal*. Beverly Hills: Sage, 209–27.

O'Brien, Jay. 1983. "The Formulation of the Agricultural Labour Force in Sudan." *Review of African Political Economy* 26:15–34.

Ogbu, John U. 1973. "Seasonal Hunger in Tropical Africa as a Cultural Phenomenon." *Africa* 43, no. 4:317–32.

Ohadike, D. C. 1981. "The Influenza Pandemic of 1918–19 and the Spread of Cassava Cultivation on the Lower Niger." *Journal of African History* 22, no. 5:379–91.

Okihiro, Gary. 1984. "Pre-Colonial Economic Change Among the Tlhaping, c. 1795–1817." *International Journal of African Historical Studies* 17, no. 1:59–80.

O'Laughlin, Bridgit. 1973. "Mbum Beer Parties: Structure of Production and Exchange in African Social Formation." Ph.D. diss. Yale Univ.

O'Laughlin, Bridgit. 1977. "Production and Reproduction: Meillassoux's *Femmes greniers et capitaux*." *Critique of Anthropology* 2:3–32.

Olivier de Sardan, Jean-Pierre. 1984. *Les sociétés Songhay-Zarma (Niger-Mali): Chiefs, guerriers, esclaves, paysans*. Paris: Karthala.

O'Mally, Pat. 1979. "Social Bandits, Modern Capitalism and the Traditional Peasantry: A Critique of Hobsbawm." *Journal of Peasant Studies* 6, no. 4:489–501.

O'Toole, Thomas. 1984. "The 1928–1931 Gbaya Insurrection in Ubangui-Shari: Messianic Movement or Village Self-Defense?" *Canadian Journal of African Studies* 18, no. 2:329–44.

Packard, Randy. 1980. "Social Change and the History of Misfortune Among the Bashu of Eastern Zaire." In I. Karp and C. Bird, eds., *Exploration in African Systems of Thought*. Bloomington: Indiana Univ. Press, 237–67.

Packard, Randy. 1984. "Maize, Cattle and Mosquitoes: The Political Economy of Malaria Epidemics in Colonial Swaziland." *Journal of African History* 25, no. 2:189–212.

Packard, Randy. 1989. *White Plague, Black Labor. Tuberculosis and the Political Economy of Health and Disease in South Africa*. Berkeley: Univ. of California Press.

Page, Melvin. 1978. "The War of Thangata: Nyasaland and the East African Campaign, 1914–1918." *Journal of African History* 19, no. 1:87–100.

Paige, Jeffrey. 1975. *Agrarian Revolution: Social Movements and Export Agriculture in the Underdeveloped World*. New York: Free Press.

Pala, Achola. 1980. "Daughters of the Lakes and Rivers: Colonization and the Land Rights of Luo Women." In M. Etienne and E. Leacock, eds., *Women and Colonization: Anthropological Perspectives*. New York: Praeger, 186–213.

Palmer, Robin. 1986. "Working Conditions and Worker Responses on Nyasaland Tea Estates, 1930–1953." *Journal of African History* 27, no. 1:105–26.

Palmer, Robin, and Parsons, Neil. 1977. *The Roots of Rural Poverty in Central and Southern Africa*. London: Heinemann.

Pankhurst, Richard. 1967. "Tribute, Taxation and Government Revenues in Nineteenth and Early Twentieth Century Ethiopia." *Journal of Ethiopian Studies* 5:37–87.

Parkin, David. 1972. *Palms, Wine and Witnesses: Public Spirit and Private Gain in an African Farming Community*. Berkeley: Univ. of California Press.

Parkin, David, ed. 1975. *Town and Country in Central and Eastern Africa*. London: International African Institute.

Pelissier, Paul. 1966. *Les paysans du Sénégal: Les civilisations agraires du Cayor à la Casamance*. Saint-Yrieix: Imprimerie Fabregue.

Pelissier, René. 1977. *Les guerres grises: Résistance et révoltes en Angola, 1845–1941*. Orgeval: Pelissier.

Pelissier, René. 1978. *La colonie du Minotaure: Nationalismes et révoltes en Angola 1926–1961*. Orgeval: Pelissier.

Pelissier, René. 1984. *Naissance du Mozambique: Résistance et révoltes anticoloniales (1854–1918)*. Orgeval: Pelissier.

Perinbaum, B. Marie. 1973. "Fanon and the Revolutionary Peasantry—The Algerian Case." *Journal of Modern African Studies* 11, no. 3:427–45.

Peters, Pauline. 1983. "Gender, Development Cycles and Historical Process: A Critique of Recent Research on Women in Botswana." *Journal of Southern African Studies* 10, no. 1:100–122.

Phimister, I. R. 1974. "Peasant Production and Underdevelopment in Southern Rhodesia, 1890–1914." *African Affairs* 73:217–28.

Phimister, I. R. 1986. "Commodity Relations and Class Formation in the Zimbabwean Countryside, 1898–1920." *Journal of Peasant Studies* 13, no. 4:240–57.

Phimister, I. R. 1987. "Zimbabwe: The Combined and Contradictory Inheritance of the Struggle Against Colonialism." *Transformation* 5:51–59.

Polanah, Luis. 1981. *The Saga of a Cotton Capulana*. Madison: Univ. of Wisconsin Press.

Popkin, Samuel L. 1979. *The Rational Peasant: The Political Economy of Rural Society in Vietnam*. Los Angeles: Univ. of California Press.

Post, Ken. 1970. "On 'Peasantization' and Rural Class Differentiation in Western Africa." The Hague: Institute of Social Studies, Occasional Papers.

Post, Ken. 1972. " 'Peasantization' and Rural Political Movements in Western Africa." *European Journal of Sociology* 13:223–51.

Post, Ken. 1977. "Peasantization in West Africa." In P. Gutkind and R. Waterman, eds., *African Social Studies: A Radical Reader*. New York: Monthly Review Press, 241–50.

Post, Ken. 1979. "The Alliance of Peasants and Workers: Some Problems Concerning the Articulation of Classes (Algeria and China)." In Robin Cohen et al., eds., *Peasants and Proletarians: The Struggles of Third World Workers*. New York: Monthly Review Press, 265–85.

Poulantzas, Nicos. 1978. *Classes in Contemporary Capitalism*. London: Verso.

Presley, Cora Ann. 1986. "Kikuyu Women in the Mau-Mau Rebellion." In G. Okihiro, ed., *In Resistance*. Amherst: Univ. of Massachusetts Press.

Price, Richard, ed. 1973. *Maroon Societies: Rebel Slave Communities in the Americas*. New York: Anchor Press.

Prochaska, David. 1986. "Fire on the Mountains: Resisting Colonialism in Algiers." In Crummey 1986:229–52.

Quandt, William B. 1969. *Revolution and Political Leadership: Algeria, 1954–1968*. Cambridge: MIT Press.

Quirin, James. 1977. "The Beta Israel (Falasha) in Ethiopian History: Caste Formation and Culture Change, 1270–1868." Ph.D. diss. Univ. of Minnesota.

Quirin, James. 1984. "A Preliminary Analysis of New Archival Sources on Daily Life in Historical Highland Ethiopia." In Sven Rubenson, ed., *Proceedings of the Seventh International Conference on Ethiopian Studies*. Uppsala, Addis Ababa, East Lansing; Michigan State Univ.

Quirin, James. Forthcoming. "The Ayhud and Beta Esra'el-Falasha in Fifteenth-Century Ethiopia: Oral and Written Traditions." *Northeast African Studies*.

Radcliffe-Brown, A. R. 1952. *Structure and Function in Primitive Society*. London: Oxford Univ. Press.

Radcliffe-Brown, A. R., and D. Forde. 1980. *African Systems of Kinship and Marriage*. London: Oxford Univ. Press.

Raikes, P. 1978. "Rural Differentiation and Class Formation in Tanzania." *Journal of Peasant Studies* 5, no. 3:285–325.

Ranger, T. O. 1967. *Revolt in Southern Rhodesia 1896–7: A Study in African Resistance*. London: Heinemann.

Ranger, T. O. 1968a. "Connections Between 'Primary Resistance' Movements and

Modern Mass Nationalism in East and Central Africa." *Journal of African History* 9, no. 3:437–54.

Ranger, T. O. 1968b. *Emerging Themes in African History*. Nairobi: East African Publishing House.

Ranger, T. O. 1977. "The People in African Resistance." *Journal of Southern African Studies* 4, no. 1:123–46.

Ranger, T. O. 1978. "Reflections on Peasant Research in Central and Southern Africa." *Journal of Southern African Studies* 5, no. 1:99–133.

Ranger, T. O. 1985. *Peasant Consciousness and Guerrilla War in Zimbabwe*. Berkeley: Univ. of California Press.

Ranger, T. O. 1986a. "Religious Movements and Politics in Sub-Saharan Africa." *African Studies Review* 29, no. 2:1–70.

Ranger, T. O. 1986b. "Resistance in Africa: From Nationalist Revolt to Agrarian Protest." In Gary Okihiro, ed., *In Resistance*. Amherst: Univ. of Massachusetts Press.

Ranger, T. O. 1988. "Chingaira Makoni's Head: Myth, History and the Colonial Experience." Hans Wolf Memorial Lecture, African Studies Program, Indiana Univ.

Rathbone, Richard. 1978. "World War I and Africa: Introduction." *Journal of African History* 19, no. 1:1–9.

Redfield, Robert. 1956. *Peasant Society and Culture: An Anthropological Approach to Civilization*. Chicago: Univ. of Chicago Press.

Reining, P. 1970. "Social Factors and Food Production in an East African Peasant Society: The Haya." In P. F. M. McLaughlin, ed., *African Food Production Systems*. Baltimore: Johns Hopkins Univ. Press, 41–90.

Rennie, J. K. 1978. "White Farmers, Black Tenants and Landlord Legislation: Southern Rhodesia, 1890–1930," *Journal of Southern African Studies* 5, no. 1:86–98.

Rey, P. P. 1973. *Les alliances des classes: Sur l'articulation des modes de production*. Paris: F. Maspero.

Rey, P. P. 1974. "Class Contradictions in Lineage Societies." *Critique of Anthropology* 2:13–14.

Rey, P. P. 1975. "The Lineage Mode of Production." *Critique of Anthropology* 3:27–29.

Reyna, Stephen. 1975. "Making Do When the Rains Stop: Adjustment of Domestic Structure to Climatic Variation Among the Barma." *Ethnology* 14, no. 4:405–17.

Reyna, Stephen. 1977. "Marriage Payments, Household Structure, and Domestic Labour Supply Among the Barma of Chad." *Africa* 47:81–88.

Richards, Audrey. 1932. *Hunger and Work in a Savage Tribe: A Functional Study of Nutrition Among the Southern Bantu*. London: Oxford Univ. Press.

Richards, Audrey. 1939. *Land, Labour and Diet in Northern Rhodesia: An Economic Study of the Bemba Tribe*. London: Oxford Univ. Press.

Richards, Audrey. 1954. *Economic Development and Tribal Change: A Study of Immigrant Labour in Present-Day Buganda: An Economic and Anthropological Survey*. Cambridge: Heffer, for the East African Institute of Social Research.

Richards, Audrey I., F. Sturrock, and J. M. Fortt. 1973. *Subsistence to Commercial Farming in Present-Day Buganda*. Cambridge: Cambridge Univ. Press.

Richards, Paul. 1983. "Ecological Change and the Politics of African Land Use." *African Studies Review* 26, no. 2:1–72.

Roberts, Richard. 1987. *Warriors, Merchants and Slaves: The State and the Economy in the Middle Niger Valley, 1700–1914*. Stanford: Stanford Univ. Press.

Roberts, Richard, and Martin Klein. 1980. "The Banamba Slave Exodus of 1905 and the Decline of Slavery in the Western Sudan." *Journal of African History* 21, no. 3:375–94.

Roberts, Andrew. 1973. *A History of the Bemba: Political Growth and Change in North-Eastern Zambia Before 1900*. Madison: Univ. of Wisconsin Press.

Roberts, Penelope. 1988. "Rural Women's Access to Labor in West Africa." In Sharon Stichter and Jane Parpart, eds., *Patriarchy and Class*. Boulder: Westview Press, 97–114.

Roberts, Richard, and Suzanne Miers, eds. 1988. *The End of Slavery in Africa*. Madison: Univ. of Wisconsin Press.

Robertson, A. F. 1987. *The Dynamics of Productive Relationships: African Share Contracts in Comparative Perspective*. Cambridge: Cambridge Univ. Press.

Robertson, Claire. 1987. "Developing Economic Awareness: Changing Perspectives in Studies of African Women, 1976–1985." *Feminist Studies* 13, no. 1:97–135.

Robertson, Claire, and Iris Berger. 1986. *Women and Class in Africa*. New York: Holmes and Meier.

Robinson, David. 1985. *The Holy War of Umar Tal: The Western Sudan in the Mid-Nineteenth Century*. Oxford: Clarendon Press.

Roche, Christian. 1976. *Conquête et résistance des peuples de Casamance*. Dakar: Les Nouvelles Editions Africaines.

Rodegem, Francis. 1974. "Une forme d'humeur contestataire au Burundi: Les Wellerismes," *Cahier d'Études Africaines* 14:521–42.

Rodney, Walter. 1968. "Jihad and Social Revolution." *Journal of the Historical Society of Nigeria* 4, no. 2:269–84.

Rodney, Walter. 1972. *How Europe Underdeveloped Africa*. London: Bogle-l'Ouverture Publications.

Rogers (Geiger), Susan. 1973. "Search for Political Focus on Kilimanjaro: A History of Chagga Politics, 1916–1952, with Special Reference to the Cooperative Movement and Indirect Rule." Ph.D. diss. Univ. of Dar-es-Salaam.

Rogers (Geiger), Susan. 1980. "Anti-colonial Protest in Africa: A Female Strategy." *Heresies* 3:222–25.

Rogers, Barbara. 1979. *The Domestication of Women: Discrimination in Developing Societies*. New York: St. Martin's Press.

Romero, Patricia, ed. 1988. *Life Histories of African Women*. New Jersey: Ashfield Press.

Rosberg, Carl, and Nottingham, John. 1966. *The Myth of "Mau-Mau": Nationalism in Kenya*. Nairobi: East African Publishing House.

Roseberry, W. 1978. "Peasant as Proletarians." *Critique of Anthropology* 11:3–18.

Rostow, Walter. 1960. *The Stages of Economic Growth: A Non-Communist Manifesto*. Cambridge: Cambridge Univ. Press.

Rotberg, R. I., and A. Mazrui, eds. 1970. *Protest and Power in Black Africa*. New York: Oxford Univ. Press.

Rotenhan, D. von. 1968. "Cotton Farming in Sukumaland: Cash Cropping and Its

Implications." In Hans Ruthenberg, ed., *Smallholder Farming and Smallholder Development in Tanzania*. Munich: Weltforum Verlag, 53–85.

Rudé, George F. E. 1964. *The Crowd in History: A Study of Popular Disturbances in France and England, 1730–1848*. New York: Wiley.

Santilli, Kathy. 1977. "Kikuyu Women in the Mau Mau Revolt: A Closer Look," *Ufamahu* 8, no. 1:143–59.

Saul, J., and Woods, R. 1971. "African Peasantries." In T. Shanin, ed., *Peasants and Peasant Societies*. London: Penguin.

Saul, John S. 1973. "Marketing Cooperatives in a Developing Country: The Tanzanian Case." In Lionel Cliffe and John Saul, eds., *Socialism in Tanzania*. Dar-es-Salaam: East African Printing House, 141–52.

Saul, John S. 1975. "The Role of the Cooperative Movement." In Lionel Cliffe et al., eds., *Rural Cooperation in Tanzania*. Dar-es-Salaam: Tanzania Publishing House, 206–11.

Saul, John S. 1979. "African Peasantries and Revolution." In *The State and Revolution in Eastern Africa: Essays by John Saul*. New York: Monthly Review Press, 297–338.

Schele, Linda, and Mary Ellen Miller. 1986. *The Blood of Kings: Dynasty and Ritual in Maya Art*. Fort Worth: Kimball Art Museum.

Scheub, Harold. 1985. "A Review of African Oral Traditions and Literature." *African Studies Review* 28, no. 2-3:1–72.

Scheub, Harold. 1987. "The Autobiography of Nongenile Masithatu Zenani." In Patricia Romero 1988:7–46.

Schildkrout, Enid. 1988. "Notes on the Life History of a Hausa Woman." In Romero 1988:78–98.

Schmidt, Elizabeth. 1987. "Ideology, Economics and the Role of Shona Women in Southern Rhodesia, 1850–1939." Ph.D. diss. Univ. of Wisconsin, Madison.

Schmidt, Elizabeth. 1988. "Farmers, Hunters and Gold-Washers: A Reevaluation of Women's Roles in Precolonial and Colonial Zimbabwe." *African Economic History* 17:45–80.

Schmidt, Elizabeth. 1991. "Patriarchy, Capitalism and the Colonial State in Zimbabwe." Signs 16, no. 4: 732–756.

Schmidt, Elizabeth. 1992. *Peasants, Traders and Wives: Shona Women in the History of Zimbabwe, 1870–1939*. Portsmouth: Heinemann.

Schoepf, Brooke Grundfest. 1987. "Social Structure, Women's Status and Sex Differential Nutrition in the Zairean Copperbelt." *Urban Anthropology* 16:73–102.

Schoffeleers, M. 1985. "Oral History and the Retrieval of the Distant Past." In Wim van Binsbergen and M. Schoffeleers, eds., *Theoretical Explorations in African Religion*. London: Kegan Paul International, 164–88.

Schroeder, Richard. 1989. "Seasonality and Gender Conflict in Irrigated Agriculture: Mandinka Rice and Vegetable Production in the Gambia." Unpublished paper.

Scott, James C. 1976a. "Exploitation in Rural Class Relations: A Victim's Perspective." *Comparative Politics* 714:489–532.

Scott, James C. 1976b. *The Moral Economy of the Peasant: Rebellion and Subsistence in Southeast Asia*. New Haven: Yale University Press.

Scott, James C. 1977a. "Hegemony and the Peasantry." *Politics and Society* 7:267–96.

Scott, James C. 1977b. "Peasant Revolution: A Dismal Science." *Cooperative Politics* 9, no. 2:231–48.

Scott, James C. 1982. "Normal Exploitation, Normal Resistance." Unpublished paper presented at the Seminar on Everyday Forms of Peasant Resistance in Southeast Asia, The Hague.

Scott, James C. 1985. *Weapons of the Weak: Everyday Forms of Peasant Resistance.* New Haven: Yale Univ. Press.

Scott, James C. n.d. "Political Analysis and the Hidden Transcript of Subordinate Groups." Unpublished manuscript.

Scott, Joan. 1986. "Gender: A Useful Category of Historical Analysis." *American Historical Review* 91, no. 5:1053–75.

Scott, Joan. 1987. "On Language, Gender and Working Class History." *International Labor and Working Class History* 31:1–13.

Searing, James. 1988. "Aristocrats, Slaves and Peasants: Power and Dependency in the Wolof States, 1700–1850," *International Journal of African Historical Studies* 21, no. 3:475–504.

Seddons, David. 1978. *Relations of Production: Marxist Approaches to Economic Anthropology.* New Jersey: Frank Cass.

Seddons, David. 1981. *Moroccan Peasants: A Century of Change in the Eastern Rif, 1870–1970.* Kent: William Dawson and Sons.

Seleti, Yonal. 1987. "Finance Capital and the Coffee Industry of Angola, 1865–1895." *Transafrican Journal of History* 16:63–77.

Sewell, W. 1985. "Ideologies and Social Revolution: Reflections on the French Case." *Journal of Modern History* 57, no. 1:57–85.

Shanin, Teodor. 1971a. "Peasantry: Delineation of a Sociological Concept and a Field of Study." *European Journal of Sociology* 12:289–300.

Shanin, Teodor. 1971b. *Peasants and Peasant Society.* Hammondsworth: Penguin.

Shanin, Teodor. 1972. *The Awkward Class: Political Sociology of Peasantry in a Developing Society: Russia, 1910–1925.* London: Oxford Univ. Press.

Shanin, Teodor. 1973. "The Nature and Logic of the Peasant Economy." *Journal of Peasant Studies* 1, no. 1:63–79.

Shanin, Teodor. 1979. "Defining Peasants: Conceptualizations and De-Conceptualizations: Old and New in a Marxist Debate." *Peasant Studies* 8, no. 4:38–60.

Shenton, R. W. 1986. *The Development of Capitalism in Northern Nigeria.* Toronto: Univ. of Toronto Press.

Shenton, R. W., and Louise Lennihan. 1981. "Capital and Class: Peasant Differentiation in Northern Nigeria." *Journal of Peasant Studies* 9, no. 1:47–70.

Shepperson, G., and T. Price. 1958. *Independent African: John Chilembwe and the Origins, Setting and Significance of the Nyasaland Native Rising of 1915.* Edinburgh: University Press.

Sheriff, Abdul. 1987. *Slaves, Spices and Ivory in Zanzibar.* London: James Curry.

Shivji, Issa. 1975. "Peasants and Class Alliances." *Review of African Political Economy* 3:10–18.

Sikitele, Gize. 1973. "Les Racine de la révolte Pende de 1971." *Etudes d'Histoire Africaine* 5:99–153.

Silberfein, Marilyn. 1978. "The African Cultivator: A Geographic Overview." In Alan Smith and Claude Welch, eds., *Peasants in Africa*. Waltham: Crossroads Press, 7–23.

Silvestre, Victor. 1974. "Differenciations socio-economiques dans une société à vocation égalitaire: Masaka dans le paysannat de l'Icyanya." *Cahiers d'Études Africaines* 53:104–69.

Simensen, Jarle. 1974. "Rural Mass Action in the Context of Anti-Colonial Protest: The Asafo Movement of Akim Abuakwa, Ghana." *Canadian Journal of African Studies* 8, no. 1:25–41.

Sklar, Richard. 1963. *Nigerian Political Parties*. Princeton: Princeton Univ. Press.

Skocpol, T. 1979. *States and Social Revolutions: A Comparative Analysis of France, Russia and China*. Cambridge: Cambridge Univ. Press.

Skocpol, T. 1982. "What Makes Peasants Revolutionary?" In Robert P. Weller and Scott Guggenheim, eds., *Power and Protest in the Countryside*. Durham: Duke Univ. Press, 156–79.

Slater, H. 1977. "Peasantries and Primitive Accumulation in Southern Africa." Centre for Southern African Studies, Collected Papers No. 2, Univ. of York.

Smith, M. G. 1954. "Slavery and Emancipation in Two Societies." *Social and Economic Studies* 3–4:239–280.

Smith, M. G. 1960. *Government in Zazzau, 1800–1950*. London: Oxford Univ. Press.

Smith, Robert. 1976. "L'administration coloniale et les villageois, les Vansi du nord de Bulungu, 1920–1940 (Zaire)." *Les Cahiers du CEDAF* 3:1–32.

Sorrenson, M. P. K. 1967. *Land Reform in the Kikuyu Country: A Study in Government Policy*. Nairobi and London: Oxford Univ. Press.

Spaulding, Jay. 1982. "Slavery, Land Tenure and Social Class in Northern Turkish Sudan." *Journal of African Historical Studies* 15, no. 1:1–20.

Spiegel, Andrew. 1980. "Rural Differentiation and the Diffusion of Migrant Labor Remittances in Lesotho." In Mayer 1980:109–68.

Spittler, G. 1979. "Peasant and the State in Niger." *Peasant Studies* 8, no. 1:30–47.

Starner, F. L. 1961. *Magsaysay and the Philippine Peasantry: The Agrarian Impact of Philippines Politics, 1953–1956*. Los Angeles: Univ. of California Press.

Staudt, Kathleen. 1985. "Rewriting Agricultural History: Women Farmers at the Center." Paper presented at the African Studies Association, New Orleans.

Staudt, Kathleen. 1986. "Stratification Implication for Women's Politics." In Robertson and Berger 1986:197–215.

Staudt, Kathleen. 1987. "Uncaptured or Unmotivated? Women and the Food Crisis in Africa." *Rural Sociology* 52, no. 1:37–55.

Stedman-Jones, Gareth. 1983. *Languages of Class: Studies in English Working-Class History, 1832–1982*. Cambridge: Cambridge Univ. Press.

Steinhart, E. 1977. *Conflict and Collaboration: The Kingdoms of Western Uganda, 1890–1907*. Princeton: Princeton Univ. Press.

Stenning, D. 1959. *Savannah Nomads*. London: Oxford Univ. Press.

Stern, Steve J. 1983. "The Struggle for Solidarity: Class, Culture and Community in Highland America." *Radical History* 27:21–45.

Stern, Steve J. 1987. *Resistance, Rebellion and Consciousness in the Andean Peasant World, 18th to 20th Centuries*. Madison: Univ. of Wisconsin Press.

Stichter, Sharon. 1975. "Women and the Labor Force in Kenya, 1895–1964." *Rural Africa* 29:45–67.

Stichter, Sharon. 1982. *Migrant Labor in Kenya: Capitalism and African Response, 1895–1975*. London: Longman.

Stichter, Sharon. 1985. *Migrant Labourers*. Cambridge: Cambridge Univ. Press.

Stoler, Ann. 1986. "Plantation Politics and Protest on Sumatra's Coast." *Journal of Peasant Studies* 13, no. 2:124–43.

Strauder, Jack. 1974. "The Relevance of Anthropology to Colonialism and Imperialism." *Race and Class* 16:29–52.

Strobel, Margaret. 1982. "African Women: A Review." *Signs* 8, no. 1:109–31.

Sturzinger, Ulrich. 1983. "The Introduction of Cotton Cultivation in Chad: The Role of the Administration." *African Economic History* 12:213–25.

Sutton, Inez. 1983. "Labour and Commercial Agriculture in Ghana in the Late Nineteenth and Early Twentieth Centuries," *Journal of African History* 24, no. 4:461–84.

Swai, Bonaventure. 1982. "Colonial Rural Development Policy and Agrarian Protest in Tanganyika Territory: The Usambara Case, 1820–1920." *Transafrican Journal of African Studies* 2:153–71.

Swantz, Marja-Liisa. 1977. *Strain and Strength Among Peasant Women in Tanganyika*. Dar-es-Salaam: Univ. of Dar-es-Salaam, Bureau of Resource Assessment and Land Use Planning, Research Paper 49.

Swindell, Kenneth. 1984. "Farmers, Traders and Labourers: Dry Season Migration From North-West Nigeria, 1900–1933." *Africa* 54, no. 1:3–19.

Tamrat, Taddesse. 1972. *Church and State in Ethiopia, 1270–1527*. Oxford: Clarendon Press.

Tareke, Gebru. 1984. "Peasant Resistance in Ethiopia: The Case of Weyane." *Journal of African History* 25, no. 1:77–92.

Tarrow, Sidney. 1988. "National Politics and Collective Action: Recent Theory and Research in Western Europe and the United States." *Annual Review of Sociology* 14:421–40.

Temu, A., and Swai, B. 1981. *Historians and Africanist History: A Critique*. London: Zed Press.

Terray, E. 1972. *Marxism and "Primitive Societies."* New York: Monthly Review Press.

Terray, E. 1974. "Long-Distance Exchange and the Formation of the State." *Economy and Society* 3, no. 3:315–45.

Terray, E. 1985a. "Sociétés segmentaires, chefferies états: Acquis et problèmes." *Canadian Journal of African History* 19, no. 1:106–15.

Terray, E. 1985b. "Une histoire du royaume Abron de Gyiaman des origines à la fin du xixe siécle." Thése d'Etat, Université Paris, V.

Tetzlaff, Rainer. 1970. *Koloniale Entwicklung und Ausbeutung: Wirtschafts-und Sozialgeschichte Deutsch Ostrafrikas, 1885–1919*. Berlin: Duncker und Humbolt.

Thelen, David. 1989. "Memory and American History." *Journal of American History* 75:117–29.

Thiele, G. 1984. "State Intervention and Commodity Production in Ugogo: A Historical Perspective." *Africa* 54, no. 3:92–107.

Thomas, Roger. 1983. "The 1916 Bongo Riots." *Journal of African History* 24, no. 1:57–75.

Thornton, John. 1983. *The Kingdom of Kongo: Civil War and Transition, 1641–1718*. Madison: Univ. of Wisconsin Press.

Throup, David. 1985. "The Origins of Mau Mau." *African Affairs* 84:399–434.

Throup, David. 1987. *Economic and Social Origins of Mau-Mau, 1945–53*. Athens, Ohio: Ohio Univ. Press.

Tilly, Charles. 1978. *From Mobilization to Revolution*. Reading, Mass.: Addison-Wesley.

Tilly, Charles. 1982. "Routing Conflicts and Peasant Rebellions in Seventeenth-Century France." In Robert P. Weller and Scott E. Guggenheim, eds., *Power and Protest in the Countryside*. Durham: Duke Univ. Press, 13–41.

Tosh, John. 1978. "Lango Agriculture During the Early Colonial Period: Land and Labour in a Cash-Crop Economy." *Journal of African History* 19, no. 3:415–39.

Tosh, John. 1980. "The Cash-Crop Revolution in Tropical Africa: An Agricultural Reappraisal." *African Affairs* 79:79–94.

Trapido, S. 1978. "Landlord and Tenant in a Colonial Economy: The Transvaal, 1880–1910." *Journal of Southern African Studies* 5, no. 1:26–58.

Trapido, S. 1980. " 'The Friends of the Natives': Merchants, Peasants and the Political and Ideological Structure of Liberalism in the Cape, 1854–1910." In A. Atmore and S. Marks, eds., *Economy and Society in Pre-Industrial South Africa*. London: Longman, 247–74.

Trapido, S. 1986. "Putting a Plough to the Ground: A History of Tenant Production on the Vereeneging Estates, 1896–1920." In William Beinart, Peter Delius, and Stanley Trapido, eds., *Putting a Plough to the Ground*. Johannesburg: Ravan Press, 336–72.

Traugott, Mark. 1978. "Reconceiving Social Movements." *Social Problems* 26, no 1:38–49.

Tronchon, Jacques. 1974. *L'insurrection malagache de 1947*. Paris: Maspero.

Trouillot, Michel-Rolph. 1988. *Peasants and Capital: Dominica in the World Economy*. Baltimore: Johns Hopkins Univ. Press.

Tuden, Arthur, and Leonard Plotnicov. 1970. *Social Stratification in Africa*. New York: Free Press.

Turner, Victor. 1957. *Schism and Continuity in an African Society: A Study of Ndembu Village Life*. Manchester: Univ. of Manchester Press.

Urdang, Stephanie. 1979. *Fighting Two Colonialisms: Women in Guinea Bissau*. New York: Monthly Review Press.

Usman, Yusufu Bala. 1981. *The Transformation of Katsina (1400–1883)*. Zaria: Ahmadu Bello Univ. Press.

Vail, David. 1972. *A History of Agricultural Innovation and Development in Teso District Uganda*. Syracuse: Syracuse Univ., East African Studies.

Vail, Leroy, ed. 1989. *The Creation of Tribalism in Southern Africa*. Berkeley: Univ. of California Press.

Vail, Leroy, 1977. "Ecology and History: The Example of Eastern Zambia." *Journal of Southern African Studies* 3, no. 2:130–55.

Vail, Leroy. 1980. *Capitalism and Colonialism in Mozambique*. Minneapolis: Univ. of Minnesota Press.

Vail, Leroy, and Landeg White. 1978. " 'Tawani Machambero!' Forced Cotton and Rice Growing on the Zambezi." *Journal of African History* 19, no. 2:239–64.

Vail, Leroy, and Landeg White. 1983. "Forms of Resistance: Songs and Perception of Power in Colonial Mozambique." *American Historical Review* 88, no. 4:883–919.

Valensi, Lucette. 1985. *Tunisian Peasants in the Eighteenth and Nineteenth Centuries*. Cambridge: Cambridge Univ. Press.

Van Allen, Judith. 1976. " 'Aba Riots' or Igbo 'Women's War'? Ideology, Stratification and the Invisibility of Women." In Nancy J. Hafkin and Edna G. Bay, eds., *Women in Africa*. Stanford: Stanford Univ. Press, 59–85.

Van Binsbergen, W. M. J. 1981. *Religious Changes in Zambia*. London: Kegan Paul International.

Van Onselen, Charles. 1990. "Race and Class in the South African Countryside: Cultural Osmosis and Social Relations in the Share-Cropping Economy of the South-Western Transvaal, 1900–1950." *American Historical Review* 95:99–123.

Vansina, Jan. 1962. "A Comparison of African Kingdoms," *Africa* 32, no. 4:324–35.

Vansina, Jan. 1966. *Kingdoms of the Savanna*. Madison: Univ. of Wisconsin Press.

Vansina, Jan. 1969. "Anthropologists and the Third Dimension." *Africa* 39, no. 1:62–68.

Vansina, Jan. 1978. *Children of Woot: A History of the Kuba Peoples*. Madison: Univ. of Wisconsin Press.

Vansina, Jan. 1985. *Oral Tradition as History*. Madison: Univ. of Wisconsin Press.

Vaughan, Megan. 1982. "Food Production and Family Labour in Southern Malawi: The Shire Highlands and Upper Shire Valley in the Early Colonial Period." *Journal of African History* 23, no. 1:351–54.

Vaughan, Megan. 1987. *The Story of an African Famine: Gender and Famine in Twentieth Century Malawi*. Oxford: Oxford Univ. Press.

Vellenga, Dorothy Dee. 1986. "Matriliny, Patriliny and Class Formation Among Women Cocoa Farmers in Two Rural Areas of Ghana." In Robertson and Berger 1986:62–77.

Vercruijsse, Emile. 1979. "Class Formation in the Peasant Economy of Southern Ghana." *Review of African Political Economy* 15–16:93–104.

Verhaegen, Benoit. 1966. *Rebellions au Congo*. Brussels: Centre de Recherche et d'Information Socio-Politique.

Verhaegen, Benoit. 1967. "Les rebellions populaires au Congo en 1964." *Cahiers d'Études Africaines* 26:345–59.

Verhaegen, Benoit. 1986. "The Method of Histoire Immédiate." In B. Jewsiewicki and D. Newbury, eds., *African Historiographies*.

Vickery, Kenneth. 1986. *Black and White in Southern Zambia*. New York: Greenwood Press.

Vidal, Claudine. 1974. "Economie de la Société Féodale Rwandaise." *Cahiers d'Études Africaines* 14:52–74.

Vincent, Joan. 1977. "Colonial Chiefs and the Making of Class: A Case Study from Teso, Eastern Uganda." *Africa* 47, no. 2:140–59.

Vincent, Joan. 1981. *Teso in Transformation: The Political Economy of Peasant and Class in Eastern Africa*. Los Angeles: Univ. of California Press.

Von Freyhold, Michaela. 1979. *Ujamaa Villages in Tanzania*. New York: Monthly Review Press.

Wallerstein, Immanuel. 1974, 1980. *The Modern World System*. Vols. 1–3. New York: Academic Press.

Wallerstein, Immanuel. 1976. "The Three Stages of African Involvement in the World Economy." In P. Gutkind and I. Wallerstein, eds., *The Political Economy of Contemporary Africa*. Beverly Hills: Sage, 30–57.

Walton, John. 1983. *Reluctant Rebels: Comparative Studies of Revolution and Underdevelopment*. New York: Columbia Univ. Press.

Watson, William. 1958. *Tribal Cohesion in a Money Economy: A Study of the Mambwe People of Northern Rhodesia*. Manchester: Manchester Univ. Press.

Watts, Michael. 1983a. "The Political Economy of Climatic Hazards: A Village Perspective on Drought and Peasant Economy in a Semi-Arid Region of West Africa." *Cahier d'Études Africaines* 89–90:37–72.

Watts, Michael. 1983b. *Silent Violence: Food, Famine and Peasantry in Northern Nigeria*. Los Angeles: Univ. of California Press.

Watts, Michael. 1987a. "Banditry, Rebellion and Social Protest in Africa: A Review." *African Economic History* 16:1230–90.

Watts, Michael. 1987b. "On Peasant Diffidence: Non-Revolt, Resistance, and Hidden Forms of Political Consciousness in Northern Nigeria, 1900–1945." In Edmund Burke, ed., *Global Crises and Social Movements*. Boulder: Lynne Reinner, 117–44.

Watts, Michael. 1988. "Struggles Over Land, Struggles Over Meaning." In Reginald Golledge, ed., *A Ground for a Common Search*. Santa Barbara: University of Santa Barbara Press, 31–51.

Watts, Michael. 1989. "Manufacturing Dissent: Culture and Production Politics in a Peasant Society." Paper presented at conference on "Political Economy and Popular Culture in Africa." Stanford: Stanford Univ. Press.

Wauchope, R., ed. 1967–76. *The Handbook of Middle American Indians*. 2 vols. Austin: Univ. of Texas Press.

Weiner, Myron, ed. 1966. *Modernization: The Dynamics of Growth*. New York: Basic Books.

Weinrich, A. 1975. *African Farmers in Rhodesia: Old and New Peasant Communities in Karangaland*. London: Oxford Univ. Press.

Weiskel, Timothy. 1980. *French Colonial Rule and the Baule Peoples: Resistance and Collaboration, 1889–1911*. London: Oxford Univ. Press.

Weiss, Herbert F. 1967. *Political Protest in the Congo*. Princeton: Princeton Univ. Press.

Welch, Claude E., Jr. 1978a. "Peasants as a Focus in African Studies." In Alan Smith and Claude Welch, eds., *Peasants in Africa*. Waltham, Mass.: Crossroads Press, 1–5.

Welch, Claude E., Jr. 1978b. "Obstacles to 'Peasant War' in Africa." In Alan Smith and Claude Welch, eds., *Peasants in Africa*. Waltham, Mass.: Crossroads Press, 121–30.

White, Christine. 1983. "Mass Mobilisation and Ideological Transformation in the Vietnamese Land Reform Campaign." *Journal of Contemporary Asia* 13, no. 1:74–90.

White, Christine. 1986. "Everyday Resistance, Socialist Revolution, and Rural Development: The Vietnamese Case." *Journal of Peasant Studies* 13, no. 2:49–63.

White, Landeg. 1987. *Magomero: Portrait of an African Village*. Cambridge: Cambridge Univ. Press.

White, Luise. 1983. "A Colonial State and an African Petty Bourgeoisie." In Fred Cooper, ed., *Struggle for the City*. Beverly Hills: Sage, 167–94.

White, Luise. 1988a. "Domestic Labor in a Colonial City: Prostitution in Nairobi, 1900–1952." In Sharon Stichter and Jane Papart, eds., *Patriarchy and Class*. Boulder: Westview Press, 139–61.

White, Luise. 1990. "Separating the Men from the Boys: Colonial Constructions of Gender in Central Kenya." *International Journal of African Historical Studies* 23, no. 1:1–26.

Whitehead, Ann. 1981. " 'I'm Hungry, Mum.' The Politics of Domestic Budgeting." In Kate Young et al., eds., *Of Marriage and the Market*. London: CSE Books, 88–111.

Wilks, Ivor. 1976. "Land, Labor, Capital and the Forest of Asante: A Model of Early Change." In J. Friedman and M. J. Rowlands, eds., *The Evolution of Social Systems*. Pittsburgh: Univ. of Pittsburgh Press, 487–533.

Williams, G. 1976. "Taking the Part of the Peasants: Rural Development in Nigeria and Tanzania." In P. Gutkind and I. Wallerstein, eds., *The Political Economy of Contemporary Africa*. Beverly Hills: Sage, 131–54.

Williams, Raymond. 1980. *Problems in Materialism and Culture*. London: Verso.

Wilmsen, E. 1983. "Iron Age Pastoralist Settlements in Botswana." *South African Journal of Science*.

Wilmsen, E. 1991. "Pastoro-Foragers to 'Bushmen': Transformations in Kalahari Relations of Property, Production and Labor." In J. Galaty and P. Bonte, eds., *Herders, Warriors and Traders: Pastoralism in Africa*. Boulder: Westview Press, 248–63.

Wilson (Hunter) Monica. 1936. *Reaction to Conquest*. London: Oxford Univ. Press.

Wilson (Hunter) Monica. 1951. *Good Company: A Study of Nyakyusa Age Villages*. London: Oxford Univ. Press.

Wilson (Hunter) Monica. 1957. *Rituals of Kinship Among the Myakua*. London: Oxford Univ. Press.

Wilson (Hunter) Monica. 1969. "The Growth of Peasant Communities." In Monica Wilson and Leonard Thompson, eds., *The Oxford History of South Africa*. Vol. 2. *South Africa, 1870–1966*. London: Oxford Univ. Press, 49–103.

Wipper, Audrey. 1977. *Rural Rebels: A Study of Luo Protest Movements in Kenya*. Nairobi: Oxford Univ. Press.

Wolf, Eric. 1966. *Peasants*. Englewood Cliffs, N.J.: Prentice Hall.

Wolf, Eric. 1969. "On Peasant Rebellions." *International Social Science Journal* 21, no. 2:286–93.

Wolf, Eric. 1969. *Peasant Wars of the Twentieth Century*. New York: Harper & Row.

Wolf, Eric. 1971. "Peasant Rebellion and Revolution." In Norman Miller and Roderick Aya, eds., *National Liberation: Revolution in the Third World*. New York: Free Press, 48–67.

Wolpe, H. 1972. "Capitalism and Cheap Labour Power in South Africa: From Segregation to Apartheid." *Economy and Society* 1:425–56.

Wolpe, H., ed. 1980. *The Articulation of Modes of Production: Essays from Economy and Society*. London: Routledge and Kegan Paul.

Worsley, P. M. 1961. "The Analysis of Rebellion and Revolution in Modern British Social Anthropology." *Science and Society* 21, no. 5.1:26–37.

Wright, Marcia. 1982. "Justices, Women and the Social Order in Abercorn, Northeastern Rhodesia, 1897–1903." In Margaret Jean Hay and Marcia Wright, eds., *African Women and the Law: Historical Perspectives*. Boston: Boston Univ. Press.

Wright, Marcia. 1983a. "Bwanikwa: Consciousness and Protest Among Slave Women in Central Africa, 1886–1911." In Claire Robertson and Martin Klein, eds., *Women and Slavery in Africa*. Madison: Univ. of Wisconsin Press, 246–67.

Wright, Marcia. 1983b. "Technology, Marriage and Women's Work in the History of Maize Growers in Mazabuka Zambia: A Reconnaissance." *Journal of Southern African Studies* 10, no. 1:71–85.

Wright, Marcia. 1984. *Women in Peril: Life Stories of Four Captives*. Lusaka: Institute for African Studies, Univ. of Zambia.

Wrigley, C. C. 1959. *Crops and Wealth in Uganda: A Short Agrarian History*. Kampala: East African Institute of Social Research.

Wrigley, C. C. 1971. "Historicism in Africa: Slavery and State Formation." *African Affairs* 70:113–24.

Wuyts, M. 1978. *Peasants and Rural Economy in Mozambique*. Maputo: Universidade Eduardo Mondlane.

Young, M. Crawford. 1965. *Politics in the Congo: Decolonization and Independence*. Princeton: Princeton Univ. Press.

Young, M. Crawford. 1986. "Nationalism, Ethnicity and Class in Africa: A Retrospective." *Cahier d'Études Africaines* 103:421–95.

Young, S. 1977. "Fertility and Famine: Women's Agricultural History in Southern Mozambique." In Robin Palmer and Neil Parsons, eds., *The Roots of Rural Poverty*. Los Angeles: Univ. of California Press, 66–81.

Zolberg, A. R. 1964. *One-Party Government in the Ivory Coast*. Princeton: Princeton Univ. Press.

Zwanenberg, R. van. 1974. "The Development of Peasant Commodity Production in Kenya, 1920–1940," *Economic History Review* 27, no. 3:442–54.

5 *William Roseberry*

Beyond the Agrarian Question
in Latin America

For all the advances made in the field of agrarian studies, we are still only beginning to understand the manifold ways whereby peasants have continuously engaged their political worlds—in apparently quiescent as well as rebellious times, as initiators of change as well as reactors to it, as peoples simultaneously disposed to "adapt" to objective forces beyond their control and to "resist" inroads on hard-won rights and achievements. Peasant political action tends still to be reduced to its most dramatic and abnormal moments—moments of rupture, defensive mobilization against harmful change, collective violence against authority. Although the literature recognizes that peasants have placed their own stamp on the political histories of their regions and countries, it shrinks such impact to moments of crisis leading to rebellion. During more normal times, peasants recede from the political picture. Politically speaking, they are an inert force—dormant, traditional, or ineffectual. This reductionism fits nicely with the image of peasants as parochial "reactors" to external forces, and with the assumption that such defensive and limited political behavior is largely inherent in the objective, "structural" condition of peasants (Stern 1987:9).

The role of the peasants themselves, their organizations, their movements, their struggles and their sacrifices, is generally underestimated if not openly neglected in the analysis of agrarian change and particularly in the study of the land-reform process. This is not surprising in view of the fact that peasants do not write their own history, and that those who do frequently look at the issues involved from the other side. Yet in

Latin America, agrarian struggles are as old as the colonization process itself, and the active participation of peasants in social and political movements of various kinds has been more widespread than is commonly assumed. . . .

But violent uprisings and revolts have not been the only or even the most common form of peasants' protest against the generalized climate of repression under which they work and live. To be sure, against violence from above, peasants have always responded to a greater or lesser extent with violence from below. But this has taken on many forms. Social banditry was long a general feature of the backward rural zones in many countries, and still appears from time to time in different areas. . . . Millenarian and messianic movements have also played an important role. (Stavenhagen 1970:371, 372)

In juxtaposing the comments of Steve Stern and Rodolfo Stavenhagen, I do not mean to suggest that Stern's criticism is unfair or inaccurate. Stavenhagen's brief comment introducing a group of essays on peasant activism in Latin America remains interesting because it was attempting to make peasant activity central to our understanding of agrarian structures and processes, was arguing—long before the present poststructuralist reconsiderations—that such activity was "generally underestimated," and was pointing to a range of activities not limited to rebellion or revolution. I do not want to push this observation too far. It would be inappropriate to suggest, for example, that Stavenhagen's comment anticipated James Scott's (1985) emphasis on "everyday forms of peasant resistance." Indeed, the two examples mentioned by Stavenhagen— banditry and millenarian movements—have their unacknowledged inspiration in Eric Hobsbawm's (1959) influential examination of prepolitical forms of peasant protest in Europe. Moreover, the construction of Stavenhagen's comment lends credence to Stern's observation that students of peasant activism have seen peasants simply as reactors to oppression rather than as actors and initiators.

Nonetheless, the juxtaposition remains interesting because it presents us with a problem. If Allen Isaacman can convincingly argue in this volume that African peasantries were invisible in the literature until quite recently, their activities subsumed within a variety of other (nationalist or tribal) movements, this was not true in Latin America. Rural toilers' existence *as peasants* was not subject to serious dispute, although anthropologists in the 1950s and 1960s could argue about the relative importance of structural and cultural factors among indigenous peasantries, and Marxists in the 1970s could complain that the peasant concept should be replaced with more precise analytical categories like "simple commodity producer." That there were large rural populations that fit most definitions of peasants could be assumed, however; indeed, much of the anthropological and sociological "discovery" (Mintz 1982) of the peasantry occurred in Latin America. Moreover, peasant discontent, agitation, and activism—especially but not exclusively in the 1960s—provided the initial context for the explosion of studies of the agrarian problem. Without it, without a variety of attempts to understand it, to prevent it in some cases, to take inspiration from it in others, to guide it or capture it in yet others, there would have been no literature on the agrarian question in Latin America.

If, some three decades into the proliferation of studies of agrarian problems in Latin America, a serious student of and contributor to that literature can argue that "we are still only beginning to understand the manifold ways whereby peasants have continuously engaged their political worlds," we need to take this observation as our central intellectual and political problem. In my view, it is not enough to attribute this failure to one of a variety of forms of structural analysis: structural-functionalism, dependency theory, or mode-of-production analysis. Our account will have to deal with these modes of analysis, their insights and their silences. But it is too easy to turn such an argument into a simplistic and self-congratulatory opposition. They ignored agency; we do not. They ignored the peasantry; we do not. They were benighted; we know better. We need to pay more serious attention to where and how they seem to have gone wrong. The various forms of structural analysis owed their success not simply to the rise and fall of academic fashions. Rather, they answered, or seemed to answer, particular intellectual and political questions. They were interventions in particular arguments. We need to pay attention to the arguments themselves, what they were about, how the questions were structured in certain ways, how they allowed certain problems to be discussed and others to be avoided. We can then examine more recent reconsiderations and criticisms in a less presentist light, explore the extent to which the arguments and questions have changed, and the manner in which some old assumptions are challenged while others remain unquestioned.

This is the subject of the present essay. In the first part ("What Was the Agrarian Question?") I take the mid-to-late 1960s as a kind of "precipice in time" (cf. Stocking 1987), from which we can attempt to reconstruct a world that now seems past, a set of intellectual and political arguments, assumptions, and agendas. In the second part ("What Is Wrong with This Question?") I examine the manner in which prevailing approaches systematically ignored central problems and relationships. In the final part ("Asking New Questions") I discuss recent trends in the anthropological and historical literature, and suggest areas for future work. As I consider these questions, I make no attempt to trace the complex lines and webs of writing and thinking within and among the centers of intellectual production in Santiago, São Paulo, Lima, Mexico City, Stanford, Austin, Madison, New Haven, Cambridge, and Paris; nor do I attempt a detailed review of modernization, dependency, world-system, and Marxist approaches to the agrarian question. Assuming a general familiarity with the history of the literature (see Stern and Cooper, this volume), I concentrate here on the *structure* of the agrarian question: What shared assumptions or questions allowed followers of one or the other theoretical approach to talk to and argue with followers of another approach? How was a common language constituted? What could and could not be talked about?

Concentration on the structure of an argument illuminates central assumptions and silences in a literature and allows us to explore key relationships and contradictions. It also imposes important limitations, however, and these need to be stressed at the beginning. First, the *structure* of an argument is not the argument itself; still less is it the rather different argument*s* that occurred in Peru, Bolivia, Chile, Brazil, Venezuela, and Mexico. At one point in the discussion that follows (pp. 331–33), I find it necessary to discuss specific arguments on the positions of indigenous peoples within the rural class structure of Mexico. Though these specific studies and interventions help us to understand a more general literature, they cannot be made to speak for the contemporaneous arguments concerning class and ethnicity that occurred in different political contexts and movements, with different social, political, and cultural registers, in Peru, Bolivia, and Chile. In this sense, I hope this essay can serve as a point of departure for critical reappraisals of local literatures and arguments.

Second, an outline of the structure of an argument provides an analysis of a *dominant* discourse. It can collaborate with the excision of those intellectual currents and initiatives that were excluded, that failed to attract a following, or that were actively suppressed in a variety of politically charged contexts. After exploring the dominant literature on the agrarian question, I consider a variety of literatures that were excluded, especially the work of various generations of anthropologists and historians who have studied local processes of social and cultural formation in detail. That there are other important bodies of work, especially by local historians who influenced other anthropologists and historians, needs to be stressed.[1]

What Was the Agrarian Question?

In Latin America the growing manifestations of rural unrest, the unsatisfactory growth of agricultural production, the increasing importation of foodstuffs, the malnutrition of the majority of the people and the acrimonious debate on agrarian reform are proof that the agrarian question has gone beyond the realm of academic discussion.

Even if it is unnecessary to document the existence of a serious agrarian problem, there is an urgent need to determine the problem's characteristics, to find out how it has put a brake on development and to adopt policies that might correct present-day defects in agrarian structure. . . .

The agrarian problem must be understood as one reflecting the very structure of the society. Control over land and labor is undoubtedly a central element in the issue, but in agrarian societies this control is equally evident at the political level. In Latin America the agrarian problem has become aggravated recently by rapid changes in population, technology and dominant social values and aspirations. Particularly since the Second World War the traditional rural production systems have become increasingly out of adjustment and political relationships have become threatened. As a result the techniques by which social and economic conflicts have historically been resolved or controlled are proving increasingly ineffective. . . .

Historically the "social equilibrium" in rural Latin America was characterized by the seigneurial system. The *patrones* (large landholders) have organized agricultural production and dominated political, economic, and social institutions during most of the last four centuries. The possibility of a campesino changing his economic function and social position or obtaining political power has always been severely circumscribed.

Unquestionably, force has been used to maintain this social order. The numerous rural uprisings since the Spanish Conquest hardly give credence to the myth of a universally respected benevolent paternalism. But an equilibrium is no less real because it is maintained by arms. Not until the present century has the dominance of the landed class in rural Latin America been seriously threatened. Social revolutions over-throwing the traditional seigneurial system, however, have now taken place in Mexico, Bolivia, and Cuba while dramatic revolutionary processes are threatening the old order throughout Latin America. (Barraclough and Domike 1970 [1966]:41–44)

So began an influential essay by Solon Barraclough and Arthur Domike, summarizing the results of a seven country study[2] conducted in the early 1960s by the Inter-American Committee for Agricultural Development (ICAD), an organizational creature of the Food and Agricultural Organization, The Economic Commission for Latin America (both units of the United Nations), the Organization of American States, the Inter-American Institute for Agricultural Sciences, and the Inter-American Development Bank. The very existence of such an organization and study indicates a crisis, or the perception of crisis. The emergence of rural *guerrillero* movements in various Latin American countries in the years following the Cuban Revolution, with the active encouragement and support of Cubans who understood that their revolution could not survive in isolation, provided the necessary context for much of the thought, organization, work, and writing on the agrarian question. For those on the left, the countryside was where the revolution would be made; the Sierra Maestra became the symbol and inspiration for what might become a continent-wide transformation. *How* this would happen, through what organizational channels, with what alliances, with what leadership, and with what strategies, were subjects for acrimonious debate. That a revolution was possible, that it would include the peasantry, and that much of it would be fought in the countryside was, however, not a subject for serious doubt.

For academics, planners, and bureaucrats less sympathetic to revolution, the Sierra Maestra and the *focos guerrilleros* established in various countries also served as a symbol. Their challenge was rural and urban development without revolutionary upheaval. However development was conceived, the agrarian problem could not be avoided. For those pursuing rural development, the stimulation of food production and agricultural output necessarily confronted the prevailing rural class structure. The "seigneurial system" described by Barraclough and Domike was seen as one that blocked any initiatives toward agricultural improvement. Tenants within such regimes were in no position to respond to or take advantage of technological inputs, and the landlords themselves were not seen as likely entrepreneurs. Whether agricultural planners favored small or large farms, then, prevailing landed regimes were perceived as an obstacle. For planners in agencies such as the Economic Commission for Latin America, who were most interested in stimulating industrial production in urban areas, the seigneurial system also constituted an obstacle to the extent that rural oligarchies controlled or dominated the state. The stimulation of industrial development required the revamping of tax policies, banking structures, currency regulations, and so forth—the transfer of income and resources from rural oligarchies to incipient industrialists or to a developmentalist state. The developmental challenge, then, involved a political balancing act—the displacement of an entrenched oligarchy so that economic resources could be directed toward rural and urban development without simultaneously unleashing the revolutionary energies that seemed to be emanating from the countryside in the decade after 1959.

Continuing the discussion of revolutionaries and developmentalists, ignoring for the moment that neither was a coherent group, that revolutionaries and developmentalists differed among themselves, and that legions of authors that seem to share one or the other basic set of assumptions would accept neither label, we can approach some preliminary observations about the agrarian question in 1960s Latin America. To begin with, it was a question posed *about* the peasantry, not necessarily *of* or *by* them, and it was most frequently posed by urban intellectuals and activists located in universities, development agencies, state bureaus, and party committees. It was asked in conferences, lecture halls, seminar rooms, and roundtables, and the conclusions were presented in memoranda, communiques, working papers, articles, monographs, and books. This does not necessarily mean that the answers would have been better had the questions been asked by or of the peasants themselves, or had the conclusions been shared more fully and collaboratively with villagers. But we need to remember that the agrarian question was simultaneously an urban, or national, or "proletarian" question, that it seemed unavoidable for groups asking other questions and pursuing other (nonrural, nonpeasant) agendas.

With this in mind, we may return to Barraclough and Domike. By the time the essay appeared, and especially by the time the volumes of data were published (for a summary, see Barraclough 1973), the theoretical and political perspectives that informed the study (the call for land reform, the particular conception of the seigneurial system) already struck many readers as excessively cautious and narrow. This was especially true with the "consumption" (F. H. Cardoso 1977) of dependency theory in the United States during the late 1960s and early 1970s. The data presented, however, and especially the manner of organizing and presenting the data in terms of land-tenure regimes, found wider acceptance and influence. Scholars who rejected the ICAD approach and conclusions could nonetheless use their data (e.g., Bartra 1974). What is more important and less obvious, however, is that we can find in the Barraclough and Domike discussion a number of assumptions and approaches to the agrarian problem that were widely shared. This does not mean that they set the terms for the discourse on the agrarian question; it would be more accurate to say that they appropriated terms and assumptions that were already in use. Nor should this imply that the basic terms were not subject to debate. Rather, the terms provided a language for disagreement and debate; they were the terms in which various versions of the agrarian question were posed and therefore helped to structure critical thought. By examining certain key phrases in the Barraclough and Domike passage, then, we can organize our discussion of the Latin American literature.

Although I shall not examine these phrases in the order in which they appear, our first phrase comes from Barraclough and Domike's opening paragraph: *"[T]he growing manifestations of rural unrest . . . are proof that the agrarian question has gone beyond the realm of academic discussion"* (1970 [1966]:41). In one sense, this statement simply underlines what has already been claimed— the urgency of the agrarian question in the context of rural unrest. This would provide the starting point of countless studies, as perceived problem or opportunity. Yet it cannot escape notice that the agrarian question remains unspecified in this passage—indeed throughout the essay. From their list of ills, we surmise that it includes the problems of unrest, low agricultural production, and malnutrition, in which case the agrarian question is actually several related but conceptually distinct questions. We shall have occasion to return to this problem after we have examined more dimensions of the structuring of the agrarian question.

"Historically, the 'social equilibrium' in rural Latin America was characterized by the seigneurial system" [3] On this point, a number of comments are necessary. First, the conception of landed regimes as being characterized by an opposition between large and small landholdings (the "latifundia-minifundia complex") and an economic, social, political, and cultural relationship between landlords and dependent tenants, was widespread in the literature of the period. It underlay the calls for land reform; it structured accounts of landed regimes in which, say, 2 percent of the population controlled 80 percent of the land; it served as the basic assumption behind analyses of political clientelism. Compare, for example, the ICAD study of agrarian structure in seven

countries with the Vicos experiment (Dobyns, Doughty, and Lasswell 1971) in self-help, in which a team of Cornell anthropologists replaced a local landlord and attempted to introduce nonservile economic, social, and cultural practices in Vicos, Peru, or with Gerrit Huizer's survey of "the revolutionary potential of peasants in Latin America" in terms of the "culture of repression" imposed by a situation in which "the great majority of these peasants are dominated by a relatively small class of large landowners" (1972:ix).

Second, implicit in this passage is the idea that the basic structure of landed property was generalized throughout Latin America. Indeed, one of the more remarkable aspects of the literature during this period is its generalizing character, its attempt to make structural statements that would characterize Latin America as a whole. Though writers necessarily paid some attention to variation, two complementary approaches to variation were deployed: (1) typologies of landed regimes and farm types, and (2) country-by-country comparisons. The two could be combined so that the typologies could be applied to various countries and subjected to statistical comparison. Consider, for example, the influential ICAD classification of farms as "subfamily," "family," "multi-family medium," and "multifamily large," and their comparison of agrarian regimes in the seven countries in terms of the relative distribution and control of land among these types (Barraclough and Domike 1970); or Alain de Janvry's (1981) more recent and detailed classification of "precapitalist estates," "subsistence farms internal to the precapitalist estates," "capitalist estates," "commercial farms," "family farms," "external subfamily farms," "subsistence farms in corporate communities," and "landless workers." De Janvry's classification and comparison represent the results of more than a decade's output of studies of agrarian problems, as well as his explicit placement within a Marxist framework. In both cases, however, the spirit is generalizing and comparative—generalizing in the attempt to broadly characterize the nature of Latin American landed regimes and comparative in its attempt to understand differentiation in terms of sociological typologies and statistical distributions. Missing in such exercises is a detailed study of social relations within particular regions, or an attempt to understand the complex economic, social, cultural, and political relations that connect and divide individuals within and between postulated farm types. Instead, it is assumed that a subfamily farm or a subsistence farm internal to the precapitalist estates in Peru is comparable with and in many ways similar to a subfamily farm or subsistence farm internal to the precapitalist estates in Chile or Argentina.

Third, it is not insignificant that the characterization of the seigneurial system begins with the word, *historically*. All characterizations of landed regimes contained a historical argument, which was usually explicit. In the most common versions, the agrarian regime was established in the colonial encounter between Spaniards and indigenous populations, implanted by colonists, and maintained by succeeding generations of oligarchical landlords. We shall let Gerrit Huizer speak for many:

The colonial period brought forms of social organization to Latin America which persist in many areas. Although there is considerable variation from country to country and from region to region, on the whole, the social system in rural Latin America is characterized by the latifundia or the *hacienda* (*fazenda* in Brazil) system. The fertile valleys or coastal lowlands, during the precolonial civilizations cultivated by the indigenous groups, were transformed into large estates belonging to the conquerors and their heirs. In some areas, they were used for pasture, elsewhere for plantation agriculture. The indigenous peasantry was in part sent as cheap labor to the mines in which the conquerors were most interested, or were driven into subsistence agriculture on the mountain slopes if they did not want to work on the estates. . . .

After the end of the colonial epoch, the local white or mestizo elite in most of the Latin American countries expanded its wealth and power in an aggressive way, mainly at the cost of the indigenous peasants. Thus, the process of pushing back the indigenous peasant population towards more remote and even more barren agricultural areas was initiated. (Huizer 1972:1)

Theoretical debates concentrated on the conceptualization of the historical foundations of the seigneurial system, whether, for example, the landed estate was to be seen primarily as a feudal institution providing for the consumption and prestige of the landlord, or a capitalist institution, "born as a commercial enterprise which created for itself the institutions which permitted it to respond to increased demand in the world or national market by expanding the amount of its land, capital, and labor and to increase the supply of its products" (Frank 1969:14). Despite debate and disagreement, many authors could agree that the basic agrarian structure in Latin America was the latifundia-minifundia complex, with admitted variations, and that the complex was established, "historically," in the colonial era, and was maintained and expanded after independence.

"Particularly since the Second World War the traditional rural production systems have become increasingly out of adjustment. . . ." The historical interpretation of the persistence of landed regimes carried with it a contention that change had begun to occur in recent decades. Barraclough and Domike's statement of this view expresses a functionalist framework, but the sense that recent changes had begun to upset structures that had lasted for centuries could be felt by those who shared neither Barraclough and Domike's functionalism nor their politics.

In general, this particular construction reflects what Frank and others writing in the 1960s criticized as a "dual economy" view—an analytical separation of the society into traditional and modern sectors which roughly correspond with rural and urban or agricultural and industrial. In this view, the rural tradition was characterized by the type of landed regime discussed earlier, but it also included a range of agricultural practices involving "traditional" techniques— oxen-drawn, iron-tipped plows and digging sticks—and "subsistence" crops such as corn, beans, squash, manioc, or potatoes; ways of village life that stressed sociality and kin ties; reproduction strategies that involved multiple offspring; and so forth. In one of the most vivid expressions of this view, George Foster began his classic ethnography of Tzintzuntzan with the observation that, "It is a paradox of our century that, at a time when some men confidently reach through outer space, others live in small, isolated communities where the way of life is only now beginning to change from that of the time of Christ" (1967:3). The modern transformation could include anything that upset "tradition"—a transformation of the landed regime, the introduction of cash crops, the investment of capital in agriculture, the out-migration of villagers, the urbanization or suburbanization of a village, or the adoption by villagers of reproduction strategies stressing fewer offspring. Because so many of the changes that upset this particular understanding of tradition occurred in the decades following World War II, especially with the developmental initiatives of the 1960s, the view that the countryside was being transformed, or that modernization was happening, or that some sort of "transition" (demographic, social, technological) was occurring, was widespread. It could be celebrated, by developmental agents for example, or its passing bemoaned, by romantic celebrants of rural virtues, or modernization and development could be seen as a necessity and challenge full of political and social danger, as in the work of people like Barraclough and Domike. But the historical divide, and the sense of recent dramatic change, seemed obvious enough.

The best-known and most dramatically stated critique of dual economy theories was expressed in the dependency theory of Andre Gunder Frank. Again and again, he contended that Latin American societies were "dialectical" rather than "dual," that backwardness, tradition, and underdevelopment were not original conditions but the results of centuries of capitalist development in Latin America and that "the regions which are the most underdeveloped and feudal-seeming today are the ones which had the closest ties to the metropolis in the past. They are the regions which were the greatest exporters of primary products to and the biggest sources of capital for the world metropolis and were abandoned by the metropolis when for one reason or another business fell off" (Frank 1969:13). This particular structure of tradition, then, was itself part of the structure of capitalist modernity. Marxist critics of Frank, especially those who contributed to the so-called mode-of-production literature, could accept Frank's view of world-historical connectedness, the contention that rural backwardness was a product of the developmental process, but they rejected Frank's definition of capitalism. Capitalism was characterized by free wage labor, and rural labor regimes in Latin America were not free and not based upon wage labor until . . . until the investment of capital in agriculture, the transformation of landed regimes, the agrarian transition. The transition could follow a landlord or "junker" path or a small farm or "farmer" path, and for understanding of the dynamics of these two paths we could turn to Lenin's *Development of Capitalism in Russia* (1974 [1899]). In the process, however, with a different language and with different political valuations, they had reconstituted the same historical dividing line: *"Particularly since the Second World War the traditional rural production systems have become. . . ."*

This does not mean that we need to return to Frank and his followers. Despite the radical appearance of the invocation of a capitalist history, the categories of tradition, backwardness, and subsistence remained historically and sociologically empty because the history ascribed to them was too general and too deeply embedded within a past that could still be seen as unchanging. The basic oppositions—tradition and modernity, rural and urban, subsistence and commerce—were unchallenged and unchanged. To a surprising degree, they remain so. Critics of development, who cannot be accused of the sins of modernization theory, may nonetheless work with the same sense of chronological development. Burbach and Flynn's *Agribusiness in the Americas* (1980) or the various works of the Food First group (Lappé and Collins 1978; Collins 1982) offer a critique of commercial agriculture that assumes and places a positive value on more traditional practices that are thought to have been more self-sufficient and subsistence-oriented. We therefore confront an implicit historical grid that seems to contain a number of analogous oppositions:

subsistence	commerce
self-sufficiency	dependence
internal market	external market
precapitalism	capitalism

If we add tradition and modernity, the circle of self-confirming assumptions is closed.

In this case, we are confronting a romantic evocation of a self-sufficient past. In other cases, we encounter a critique of that past in contrast with the virtues of a developmentalist present. Such radically different valuations matter less than the static and oppositional reading of history, a reading established with the developmentalist reading of the agrarian question and reproduced in surprising ways by even their most vociferous critics.

One is reminded of Raymond Williams' observation in *The Country and the City* (1973) that various moments in English literature have produced requiems for a changing, disappearing countryside. For whatever moment one chose, however, writers contended that the ways of life and livelihood whose disappearance they mourned had disappeared only recently, or within the memory of those now living. As one read further back, one encountered a constantly receding, constantly disappearing rural idyll. Although Williams was evaluating romantic constructions of rural life in opposition to urban or industrial society, his commentary can guide us in our consideration of a wider variety of political evaluations of a changing countryside. The view of a recently changing, disappearing, or "out-of-adjustment" countryside necessarily carries with it a historical interpretation and a political construction, both of which might be implicit. We can render the interpretation explicit by exploring the identifying characteristics of the perceived moment of transformation. In this sense, it does not matter whether the view of recent fundamental change is true: it *is*. The myriad of developmental initiatives in the 1960s—from community development programs that built roads, irrigation dams, or houses, or extended electricity or potable water to villages, or introduced public health clinics, or introduced new strains of coffee, corn, or potatoes, to land reform initiatives of various types—these did indeed represent profound transformations. But so were the changes associated with urbanization and other forms of migration, which began in some countries before World War II, in others after. So were the changes precipitated by the collapse of the world market in the 1930s. So were the changes associated with the flurry of road and railroad building during the "dance of the millions" of the 1920s in places like Colombia and Peru. So were the changes instituted by the Mexican Revolution. So were the changes that occurred in coffee-growing regions from the 1870s to the 1930s. And so on. This does not mean that change has been constant and that all changes have been equally important. But we need to pay more attention to the analytic process by which certain changes are selected and designated as historical markers or moments of transformation. We structure our historical accounts around changes that we think are more significant, and we assign significance in terms of a larger narrative. When an anthropologist like George Foster contrasts men on the moon with villagers emerging from ways of life established at the time of Christ, we see, more vividly than in other accounts, an ideology and a history. But there is also an ideology and history in Barraclough and Domike's view of fundamental changes since World War II, or in Burbach and Flynn's (1980) analysis of the implantation of North American agribusiness in the Americas, or in Frances Moore Lappe's opposition between subsistence and cash cropping (Lappé and Collins 1978). In each, a moment of change marks a dividing line between a period without history, or a period when economic, political, and social structures were more stable, and a period of profound change and transformation.

   "The agrarian problem must be understood as one reflecting the very structure of society." This simple statement provoked little controversy; debate concentrated on the nature and character of the "very structure of society," the connecting threads between the rural village and the commanding heights of society. Nor should such a statement provoke controversy. As with reference to

recent changes, so with reference to structural connections and determinations; the statements were "true." The manner in which structural connections were asserted and examined had consequences for the conception and resolution of the agrarian question, however. Here I briefly indicate a range of approaches to structural connections and determinations, and indicate some of the more general consequences of the structural studies.

For developmentalist authors such as Barraclough and Domike, the postulated connection is located at the upper end of the class structure. The landlords who had controlled the land for centuries also controlled or dominated the state. They blocked any sort of development—be it expansion of food production, infrastructural construction, industrial development, or the expansion of social services. All such changes threatened their entrenched economic and political position. The challenge of land reform involved a dual displacement of the landlord class—their displacement from political power and their displacement from control of land. This was not always admitted by state planners and development agents; the kinds of structural change necessary for such reforms were often not possible politically without a major social upheaval. The history of land reform movements is therefore inseparable from the recent political history of Latin American countries (see de Janvry 1981:202–23). The reforms themselves and the political history remain outside the scope of this essay; here it is only necessary to stress that the structural connections were sought at the commanding heights. The tenants, peasants, and rural laborers themselves received less attention. This is not to say they were ignored. Community development programs of various sorts engaged local producers, but most of these programs attempted to place themselves outside of, or to set aside, the "very structure of society." Applied development programs brought to apparently isolated rural villages some of the benefits of modernity: new seeds, better latrines, roads, potable water, radios. To the extent, then, that developmentalists considered the structure of society, they ignored villagers; to the extent that they engaged with villagers, they ignored the structure of society.

The more radical writers—the dependency theorists and Marxists—tended to pay more attention to the entire agrarian structure in their analyses. With their often explicit commitment to a socialist transformation, their structural analyses necessarily considered powerholders and dominated alike. In practice, this took the form of class analysis, the placement of various urban and rural sectors within a postulated hierarchy of classes and class fractions. Such placements ranged from the relatively simple to the complex. In Frank's extreme version of dependency theory, everything had been capitalist since the sixteenth century. His critique of dual economy theories and the presumed feudal character of the countryside led him to see rural landlords as a rural detachment of the comprador bourgeoisie. Peasants and tenants, on the other hand, were the real proletariat, the true revolutionary hope (see, for example, Frank 1969:350–61).

Cardoso and Faletto (1979) link their class analyses to a historical argument that allows more room for variation in time and space. In their historical analysis, they concentrate on the consequences of the period of outward expansion in the nineteenth century, the establishment of export economies generally organized around agricultural exports. Ignoring the question of feudalism versus capitalism but also avoiding the trap of a dualistic assumption that might remove rural society from its historically established social, economic, and political connections with developmental processes, they explore the nature of a variety of "bourgeois-oligarchic" pacts—the connections among urban agro-exporting elites and rural landholders during a period of agricultural expansion. For this period, their primary distinction contrasts "enclave" economies, in which the local bourgeois-oligarchic groups lost control to foreign interests, with those countries in which local bourgeois-oligarchic groups were able to retain control of the export sector and state. The political and economic development of the twentieth century has been the development of an internal market, the expansion of "middle" social sectors that benefit from and participate in that market, and the demand for an opening of the political system to these groups, the displacement of those involved in the bourgeois-oligarchic pact from their exclusive hold on power. The class analysis and political history Cardoso and Faletto conduct contrasts the various paths these middle groups have taken to power, the nature of the states and the political alliances that have resulted, and the new forms of economic dependence and multinational domination that have emerged. Satisfying as this analysis is in comparison with the catastrophism of a Frank, problems remain. Despite the attention to variation, different countries are still being fit into a fairly general scheme. Moreover, it cannot escape notice that rural villagers disappear from the analysis altogether, except as they join the "middle" classes—who sustain an urban character.

Here we need to consider a range of Marxist attempts to place rural people within class analysis. Although the focus of this discussion remains fixed on the larger structure of argument, a careful examination of the strengths and weaknesses of rural class analysis requires that we examine specific studies and debates in detail. I concentrate here on the Mexican literature of the late 1960s and early 1970s, the specificity of which needs to be stressed. Despite this specificity, despite the fact that Peruvian or Brazilian analyses and debates did not simply replicate the assumptions and arguments of the Mexican literature, a brief examination of literature from a single area illuminates more general problems with the literature on rural class analysis. We might begin with Rodolfo Stavenhagen's *Las Clases Sociales en las Sociedades Agrarias* (1969), an explicitly Marxist attempt to conduct a class analysis of Latin

American and other peasantries. Of special interest in Stavenhagen's treatment is its eclectic character—its attempt to conduct a structural class analysis that took account of the advances of dependency literature and its attempt to pay attention to anthropological literature on indigenous communities in Mexico and Guatemala. His book is really three loosely related essays. A first essay on class structure in agrarian societies undertakes a general contribution to the concept of class and a specific analysis of particular countries, in which the class analysis is largely a list of structural terms. For Mexico, for example, he identifies four groups of private landholders: minifundistas, middle peasants, a peasant bourgeoisie, and large landowners. He then classifies a group of *ejidatarios,* seen as similar to minifundistas and middle peasants, and various groups of agricultural workers, including migrant laborers. He also places these groups within a distinction between modern and traditional structures and attempts a statistical distribution (1969:96, passim). This structural breakdown is repeated for various other countries and regions. A second essay deals with commercial agriculture and class structure in the Ivory Coast; a third considers class and ethnicity in Mesoamerica. In an evaluation and reanalysis of much anthropological literature, Stavenhagen sets aside the structural distinctions and statistical distributions and interprets a centuries-long historical process in which indigenous communities had been incorporated within the colonial structure, and in which ethnic distinctions were simultaneously class distinctions. He then considers postcolonial developments in which the congruence between class and ethnicity is broken, the ethnic character of indigenous communities retains importance, yet class distinctions and determinations continue to develop, imposing two systems of stratification.

The distinct forms of class analysis contained in parts 1 and 3 of Stavenhagen's book suggest a kind of tension that was resolved by later writers in favor of the style presented in part 1. That is, the extent to which particular historical experiences, regional variation, or ethnic identification imposed a different character on class structures or on social and political processes was largely ignored. Instead, just as Velazco's regime declared that Indians were thenceforth peasants in Peru after 1968, radical social scientists could proudly subsume ethnicity within class labels. As they did so, however, most writers were unsympathetic toward Stavenhagen's style of structural categorization, which remained essentially rural, classifying various sorts of rural groups. Of more interest for the next group of Marxists was a placement of rural groups within a wider, national structure of classes. Ricardo Pozas and Isabel de Pozas' study of *Los Indios en las Clases Sociales de México* (1971), for example, not only sidestepped the ethnic question altogether, but quickly placed rural villagers within larger classes, situating rich and middle peasants within bourgeois and petty bourgeois classes and considering poor peasants, minifundistas, and others a detachment of the proletariat. That the bourgeois and proletarian labels carried modifiers like *rural, agrarian,* or *agricultural* was less significant than the fact that various groups of people were being placed in a capitalist two-class scheme.

Roger Bartra's influential analysis (1974) attempted to avoid either a dualistic analysis of traditional and modern sectors or a simple subsumption of rural villagers within capitalist classes by adopting a model of articulating modes of production. In his view, Mexico was subcapitalist, a situation characterized by the articulation of a capitalist and a simple commodity mode of production, the latter of which included a numerous peasantry. The simple commodity mode did not exist in isolation, however; peasants produced commodities that entered capitalist circuits of circulation and were exploited by merchants, usurers, and landlords—the same rural bourgeoisie that was exploiting rural laborers. The mechanisms through which peasants were exploited tended to promote differentiation into comfortable, middle-level and poor or semiproletarian statuses, undermining the very basis for their reproduction. Thus, "unlike the situation of the proletarian, the exploitation of the peasant does not tend to reproduce the conditions for the extraction of surplus labor. On the contrary it tends to make them disappear, to transform them into an authentic extraction of surplus value; that is, it tends to proletarianize the peasant" (Bartra 1974:84).

This conclusion was controversial, provoking criticisms from "peasantist" scholars who might share the view that Mexico was characterized by a distinction between capitalist and noncapitalist (peasant or simple commodity) modes of production but would contend that Bartra and others who followed that line of analysis were too quick to subsume the dynamics of the noncapitalist mode within capitalism, ignoring the resources, dynamics, and potential for reproduction and expansion of the noncapitalist mode. In both his more general essays and his magisterial *We come to object* (1981), the result of a collaborative study of peasant villages in Eastern Morelos, Arturo Warman was perhaps the most persuasive Mexican scholar arguing against a "proletarianization" perspective.

Much of the literature on peasants that emerged over the succeeding decade and a half, in Mexico and elsewhere, was concerned with this debate. Given a structural disjunction between noncapitalist and capitalist spheres, what was the fate of the peasantry in such a situation of structural inequality and exploitation? Should it be analyzed "on its own terms," as a group capable of a certain resilience, capable of reproducing itself at once outside of and in relation to a dominant capitalist sector? Or should the peasantry be seen as a "class or a fraction of a class within different modes of production—a class that is essential in modes like feudalism and transitory (and hence only a fraction of a class) in others, like capitalism" (de Janvry 1981:106). Although various authors on both sides (such as de Janvry in the passage cited) rejected the concept of "articulation of modes of production," the initial problem and debate arose from it.

The debate is now frequently seen as one between Chayanov and Lenin—or, more accurately, between followers of Chayanov or Lenin. To a certain extent this is true. Those who were most interested in the internal dynamics of peasant agriculture might turn to Chayanov's model of the peasant household, the linkage of peasant decision making with the developmental cycle of the household, and the process of "demographic differentiation" (Chayanov 1966 [1925]). Those interested in proletarianization might draw their inspiration from Lenin's *Development of Capitalism in Russia* (1974 [1899]) or Kautsky's *The Agrarian Question* (1974 [1899]). It is worth noting, however, how many scholars used both Chayanov and Lenin. While writing a largely Leninist analysis of the disappearance of the peasantry, for example, Bartra (1974) used Chayanov in his discussion of peasant agriculture (having earlier written an introduction for a Spanish edition of Chayanov's work), and used Chayanov's concept of "self-exploitation" as a central element in his analysis of the exploitation of peasant households.

Of greater importance, however, is the generalized appropriation of these Russian and German writers on the agrarian question in Europe in the late nineteenth and early twentieth centuries for the analysis of an agrarian question in the last third of the twentieth century in Latin America. As sources of ideas, models, and inspiration, such appropriation requires little comment. But the appropriations were generally much more than that. They served as filters through which the "Mexican reality" (say) was to be viewed; they provided the central concepts and categories. By the late 1970s, a textual strategy such as that followed by Bartra was common, in which the author could move quickly from a statement of a desire to produce a class analysis of the Mexican countryside to a detailed summary of "Lenin's scheme" and "Marx's scheme," or could begin virtually every chapter with a theoretical discussion that was based on a discussion of Marx's or Lenin's texts. From these texts (and from Chayanov), an array of sociological categories is generated, which can then be applied to "the Mexican reality." Certain distinctive features such as the *ejido* can then be mentioned, and one can find occasional reference to Mayans, for example. But both the *ejidos* and the Mayans finally disappear into the structural categories of comfortable, middle, and poor peasants. We then have a bibliography that is full of references to classic Marxist texts, or texts from the literature on the agrarian question in early twentieth-century Europe, texts from contemporary political debate, and statistical studies of conditions in the Mexican countryside. Anthropological or historical studies of particular regions, communities, or peasantries are notable for their absence.

This is not to say that the "peasantists" are any less guilty in this regard.

Rare are the studies such as Warman's careful study of the peasants of Eastern Morelos, which combines sociological sophistication with a richly detailed examination of peasant households and villages, and their unfolding relations with landlords and the Mexican state. Yet it is disconcerting to see how many of the field studies that were published by Warman's ethnographic collaborators and students began their accounts with simple assertions regarding the centrality of the peasant household, followed not by an examination of the formation of particular kinds of peasant households in eastern Morelos but by a casual reference to Chayanov, as if that settled all questions. The more the peasantists broke loose from specific regions like eastern Morelos and moved toward more theoretical studies, the more pronounced this tendency became. The analysis of peasantries was hardly conducted "on their own terms;" it was conducted on, or through, Chayanov's terms.

We need to concentrate on the act of appropriation as a problem. We have already considered the political nature of the agrarian question in the 1960s and 70s, and the fact that the agrarian problem arose in the context of a threatened, or perceived, or hoped-for socialist transformation. As intellectuals, many of the contributors to the literature on, say, rural Mexico, were active socialists. It is unsurprising, then, that the classics of the socialist literature on the agrarian question in the early twentieth century would be republished or made more widely available in Latin America, North America, and Europe, and that intellectuals would turn to these classics for theoretical and political inspiration and guidance. In their consideration of an agrarian question, these early twentieth-century writers seemed to be addressing a series of questions that were broadly similar to the ones facing Latin American intellectuals and activists. There were also some important differences, however. To consider them, we need to return to the question that begins this section. Having discussed certain structuring assumptions in the literature, we are now able to consider the question, "What was the agrarian question?"

As already indicated, the agrarian question was actually a number of related but distinct questions, not only because intellectuals and activists working from different positions and for different agendas were asking it. Even from a single political vantage point, the agrarian question was multiple. It was simultaneously a set of political and economic questions. Among the political questions were these: Who were the peasants? What were their agendas, commitments, and loyalties? Could they serve as a revolutionary force, or could they only be mobilized in alliance with other groups? Was a "worker-peasant alliance" possible? The economic questions included the following: What was the nature of economic development in the countryside? How were peasants incorporated within the larger society? For both sets of questions, a variety of more or less prescriptive queries might emerge, depending on the agendas and assumptions of those posing the questions. For the developmentalist, for example, the economic question concerned the manner in which developmental initiatives could be introduced without precipitating major political upheavals. For the socialist, the economic question might concern the nature of capitalist development in the countryside, the extent to which peasants had been incorporated within capitalist circuits of production and circulation, and therefore the structural bases for a class alliance between workers and peasants. The debate between dependency and mode-of-production theorists on capitalist development therefore had directly political consequences.

The agrarian question was not only a set of political and economic questions, however; at another level, it was a political question that was given a primarily economic answer. To know who the peasants were and how they would act in a political upheaval, or how they could be incorporated within an urban-directed socialist movement, one had to analyze their class position, their role and fate in capitalist development, their relation to the state. What linked the political and economic questions was class analysis, and one of the constants in the literature across various political and theoretical currents is the attempt to analyze the social class structure of the countryside—from the ICAD distinctions among subfamily, family, and multifamily farms to Bartra's placement of peasants in a simple commodity mode of production articulated with a capitalist mode within an overall structure of "subcapitalist" accumulation. The agrarian question began, then, with the activity or threatened/potential activity of the peasantry and quickly moved to a consideration of "the very structure of society," conceived as a class structure.

There is nothing necessarily wrong with this; the two questions are *necessarily* linked. Nonetheless, it was in this movement, in the very manner in which the class analysis was conceived, that we came to understand so poorly "the manifold ways whereby peasants have continuously engaged their political worlds" (Stern 1987:9). The shared language of analysis, an analysis that perceived a political movement and problem and saw the need to consider that problem as part of the "very structure of society," a structure based on a seigneurial system established "historically" in the colonial encounter, dictated the displacement of peasants from the very structure and history that seemed to make sense of them.

What is Wrong with This Question?

In fact, it was especially in the aftermath of the Cuban Revolution that such questions began to be posed clearly for Latin America, and it may have been inevitable that the Cuban case would generate large numbers of kremlinologists in sombreros, eager to apply and misapply their knowledge of East European political history to a wholly new situation. One of the major stumbling-blocks in such exercises—though by no means the only one—was the general lack of understanding of Latin American rural life, and the uncritical transfer of such concepts as "the peasantry" from Europe to the Americas. The term "peasant" has often been used, and is sometimes still used, both for Latin America and elsewhere, to describe agrarian folk without distinction. It may carry pejorative overtones of illiteracy, backwardness, conservatism, or stupidity, even when it is purportedly being used sympathetically. Sometimes rural Latin America has been described as populated entirely by "peasants." When such loose usage has occurred in attempts to depict a society such as pre-revolutionary Cuba, the resulting interpretations of political events have been misleading (Mintz 1974a:292–93).

Sidney Mintz's complaint, which appeared relatively early in the explosion of the literature on peasantries (appearing in volume 1 of the *Journal of Peasant Studies*) took the early literature on the Cuban Revolution as a case study of the misunderstanding of rural life in Latin America. Exploring misperceptions of the "peasant" character of the countryside and of the rural toilers who participated in the revolution, Mintz demonstrates that they failed to consider the capitalist character of the sugar estates or the long-established rural proletariat that worked on them. He then raised a series of questions that place us in good position to move beyond Cuba and consider certain problems with the literature on the agrarian question in Latin America.

The structure of Cuban rural society had been shaped during the nineteenth century by the continual growth of the sugar industry, and by substantial changes in the distribution of land, capital, and work opportunities, as well as by a heavy importation of labor, in ethnic and racial succession, both before Emancipation and after. Without much more data on the character of rural life in that country before 1959, effective and convincing analyses of the roles of different classes in the making of the revolution will be difficult to develop. The very definition of the peasantry in the Cuban case can prove to be a puzzle. If one means by "peasantry" the *colono* class of independent cane producers whose security of tenure was won by legislation in the 1930s, then "peasant" here should probably read "farmer," in Wolf's usage (1969:xiv–xv), and members of this group probably never assumed a pro-revolutionary posture. If one means those other small-scale landholders of the sort who inhabited the Sierra Maestra, within which the major guerrilla *foco* (center, area of control) was sustained, then preliminary distinctions would have to be drawn according to security of tenure, size of holding, principal crop and other criteria. Even though we know something of the role of such people in supporting the *foco* and serving in its ranks, we are not able to go much further in specifying their pre-revolutionary social and economic position in regional rural life. Again, if one refers to the agricultural squatters (*precaristas*) common in the Sierra Maestra, and struggling to hold land in the periphery of a large plantation zone, these folk do not effectively qualify as a peasantry—or barely. They may indeed have played an important part, however, in sustaining the revolution.

Finally, we are left with the class of landless wage-earning workers, numerous and strong in Oriente, and soon providing a good deal of the manpower of the *foco* even while peasant recruitment lagged (Wolf 1969:270). How important these workers may have been in fuelling the Revolution, particularly after the guerrilla *focos* had become militarily defensible, remains a largely unanswered question (ibid.:296).

Although the entire thrust of Mintz's discussion differs from that of the other approaches to the agrarian question encountered earlier, a number of simplistic ways of characterizing that difference are denied us. It would be inaccurate to claim, for example, that the earlier studies were too structural. Mintz's questions are profoundly structural. Nor would it be fair to say that Mintz paid more attention to history or to the particular than did other analysts. We have already encountered historical constructions in other modes of proposing an agrarian question. And although we have encountered a number of theorists who showed little interest in local detail (Huizer's [1972:1] dismissal—"Although there is considerable variation from country to country and from region to region, on the whole . . ."—serves as a paradigmatic statement of this style of generalizing sociology), many others did. The analyses of Stavenhagen, Pozas and Pozas, and Bartra were attempts to understand the class structure of the Mexican countryside, just as, in an earlier period, Kautsky's, Lenin's, and Chayanov's studies were attempts to understand the structure and dynamics of the German and Russian countryside. Nonetheless, the conceptions of structure and history differ profoundly in these examples, as does the understanding of what is required for an analysis of a particular situation. We can explore these differences by leaving Mintz and Cuba for the moment and returning to Lenin and Chayanov in Russia.

Neither Lenin's nor Chayanov's studies of the Russian countryside could have been conducted outside of a particular historical context: the land reforms of 1861, marking the demise of the junker estates and the expansion of peasant agriculture, organized through households and community (*mir*) landholding and land distribution units. By the 1870s, a census and statistical apparatus had been set up through local assemblies (the *zemstvos*), which produced a wealth of detailed statistical materials on households and farms in the Russian countryside. The dynamics and fate of those peasants were the subject of a late nineteenth-century agrarian question raised among two groups of Marxists, a populist group who saw the peasant community as a bridge toward socialism that would allow Russia to bypass the capitalist stage, and another group, for whom Lenin was to become the most vigorous spokesman, who saw the same laws of capitalist development working in Russia that had worked in England, and who examined the dynamics of capitalist development in the countryside. By the early twentieth century, a "neopopulist" group had emerged that set the larger political and economic questions aside and attended to those organizational and structural features of the peasant household thought to characterize peasant agriculture regardless of the larger societal structure in which the household operated or the political and economic dynamics and demands that pressed upon it.

The statistics gathered by late nineteenth-century economists, and in the early twentieth century by the neopopulist Organization and Production

School, provided the basic material analyzed in the writings of Lenin, Chayanov, and others who contributed to the debate on the fate of the Russian peasantry. They lend the works an appearance of specificity, the application of theory to practice, or the analysis of empirical materials in a theoretically informed and sophisticated way. Their most important problem, however, is that they are not really about the Russian peasantry at all. They invoke a particular peasantry without confronting that peasantry's particularity.

Let us take Lenin as an example. His *Development of Capitalism in Russia* (1974 [1899]) weds a historical analysis of feudalism and capitalism with a detailed (but consistently synchronic) analysis of *zemstvo* statistics for particular regions, demonstrating the differentiation among the peasantry since the land reforms, the emergence of large peasant farms and pauperized masses, and so on. A number of his observations are insightful, especially his criticism of the use of statistical averages and aggregates in ways that conceal fundamental differences and his argument that the presence of small-scale landholding often fools observers into ignoring the reality of wage work and proletarianization that characterizes poor peasants' lives. Yet his historical account is a universal history, given Russian markers. It is structured by an overarching opposition between natural economy and commodity economy, from which virtually everything else follows. Certain aspects of the social division of labor, of the process of accumulation and class formation, are thought to be inevitable with the development of commodity economy unless artificial political barriers are constructed in the doomed attempt to prevent the laws of commodity economy from operating. In this view, such obstacles only worsen the condition of direct producers, who suffer even more from the incompleteness of capitalist development than from its full operation. The 1861 reforms are then cited to mark the transition in Russia from feudalism to capitalism, and *zemstvo* statistics are used to demonstrate the development of capitalism in the countryside despite the continued existence of political obstacles and prohibitions.

In Kautsky's *Agrarian Question* (1974 [1899]), we find a sophisticated examination of census materials from England, France, Germany, and the United States, and once again we encounter a number of insightful observations—in this case, a careful treatment of the situation of small-scale producers trying to reproduce their farms and households within mercantile circuits of capital circulation and accumulation. Moreover, his project has a more comparative intent. He proposes to study "all the transformations in agriculture under the capitalist mode of production. That is, to determine "*if and how capital takes control of agriculture, transforms it and makes untenable the old forms of production and property, and creates the necessity of new ones*" (Kautsky 1974 [1899]: 12, emphasis in original). Yet once again the statistics are examined in terms of a universal historical narrative organized around centuries-long historical epochs; the "old forms" are feudal, and the fundamental transition is one from feudalism to capitalism. On feudal agriculture, Kautsky offers a much more detailed sociological analysis of peasant agriculture, exploring classic three-field rotation schemes, their consequences for village life and household strategies, and the social and economic consequences for peasants of the demise of open-field agriculture. Nonetheless, the peasant remains transhistorical, and one of Kautsky's opening chapters posits a prior union of agriculture and manufacture within the peasant household, exploring the consequences for peasants of the rupture of the presumed prior union, turning the peasant household into a primarily agricultural household.

Chayanov's (1966 [1925]) concentration on the organizational features and dynamics of the peasant household also contained a universal historical assumption in his contention that through such concentration he was uncovering "our economic past," a past characterized by natural economy. Indeed, the images of the self-sufficient household in natural economy are remarkably similar in Lenin, Kautsky, and Chayanov. The rest of Chayanov's work attempts to set all history aside. Despite its use of statistics on Russian peasants, then, it is not about the Russian peasantry at all, as it makes no attempt to determine how this peasantry is like or unlike other peasantries, or what effects the land reforms of 1861 or the Stolypin Reforms after the 1905 Revolution might have had on peasant households in this or that region.

It is interesting to contrast, then, Marx's own attempt (in Shanin 1983) toward the end of his life to understand the Russian peasantry. Asked by populist Russian Marxists to communicate his opinion on their view that the peasant commune might serve as a bridge toward socialism, Marx attempted to answer them historically and sociologically. He taught himself to read Russian and studied works by economists and political activists on the peasant commune, the landlord economy, the reforms of 1861, the expansion of peasant agriculture, the relationships between peasant villagers and merchants, former landlords, and the state. He then wrote a number of drafts before settling on a brief, noncommittal published response. The drafts and the final response have recently been gathered in English (with commentaries by Derek Sayer, Philip Corrigan, and others) by Teodor Shanin (1983), but the texts themselves have been available in a variety of languages, including French and Spanish, for a number of years (e.g., Godelier 1969, 1970), and were therefore available to the same writers who were appropriating the texts of Lenin and Kautsky. I would disagree with Shanin's contention that the texts indicate a "late Marx" who rejected his earlier evolutionistic and universalistic analyses of capitalism. I think we can find much the same historical sensibility in Marx's attempts to understand the emergence of Bonapartism in mid-nineteenth-century France, especially *Class Struggles in France* (1974a [1850]) and *The Eighteenth Brumaire of Louis Bonaparte* (1974b [1852]). I agree, however, with Shanin's assessment of the Marxism that emerges from these texts and its radical disjunction with the Marxisms of the Second, Third and Fourth Internationals. Here, Marx's specific observations and conclusions in the various texts of his response to the Russian populists are less important than his methodological stance, one that rejected a universal history and contended that

thus events of striking similarity, taking place in different historical contexts, led to totally disparate results. By studying each of these developments separately, and then comparing them, one may easily discover the key to this phenomenon. But success will never come with the master-key of a general historico-philosophical theory, whose supreme virtue consists in being supra-historical (quoted in Shanin 1983:136).

This served as a point of departure, a founding assumption. Politically, and therefore intellectually, it was untenable to attempt to resolve the agrarian question in Russia by applying a body of statistics to a universal historical scheme. For Marx, the only conceivable response was one that attempted to grasp what was historically, socially, and politically particular about the Russian countryside in the 1870s and 80s.

If we examine his earlier texts on France, we see the same interest. His comments on the French peasantry as forming an immense, homogeneous mass of isolated households with no relations among themselves, a sack of sociological potatoes, are clearly intended to characterize French peasants in the mid-nineteenth century and are linked to an analysis of the demise of the landlord class after the French Revolution, the creation of a small-scale peasantry and the subsequent capture of that peasantry by usurious merchants and a taxing state. Subsequent appropriations of Marx's text by Marxists have left out the historically particular analyses by Marx and elevated the sociological conclusions to the status of a universal truth about peasants.

Again, what matters is less the specific conclusions and more the historical and sociological sensibility. This split between a transhistorical, universal Marxism and a historical materialism that sees the analysis of specific historical conjunctures as a necessary starting point for political and economic analysis constitutes a crucial political and intellectual divide. One of the most important problems with the Marxist literature on the agrarian question in Latin America in the 1960s and 1970s was that its most visible spokesmen worked with a transhistorical Marxism. Their attempts to analyze, say, the Mexican peasantry historically and structurally therefore placed that peasantry within a "general historico-philosophical theory, whose supreme virtue consists in being supra-historical." As they did so, they were able to communicate with a variety of non-Marxist social scientists writing on the agrarian question, who might reject the Marxists' specific conclusions and labels but would share a similar generalizing, transhistorical approach. They spoke a common language.

Let us return, then to the questions Mintz posed regarding rural Cuba, and consider how different they are from then prevailing models for addressing the agrarian question, and how similar they are to the questions Marx posed concerning Russia. The history they interrogate is no longer the epochal history of the transition from feudalism to capitalism or of the seigneurial system established in the colonial era. Instead, they consider the prerevolutionary and revolutionary experiences of particular groups of people in specific regions— the *colonos* in the cane zone, the smallholders and squatters of the Sierra Maestra, and the rural proletarians in Oriente. Such questions and considerations do not preclude structural analysis; we are not working with an opposition between structuralist approaches, on the one hand, and historical studies on the other. Indeed, in the very article in which Mintz criticizes the uncritical application of European concepts like "peasantry" to vast stretches of the Latin American countryside, he defends the use of sociological typologies of rural peoples:

Typologies of classes and of enterprises, particularly for the rural sectors of agrarian societies, are not mere cubbyholes of classification. Study of the relationships among rural groups in specific socio-historical contexts is not circumvented by a typological approach; instead, this approach aims at clarifying the possible range of such relationships. The specification of class, ethnic, "racial" and other dimensions of group assortment, then, should enable the observer to understand the interplay of groups and of group interests more clearly. The typology, in short, is not a reification of social reality, but rather an experimental attempt to deal with that reality (Mintz 1974a:298).

In this view, the crucial distinction is not one between a "structural" approach and one dealing with "real people doing real things;" even less is it one between something called *structure* and something called *agency*. Mintz clearly recognizes that avowedly non- or antistructural approaches carry an implicit understanding of structural relationships or "reduce group behaviour to an infinite range of individual variation, [avoiding] the need to examine the contradictory quality of relationships between and among groups" (Mintz 1974a: 299). The critical distinction here, then, is between structural concepts and typologies that are historically and sociologically empty and those that have historical and sociological content.

For the second kind of typology, we need careful and detailed studies of squatters and smallholders in the Sierra Maestra, or rural cane cutters and carters in Oriente or the south coast of Puerto Rico; of the colonial encounter between Spaniards and indigenous communities in the Central Valley of Mexico, Oaxaca, or Yucatan, or in Cuzco, Ayacucho, or Huarochiri; of the effects of the expansion of coffee cultivation on rural toilers in São Paulo, Cundinamarca, Antioquia, or the Central Mesa of Costa Rica; and so on. We need such studies both for what they tell us of specific experiences of a colonial and modern world and for the material they provide, the problems they pose, and the contrasts they present for a truly comparative and generalizing social science.

Rather than building typologies from categories amenable to statistical calculation (subfamily, family, multifamily, for example), such studies facilitate and
require a rural sociology that can connect with a variety of Latin American
experiences. To give Mintz the platform once again: "Anthropology on the
level of rural regional or community study *must* be historical and particular, if it
aspires to be sociological and generalizing. (I daresay the other social sciences
might benefit from a similar confinement)" (1982:187).

Asking New Questions

Given that we have considered the appropriation of certain literatures by authors
pondering the agrarian question, however, it is remarkable how few works by
anthropologists and historians appear in the more programmatic theoretical
statements. The writings of Lenin, Kautsky, and Chayanov might be much
more frequently cited and seriously discussed than those of, say, Redfield,
Wolf, Gibson, or Womack. Or, if specific anthropologists or historians make
it into a bibliography, it is more often for their general than for their particular studies: Stein and Stein's *Colonial Heritage of Latin America* (1972) but
not Stein's *Vassouras* (1985 [1957]; Gibson's *Spain in America* (1966) but not
his *The Aztecs under Spanish Rule* (1964). Even more remarkable, given the
interest in peasant activity and resistance, is the relative lack of influence by,
or citation of, the important studies of Womack and Wolf. Womack's *Zapata
and the Mexican Revolution* (1969) was widely read and admired, but its very
particularity, its concentration on Morelos, could frustrate those whose more
generalizing bent caused them to approach regional studies with impatience.
Or consider Theda Skocpol's appraisal of Wolf's *Peasant Wars of the Twentieth
Century* (1969): she admires it, but complains that it is "too complex and vague
to be more than a set of analytic pointers" (Skocpol 1982:166) and that Wolf
wrote the "least theoretically" of the contributors to the literature on peasant
rebellions (1982:178).

This claim demands modification. First, it ignores those contributors to the
literature who engaged the work of anthropologists and historians. Stavenhagen's whole argument in section 3 of *Las Clases Sociales en las Sociedades
Agrarias* (1969), for example, pursued an engagement with and reanalysis of
anthropological community studies in Mesoamerica. Second, it ignores the
large number of young anthropologists and historians who contributed to the
literature on peasantries, many of whom were also more apt to discuss Lenin or
Chayanov than Redfield or Lewis. Third, it ignores the great body of community studies by anthropologists that provide little help in thinking historically,
structurally, or comparatively about rural peoples in Latin America.[4]

Nonetheless, the problematic relationship between the literature on the
agrarian question and the works of anthropologists and historians was critical

in at least two senses. First, important studies appeared, beginning especially in the 1950s, that deserved more attention and discussion in the theoretical literature than they received. Second, historians and anthropologists writing in the 1970s and 1980s, especially but not exclusively from a younger generation, took the problems posed by the literature on the agrarian question and applied them to regional and community studies. The results of these researches, and the new studies and questions they have provoked, have made it possible to move well beyond the simplistic invocation of Chayanov or Lenin.

Concerning the first point, I concentrate here on only one line of work, although there were others. In a helpful essay on the peasant concept in anthropology, Sydel Silverman (1979) delineates two broad traditions. The first was associated with Robert Redfield (1930, 1940, 1953) and concentrated on local community studies, usually without connecting the communities with a larger society or history. To the extent that a larger structure was engaged, it was conceived in a dualistic sense—the great versus the little tradition, the urban versus the folk—which also provided the foundation for a dualistic reading of history. The second was associated with Julian Steward and was explicitly interested in addressing structural and historical questions and pursuing community studies that could be compared in terms of structure and history. This was more clear in the well-known Puerto Rico project, directed by Julian Steward and conducted by Robert Manners, Sidney Mintz, Elena Padilla, Raymond Scheele, and Eric Wolf when they were graduate students. The resulting book (Steward et al. 1956) outlined a "culture historical" approach that conducted community studies but placed each community chosen within a political and economic history of Puerto Rico. A coffee-producing municipality studied by Wolf could be compared with a sugar cane plantation community studied by Mintz in terms of their different geographical and ecological placements on the island, as well as their different experiences in the history of Puerto Rican agriculture, and their different class structures and social organization.[5]

This comparative culture historical approach provided the foundation for a number of influential typological essays by Wolf, Mintz, and others in the 1950s—on haciendas and plantations (Wolf and Mintz 1957), on types of plantations (Rubin 1959), on types of peasantry in Latin America (Wolf 1955), and so on. As these typologies were appropriated by anthropologists and other social scientists, they were subject to a good bit of reification, but they also organized and inspired interesting work. Let us consider, for example, Wolf's typology of Latin American peasantries (1955). Unlike later typologies that were based on farm size or their connection to precapitalist or capitalist estates, Wolf began his typology with differential colonial and postcolonial experiences. The concept of the "closed corporate community" was used to designate those indigenous villagers in the "nuclear" areas of Latin America— Mesoamerica and the Central Andes—where indigenous populations had been densely settled under state regimes before the conquest, and where the Spanish colonial regimes created *repúblicas de indios* as instruments of colonial protection and as sources of labor and tribute. "Open" peasantries also referred to a particular kind of historical experience—the expansion of export agriculture in the nineteenth century and the migration of rural folk into frontier tropical and subtropical regions to plant export crops.

For each of these types, we now need a more fine-grained typology because we know more about the different social-historical experiences of indigenous communities during the colonial period and rural pioneers in the nineteenth century.[6] I wish to emphasize here, however, the uniqueness of this contribution and the other typological essays of the 1950s. In contrast to a then-prevailing anthropology, Wolf was trying to move beyond a myopia that stressed the cultural distinctiveness of each community or indigenous grouping. In his words, he was pursuing a "structural" rather than a "cultural" approach, language that often seems strange to a poststructural generation of students but that needs to be read in terms of then-prevailing conceptions of structure and culture. In contrast to other typologies encountered in this essay, Wolf's exercise was built upon and attempted to illuminate studies of local communities and situations, and the types themselves were designed to capture distinct experiences of colonization and settlement. The types were neither sociologically nor historically empty. They have therefore provided a touchstone against which others may apply or test their own concepts or understandings of peasant experiences in Latin America (see, e.g., Stern 1983 or Wolf 1986). The typology is an example of generalizing and sociological analysis that depends upon the historical and particular.

By the 1970s, a new generation of anthropologists and historians began to address and expand upon some of the questions and concerns raised by the culture historians of the 1950s, drawing unevenly upon that earlier work. Before considering this new generation, however, a modifying comment is necessary. The generational focus is not meant to deny the continuing activity and influence of scholars who had framed the very questions this new generation began to consider. If, however, we start from the observation that the agrarian question was a question posed by intellectuals and others about peasants, then the formation of intellectuals and the structural conditions in which intellectual work is produced become important areas for inquiry. The reference to a younger generation here is a reference to a generation of graduate students who took from seminars and discussions a series of debates concerning dependency theory, modes of production, dual economies, and the like, as well as an engagement with a literature on an area (Mesoamerica, the Central Andes), and fashioned dissertation topics designed to address perceived weaknesses, gaps, or unresolved problems in both theoretical and areal literatures. They then took these concerns and projects to the field, where they encountered complexly structured and differentiated social relations, as well as communities of scholars and activists turning to increasingly detailed questions and examinations. The move toward a regional agrarian history came out of this particular conjuncture (of theoretical preoccupation and historical or anthropological research) in the intellectual formation of a generation of historians and anthropologists. The argument privileges the dissertation, not as the sole source of intellectual innovation (this would be absurd) but as a marker of certain intellectual conjunctures, a statement of what is perceived to be problematic or troublesome at a certain moment.

The movement toward regional studies took distinct forms among historians and anthropologists. Among historians, one of the initial moves toward a more complex rural sociology came via an exploration of noncentral regions. Building upon Gibson's pioneering work on central Mexico, William Taylor (1972) studied landlord-peasant relations in colonial Oaxaca and found that the large hacienda had not held the dominant, monopolistic position that had characterized northern Mexico. Instead, indigenous villagers and villages continued to control lands alongside more modest haciendas throughout the colonial period. Both in his 1972 book and in a 1974 article, he used the Oaxaca case to criticize the popular image of the pervasive domination of the hacienda in colonial Mexico, an image given scholarly support by Chevalier's (1963 [1952]) classic study. Contending that Chevalier had based his argument on northern materials, Taylor suggested a basic opposition between the mining north, where large haciendas prevailed, and the indigenous south, which was less central to the colonial economy, where the colonial presence was maintained primarily through urban commercial, administrative, and ecclesiastical channels. In the same year, an article by Friedrich Katz (1974) moved beyond the colonial period to the late nineteenth-century Porfiriato, another period when the hacienda was thought to have expanded and dominated throughout Mexico. Katz suggested a much more detailed and complex regional variation in forms of landholding, labor exploitation, and rural class relations, connecting this variation with differential peasant participation in the revolution in distinct regions. Simultaneously, historians of Andean Peru, building upon the classic ethnohistorical work of Murra, paid more careful attention to indigenous encounters with Spanish colonists and began to question both the chronology and regional distribution of haciendas, placing their development here in the eighteenth century, there in the late nineteenth and early twentieth (e.g., Morner 1978; Spalding 1984).

Anthropologists, on the other hand, had long been committed to the local and particular. In this period, radical anthropologists' engagement with dependency and mode-of-production theories reflected dissatisfaction with prevailing anthropological approaches to community studies. The aim of their work was to link local communities with larger (regional, national, global) historical processes. Their resolutions of this problem tended to retain an ethnographic focus (necessarily an engagement with local and particular situations) and look outward or upward toward the region or nation, examining the linkages historically. Consider here the work of Warman in Morelos (1981), Cook and Diskin in Oaxaca (1975), Wasserstrom in Chiapas (1983), C. Smith in Guatemala (1984), Roseberry in Venezuela (1983), and Orlove (1977) or G. Smith (1989) in Peru. In their move toward the region as an effective frame of reference for studies of community formation and linkage with a wider world, and in their conceptualization of that linkage in historical terms, they met a generation of historians who were also discovering the region (Taylor 1972; Spalding 1984; Larson 1988; Stern 1982; Mallon 1983; Joseph 1982; Weinstein 1983). We find here the basis for a new intersection between anthropology and history, with clear antecedents in earlier intersections based on the work of Wolf (1959), Mintz (1974b), Murra (1975), Rowe (1957), Gibson (1964), Stein (1985 [1957]), and Womack (1969).

As a younger generation of scholars and activists began to conduct their field research in the early 1970s, then, they took with them many of the questions posed by the literature on the agrarian question. They were interested in the establishment and formation of basic land and labor institutions, the connections between these institutions and the "very structure of society," the dynamics of capitalism in the countryside, and the participation of rural toilers in protests, riots, rebellions, and revolutions. Yet they were also aware, sometimes more keenly than earlier generations had been, of the regional diversity that characterized these relations and processes, and of the political importance of that diversity for processes of class formation. As they began to make particular regions the objects and subjects of their studies, they uncovered new archival sources and explored the possibilities of oral history. By the late 1970s and early 1980s, their studies began to appear, stimulating a wealth of detailed and sophisticated investigations of Latin American rural sociology and history.

Some of these works offered explicit challenges to earlier anthropological and historical studies, just as Taylor had used his research on Oaxaca to challenge Chevalier's model of the colonial Mexican hacienda. Robert Wasserstrom's (1983) historical study of Indian-white relations over a four-hundred-year period in Chiapas, for example, was offered as a critique of an entire body of anthropological community studies in Zinacantan, Chamula, and other Chiapas municipalities (see also Favre 1973). Chance and Taylor's (1985) ongoing work on regional and temporal differentiation in civil-religious hierarchies in colonial and nineteenth century Mexico also challenges long-standing images of the continuity and stolidity of such hierarchies. Other works have offered less explicit challenges but extended the range of our knowledge to regions of Puerto Rico, El Salvador, Costa Rica, Colombia, or Venezuela, where historiographical or rural sociological traditions had been weakly developed.

These studies underscore the profound complexity of class and ethnic relations in rural Latin America, defying and confounding most attempts at typology. In one sense, we see this complexity in the increasing geographical scope of our knowledge. We see it in new studies of haciendas in Mexican peripheries—in the extreme north (Katz 1976; Wasserman 1984; Nugent 1987; Alonso 1988) and in Yucatan (Farriss 1984; Patch 1985; Joseph 1982), where we also encounter a rather different process of indigenous/Spanish encounter and conquest, one that does not begin to fit into a north/south divide. We see it also in studies that extend our knowledge of Alto Peru beyond Cuzco, to Huamanga (Ayacucho), to the Mantaro and Yanamarca valleys, or to Cochabamba (Stern 1982; Mallon 1983; Larson 1988); in treatments of regional differentiation in Colombian coffee zones (Palacios 1983; Machado 1977; Bergquist 1978). We also find extraordinary differences within regions. The "colonial spaces" outlined by Assadourian (1983) give way to a much more complex microsociology as we learn more about intraregional and parish level differences in *mita* mobilization for the mines at Potosí and in the incidence of *forastero* settlement (Morner and Trelles 1987). In Morelos, Mexico, we encounter important differences between highland and lowland villages in terms of their relationships to and encroachment by expanding sugar haciendas, and even within highland and lowland regions, we find differences among municipalities in terms of their respective fates during periods of hacienda expansion (for example, during the Porfiriato) (de la Peña 1982; Martin 1985; Warman 1981).

We also begin to learn more about the complexity of regionally distinct Spanish conquests in studies such as Stern's of Huamanga (1982), Larson's of Cochabamba (1988), Spalding's of Huarochiri (1984), or Farriss's of Yucatan (1984). Here we begin to view the conquests as contradictory and protracted processes, in which a colonial state-in-formation maintained an illusion of strength and extensive control through a complex bureaucratic apparatus but exercised that control through individual agents, officers, and governors who contracted their services to the Spanish Crown and who often pursued their own interests and agendas. The state was not so much weak as it was thinly and unevenly distributed, despite the appearance of density and strength on paper, leaving room for individual and group maneuver on the part of colonial officers, merchants, landowners, mining entrepreneurs, and villagers. Indigenous peoples came to the colonial encounter with their own interests and understandings, entering readily and willingly into trade arrangements that seemed to benefit them, for example, and yet finding that these arrangements brought with them unanticipated and unintended consequences (Stern 1982). We see indigenous villages creating spaces in which they could control their own resources and activities, as in Farriss's treatment of the community treasuries and the conflicts over their control among communities, the Church, and state officials (finally resolved in favor of the Church in the late eighteenth century).

Moreover, just as the encounters were decades- and centuries-long processes in which multiple and contradictory interests were placed in conflict and unintended consequences emerged, they also produced the progressive blurring of "Spanish" and "indigenous" categories, because of the internal social differentiation within these groups (*caciques* or *kurakas* and commonors, for example) and the emergence of new groups—peninsular versus American-born Spaniards, persons born of mixed Spanish and indigenous, or Spanish and African, or indigenous and African parentage, and so on.

"The colonial hacienda" also emerges as several different kinds of social institution and economic enterprise, depending upon the location of the region in colonial economic and political space (relative distance from markets, relative isolation from or incorporation with colonial administrative centers, the density and social organization of the indigenous population— whether the hacienda depends upon resident laborers or neighboring villagers, whether the resident laborers come from neighboring villages or from other regions altogether, whether laborers are impressed, either through colonial schemes of labor appropriation [*repartimiento, mita,* etc.], through the importation of African slaves, or through some form of debt peonage—and so on). One of the first historians to signal that the hacienda did not easily correspond with popular imagery was Charles Gibson (1964). In his study of indigenous villages in the Valley of Mexico, he showed that one source of indigenous labor for emerging *hacendados* was composed of villagers escaping tribute and labor obligations to the colonial administration. Tribute and labor obligations were assessed and collected by and through villages, and villagers could escape the exactions by leaving the village and taking up residence in another village, where they would enjoy none of the rights and protections of a member of a *república de indios* but also would be subject to none of the obligations. Neighboring or distant haciendas also offered protection, escape, and a livelihood in return for labor on the hacienda. Similar studies in Alto Peru show the importance in some regions of *forasteros* (outsiders) escaping *mita* labor obligations in Potosí and taking up residence in other indigenous villages or on emerging haciendas. In both cases, they served as a potential labor force—for the *caciques* or *kurakas* operating haciendas or *obrajes* (factories) in indigenous villages or for Spanish hacendados (see Rowe 1957; Spalding 1984; Stern 1982; Larson 1988).

With this, images of widespread debt peonage, the use of usurious debts to tie resident laborers to the hacienda and prevent escape, are undercut, and we now have a wide literature questioning its importance in both colonial and nineteenth-century haciendas, except in particular regions. Such revisionism does not constitute apologetics for the hacendado or an attempt to give the hacienda a human face. Rather, it recognizes that haciendas emerged in particular, complexly structured fields of power, that the forces that attracted or forced or held laborers on haciendas in particular regions were contradictory, that haciendas operated in a wider field of force including competing colonial forces and interests and a variety of resources and actions from the laborers and potential laborers themselves.

The most interesting recent studies of colonial landed regimes have been those that attempt to reconstruct that field of force and place their analysis of hacienda development within it. In Cheryl Martin's study of haciendas in Morelos (1985), for example, we find an important distinction between lowland and highland villages in relationship to the lowland development of sugar estates in the seventeenth century. She draws a contrast between lowland villages that lost lands, experienced the settlement of large numbers of mestizos and other nonindigenous people, and provided resident laborers for the estates, as opposed to highland villages that entered into more symbiotic relations with the estates, providing corn, wood, and other goods for the estates as well as seasonal laborers.

Nancy Farriss's exploration of Mayan responses to colonial rule in Yucatan (1984) also pays attention to the Yucatecan field of power, one that was characterized for most of the colonial period by Yucatan's peripheral position within colonial economic and political spaces. In her examination of colonial estates and enterprises and indigenous relations with the church, Farriss stresses Mayan control over resources, their holding of village lands and *cenotes* (large water holes, crucial resources in the limestone-studded peninsula), their control over village treasuries and the actual practice of Catholic and Mayan ritual, and their work on emerging colonial farms while residing in village lands. A crucial aspect of Yucatecan social and political space was a vast unconquered frontier to the east and south, to which villagers could escape if colonial exactions became too severe. She also treats the expansion of corn and cattle haciendas in the late eighteenth century, the colonial capture of village treasuries and the hacendados' control of *cenotes,* a period during which, in Farriss's view, something like a closed corporate community emerged as certain resources (especially the dispersal option) were closed off.

Perhaps the most impressive of recent studies, the one that most closely approximates Charles Gibson's work in scope and richness of detail, is Brooke Larson's study of Cochabamba (1988). In addition to a closely observed analysis of the colonial encounter in the sixteenth century, one that pays special attention to the ethnically and politically diverse precolonial character of the Cochabamba valley in its relationships with Aymara lords and the colonial severing of these relationships and conversion of the valley, in part, into a provisioner of grain for Potosí, she explores the structure and dynamics of the eighteenth-century hacienda economy. Here she pays special attention to the mestizo peasantry within the hacienda. She describes a local field of power in which hacendados had found it convenient and expedient to turn over commercial production as well as food production to those indigenous peoples and mestizos who settled on hacienda lands or lived on lands claimed by the hacienda. Content to collect rent from peasant producers, hacendados then found it difficult to capture the produce from a thriving peasant economy during crisis years, to take control over production.

Here we see the importance of examining the peasantry within haciendas, of including within the field of power the areas of strength and weakness associated with peasant livelihood. Had hacendados turned food production associated with the tenants' livelihoods over to the tenants themselves? In most cases, hacendados did, and the full implications of this concession—an obviously convenient one for the hacendados—for the structure and dynamics of the hacienda and for the tenantry remain to be explored in other regions. Did the hacendado control commercial production, using tenants as laborers, or turn commercial production over to the tenants themselves, collecting rent from a peasant tenantry? Answers to such questions will vary spatially and temporally, as the needs of hacendados change, as markets expand and contract, prices rise and fall, colonial policies change, and population becomes more or less dense. The questions mark out areas of potential and actual conflict, fault lines in a structure of domination. And they allow us to place peasants' activities and resources at the center of our understanding of the constitution of social and political structures without assuming that these activities necessarily constitute resistance—everyday or otherwise.

The colonial encounter emerges, then, not as a single shock in the sixteenth century, establishing a remarkably stable seigneurial regime, but as an ongoing process, a series of encounters, exactions, colonial adjustments (sometimes having to do with the Crown's attempts to limit the power of colonial entrepreneurs and increase revenues, but with immediate consequences for indigenous villagers), population relocation and settlement schemes, indigenous group and individual flight from colonial tribute, hacienda expansion and contraction, mining and factory expansion and contraction, and so on, all occurring in unevenly developing colonial spaces organized around shifting centers and peripheries.

As we move toward the nineteenth century, we also encounter unevenly developing spaces and shifting centers and peripheries. In the first place, although some regions were characterized by a settled and seemingly stable colonial society confronting the challenges of independence, other regions remained sparsely settled or unconquered. The conquest, the encounter between civilization and barbarism, was to continue through the nineteenth century and into the present. Alexander von Humboldt's early nineteenth-century reference to "the sinuousities of that interior shore, on which barbarism and civilization, impenetrable forests and cultivated land, touch and bound each other" (1818, 3:422) gives expression to the conquest as an unfinished project. In the second place, the expansion of agricultural production for export markets in the late nineteenth century entailed the displacement of former centers and the emergence of former peripheries as economic growth poles. The expansion of São Paulo in Brazil, the Western Andes in Venezuela, Antioquia in Colombia, or the Central Mesa in Costa Rica, all in association with coffee production, provide dramatic examples of this. In each case, frontiers were settled and transformed, roads and railroads built, towns and parishes established, and political arrangements and alliances shattered. We might briefly consider recent research on these coffee regions as an example of the range of processes and relations that emerged in late nineteenth-century Latin American regions. The expansion of coffee production in Brazil, first in Rio and later in São Paulo, was thoroughly dominated by a planter aristocracy. The settlement of the western frontier involved a continual displacement of squatters (who in turn had displaced indigenous peoples) by large planters who attempted to recreate in the southern and western interior the plantation society of the northeast and the coast. They maintained slavery for decades after the slave trade itself had been cut off. With abolition in 1888, the state of São Paulo, acting as an instrument of the planters who controlled them, instituted a massive program of subsidized immigration, in which foreign laborers—especially Italian but also Portuguese, Japanese, and others—received free passage to São Paulo and free railroad trips to the coffee-growing areas. There they contracted with individual planters for annual labor agreements. The *colonato,* as described by Warren Dean (1976), Thomas Holloway (1980), Verena Stolcke (1988), and Mauricio Font (1990), marks a labor regime in which immigrant families would be hired to tend and harvest a patch of coffee trees for an annual cycle. Their compensation consisted of a three-part package. They would receive a set sum of money for tending the trees during the year; they would be paid wages during the harvest, the sum paid dependent on yield; and they would be granted a plot of land on which they could grow food. At the end of the year, accounts were settled, and the contract could be renewed, or the *colono* family could be dismissed or decide to seek its fortunes elsewhere. The system encouraged extraordinary spatial mobility, as *colonos* changed farms at the end of each year, moving further to the west. Despite this apparent instability in the labor force, the immigrant stream itself and the São Paulo state's willingness to provide transport for the laborers to the estates assured the planters of a labor supply during the last decade of the nineteenth century and the first two decades of the twentieth.

A number of features in this labor system require comment. First, planters insisted on hiring families rather than individual workers. As the *Bulletin of the Department of Agricultural Labor* observed in 1932, "Coffee growing demands not the contribution of casual labour but, indeed, that of 'well constituted' families, of at least three hoes" (quoted in Stolcke 1988:208). Verena Stolcke has explored some of the implications of this decision with great sensitivity, noting the "exploitation of family morality." Second, despite unquestioned planter domination, given its most vigorous expression in the state's subsidy of some of their more important labor costs, planter concessions of food plots to *colonos* could have important effects. Although they gave the planters greater flexibility during crises, allowing planters to cut wages, they also conceded to workers a certain control over their own reproduction. Holloway (1980), among others, has argued that this provided a basis for *colono* mobility, allowing some *colonos* to accumulate resources and escape the *colonato*, establishing small farms in the west and eventually serving as the social base for an urban, industrial bourgeoisie. The ensuing debate about the mobility of *colonos* and the origins of the São Paulo bourgeoisie need not concern us here (Font 1987, 1989, 1990; Stolcke 1989; Love 1989). What does deserve attention is the importance of small-scale production within the large estate—both in the concession of food plots and in the organization of labor in the coffee patches.

In Colombia, the three regions that turned to coffee were characterized by three different land and labor regimes (see Palacios 1983; Machado 1977; Arango 1977). In Santander, in the northeast, the first region to turn to coffee, a form of sharecropping predominated in which landlords contracted with tenants to work their coffee patches and turn over a portion of their coffee and food crops after the harvest. In Cundinamarca and Tolima in the center, land was held by absentee landlord/merchants who resided in Bogotá and other centers, turning their estates over to administrators who contracted with tenants. Tenants would be given access to food plots to maintain their households in exchange for obligatory work in coffee patches, tending the trees during the year and picking the coffee (along with hired labor from off the estate) during the harvest. In Antioquia, which had been much less densely settled and attracted a famous process of frontier migration and settlement, a group of small-scale coffee farmers emerged alongside large farms, and much of the coffee economy was oriented toward provincial towns and the emerging city of Medellín, where merchants bought up, processed, and exported the coffee produced by small farmers, to whom they also provided credit. As in Brazil, we find the importance of small-scale production even in regions dominated by landlords. Marco Palacios has written of the "cellular" structure of the hacienda (1983), the presence of the peasantry within haciendas and the importance of their control over food production, including sugar and livestock, within the estates. Both Palacios and Michael Jimenez (1989) have argued that this tenant control was one of the most important sources of weakness for landlords, and proved to be the fissure that brought the collapse of the landlord economy of Cundinamarca in the 1920s and 30s.

Guatemalan plantation owners in piedmont zones were much less dependent upon a resident tenantry, calling upon indigenous villagers from highland zones to work on their estates for short or extended periods and return to their villages. To enforce the migration of villagers to the estates, planters were able to call upon the state after Rufino Barrios' liberal revolution. Through a series of vagrancy laws, the state instituted a system requiring indigenous villagers to carry identification and work books. Villagers who could demonstrate that they had enough work or resources in the highlands, as certified by their employers or the local *jefe político,* were exempted from work on the estates. Those who could not were required to travel to the estates and work; evidence of work and payment would then be noted in their books. As in Brazil, then, estate owners enjoyed extraordinary control of the state and were able to make state machinery serve as an engine of production. David McCreery (1976, 1983) has written the most detailed and careful descriptions of this system, outlining the structure and operation of the *mandamiento* (obligatory labor) system, the power of the landlords, conditions on the estates themselves, the process of estate expansion, and the effects of forced migrant labor on village agriculture. McCreery has also provided insightful discussion of indigenous resistance— not in the form of rebellion or other overt actions and protests, which would have provoked an immediate state response, but in the form of temporary flight, the hiding of resources and people, and other means of obstructing the work of the labor contractor and the jefe político.

Contrast this sort of situation with that in Costa Rica. A relatively peripheral and sparsely settled region during the colonial period, Costa Rica was one of the first Latin American countries to turn toward coffee production. As it did so, it precipitated a process of migration and settlement in the Central Mesa. As historians and geographers such as Carolyn Hall (1976), Mario Samper (1990), Victor Hugo Acuña Ortega (1985), and Lowell Gudmundson (1986) have demonstrated, Costa Rica's coffee economy was not dominated by large landowners. Although some large farms existed, the coffee economy of the Central Mesa was characterized by small-scale production. Small producers were, in turn, indebted to processor-merchants, who provided credit, bought, and processed their coffee. While there is general agreement about the importance of small producers in the coffee economy (see Seligson 1980 for a dissenting view), there has been less agreement about the basic structure and dynamics of the rural society into which coffee was originally introduced. In one of the most provocative and interesting recent treatments, Gudmundson has argued that colonial Costa Rica had been characterized by a village economy, with most of the population living in small towns and villages, farming the surrounding lands. The move toward coffee was simultaneously a move toward the countryside, a kind of ruralization of the landscape with the establishment of a peasantry in homesteads on newly created coffee farms.

The contrasts among coffee regions can be extended to Puerto Rico (Picó 1979, 1981; Bergad 1983), Venezuela (Carvallo and Hernandez 1979; Roseberry 1983), Haiti (Trouillot 1982), and so on. We find in these regions an extraordinary range of landed regimes and class experiences, each of which needs to be understood in terms of local processes of class formation, the local contexts in which export production zones were created (see Roseberry 1991; forthcoming; Roseberry and Gudmundson, forthcoming). If we were to extend our survey of class relations beyond the coffee zones, our appreciation of diversity would be further deepened as we encountered rural zones producing other export crops, zones relatively isolated from commercial production, escape zones from more commercial areas, cattle-ranching haciendas, small-scale food-crop zones in the environs of cities, haciendas and communities in the environs of new mining zones, and so on. Rather than surveying this research and further cataloging some of the documented diversity in agrarian relations, however, I shall take the recent research on coffee zones to suggest certain implications of the new studies and directions for further work.

Scholars are drawing increasing attention to the importance of small-scale production within and outside of large farms. Despite the structure of land-holding, the organization of work might be shifted downward, giving the hacienda or plantation a cellular structure. Regardless of whether the cellular structure embraced the commercial crop, it frequently organized food production as landlords found it expedient to leave the reproduction of a labor force to the laborers themselves. As we pay more attention to this cellular structure, a number of problems come into sharper focus. For one thing, the concession of food production to tenants, *colonos,* and others was important economically and politically. Economically, food production could provide the basis for an alternative and competing economy within the hacienda, in, for example, eighteenth-century Cochabamba (Larson 1988) or early twentieth-century Cundinamarca and Tolima (Jimenez 1989). As in our earlier criticism of the opposition between subsistence and commercial production, so in the present discussion of food versus commercial or export crops. Until the past three decades, most export agricultural sectors were not really monocrop zones (Stolcke 1988). Export-based haciendas and plantations had to reproduce their labor force, and provide feed for cattle and the mules necessary for hauling goods to market, with locally or regionally produced resources—either within the estate itself or from nearby zones. The lowland sugar estates of Morelos entered into symbiotic relations with highland villages not only for seasonal labor but also for corn, beans, and pasture (Martin 1985). A coffee hacienda in late nineteenth-century Colombia, for example, seldom devoted as much as 10 percent of its land to coffee. Most of the land would be planted in pasture, sugar, corn, beans, and manioc, all necessary for the maintenance of the hacienda as a commercial farm, and much of the control of this complementary sector was in the hands of tenants (Palacios 1983). The reproduction of a tenantry provided ample base for a non-export-based commercial economy. Fields planted in corn, beans, sugar, and pasture provided fungible resources; cattle, horses, and mules were items and sources of wealth; trade stores established within the hacienda provided sources of accumulation and differentiation. These sources and the competing economy they supported provided a basis of potential political strength for tenants, both in periods of agitation, such as in Colombia in the 1920s, and in relatively quiet periods in which the tenantry could constitute a group captured in one sense (they worked for the landlord on the export crop) but uncaptured in another (they controlled much of the reproduction of the hacienda).

The reproduction of a commercial estate need not depend solely on the tenantry within, however. Resources could also be purchased in nearby villages and towns, providing opportunities for small-scale producers who would grow food crops for use and sale, and perhaps work seasonally on the hacienda. It is inadequate to view these small farms solely as the minifundistas in a presumed latifundia/minifundia complex. As in the case of the tenantry, small-scale food production could provide ample opportunity for accumulation and social differentiation. Nor should we limit our understanding of peasant commercial production to so-called food crops complementary to export production on large estates. As Gudmundson (1986) has shown in Costa Rica, and as studies of other coffee-producing regions in Antioquia, western Venezuela, and Puerto Rico (Machado 1977; Palacios 1983; Roseberry 1983; Picó 1981) have demonstrated, independent small producers could become the primary producers of export crops. In such cases, the apparently independent producer would be indebted to town-based merchant processors, signifying a rather different type of class relation than the sort that emerges when we concentrate solely on land distribution, and one that has so far received little attention (but see Machado 1977; Palacios 1983; Acuña Ortega 1985; Hall 1976; Samper 1990; Roseberry 1983).

The studies of peasant commercial production in coffee regions are part of a growing group of studies of small-scale commercial production in a variety of contexts (see, e.g., Mallon 1983, Schryer 1980). Such small farmers have remained relatively invisible partly because they did not fit into prevailing models of "seigneurial regimes" established "historically" from the colonial encounter, imposing themselves in the "very structure of society." We may find that such peasantries were more widespread than had been thought, once we know how and where to look for them. For example, important research presently being conducted in El Salvador explores the extent to which smallholding figured in late nineteenth-century coffee production and suggests that the transition to large-scale production may have been more protracted than generally thought.[7] As studies of independent peasantries accumulate, we will need to link them with studies of peasants within the cellular structure of haciendas and plantations. One feature that both kinds of analyses have in common is that they treat the *formation* of peasantries as a historical problem. If we link them with those studies of colonial encounters discussed earlier, we see this concentration on "peasantization" as a process to be a common theme. As we study more of these processes, exploring the emergence of a variety of peasantries within particular fields of power, new questions begin to emerge.[8]

For one thing, it becomes impossible to simply assert the centrality of the household in peasant agriculture, cite Chayanov, and retreat. If particular kinds of peasantry have emerged in historically contingent fields of power, so have particular kinds of households and household economies. Once the peasant household is taken as a historical problem, studies of gender relations in the household move to a new plane. Clear advances have been made over the past two decades in the study of gender among peasantries in Latin America. When the household was no longer taken as an acting, thinking unit and attention was paid to adversarial, exploitative relations among individuals within the household, Chayanov's concept of "self-exploitation" in the peasant household could be given its important, gendered dimension. This represented an obvious advance and has made possible all further rethinking of the peasant household. In some early studies, however, the household could still be taken for granted historically; the formation of different kinds of households in different colonial encounters, or in different cellularly structured haciendas, would not be taken as a problem (see Young 1978 for an early exception). Instead, the household could be placed in the same transhistorical scheme that captured the peasantry. Before capitalism, gender relations in households could be thought to be one way (for example, the household might be both a production unit and a consumption unit, giving women's work a less privatized, alienated character); after capitalism, gender relations in households were transformed (for example, the household was now primarily a unit of consumption, devaluing women's labor). This problem was less immediately important for sociological or ethnographic studies of present-day gender relations, and we therefore have a rather good collection of studies of the present (Deere 1990; Deere and Leon de Leal 1987; Nash and Safa 1976, 1986; Crummett 1987). Nonetheless, as argued earlier, our studies of the present carry with them implicit historical assumptions.

More recently, a number of authors have subjected the household economy to more detailed historical scrutiny, following the pioneering suggestions of Olivia Harris (1981, 1982; see, e.g., Mallon 1986; Collins 1986; Deere 1986; Stolcke 1988; Roseberry 1986). Unfortunately, unlike its development in Europe, family history has been weakly developed in Latin America. As authors raise new questions about the household, they find little help in the secondary literature. While we might find thoroughly detailed studies of the colonial encounter, village resettlement, ethnic redefinition, hacienda formation and expansion, and so forth, the formation and transformation of peasant households within these more finely sketched encounters and transformations have seldom been treated as historically problematic. This constitutes, then, one of the most important areas for primary historical and anthropological research on Latin American peasantries.

Conclusion

Let us return to the problem with which we began—our understanding of the "manifold ways whereby peasants have continuously engaged their political worlds." In surveys of scholarship on rural peoples over the past decade, our lack of understanding of such engagements is often identified as a problem with studies and paradigms that are too "structural" or "capital-centric," or with histories that are written "from above." Given this definition of a problem, the evident resolution is to write histories "from below" and to uncover and investigate the variety of ways in which working peoples have been conscious of and resisted the orders of domination that press upon them.

As this resolution took shape over the past fifteen years, two rather different studies were especially influential. Although it was an examination of Southeast Asian peasant protest and rebellion, James Scott's *Moral Economy of the Peasant* (1976) served as inspiration and guide for much work in Latin America on peasant politics and consciousness. Scott argued that peasants evaluate the social orders in which they live in terms of the extent to which those orders, and the elites that dominate them, offer survival guarantees. To the extent that landlords, colonial officers, merchants, and priests guarantee or protect peasant livelihood in exchange for the tribute, produce, or labor they extract, peasants value and support them, or accommodate themselves to elite demands. The spread of industrial capitalism or of the more rationalistic colonial regimes of the late nineteenth century, however, undermined the preexisting balance of more traditional orders of domination and eroded the bases of livelihood and survival guarantees on which peasants had depended, providing rural villagers with the basis for a moral critique of and opposition to the new regimes.

Michael Taussig's *Devil and Commodity Fetishism in South America* (1980) also explores the bases for moral critique on the part of rural peoples and first-generation proletarians caught in the spread of capitalist relations. Rather than exploring preexisting orders of domination, however, Taussig weds his insightful model to an opposition between reciprocity and nonreciprocity, or use-value and exchange-value regimes. Rural peoples and first-generation proletarians evaluate the bizarre expectations and demands of an expanding capitalism in terms of their own experience of reciprocity and use-value production. Where Scott's work provided a model for understanding peasant consciousness and political activity, however, Taussig's drew our attention to previously unexplored political dimensions of fantasy and magic, devil imagery and propitiation, shamanism and cosmology.

Both authors offer refreshing challenges to the more extreme "capital-centric" statements of the agrarian question. Their influence has been evident in recent years, even in studies that do not explicitly cite them. Their earliest statements of their models, however, suffer from some of the same problems alluded to above: they were sociologically and historically empty. Their conceptions of peasantries were based on imputed characteristics derived from a sociological model (Scott's emphasis on a livelihood or survival orientation; Taussig's on use-value or reciprocal regimes), and their conceptions of capitalism were broad and epochal. Their works seemed to draw our attention to the thoughts and actions of ordinary people, and they seemed to write a history from below, but the history was strongly inflected by and permeated with the thoughts, preoccupations, moral vision, and consciousness of James Scott or Michael Taussig (but see Scott's more recent *Weapons of the Weak* [1985], based on village ethnography). This is not to suggest that we need to reject Scott's or Taussig's works out of hand. As with the studies encountered above, so with the earlier work of Scott and Taussig. The critical distinction remains one between models that are historically and sociologically empty and those that have historical and sociological content. Unless we move toward detailed local studies, we are left with the romance of resistance rather than "the manifold ways whereby peasants have continuously engaged their political worlds." That some of these questions can be applied to regional history is clear from Scott's subsequent work, as well as in some of the work influenced by him or Taussig (on Scott, see Roseberry 1989:55–79; on Taussig, see ibid.: 218–22).

One of the effects of the study of the historical formation of particular peasantries in locally configured fields of power is that we are in a much better position to ask such questions. Consider, for example, three recent studies of rural politics. In her comparison of two Peruvian regions in the late nineteenth century, Florencia Mallon (1987) explores the regional sociology of the central highlands, especially the Mantaro and Yanamarca Valleys, and the northern highlands, especially Cajamarca, during the period before, during, and after the War of the Pacific. Describing distinct placements within economic, social, and political networks, distinct class relations among villagers and between villagers and landlords or merchants in the two regions, she is able to examine different positions within and attitudes toward emerging state institutions, different types of and roles for local and state politics. The responses of local villagers, landlords, and merchants to the War of the Pacific and its aftermath depend in part on the two regions' different prior histories but also upon their different experiences of and types of participation in the war itself.

In his study of long-standing patterns of community activism and resistance in Huasicancha, Peru, Gavin Smith (1989) writes a detailed history of relations between the pastoral villagers and the neighboring hacienda, a history that traces changing forms of herding tenantry as well as moments of resistance. Moreover, he offers a detailed history and sociology of migration from

Huasicancha to Lima and other towns and cities, providing a careful analysis of various kinds of kin and community-based confederations of households linking pastoral activities in the highlands with small-scale fruit selling in Lima. One of the strengths of his analysis is Smith's linkage of a study of changing modes of livelihood and economic cooperation with an examination of the microlevel politics of community formation and resistance.

In his recent *To Lead as Equals* (1990), Jeffrey Gould studies a variety of pre-Sandinista forms of rural organization and resistance in Chinandega, Nicaragua. The centerpiece of his study is a detailed examination of the mobilization of villagers from San José del Obraje, a village of rural workers living on the margins of estates during a period of export expansion. Though the villagers come from diverse backgrounds and regions, they are united by their common position in relation to the estates, working for them and trying to obtain land for food crops. Gould's account of their attempt to claim and secure such land is a history of the villagers' engagement with, adaptation to, and transformation of the institutions of the Somocista state. Because of the rich detail in Gould's analysis, we gain a more sophisticated understanding of both the villagers and the Somocista state itself. Among the villagers, we see a constant effort to overcome internal differences, to experiment with new forms of struggle, or new terms in which to define their struggle (including an attempt to take advantage of state protection for indigenous populations by claiming to be an indigenous community). At the level of the state, we are made aware of differentiation and internal contradictions, of attempts to accommodate and repress, or to satisfy multiple and competing rural interests while solidifying a ruling bloc. Attention to villagers' actions and to local and state government responses to these actions helps us to see both village life and state politics in more dynamic and dialectical terms.

What makes each of these studies possible is that they begin with detailed local knowledge of class relation and structure, both of which are understood in dynamic terms, as emerging within distinct fields of power and changing through specific and interactive patterns of conflict and force. Villagers act within and against structural positions, but neither their actions nor their consciousness can be imputed from those structural positions. Instead, the landlords have names and faces: María Luisa Chavez or Manuel Pielago in Peru, Doña Tesla or Edmundo Deshon in Nicaragua. Villagers have leaders: Elías Tacunan or Demetrio de la Cruz Lazo in Peru, Regino Escobar or Juan Suazo in Nicaragua. The leaders have opponents, and the villagers engage in arguments over tactics, terms, resources, and intentions. Capitalism takes the form of a mining complex or expanding cotton or sugar estates, of a market depression or export boom. The state takes the form of state marketing boards, property law, protectionist institutions, the army, or the national guard—vigorously present in the countryside in one place at one moment, confined to a city in another.

In sum, we understand peasants' engagements with their political worlds in terms of much more complex and dynamic structures and relations of domination and control, resistance and accommodation. These studies point the way toward new ways of posing agrarian questions, and of listening to and understanding those rural voices who pose their own questions and seek their own answers.

Notes

I thank Fred Cooper, Mauricio Font, Florencia Mallon, Nicole Polier, and Steve Stern for their detailed criticisms and suggestions concerning an early draft of this essay. I also thank students and faculty at the University of Connecticut, The Johns Hopkins University, and the New School for Social Research for their comments and questions when I presented these ideas in public lectures. I regret that I have not been able to follow all of their suggestions or respond to all of their questions.

1. See, e.g., Sotelo Inclán 1943 and Andrade 1964. I thank Florencia Mallon for these important observations. For a model history of ideas that pays careful attention to both dominant and "subterranean" texts, with special emphasis on the multiple political contexts that influence work that is accepted and work that is rejected, work that is reviewed and work that is ignored, and so on, see Vincent 1990. One of the ways that we can explore dominant and subterranean trends is to engage in cohort analysis, marking particular generations of intellectuals in particular places, the works they read and argued about, the ideas they embraced, the projects they pursued (Roseberry 1990).

2. Argentina, Brazil, Colombia, Chile, Ecuador, Guatemala, and Peru.

3. All of these italicized quotations are from the material cited at the opening of this section (Barraclough and Domike 1970 [1966]: 41–44).

4. William Taylor's complaint in footnote 22 to his essay on "Landed Society in New Spain" (1974:397), concerning the lack of historical awareness and sensitivity on the part of most ethnographers of rural Mexico, states the problem clearly and concisely enough.

5. The most serious critical study of this project and the texts that emerged from it has been written by Antonio Lauria (1989).

6. Research in what Wolf called "open" villages was decidedly underdeveloped when Wolf wrote his essay.

7. This research is being conducted by Aldo Lauria Santiago, a Ph.D. candidate in history at the University of Chicago.

8. One such problem, the resolution of which lies beyond the scope of this essay, is the continued use of the concept and label *peasant* itself. If our emphasis is on the complexity and diversity of processes of formation and fields of power that situate particular peasantries, there is little to be gained from elaborate theorization of peasant typologies, complete with imputed political and moral orientations, historical origins and trajectories, and the like. Unfortunately, the literature is so burdened with such theorizations that the simple use of the term *peasant* can seem to invoke them. My own use of the word *peasant* is much more matter-of-fact, as evidenced by my frequent use of words or phrases like *peasant, villager, rural worker,* and *rural population,* as if they were interchangeable. Here I have been influenced by

Jeff Gould's (1990) adoption of the term *campesino* in his depiction of a diverse rural population in Chinandega, Nicaragua. The word means, simply, "country person," and is maddeningly vague. Gould is able to provide greater analytical precision in his examination of specific villagers and their activities while retaining the more vague and inclusive label, used by the country people themselves, in his study of the formation of a rural (*campesino*) movement composed of smallholders, rural proletarians, and tenants. I would similarly argue that analytical precision can only be provided in the context of specific situations and formations, and I retain the word *peasant* as a matter-of-fact way of talking about rural villagers, agriculturalists, tenants, and smallholders, making no claims and drawing no inferences about their historical trajectories, moral and ethical dilemmas, political capacities and incapacities. As I argue in the text, such claims and inferences depend upon an understanding of specific fields of power in which various peasantries have been formed.

References

Acuña Ortega, V. H. 1985. "Clases Sociales y Conflicto Social en la Economía Cafetalera Costarricense: Productores Contra Beneficiadores: 1932–1936." *Revista de Historia* (Número Especial), 181–212.

Alonso, Ana María. 1988. " 'Progress' as Disorder and Dishonor." *Critique of Anthropology* 8, no. 1:13–33.

Andrade, Manuel Correia de. 1964. *A Terra e o Homen no Nordeste*. São Paulo: Editora Brasiliense.

Arango, M. 1977. *Café e Industria: 1850–1930*. Bogotá.

Assadourian, Carlos Sempat. 1983. *El Sistema de la Economía Colonial: El Mercado Interior. Regiones y Espacio Económico*. Mexico City: Editorial Nueva Imagen.

Barraclough, Solon L., ed. 1973. *Agrarian Structure in Latin America: A Resume of the CIDA Land Tenure Studies of Argentina, Chile, Colombia, Ecuador, Guatemala, Peru*. Lexington, Mass.: Lexington Books.

Barraclough, Solon, and Arthur L. Domike. 1970 [1966]. "Agrarian Structure in Seven Latin American Countries." In Rodolfo Stavenhagen, ed., *Agrarian Problems and Peasant Movements in Latin America*. New York: Doubleday/Anchor, 41–94.

Bartra, Roger. 1974. *Estructura Agraria y Clases Sociales en México*. Mexico City: ERA.

Bergad, Laird. 1983. *Coffee and the Growth of Agrarian Capitalism in Nineteenth-Century Puerto Rico*. Princeton: Princeton Univ. Press.

Bergquist, Charles. 1978. *Coffee and Conflict in Colombia, 1886–1910*. Durham: Duke Univ. Press.

Burbach, Roger, and Patricia Flynn. 1980. *Agribusiness in the Americas*. New York: Monthly Review Press.

Cardoso, Ciro F. S. 1975. "Historia Económica del Café en Centroamerica: Estudio Comparativo." *Estudios Sociales Centroamericanos* 4, no. 10:9–55.

Cardoso, Fernando Henrique. 1977. "The Consumption of Dependency Theory in the United States." *Latin American Research Review* 12, no. 3:7–24.

Cardoso, Fernando Henrique, and Enzo Faletto. 1979. *Dependency and Development in Latin America*. Berkeley: Univ. of California Press.

Carvallo, Gastón, and Josefina Ríos de Hernandez. 1979. *Agricultura y Sociedad: Tres Ensayos Históricos*. Caracas: CENDES.

Chance, John, and William Taylor. 1985. "Cofradías and Cargos: An Historical Perspective on the Mesoamerican Civil-Religious Hierarchy." *American Ethnologist* 12:1–26.

Chayanov, A. V. 1966[1925]. *The Theory of Peasant Economy*. Homewood, Ill.: Richard D. Irwin.

Chevalier, François. 1963[1952]. *Land and Society in Colonial Mexico: The Great Hacienda*. Berkeley and Los Angeles: Univ. of California Press.

Collins, Jane. 1986. "The Household and Relations of Production in Southern Peru." *Comparative Studies in Society and History* 28:651–71.

Collins, Joseph. 1982. *What Difference Could a Revolution Make? Food and Farming in the New Nicaragua*. San Francisco: Food First.

Cook, Scott, and Martin Diskin, eds. 1975. *Markets in Oaxaca*. Austin: Univ. of Texas Press.

Crummett, María de los Angeles. 1987. "Class, Household Structure, and the Peasantry: An Empirical Approach." *Journal of Peasant Studies* 14: 363–379.

Dean, Warren. 1976. *Río Claro: A Brazilian Plantation System, 1820–1920*. Stanford: Stanford Univ. Press.

Deere, Carmen Diana. 1986. "The Peasantry in Political Economy: Trends of the 1980s." Unpublished paper presented in the symposium, "Peasant Studies: Obstacles to Theoretical Advances." Meeting of the Latin American Studies Association. Boston.

Deere, Carmen Diana. 1990. *Household and Class Relations: Peasants and Landlords in Northern Peru*. Berkeley: Univ. of California Press.

Deere, Carmen Diana, and Margarita Leon de Leal, eds. 1987. *Rural Women and State Policy: Feminist Perspectives on Latin American Agricultural Development*. Boulder: Westview.

de Janvry, Alain. 1981. *The Agrarian Question and Reformism in Latin America*. Baltimore: The Johns Hopkins Univ. Press.

de la Peña, Guillermo. 1982. *A Legacy of Promises*. Austin: Univ. of Texas Press.

Dobyns, Henry F., Paul L. Doughty, and Harold Lasswell. 1971. *Peasants, Power, and Applied Social Change: Vicos as a Model*. Beverly Hills: Sage.

Farriss, Nancy. 1984. *Maya Society under Colonial Rule: The Collective Enterprise of Survival*. Princeton: Princeton Univ. Press.

Favre, Henri. 1973. *Cambio y Continuidad entre los Mayas de México: Contribución al Estudio de la Situación Colonialista en América Latina*. Mexico City: Siglo XXI.

Font, Mauricio. 1987. "Coffee Planters, Politics, and Development in Brazil." *Latin American Research Review* 22, no. 3:69–90.

Font, Mauricio. 1989. "Perspectives on Social Change and Development in Sao Paulo: A Reply." *Latin American Research Review* 24, no. 3:143–57.

Font, Mauricio. 1990. *Coffee, Contention, and Change in the Making of Modern Brazil*. Cambridge, Mass.: Basil Blackwell.

Foster, George. 1967. *Tzintzuntzan: Mexican Peasants in a Changing World*. Boston: Little, Brown.

Frank, Andre Gunder. 1969. *Latin America: Underdevelopment or Revolution*. New York: Monthly Review Press.

Gibson, Charles. 1964. *The Aztecs Under Spanish Rule: A History of the Valley of Mexico, 1519–1810*. Stanford: Stanford Univ. Press.

Gibson, Charles. 1966. *Spain in America*. New York: Harper and Row.

Godelier, Maurice. 1969. *Sobre el Modo de Producción Asiático*. Barcelona: Ediciones Martinez Roca.

Godelier, Maurice. 1970. *Teoría Marxista de las Sociedades Precapitalistas*. Barcelona: Ediciones LAIA.

Gould, Jeffrey L. 1990. *To Lead as Equals: Rural Protest and Political Consciousness in Chinandega, Nicaragua, 1912–1979*. Chapel Hill: Univ. of North Carolina Press.

Gudmundson, Lowell. 1986. *Costa Rica Before Coffee: Society and Economy on the Eve of the Export Boom*. Baton Rouge: Louisiana State Univ. Press.

Hall, Carolyn. 1976. *El Café y el Desarrollo Histórico-Geográfico de Costa Rica*. San José: Editorial Costa Rica.

Harris, Olivia. 1981. "Households as Natural Units." In Kate Young, Carol Wolkowitz and Roslyn McCullagh, eds., *Of Marriage and the Market*. London: CSE Books, 49–68.

Harris, Olivia. 1982. "Households and Their Boundaries." *History Workshop Journal* 13:143–152.

Hobsbawm, Eric. 1959. *Primitive Rebels*. New York: Norton.

Holloway, Thomas. 1980. *Immigrants on the Land: Coffee and Society in São Paulo, 1886–1934*. Chapel Hill: Univ. of North Carolina Press.

Huizer, Gerrit. 1972. *The Revolutionary Potential of Peasants in Latin America*. Lexington, Mass.: D. C. Heath/Lexington Books.

Humboldt, Alexander von. 1818. *Personal Narrative of Travels to the Equinoctial Regions of the New Continent During the Years 1799–1803*. London: Longman, Hurst, Rees, Orme, and Brown.

Jimenez, Michael. 1989. "Traveling Far in Grandfather's Car: The Life Cycle of Central Colombian Coffee Estates. The Case of Viotá, Cundinamarca (1900–1930)." *Hispanic American Historical Review* 69:185–219.

Joseph, G. M. 1982. *Revolution from Without: Yucatan, Mexico, and the United States, 1880–1924*. New York: Cambridge Univ. Press.

Katz, Friedrich. 1974. "Labor Conditions on Haciendas in Porfirian Mexico: Some Trends and Tendencies." *Hispanic American Historical Review* 54:1–47.

Katz, Friedrich. 1976. "Agrarian Changes in Northern Mexico in the Period of Villista Rule, 1913–1915." In James W. Wilkie et al., eds., *Contemporary Mexico: Papers of the IV International Congress of Mexican History*. Berkeley: Univ. of California Press.

Kautsky, Karl. 1974[1899]. *La Cuestión Agraria*. Mexico City: Ediciones de Cultura Popular.

Lappé, Frances Moore, and Joseph Collins. 1978. *Food First: Beyond the Myth of Scarcity*. Rev. ed. New York: Ballantine.

Larson, Brooke. 1988. *Colonialism and Agrarian Transformation in Bolivia: Cochabamba, 1550–1900*. Princeton: Princeton Univ. Press.

Lauria, Antonio. 1989. *A Study in Historical and Critical Anthropology: the Making of*

The People of Puerto Rico. Unpublished Ph.D. diss. New York: New School for Social Research.

Lenin, V. I. 1974[1899]. *The Development of Capitalism in Russia.* Moscow: Progress Publishers.

Love, Joseph L. 1989. "Of Planters, Politics and Development." *Latin American Research Review* 24, no. 3:127–35.

Machado, Absalón. 1977. *El Café: de la Aparcería al Capitalismo.* Bogotá: Punta de Lanza.

Mallon, Florencia. 1983. *The Defense of Community in Peru's Central Highlands: Peasant Struggle and Capitalist Transition, 1860–1940.* Princeton: Princeton Univ. Press.

Mallon, Florencia. 1986. "Gender and Class in the Transition to Capitalism: Household and Mode of Production in Central Peru." *Latin American Perspectives* 13, no. 1:147–74.

Mallon, Florencia. 1987. Nationalist and Antistate Coalitions in the War of the Pacific: Junín and Cajamarca, 1879–1902. In Steve J. Stern, ed., *Resistance, Rebellion, and Consciousness in the Andean Peasant World.* Madison: Univ. of Wisconsin Press, 232–79.

Martin, Cheryl English. 1985. *Rural Society in Colonial Morelos.* Albuquerque: University of New Mexico Press.

Marx, Karl. 1974a[1850]. "The Class Struggles in France, 1848–1850." In David Fernbach, ed., *Surveys from Exile.* New York: Random House/Vintage, 35–142.

Marx, Karl. 1974b[1852]. "The Eighteenth Brumaire of Louis Bonaparte." In David Fernbach, ed., *Surveys from Exile.* New York: Random House/Vintage, 143–249.

McCreery, David. 1976. "Coffee and Class: The Structure of Development in Liberal Guatemala." *Hispanic American Historical Review* 56:438–60.

McCreery, David. 1983. "Debt Servitude in Rural Guatemala, 1876–1936." *Hispanic American Historical Review* 63:735–59.

Mintz, Sidney. 1974a. "The Rural Proletariat and the Problem of Rural Proletarian Consciousness." *Journal of Peasant Studies* 1:290–325.

Mintz, Sidney. 1974b. *Caribbean Transformations.* Chicago: Aldine.

Mintz, Sidney. 1982. "Afterword: Peasantries and the Rural Sector—Notes on a Discovery." In Robert P. Weller and Scott E. Guggenheim, eds., *Power and Protest in the Countryside: Studies of Rural Unrest in Asia, Europe, and Latin America.* Durham: Duke Univ. Press, 180–88.

Morner, Magnus. 1978. *Perfil de la Sociedad Rural del Cuzco a Fines de la Colonia.* Lima.

Morner, Magnus, and Efain Trelles. 1987. "A Test of Causal Interpretations of the Tupac Amaru Rebellion." In Steve J. Stern, ed., *Resistance, Rebellion, and Consciousness in the Andean Peasant World, 18th to 20th Centuries.* Madison: Univ. of Wisconsin Press, 94–109.

Murra, John. 1975. *Formaciones Económicas y Políticas del Mundo Andino.* Lima: Instituto de Estudios Peruanos.

Nash, June, and Helen Safa, eds. 1976. *Sex and Class in Latin America.* New York: Praeger.

Nash, June, and Helen Safa, eds. 1986. *Women and Change in Latin America*. South Hadley, Mass.: Bergin and Garvey.

Nugent, Daniel. 1987. "Mexico's Rural Populations and *La Crisis*: Economic Crisis or Legitimation Crisis?" *Critique of Anthropology* 7, no. 3:93–112.

Orlove, Benjamin. 1977. *Alpacas, Sheep, and Men: The Wool Export Economy and Regional Society of Southern Peru*. New York: Academic Press.

Palacios, Marco. 1983. *El Café en Colombia, 1850–1970: Una Historia Económica, Social y Política*. 2d ed. Mexico City: El Colegio de México.

Patch, Robert. 1985. Agrarian Change in Eighteenth-Century Yucatan. *Hispanic American Historical Review* 65:21–49.

Picó, Fernando. 1979. *Libertad y Servidumbre en el Puerto Rico del Siglo XIX: Los Jornaleros Utuadeños en Vísperas del Auge del Café*. Río Piedras: Ediciones Huracán.

Picó, Fernando. 1981. *Amargo Café (Los Pequeños y Medianos Caficultores de Utuado en la Segunda Mitad del Siglo XIX)*. Río Piedras: Ediciones Huracán.

Pozas, Ricardo, and Isabel de Pozas. 1971. *Los Indios en las Clases Sociales de México*. Mexico City: Siglo XXI.

Redfield, Robert. 1930. *Tepoztlán, a Mexican Village: A Study of Folk Life*. Chicago: Univ. of Chicago Press.

Redfield, Robert. 1940. *The Folk Culture of Yucatan*. Chicago: Univ. of Chicago Press.

Redfield, Robert. 1953. *The Primitive World and its Transformations*. Ithaca, N.Y.: Cornell Univ. Press.

Roseberry, William. 1983. *Coffee and Capitalism in the Venezuelan Andes*. Austin: Univ. of Texas Press.

Roseberry, William. 1986. "The Ideology of Domestic Production." *Labour, Capital and Society* 19:70–93.

Roseberry, William. 1989. *Anthropologies and Histories: Essays in Culture, History, and Political Economy*. New Brunswick: Rutgers Univ. Press.

Roseberry, William. 1990. "Latin American Contexts for Historical Anthropology." Unpublished paper presented in the symposium, "Culture, History, Place," at the Annual Meeting of the American Anthropological Association. New Orleans.

Roseberry, William. 1991. "*La Falta de Brazos*: Land and Labor in the Coffee Economies of Nineteenth-Century Latin America." *Theory and Society* 20:351–82.

Roseberry, William. Forthcoming. "Introduction." In William Roseberry and Lowell Gudmundson, eds., *Coffee, Society, and Power in Latin America*.

Roseberry, William, and Lowell Gudmundson, eds. Forthcoming. *Coffee, Society, and Power in Latin America*.

Rowe, John. 1957. "The Incas under Spanish Colonial Institutions." *Hispanic American Historical Review* 37:155–99.

Rubin, Vera, ed. 1959. *Plantation Systems of the New World*. Social Science Monograph No. 7. Washington, D.C.: Division of Social Science Department, Pan American Union.

Samper, Mario. 1990. *Generations of Settlers: Rural Households and Their Markets on the Costa Rican Frontier*. Boulder: Westview.

Schryer, Frans J. 1980. *The Rancheros of Pisaflores: The History of a Peasant Bourgeoisie in Twentieth-Century Mexico*. Toronto: Univ. of Toronto Press.

Scott, James C. 1976. *The Moral Economy of the Peasant*. New Haven: Yale Univ. Press.

Scott, James C. 1985. *Weapons of the Weak: Everyday Forms of Peasant Resistance.* New Haven: Yale Univ. Press.

Seligson, Mitchel. 1980. *Peasants in Costa Rica and the Development of Agrarian Capitalism.* Madison: Univ. of Wisconsin Press.

Shanin, Teodor. 1983. *Late Marx and the Russian Road: Marx and the Peripheries of Capitalism.* New York: Monthly Review Press.

Silverman, Sydel. 1979. The Peasant Concept in Anthropology. *Journal of Peasant Studies* 7:49–69.

Skocpol, Theda. 1982. What Makes Peasants Revolutionary? In Robert P. Weller and Scott E. Guggenheim, eds., *Power and Protest in the Countryside: Studies of Rural Unrest in Asia, Europe, and Latin America.* Durham: Duke University Press, 157–79.

Smith, Carol A. 1984. "Local History in Global Context: Social and Economic Transitions in Western Guatemala." *Comparative Studies in Society and History* 26:193–228.

Smith, Gavin. 1989. *Livelihood and Resistance: Peasants and the Politics of Land in Peru.* Berkeley: University of California Press.

Sotelo Inclán, Jesús. 1943. *Raíz y Razon de Zapata.* Mexico City: Etnos.

Spalding, Karen. 1984. *Huarochirí, An Andean Society under Inca and Spanish Rule.* Stanford: Stanford Univ. Press.

Stavenhagen, Rodolfo. 1969. *Las Clases Sociales en las Sociedades Agrarias.* Mexico City: Siglo XXI.

Stavenhagen, Rodolfo. 1970. "Introduction to Part 3." In Rodolfo Stavenhagen, ed., *Agrarian Problems and Peasant Movements in Latin America.* New York: Doubleday/Anchor, 371–73.

Stein, Stanley J. 1985[1957]. *Vassouras, A Brazilian Coffee County, 1850–1900: The Role of Planter and Slave in a Plantation Society.* 2d ed. Princeton: Princeton Univ. Press.

Stein, Stanley J., and Barbara Stein. 1972. *The Colonial Heritage of Latin America.* New York: Oxford Univ. Press.

Stern, Steve J. 1982. *Peru's Indian Peoples and the Challenge of Spanish Conquest: Huamanga to 1640.* Madison: Univ. of Wisconsin Press.

Stern, Steve J. 1983. "The Struggle for Solidarity: Class, Culture, and Community in Highland Indian America." *Radical History Review* 27:21–45.

Stern, Steve J. 1987. "New Approaches to the Study of Peasant Rebellion and Consciousness: Implications of the Andean Experience." In Steve J. Stern, ed., *Resistance, Rebellion, and Consciousness in the Andean Peasant World, 18th to 20th Centuries.* Madison: Univ. of Wisconsin Press, 3–25.

Steward, Julian, Robert Manners, Eric Wolf, Elena Padilla, Sidney Mintz, and Raymond Scheele. 1956. *The People of Puerto Rico.* Urbana: Univ. of Illinois Press.

Stocking, George W., Jr. 1987. *Victorian Anthropology.* New York: Free Press.

Stolcke, Verena. 1988. *Coffee Planters, Workers, and Wives: Class Conflict and Gender Relations on São Paulo Plantations, 1850–1980.* New York: St. Martin's Press.

Stolcke, Verena. 1989. "Coffee Planters, Politics, and Development in Brazil: A Comment on Mauricio Font's Analysis." *Latin American Research Review* 24, no. 3:136–42.

Taussig, Michael. 1980. *The Devil and Commodity Fetishism in South America*. Chapel Hill: Univ. of North Carolina Press.

Taylor, William. 1972. *Landlord and Peasant in Colonial Oaxaca*. Stanford: Stanford Univ. Press.

Taylor, William. 1974. "Landed Society in New Spain: A View from the South." *Hispanic American Historical Review* 54:387–413.

Trouillot, Michel-Rolph. 1982. "Motion in the System: Coffee, Color, and Slavery in Eighteenth-Century Saint-Domingue." *Review* 5:331–87.

Vincent, Joan. 1990. *Anthropology and Politics: Visions, Traditions, Trends*. Tucson: Univ. of Arizona Press.

Warman, Arturo. 1981. *We Come to Object: The Peasants of Morelos State and the National State*. Baltimore: The Johns Hopkins Univ. Press.

Wasserman, Mark. 1984. *Caciques, Capitalists, and Revolution: The Native Elite and Foreign Enterprise in Chihuahua, Mexico, 1854–1911*. Chapel Hill: Univ. of North Carolina Press.

Wasserstrom, Robert. 1983. *Class and Society in Central Chiapas*. Berkeley: Univ. of California Press.

Weinstein, Barbara. 1983. *The Amazon Rubber Boom, 1850–1920*. Stanford: Stanford Univ. Press.

Williams, Raymond. 1973. *The Country and the City*. New York: Oxford Univ. Press.

Wolf, Eric. 1955. "Types of Latin American Peasantries: A Preliminary Discussion." *American Anthropologist* 57:452–71.

Wolf, Eric. 1959. *Sons of the Shaking Earth*. Chicago: Univ. of Chicago Press.

Wolf, Eric. 1969. *Peasant Wars of the Twentieth Century*. New York: Harper & Row.

Wolf, Eric. 1986. The Vicissitudes of the Closed Corporate Peasant Community. *American Ethnologist* 13:325–29.

Wolf, Eric, and Sidney Mintz. 1957. "Haciendas and Plantations in Middle America and the Antilles." *Social and Economic Studies* 6:386–412.

Womack, John. 1969. *Zapata and the Mexican Revolution*. New York: Knopf.

Young, Kate. 1978. "Modes of Appropriation and the Sexual Division of Labour: A Case from Oaxaca, Mexico." In A. Kuhn and A. Wolpe, eds., *Feminism and Materialism*. London: Routledge and Kegan Paul, 124–84.

PART 3
Cycles of Reverberation?

6 *Florencia E. Mallon*

Dialogues Among the Fragments:
Retrospect and Prospect

This book is the product of a generational encounter with Africa and Latin America. Its authors came of academic age in the 1970s and entered their productive maturity in the 1980s. In twenty years, we have lived through two fairly dramatic intellectual and political transitions, both of which have had an important effect on our work. The first of these was the revival of world radicalism in the 1960s, which inspired and challenged us, as well as other intellectuals in our cohort, to combine local research with radical theories and methods that focused on the "common folk." Such a combination, we hoped, would begin to produce complex case studies that challenged the reductionism, political conservatism, and imperial assumptions built into the overarching paradigms of an earlier, intellectually more orthodox and unified era. So in the 1970s and early 1980s, we contributed numerous examples of this "new social history" to the local literatures in various African and Latin American countries. By the second half of the 1980s, however, the second major transition was upon us, combining the crisis of Marxism and socialism with the resuscitation of subjectivity present in feminism and postmodernism/poststructuralism. This second transition has not only called into question the overarching theories we were already criticizing, but also challenged us radically to rethink many of the megascripts we had been using as alternatives. Within two short decades, then, our experiences with the new social history have blended with the critiques of metanarrative to place us at a crossroads.

One side of this crossroads emerges from our generational journey into the field. Throughout Africa and Latin America, local and foreign researchers went out into the countryside, both concretely and metaphorically, in the 1970s. They did not, of course, begin their journeys with a blank intellectual slate. Some carried volume 1 of *Capital* under their arms, others *Reading Capital*. Larger numbers traveled in the company of E. P. Thompson, E. J. Hobsbawm, or Antonio Gramsci.[1] Some attempted to fit all these texts and many more into their knapsacks. As is the case with all journeys, these excursions were marked, in important ways, by the choice of traveling companions. But they were defined as well by the encounter with complex local realities, and by the failure of any one text or approach adequately to encompass or explain them. The authors writing in this volume have all been part, in their own ways, of this generational experience: the explosion of regional and local studies of histori- cal experience, in Africa and Latin America, that multiplied and fragmented supposedly unified national or continental narratives.

Yet the other side of the crossroads is that we still have before us the challenge of how and if it will be possible to reconstruct. Can we reestablish a dialogue, at a sufficiently general level of abstraction, among the fragments of the multi- leveled and conflictual local and regional realities we have been uncovering? The task at hand, it seems to me, is not the building of new, hard-and-fast, "correct" paradigms—understood as attempts to dismiss troublesome anoma- lies and questions as unimportant externalities—but rather the redefinition of paradigms as open-ended yet committed attempts to find principles of unity, patterns of meaning, among the fragments. This involves, on the one hand, a continuous emphasis on the ongoing, intellectually skeptical, and flexible quality of the dialogue with which we wish to infuse paradigms and theories. But on the other hand, it also means a recommitment, on redefined terms, to the importance of understanding broader narratives, structures, and power relations. If our previous versions of these narratives and structures were too rigid, recent treatments of discourse and culture have sometimes treated power and narrative line as if they were endlessly variable and diffuse. In this volume we move to claim an intermediate space in which to confront our constructed regional "stories" and the broader scripts we wish to rewrite. As Fred Cooper points out in the new postscript to his essay, the development of capitalism— and one might add, as analogous and sometimes related scripts, of colonial- ism and nation-state formation, labor and the development of a world system, peasants in the making of modern politics, the historical constructions of gender and racial/ethnic hierarchies—are processes that still need to be under- stood, both locally and more generally. These issues will not go away, even if our approaches need major rethinking.

My purpose in this conclusion, then, is to take the various stories contained in the essays in this volume and suggest some broader patterns by placing them together on a few larger narrative and theoretical canvases. As often happens with a cubist painting, the patterns of meaning—of line, color, angle, composition—will vary with the distance from the canvas, and the direction of the gaze. I begin with selective summaries of the main points of overlap and difference among the essays, establishing my own dialogue among them to elucidate their broader and enduring contributions to our understandings of agrarian transformations and the development of the world system. I then take a step back to place the book's essays on a broader canvas, where some of the commonalities and differences between the African and Latin American scholarly literatures of the past generation can be seen in the context of the distinct colonial and postcolonial histories of the two regions. A step to the side next permits me to bring into focus earlier reverberations between African and Latin American literatures, around analyses of dependency, articulation of modes of production, gender, and the intersections between class and politics. And a final step back suggests future directions for dialogue concerning questions of ethnicity, gender and generation, culture and politics, and the meaning of nationalism in "Third World" areas. These themes constitute a field of potential reverberations among the literatures for Asia, Africa, and Latin America.

Capitalism, Rural Peoples, and the World Economy

Written nearly a decade apart, the essays by Cooper and Stern differ quite markedly in purpose and context. Originally commissioned as a review of existing literature on Africa and the world economy, Cooper's essay summarizes a generation of the most creative and extensive academic production on African economic history and economic anthropology. It is inclusive rather than selective; its general project is to get beyond a vision of capitalism "as an implacable entity redefining social structures through its own requirements." Whether this "deterministic view of exchange" is held by developmentalists, who "joyfully add up cocoa shipments," or by dependency theorists, who indignantly might add up surpluses drained, Cooper argues that the specificities of culture, politics, and production get lost. It is only by reestablishing a dialogue between the broad theoretical and comparative questions, and the particularities of place, time, culture, perception, and conflict, that the realities of Africa's place in the world economy will be better understood. From an examination of process rather than periodization, which allows for a more flexible approach to local variation and contestation, he concludes that the general "underlying issue is still the general process of capital accumulation and its limitations."

Initially a paper about the significance of Immanuel Wallerstein's work for Latin America, Stern's essay is more selectively focused, analyzing colonial mining and plantation slavery as tests for Wallerstein's theories on labor relations in the periphery. In the process of constructing his argument, however, Stern moves far beyond testing Wallerstein to an ambitious overview of Latin American literatures on dependency and modes of production, and concludes with his own alternative explanation for the evolution of relationships in the Iberian colonies. Tying this evolution to three "grand motors"—the world system, popular strategies of resistance and survival in the periphery, and mercantile or elite interests tied to American "centers of gravity"—Stern provides us with an initial map to the ways in which "local conditions . . . molded the options, constraints, and opportunities faced by the 'world-system.' "

Despite the differences between the essays, therefore, both authors share a deep skepticism about using world-system approaches as overarching explanations for events, trends or relationships in Africa or Latin America. Both emphasize the original creativity of Latin American structuralists and dependency theorists, who by the 1940s, 1950s, and early 1960s were already asking the questions that would become so current—and in many ways simplified— in the literature of the late 1960s and 1970s. Stern points as well to an original literature on colonial modes of production created by Latin Americans as of the mid-1970s, which took us far beyond the question of dependency in the world economy, but was never translated and hardly noticed by scholars in the United States. In the end, therefore, both authors demonstrate how, with "peripheral vision" (to borrow a phrase from Stern), researchers working on Latin America and Africa creatively engaged the paradigms being developed or appropriated in Europe and the United States, confronting and contesting their boundaries through empirical as well as critical theoretical work. They show that unequal exchange is not only a key concept in the theory of the world system, but also a power relationship within the academy that gets reproduced even in approaches that claim to move beyond it. Excavating the realities of power in our own midst must thus form a crucial part of our ongoing confrontations with existing and evolving historical paradigms.

Beyond these similarities in perspective, however, the two essays construct their general stories of colonialism in significantly different ways. While for Cooper, as we have seen, the underlying script is the accumulation of capital and the development of capitalism—with all the dead-ends and peculiar pathways it possessed in Africa—for Stern the core of the story is composed of a noncapitalist colonialism intimately related to the development of capitalism in Europe. Of course, part of this difference has to do with the distinct historical moments at which the two colonial encounters occurred: Latin America, at a conjuncture of crisis in and transition from European feudalism; Africa, at the moment of European capitalism's greatest initial expansion. The end result, however, is that, even as authors emphasize the centrality of popular resistance strategies and local entrepreneurial interests in shaping the contours of colonial projects, the theoretical implications of these processes—and of the analyses of the two authors—emerge as quite distinct. In Stern, the script of capitalism is distant, both in space and time; meanwhile, the creativity of alternative modes-of-production analyses can be more systematically explored, especially the work of Latin Americans on colonial or colonial slave modes of production, and on colonial social formations. In Cooper, by contrast, the scripts of capitalism and colonialism overlap so substantially that analyses of noncapitalist formations get much shorter shrift, criticized more readily and easily for their shortcomings.

Given the stated goals of each of the authors, both essays are relatively short on political analysis. While mentioning the role of colonial states and their officials in the reorganization of production and labor systems, Stern affords little attention to the internal contradictions of colonial politics when assessing the validity of Wallerstein's paradigm for colonial mining and plantation slavery. Cooper, for his part, addresses the contradictions within colonial states, especially with regard to labor control, and consistently brings up the role of social conflict in the transformation of particular forms of surplus extraction. Yet in the end, he is less than comfortable with a politically centered analysis of tensions among capitalists, preferring to Poulantzas's concept of class fractions the more basic Marxist distinction between absolute and relative surplus value. And while he is right that the particular renditions of class fractions given by scholars of African social formations were less than helpful, the concept itself is something else again, potentially permitting us to conceptualize conflicts over state power as more than reflections of contradictions in the productive sphere.

Isaacman and Roseberry's companion essays on peasant studies in Africa and Latin America review extremely rich yet quite distinct literatures on rural production and politics. For Isaacman, the African peasant studies field remained in relative infancy through the 1970s, despite dramatic developments in African studies more generally. All the approaches used from the 1950s forward, he argues—including modernization theory, nationalist historiography, dependency and modes of production theories—tended to render peasants politically invisible. It was only in the 1980s, with new emphases on gender and politics, that the peasants themselves emerged clearly as actors. By contrast, Roseberry argues that peasants were not invisible in Latin America by the 1960s, largely because rural mobilizations and debates over agrarian reform put rural people squarely in the center of both scholarly and policy-oriented discussions. He emphasizes, however, that the "agrarian question" was posed about, not by, the peasantry; and partially as a result of this, a political question was given a primarily economic answer. Intellectuals sought to discover whether peasants could or would play an important role in revolutionary change through an economic class analysis of "the very structure of society," displacing peasants from the political stage.

Since the essays treat debates on peasants and politics as they emerged within their respective fields, reading the two together may well exaggerate the difference between African and Latin American renditions of peasants over these years. Invisibility, in this context, may be in the eye of the beholder, defined according to lines of conflict more readily discernible to the regional specialist. From a more general comparative angle, important similarities emerge as well. In Africa as well as Latin America, the 1960s saw the dramatic involvement of rural peoples in movements for social change, as well as attempts by local and foreign intellectuals to make sense of that involvement. In both cases, too, questions about the political participation or relevance of peasants were asked *about* them, by activists or politicians with other agendas, rather than by peasants themselves or from a peasant-centered perspective. Differences were more in the context in which the questions were asked, and in the particular image of peasant politics that emerged in each case.

In Latin America, the focus on peasants began in the 1950s and 1960s, when rural unrest generated concern with the "backwardness" and "feudal" character of the countryside. Though active in a series of movements that sought the redistribution of land, and differentiated among themselves in a variety of ways, peasants and their communities were viewed as seamless and traditional. Scholars and activists wished to transform them, either through an agrarian reform that would integrate them into the "modern" world, or through an impending process of proletarianization that would facilitate their organization as rural workers. In either case, "traditional" peasant politics had negative connotations, and it was hoped that they would be transformed through modernization or a worker-peasant alliance. Only in the 1970s, with the renewed influence of Chayanovian perspectives on the peasant family economy, was this debate reorganized between the "campesinistas," who glorified peasant culture and politics, and the "proletaristas," who argued for the advancing disappearance of the peasantry into a capitalist class system.

In the African nationalist literature of the 1960s, with the primary focus on the anticolonial mandate of the nationalist parties, peasants tended to be treated as "prepolitical" precursors or junior partners. Here as well, despite a variegated history of economic participation, differentiation, and political activism, rural communities were seen as seamless and traditional. The main difference with Latin America was that, in the context of anticolonialism, supposedly precolonial cultures were viewed as positive. So were early forms of resistance to colonialism, which several authors argued would need to be integrated into nationalist movements if the latter were to garner effective popular support (Lonsdale 1968; Ranger 1968).

Both authors point out that by the 1980s the literatures on peasants had moved far beyond their origins in parallel though distinct discourses of national development. In both areas, more abstract and top-down approaches gave way to empirically grounded regional and local studies in which specific peasantries and political movements claimed the space and analytical attention they deserved. From a comparative vantage point, and building on the perceptions and perspectives of both authors, it is interesting to note, however, that the path and endpoint of revision was different on each continent. In Africa, agrarian struggles and their protagonists came more fully into focus only after the analytical wheel had taken two full turns: first, a critique of nationalist analyses grounded in dependency theory; and second, a new focus on politics in the postdependency and post-modes-of-production era. Given the more political and nationalist emphasis of the earlier "resistance" literature in Africa, revisionists radically questioned the capacity of any nationalist movement or ideology truly to incorporate the popular classes, giving their writings a strong "postnationalist" flavor. In Latin America, by contrast, many of the 1980s revisions attempted to vindicate the place of peasant movements in national political arenas and, while sharing with the Africanist literature a strong empirical grounding in specific regions, ended up sounding more like the earlier Africanist resistance literature in their celebrations of nationalism from below.

This difference in the extent to which nationalist scripts were questioned facilitated, in my view, the earlier incorporation of gender and ethnicity into the study of peasant politics in Africa. In Latin America, intellectuals have longer harbored the hope of reintegrating the stories of peasants, women, or people of color into national metanarratives, resisting the radical modifications that a focus on gender and ethnicity demands. Indeed, these are occurring later and more painfully in the Latin American literature. For Africa, when Isaacman calls in his essay for a more detailed consideration of the labor process and its effect on peasant options, he is arguing from an already variegated and sophisticated position about labor that includes an analysis of gender. In Latin America, on the other hand, Roseberry points out that the gender analysis of households and the distinction between ethnicity and class are less fully developed themes, in need of immediate and urgent research.

Despite the different trajectories they signal, Roseberry and Isaacman have generally similiar visions of where future study of peasants should head in Latin America and Africa. Both underline the importance of understanding peasant political cultures on the ground, as well as their insertion into broader oppositional or hegemonic movements. Building from recent work that traces peasant discourses historically and locally, both authors welcome trends that, in Roseberry's phrase, "name the names" of the actors in local political processes, while at the same time showing the impact of the local on the emergence of regional and national coalitions. Yet once again, even as the two authors point in the same general direction, they chart distinct paths.

As a corrective to the heavily economistic tendencies in the literature on Latin American peasants, Roseberry concludes his piece with a call for more work on "the historical formation of particular peasantries in locally configured fields of power." Through historically and theoretically deep immersion in specific regions and locales, he suggests, where the particularities of production and social conflict merge with specific intra- and interclass political struggles and alliances, we can begin to understand "the 'manifold ways whereby peasants have continuously engaged their political worlds.' " For Isaacman, on the other hand, the task at hand holds other twists: a decade of Africanist work on particular peasantries has illuminated many cases of peasant political engagement, yet left scholars still unclear on how to reconnect these specific realities to the broader cultural, social, and economic contexts in which rural cultivators produce and reproduce their livelihood. "By focusing on historically specific forms of the labor process," a concept he expands to include gender relations and cultural elements, Isaacman challenges us to ground our more sophisticated views of rural power struggles and political alliances in the recognition that their daily conditions of life afforded peasants a comparatively greater degree of autonomy than that attained by rural or urban workers.

In calling for a reintegration of labor processes into our analysis of rural struggles, Isaacman points to a general problem. Many of us feel uneasy about how best to reconnect apparently economic concepts—the labor process, capital accumulation, absolute versus relative surplus value—to our increasingly complex and multilayered understandings of politics. To do so in a way that gives each layer its due is probably impossible for any single author; yet recognizing the centrality of the overall project is crucial. A promising place to start is with a dual recognition: first, that class is not reducible to a particular point in the process of production; and second, that political action and consciousness is not reducible to class position. Taken together, the essays in this book move us in this direction by examining the interactions, overlap, and contradictions between evolving systems of production, and the processes of political conflict, alliance, and contestation within and between classes that precede, accompany, and transform those production systems.

A First Step Back from the Canvas:
Africanist and Latin Americanist
Reverberations in Historical Perspective

Beyond their specific content and potential reverberations, the four essays also capture the different histories and political contexts of intellectual debates in Africa and Latin America, suggesting parallelisms or similarities in the timing and issues involved. On both continents, for example, the period after World War II became the era of modernization; it was time to bring these "backward" regions into the modern world. In Africa, modernization was experienced— from the late 1930s through the 1950s—as "responsible" colonialism, when the social engineering of modern colonial states would create a proletariat and a capitalist agriculture in the European image. In Latin America, by contrast, modernization was constructed over the same general period as national development, with activist states fomenting industrialization through import substitution, and integration through education and public works construction. In both regions, however, it was this period of modernization that yielded the mainstream paradigms on whose criticism a generation cut its intellectual and political teeth.

Both modernization projects failed by the 1960s. The "second colonization" of Africa was resisted by many groups and factions, setting into motion a series of social, economic, and political contradictions and mobilizations that, in myriad combinations, fed into nationalist independence movements. As we have seen, peasant politics were submerged in this context, becoming a subtext of the nationalist "master narratives" constructed ex post facto by academics and some activist intellectuals. In Latin America, rural struggles also became a subplot within a nationalist drama, whose title could easily have been "Development: Agrarian Reform or Revolution?" Throughout the continent, young radicals unhappy with the gradualist approaches of reformist and Marxist political parties took seriously the "guerrilla foco" theory of the Cuban revolution, marching out into the countryside to ignite their own radical transformations. At the same time, Latin American and U.S. state officials, hoping to outflank peasant activists and their erstwhile urban allies and thus avoid a repeat of Cuba 1959, hastily wrote up plans for agrarian reform. And once again, by the early 1970s, the two nationalist dramas—one anticolonial and the other decidedly postcolonial—were hopelessly entangled in their own contradictions.

In Africa, interest in dependency theory and articulation of modes of production emerged from the disillusionment with nationalist movements and nationalist promises. Transitions from colonial rule left poverty and economic dependence pretty much intact, and led to discussions about the underdevelopment inherent in colonialism, the lack of an autonomous African bourgeoisie, the problems with building healthy national economies on the basis of unequal exchange. In this context, the discussions and debates of Latin America's post–World War II policymakers—who had been attempting to deal with the problematic reintegration of that region's economies into a world system dominated by the United States—suddenly made a great deal of sense. So did the discussions emerging among French and Latin American intellectuals, inspired by an Althusserian structural Marxism, about the problematic, violent, and long-lasting articulation of capitalist and precapitalist modes of production. As had always been the case, however, the meaning of these concepts in an African context was quite distinct; for in a situation where colonialism and capitalism had been companion scripts, the possibility of autonomous capitalist development, or of a complete transition to advanced capitalism at the other end of articulation, rang more immediately and completely hollow than it had in Latin America.

In Latin America, meanwhile, the promises of populist developmentalists and violent revolutionaries were coming unraveled at about the same time. Between the Brazilian military coup of 1964 and the Chilean bloodbath of 1973, violent authoritarian regimes spread throughout the continent. Agrarian reforms were pronounced dead, stopped, or reversed. And by 1968 the failure of a variety of attempted guerrilla movements, symbolized most dramatically by the death of Che Guevara in Bolivia, had also demonstrated the impossibility of cloning the Cuban Revolution. Here, too, the attraction of overdetermined, outside explanations grew apace; dependency and the articulation of modes-of-production approaches—often, as both Stern and Cooper have shown in this volume, in simplified form—increased in popularity.

And yet the growth of intellectual generations does not mirror, in a parallel or simplistic way, the paths of change in society as a whole. Even as the influence of structuralist and overdetermined explanations was increasing, scholars who had grown up at the intersection of the student movements of the 1960s and the heady promises of "Third World" revolutions went out into the field. Our experiences in the classroom and in the world at large had taught us to search out and recognize human agency and creativity, in field and archives—and we found it. But the problem became how to fit these findings back into existing structuralist paradigms: if one pushed and strained hard enough, would it be possible—just barely—to close the lid? Sometimes it was possible to do so, at least in the short run. Sometimes a deeper partial revision was in order, with a serious sense of human agency and its consequences being used to temper the rigidity of overdetermined explanations. Yet by the end of the 1980s, feminisms, a series of "post-isms," and events in the Third and socialist worlds all contributed to blowing most paradigmatic lids off permanently.

It is out of this conflictual, painful, and extremely rich process of intellectual and political discovery that the present scholarly conjuncture—the now familiar focus on the politics and contestation of knowledge, discourse, and culture—has emerged. But in Africa and Latin America, the confrontation with postmodern concerns around cultural analysis, discursive patterns, and diffuse and decentered power occurs in quite a different context from that in Europe or the United States. If, as Kwame Anthony Appiah suggests, "the project of transcending some species of modernism" means that "the rationalization of the world can no longer be seen as the tendency either of the West or of history" (1991:343), then postmodernism may easily take on an anti-imperialist flavor. In this guise it would explode the master narratives that constructed the colonial, neocolonial, and postcolonial "Third Worlds" as backward "others" to be rescued and modernized by the rational and civilized West. If, on the other hand, the intellectual and political practices that shape postmodernism become the exclusive province of the intelligentsia of late capitalism in the so-called advanced countries, the implications look quite different. In the latter context, postmodernism is likely to erect another correct paradigm on the ruins of previous ones, thus initiating a new epoch in which truth and subjectivity are still the "tendency of the West," and thereby recreating, with new packaging, the imperialisms and power differentials of the past.

An example of these potential dangers and complexities is a debate that occurred several years ago among some of the participants in a conference on the nation-state in the Andes. Several French scholars dismissed ongoing attempts by Andean intellectuals to incorporate their countries into a nationalist metanarrative by declaring summarily that such narratives, if they had a basis in reality, applied to nineteenth-century Europe only; thus they could not be applied to twentieth-century Latin America. The fact that inclusive national projects and metanarratives had generally failed in the Andes, but still represented to many a vital intellectual and political challenge, was suddenly irrelevant.[2] Sensitive to these possible variations and implications, the authors in this volume call for a judicious reading and application of theories and texts; a recognition of the contributions made by Latin Americans and Africans to empirical, analytical, theoretical, and political understandings of their own and other societies; and the need for present and future work to avoid falling into the trap of "we" are right, and "they" were wrong—whoever *we* and *they* might represent at any given moment.

Past Reverberations in Individual Perspective: Three Intellectuals on Dependency, Modes of Production, Gender, and Politics

In keeping with this general spirit, I now take a step to the side in order to observe the canvas from another angle, thereby to ponder more fully the earlier reverberations between African and Latin American literatures and their interactions and intersections with literatures produced in Europe. We have already seen some of the ways in which dependency perspectives got formed and reproduced, in multileveled interactions between and among Latin American policymakers, critical intellectuals on both continents, and their European and North American interpreters. But there are many other ways in which similar interactions have occurred, not only in the world-system literatures, but also in discussions of articulation of modes of production, gender, and class and politics. By stepping to the side, therefore, I would like to reconsider some of these earlier reverberations by focusing on the individual trajectories of three specific intellectuals: Walter Rodney, Maxine Molyneux, and Ernesto Laclau. The three obviously do not exhaust the potential list of individual paths of interaction and reverberation. But given their particular forms of intellectual movement, across the boundaries of supposedly balkanized geographies, theories, and topics, and the broad influence their evolving work has had on others working on related subjects, these three scholars taken together constitute an excellent organizing core for my discussion.

Stern has already addressed, for the dependency literature, how the manuscript of Cardoso and Faletto's important text was circulating in Latin American intellectual circles by the mid-1960s, helping to delineate the context and issues that would be addressed by Andre Gunder Frank. Other developments, some mentioned in the essays reproduced here and some not, also tied together the various strands of debate around dependency. An excellent example of such ties can be seen in the life and work of Walter Rodney, prominent Guyanese activist and politician. Rodney was formed by and struggled in the kind of multicultural and multiethnic reality constructed by colonialism and the world system in the Caribbean, whose history (as Rodney and Stern remind us in different ways) was deeply furrowed by popular strategies of resistance and survival. His political vision—which ultimately led to his assassination—was of a united popular movement in which Guyanese people from African and Asian backgrounds could come together to claim their common rights. Yet as he experienced the intense ethnic, racial, and class contradictions of building a counterhegemonic consensus, he, too, was tempted by overdetermined answers. In 1972 he published the groundbreaking *How Europe Underdeveloped Africa*, which became a flagship text in the dependency-oriented critique of African nationalist historiographies. His later work on Guyana, especially *A History of the Guyanese Working People* (1981), went far beyond the more abstract world-system position, moving us into the villages of ex-slaves on the Guyanese plantation-dominated coast, examining close up their variegated strategies of survival, resistance, and confrontation. And yet among Africanists (rather than Caribbeanists), Rodney continues to be known best for his earlier text.

Almost concurrently with the development of dependency perspectives, both Cooper and Stern remind us, the approach focusing on the articulation of modes of production also began to gain influence. This theory had a complex origin in dialogues between and among French Althusserian Marxists, scholars working in and on Africa, and Latin American activists and intellectuals. Though the issues had already been debated in the French-oriented literature for Africa since the late 1960s, it was the work of Claude Meillassoux (1972) and Pierre-Philippe Rey (1973) that had the greatest impact in Latin America. Latin American scholars and activists also found in the approach some interesting potential for getting beyond the interpretation of Latin American "feudalism," common at that point in both scholarly Marxist and politically communist analyses of the continent. By the mid-1970s as well, Latin American colonial historians and activist intellectuals had begun to experiment with the concept of the articulation of modes of production. Among historians, this led to the various formulations of the colonial mode of production discussed by Stern. Among politically active intellectuals such as Roger Bartra, it resulted in an expanded consideration of the Asiatic mode of production and of articulation (Bartra 1976), challenging the more doctrinaire forms of Marxist theory that had dominated until that time. Through the work of Argentine intellectual Ernesto Laclau (1971), among others, the modes-of-production approach would be used as a corrective to and critique of the more reductionist forms of dependency theory.[3]

In Latin America as well as Africa, in encounters with scholarly as well as activist issues, new questions and critiques began to be heard along the edges of modes-of-production approaches by the last years of the 1970s. One of the inspirations for these was political, and came once again from the Caribbean— that melting pot of American, European, African, and Asian influences. The Cuban Revolution, and most importantly the intense debates on gender inspired by and contained within it by the end of the 1970s, prompted women intellectuals throughout Latin America to use Cuba as a starting point and organizing principle for their critiques of class-centered theories of domination. In Europe and the United States, feminist intellectuals involved themselves in dialogue between the experiences of their own new women's movements and those of women in the so-called "Third World." As women's participation in violent guerrilla struggles for national liberation—in Angola, Mozambique, Vietnam, and Zimbabwe (1975–1980)—yielded initial optimism about a transformation of gender roles, which was fairly quickly reversed in the years of reconstruction after the violent phase, the seeming contradiction between feminist demands and social justice became an additional and controversial topic of debate. And here also the reverberations among these various gender debates crossed the boundaries of apparently balkanized arenas, as is well represented by the work of Maxine Molyneux.

In 1977, Molyneux published an article entitled "Androcentrism in Marxist Anthropology," where she took on the work of Marxist anthropologists such as Emmanuel Terray for contending that West African societies were egalitarian because they had no classes. Using the case of the Gouru, she argued convincingly for a previous hierarchy based on gender and generation, in which older men controlled younger men through their control of women and marriage strategies. Though beginning from a very specific and specialized case, Molyneux's article was meant as a broad critique of Marxist class analysis for its inability fully to understand the internal dynamics of human hierarchies. Part of a broader tendency toward feminist critiques of modes-of-production theories (see also the other essays in *Critique of Anthropology* 1977; Hartmann 1981; and *Feminist Review* 1979, dedicated to the Cuban Revolution), this article formed part of Molyneux's own broader attempt to deal with the question of gender and socialism (see also Molyneux 1982, 1985a). Indeed, by the mid-1980s her attempts at confronting gender and class yielded some of the most interesting and critical readings of gender in the Nicaraguan revolution (Molyneux 1985b). At the same time, the Africa-centered side of Molyneux's intellectual project—that is, her use of gender analysis to criticize class reductionist perspectives on African societies—was shared by other Africanist authors since the mid-1970s (e.g., Wright 1975, O'Laughlin 1977), and fed into a rapidly expanding literature in the 1980s. Indeed, as the most recent work on East Africa suggests (e.g., Schmidt 1987, Feierman 1990, Mandala 1990) the existence of a well-developed Africanist literature on gender has facilitated a particularly sophisticated and multileveled treatment of power relations in the African countryside.

Another fascinating personal trajectory that helps us trace the reverberations among literatures and continents is that of Ernesto Laclau. After his use of a mode-of-production approach to critique Frank (Laclau 1971), he moved on to engage European theorists of the state, especially Nicos Poulantzas, and contributed a provocative intervention to the Poulantzas/Miliband debate (Laclau 1975). In this essay he previewed one of the important conclusions of his 1977 book on *Politics and Ideology in Marxist Theory*, namely that Althusserian Marxism's reliance on articulation among levels of a mode of production was simply a game of mirrors to avoid admitting that class was not only, not even primarily, an economic category. In fact, the essays in *Politics and Ideology* give us the broad view of Laclau's intellectual production during the 1970s, beginning with his essay on Frank, reproducing his essay on the Poulantzas/Miliband debate, and finishing with new and groundbreaking discussions of fascism and populism. These last two essays move us into political territory in which consciousness does not have a class belonging, and all forms of politics involve class alliance as well as class conflict. From a long perspective, therefore, Laclau represents as well as anyone the multiple dialogues occurring during the 1970s.

Indeed, the frosting on this particular cake comes in the use to which Laclau's work was put by Africanist John Saul in his essay "The Dialectic of Class and Tribe" (1979). In this essay, Saul used Laclau's conceptualization of the relative autonomy of class and politics, in particular the idea of the "national-popular" as a tradition of struggle by "the people" against state power that does not belong to any particular class, to reexamine the question of ethnicity and tribalism in Africa. He suggested that ethnicity or tribe should be understood as part of the national-popular: a form of cultural politics and struggle against power that has a strong popular content, even as it is autonomous from class relations. If this is true, he concluded, the cultural power of ethnicity or tribalism is not only a power of domination, but also of contestation; and

Marxist scholars should give renewed attention and legitimacy to an analysis of ethnic hierarchies as separate from, though interrelated with, class. In my view, the importance of Saul's conclusion lies not in its overall innovation— non-Marxist students of ethnicity had been saying similar things for years— but in his attempt to open up a systematic field of inquiry on ethnicity that began from Marxism, yet did not make the common Marxist assumption that ethnic hierarchies were simply a proxy for class relations.[4]

Seen through the work of Rodney, Molyneux, and Laclau, the 1970s and 1980s were a time of rich debate and reverberation between Latin American and African literatures and scholars, with a unifying line traced through on-going dialogues with, and unfolding critiques of, Marxist theory. Even as structural or overdetermined versions of Marxism and dependency theory gained influence, critiques of their limitations for understanding politics, ethnicity, and gender also emerged. These trends stood consistently at the interstices between political events and academic discourse, revolution and theoretical framework, human agency and conceptual abstraction. The role of African and Latin American intellectuals, both academics and activists, was central throughout. From this perspective, it is perhaps easier to see that postmodernism and all its accompanying post-isms cannot claim to have invented the fragmentation of the various "Western" metascripts; these had been actively fragmented, exploded, and deconstructed in Africa and Latin America since the early 1970s. From a "Third World" perspective, then, postmodernism is perhaps not all that much more fragmented and decentered a script than modernism has turned out to be. To frame the matter somewhat differently, the prescribed practices of postmodernism may turn out to be as power-laden and Eurocentric as those for which we have criticized modernism. Mindful that all theoretical and analytical perspectives developed in the so-called advanced West must be used with caution when applying them in colonial, neocolonial, and postcolonial regions, let us take a final step back from the canvas to ponder the future possibilities for dialogue among these multiple "Third World" fragments.

A Final Step Back: A Proposal
for Future Reverberations
in Africa, Latin America, and Asia

A common quest underlies the dialogues among the essays in this book and the perspectives gleaned from an examination of Rodney, Molyneux, and Laclau: we have all sought to understand the process of European expansion in an emerging world system, and how the process facilitated and constricted the development of world capitalism. We have all discovered as well that the confrontation with peoples and social formations in Africa and Latin America

resulted in multiple forms of conflict and interaction that significantly transformed not only colonizers and colonized but the nature of the world system
as well. Scholars interested in Africa, Latin America and Asia have, since at
least World War II, been applying different scripts to this unfolding drama,
changing stage directions here, bit parts there; each particular script has been
found wanting, and has also been transformed through the act of trying it out.
A realization that has informed the effort of compiling this volume is that we
are now beyond the tinkering, to the point where the main story lines and characters need major rewriting. And yet the basic drama is still there, waiting for
us to try, once again, to "get it right."

Getting it right, however, cannot mean—and in reality never has meant—
closing debate. The challenge before us is to make the processes of debate
and generalization ever more open-ended, to confront directly the perceptions
gleaned by other intellectuals, under other historical, political and research
conditions, and to do so without closing off discussion. Discerning the patterns, while resisting the temptation to homogenize and unify it all: this is the
way to insure that defining and answering "the fundamental questions" (as
Cooper puts it) will remain "open and contested" intellectual labor. Remaining
open-ended will insure as well that we can maintain an expansive and flexible,
changing and creative view of what these fundamental questions may become
in the future.

With this last step back from the canvas, I would like to bring together some
of the perceptions emerging from our discussions of Africa and Latin America,
and place them next to analogous concerns emerging in some of the literature
on Asia. I do not wish to argue that perspectives developing in Asia can simply
be applied in Latin America or Africa, nor vice-versa. Attempts to do so would
impoverish rather than enrich our dialogues. Rather, it now seems possible to
contemplate a new cycle of reverberations that will allow us to tie earlier perceptions about the capitalist world system, labor, and peasantries to emerging
concerns about culture and power. In this context, I will concentrate on four
specific subject areas where future dialogues may prove particularly rich: culture and politics, the meaning of nationalism in "Third World" areas, ethnicity
and the construction of power relations, and gender and generation. In keeping
with the spirit of this essay and of the volume as a whole, I do not wish to
define a future agenda in any hard and fast way, but rather to reemphasize the
need consciously to expand our multiple mutual dialogues, while suggesting
some possible lines of future reverberation.

A starting point for our analysis of culture and politics is provided once again
by Ernesto Laclau. Laclau and his recent coauthor Chantal Mouffe have been
key figures in facilitating engagement with new perspectives in Latin America
(see Labastida 1985, 1986). In their book *Hegemony and Socialist Strategy*
(1985), Laclau and Mouffe attempt to move beyond reductionist and evolu-

tionist explanations for social change by exploding all separation between base and superstructure. What remains, for them, is discourse: the intellectual and political practices that make sense of events, objects, and relationships. Ideas ("elements") are articulated in a discursive field along two dimensions: equivalence, which emphasizes the commonalities among them and connects them to each other; and antagonism, which emphasizes their differences and partially fixes a frontier between them. What provides this seemingly eternal process of articulation, dispersion, and recomposition with some political meaning is the concept of hegemony. In critical dialogue with Gramsci, Mouffe and Laclau define hegemony as the historically contingent, socially "open," and conscious process by which human beings articulate discourses. The practice of hegemony seeks to recompose the frontiers of antagonism at new points, creating new and broader fields of equivalence. It is through hegemony that human beings create social movements, political alliances, power relations, and new forms of politics. By using the concept, Laclau and Mouffe introduce a historical dimension into their analysis, connecting it to discussions of hegemony and culture inspired by other currents (Gramsci 1971; Williams 1977; Scott 1985; Corrigan and Sayer 1985), though they themselves only recognize explicitly the connection to Gramsci.

The repetition of hegemonic practices through time creates patterns of discursive meaning which, as they accumulate, seem to condition the range of possible antagonisms and equivalences at any particular historical moment. Only in this way can we understand the importance Mouffe and Laclau give to the "democratic revolution," which between the seventeenth century and the French revolution made available a new discourse of liberty and equality to the world, opening up new possible articulations of equivalence between previously dispersed elements. Through their concept of the democratic revolution as a watershed, Mouffe and Laclau divide historical time into two large blocks. In premodern, or precapitalist, time, social struggle obeyed a different dynamic because social identities were stable and given. As a result contradictions and antagonisms were clearer, and political struggle did not require hegemony. One cannot escape the conclusion, in this context, that it was the emergence of modern class struggle that made hegemony necessary.

Even as they give historical and political dynamism to their analysis through the concept of hegemony, therefore, Laclau and Mouffe use the concept of the democratic revolution to remove complexity from all precapitalist social struggles, recreating, for precapitalist formations, precisely the kind of essentialist language and epistemology—the class reductionist notions and "logic of capital" arguments—they set out to critique in their treatment of capitalist societies and times. In so doing they recreate a colonial "Other," for only when Western European capitalism brings the rest of the world into modernity will "other" people require the complex forms of agency contained in the practice of hegemony. Until then, their "simpler" social struggles will be organized around the kind of "pure" antagonisms found in millenarian movements, where the "distance between the two communities is something immediately given and acquired from the beginning, and it does not suppose any articulatory construction" (Laclau and Mouffe, 1985:136); or in the still simplified if slightly more complicated arena of the "national-popular" (131).

In addition to denying non-Europeans the complex agency of hegemony, Laclau and Mouffe also relegate gender, race, and ethnic relations to the category of "secondary contradictions." Gender, race, and ethnicity become important only once the discourse of the democratic revolution, based on the class transformations associated with capitalism, brings them out of their slumber as unconscious "relations of subordination" by articulating them to the promise of democracy, thus transforming them into "relations of oppression" (152–56). But surely this denies all complexity and conscious agency to precapitalist gender, ethnic, and racial struggles, relocating the barrier between the primordial and historical in a different place rather than questioning its existence altogether.

The key, it seems to me, is to retain the openness of analysis provided by Mouffe and Laclau's deconstructions of the base/superstructure dichotomy, and the richness of texture made possible by their analyses of political alliances as discursive practice, while exploding the dualisms inherent in their historical division between capitalism and noncapitalism. In this way, and in keeping with the overall spirit and project of the work compiled in this volume, we will be able to bring gender, race, and ethnicity more fully into the analysis, and also more fully historicize the politics of noncapitalist and "Third World" peoples. As a part of this general project, the contribution of the Indian *Subaltern Studies* school to our understanding of popular culture, resistance, and colonialism (Guha 1983, 1982–85) cannot be overestimated. Like Mouffe and Laclau, the scholars represented in the Subaltern School began from a critical rereading of Gramsci. But in contrast to Laclau and Mouffe, who applied their insights to an understanding of late, developed capitalism, these other scholars read Gramsci against the backdrop of colonial and postcolonial India. The results were quite distinct: rather than exploding the base/superstructure dichotomy, they unmasked the dualisms constructed between peasant resistance and elite politics, European "rationality" and colonial "otherness." By placing the politics and struggles of peasants and other subalterns at the center of anticolonial movements, authors in the Subaltern School revitalized and expanded our understanding of the counterhegemonic impulses and pressures that crosscut and articulate all political processes.

As Roseberry and Isaacman's essays in this volume make clear, one of the keys to understanding popular culture and counterhegemonic movements is the combination of close local readings of discourse and contestation, with a broad

commitment to the political and historical understanding of resistance and ac-
comodation. In this way it is possible to uncover and analyze popular political
action, without reifying or romanticizing popular struggle. In my view, this
is precisely what can be accomplished through an analysis of hegemony, discourse, and politics as represented in the combination of Laclau and Mouffe
with the Subaltern School. Some Africanist and Latin Americanist studies of
peasant and popular politics have begun to move in this direction (Feierman
1990; Joseph 1990; Nugent 1988, 1989; an inspiration here was Scott 1985);
but as they do, they begin from very different points of departure.

In Africa, as we have seen, initial considerations of peasants and politics
emerged in the old and relatively linear "resistance studies" tradition (e.g.,
Ranger 1968; Lonsdale 1968) that accompanied the nationalist movements of
the 1960s. The promises of national liberation associated with these movements, however, whether socialist or not, tarnished quickly and dramatically.
As a result, the resistance studies tradition was strongly criticized and almost
abandoned by the 1970s. One trend in work from the 1980s has been to use
perspectives on hegemony, discourse, and culture to deconstruct national-level
claims while building regionally grounded, postnational, and postcolonial perspectives on the role of popular resistance in socioeconomic and political
change (Feierman 1990; Fields 1985; Comaroff 1985; Lonsdale 1990; White
1990; Beinart and Bundy 1987; Cooper 1989). In Latin America, on the other
hand, the prestige of resistance studies has been more enduring. Nurtured by a
long history of popular upheaval, from the late colonial revolts in the Andes,
Mexico, and the Caribbean to the twentieth-century revolutionary tradition that
began in Mexico (1910) and continued in Bolivia (1952), Cuba (1959), and
Nicaragua (1979), studies of popular resistance have helped articulate counterhegemonic politics to the promises of national liberation contained within each
of these revolutions. In contrast to the situation in Africa, moreover, promises
of national liberation have tarnished more slowly, leaving stronger and more
enduring legacies and hopes for legitimacy. In this context, it is not surprising
that discourse and cultural analysis has been more influential in anthropology
and literary criticism (examples are Franco 1989; Taussig 1986; Poole 1988a,
1988b), but used less to deconstruct the national scripts contained in historical or resistance studies (but see Nugent 1988, 1989; Koreck 1988; Alonso
1988a, 1988b).[5]

Given their almost opposite evolutions, I think the potential for future reverberation between the African and Latin American literatures on nationalism
and peasant politics is particularly rich. Latin Americanists would benefit
greatly from a dose of the skepticism with which Africanists regard all nationalist narratives, while Africanists would benefit from a revival (though in new
form) of the concern with national projects and power that informed earlier
studies of peasants within the resistance tradition. And here again, as with

Laclau and Mouffe, scholars from other "Third World" areas would benefit from a confrontation with scholars from the Subaltern School, especially
Partha Chatterjee and David Hardiman, who have produced some of the most
interesting recent work on nationalism in the colonial world (Chatterjee 1986;
Hardiman 1981) and opened up theoretical and political space for subalterns
within the process. I would like to explore some of the possible directions such
interactions might take by focusing on three cases: Chatterjee's study of India
(1986); Feierman's study of Tanzania (1990); and the recent debate on the
intersections between nationalism and peasant politics in nineteenth-century
Peru (Bonilla 1978, 1979, 1987; Favre 1975; Mallon 1983, 1987a; Manrique
1981, 1988).

In *Nationalism and the Colonial World*, Partha Chatterjee is interested in
examining the implications of India's nationalist revolution for our understanding of nationalism more generally. Though he begins from the assumption
that nationalism is a "derivative discourse" in the colonial world—that is, it
originates in Europe—Chatterjee nevertheless gives the discourse a great deal
of internal dynamism and allows for possible radical modifications within it
during the process of its adoption by or diffusion to "Third World" areas. He
argues that from the start there was a basic contradiction, at the discursive
level, within nationalist discourse. At the level of its "problematic"—that is,
its identification of the historical possibilities and programs for action contained within nationalist thought—the discourse was universal, for it posited
the basic equality of all peoples, and people, in the world, granting all the right
to dignity and autonomy. At the level of its "thematic," on the other hand—its
ethical and epistemological framework of knowledge—nationalist discourse
was bounded by the limits of post-Enlightenment western thought, with its
colonial constructions of Reason and Other, West and East. This contradiction between a universalizing problematic and a eurocentric thematic became
an important source of tension and dynamism in how nationalist discourses
and movements were constructed in history. On the one hand, the thematic
placed important limits on what was even considered possible within nationalist politics. Yet on the other hand, the dynamic tension between the thematic
and the problematic, worked out in the context of specific political movements
and alliances, at times threatened to transcend the eurocentric boundaries of
original nationalist thought and open up the potential for liberation it contained (Chatterjee 1986:43). These moments of near-transcendence occurred,
for Chatterjee, when nationalist leaders such as Gandhi articulated popular
and peasant traditions of resistance to an evolving nationalist movement, and
in so doing created the conditions under which the universal problematic of
nationalist discourse might break open its exclusionary thematic.

In his book on peasant intellectuals, Steven Feierman (1990) examines an
analogous moment in the genesis of the anticolonial movement in Tanzania.

In the period of transition toward a postcolonial state, there is a moment of near-transcendence in which the peasant intellectuals who had articulated rural discourses on healing the land, antislavery, and democracy become dynamic partners in the formation of a nationalist coalition. Some of the rural discourses, such as healing the land, were old and enduring, constantly reorganized at moments of political transition to signify or mark the reciprocal relationship between power and responsibility. Others, such as democracy and antislavery, were new to the colonial process. Taken together, reorganized and modified by peasant intellectuals, they became regional emancipatory discourses and formed the very core of what was dynamic in the Tanzanian independence movement. Yet because peasant leaders did not possess the bureaucratic skills to position themselves strategically during the final scramble for state power, they lost out when that power was ultimately distributed.

Though concerned with very similar subjects and periods, Feierman and Chatterjee approach their inquiries from exactly opposite perspectives. Feierman is interested in investigating the actual content and dynamic articulation of the rural discourses themselves: his book is thick with the voices of peasant intellectuals, gathered over two decades of fieldwork. That these discourses existed at all, that they were central to peasant consciousness and internally diverse and contested—all this knowledge we owe to Feierman's deep engagement with and commitment to the people who produced them. By contrast, Chatterjee's main project seems to be the demystification of Mohandas Karamchand Gandhi and Jawaharlal Nehru. In this context, the content of rural discourses matters much less than what was done with them at the regional and emerging national levels. Chatterjee's is not a story of complex and internally contested local discourses giving impulse to a nationalist movement, only to have their producers lose their way in the bureaucratic maze of national power politics: it is a story of undeconstructed "popular culture" sold down the river by unscrupulous or tortured national allies interested in building a new hegemony. As an Africanist steeped in the rejection of the nationalist tradition, Feierman seems less interested in what his rich analysis might mean to a reconstruction of a nationalist story; as a member of the Subaltern School submerged in the decolonization of Gramsci and poststructuralist theory, Chatterjee cares less about the internal composition and contradictions of subaltern culture. That a combination of the two perspectives might be extremely fruitful becomes clear from their application to the existing debate on Peruvian peasant nationalism.

Ongoing since 1979, the main contours of the debate on Peruvian peasant nationalism have developed out of the dialogue and confrontation among four authors—Heraclio Bonilla and Henri Favre, Nelson Manrique and myself—over how to interpret events during the War of the Pacific (1879–1884). The main bone of contention has been how to interpret the lack of a united and effective Peruvian response to the Chilean invasion and occupation of their country. Bonilla has, over the course of his various writings (1978, 1979, 1987), posed the question in the clearest and most theoretically consistent way and, by placing the Peruvian case squarely in the Marxist metanarrative on nationalism, provided the simplest answer. Because Peru did not have a unified national bourgeoisie which could have organized and led a national resistance movement, the country degenerated into a series of regions and racial factions, with the Chilean occupation providing the excuse for the redress of more primitive and atavistic grievances that were the legacy of a colonial experience carried into postcolonial times. Building from the specific case of the Peruvian central highlands, Manrique and I have attempted to counter this argument by demonstrating empirically that a nationalist peasant movement did evolve in the course of the Chilean occupation, and was repressed by its former allies in the postwar period because it was too radical and autonomous. The problem with all of the work up until now is that it has not systematically and consistently questioned the Marxist version of Western nationalist scripts: if nationalism was not elaborated by a national bourgeoisie at a particular point in the development of capitalism, how could it otherwise evolve?

Several years ago, I attempted to find a new path by using the work of Zionist socialist Ber Borochov (Mallon 1987a). Following Borochov, I argued that nationalist consciousness is relatively autonomous from class relations because it evolves from a connection to the conditions of production—a particular territory, material culture, language, and other traditions and patterns of interaction—that help constitute each particular society. In this context, any social class might develop nationalism under specific conditions, especially when a national question—a particular conflict between peoples—emerges. From my present vantage point, however, such an approach continues to be confined by the categories of class analysis. Rather than elaborating an alternative script that placed peasants at the center, relying on Borochov resulted in just one more attempt to "add peasants and stir."

A more promising future direction for Latin Americanist literature on peasants and politics (see Albó 1987; Platt 1982, 1987; Stern 1987; Gould 1990; Guardino 1991; Koreck 1988; Alonso 1988a,b; Nugent 1988, 1989; Joseph 1990; Smith 1989) is the attempt to combine the sensitivity to popular culture and discourse present in Feierman's work, with the complex attention to regional and national power relations that marks Chatterjee's contribution. Only in this way will it be possible finally to move beyond existing national and nationalist metanarratives and ultimately to reconstruct national stories more sensitive to regional or local variation, as well as to inequality and repression. At the intersections of these different tendencies in "Third World" literatures, it might be possible for scholars from all three areas to move beyond the limitations imposed by their own region's dialogue between past and present, while at the same time recognizing and expanding on the particular strengths of their own literature's overall contribution. Indeed, these broad forms of comparative dialogue might serve as a good reminder to all of us that the integration of peasant, or more generally subaltern, politics into national trends is a difficult and risky proposition. Combining the study of popular political cultures with an analysis of state formation has the makings of a good marriage, in the sense that it can change both partners in a positive direction. Yet as is the case with most marriages, it will prosper best if each partner partially retains his or her own identity.

Though treated less systematically by the essays in this volume, the literatures on ethnicity and on gender and generation are further examples of how much one continent's historiography could benefit from future interaction with the others. Given the centrality of decolonization processes in Africa and Asia to the new debates on ethnicity developing after World War II, it is perhaps not surprising that the most stimulating debates on the subject should have initially occurred on these two continents. This has continued to be the case until the present day, with scholars who work on Asia and Africa pioneering a series of more historical, flexible, and power-oriented approaches to the formation and transformation of ethnic identities (Bentley 1987; Brass 1985; Cohen 1978; Enloe 1980a, 1980b; Lonsdale 1977; Norton 1984; Saul 1979). Recent Asianist literature has also addressed in interesting ways the role of gender in constructing ethnic and racial categories (Stoler 1989; Chatterjee 1989). In Latin America, while pioneering work on gender, race and class was done by Verena Martínez-Alier (1974), much of the literature still tends to be caught in the old quandary between ethnicity and class, with the newest literature analyzing the dynamic between the two (Manrique 1988; Schryer 1990; but see also Gutiérrez 1991; Warren 1978; Smith 1990; Urban and Sherzer 1991 for promising alternative directions).

In Latin America especially, then—though clearly throughout the "Third World"—future discussions of ethnicity would benefit greatly from reverberation among these various recent approaches, with their emphases on historicity, ideology, power, exploitation, and the internal dynamics of ethnic groups. The most productive direction for future studies would be to ground them historically in specific moments and cases of ethnic conflict or change. The key analytical element here would be the organization, reproduction, and reorganization of power relations, both during periods of relative continuity and moments of dramatic change for, as Gerald Sider (1987) points out, the relationship between power and ethnic differentiation is ambiguous. On the one hand, the exercise of power through domination seeks both to generate and destroy difference; on the other, dominated ethnic peoples both resist and adapt to or collude with their dominators. It is this complex historical dynamic, in which any relationship has two sides and is in motion through time, that we must locate our understanding of ethnicity, both as identity and struggle. And as is true in any serious attempt at analyzing or writing history, "the paradoxes, contradictions, and disjunctions . . . , rather than being obstacles to our understanding, are the keys to getting inside" (Sider 1987:4).

On the importance of gender and generation for understanding peasant society and peasant politics, the African literature has clearly led the way. From the mid-1970s, when Marcia Wright published "Women in Peril" (1975) the question of women's subordination and of the exchange of women among ethnic groups was squarely on the Africanist agenda. Though a Latin Americanist literature on women and the transition to capitalism began to take shape about the same time (Deere 1976, 1977; Deere and León de Leal, 1982; *Latin American Perspectives* 1977; Nash and Safá, 1980, 1986; Fernández Kelly, 1983), the question of women's subordination in indigenous and peasant societies and the role of gender in peasant politics remained on the back burner until well into the 1980s (Mallon 1987b, 1990; Collins 1986; Deere 1990; Gould 1990). In the *Subaltern Studies* school as well, the issue of gender hierarchies within popular cultures was not directly addressed (see Spivak 1988 for a critique; but see also Chatterjee 1989). Future studies of gender in "Third World" areas would therefore benefit greatly from the comparatively mature discussion the issue has generated in Africa, especially for our understanding of the intersections between the constructions of gender and ethnic identities (see also Stoler 1989).

Finally, reverberations among Asianists, Africanists, and Latin Americanists also promise to be particularly rich around the general question of theorizing gender and politics. Though the literature on gender and revolution, feminism, and socialism, has quite a long and distinguished pedigree by this point (for a recent contribution, see Kruks, Rapp, and Young 1989), an important strand of political analysis that places gender and generation at the center of our understanding of revolution (Stacey 1983) has yet to be adequately digested by scholars in other parts of the "Third World." Stacey argues that Chinese revolutionary policy on gender and family issues emerged from a negotiation between the expectations of radical party cadres and rural peasant patriarchal values and practices, and resulted in a form of democratic or socialist patriarchy in which male rights and privileges were more evenly distributed among men, regardless of age and class, while women still remained, in important respects, second-class citizens. Recently, and in dialogue with some additional authors who have conceptualized the patriarchal practices and content of radical political movements or ideologies (Scott 1988; Enloe 1983; Elshtain 1987), I have attempted to apply Stacey's concept of generational and gender negotiations among men in periods of revolutionary change to nineteenth-century Latin America (Mallon 1990). Ilene O'Malley (1986) has applied an analogous perspective to the institutionalization of the 1910 Mexican revolution, exploring the various forms of patriarchal relations, imagery, and language at play within revolutionary politics and postrevolutionary consolidation. In the future, I suspect that this line of inquiry will have much to recommend it, not only for our understanding of socialist revolutions in the Third World, but also for our broader analyses of nationalism and other political movements.

By way of conclusion, let me retrieve, one last time, the broad narrative thread that connects all the pieces in this volume, as well as the additional texts and inquiries with which I have been conversing in this essay. That thread is itself composed of two interlocking strands: one the story of capitalist and imperial expansion; the other a tale of subaltern responses and initiatives that defy linear metanarratives of modernization, capitalist expansion, or dependency. When woven together, these strands provide us with a "peripheral vision" of historical processes in the world, and recast conventional stories of how a world system was made, markets and wage labor extended, colonies created and destroyed, ethnic and gender hierarchies contested and reconstructed, political coalitions and conflicts fought and resolved, discourses articulated and transformed, nationalisms made and repressed. In many ways, our ongoing quest is still to chronicle this broad process, yet in contexts and with scripts that no longer prevent important characters from claiming their space on center-stage.

My central line of inquiry has been to explore the reverberations, past and future, that may permit us to rewrite the plot of this story without recreating (as Roseberry also warns we must not do) the frozen dualisms of the past: before capitalism and after capitalism; before rationality and after rationality; before class struggle and after class struggle. To maintain some sense of narrative line without becoming linear, to maintain a sense of diachronic process and transition without becoming dualistic, to rebuild a sense of explanation and causation without silencing important stories—these are the juggler's or tightrope walker's acts we have before us. The core of the challenge we face is, in my opinion, to make our scripts more flexible and dynamic by rewriting the plots and main cast of characters to include, alongside class, questions of culture, colonialism, politics, ethnicity, and gender and generation. Two earlier cycles of reverberation in "Third World" scholarship—on world capitalism, labor, and peasantries; and on gender, race, and modes of production—provided us with rich new suggestions that have gone far toward changing the paradigmatic story and cast of characters. I hope I have demonstrated, through a partial, initial, and experimental doing of it, how a renewed cycle of open-ended dialogues among the fragments of "Third World" literatures can help us further refine, improve, and move closer to "getting right" the large and small stories many of us still feel the need to tell. I trust that this volume, by picking up and redefining the earlier cycles of dialogue and suggesting the contours for a cycle yet to be played out, will contribute to the constant reworking and rewriting of the metanarratives of capitalism and the "peoples without history".[6] Only by so doing can we insure that history will be the province and right of all. May it always be so.

Notes

This essay was written while I was a fellow at the Center for Advanced Study in the Behavioral Sciences, Stanford, California, 1990–91. Funding for my year was provided by the Center and by NEH. I wish to thank coauthors Frederick Cooper, Allen Isaacman, and Steve J. Stern for their comments on the first draft of this essay. Cooper and Stern offered particularly hard-hitting comments that forced me to rethink and reformulate in important ways. Stern also took the time to read and critique a second draft, which helped immeasurably in making the final product intelligible and readable. Cooper and Isaacman, respectively, pointed out the remaining problems in the third and fourth drafts. While each time I was dismayed to learn I did not have a final version in hand, each revision—thanks to my colleagues—was notably better than the one before.

1 I am referring here to the following texts: Marx 1967; Althusser and Balibar 1970; Thompson 1968, 1971; Hobsbawm 1959; and Gramsci 1971.

2 This discussion and debate occurred in Deler and Saint-Geours 1986:419–33.

3 In several conversations with Roger Bartra over the past five years, the issue of the Asiatic mode of production and how it came to symbolize resistance in official Marxist circles, both in Mexico and Cuba, has come up.

4 This was especially important in the African literature, where the class-first approach of Marxists had been particularly rigid. See also Kahn 1981; Mamdami 1976; Leys 1975; Saul 1979; Sklar 1967; and Mafeje 1971.

5 Interestingly, and as further support for my contention here, Ana María Alonso, María Teresa Koreck, and Daniel Nugent were all trained at the University of Chicago, where they worked with Africanist anthropologists Jean and John Comaroff.

6 This phrase, though it has a long Marxist genealogy, was creatively appropriated and popularized by Eric Wolf in his book *Europe and the People Without History* (1982).

References

Albó, Xavier. 1987. "From MNRistas to Kataristas to Katari." In Stern, ed. 1987:379–419.

Alonso, Ana María. 1988a. "The Effects of Truth: Re-presentations of the Past and the Imagining of Community." *The Journal of Historical Sociology* 1, no. 1:33–57.

Alonso, Ana María. 1988b. "'Progress' as Disorder and Dishonor: Discourses of *Serrano* Resistance." *Critique of Anthropology* 8 no. 1:13–33.

Althusser, Louis, and Etiene Balibar. 1970. *Reading Capital*. London: New Left Books.

Appiah, Kwame Anthony. 1991. "Is the Post- in Postmodernism the Post- in Post-Colonial?" *Critical Inquiry* 17 (Winter):336–57.

Bartra, Roger. 1976. "Sobre la articulación de modos de producción en América Latina." In *Modos de producción en América Latina*. Lima: Delva Editores, 5–19.

Beinart, William, and Colin Bundy. 1987. *Hidden Struggles in Rural South Africa*. Berkeley: Univ. of California Press.

Bentley, G. Carter. 1987. "Ethnicity and Practice." *Comparative Studies in Society and History* 29 (January):24–55.

Bonilla, Heraclio. 1978. "The War of the Pacific and the National and Colonial Problem in Peru." *Past and Present* 81:92–118.

Bonilla, Heraclio. 1979. "A propósito de la guerra con Chile." *Histórica* 3 (July):133–38.

Bonilla, Heraclio. 1987. "The Indian Peasantry and 'Peru' during the War with Chile." In Stern, ed. 1987:219–31.

Brass, Paul, ed. 1985. *Ethnic Groups and the State*. London: Croom Helm.

Chatterjee, Partha. 1986. *Nationalism and the Colonial World. A Derivative Discourse?* London: Zed Books.

Chatterjee, Partha. 1989. "Colonialism, Nationalism, and Colonialized Women: The Contest in India." *American Ethnologist* 16 (November):622–33.

Cohen, Ronald. 1978. "Ethnicity: Problem and Focus in Anthropology." *Annual Review of Anthropology* 7:379–403.

Collins, Jane. 1986. "The Houschold and Relations of Production in Southern Peru." *Comparative Studies in Society and History* 28:651–71.

Comaroff, Jean. 1985. *Body of Power, Spirit of Resistance: The Culture and History of a South African People*. Chicago: Univ. of Chicago Press.

Cooper, Frederick. 1989. "From Free Labor to Family Allowances: Labor and African Society in Colonial Discourse." *American Ethnologist* 16 (November):745–65.

Corrigan, Philip and Derek Sayer. 1985. *The Great Arch. English State Formation as Cultural Revolution*. New York: Basil Blackwell.

Critique of Anthropology. 1977. Autumn issue.

Deere, Carmen Diana. 1976. "Women's Subsistence Production in the Capitalist Periphery." *The Review of Radical Political Economics* 8, no. 1:9–17.

Deere, Carmen Diana. 1977. "Changing Social Relations of Production and Peruvian Peasant Women's Work." *Latin American Perspectives* 4, nos. 1 and 2:58–69.

Deere, Carmen Diana. 1978. "The Development of Capitalism in Agriculture and the Division of Labor by Sex." Ph.D. diss. Univ. of California, Berkeley.

Deere, Carmen Diana. 1990. *Household and Class Relations: Peasants and Landlords in Northern Peru*. Berkeley: Univ. of California Press.

Deere, Carmen Diana, and Magdalena León de Leal. 1982. *Women in Andean Agriculture: Peasant Production and Rural Wage Employment in Colombia and Peru*. Geneva: International Labour Organization.

Deler, Jean-Paul, and Yves Saint-Geours, eds. 1986. *Estados y naciones en los Andes: Hacia una historia comparativa*. Vol. 2. Lima: Instituto de Estudios Peruanos/Instituto Francés de Estudios Andinos.

Elshtain, Jean Bethke. 1987. *Women and War*. New York: Basic Books.

Enloe, Cynthia. 1980a. *Ethnic Soldiers: State Security in Divided Societies*. Athens, Ga.: Univ. of Georgia Press.

Enloe, Cynthia. 1980b. *Police, Military and Ethnicity: Foundations of State Power*. New Brunswick, N.J.: Transaction Books.

Enloe, Cynthia. 1983. *Does Khaki Become You? The Militarization of Women's Lives*. London: Pluto Press.

Favre, Henri. 1975. "Remarques sur la lutte des classes au Pérou pendant la guerre du Pacifique." In *Littérature et Societé au Pérou du XIXème Siècle à Nos Jours*. Grenoble: Association Française pour l'Etude et la Récherche sur les Pays Andins, Université des Langues et Lettres.

Feierman, Steven. 1990. *Peasant Intellectuals: Anthropology and History in Tanzania*. Madison: Univ. of Wisconsin Press.

Feminist Review. 1979. Numbers 2 and 3.

Fernández Kelly, Patricia. 1983. *For We Are Sold, I and My People: Women and Industry on Mexico's Frontier*. Albany: SUNY Press.

Fields, Karen. 1985. *Revival and Rebellion in Colonial Central Africa*. Princeton: Princeton Univ. Press.

Franco, Jean. 1989. *Plotting Women: Gender and Representation in Mexico*. New York: Columbia Univ. Press.

Gould, Jeffrey. 1990. *To Lead As Equals: Rural Protest and Political Consciousness in Chinandega, Nicaragua, 1912–1979*. Chapel Hill: Univ. of North Carolina Press.

Gramsci, Antonio. 1971. *Selections from the Prison Notebooks*. Trans. Quintin Hoare and Geoffrey Nowell Smith. New York: International Publishers.

Guardino, Peter. 1991. "Peasants, Politics, and State Formation in Early 19th-Century Mexico: Guerrero, 1800–1855." Ph.D. diss. (History). Univ. of Chicago.

Guha, Ranajit. 1983. *Elementary Aspects of Peasant Insurgency in Colonial India*. Delhi: Oxford Univ. Press.

Guha, Ranajit, ed. 1982–85. *Subaltern Studies*. 4 Vols. Delhi: Oxford Univ. Press.

Gutiérrez, Ramón A. 1991. *When Jesus Came, the Corn Mothers Went Away: Marriage, Sexuality, and Power in New Mexico, 1500–1846*. Stanford: Stanford Univ. Press.

Hardiman, David. 1981. *Peasant Nationalists of Gujarat: Kheda District, 1917–1934*. Delhi: Oxford Univ. Press.

Hartmann, Heidi. 1981. "The Unhappy Marriage of Marxism and Feminism: Towards a More Progressive Union." In Lydia Sargent, ed., *Women and Revolution*. Boston: South End Press.

Hobsbawm, Eric J. 1959. *Primitive Rebels*. New York: Norton.

Joseph, Gilbert. 1990. "On the Trail of Latin American Bandits: A Reexamination of Peasant Resistance." *Latin American Research Review* 25, no. 3:7–53.

Kahn, Joel S. 1981. "Explaining Ethnicity: A Review Article." *Critique of Anthropology* 4, no. 16:43–51.

Koreck, María Teresa. 1988. "Space and Revolution in Northeastern Chihuahua." In Nugent, ed. 1988:127–48.

Kruks, Sonia, Rayna Rapp, and Marilyn B. Young, eds. 1989. *Promissory No s: Women in the Transition to Socialism*. New York: Monthly Review Press.

Labastida Martín del Campo, Julio, ed. 1985. *Hegemonía y alternativas políticas en América Latina*. Mexico City: Siglo XIX Editores.

Labastida Martín del Campo, Julio, ed. 1986. *Los nuevos procesos sociales y la teoría política contemporánea*. Mexico City: Siglo XXI Editores.

Laclau, Ernesto. 1971. "Feudalism and Capitalism in Latin America." *New Left Review* 67 (May–June):19–38.

Laclau, Ernesto. 1975. "The Specificity of the Political: Around the Poulantzas-Miliband Debate." *Economy and Society* 4 (February):87–110.

Laclau, Ernesto. 1977. *Politics and Ideology in Marxist Theory*. London: New Left Books.

Laclau, Ernesto, and Chantal Mouffe. 1985. *Hegemony and Socialist Strategy: Toward a Radical Democratic Politics*. London: Verso.

Latin American Perspectives. 1977. *Special Issue on Women and Class Struggle* 4 (Winter and Spring).

Leys, Colin. 1975. *Underdevelopment in Kenya*. London: Heineman.

Lonsdale, John. 1977. "When Did the Gusii (or Any Other Group) Become a 'Tribe'?" *Kenya Historical Review* 5:123–33.

Lonsdale, John. 1968. "Some Origins of Nationalism in East Africa." *Journal of African History* 9, no. 3:119–46.

Lonsdale, John. 1990. "Mau Maus of the Mind: Making Mau Mau and Remaking Kenya." *Journal of African History* 31:393–421.

Mafeje, Archie. 1971. "The Ideology of 'Tribalism'." *The Journal of Modern African Studies* 9, no. 2:253–61.

Mallon, Florencia E. 1983. *The Defense of Community in Peru's Central Highlands: Peasant Struggle and Capitalist Transition, 1860–1940*. Princeton: Princeton Univ. Press.

Mallon, Florencia E. 1987a. "Nationalist and Anti-State Coalitions in the War of the Pacific: Junín and Cajamarca." In Stern, ed. 1987:232–79.

Mallon, Florencia E. 1987b. "Patriarchy in the Transition to Capitalism in Central Peru, 1830–1950." *Feminist Studies* 13 (Summer):379–407.

Mallon, Florencia E. 1990. "Constructing Third World Feminisms: Lessons from Nineteenth-Century Mexico (1850–1874)." Women's History Working Papers Series, no. 2. Madison: Wisconsin.

Mamdami, Mahmoud. 1976. *Politics and Class Formation in Uganda*. New York: Monthly Review Press.

Mandala, Elias. 1990. *Work and Control in a Peasant Economy*. Madison: Univ. of Wisconsin Press.

Manrique, Nelson. 1981. *Campesinado y nación: Las guerrillas indígenas en la guerra con Chile*. Lima: Centro de Investigación y Capacitación-Ital Perú, S.A.

Manrique, Nelson. 1988. *Yawar mayu. Sociedades terratenientes serranas, 1879–1910*. Lima: Instituto Francés de Estudios Andinos/ DESCO.

Martínez-Alier, Verena. 1974. *Marriage, Class and Colour in Nineteenth-Century Cuba*. Cambridge: Cambridge Univ. Press.

Marx, Karl. 1967. *Capital*. Vol. 1. New York: International Publishers.

Meillasoux, Claude. 1972. "From Reproduction to Production." *Economy and Society* 1 (February):93–105.

Molyneux, Maxine. 1977. "Androcentrism in Marxist Anthropology." *Critique of Anthropology* 3 (Autumn):55–81.

Molyneux, Maxine. 1982. "Socialist Societies Old and New: Progress Toward Women's Emancipation?" *Monthly Review* (July/August):56–100.

Molyneux, Maxine. 1985a. "Family Reform in Socialist States: The Hidden Agenda." *Feminist Review* 21 (Winter):47–64.

Molyneux, Maxine. 1985b. "Mobilization Without Emancipation? Women's Interests, the State, and Revolution in Nicaragua." *Feminist Studies* 11 (Summer):227–54.

Nash, June, and Helen Safá. 1980. *Sex and Class in Latin America*. 2d. ed. South Hadley, Mass.: Bergin and Garvey.

Nash, June, and Helen Safá. 1986. *Women and Change in Latin America*. South Hadley, Mass.: Bergin and Garvey.

Norton, Robert. 1984. "Ethnicity and Class: A Conceptual note with Reference to the Politics of Post-Colonial Societies." *Ethnic and Racial Studes* 7 (July):426–34.

Nugent, Daniel, ed. 1988. *Rural Revolt in Mexico and U.S. Intervention*. San Diego: Center for U.S.-Mexican Studies.

Nugent, Daniel. 1989. " 'Are We Not (Civilized) Men?': The Formation and Devolution of Community in Northern Mexico." *The Journal of Historical Sociology* 2, no. 3:206–39.

O'Laughlin, Bridgit. 1977. "Production and Reproduction: Meillassoux's *Femmes greniers et capitaux*." *Critique of Anthropology* 2:3–32.

O'Malley, Ilene V. 1986. *The Myth of the Revolution: Hero Cults and the Institutionalization of the Mexican State, 1920–1940*. Westport, Conn.: Greenwood Press.

Platt, Tristan. 1982. *Estado boliviano y ayllu andino: Tierra y tributo en el Norte de Potosí*. Lima: Instituto de Estudios Peruanos.

Platt, Tristan. 1987. "The Andean Experience of Bolivian Liberalism, 1825–1900: Roots of Rebellion in 19th-Century Chayanta (Potosí)." In Stern, ed. 1987:280–323.

Poole, Deborah. 1988a. "A One-Eyed Gaze: Gender in 19th-Century Illustration of Peru." *Dialectical Anthropology* 13:333–64.

Poole, Deborah. 1988b. "Landscapes of Power in a Cattle-Rustling Culture of Southern Andean Peru." *Dialectical Anthropology* 12:367–98.

Ranger, Terence O. 1968. "Connections Between 'Primary Resistance' Movements and Modern Nationalism in East Africa." *Journal of African History* 9, no. 3:437–53; 9, no. 4:631–41.

Rey, Pierre-Philippe. 1973. *Les alliances des classes: Sur l'articulation des modes de production*. Paris: F. Maspero.

Rodney, Walter. 1972. *How Europe Underdeveloped Africa*. London: Bogle-l'Ouverture Publications.

Rodney, Walter. 1981. *A History of the Guyanese Working People, 1881–1905*. Baltimore, Md.: The Johns Hopkins Univ. Press.

Saul, John. 1979. "The Dialectic of Class and Tribe." *Race and Class* 20, no. 4:347–72.

Schmidt, Elizabeth. 1987. "Ideology, Economics and the Role of Shona Women in Southern Rhodesia, 1850–1939." Ph.D. diss. (History). Univ. of Wisconsin, Madison.

Schryer, Frans J. 1990. *Ethnicity and Class Conflict in Rural Mexico*. Princeton: Princeton Univ. Press.

Scott, James C. 1985. *Weapons of the Weak: Everyday Forms of Peasant Resistance*. New Haven: Yale Univ. Press.

Scott, Joan Wallach. 1988. *Gender and the Politics of History*. New York: Columbia Univ. Press.

Sider, Gerald. 1987. "When Parrots Learn to Talk, and Why They Can't: Domination, Deception, and Self-Deception in Indian-White Relations." *Comparative Studies in Society and History* 29 (January):3–23.

Sklar, Richard. 1967. "Political Science and National Integration—A radical approach." *The Journal of Modern African Studies* 5, no. 1:1–11.

Smith, Carol A., ed. 1990. *Guatemalan Indians and the State, 1540 to 1988*. Austin: Univ. of Texas Press.

Smith, Gavin. 1989. *Livelihood and Resistance: Peasants and the Politics of Land in Peru*. Berkeley: Univ. of California Press.

Spivak, Gayatri Chakravorty. 1988. "Subaltern Studies: Deconstructing Historiography." In Spivak, *In Other Worlds: Essays in Cultural Politics*. New York: Routledge, 197–221.

Stacey, Judith. 1983. *Patriarchy and Socialist Revolution in China*. Berkeley: Univ. of California Press.

Stern, Steve J., ed. 1987. *Resistance, Rebellion and Consciousness in the Andean Peasant World: 18th to 20th Centuries*. Madison: Univ. of Wisconsin Press.

Stern, Steve J. 1987. "Introductions to Parts III and IV." In Stern, ed. 1987:213–18, 327–33.

Stoler, Ann. 1989. "Making Empire Respectable: The Politics of Race and Sexual Morality in 20th-Century Colonial Cultures." *American Ethnologist* 16 (November):634–60.

Taussig, Michael. 1986. *Shamanism, Colonialism and the Wild Man: A Study in Terror and Healing*. Chicago: Univ. of Chicago Press.

Thompson, E. P. 1968. *The Making of the English Working Class*. 2d ed. Harmondsworth, Eng.: Penguin.

Thompson, E. P. 1971. "The Moral Economy of the English Crowd." *Past and Present* 50 (February):76–136.

Urban, Greg, and Joel Sherzer, eds. 1991. *Nation-States and Indians in Latin America*. Austin: Univ. of Texas Press.

Warren, Kay B. 1978. *The Symbolism of Subordination: Indian Identity in a Guatemalan Town*. Austin: Univ. of Texas Press.

White, Luise. 1990. "Separating the Men from the Boys: Constructions of Gender, Sexuality, and Terrorism in Central Kenya, 1939–1959." *International Journal of African Historical Studies* 23, no. 1:1–27.

Williams, Raymond. 1977. *Marxism and Literature*. Oxford: Oxford Univ. Press.

Wolf, Eric R. 1982. *Europe and the People Without History*. Berkeley: Univ. of California Press.

Wright, Marcia. 1975. "Women in Peril: a Commentary on the Life Stories of Captives in Nineteenth-Century East-Central Africa." *African Social Research* 20 (December):800–19.

Index

Index

Accumulation. *See* Primitive accumulation

Accumulation on a World Scale (Amin), 109

Acuña Ortega, Victor Hugo, 354

Africa: historical scholarship on, 3, 9–13, 15–16, 84–186, 378–81, multidisciplinary nature of, 9–10, 218, since the 1970s, 187–201; nationalist movements in, 4; as underexploited nation, 146–49. *See also* Africanists; Africans; African Studies; Development; Labor; Peasant(s); Resistance; *Names of nations, regions, peoples, precolonial states in*

"Africa bashing," 189

African agency paradigm, 209, 212–13

African Economic History (Austen), 232

Africanists: changing assumptions of, 10, 11–12, 14, 84–85; definitions of peasants by, 205–6; studies by, 205–317. *See also* Reverberations

Africans: as slaves, 36, 43, 45–46, 48, 49, 59*n26*, 68*n89*, 110; in Brazil, 46–47; importance of emphases set by, 381. *See also* Men; Peasant(s); Slavery; Women

African Studies: changing concerns of profession of, 212, 215–16, 278–81, 389. *See also* Historical profession

Agrarian Question, The (Kautsky), 334, 339–40

Agrarian studies: in Latin America, 25, 318–62, 375; and rural protest in Africa, 215–74; of precolonial peasants in Africa, 228–35; application of Russian and German theories to Latin American, 334–36, 338–42; directions for

future research in, 377–78. *See also* Peasant(s)

Agribusiness in the Americas (Burbach and Flynn), 328

Agricultural extension agents, 126, 127, 128, 212; women's opposition to, 241, 253. *See also* Development

Agriculture: under colonialists, 121–31; and industry, 136. *See also* Agricultural extension agents; "Coerced cash-crop labor"; Food production; Forced cultivation; Labor; Peasant(s); Women: and agriculture; *Names of specific crops*

Algerian War, 4, 12, 266*n13*

All African Convention, 259

Alliance for Progress, 12, 18*n8*

Alpers, E. A., 85, 98, 213

Althusser, Louis: Marxism of, 100–101, 379–80, 382, 384

Amin, Idi, 143

Amin, Samir, 84, 94–95, 97, 98, 109, 130, 147, 213

"Analysis of a Social Situation in Modern Zululand" (Gluckman), 211

ANC, 259

"Androcentrism in Marxist Anthropology" (Molyneux), 383

Angola, 123, 125, 217, 219; rural-based struggles in, 215, 237, 244, 255, 383

Annales historians, 6, 218

Anthropology, 343–58; ahistoricism of, 210–12. *See also* Ethnography; Structural-functionalist paradigm

Antierosion schemes, 125, 208, 240, 241, 253, 255, 257, 260, 262

Antioquia region, 353, 356

405